Davidson
2016

Staging Scripture

»LUDUS«

Medieval and Early Renaissance Theatre and Drama

Edited by

Peter Happé
Wim Hüsken

Volume I:	*English Parish Drama*
Volume II:	*Civic Ritual and Drama*
Volume III:	*Between Folk and Liturgy*
Volume IV:	*Carnival and the Carnivalesque*
Volume V:	*Moving Subjects*
Volume VI:	*Farce and Farcical Elements*
Volume VII:	*Cyclic Form and the English Mystery Plays*
Volume VIII:	*Performance and Ritual*
Volume IX:	*Interludes and Early Modern Society*
Volume X:	*The St Gall Passion Play*
Volume XI:	*Spectacle, Rhetoric and Power*
Volume XII:	*Les Mystères: Genre, Text and Theatricality*
Volume XIII:	*Staging Vice*
Volume XIV:	*Staging Scripture*

VOLUME 14

The titles published in this series are listed at *brill.com/lud*

Staging Scripture

Biblical Drama, 1350–1600

Edited by

Peter Happé
Wim Hüsken

BRILL
RODOPI

LEIDEN | BOSTON

Cover illustration: "De Kruisiging des Heeren" ('The Crucifixion of the Lord'), by Lodewijk Grootaers, pen drawing from 1851 (Mechelen, Hof van Busleyden, inv. nr. G/103).

Library of Congress Cataloging-in-Publication Data

Names: Happé, Peter, editor.
Title: Staging scripture : biblical drama, 1350-1600 / edited by Peter Happé, Wim Husken.
Description: Boston : Brill-Rodopi, 2016. | Series: Ludus : medieval and early Renaissance theatre and drama, ISSN 1385-0393 ; VOLUME 14 | Includes bibliographical references and index.
Identifiers: LCCN 2016008199 (print) | LCCN 2016015285 (ebook) | ISBN 9789004313941 (hardback : alk. paper) | ISBN 9789004313958 (E-book)
Subjects: LCSH: Bible plays--History and criticism. | Religious drama--History and criticism. | Drama, Medieval--History and criticism. | Religious drama--Presentation, etc.
Classification: LCC PN1880 .S77 2016 (print) | LCC PN1880 (ebook) | DDC 792.1/6--dc23
LC record available at https://lccn.loc.gov/2016008199

Want or need Open Access? Brill Open offers you the choice to make your research freely accessible online in exchange for a publication charge. Review your various options on brill.com/brill-open.

Typeface for the Latin, Greek, and Cyrillic scripts: "Brill". See and download: brill.com/brill-typeface.

ISSN 1385-0393
ISBN 978-90-04-31394-1 (hardback)
ISBN 978-90-04-31395-8 (e-book)

Copyright 2016 by Koninklijke Brill NV, Leiden, The Netherlands.
Koninklijke Brill NV incorporates the imprints Brill, Brill Hes & De Graaf, Brill Nijhoff, Brill Rodopi and Hotei Publishing.
All rights reserved. No part of this publication may be reproduced, translated, stored in a retrieval system, or transmitted in any form or by any means, electronic, mechanical, photocopying, recording or otherwise, without prior written permission from the publisher.
Authorization to photocopy items for internal or personal use is granted by Koninklijke Brill NV provided that the appropriate fees are paid directly to The Copyright Clearance Center, 222 Rosewood Drive, Suite 910, Danvers, MA 01923, USA. Fees are subject to change.

This book is printed on acid-free paper and produced in a sustainable manner.

Contents

List of Figures   VII

Introduction   1
 Peter Happé

1 Performing the Scriptures: Biblical Drama after the Reformation   12
 Sarah Carpenter

2 Blurred Lines? Religion, Reform, and Reformation in Sir David Lyndsay's *Ane Satyre of the Thrie Estaitis*   42
 Greg Walker

3 Play Titles without Play Texts: What Can They Tell Us, and How? An Investigation of the Evidence for the Beverley Corpus Christi Play   68
 Diana Wyatt

4 The Bible and the *Towneley* Plays of *Isaac* and *Iacob*   92
 Philip Butterworth

5 The Norwich Grocers' Play(s) (1533, 1565): Development and Changes in the Representation of Man's Fall   125
 Roberta Mullini

6 Preaching Penance on the Stage in Late Medieval England: The Case of John the Baptist   149
 Charlotte Steenbrugge

7 "Have here a Drink full good": A Comparative Analysis of Staging Temptation in the Newcastle Noah Play   166
 Katie Normington

8 Dramatizing the Resurrection   182
 Peter Happé

9 Seeing and Recognizing in the Sacred and New: The Latin Scriptural Plays of Nicholas Grimald   204
   Elisabeth Dutton and Stephanie Allen

10 Staging and Liturgy in *The Croxton Play of the Sacrament*   235
   David Bevington

11 Herod's Reputation and the Killing of the Children: Some Theatrical Consequences   253
   Bob Godfrey

12 Passion Play: Staging York's *The Conspiracy* and *Christ before Annas and Caiaphas*   279
   Philip Crispin

13 "Alle out of hir self": Mary, Effective Piety and the N-Town *Crucifixion*   309
   James McBain

14 Memory and Remembering: Sacred History and the York Plays   334
   Clifford Davidson

15 Audience Responses and the York Corpus Christi Play   360
   Margaret Rogerson

16 "Be ye thus trowing": Medieval Drama and Make-Belief   384
   Garrett P.J. Epp

   Index   407

List of Figures

3.1　Beverley Pageant Assignments to Guilds, c. 1510–20　70
3.2　Carvings on the tomb of Henry Fitzroy, Duke of Richmond　80
3.3　Adam holding a spade with Mary sitting beside him　81
3.4　Adam delving and Eve spinning (with the Expulsion?)　82
3.5　Adam and Eve delving and spinning　83
3.6　Adam and Eve delving and spinning　84
12.1　Jesus blindfolded and seated on a low stool　290
12.2　A torturer upending a chamber pot over the Saviour's head　291
12.3　Christ defiled　292
12.4　An example of gestural acting　298
12.5　An electric torch shining blindingly onto Christ　302
12.6　Blocks in the traverse ground-level space to allow the public to remain involved in the action　304
12.7　An example of iconic 'framing': Pilate with the Temple authorities flanked on either side　305

Introduction

Peter Happé

1   **The Bible and Drama**

The target of this collection of essays about biblical drama is broad and it is concerned with about two and a half centuries.[1] Such a long period inevitably includes many changes, but this particular one is outstanding in that it saw a revolution in Christian belief in Europe. Such developments in religious experience were intensified and promoted by political and social factors, as well as by one very specific and influential technological invention in the establishment of printing. The Bible, in what may now seem a somewhat bewildering variety of forms, was at the centre of these changes, as it was, at different times, an authority, a repository of belief and an emotional experience, a source of controversy, and a weapon.[2] During this period the status of the Bible as a text changed as the recovery of ancient versions together with translations from them, and availability through printing made it available, in some form or other, to far more readers than ever before. In previous times its contents had reached much of its audience through visual, but non-verbal means, through the music of the liturgy, and through exegesis by the clergy in sermons.[3] But with the Reformation it now became much more available through reading, both in public contexts and in private ones. Such a change, while positively received by some, was perceived by others as a threat which had to be overcome by legislation and restraint.[4] Nevertheless it is clear that in some form or other the Bible provided access to the divine for both Catholics and Protestants.[5]

---

1   For a comprehensive international documentation see Lynette Muir, *The Biblical Drama of Medieval Europe* (Cambridge: Cambridge University Press, 1995).
2   Besides these purposes the biblical drama was also a place for doubt. See Erin E. Kelly, "Doubt and Religious Drama across Sixteenth-Century England, or Did the Middle Ages believe in Their Plays?", in *The Chester Cycle in Context 1555–1575*, ed. Jessica Dell, David Klausner and Helen Ostovich (Farnham: Ashgate, 2012), 47–63.
3   Theodore K. Lerud, *Memory, Images and the English Corpus Christi Drama* (New York: Palgrave Macmillan, 2008), 63–67.
4   Paul Whitfield White, "The Bible as Play in Reformation England," in *The Cambridge History of British Theatre*, vol. 1: *Origins to 1660*, ed. Jane Milling and Peter Thomson (Cambridge: Cambridge University Press, 2004), 88, suggests that the increase in Bible reading "did not curtail but rather generated new interest in biblical drama."
5   Heather Hill-Vásquez, *Sacred Players: The Politics of Response in the Middle English Drama* (Washington, D.C.: Catholic University of America Press, 2007), 208.

At the same time the drama itself changed in many ways. The alterations in the status of the Bible may have fuelled these but the process was reciprocal because drama came to embody a growing and illuminating experience of the contents of the Bible for many. One of the primary manifestations of these new forms of drama was the invention of large-scale dramatic sequences in cyclic form and these must be part of the subject matter of this collection. But our experience and knowledge of medieval drama is currently changing. In spite of the fact that in England, France, Germany, Italy, the Netherlands and Spain many biblical cycles in dramatic form were created, particularly in the fifteenth century, it is now clear that there were other ways of using the Bible and its contents in dramatic forms and there were many of them. In particular in England the occurrence of cyclic drama like that at York, Beverley and Chester has been found to be less extensive than was previously thought. It has also become apparent that the extant texts of cycle plays embody a variety of differing dramatic styles within them, and in doing so they leave us with problems about their interpretation. However, we do have two complete cycles in the surviving manuscripts from York and Chester, which can be located in time and place. To these we can add the N-Town manuscript and the Towneley plays, but these two collections are curiously similar in that they are both eclectic collections containing plays with differing provenances and acting styles.[6] They were both put together in a way which suggests a full scale cyclic method but there is little probability that they were ever performed in the way the whole manuscripts suggest. Nevertheless the fact that they were so assembled suggests that it was felt that there was some value or need for cycles like those of York and Chester to be generated.[7] The variety of these and other dramatic forms was in part a reaction to the changes in status and interpretation of the Bible which were taking place as proponents of different kinds of faith saw the Bible in their own conflicting ways. This broadening into many kinds of drama is reflected in the scope of the present collection, and it is clear that we should not look at biblical drama solely in terms of the cycle plays.

The individual essays reflect some of the changes in belief and practice, but they also respond to development and innovation in dramatic forms. Beyond this, some of the plays are considered in terms of the religious and social exploitation of the Bible, as well as there being approaches to the controversies

---

6   The eclectic nature of N-Town and its textual diversity has recently been emphasised by Alexandra F. Johnston, "The Puzzle of the N.Town Manuscript Revisited," *Medieval English Theatre* 36 (2014): 104–23.

7   Other cities where there is some evidence – of varying strength and credibility – for cycle plays include Beverley, Coventry, Hereford, Lincoln, Newcastle-upon-Tyne and Norwich.

which enveloped them and which had an effect on how they were interpreted and used. The interaction between bibles and dramatic form brings into question the varied nature of the dramatic texts which are considered here. Whilst a dramatic text always implies a performance, the actual relationship between a given text and any performances which relate to it may be weighted towards giving instruction about how to perform it. The text may be a record of the details of a performance; or it may be expressly created to give priority to reading or studying the text, leaving the actual performance more to the readers' imaginative visualization of a performance.[8] But even beyond this latter state the text of a play may become iconic in its religious and social implications.

As far as the Bible is concerned the changes in the use of it were profound. Whereas for many years the Bible was presented in Latin to congregations, the translations into the vernacular at the Reformation, as well as the re-editing of the text itself, made it more possible for the individual Christian to study the Bible without the intermediary of the learned clergy. This gave great priority to the words themselves and was much encouraged by most Protestants. Complementary to this were the iconoclastic attacks on visual representations in churches and the evolution of a new liturgy which replaced the previous form largely based on musical settings of words from the Vulgate.

But such changes were not simple or comprehensive because ecclesiastical policy and governance took different directions over many years during which there were political alterations and reversals. In the fifteenth century the impact of Wycliffite criticism had been countered in England by the promulgation of Arundel's *Constitutions* (1409) which sought to preserve and increase the role and function of the clergy in the interpretation of theology and to reduce the role of the laity in establishing and interpreting matters of belief. The provisions of this directive included an attempt to restrain the use of the vernacular. As far as the biblical drama is concerned this attempt was not very successful since much of the invention and development of the cycle plays at York, Chester and Beverley appears to have followed.[9] However, in the middle of the sixteenth century, following Henry VIII's break with Rome, the effects upon the cyclic drama were greater. Some of the Protestant changes in belief and church practice which had been started by Henry VIII, and intensified

---

8 For a Protestant interest in modifying texts for reading rather than performance: see Tamara Atkin, "Playing with Books in John Bale's *Three Laws*," *The Year's Work in English Studies* 43 (2013): 244–46.

9 For one particular example of these changes in belief see Peter Happé, "Genre and the Fifteenth-century Drama: The Case of Thomas Chaundler's *Liber Apologeticus*," *Medium Aevum* 82 (2013): 66–80.

during the reign of his son, were reversed by Queen Mary, and then restored under Elizabeth I. The alterations to the text of the York Plays are notable for their reflection of these changes of official policy.[10] The Protestant, or rather the Calvinist objections to traditional elements in this form of drama were particularly apparent in Chester in 1572.[11] Nevertheless there was support for biblical drama as in York and Chester where the traditional plays continued to be performed and supported until the 1570s, and we may note the Protestant view expressed by Martin Bucer, Regius Professor of Divinity at Cambridge under Edward VI. He described the power of drama to

> strengthen faith in God, arouse love and desire of God and to create and increase not only admiration of piety and justice but also the horror of impiety and the sowing and fostering of every kind of evil.

But plays were to be monitored before performance "that nothing frivolous or theatrical be allowed."[12]

2 History and Politics

Most of the conflict arising over the uses and status of the Bible came relatively late in the period under review. The interest in Bible narratives and in characters familiar from biblical contexts showed itself in plays about Hester, Mary Magdalene, Jacob and Esau, and Susanna, as Sarah Carpenter notices in her essay. These plays are part of the sixteenth-century development of interludes as polemical weapons in which a didactic mode is significant and they are determined by ideological intentions. Carpenter brings out that in form these examples were very different from one another, but they all reflected a growing lay interest in the use of biblical characters and narratives. They were not, however, necessarily close to the source narrative and the dramatists were selective in their attention to these stories. Political and sectarian interests played their

---

10 See *The York Plays: A Critical Edition of the York Corpus Christi Play as recorded in British Library Additional MS 35290* ed. Richard Beadle, 2 vols., EETS s.s. 24 and 34 (Oxford: Oxford University Press, 2009–13), 2: 416–17.

11 Christopher Goodman's letter to the Archbishop of York specifies a list of what he calls "absurdities" of the old form of drama. See *REED: Cheshire including Chester*, ed. Elizabeth Baldwin, Lawrence M. Clopper and David Mills, 2 vols. (Toronto: The British Library and University of Toronto Press, 2007), 1: 144–6.

12 English version of *De Honestis Ludis* (1551) in Appendix C of Glynne Wickham, *Early English Stages, 1300–1660*, 3 vols. in 4 (London: Routledge, 1963), 2.1: 329–31.

part in the design, as in the case of *Godly Queen Hester*, which has been interpreted as a political satire on Wolsey, and in several plays in this category the dramatists expressed themselves by mixing abstract characters, drawn no doubt from precedents in the morality plays, with those in the biblical source. Carpenter's analysis reflects an uneasy relationship between the Bible and the plays, a feature which is probably determined by the delicacy, if not the inherent danger in the changing political situations which they reflected.

Greg Walker's essay has a similar interest in a political context, this time in connection with Lyndsay's *Ane Satyre of the Thrie Estaitis* in Scotland in the 1550s. The authority of the Vulgate is still a feature, and Lyndsay's attention to it is part of his presentation of the need for reform in Scottish religious affairs. His intention, however, was to incorporate such reform within traditional Catholic culture rather than to adopt a radical Protestant stance. But such a policy was difficult to bring about within the existing state of affairs, and it required political sensitivity. Walker shows that in addition Lyndsay's play reveals uneasiness about royal authority even though it is a necessary element in the improvement of religious practices. Lyndsay is exercised to preserve much of traditional Catholicism in Scotland, but his satirical intention leads him to present a grim picture of the way abuses were undermining the inherent value of the traditional faith.

3 Cycle Plays

The English cycle plays, as we have noticed, show significant interest in the Bible narratives and they are the result of great creativity in their use of them. Though only a few survive, and the number lost is hard to determine, the extant English examples share with many plays from the rest of Europe a kind of dialogue with the biblical narrative. They are the result of the work of many individual writers, most of whom probably had a clerical training and background.[13] In the surviving examples there is frequently a concern about the inclusion of non-biblical material, some of which had a longstanding place alongside the details of character and narrative which are found in the Bible. This is no doubt related to a pervasive concern about the reliability of evi-

---

13   This can be demonstrated for Arnoul Gréban's *Passion* (c. 1450), and Jean Michel's revision and expansion of it (1485). See also Johnston, "The Puzzle of the N.Town Manuscript Revisited," 118.

dence. In both Catholic and Protestant interpretations we find defence of material added to the Bible accounts.[14]

Though there are no dramatic texts surviving from Beverley, Diana Wyatt's investigation into the records and the pageant list reveals that its lost cycle had some similarities with other survivals, coming as it does from near York. She brings out local analogues and by using some iconographic parallels suggests local interests. Her results also indicate that there were some distinctive features setting some plays apart from other examples and these may be linked to such interests as they were developed around the biblical core.

The essay by Philip Butterworth on two of the *Towneley* plays about Isaac and Jacob brings out that these authors could keep very close to the biblical narratives. Working with details from the Wycliffite, Coverdale and Geneva bibles, he shows that theatrical considerations are evident in the preparation of these texts and he pays particular attention to the objectives that governed the stage directions found in them. In spite of this his observations suggest that for these two episodes at least there was a palpable theatrical purpose.

Although Butterworth does not find much that could be said to reflect sectarian demands in the plays he discusses, there is a significant contrast in the pressures which are found in some other work in this genre. The essay by Roberta Mullini on the two surviving texts (A & B) of the Norwich Grocers' Play about Adam and Eve relates to contemporary issues. Though these are the only surviving texts from what appears to have been a large-scale cycle, they were written at different times and from opposing sides of the religious divide. Both show didactic intention in their Prologues, but the later Text B is much more particular about its polemical intentions. Its title-page is explicit in pointedly asserting that the play is written "accordynge unto the Skripture," and Mullini's analysis brings out the Calvinist influence on this text, including predestination, and she identifies a concern for the readers which she does not find in Text A. It is an interesting reflection that here at Norwich the spread of Protestant interpretation was urgent enough to prompt what amounts to a re-writing of the original Catholic play, but unfortunately we do not know whether this happened for the remainder of the cycle. It may be that its disappearance

---

14   Richard Beadle has described the Catholic view in "'Devoute ymaginacioun' and the Dramatic Sense in Love's *Mirror* and the N-Town Plays," in *Nicholas Love at Waseda: Proceedings of the International Conference, 20–22 July, 1995*, ed. Shoicho Oguro, Richard Beadle and Michael G. Sargent (Cambridge: D.S. Brewer, 1997), 1–17. The Protestant justification can be found in the defence by the presenter called Appendix in *The Resurrection of Our Lord*, ed. J.D. Wilson, B. Dobell and W.W. Greg, Malone Society Reprint (Oxford: Oxford University Press, 1913), 611–15, where he admits to having "shewed our ymagenation."

is part of the story. However, in addition to the consideration of the sectarian divide, Mullini is able to draw attention to some continuity in theatrical practice.

The didactic element in the biblical plays forms part of Charlotte Steenbrugge's account of preaching in them. By fixing upon episodes about John the Baptist, who preached in the Bible narrative, she shows that there appears to have been some anxiety about having sermons on the stage, probably as a result of Arundel's *Constitutions* which were aimed in part at unlicensed preaching. Referring to French practice, she observes that the *Mystères* did indeed include sermons preached by the Baptist. This was followed in N-Town, but York and Towneley seem to embody a reluctance to do so. The difference may be the result of inconsistencies in the states of the texts. However, it does appear that at York the intentions underlying the *Constitutions* may have had some effect, especially as the only text we have dates from the 1470s and the political/religious features of that context, rather than from the sixteenth century when the Catholic-Protestant divide became more pronounced.

Newcastle is another city having limited survivals of what appears to have been a cycle. Katie Normington observes some traditional theatrical practices in the Noah play which unusually contains a temptation of Noah's Wife by Satan. Her consideration of the behaviour of the devils shows that this dramatist was aware of conventional elements in their behaviour, including their part in the Fall and the biblical episode of Pilate's Wife, which are found in some other cycles, but that there was also room for innovation. Indeed the latter is significant in the study of the biblical drama because it exemplifies one of the ways that dramatists used material which was not strictly biblical, but which could be used to enlarge upon it. Normington's essay calls attention to the way this play is concerned about the dangers of temptation and its possible effect on the audience.

The inclusion of non-biblical material is noticeable in Peter Happé's essay on plays about the Resurrection. He points out that although this is a very common topic in English and European drama, it is treated rather briefly in many of the biblical accounts and that a good deal of non-scriptural matter has traditionally been incorporated in the plays, as well as in iconographic representations. The plays discussed show a selection of ways of presenting this central event, but there remains an element of mystery about it which was probably deliberate. The episode is often concerned about the proof that the Resurrection really did take place, and this was clearly an important issue in the biblical accounts, which contained both human and supernatural evidence.

4   Dramatic Styles

Though there is still no doubt that biblical drama came in the form of large-scale plays performed in some cities, some of the essays here offer an insight into other kinds of dramatic experience which were closely or mainly associated with the Bible but had their own theatrical objectives and methods. Here the quantity of lost plays needs to be noted. It is now apparent that many kinds of local or parish plays have been lost, and a corpus of saints plays was destroyed at the Reformation. Among the extant plays we have already noticed some interludes are centred on characters from the Bible, and these form a different kind of theatrical experience because of the allegorical elements they depend upon, the types of plot they incorporate, and because they have specific, if narrower objectives. Unlike some of the cycle plays, which were closely tied to civic authority and reputation, interludes often were written about specific social issues of individual wrongs.

In marked contrast the two plays of Nicholas Grimald discussed by Stephanie Allen and Elisabeth Dutton were created in Oxford and are deeply influenced by classical models, tragic and comic, as applied to the biblical core. Their analysis brings out ways in which classical rhetoric could be used to turn the attention of the viewers inwards. The important theme of witness and testimony is underlined by the psychological complexity of some of the characters and the linguistic characteristics of their speeches. Theological issues appear in the revelation of human depravity, and the selection of scriptural detail gives emphasis upon the value of Christ's body. In these learned plays Grimald adds to such detail and shows that he thought it was acceptable to adapt the biblical material to his own objectives. It is noticeable that his methodology contrasts greatly with much other biblical drama and that he pursues his ends with rigour.

The orientation of *The Croxton Play of the Sacrament* is so remarkable and inventive that one might understandably be eager to know whether there were others like it in its original combination of theatrical experiences. David Bevington shows that some of its comic elements are linked to the Bible and that its action parodies the Crucifixion. Central to it is the contemporary concern about the Real Presence. The play relies on an awareness of the scriptural narrative and alludes to it in places, including the miracle of the Resurrection. In common with some other plays treated in this collection, it is concerned about scepticism, and the threat of heresy. The links with theatrical practices elsewhere, including the quack doctor, are palpable and Bevington analyses the staging which had three areas of action, as well as the spaces between them. He pointedly associates the final conversion of the Jews with the liturgy, noting that the dramatist was working with an interaction of liturgy and drama.

The performance reading by Bob Godfrey of two episodes from the Towneley plays involving Herod gives a theatrical view of these plays and demonstrates the versatility which could be exercised in the treatment of biblical material. The individual episodes in the Towneley collection are remarkable for the variety in their different staging methods which are adopted by individual dramatists, and these two plays are no exception. Centring on the character of Herod, Godfrey is able to demonstrate the complex staging required together with the comic effectiveness, in a farcical mode, of the audience's superior knowledge which is based upon their biblical awareness. He is particularly interested in the self-presentation by Herod in the course of which the language and verse he uses help to intensify his isolation as a phoney king. Although this tyrant is evil and dangerously duplicitous, Godfrey argues that in this case the characterisation points to human fallibility and that this is in marked contrast to the tradition manifest in other plays.

The actualities of performance are a significant element in Philip Crispin's analysis of two York plays he produced in the Holy Trinity Church, Hull. Using an approach through a number of modern theories about the nature of theatrical embodiment, he shows that these texts deal with violence and power and the rhetoric associated with it. He sees the two plays as bringing together devotional and political experience and he shows that his directorial decisions sought to link the medieval and the modern in ways which destabilized the practice and abuse of power. His discussion interrogates the nature of the medieval exploitation of the festive and carnivalesque and he reflects in particular upon the ways in which characters drawn from the biblical account embody persistent religious and social functions.

In his essay on parts of the N-Town Passion sequence James McBain is concerned with the dramatization of Mary. Her interaction with other characters shows both the generation of affective piety and the ways in which this particular dramatist shapes his play as he seeks to manage its effect upon the audience. McBain perceives that the response generated in the audience is different from that of the characters who talk to Mary. The development of source material from Nicholas Love's *Mirror of the Blessed Life of Jesus Christ* is managed with acute theological awareness and with an awareness of dramatic coherence which goes beyond that of the other texts dealing with this situation.

5 Audience

Clifford Davidson's approach is largely through the impact of biblical drama on the audience. The evocation of memory, collective or individual, is seen as a having a key function in the way people respond to the Bible. Through the perception of what was already familiar, links between the past and present are generated. In this network iconographical material has a significant function in reinforcing the awareness. The involvement of the audience, made up, as it is, of many individuals, is such that they may be considered not so much as bystanders as having complicity with what is portrayed through the characterisation and action. The view of history presented to the audience included Doomsday.

The complexity in the composition of audiences is noted by Margaret Rogerson in her discussion of the interrelationship between them and the actors. She takes account of the emotional effect and the close association of some witnesses to the events and experiences portrayed in the plays. It is as though some were living the events and the visual experience could stimulate meditation, including the practice of *imitatio Christi*. But this intimate response goes along with shock over crude comedy and laughter over justice. She considers hostile reaction, especially that of Christopher Goodman at Chester in his attack upon them from a Protestant standpoint in 1571–72, at a time when the tradition of the cycle plays was well established and the attack upon it was becoming more vociferous.

The complexity of audience response is further examined by Garrett Epp, who sees in it a capacity to create experience of theology, as well as generating belief. Although he notices there was some traditional objection to drama, his emphasis upon how performance enhances religious experience by enacting the biblical material embraces a number of processes including the creation of illusion and meditation and the stimulation of affective piety. But he shows there is separation from the enacted material brought about by didactic and meditative distancing. His interest in how belief is induced is fundamental to the experience of the audience.

6 Staging Scripture

In spite of the loss of so many plays from the period under review this collection of essays may give some insight into the complexities of the ways in which dramatists responded to and used biblical material. Because of the centrality of the Bible in Christian thought and experience it was inevitable that it should provide subject matter that was vital and irresistible but also that dramatists should aspire to mould its contents to suit their requirements.

To bring together the complexities of 'the Bible' and 'drama' is a Herculean task. The editors would like to thank the contributors for their willingness to commit themselves to exploring the relationship between them.

Bibliography

Atkin, Tamara. "Playing with Books in John Bale's *Three Laws*." *The Year's Work in English Studies* 43 (2013): 243–61.

Baldwin, Elizabeth, Lawrence M. Clopper and David Mills, eds. REED: *Cheshire including Chester*, 2 vols. Toronto: The British Library and University of Toronto Press, 2007.

Beadle, Richard. "'Devoute ymaginacioun' and the Dramatic Sense in Love's *Mirror* and the N-Town Plays," 1–17. In *Nicholas Love at Waseda: Proceedings of the International Conference, 20–22 July, 1995*, edited by Shoicho Oguro, Richard Beadle and Michael G. Sargent. Cambridge: D.S. Brewer, 1997.

———, ed. *The York Plays: A Critical Edition of the York Corpus Christi Play as recorded in British Library Additional MS 35290*, 2 vols., EETS s.s. 23–24. Oxford: Oxford University Press, 2009–13.

Happé, Peter. "Genre and the Fifteenth-century Drama: The Case of Thomas Chaundler's *Liber Apologeticus*." *Medium Aevum* 82 (2013): 66–80.

Hill-Vásquez, Heather. *Sacred Players: The Politics of Response in the Middle English Drama*. Washington, D.C.: Catholic University of America Press, 2007.

Johnston, Alexandra F. "The Puzzle of the N.Town Manuscript Revisited." *Medieval English Theatre* 36 (2014): 104–23.

Kelly, Erin E. "Doubt and Religious Drama across Sixteenth-Century England, or Did the Middle Ages believe in Their Plays?", 47–63. In *The Chester Cycle in Context 1555–1575*, edited by Jessica Dell, David Klausner and Helen Ostovich. Farnham: Ashgate, 2012.

Lerud, Theodore K. *Memory, Images and the English Corpus Christi Drama*. New York: Palgrave Macmillan, 2008.

Muir, Lynette. *The Biblical Drama of Medieval Europe*. Cambridge: Cambridge University Press, 1995.

White, Paul Whitfield. "The Bible as Play in Reformation England," 87–115. In *The Cambridge History of British Theatre*, vol. 1: *Origins to 1660*, edited by Jane Milling and Peter Thomson. Cambridge: Cambridge University Press, 2004.

Wickham, Glynne. *Early English Stages, 1300–1660*, 3 vols. in 4. London: Routledge, 1963.

Wilson, J.D., B. Dobell and W.W. Greg, eds. *The Resurrection of Our Lord*. Malone Society Reprint. Oxford: Oxford University Press, 1913.

CHAPTER 1

Performing the Scriptures: Biblical Drama after the Reformation

Sarah Carpenter

Abstract

From the late 1530s, when the translation of the Scriptures into English was authorised, there rapidly developed a new body of lay Bible-readers with new practices of reading and interpretation of the Bible. While the traditional biblical drama of the late middle ages was gradually suppressed or abandoned, a new generation of plays on scriptural subjects emerged, written by and addressed to these new readers. This paper explores the ways in which mid-sixteenth-century playwrights responded to the lively culture of Bible-reading in the early years of the Reformation. Increased focus on the literal, social and ethical implications of biblical stories guided playwrights towards a greatly expanded body of powerful narratives, which raised challenging human issues, allowing strong theatrical interpretation in relation to contemporary concerns. But the new theatrical strategies do not always sit quite comfortably with the special status accorded by Protestantism to the Bible as the word of God. These Reformation plays begin to suggest crucial tensions between drama and doctrine, inadvertently reinforcing the gradually increasing Protestant unease with the stage as a forum in which to address the Bible.

Keywords

theatre and the bible – biblical interludes – reformation – lay bible-reading – protestant theatre – mid-sixteenth century plays

Introduction

> That moste precious iuell, the worde of God is disputed, rimed, song, and iangeled in every Alehouse and Tauerne.
> (HENRY VIII, 1545)[1]

---

1 Henry VIII's speech in Parliament, 24 Dec. 1545: Edward Hall, *The Vnion of the Two Noble and Illustre Famelies of Lancastre [and] Yorke* (London: Richard Grafton, 1548), fol. xxx.iiii[r].

With gods word was euery mans mouth occupied, of that were all songes, enterludes, & plaies made.

(ROBERT VAUX, *1582*)[2]

Comments and memories like these frame the Reformation as a time of new and vibrant public engagement with the Bible that, for good or ill, animated drama along with all cultural interaction. Henry VIII in his 1545 address to parliament reflected anxiously on the popular liberties taken since the vernacular Scriptures were made widely available, while Robert Vaux looked back nostalgically to what he saw as a golden age in the reigns of Henry and his son Edward. It is hard for us to judge now quite what the theatrical scene of this period offered, since only a tiny proportion of its plays survive.[3] But we have enough to suggest that playwrights did, indeed, begin to use the Bible in different and sometimes newly provocative theatrical ways. A number of the new biblical plays written from 1530 onwards engaged directly, often vehemently, with the ideological issues of the Reformation, and these have been explored in valuable work which has been done on the drama as an active instrument of religious and political debate.[4] But Bible stories also formed the basis for a range of plays with a less explicit, or less combative interest in promoting religious reform. In this paper I aim to explore what the scriptural plays of the mid-sixteenth century can reveal, not about Reformation polemics, but about the changing modes of lay engagement with the Bible, that "central cultural text of the Reformation."[5]

---

[2] Robert Vaux's Preface to Martin Chemnitz, *A Discouerie and Batterie of the Great Fort of Vnwritten Traditions* (London: Thomas Purfoot and William Pounsonbie, 1582), fol. Nii^r.

[3] References to the activities of court interluders, in particular, testify to a flourishing dramatic scene whose repertoire is now unknown. Revels accounts, as well as diplomatic correspondence and Hall's *Chronicle*, record many play performances about which we have no information.

[4] See for example the influential studies by David M. Bevington, *Tudor Drama and Politics: A Critical Approach to Topical Meaning* (Cambridge, MA: Harvard University Press, 1968); Paul Whitfield White, *Theatre and Reformation: Protestantism, Patronage, and Playing in Tudor England* (Cambridge: Cambridge University Press, 1993). For a wider survey of biblical plays see Ruth Blackburn, *Biblical Drama under the Tudors* (The Hague: Mouton, 1971).

[5] Bruce Gordon, "The Changing Face of Protestant History and Identity in Sixteenth Century Europe," in *Protestant History and Identity in Sixteenth Century Europe: The Later Reformation*, 2 vols., ed. Bruce Gordon (Aldershot: Ashgate, 1996), 1: 4.

2   Reading the Bible

Since both playwrights and audiences brought their own experiences of the Bible to sixteenth-century plays, we should consider the climate of Bible-education that led to the noisy discussion Henry VIII and Vaux seem to have perceived. In the first decades of the sixteenth century, humanist scholarship and early Protestant theology were already influencing the understanding and reception of the Scriptures among European clerics and scholars.[6] But for most lay people in England probably the most significant and noticeable change from late-medieval practice was the translation of the Bible into the vernacular and the rapidly spreading encouragement to read it. It is of course tempting to imagine a tidy step-change from a Roman Catholic model in which lay people learned of the Latin Vulgate Bible primarily through clerical paraphrase and devotional commentary,[7] imagery, theatre, and liturgy, to a Protestant model in which individual readers encountered English translations of the Scriptures and interpreted for themselves the words they found, without intervention by a Church hierarchy. But while this may characterise retrospectively some important elements of truth, the picture at the time was inevitably far more complicated and uncertain, more partial, gradual, blurred and shifting, than such a simplified oppositional account suggests.

Like the Reformation itself, the official spread of direct access to the English Bible during the sixteenth century was somewhat fitful. In 1529 'heretical books', including Tyndale's English translations of the Scriptures, were banned.[8] By the following year Henry VIII was already beginning to consider an approved English translation,[9] and in 1536 the clergy were formally enjoined to make "the hole Byble, bothe in Latin, and also in Englyshe" available in every parish church "for euery man that wyll, to loke and rede theron, and shal discourage no man from the reding of any part of the Bible, either in Latin or in Englishe,

---

6   For a helpfully concise overview of Reformation biblical scholarship see Alister E. McGrath, *Reformation Thought: An Introduction* (Oxford: Blackwell, 1999 [3rd ed.]), Chapter 8: "The Return to Scripture," 145–65.

7   The best example of devotional paraphrase is Nicholas Love's early fifteenth-century English translation of the widely popular *Meditationes Vitae Christi*, *The Mirror of the Blessed Life of Jesus Christ*, which continued to be circulated up to the eve of the Reformation, with eight printed editions between 1484 and 1525.

8   *Tudor Royal Proclamations*, 3 vols., ed. Paul L. Hughes and James F. Larkin (New Haven and London: Yale University Press, 1964), 1: no. 122, 181–86.

9   Ibid., 1: no. 129, 193–97, where Henry VIII states, at page 196, that once controversy is controlled he may be minded to consider a vernacular translation.

but rather comforte exhorte, and admonishe euery man to rede the same."[10] Parishioners should be urged, however, that "they doo in no wyse styffely or eygrely contende or stryue one with an other about the same, but referre the declaration of those places, that be in controuersie, to the iudgement of them that be better lerned." This became the basis of a long series of injunctions to the clergy promoting the accessibility of the English Bible through the rest of the century. It contains three key proposals: that the Bible in English should be freely available in parish churches; that the clergy had a duty to encourage all to read; but that readers should not enter into controversy about the Scriptures.

These provisions are repeated throughout the reigns of Henry, Edward and Elizabeth although with notable changes of emphasis, as the balance shifted between free encouragement and a cautiously restrictive approach to personal reading. The early Protestant reformers, although eager to promote individual vernacular Bible-reading, had very soon come to distrust individual Bible-interpretation by the new lay readers.[11] Under Henry VIII, readers were increasingly warned against such personal interpretation of the Scriptures; Cranmer's 1540 Preface to the Great Bible, the first authorised English translation, asserted "It is not fitte ... for euery man to dispute the hygh questions of diuinite" and urged any puzzled reader to "submyt thy selfe to the iudgement of those that are godly learned in Christ Iesus."[12] In 1543 the range of those permitted to read the English Bible was seriously restricted, the Act for the Advancement of True Religion laying down that "no woomen [noble and gentlewomen excepted] nor artificers prentises journeymen serving men of the degrees of yeomen or undre, husbandemen nor laborers shall reade ... the Byble or Newe Testament in Englishe, to himselfe or any other pryvatelie or openlie."[13] While Edward VI repealed this measure in 1547, his own injunctions laid down that Erasmus's Gospel *Paraphrases* should be placed in churches alongside the English Bible, thus tacitly acknowledging the need for an

---

10   *Iniunctions gyuen by th* [sic] *auctoritie of the kynges highnes to the clergie of this his realme* (London: Thomas Berthelet, [1538?]), fol. 3ʳ.
11   See McGrath, *Reformation Thought*, 161–65.
12   Thomas Cranmer, *The Byble in Englyshe that Is to saye the content of al the Holy Scrypture, both of the Olde, and Newe Testament, with a Prologe therinto, made by the Reuerende Father in God, Thomas Archbysshop of Cantorbury* (London: Rychard Grafton, 1540), Prologue, fol. +iiᵛ.
13   *The Statutes of the Realm Printed by Command of His Majesty King George the Third ... from Original Records and Authentic Manuscripts*, 4 vols., ed. Great Britain Record Commission (Medieval and Early Modern Sources Online, 2007), 3 (1509–45): 896, accessed, 19 April 2015, on the TannerRitchie publishers page, <http://www.tannerritchie.com/memso.php>.

approved commentary to interpret the Scriptures to independent readers. Following Mary Tudor's Roman Catholic reign, Elizabeth reinstated Edward's provisions on her accession; these then remained in force unchanged throughout her 45-year reign, suggesting that lay Bible-reading gradually stabilised as royal intervention waned. Nonetheless, anxieties about how individuals might and should engage with the Scriptures continued, from the Protestant clergy if not from the throne. Kate Narveson offers evidence "of ongoing, earnest but anxious attempts to delimit [lay Scripture reading's] proper scope, to provide tools to ensure proper edification, and yet at the same time to close off unsuitable avenues and discourage presumptuous ventures."[14] By the end of the sixteenth century, then, personal access to the Scriptures appears to have become readily accepted, but personal interpretation remains much more suspect. Bible-reading is hedged about with guidance and instruction, persuasion and advice.

For the biblical drama, the nature of this guidance may be at least as important as the direct accessibility of the Scriptures. It is therefore worth exploring how the new readers of the English Bible were encouraged to read, and how that encouragement might differ from pre-Reformation Bible-teaching. The emphasis of advice, and assumptions about readers, clearly change in the early sixteenth century under the pressure of the Reformation, a shift that is plain if we compare two key vernacular paraphrases. Nicholas Love, the fifteenth-century English translator of the hugely popular *Meditationes Vitae Christi*, explained the aim of its devotional meditations on the gospel narratives, which was to

> sette in mynde þe ymage of crystes Incarnacion passion & Resurreccion so that a symple soule þat kan not þenke bot bodyes or bodily þinges mowe haue somwhat accordynge vnto is affecion where wiþ he maye fede & stire his deuocion.[15]

The Prologue urged readers "þat coueytest to fele treuly þe fruyt of þis boke, þou most with all þi þought & alle þin entent, in þat manere make þe in þi soule present to þoo þinges þat bene here writen seyd or done of oure lord

---

14   Kate Narveson, "'Their Practice Bringeth Little Profit:' Clerical Anxieties About Lay Scripture Reading in Early Modern England," in *Private and Domestic Devotion in Early Modern Britain*, ed. Jessica Martin and Alec Ryrie (Farnham: Ashgate, 2012), 166.

15   Nicholas Love, *The Mirror of the Blessed Life of Jesus Christ: A Full Critical Edition*, based on Cambridge University Library Additional MSS 6578 and 6686 with Introduction, Notes and Glossary, ed. Michael G. Sargent (Exeter: University of Exeter Press, 2005), 10.

Jesu."[16] The purpose of reading is thus presented as affective and devotional: the reader is to cultivate an emotive and empathetic projection of the self into the image the text presents. Love is even explicit that it is appropriate to "ymagine & þenk diuerse words & dedes of him & oþer, þat we fynde not written" in order to stir "symple soules to þe loue of god."[17] Nicholas Udall's 1548 preface to the English translation of Erasmus's *Paraphrases* of the New Testament offers a very different view of the aim of Gospel paraphrase. It is to "make the sentence open, cleare, plaine, & familiar, whiche otherwise should perchaunce seme bare, vnfruitful harde, straunge, tough, obscure, & derke to be vnderstanded."[18] Udall assumes the reader is searching the text for intellectual understanding, for "pure & perfeict knowlage of Gods worde."[19] The aim is not so much an affective devotional experience, as 'the priuate edifying of euery one particularely, and also for the enstruccion & teaching of eche other in common."[20]

A new suspicion of text as image, and of affective rather than rational responses, thus seems to inflect the ways in which lay sixteenth-century readers are encouraged to approach the Scriptures. Tyndale had already argued that the Bible was there for 'use': "Though we read the scripture and babble of it never so much, yet if we know not the use of it ... it profiteth us nothing at all."[21] Various metaphors support this utilitarian vision, Cranmer's Preface in particular arguing: "as mallettes, hammars, sawes, chesylles, axes, and hatchettes, be the tooles of [craftsmen's] occupacyon. So bene the bokes of the prophetes, & apostelles, & all holye wryte inspired by the holy ghost, the instrumentes of oure saluacyon."[22] Salvation was the prime function of these tools:

---

16   Ibid., 12–13.
17   Ibid., 10–11. For further discussion see Richard Beadle, "'Devoute ymaginacioun' and the Dramatic Sense in Love's *Mirror* and the N-Town Plays," in *Nicholas Love at Waseda: Proceedings of the International Conference, 20–22 July, 1995*, ed. Shoicho Oguro, Richard Beadle, and Michael G. Sargent (Cambridge: D.S. Brewer, 1997), 1–17.
18   Nicholas Udall, "Translator to the Reader," in Desiderius Erasmus, *The First Tome or Volume of the Paraphrase of Erasmus Vpon the Newe Testamente*, ed. Nicholas Udall (London: Edward Whitchurche, 1548), fol. xiiii^r.
19   Ibid., fol. xiii^v.
20   Ibid., fol. xiiii^r.
21   William Tyndale, "A Prologue Showing the Use of the Scripture," in *Tyndale's Old Testament: Being the Pentateuch of 1530, Joshua to 2 Chronicles of 1537, and Jonah*, ed. David Daniell (New Haven and London: Yale University Press, 1992), 7.
22   Cranmer, *Byble in Englyshe*, fol. +i^v. Erasmus, *Paraphrase*, fol. Ciii^v, compares the Bible to works "concernyng the preseruacion or restoryng of health, or the waye to increace worldely substaunce, or touchyng any other facultie whiche maketh only for worldly commodities," presenting it as the ultimate self-help book.

Protestant doctrine asserted that salvation came by faith rather than works and that faith was found, *sola scriptura*, in the words of the Bible. But this emphasis on practical use, combined with a suspicion of the imagery and allegorical interpretations of the middle ages, also led to a focus on the purity and accessibility of literal meaning, the "one simple literal sense whose light the owls cannot abide."[23] The emphasis on the literal accompanies an increasing stress on the social and ethical, as much as the spiritual, edification of Bible-reading. Doctrinally, readers were encouraged to be passive, accepting interpretation offered by the authorities and avoiding debate about the Bible's meaning.[24] But at a more literal level they should actively seek in the Scriptures examples of how they should live their own lives in the world.

The obligations imposed on readers by the royal injunctions placing Bibles in churches are explicitly indicative of this purpose. All Christians should read the Bible so that "they may the better knowe their dueties to God, to their souereigne lord the Kyng, and theyr neighbour."[25] God may come first, but duties as obedient and socially productive citizens are very close behind. Readers were advised to take the figures of Old and New Testament narratives as exempla, showing them how to behave and what to avoid. Cranmer's Preface to the Great Bible is eloquent on the social lessons it provides:

> Herin maye princes learne howe to gouerne their subiectes: Subiectes obedience, loue & dreade to their princes. Husbandes, howe they shuld behaue them vnto their wyfes: howe to educate their chyldren & seruauntes. And contrary, the wyfes, chyldren, & seruauntes may knowe theyr dutye to their husbandes, parentes & masters.[26]

The Bible is presented as a guide to life in this world as much as it is to the next. Individual readers are exhorted to take its lessons personally, as Tyndale urges: "As thou readest therefore think that every syllable pertaineth to thine own self."[27] While this partly echoes the advice of the *Meditationes* to "make þe in þi soule present" to the events of the biblical narrative, the process now envisaged is more didactic, less emotionally performative and more consciously

---

23   Tyndale, "To the Reader," in Daniell, *Tyndale's Old Testament*, 3.
24   See Narveson, "Clerical Anxieties," 167–68.
25   *Iniunccions Geuen by the Moste Excellent Prince, Edward the Sixte by the Grace of God, Kyng of England, Fraunce, and Irelande: Defendor of the Faythe, and in Earthe Vnder Christ, of the Churche of Englande and of Ireland the Supreme Hedde: to all and singuler his louyng subiectes, aswell of the Clergie, as of the Laietie* (London: Richard Grafton, 1547), fol. bi[r].
26   Cranmer, *Byble in Englyshe*, fol. +ii[r].
27   Tyndale, "Prologue," in Daniell, *Tyndale's Old Testament*, 8.

ethical. Readers are not invited to imagine and project themselves into the affective experience of biblical figures, but to learn ethical lessons by making reasoned comparisons of the implications for their own lives.

These lessons were not only personal. As scholars have suggested, this is an age in which the Bible came to be understood as providing newly direct parallels to current social and political situations.[28] Ordinary readers of the Scriptures were guided to read contemporary events through the lens of the Bible. Tyndale insisted:

> go to and read the stories of the Bible ... for according to those examples shall it go with thee and all men until the world's end. ... As it went with their kings and rulers, so shall it go with ours. As it was with their common people, so shall it be with ours.[29]

Readers are invited to see biblical narratives as echoing contemporary situations. This is the age in which Henry VIII and Edward VI were regularly addressed as Josiah or Hezekiah, as Elizabeth was later imaged as Deborah; or where, at the other end of the spectrum, a sample law case illustrating complex inheritance issues between twins might be named 'Jacob and Esau'.[30] Lay readers will have found biblical exempla giving imaginative shape to many aspects of their lives, testifying to what Bruce Gordon has named an "existential bond which early modern people felt with the characters of biblical narratives."[31]

All this suggests a body of playwrights and audiences with a lively knowledge of Bible stories and teaching, but with a different kind of engagement with that knowledge from earlier times. The broad shift in emphasis from image to word, the affective to the reasoned, divine mystery to social ethics, clearly had implications for new forms of drama. The changes must have happened gradually and partially, and there will have been for much of the sixteenth century wide variation in individuals' relationship with the Bible. But it would not be surprising if the new biblical plays started to offer different

---

28 See for example: Gordon, "Changing Face;" Peter Matheson, "The Reformation," in *The Blackwell Companion to the Bible and Culture*, ed. John F.A Sawyer (Oxford: Blackwell, 2006), 69–84.
29 Tyndale, "Prologue," in Daniell, *Tyndale's Old Testament*, 11.
30 Christopher Bradshaw, "David or Josiah? Old Testament Kings as Exemplars in Edwardian Religious Polemic," in Gordon, *Protestant History*, 2: 77–90; *Readings and Moots at the Inns of Court in the Fifteenth Century*, 2 vols., ed. Samuel E. Thorne and J.H. Baker (London, Selden Society, 1990), 2: 17.
31 Gordon, "Changing Face," 4.

theatrical experiences of scriptural material from the drama that had evolved through the later middle ages.

3   Biblical Drama

The first flurry of new Bible plays, unsurprisingly, rode on the movement towards religious reform. Biblical drama was drawn into a new combative role in the 1530s, as part of Thomas Cromwell's campaign against the papacy. Recognising that Roman Catholic teaching was successfully spread partly through being "plaied in playes before the ignoraunt people," Cromwell adopted drama as an important channel of anti-papal persuasion for those same audiences.[32] The most prolific of the playwrights he patronised for this purpose was John Bale, whose fiercely anti-Catholic plays of the 1530s included many which were scripturally based. Of those that survive, one, the *Three Laws of Nature, Moses and Christ*, offers a strikingly new kind of biblical dramaturgy: rather than enacting a Bible narrative, it develops a lively satiric allegory drawing on various popular theatrical forms, to present a unified Protestant overview and interpretation of the teaching of the Bible as a whole.[33] But while this play offers a new approach to dramatizing the Bible, many of Bale's scriptural interludes follow more traditional dramatic strategies: titles of his lost plays suggest a series on Christ's life echoing the medieval 'cycle', and the surviving *God's Promises*, *John Baptist's Preaching* and *The Temptation of our Lord* all dramatize episodes familiar from popular late-medieval drama.[34] These plays, however, are distinctly less narrative in focus than the traditional drama; far more striking are the doctrinal polemic informing the dialogue, and the satiric identification of the Roman Catholic clergy with the opponents of Christ. Many other Reformist plays similarly co-opt Bible narratives to challenge and attack their confessional opponents. At around this time, Scotland also saw performances of what sound like traditional New Testament plays adapted for Reformist purposes. In Stirling in the mid-1530s a "Historye of Christis Passioun" was played in which, according to John Knox, "all thingis war so levely expressed" that "the verray

---

[32]   Sydney Anglo, "An Early Tudor Programme for Plays and Other Demonstrations against the Pope," *Journal of the Warburg and Courtauld Institutes* 20 (1957): no. 1/2, 176–79; for Cromwell's campaign see White, *Theatre and Reformation*, 13–15.

[33]   John Bale, *Three Laws*, in *The Complete Plays of John Bale*, 2 vols., ed. Peter Happé (Cambridge: Brewer, 1985), 2: 65–124; for dramaturgy see White, *Theatre and Reformation*, 30–32.

[34]   See Blackburn, *Biblical Drama*, 36–63; Happé, *Complete Plays of John Bale*, 1: 12–13.

sempill people understood ... that as the ... obstinate Pharisyes persuaded the people to refuise Christ Jesus ... so did the Bischoppes, and men called Religious, blynd the people."[35]

After the 1530s, however, biblical playwrights mostly moved away from the existing models, although there are some signs of Protestant moves to recuperate the traditional civic drama. This is perhaps most explicitly laid out in the "Late Banns" written for the 1575 revival of the Chester plays. These Banns apologetically excuse the early playwright for departing from the Scriptures, in "interminglinge ... some thinges not warranted by anye wrytte," while justifying the original role of the earlier plays in giving access to the Bible since:

> These storyes of the testament at this tyme, you knowe,
> In a common Englishe tonge [were] never reade nor harde. (ll. 21–22)[36]

There were, too, at least some continuing initiatives to rewrite traditional biblical drama. Thomas Ashton, for example, the reforming headmaster of Shrewsbury Grammar School, wrote a number of plays performed in the 1560s, including one referred to as *The Passion of Christ*.[37] Since this was performed in the traditional playfield outside the town to a public audience of thousands, and apparently extended across "all the holly daies" of Whitsun, it seems to have deliberately imitated the forms, location and occasion of Shrewsbury's pre-Reformation drama.[38]

No known text of Ashton's play survives; but a possible candidate, or at least an analogy, might be found in an incomplete late sixteenth/early seventeenth-century manuscript now published as *The Resurrection of Our Lord*.[39]

---

35   Anna Jean Mill, *Mediaeval Plays in Scotland* (Edinburgh, William Blackwood and Sons, 1927), 291. At Dundee a little later a play of the beheading of John the Baptist also "carped roughlie the abuses and corruptions of the Papists." Ibid., 175.

36   "The Late Banns," in R.M. Lumiansky, David Mills, and Richard Rastall, *The Chester Mystery Cycle: Essays and Documents* (Chapel Hill and London: University of North Carolina Press, 1983), 285–95, ll. 11–12, 21–22. For processes of Protestant revision, see ibid., 37–40.

37   *Records of Early English Drama: Shropshire*, 2 vols., ed. J. Alan B. Somerset (Toronto: University of Toronto Press, 1994), 1: 379–80.

38   Ibid., 1: 214.

39   *The Resurrection of Our Lord*, ed. John Dover Wilson, Malone Society Reprints (London: Oxford University Press, 1912) references to this edition; Karen Elaine Sawyer, "The Resurrection of Our Lord: A Study and Dual-Text Edition" (PhD thesis, University of Toronto, 2001). Sawyer observes the analogy and helpfully discusses the first known provenance of the manuscript which, although reaching back only to the mid-nineteenth century, was from a bookseller in Oswestry, near to Shrewsbury. It has not, as far as I know, previously

Its fragments record parts of the "first dayes playe" and "Seconde dayes playe" of a drama whose cast-list and narrative broadly resemble those of plays from the Chester, York and N-Town manuscripts. The dialogue, however, articulates elements of Reformed doctrine and its expositor, Appendix, offers explicitly Protestant commentary on the play's and the audience's relationship with the Bible. Commenting on the stratagems of the "Bishopps" Annas and Caiaphas, for example, Appendix reflects on the need for direct access to the Scripture, without the mediation of clerics:

> woulde God their were non such now wch doth plaie ye same
> which diswayes ye people, for reading of the scripture
> lest it make them Heretikes vnlesse they have a *Doctor*
> ...
> when the worde yt selfe, doth ravishe much better
> then the words of them doe, which doe expounde ytt. (ll. 311–17)

The relationship of the play to "the worde yt selfe" is later carefully explained, to prevent any misunderstanding by the audience. After a scene showing Christ's appearance to Peter, Appendix intervenes:

> We nowe have noe scripture, doth teach vs such appearance
> as we have made of Christ (to *Peter*) in this order
> but that we gather this, even of the circumstance
> both of St *Luke* his wordes, and of St *Paules* together
> ...
> The rest you must then attribute, vnto our invention. (ll. 590–612)

Though traditional in form, this play is thus far more concerned than earlier drama to alert its audience to the distance between its own representation and the word of God in the New Testament. It even seems to expect that spectators might cross-check what they see on stage against the biblical narrative and spot divergences. As far as we can tell from the incomplete manuscript, the play appears to concentrate on conveying to the audience the accuracy of scriptural events and doctrinal explanations of their significance, while offering little of the affective engagement of the spectators in the grief of the Magdalen, or in Thomas's tactile encounter with Christ's wounds, that earlier

---

been suggested that it might contain parts of Ashton's play but its style, date and provenance are all suggestive.

Bible plays worked hard to arouse.[40] Very similar dramatic forms are therefore generating a different mode of understanding and of relating to the Scriptures.

Most of the surviving biblical drama of the sixteenth century, however, moves away from these traditional forms, developing different strategies to address the new purposes, as we find in the heightened debate and active controversy of the 1530s. In 1538 John Hussee, the steward of Lord Lisle, the Governor of Calais, undertook to source a play-script and costumes for an interlude for the Lisles' household. He was dubious about one specific request from Lady Lisle – "these new ecclesiastical matters will be hard to come by" –, explaining a day or two later that "I will do my best to get some of these new Scripture matters, but they be very dear; they asketh above xx^s for an Interlude."[41] We know nothing more about these "Scripture matters," although the date might suggest that they were part of Cromwell's anti-papal propaganda. This picture is complicated, however, by the sympathies of Lady Lisle, who initiated Hussee's search: it was well-known that she was "given to be a little papish," making it unlikely that she would willingly patronise plays like those of Bale.[42] It is possible that biblical plays were deployed on both sides of the religious debate, although official pressure would certainly have been on Lady Lisle to avoid any overtly Roman Catholic interlude. More probably, as with many aspects of the early Reformation, the discussion was less firmly polarised than it appears in retrospect. What does seem clear from Hussee's remarks is that the new drama presenting "Scripture matters" was seen as much talked-about, innovative, fashionable, and probably controversial.

The theatrical context of Hussee's commission is also suggestive: these are interludes, apparently designed and expensively marketed for performance in private households or other indoor settings, with the Bible dramatized not as in the past, primarily to promote traditional and consensual issues of faith, but to explore new territory and challenges. And this sets a model for most of the sixteenth century. The surviving sixteenth-century biblical plays suggest the dominance of relatively brief and portable interludes, offered to relatively small and selected audiences. As the century progresses the focus of these plays diversifies: Protestant doctrines and theology may be expounded, moral

---

40 See, for example, the speeches in the York plays of the Carpenters (ll. 270–87), the Winedrawers (ll. 110–25) and the Scriveners (ll.97–124, 169–86) in *The York Plays: A Critical Edition of the York Corpus Christi Play as Recorded in British Library Additional MS 35290*, 2 vols., ed. Richard Beadle, EETS s.s. 23–24 (Oxford: Oxford University Press, 2009–13).

41 *The Lisle Letters*, ed. Muriel St Clare Byrne, 6 vols. (Chicago: University of Chicago Press, 1981), 5: no. 1242.

42 Ibid., 4: 408. See Diarmaid MacCulloch, *Thomas Cranmer: A Life* (New Haven, CT, and London: Yale University Press, 1996), 111, 198.

or legal issues explored, theatrically compelling stories dramatized. These interludes draw on the Bible to engage not so much with the unquestioned and unchanging mysteries of a universal faith as with more particular questions and conflicts of the here and now.

In the new climate we might expect questions to have arisen about the propriety of putting the Scriptures on stage. But the early Reformers, including Luther himself, were not comprehensively antagonistic either to drama itself, or to the dramatization of the Bible.[43] Mid-century English legislation, brought in to control the content of new interludes, never mentions the Bible itself as theatrically problematic, a contrast with the situation in Scotland where a Kirk injunction of 1574 declares "no Clerk playes, comedies or tragedies be made of the Canonicall Scripture," since performance "induceth and bringeth with it a contempt and profanation of the same."[44] In England, however, general Protestant opinion was not against the performance of biblical drama, although cautious about how it handled its material. This may lie behind the strikingly new choice of scriptural subjects. Medieval biblical plays tended to dramatize a very select group of stories, focusing largely on the life of Christ, especially the Passion.[45] The new interludes, conversely, are dominated by Old Testament stories. Of some twenty-six lost and surviving plays whose titles indicate biblical topics, fifteen present Old Testament episodes.[46] Ranging more widely through the Bible, these plays tend to choose previously unfamiliar episodes: apart from plays on *Abraham's Sacrifice* (an English translation of Beza's French original) and *Jacob and Esau*, all the Old Testament subjects appear new to English drama. The playwrights also disproportionally favour episodes drawn from books which had recently come to be classified as apocryphal; of the five surviving Old Testament interludes in English, three are

---

[43] For Reformist attitudes to drama see Howard B. Norland, *Drama in Early Tudor Britain, 1485–1558* (Lincoln, NE, and London: University of Nebraska Press, 1995), 128–45. Tyndale even speaks admiringly of episodes of the Old Testament which present "the circumstances and virtue of [Christ's] death so plainly as if we should play his passion on a scaffold or in a stage play openly before the eyes of the people" (Daniell, *Tyndale's Old Testament*, 146).

[44] Mill, *Mediaeval Plays in Scotland*, 93, n. 2.

[45] See Pamela M. King, *The York Mystery Cycle and the Worship of the City*, Westfield Medieval Studies, 1 (Cambridge: D.S. Brewer, 2006), 31–36.

[46] This information is based on the helpful charts in White, *Theatre and Reformation*, 174–80. I have excluded Bale as his prolific output distorts a relatively small sample. The same bias is evident in broadside ballads of the sixteenth century.

drawn wholly or partly from books the Great Bible designates as "Hagiographa."[47] Its account of their status may be significant: "generally of all the bokes called Hagiogripha ... men maye reade them to the edifying of the people: but not to confyrme & strengthen the doctrine of the Churche."[48] These are books which are morally, rather than doctrinally valuable.[49] Choosing subjects from them may signal something about the prime purpose of the plays: they are not concerned, like the traditional drama, directly with matters of faith, but with a more secular kind of edification.

This may also inflect the dramatic strategies of the new biblical interludes. Chosen forms include classical dramatic models: Greek tragedy, in the Latin plays such as George Buchanan's *Jephthes* or Watson's *Absolom*, or Terentian comedy in the vernacular *Jacob and Esau*.[50] The pre-Christian classical drama offered rich new literary and intellectual modes for exploring biblical narratives; but it also inevitably complicated the exploration of questions of a faith based directly on the Scriptures. Another innovation adopted by vernacular playwrights was the incorporation into the biblical stories of characters and theatrical motifs from the rapidly developing allegorical drama. Many of the new scriptural interludes feature characters personifying virtuous or vicious qualities, usually embodying forces at play in or on the mind, soul or society of the biblical characters. These personifications may provide exposition of moral or spiritual lessons, or lively theatricality in the familiar comic routines of the Vice roles. Either way, they tend to encourage audiences to engage with the social, psychological and ethical implications of the scriptural exempla they present, rather than directly or affectively with the truths of the faith.

Tamara Atkin has recently reminded us of the significance for drama of the iconoclasm of Edward VI's 1547 *Injunctions*.[51] They directed that the clergy should teach their parishioners "that Images serue for no other purpose, but to be a remembraunce, whereby, men may be admonished, of the holy liues and

---

47 The five English interludes are: *Godly Quene Hester**, *King Darius**, *Abraham's Sacrifice*, *Virtuous and Godly Susanna**, and *Jacob and Esau*. Plays marked * are drawn wholly or partly from the apocryphal books.

48 *Byble in Englyshe*, fol. Aaai^v.

49 *The Byble in Englyshe* advises that "when thou wilt maynteyne any thynge for certen, rendryng a reason of thy fayth || take heade to procede therin by the lyuynge and pyitthye Scriptures," rather than the apocryphal books (ibid.).

50 For the adaptation of classical drama see the essay on Nicholas Grimald by Stephanie Allen and Elisabeth Dutton in the present volume.

51 Tamara Atkin, *The Drama of Reform: Theology and Theatricality, 1461–1553* (Turnhout: Brepols, 2013), 101–25.

conuersacion of theim that the saied Images do represent."[52] The new biblical plays, which continue to present images of patriarchs, saints and other holy figures, seem similarly to focus on admonitory remembrance of their lives and conversation, rather than encouraging devotional engagement with the Bible stories and characters. This approach informs the increasing range of topics addressed by biblical interludes; not only the doctrinal and confessional, but also political, ethical, educational and legal. Overall, the new biblical drama is more likely to encourage reflection on behaviour and ethics, than on the mysteries of God or of the faith. A closer look at some specific interludes may now serve to explore more sharply the dramatic strategies by which individual playwrights engaged with these topics and responded to the new attitudes to the Bible.[53]

4   *Godly Queen Hester*

This anonymous interlude, based on the Book of Esther, has attracted considerable attention for its striking political topicality: in spite of the insistence of the 1561 printing that it is a "newe enterlude drawen oute of the holy scripture … newly made and imprinted, this present yere," it has been persuasively located in the reign of Henry VIII, referring to the fall of Wolsey, and especially relevant to the situation of 1529.[54] If we accept this date, the play becomes a remarkable example of changing dramatic use of the Bible. 1529 precedes not only the authorised circulation of the English Bible, but also Henry VIII's moves to separate his country from the authority of the Pope. Free from such

---

52   *Iniunccions*, fol. aiii^v.

53   There is a caveat in examining the specific contexts of these plays. Sixteenth-century interlude drama has survived largely in printed editions, and their publication dates are generally a poor guide to composition or performance date. There was clearly a surge in the printing of biblical plays in the early years of Elizabeth's reign, the 1560s and 1570s, but the particular interests of the plays often suggest that they originally derive from considerably earlier, from the reigns of Edward VI and even Henry VIII.

54   *The Enterlude of Godly Quene Hester*, in *Medieval Drama: An Anthology*, ed. Greg Walker, Blackwell Anthologies (Oxford: Blackwell, 2000), 409–31; all references to this edition. For discussion of dating, see Bevington, *Tudor Drama and Politics*, 87–95; Janette Dillon, "Powerful Obedience: *Godly Queen Hester* and Katherine of Aragon," in *Interludes and Early Modern Society: Studies in Gender, Power and Theatricality*, ed. Peter Happé and Wim Hüsken, Ludus: Medieval and Early Renaissance Theatre and Drama, 9 (Amsterdam: Rodopi, 2007), 117–39; Greg Walker, "'To Speak before the King, It Is No Child's Play:' *Godly Queen Hester* in 1529," *Theta* 10 (2013): 69–96.

formal Reformation pressures on reception of the Bible, it nonetheless shows many of the new developments in biblical dramaturgy. This confirms the fluidity of the religious climate: changing attitudes to the Scriptures were clearly not restricted to religious reform.

The play dramatizes the story of Esther, to figure the political situation of its own time. Aman (Haman), the evil counsellor, represents Wolsey, thus casting King Assuerus (Ahasuerus) as Henry VIII, misled by his proud and grasping chancellor. If 1529 is accepted, Hester's (Esther's) protection of the Jews would present Katherine of Aragon attempting to defend the monasteries against dissolution. We should not underestimate the innovation of this sustained political allegory. Although medieval political satire was always rich in biblical reference, this generally took the form of suggestive allusion rather than re-told biblical narrative. The late-medieval biblical drama equally at times alluded critically to political or social conditions, but did not present a sustained narrative re-imagining of a recognisably current situation. In *Godly Queen Hester* the Bible story represents not so much itself, as events and people of the first audience's here and now, using the Scriptures to provide authority and force to political analysis and comment, rather than for spiritual purposes. Early as its date appears to be, the interlude is already drawing confidently and with sophistication on the new kinds of biblical engagement.

In spite of its apparently Roman Catholic sympathies with the monasteries, the interlude reveals many of the strategies we think of as belonging to the Reformation. Like many subsequent plays, it takes its subject from the Old Testament, even from a book which Luther would have liked to exclude from the canon altogether.[55] It develops that subject for political rather than spiritual ends, focusing on the morality of government rather than on matters of faith. Jo Carruthers suggests this was a characteristic Protestant response to the story: in reformed commentaries and sermons, "Esther's significance is narrowed from any wide theological application to much narrower concerns: it becomes a site through which to comment upon monarchy, female nature or response to threat."[56] This is exactly what we see in the interlude, which is concerned with issues of royal rule and counsel, with the political role of queens, with relations between Church and State. The story is socially exemplary, showing, as Tyndale had claimed: "As it went with their kings and rulers, so shall it go with ours." If it was, as various scholars suggest, designed for court

---

55 See Jo Carruthers, *Esther through the Centuries* (Oxford: Blackwell, 2008), 28. Several of the books of Esther were transferred to the apocrypha in the Great Bible.
56 Carruthers, *Esther*, 12.

performance, then Cranmer's observation also comes into play: "Herein may princes learn how to govern their subjects."

This is all enhanced by the other key innovative feature of its dramaturgy. The story of Esther, selectively compressed and adapted but fairly straightforwardly repeated from the Bible, is interspersed with allegorical scenes in which three personifications of political corruption – Pride, Adulation and Ambition – lament that Aman has appropriated all their qualities, leaving them unemployed. In another addition the Vice Hardy Dardy acts as a comic 'wise fool' with licence to challenge the supposed wisdom of Aman, and even Assuerus. In different ways both sets of characters make comically explicit many of the political warnings the playwright draws from the narrative. This is a very early instance of combining the established comic techniques of the allegorical theatre with scriptural narrative. Audiences would be familiar with the kinds of comic routine presented by Hardy Dardy and the vices; much less so with seeing these interact with and interpret biblical figures. This may account for the play's striking separation of the three vices from the human characters; their comic laments expose the corruption of Aman/Wolsey, but they never meet on stage, thus protecting the biblical characters from direct interaction with contemporary satire. The play provides a vivid example of how the Bible could be dramatized to illustrate political rather than religious issues. Its printing thirty years later further reinforces this more pragmatic, utilitarian approach to biblical material. The action of the interlude focuses not primarily on Hester but on Aman, making his fall central. By 1561, however, Wolsey's downfall is no longer immediately topical; but following Elizabeth's accession an interest in biblical heroines is developing. *Godly Queen Hester* probably acquired its title, and an admonitory epigraph recommending it as an example to "vertuous matrons and women kind," to reflect these changing priorities. The Bible can provide a story which shows how "wives … may know their duty to their husbands," as well as how princes may "learn how to govern their subjects."

5 Lewis Wager, *The Life and Repentaunce of Marie Magdalene*

Not all of the new biblical drama was so overtly secular in focus. Lewis Wager's *Marie Magdalene* is a prime example both of the direct performance of religious belief, and of changing attitudes to the Bible. Though printed in 1566, evidence suggests it was originally an Edwardian play, committed to the more explicit circulation of Protestant doctrine in that reign.[57] It performs only a

---

57 Lewis Wager, *A New Enterlude, Neuer before This Tyme Imprinted, Entreating of the Life and Repentaunce of Marie Magdalene* (London: John Charlewood, 1566); all references to this

brief section of the composite biblical and medieval lives of Mary Magdalene: her supposed early life in sin and her repentance, culminating in the gospel episode of the washing and anointing of Christ's feet.[58] This highly reduced extract from the wealth of scriptural and hagiographical material available is itself significant. Unsurprisingly, Wager ignores the legendary accounts of the Magdalen's later life; but he also omits her central gospel role as witness to the Resurrection, the chief focus of earlier drama. In fact most of the interlude centres on an allegorization of Mary's fall and repentance, with biblical material taking up less than half its action. And while the Prologue asserts that with "Authoritie of Scripture … we shall rehearse a fruietfull story," this is only "the storie of a woman that was right sory"[59]: Mary is not a Roman Catholic saint but simply an individual sinner, promised salvation by Christ.

In this, Wager dramatizes the shifting current of Protestant thinking about sainthood.[60] If his play is indeed Edwardian it coincides with a telling liturgical development. Frank Henderson draws attention to the removal of the feast of Mary Magdalene from the 1552 *Book of Common Prayer*.[61] He further points out that the 1549 *Book*, which had already excluded all post-biblical saints, included the feast only with a significantly revised collect. The Sarum Use had prayed that "as blessed Mary Magdalene by loving thy Only-begotten One above all things, obtained pardon of all her sins, so she may secure for us everlasting blessedness;" whereas the new collect asks that, "we maye truly repent, and lament [our offences], after the example of Mary Magdalene, and by lyuelye faythe obtayne remission of all oure sinnes." Mary is no longer a Roman Catholic intercessor but a Protestant 'example', the salvific efficacy of her devoted love transferred to the individual believer's own faith.[62] This is the

---

edition. For dating, see White, *Theatre and Reformation*, 80–81.

[58] For the composite biblical and legendary figure of the Magdalen see Katherine Ludwig Jansen, *The Making of the Magdalen: Preaching and Popular Devotion in the Later Middle Ages* (Princeton: Princeton University Press, 2000).

[59] Wager, *A New Enterlude*, fols. Aii^v-iii^r.

[60] See Peter Happé, "The Protestant Adaptation of the Saint Play," in *The Saint Play in Medieval Europe*, ed. Clifford Davidson (Kalamazoo, MI: Medieval Institute Publications, 1986), 226–34.

[61] J. Frank Henderson, "The Disappearance of the Feast of Mary Magdalene from the Anglican Liturgy," accessed 19 April 2015, <http://www.jfrankhenderson.com/pdf/Disappearance_Feast_MaryMagdalene.pdf>.

[62] As a 1550 exhortation on the Magdalen urged: "folowe good Mary Magdalene in this point, & cry not, cal not vnto her, prai for vs, prai for vs." Roger Hutchinson, *The image of God, or laie mans boke in which the right knowledge of God is disclosed* (London: John Day and William Seres, 1550), fol. 76^v.

Mary that Wager presents: a faulty woman who offers the audience an example of penitence, showing how personal faith can lead to salvation.

This dramatization of the biblical Magdalene has a vivid effect on the staging of the interlude. Its extended opening sequence presents Mary in remarkably naturalistic terms as a spoiled, self-indulgent and pleasure-seeking young woman, "triflyng with her garments" and offering a detailed picture of contemporary social behaviour in a domestic setting.[63] The vices persuade her towards a sharply realised provocative fashion regime: she should curse her dressmakers, dress revealingly, curl her hair with a hot needle, dye it with gold, and loose it seductively, since "yong men to your loue it will allure."[64] Although clearly not biblical, this draws on biblical commentary: Erasmus's *Paraphrases*, recently made available in churches, explains how the Magdalen had "customablye vsed [her hair]for the delycate and sensuall pleasure of the fleashe, to enoynt with swete perfume, to dye with coloures, to kembe, and to brede with wrythes of golde enterlaced emong it."[65] But Erasmus presents this retrospectively as the penitent motivation for drying Christ's feet with her hair; Wager enacts it, in engrossingly comic detail, encouraging spectators to recognise in it a reflection of their own contemporary manners. The immediacy of the example is enhanced by graphic erotic flirtation between Mary and the vices, expressed both in promiscuous kissing and explicit verbal provocation. There is no trace of the devotional reverence of earlier drama, but an inescapably warning example of morally dangerous social behaviour.

This lifelike immediacy reinforces Mary's status as contemporary exemplum for the audience. But the play then introduces a series of allegorical figures to stage a detailed articulation of the Protestant doctrine of justification by faith. Following the portrayal of her sin, a sequence of personifications spells out the stages involved in Mary's fall and conversion. Theatrically, this strand of the play is openly expositional: Paul Whitfield White has demonstrated how extensively and explicitly the personifications echo the doctrinal tenets of Calvin's *Institutes*.[66] The closing moments of the play summarise her process of enlightenment simply by listing the "persons we introduce into presence":[67] *The Lawe* declared the sinful Mary damned, bringing her

---

63 Wager, *A New Enterlude*, fol. Aiiii[r]. White, *Theatre and Reformation*, 84–86, suggests Mary is staged to appeal especially to an audience from a noble household.
64 Wager, *A New Enterlude*, fol. Ciiii[r].
65 Erasmus, *Paraphrase*, fol. lxxxv[v].
66 Paul Whitfield White, "Lewis Wager's *The Life and Repentaunce of Mary Magdalene* and John Calvin," *Notes and Queries* 226 (1981): 508–12.
67 Wager, *A New Enterlude*, fol. Iiii[r].

Knowledge of Sinne; Christ's preaching brought in *Fayth* and *Repentaunce* who were finally followed by *Justification* which engendered *Love*. Each personification explained its concept and role, insisting that they had no physical existence but "inuisibly in your heart we will remayne."[68]

The play thus offers the audience a highly interpreted account of the biblical narrative. The central gospel action, Mary's penitent washing of Christ's feet, is briefly enacted in silent mime: Christ, and the extensive parade of personifications, provide a meticulous doctrinal exposition of what this biblical moment means. Following contemporary theological debates they insist that sin is inevitable, that the law can only condemn, that man cannot deserve mercy, that Mary was not saved by her love for Christ, and that only faith, granted by God, can bring justification and salvation.[69] Medieval drama had presented the Magdalen as a primarily affective figure, drawing the audience emotively into her own tearful and penitent love for Christ.[70] Wager's dramaturgy allows the audience to engage with Mary only as a negative exemplum. The biblical episode is protected from the dangerously empathetic fictions of the stage by a doctrinal commentary that distances it, focusing the audience on understanding the processes of salvation rather than on direct emotional engagement with Mary or the events of the gospel.

6 *Jacob and Esau*

The "Comedie or Enterlude … of Jacob and Esau," entered on the Stationers Register 1557–58 and surviving in a printed edition from 1568, employs a very different theatrical mode that raises new questions about dramatizing the

---

68 Ibid., fol. Gii^r.

69 These are all concepts expounded in contemporary Protestant thinking. Apart from White's identification of Calvin, see e.g. Tyndale's comment that Scripture contains "first the law to condemn all flesh: secondarily the gospel, that is to say promises of mercy for all that repent and knowledge their sins at the preaching of the law" (*Tyndale's Old Testament*, 628); Hutchinson, *Image of God*, fol. 76^r: "we may not thinke that loue causeth remission of sins, but that remission of sinnes causeth loue. For that our loue foloweth, and goeth not before."

70 For an insightful discussion of theatrical affect see Meg Twycross, "Playing the Resurrection," in *Medieval Studies for J.A.W. Bennett, Aetatis Suae LXX*, ed. Peter Heyworth (Oxford: Clarendon Press, 1981), 283–87; also Theresa Coletti, *Mary Magdalene and the Drama of Saints: Theater, Gender, and Religion in Late Medieval England* (Philadelphia: University of Pennsylvania Press, 2004), 204–13.

Bible.[71] This interlude is related to a humanist tradition of biblical plays in Latin imitating classical drama: Watson's *Absolom*, Grimald's *Christus Redivivus* or Buchanan's *Jephthes* and *Baptistes*. *Jacob and Esau* chooses the model of Terentian comedy for a vernacular drama which is seemingly designed for schoolboy performance.[72] This pedagogic form has significant implications for staging, determining not only such formal features as act and scene division, but also the nature of characterisation and stage action. *Jacob and Esau* presents its biblical characters with the formalised naturalism of its model, introducing comic servants derived from Roman comedy, with "Mido, a little Boy" and "Abra, a little wench" charmingly adapted for child performance. It avoids not only allegorical or commentating figures, but also the kinds of direct address and acknowledgement of the audience which allows for doctrinal or moral commentary in many other biblical interludes. This throws extra weight on the action and characterisation to engage the audience in the ideas the playwright wishes to convey.

The play presents two episodes from Genesis: Esau losing first his birthright, and then his father's blessing, to his twin brother Jacob. The Jacob and Esau story had become a key text in Protestant discussion of predestination, developing Paul's text: "As it is wrytten: Iacob haue I loued, but Esau haue I hated," a divine decision made "yer the chyldren were borne, when they had nether done good nether bad (that the purpose of God by eleccion, myghte stande)."[73] It is clear that the playwright wishes to focus his audience's attention on this issue, citing Paul's words explicitly, and commenting on them in both the Prologue and Epilogue. But the doctrine, as illustrated in this biblical story, in spite of extensive discussion among commentators continued to provoke difficulty because of its clear unfairness in terms of human morality.[74] This led many Protestant writers, from Tyndale onwards, to stress the unknowability of God's justice and urge readers not "to search ye bottomlesse secretes

---

71   *Jacob and Esau*, ed. John Crow and F.P. Wilson, Malone Society Reprints (Oxford: Oxford University Press, 1956); all references to this edition.

72   For discussion of potential author and auspices see White, *Theatre and Reformation*, 118–19.

73   Epistle of Paul to the Romans 9:11–13 (*The Byble in Englyshe*, fol. Hhvii^v).

74   See John Curran, "*Jacob and Esau* and the Iconoclasm of Merit," *Studies in English Literature, 1500–1900* 49:2 (2009): 285–309; Arnold Ledgerwood Williams, *The Common Expositor: An Account of the Commentaries on Genesis, 1527–1633* (Chapel Hill: University of North Carolina Press, 1948), 169–73.

of Gods predestination."[75] The interlude's Epilogue similarly concludes: "How unsearchable are his ways to mans reason" (l. 1814).

This unimpeachable conclusion is, however, potentially compromised by the playwright's chosen dramaturgy. Performance, by presenting the spectators with an embodied story, inevitably challenges them to respond to and interpret what they see. The relatively naturalistic characterisation of *Jacob and Esau*, without any easy opportunity for onstage exposition of divine purpose, makes it hard to dissuade the audience from making human judgements of the Bible narrative. This is especially the case since the playwright develops the characterisation away from the neutrally non-judgmental account of Genesis, following both the strategy of Roman comedy, and the practice of other scriptural interludes, to focus more on the ethical and social aspects of the narrative than on God's mystery. Theatrically, this is certainly effective. There is a deft touch with imaginatively colloquial dialogue which draws the audience in to the engaging realism of the play: so Esau mocks his stay-at-home younger brother who must "tarrie and sucke mothers dugge at home" (l. 99), or curses the aged Deborah as a witch "as white as midnights arsehole" (l. 1572); while the little servant maid, Abra, trusts to make broth so tasty that "God almighty selfe may wet his finger therein" (l. 1171). To this end, too, the play develops the character of Esau into a loutish and inconsiderate figure, roughly dismissive of his brother and despised by most of the community for his antisocial behaviour. As such he reflects the unregenerate protagonists of many Protestant education plays, contrasted by the pious and submissive Jacob. Their relative roles, theatrically lively and engaging, echo those of *Nice Wanton* and other plays which invite the audience to approve of the well-behaved and consign the ill-mannered to damnation.

But this characterisation problematizes the doctrine of predestination, which specifically asserts that salvation and damnation have no relation to good works but depend entirely on God's grace. The audience is theatrically drawn by the play into making human judgements of the behaviour of the two brothers, yet are told that this has no bearing on the divine judgement that is passed upon them. Both brothers present problems, setting the social morality of the action against the divine understanding expressed in the Prologue, Epilogue and Songs of the play. If Esau is riotous and churlish, Jacob seems self-righteous and hypocritical in his readiness to accept as God's will the apparently self-seeking deceptions proposed by his mother Rebecca, who herself cannot

---

75 William Tyndale, *A compendious introduction, prologue, or preface vnto the Epistle to the Romains* (London: John Charlewood, 1564), fol. Evii[r]. Curran, "Jacob and Esau," 288–90, explores these views more fully.

but seem in human terms a culpably partial and manipulative mother. Partly because of the Protestant stress on family, education, and social behaviour, Jacob and Rebecca's readiness to pre-empt God's will and align it with their own, by setting traps for Esau, seems at best distasteful. The ethically naturalistic characterisation is thus set against the doctrinal purpose of the play, offering the audience an entertaining but rather incoherent theatrical experience of the biblical narrative.

This difficulty has been noted by many critics who have offered various suggestive interpretations of the play's purposes and effects.[76] Yet beyond their perceptive readings, what may also be in play is a problem posed by Protestant habits of Bible reading and their transition into theatre. Direct access to the Scriptures had fostered encouragement toward literal and ethical reading. Teaching of the faith was a rather different activity: as Narveson suggests, the laity "were being called to read [the Bible] in order to confirm the grounds of doctrine already laid down elsewhere."[77] The interlude seeks to present ideas both of faith and of ethics, yet *Jacob and Esau* chooses a dramatic mode which allows little opportunity for laying down the doctrine by which to understand its story. Influential commentators, including Calvin, were able to criticise Jacob and Rebecca's deceptions while offering positive teaching about predestination and exhortation to accept the mysteries of God.[78] But this course is hard to follow for a playwright committed to a dramatic form that prioritises the ethically naturalistic. Engaging as it is theatrically, *Jacob and Esau* may suggest crucial tensions between drama and doctrine, and inadvertently reinforce

---

[76] Blackburn, *Biblical Drama*, 152, understands the problem as a miscalculation by the playwright who "displays a certain moral obtuseness in the development of his characters." White, *Theatre and Reformation*, 122–23, is readier to accept that this may be an anachronistic perception of 'the modern reader', arguing that the play "illustrates the validity of predestination chiefly through the contrasting characters of the elect Jacob and his reprobate brother." Like Bevington, *Tudor Drama and Politics*, 112, he sees this characterisation also supporting a radical political purpose, in justifying "unseating corrupt authority." In a subtle discussion that addresses the problems posed by the twin brothers more directly, Curran, "*Jacob and Esau*," 285, argues that the playwright deploys the moral difficulties of characterisation deliberately, challenging the audience to realise that "viewing the elect as deserving and the reprobate as undeserving is a trap into which we all too easily can fall."

[77] Narveson, "Clerical Anxieties," 167–68.

[78] See Ledgerwood Williams, *Common Expositor*, 169–73.

the gradually increasing Protestant unease with the stage as a forum in which to address the Bible.[79]

7   Susanna

Thomas Garter's *Commody of the moste Vertuous and Godlye Susanna*, printed in 1578, ostensibly avoids such issues of doctrine, while demonstrating how a biblical story might address a broad range of contemporary social and ethical issues.[80] Although plainly concerned with piety, through the "Godlye" life of his heroine, Garter's focus is primarily on the human. His apocryphal material presents the story of the virtuous wife trapped while bathing and slanderously accused of adultery by two corrupt Elders, who is saved from death by the divinely inspired intervention of the child Daniel.[81] The play expands this scriptural account with a good deal of domestic and characterising detail. While the cast list suggests Garter has also introduced an allegorical strand to expound the moral or spiritual concepts at stake, it quickly becomes clear that Sensualitas and Voluptas are not conceptual personifications, but simply names given to the two lecherous Elders or Judges, labelling them rather in the mode of Jonsonian humours. The comic Vice Ill Report, deployed by Satan to 'overthrow' Susanna, is more fully allegorical; but as his name suggests the quality he represents feeds into the social, rather than the religious, drivers of the action.

Garter takes pleasure in presenting a compelling story, but he does not show any particular doctrinal purpose. The Prologue explains that the play "sheweth forth how prone God is, to helpe such as are iust" (l. 8), thus presenting it as a consoling "ensample good" (l. 22) rather than an exploration of God's word.

---

[79] Anthony Munday's complaint, although unlikely to be aimed at plays such as *Jacob and Esau*, characterises this growing anxiety: "The reuerend word of God, & histories of the Bible set forth on the stage by these blasphemous plaiers, are so corrupted with their gestures of scurrilitie, and so interlaced with vncleane, and whorish speeches, that it is not possible to drawe anie profite out of the doctrine of their spiritual moralities" (*A Second and Third Blast of Retrait from Plaies and Theaters ... by a Worshipful and Zealous Gentleman Now Aliue: ... Showing ... the Abhomination of Theaters in the Time Present* [London: Henrie Denham and William Seres, 1580], 103.)

[80] Thomas Garter, *The Most Virtuous & Godly Susanna*, ed. B. Ifor Evans, Malone Society Reprints (London: Oxford University Press, 1937); all references to this edition.

[81] The story of Susanna became widely popular in art, literature and drama of the sixteenth century. See e.g. Dan W. Clanton, *The Good, the Bold, and the Beautiful: the Story of Susanna and its Renaissance Interpretations* (New York: T & T Clark, 2006).

This indeed seems to be the prime motivation of the play; Meg Twycross has shown persuasively how richly varied a series of behavioural exempla it offers for contemporary audiences.[82] Susanna frequently appears in commentaries as an example of beleaguered faith saved by trust in God.[83] Garter's warmly naturalistic development of the story also presents her as a social example – of good parental education, model housewifery, modest chastity, filial and spousal loyalty, and pious faith in God's guidance. The corrupt Judges, meanwhile, are warning examples, first of lechery and then of the perversion of justice.

This last topic contributes to the play's more extended exploration of the administration of justice and of legal process. Before Susanna herself appears, her husband Joachim, in a role much extended from the Scripture, is introduced as a concerned and conscientious magistrate troubled by the human responsibilities of executing justice. He laments these difficulties with a newly psychological realism, explaining his anxieties to the corrupt Judges: "when I am in place alone … I cannot rid out of my brayne the charge of our degree" (ll. 299–300), and praying fervently for God's guidance while they pore over legal books. This develops a serious human context for the story's crux, Daniel's exposure of the Judges' conspiracy by deploying the legal 'two witness rule' that reveals their inconsistent evidence as false.[84] Garter embeds this moment, which the biblical narrative presents as a quasi-miraculous gesture, in a framework of social and legal concern that offers yet another contemporary exemplum for the citizens of his audience.

The play's extended variety of social and ethical exempla is performed with lively human touches, a sharp eye for theatrical action, and considerable comic by-play especially by the Vice. There is little doctrinal teaching, although the play shows its Protestant heritage in the focus on domestic piety and the constant invocation of God's grace. But its development of the biblical story nonetheless raises questions. Garter's dramatization focuses the audience primarily on the ethics of human behaviour. Yet, as Lorna Hutson reminds us, the play's crisis is not resolved through such human action but by an unheralded moment of divine intervention when "God rayseth the spirite of Danyell" (l. 1060).[85] While presenting a reassuring response to Susanna's submissive piety,

---

82   Meg Twycross, "*Virtuous and Godly Susanna*: Exemplum and Allegory," *Medieval English Theatre* 34 (2012), 96–145.

83   See e.g. Thomas Becon, *A comfortable epistle* (Strasburg: J. Lambrecht [?], 1554), fol. Cvii^v; John Fisher, *A spirituall consolation* (London: W. Carter, [1578?]), fol. Hiii^v.

84   For a valuable account of this legal principle and its operation in *Susanna* see Olga Horner, "Susanna's Double Life," *Medieval English Theatre* 8:2 (1986): 76–102.

85   Lorna Hutson, "Imagining Justice: Kantarowitz and Shakespeare," *Representations* 106:1 (2009): 118–42, explores the tensions in drama of the time between divine and human action.

it runs into danger of theological over-simplification. The theatrical conclusion inevitably implies a causal relationship between Susanna's virtue and God's intervention that sits a little uneasily with Protestant theology, while turning Susanna into an example of a rather crude notion of God's providence: "Let myne example comfort you in all kinde of distresse, || That if you suffer for His sake, He will your cares release" (ll. 1107–08). In a fictional comedy this could be powerfully effective; but as a reading of a biblical narrative it might seem potentially reductive.

8 Conclusion

As these four examples show, Reformation biblical playwrights engaged creatively with changing modes of Scripture-reading, in ways that expanded the possibilities of drama while at times also revealing a newly uneasy relationship between theatre and the Bible. The centrality of the Bible in Protestant thinking, combined with hugely expanded direct lay access, led to distinctive practices of Bible-reading. These practices guided playwrights towards a greatly expanded body of powerful narratives, which raised challenging human issues, allowing strong theatrical interpretation in relation to contemporary concerns. But while these interludes themselves show little anxiety about dramatizing the Scriptures, their new theatrical strategies do not always sit quite comfortably with the special status accorded to the Bible as the word of God. As Puritans later argued more passionately, embodied performance can prove a challenging, or reductive, medium for doctrinal truth. While the excitement of "gods word [in] euery mans mouth" invigorated dramatic practice, it is perhaps not surprising that as the Reformation proceeded, the theatre gradually moved away from the long tradition of plays based on the Bible.

Bibliography

Anglo, Sydney. "An Early Tudor Programme for Plays and Other Demonstrations against the Pope." *Journal of the Warburg and Courtauld Institutes* 20 (1957): no. 1/2, 176–79.

Atkin, Tamara. *The Drama of Reform: Theology and Theatricality, 1461–1553*. Turnhout: Brepols, 2013.

Bale, John. *The Complete Plays of John Bale*, 2 vols., edited by Peter Happé. Cambridge: Brewer, 1985.

Beadle, Richard. "'Devoute ymaginacioun' and the Dramatic Sense in Love's *Mirror* and the N-Town Plays." In *Nicholas Love at Waseda: Proceedings of the International*

Conference, 20–22 July, 1995, edited by Shoicho Oguro, Richard Beadle, and Michael G. Sargent, 1–17. Cambridge: D.S. Brewer, 1997.

———, ed. *The York Plays: A Critical Edition of the York Corpus Christi Play as Recorded in British Library Additional MS 35290*, 2 vols. EETS s.s. 23–24. Oxford: Oxford University Press, 2009–13.

Becon, Thomas. *A comfortable epistle*. Strasburg: J. Lambrecht [?], 1554.

Bevington, David M. *Tudor Drama and Politics: A Critical Approach to Topical Meaning*, Cambridge, MA: Harvard University Press, 1968.

Blackburn, Ruth. *Biblical Drama under the Tudors*. The Hague: Mouton, 1971.

Bradshaw, Christopher. "David or Josiah? Old Testament Kings as Exemplars in Edwardian Religious Polemic." In *Protestant History and Identity in Sixteenth Century Europe: The Later Reformation*, 2 vols., edited by Bruce Gordon, 2: 77–90. Aldershot: Ashgate, 1996.

Carruthers, Jo. *Esther through the Centuries*. Oxford: Blackwell, 2008.

Chemnitz, Martin. *A Discouerie and Batterie of the Great Fort of Vnwritten Traditions*. London: Thomas Purfoot and William Pounsonbie, 1582.

Clanton, Dan W. *The Good, the Bold, and the Beautiful: the Story of Susanna and its Renaissance Interpretations*. New York: T & T Clark, 2006.

Coletti, Theresa. *Mary Magdalene and the Drama of Saints: Theater, Gender, and Religion in Late Medieval England*. Philadelphia: University of Pennsylvania Press, 2004.

Cranmer, Thomas. *The Byble in Englyshe that Is to saye the content of al the Holy Scrypture, both of the Olde, and Newe Testament, with a Prologe therinto, made by the Reuerende Father in God, Thomas Archbysshop of Cantorbury*. London: Rychard Grafton, 1540.

Crow, John, and F.P. Wilson, eds. *Jacob and Esau*. Malone Society Reprints. Oxford: Oxford University Press, 1956.

Curran, John. "*Jacob and Esau* and the Iconoclasm of Merit." *Studies in English Literature, 1500–1900* 49:2 (2009): 285–309.

Daniell, David, ed. *Tyndale's Old Testament: Being the Pentateuch of 1530, Joshua to 2 Chronicles of 1537, and Jonah*. New Haven and London: Yale University Press, 1992.

Dillon, Janette. "Powerful Obedience: *Godly Queen Hester* and Katherine of Aragon." In *Interludes and Early Modern Society: Studies in Gender, Power and Theatricality*, edited by Peter Happé and Wim Hüsken, 117–39. Ludus: Medieval and Early Renaissance Theatre and Drama, 9. Amsterdam: Rodopi, 2007.

Erasmus, Desiderius. *The First Tome or Volume of the Paraphrase of Erasmus Vpon the Newe Testamente*, edited by Nicholas Udall. London: Edward Whitchurche, 1548.

Fisher, John. *A spirituall consolation*. London: W. Carter, [1578?].

Garter, Thomas. *The Most Virtuous & Godly Susanna*, edited by B. Ifor Evans. Malone Society Reprints. London: Oxford University Press, 1937.

Gordon, Bruce. "The Changing Face of Protestant History and Identity in Sixteenth Century Europe." In *Protestant History and Identity in Sixteenth Century Europe: The Later Reformation*, 2 vols., edited by Bruce Gordon, 1: 1–22. Aldershot: Ashgate, 1996.

Hall, Edward. *The Vnion of the Two Noble and Illustre Famelies of Lancastre [and] Yorke*. London: Richard Grafton, 1548.

Happé, Peter. "The Protestant Adaptation of the Saint Play." In *The Saint Play in Medieval Europe*, edited by Clifford Davidson, 205–40. Kalamazoo, MI: Medieval Institute Publications, 1986.

Henderson, J. Frank. "The Disappearance of the Feast of Mary Magdalene from the Anglican Liturgy." Accessed 20 April 2015. <http://www.jfrankhenderson.com/pdf/Disappearance_Feast_MaryMagdalene.pdf>.

Horner, Olga. "Susanna's Double Life." *Medieval English Theatre* 8:2 (1986): 76–102.

Hughes, Paul L., and James F. Larkin, eds. *Tudor Royal Proclamations*, 3 vols. New Haven and London: Yale University Press, 1964.

Hutchinson, Roger. *The image of God, or laie mans boke in which the right knowledge of God is disclosed*. London: John Day and William Seres, 1550.

Hutson, Lorna. "Imagining Justice: Kantarowitz and Shakespeare." *Representations* 106:1 (2009): 118–42.

Iniunccions Geuen by the Moste Excellent Prince, Edward the Sixte by the Grace of God, Kyng of England, Fraunce, and Irelande: Defendor of the Faythe, and in Earthe Vnder Christ, of the Churche of Englande and of Ireland the Supreme Hedde: to all and singuler his louyng subiectes, aswell of the Clergie, as of the Laietie. London: Richard Grafton, 1547.

Iniunctions gyuen by th [sic] *auctoritie of the kynges highnes to the clergie of this his realme*. London: Thomas Berthelet, [1538?].

Jansen, Katherine Ludwig. *The Making of the Magdalen: Preaching and Popular Devotion in the Later Middle Ages*. Princeton: Princeton University Press, 2000.

King, Pamela M. *The York Mystery Cycle and the Worship of the City*. Westfield Medieval Studies, 1. Cambridge: D.S. Brewer, 2006.

Ledgerwood Williams, Arnold. *The Common Expositor: An Account of the Commentaries on Genesis, 1527–1633*. Chapel Hill: University of North Carolina Press, 1948.

Love, Nicholas. *The Mirror of the Blessed Life of Jesus Christ: A Full Critical Edition, based on Cambridge University Library Additional MSS 6578 and 6686 with Introduction, Notes and Glossary*, edited by Michael G. Sargent. Exeter: University of Exeter Press, 2005.

Lumiansky, R.M., David Mills, and Richard Rastall. *The Chester Mystery Cycle: Essays and Documents*. Chapel Hill and London: University of North Carolina Press, 1983.

Matheson, Peter. "The Reformation." In *The Blackwell Companion to the Bible and Culture*, edited by John F. A Sawyer, 69–84. Oxford: Blackwell, 2006.

MacCulloch, Diarmaid. *Thomas Cranmer: A Life*. New Haven, CT and London: Yale University Press, 1996.

McGrath, Alister E. *Reformation Thought: An Introduction*. Oxford: Blackwell, 1999 (3rd ed.).

Mill, Anna Jean. *Mediaeval Plays in Scotland*. Edinburgh: William Blackwood and Sons, 1927.

Narveson, Kate. "'Their Practice Bringeth Little Profit:' Clerical Anxieties About Lay Scripture Reading in Early Modern England." In *Private and Domestic Devotion in Early Modern Britain*, edited by Jessica Martin and Alec Ryrie, 165–87. Farnham: Ashgate, 2012.

Norland, B. *Drama in Early Tudor Britain, 1485–1558*. Lincoln, NE and London: University of Nebraska Press, 1995.

Sawyer, Karen Elaine. "The Resurrection of Our Lord: A Study and Dual-Text Edition." PhD thesis, University of Toronto, 2001.

Second and Third Blast of Retrait from Plaies and Theaters, A, … by a Worshipful and Zealous Gentleman Now Aliue: … Showing … the Abhomination of Theaters in the Time Present. London: Henrie Denham and William Seres, 1580.

Somerset, J. Alan B., ed. *Records of Early English Drama: Shropshire*, 2 vols. Toronto: University of Toronto Press, 1994.

St Clare Byrne, Muriel, ed. *The Lisle Letters*, 6 vols. Chicago: University of Chicago Press, 1981.

Statutes of the Realm Printed by Command of His Majesty King George the Third, The, … from Original Records and Authentic Manuscripts, edited by Great Britain Record Commission, 4 vols. Medieval and Early Modern Sources Online, 2007. Accessed, 20 April 2015 on the TannerRitchie publishers page. <http://www.tannerritchie.com/memso.php>.

Thorne, Samuel E., and J.H. Baker, eds. *Readings and Moots at the Inns of Court in the Fifteenth Century*, 2 vols. London: Selden Society, 1990.

Twycross, Meg. "Playing the Resurrection." In *Medieval Studies for J.A.W. Bennett, Aetatis Suae LXX*, edited by Peter Heyworth, 273–96. Oxford: Clarendon Press, 1981.

———. "*Virtuous and Godly Susanna*: Exemplum and Allegory." *Medieval English Theatre* 34 (2012): 96–145.

Tyndale, William. *A compendious introduction, prologue, or preface vnto the Epistle to the Romains*. London: John Charlewood, 1564.

Wager, Lewis. *A New Enterlude, Neuer before This Tyme Imprinted, Entreating of the Life and Repentaunce of Marie Magdalene*. London: John Charlewood, 1566.

Walker, Greg, ed. *Medieval Drama: An Anthology*. Oxford: Blackwell, 2000. Blackwell Anthologies.

———. "'To Speak before the King, It Is No Child's Play:' Godly Queen Hester in 1529." *Theta* 10 (2013): 69–96.

Whitfield White, Paul. "Lewis Wager's *The Life and Repentaunce of Mary Magdalene* and John Calvin." *Notes and Queries* 226 (1981): 508–12.

———. *Theatre and Reformation: Protestantism, Patronage, and Playing in Tudor England*. Cambridge: Cambridge University Press, 1993.

Wilson, John Dover, ed. *The Resurrection of Our Lord*. Malone Society Reprints. London: Oxford University Press, 1912.

CHAPTER 2

Blurred Lines? Religion, Reform, and Reformation in Sir David Lyndsay's *Ane Satyre of the Thrie Estaitis*

Greg Walker

Abstract

This article examines Sir David Lyndsay's treatment of religious reform in *Ane Satyre of the Thrie Estaitis*. It begins by examining the play's representation of the Bible, but subsequently widens the perspective to look at the complexities and apparent contradictions evident in the play's discussion of clerical wealth and immorality and the failure of clerics to preach and teach those in their cure. Rather than accepting the once conventional line that the playwright was advancing a proto-protestant position in the play, this essay sets his careful negotiation of questions of clerical corruption and failure in the context of the programme of progressive catholic reform led by Archbishop John Hamilton in the early 1550s. It suggests that, rather than advancing a radical confessional agenda, the play reflects the fluid state of religious politics in the Scotland of the 1550s on the eve of the Reformation.

Keywords

David Lyndsay – John Hamilton – religion – reformation – representation of the bible – clerical wealth – immortality – corruption

1   Introduction

As Sarah Carpenter has recently suggested, the place and role of bibles, and of the Bible, in Sir David Lyndsay's *Satyre of the Thrie Estaitis* is both seemingly self-evident and fundamentally puzzling.[1] When Veritie enters, carrying a biblical text that the Vice, Flatterie, identifies as "the New Testament, || In Englisch

---

[1] Sarah Carpenter, "Verity's Bible: Books, Texts, and Reading in *Ane Satyre of the Thrie Estaitis*," *Medieval English Theatre* 33 (2011): 58–74.

toung, and printit in England!" (ll. 1153–54),[2] it seems clear that Lyndsay is deploying a recognisable evangelical polemical trope. Here, we might assume, is the playwright signalling his own affiliations, representing Truth as an evangelical bible-reader and, by implication, her enemies as traditional Catholics eager to restrict access to the biblical Word. And this assumption seems confirmed when Flatterie, a friar (suggesting an equally recognisable stereotype of corrupt Catholicism) immediately condemns Veritie with a knee-jerk accusation of heresy ("Heresie, heresie; fire, fire, incontinent!" [l. 1155]). Such a reading would fit well with the conventional view of Lyndsay as an anticlerical, proto-protestant author at odds with the ecclesiastical authorities of his time – a view cemented as early as 1568 in the preface to Henry Charteris's edition of the writer's *Warkis* (which did not contain *The Thrie Estaitis*). There, Charteris claimed that the playwright, "ernist and vehement" against the established church, and a "professit enemie to thame", wrote the *Satyre* to give them "ane spring", and succeeded thereby in provoking their implacable enmity:

> This play did enter with sic greif in thair hartis, that thay studyit be all menis to be avengit thairof. Thay convenit thair provinciall counsellis, thay consultit how thay suld best sustene thair kingdome inclynand to ruyne, quhilk laitlie had gottin sa publict ane wound: thay ȝeid about to have his haill warkis condempnit for hereticall, and cessit not in kirk and market, publictlie and privelie, to rage and rayll againis him, as ane Heretike ...[3]

There would seem to be little room for doubt about either Lyndsay's own religious position or his place in the confessional politics of his time. And yet, as Carpenter demonstrates, things are not quite that simple. Exactly which version of the English New Testament Veritie carries is never revealed; thus the precise degree of her affiliation to reformist Protestantism is left unexplored. For neither she nor her tormenters ever reads from her book in the course of the play. A number of bibles *are* quoted from, both directly and seemingly from

---

2   All quotations from Lyndsay's play are from, *Medieval Drama: An Anthology*, ed. Greg Walker, Blackwell Anthologies (Oxford: Blackwell, 2000).

3   Henry Charteris, "Preface to the Reidar," in *The Warkis of the famous and [w]orthie knicht, Sir David Lyndesay of the Mount* (Edinburgh: Henry Charteris, 1568), sig ii(v)-iii. See also Charteris's verse reiteration of the claim in his "Adhortatioun of All Estatis To the Reiding of Thir Present Warkis," in *Warkis*, sig. Aii [17–24]: "Yit never Poeit of our Scottische clan || Sa cleirlie schew that Monstour with all his markis, || The Romane God, in quhome all gyle began, || As dois gude David Lyndesay in his warkis". For an argument for Lyndsay's Catholicism, see Brother Kenneth, "Sir David Lyndsay, Reformer," *Innes Review* 1 (1950): 79–91.

memory, but not this one. Veritie herself, when quoting a biblical passage, cites only the Latin Vulgate version, or paraphrases it in a Scots translation seemingly of her own devising. Gude Counsall, another virtuous character, also produces a copy of the New Testament, seemingly a different edition (as it is in Latin), from which he reads directly a passage from St Paul's account of the desiderata of a good bishop in 1 Timothy 3:1–3. He then translates that passage into English, whether supposedly reading from a parallel text edition or by translating extemporarily is not clear. "Counsall sall read thir wordis on ane Buik", reads the stage direction, and the actor declares:

> *Fidelis sermo, si quis Episcopatum desiderat, bonum*
> *opus desiderat. Oportet [ergo], eum irreprehensibilem*
> *esse, unius uxoris virum, sobrium, prudentem,*
> *ornatum, pudicum, hospitalem, doctorem:*
> *non vinolentum, non percussorem, sed modestum.*
>
> That is: "This is a true saying, If any man desire the office of a Bishop, he desireth a worthie worke: a Bishop, therefore, must be unreproveable, the husband of one wife, etc. ..." (ll. 2916–24)[4]

Here again, a virtuous character associated with reform bases his appeal to the authority of the biblical text, not on a protestant English translation but on the vulgate Latin. But, as Carpenter observes, what is still more interesting here is that the English translation offered, as it appears in the earliest printed text of the play (the 1602 Edinburgh edition published by Robert Charteris), *is* drawn from an explicitly protestant text, but one which Lyndsay himself could not have cited, the 1560 'Geneva Bible', which appeared some six years after the later of the two performances to which the Charteris text seems to relate, and five years after Lyndsay's death.[5] The translation, then, must seemingly have been added to Lyndsay's text posthumously, whether by Charteris or the unknown scribe of his exemplar. Perhaps Lyndsay's script did not call for Gude

---

4 The Douay-Rheims translation of the Vulgate gives the relevant passage as follows: "A faithful saying: if a man desire the office of a bishop, he desireth a good work. It behoveth therefore a bishop to be blameless, the husband of one wife, sober, prudent, of good behaviour, chaste, given to hospitality, a teacher, not given to wine, no striker, but modest, not quarrelsome, not covetous, but one that ruleth well his own house, having his children in subjection with all chastity" (See "Douay-Rheims Bible + Challoner Notes," <http://www.drbo.org/chapter/61003.htm [Accessed December 11, 2014])>.

5 *The Bible and Holy Scriptvres Conteyned in the Olde and New Testament, Translated according to the Ebrue and Greke, and Conferred with the Best Translations in Diuers Languages* (Geneva: Rowland Hill [=Hall, WH], 1560).

Counsall to translate the Latin at all, or perhaps it did, but used a translation that Charteris or his source found unsatisfactory, and so they silently replaced it with one more doctrinally acceptable at that moment (the Geneva Bible had been adopted by the reformed *kirk* in 1560).[6] Either way, it is striking that the one direct quotation from an English bible in a play frequently assumed to be evangelical in inspiration seems not to have been one intended by the playwright.

This seemingly minor anomaly is significant for two reasons, one textual, the other political and theological. It draws attention to the problematic and still rather mysterious textual history of the *Satyre,* suggesting how little we really know about the relationship between the two surviving early-modern texts – the partial version copied into the Bannatyne Manuscript in the 1560s, and the equally (but differently) incomplete Charteris printed version[7] – and what was actually played at the two known performances: that in Lyndsay's home town of Cupar, Fife, on June 7, 1552, and that on the Greenside, Calton Hill, Edinburgh, probably on August 12, 1554. But it also, as Carpenter argues,[8] suggests the complexity of Lyndsay's own religious position, and demonstrates the care with which he navigates the fraught doctrinal controversies of mid-century Scotland in the *Satyre*. From very soon after his death, as we have seen, reformers were claiming the playwright as a forerunner of the protestant cause. But, as we shall see, in the *Satyre,* his most public work, his position was much more nuanced than that claimed by Charteris. And, on closer inspection it becomes clear that the play was tied much more intimately to the shifting agendas and mundane frustrations of catholic religious reform, and indeed to the conclusions of those same provincial councils that Charteris claimed condemned the playwright and his works, than it was to the currents of continental Protestantism.

In one sense, perhaps, we should not be surprised by Lyndsay's seeming preference for the Latin Vulgate over the vernacular, and his tendency to cite and paraphrase it rather than any contemporary translation. The Vulgate was

---

6 Charteris may have used the 1579 Edinburgh edition, *The Bible and Holy Scripture conteined in the Olde and Newe Testament,* printed by Alexander Arbuthnot and Thomas Bassandyne.

7 For the texts, see J. Derrick McClure, "A Comparison of the Bannatyne MS and the Quarto Texts of Lyndsay's *Ane Satyre of the Thrie Estaitis*," in *Scottish Language and Literature, Medieval and Renaissance,* ed. Dietrich Strauss and Horst W. Drescher (Frankfurt am Main: Peter Lang, 1986), 409–22.

8 Carpenter, "Verity's Bible," 70. See also Alec Ryrie, "Reform without Frontiers in the Last Years of Catholic Scotland," *English Historical Review* 119 (2004) nr. 480: 27–56, and Carole Edington, *Court and Culture in Renaissance Scotland: Sir David Lyndsay of the Mount* (Amherst: University of Massachusetts Press, 1994), 146–47.

the text that he would have heard read aloud and learned in childhood and with which he had grown up, so it was probably the text that came naturally to mind when he thought about the scriptural Word. It is interesting to compare his approach here with that of another roughly contemporary figure, John Knox. He, while clearly polemically evangelical and protestant, was also inclined, as David Wright has shown, to quote the scriptures from memory from the Vulgate, and, when translating passages extemporarily he tended to Anglicize the Vulgate rather than reach for the translations of Tyndale, Coverdale, or the Genevan exiles.[9] So, perhaps we should not expect reformers of Lyndsay's generation to quote readily any of the protestant translations of the bible then available. For them the biblical text par excellence remained the Vulgate, however many intellectual and theological reservations they might have held about its authority or the implications of its more contested readings. But Lyndsay's use of the Vulgate, I would argue, is more pointed than that, and more revealing. Habitual it may have been (and his very use of the Latinate name "Veritie" rather than the more Anglophone 'Truth' for his figure of scriptural authority would suggest that such habits ran deep),[10] but it was also strategic, a signalling of his broad allegiance to a project of progressive catholic reform rather than anything more extreme. He clearly wanted the biblical Word to be available to the Scottish people in their own language, but it was a vernacularisation of the Vulgate that he seems to have wanted rather than a new text which contested the details and emphases of the Latin work. Hence his embodiment of reformation in the *Satyre*, Divine Correctioun, is open-minded about just who should do the preaching that would reveal God's Word to the people, rather than determined to find scholars who would push a particular confessional agenda. When Diligence asks him, "Quhat gif I find sum halie provinciall || Or minister of the gray freiris all, || Sall I bring them with me in cumpanie?" (ll. 3183–85), he replies,

Cair thou nocht quhat estait sa ever he be,	
Sa thay can teich and preich the veritie.	[so long as]
Maist cunning clarks with us is best *beluifit*,	[beloved]
To *dignitie* thay salbe first *promuifit*.	[office; promoted]
Quhidder thay be munk, channon, preist or freir,	[whether]

---

9   David Wright, "John Knox's Bible," in *The Bible as Book: The Reformation*, ed. Orlaith O'Sullivan (London and New Castle, DE: The British Library and Oak Knoll Press, 2000), 52. John Bale was another reformer who cited the Vulgate rather than any reformed text. I am very grateful to Peter Happé for this last point.

10 Ibid., 53.

Sa thay can preich, faill nocht to bring them heir. (ll. 3186–91)

It is learning: the ability to read, understand, and reveal the Word that Correctioun prizes. He is not calling for a cadre of reformist preachers to counter the malign influence of the established church and its teachings (the absence of any reference to 'superstition', 'popish ignorance', or similar phrases redolent of protestant propaganda is telling here). It is not that current preaching and teaching are wrong, in his view, but that hitherto the clergy have not preached or taught at all, and the bishop, Spirituality, has never read the Bible, so it is no wonder that the people are ignorant. And, significantly, the one example of reformed preaching that the play represents, the Doctor of Divinity's sermon (ll. 3474–551), proves to be an entirely conventional exposition of Christ's injunctions to love God and one's neighbours and the need for good works. Lyndsay's attacks upon the 'ignorance' of the clergy and people seem, then, not to be a coded critique of Catholicism, as they would be in the hands of a Knox or John Bale, but frustration at the literal ignorance of parishioners who did not know the contents of the New Testament or the fundamentals of the faith, and at the clergy who would or could not enlighten them. And here, as we shall see, his position was entirely in line with current thinking among the more progressive elements of the Scottish ecclesiastical elite.

Crucially, Lyndsay seems to have been far more enthusiastic about making the biblical word available through preaching and teaching than through ensuring the universal accessibility of the written word itself.[11] Hence there is almost nothing in the *Satyre* about biblical translators and printers, but a great deal about preachers and teachers. In this he was markedly less scripture-centred than most contemporary evangelical reformers, and somewhat more conservative than even a catholic reformer such as Erasmus, with his vision of a bible in the hands of every ploughman. But if we turn now to a detailed examination of the ways in which the *Satyre* addresses religious and doctrinal issues, the precise nature of the playwright's concerns and affiliations will become clearer.

2   Reform of the Church in *The Thrie Estaitis*

There can be no argument with the claim that the *Satyre* criticises the clergy: it does so vehemently and often. Lyndsay deploys a number of potent voices in a

---

[11]   Carpenter, "Verity's Bible," 64.

seemingly unremitting chorus of complaint and protest against Spirituality and his fellow churchmen, ranging from eloquent members of the distressed poor (Pauper, the Sowtar and Tailor) and the embodiment of the commonwealth (John the Commonweal) to personifications of Gude Counsall and Divine Correctioun (a representation of St Michael, God's angel of punishment). But the central planks of its strident anticlericalism are not doctrinal but moral and pastoral. These voices descant on only two primary themes, the sexual and financial abuses of the clergy and their failure to enlighten their congregations through preaching and teaching. Similarly, the reforms enacted by the three Estates purge the church of sexual incontinence, strip away the financial prerogatives of the clergy, take away their opportunities to exploit their landed estates for profit, and enforce a rigorous test of clerics' capacity to fulfil the responsibilities of their offices (which are defined almost exclusively as the obligation to preach and teach wholesome matter). There is nothing in their programme which touches on the central doctrinal pillars of the catholic faith – no criticism of the mass or of prayers to saints, no doubts about Purgatory, no mention of the means of Justification beyond exposition of the primary Commandments – and nothing either which challenges those aspects of catholic practice which had been dismissed as superstitious in England over the previous decade such as pilgrimages, image worship, or the existence of shrines.

Even when the play does flirt with radical ideas, as with the proposal to dissolve the Scottish nunneries, or the advocacy of clerical marriage, these things are justified on eminently practical rather than doctrinal grounds, combining criticism of alleged clerical immorality and sensuality with more pragmatic matters. Thus while nuns are declared to be 'not necessary', it is seemingly not because prayers and services for the dead are deemed non-efficacious, as monks and friars are tacitly allowed to continue, albeit with many of their privileges curtailed. What is 'unnecessary' about nuns would seem to be their inability to preach and teach. In Lyndsay's vision of a reformed church such things were men's responsibilities. Similarly, clerical marriage is discussed in very pragmatic terms. Slipped into the list of Acts without prior discussion, seemingly as the herald, Diligence's own idea, it is justified as it will end the need for concubines and allow the clergy to marry their children among themselves ("As Bischop Annas in Scripture we may se || Maryit his dochter on Bischop Caiphas" [ll. 3972–73] as Diligence wryly observes). And, if Alec Ryrie is correct, such pragmatic reasoning may well have commended the measure to some at least of Lyndsay's aristocratic spectators, especially "those noble and lairdly younger sons who wished both to hold lucrative ecclesiastical appointments and to have legitimate children."[12] All of this aligns the play's religious stance, not with John Knox and the protestant exiles, but more squarely with the contemporary reforming movement within the Scottish church led by Archbishop John Hamilton of St Andrews, coupled with some attitudes towards ecclesiastical and legal reform set in train in the reign of James V, and promoted by the king himself.

In a series of general provincial councils, the most important of which in Lyndsay's lifetime were held in 1549 and 1552, Hamilton and his allies introduced a swathe of measures designed to purge the clergy of corruption and shore up the church against its evangelical critics. As Ryrie elegantly sums it up, Hamilton's

> central concern was to confirm the laity in the faith through building an active preaching ministry, through restoring respect for the clergy, and, critically, through striving to make that faith palatable to those who might be inclined to doubt it.[13]

The 1549 council, held in Edinburgh from November 27, thus passed legislation for the tighter enforcement of clerical celibacy, the regulation of clerical households, the dress, physical appearance, and lifestyles of the clergy, and also provided the groundwork for a preaching ministry by establishing lectureships in theology in cathedrals and collegiate churches, and insisting on regular preaching in all parishes based on Scripture and the fundamentals of the faith, while the 1552 council issued a comprehensive book of guidance, 'Hamilton's Catechism', to aid less able priests to deliver such sermons. Both the language and the details of the councils' exposition of their statutes map with striking accuracy onto the argumentative structure and narrative detail of the *Satyre*. The 1549 session, for example, announced its intentions in terms that both echo the grounds for summoning the three Estates in the play and agree with its broad diagnosis of the failings of the clergy. It would, it declared,

> Follow the example of the prudent physician, and first of all seek by careful study to discover the causes and occasions of the sore maladies wherewith the morals of churchmen have now for a long time been

---

12 Alec Ryrie, *The Origins of the Scottish Reformation* (Manchester: Manchester University Press, 2006), 36.

13 Ibid., 97. See also James K. Cameron, "Humanism and Religious Life," in *Humanism in Renaissance Scotland*, ed. John MacQueen (Edinburgh: Edinburgh University Press, 1990), 161–77.

corrupted, and thereafter take thought for and provide suitable remedies. And whereas there appear to have been mainly two causes and roots of evils which have stirred up among us so great dissensions and occasions of heresies, to wit, the corruption of morals and profane lewdness of life of churchmen of almost all ranks, together with crass ignorance of literature and of all liberal arts – and from these two sources principally spring many abuses, this holy synod and provincial council has determined to ... put a check on these mischiefs so far as it can adequately to the exigency of the times.[14]

A similar determination to proceed carefully, by close enquiry, to determine the causes of deep-seated abuses colours the opening of Lyndsay's parliament in the second half of his play, which is heralded by the striking image of the three Estates processing backwards to the meeting. When Rex proposes immediately to confront them about their misordered behaviour, Gude Counsell advises him rather to act only after he has discovered by careful observation and questioning the root causes of their behaviour (ll. 2347–58). And, although this enquiry discovers a range of abuses practised by the secular estates, it is to the failings of the clergy that the play devotes the vast majority of its time and attention, and here too the dramatic action follows closely the emphases of the reforming councils.

A central strand of Hamilton and his allies' reformation of clerical morals was the enforcement of celibacy and the punishment of concubinage. The 1549 council endorsed the decree of the Council of Basel, *De Concubinariis*, stipulating that any priest, "even though he be of Episcopal or other kind of pre-eminence whatever, who shall be notoriously the keeper of a concubine," shall, after due warning, be suspended for three months, and enjoined to put away his concubine, on pain of formal suspension from office. And those superiors who were lax in enforcing these stipulations should themselves be punished.[15] That Hamilton himself kept a mistress might imply that these measures paid merely lip service to the idea of reform. But, as Ryrie suggests, the sustained attention focused on the issue by successive general councils gives the strong impression that the administration was determined to cut out abuses – at least everywhere beyond Hamilton's own household.[16] And a simi-

---

14   *The Statutes of the Scottish Church, 1225–1559: Being a Translation of the Concilia Scotiae*, ed. David Patrick, Publications of the Scottish History Society, 54 (Edinburgh: University Press, 1907), 84.
15   Ibid., 89.
16   Ryrie, *Origins*, 95.

lar determination colours the *Satyre* throughout. Every one of the clerical figures satirised in the play proves to be wedded to Sensuality and unwilling to reject her, even when Chastitie literally comes knocking at their doors to remind them of their vows (see ll. 1212–79). Spirituality boasts that "concubeins I have had four or fyfe, || And to my sons I have givin rich rewairds || And all my dochters maryit upon lairds" (ll. 3388–90). The Abbot similarly talks of his paramours "baith als fat and fair, || As ony wench into the toun of Air", sends his sons to Paris to the Schools, and provides good dowries for his daughters (ll. 3433–38), while the Abbasse confesses that she would have taken up Chastitie, but her "complexioun thairto wald nat assent" (l. 3454). All of these sexual offenders are expelled from the play's reformed *kirk* and replaced by more prudent pastors.

Given the play's pointed suggestion that the wealthy are always able to evade such laws through the payment of bribes (see ll. 2845 and 2660–73), it is also noteworthy that the 1549 statute stipulated that punishment could not be commuted to a money payment, condemning the practice in no uncertain terms:

> Now, whereas some who have ecclesiastical jurisdiction in certain countries do not blush to receive money payment from concubinaries, allowing them meanwhile to wallow in such filthiness, wherefore this holy synod enacts, under pain of eternal anathema, that they never hereafter tolerate or overlook such crimes in any manner of way in consequence of any compact, composition, or hope of any returns in money.[17]

In both play and council too, the attention to clerical sexual offences is grounded on social and economic as well as moral grounds. The stresses placed on the social hierarchy by the principal consequence of the clergy's unchastity, the existence of their illegitimate offspring, is a preoccupation of the *Satyre*. Both the Abbot and Spiritualitie, as we have seen, boast of the good marriages that they have achieved, or aim to achieve, for their children. Meanwhile, the secular lord, Temporalitie, laments the consequences for his own class of a marriage market flooded with the bastard children of manse and monastery.

> Sir, we beseik Your Soverane Celsitude
> Of our dochtours to have compassioun,
> Quhom wee may na way marie, *be* the Rude, [by]

---

17   Patrick, *Statutes*, 91.

> Without wee mak sum alienatioun
> Of our land for thair supportatioun.
> *For quhy* the markit raisit bene sa hie [because]
> That prelats dochtours of this natioun
> Ar maryit with sic superfluitie
> Thay will nocht spair to gif twa thowsand pound
> With thair docthtours to ane nobill man,
> In riches sa thay do superabound. (ll. 3194–204)

As a result the Estates agree upon an Act forbidding the offspring of clerics from intermarrying with the laity (ll. 3958–62).

Far from emerging from nowhere, this issue was also a matter of concern for the Council of 1549, which legislated that,

> This synod exhorts that neither prelates nor their subordinate clergy keep their offspring born of concubinage in their company, nor suffer them directly or indirectly to be promoted to their churches, nor under any colour of any pretext to marry their daughters to barons or make their sons barons out of the patrimony of Christ.[18]

Rather than representing a direct challenge to the ecclesiastical hierarchy, then, Lyndsay's focus on the sexual immorality, fecundity, and nepotism of the clergy directly reflected the initiatives of the contemporary provincial councils.

A second area of concern in both drama and synod concerned the workings of the ecclesiastical courts, and their tendency to favour those who could pay to manipulate the system over those who could not. Pauper's anguished account of the delays and impoverishment that he has suffered in seeking justice in the Consistory court (ll. 3072–91), finds echoes in the statutes, which sought to ban obstructive, time-wasting tactics designed to slow down due process in the church courts.

> Item, no one shall insist on longer delays than the necessity of the case demands, plead false excuses of his own remissness, or trickery with intent to prolong the suit … hinder the execution of decreets through the

---

18 Ibid., 92.

disappearance of [documents] ... or let law suits sleep through counsel on either side acting in collusion with each other.[19]

The issue resurfaced in the catechism propounded by the 1552 council and published by Hamilton later in the same year. There, among the perverters of justice who are said to offend against the commandment condemning theft, are listed,

> speciallie Advocatis, Procuratours, and Scrybis, quhidder they be of temporal court or spirituall, [who] braikis [th]is command twa maner of ways. First quhen [th]ai tak wagis to procure or defende a cause quhilk [th]ai ken [i.e., *which they know*] is unlauchfull and aganis justice. Secundlie, quhen for their wagis that tak on hand an lauchfull cause, bot for lucre of geir thay differ [i.e., *defer*] and puttis of[f] the executioun of justice fra day to day, and oft tymes fra ʒeir to ʒeir to the gret skaith and herschyppe [i.e., *hardship*] of thaim quhilk hes ane rycht action of the pley.[20]

For all Spiritualitie's bluster against Pauper's complaints (see ll. 3102–04), then, Lyndsay's satire was knocking at an open door in terms of ecclesiastical willingness to acknowledge the failings of the legal system and to address them.

Another particular area of shared interest between playwright and synod concerned the use of church lands, and specifically the practice of leasing out lands in the forms of tenure known as the feu-farm and tack to those who would manage them for personal profit rather than for the good of the parish or commonweal (2575–2605, 2688–2703). The statutes of 1549 share the *Satyre's* concern at the abuses created by the clergy leasing out their glebe lands and other estates for short-term profit via these instruments:

> Lest by the non-residence of vicars, rectors, and prebendaries the function of those who minister in the cure of souls and the sacraments of the church be neglected, it is enacted that no infestments or leases in feu-farm, or tacks for a long time, of any manner of glebes or church lands, or vicarages be henceforth granted by the rectors or vicars in person, unless for good reasons previously considered ... in general or provincial synod,

---

19   Ibid., 130 and 131–34. See also 129–30.
20   *The Catechisme: That is to say, ane com[m]une and catholik instructioun of the christin people in matteris of our catholik faith and religioun, quhilk na gud christin man or woman suld misknaw* ... (s.n. [= St. Andrews], 1552), fol. lx(v).

and found to tend to the benefit of these same churches, and not only to the private advantage of the individual possessors.[21]

3 Preaching the Word

It is hard, then, to avoid the conclusion that, far from being dangerously incendiary in its satirical agenda, Lyndsay's play was modelling its allegations against the clergy very closely on the issues identified and legislated against by the councils of 1549 and 1552, and the abuses castigated in Hamilton's catechism.[22] Even such seemingly throwaway details as the Parson's comments about the fashionable hats currently worn by the parish clergy ("Our round bonats we mak them now four-nuickit, || Of richt fine stuiff, gif yow list cum and luik it" [ll. 3445–46]) echo an issue legislated for by the 1549 council, which decreed that, under penalty of suspension, "beneficed churchmen and clerks in holy orders shall according to the ancient custom of the clergy wear only round birettas, and shall always take off their caps in churches," as part of an attempt to stop them dressing like laymen ("as for example, in top-boots, and double-breasted or oddly cut coats, or [coats] of forbidden colours, as yellow, green, and such kinds of parti-colour"[23]).

But far and away the most important thrust of the 1549 statutes, reemphasised in the council of 1552, was the need to educate the clergy in order that they should preach and teach the laity in the essentials of the faith. Here again they are echoed emphatically in the *Satyre*'s wry reflections on the ignorance of the clergy, the lack of preaching received in the parishes, the unwillingness or inability of bishops and subordinate clerics to preach, and the need for a

---

21   Patrick, *Statutes*, 97.
22   In a less serious register, it is tempting to see in the scurrilous mock divorce provided for the Sowtar and his wife by the corrupt pardoner, Robert Rome-Raker, a wry comment on the issue legislated for by the 1552 Council: "… whereas it happens that causes relating to matrimony are too lightly despatched in court, albeit they are in their own nature eminently serious and difficult questions, and are of right reserved exclusively to bishops, therefore it is statute by this holy convention … that, in matrimonial causes tending towards divorce, no decreets shall be given henceforth … unless such processes and the merits of their claims have been discussed and lawfully weighted by the ordinaries in person" (Patrick, *Statutes*, 138). It is not hard to see the 'divorce' performed by Robert, performed in return for a payment in cash and kind, concluded after the most perfunctory of examinations, and enacted by the couple kissing each other's arses, as a parody of the solemnity and seriousness enjoined here.
23   Ibid., 92.

new, educated clergy to push forward the reforms enacted by Correction, Rex, and the Estates (see, for example, ll. 2754–55, 4468–73). Noting that preaching "is the principal duty of bishops,"[24] the 1549 synod enjoined that every bishop and local ordinary (those with law-enforcing powers within the church) should preach in person the Word of God to their flock at least four times a year. And any bishop who has "hitherto exercised themselves too little in preaching, they shall fit themselves as soon as they may for the discharge of their duty, both by their own application and the help of others who are skilled."[25] In addition,

> Every ordinary shall have a care that throughout his diocese rectors of parishes and other ecclesiastical persons shall strive with all their might that the word of God be expounded to their flocks purely, sincerely, and in a catholic sense, that the true uses of the church's ceremonies be moderately, soberly, and discreetly explained; [and] that false opinions be prohibited, denounced, and confuted.[26]

As Ryrie suggests, Hamilton's agenda was to galvanize the church into a preaching ministry in order both to educate the population at large in the necessary fundamentals of the faith and to counter the influence of heretical ideas by elucidating orthodox doctrine. He and his allies were prepared to acknowledge the failings of the clergy at all levels as the first steps in a process of renewal echoing the initiatives of the opening sessions of the Council of Trent (1545–63), and contemporary reforms in the archdiocese of Cologne. Hence even Gavin Dunbar, the Archbishop of Glasgow, was provoked to apologise publically for his failure to preach regularly, and to promise to do so more assiduously in the future.[27]

When Lyndsay has Diligence declare to Folly, toward the end of the *Satyre*, that "Our new bischops hes maid ane preiching, || Bot thou heard never sic ane pleasant teiching: || Yon Bischop will preich throch the cost," and Folly reply, "Than stryke ane hag [i.e., *nail*] into the poast; || For I hard never in all my lyfe || Ane bischop cum to preich in Fyfe" (ll. 4468–73), he was doing no more, then, politically speaking, than adding comic emphasis and impetus to self-criticisms already set on record by the church authorities, and giving dramatic embodiment to Hamilton's ambitions for a renewed, preaching episcopate.

---

24 Ibid., 101.
25 Ibid., 98.
26 Ibid., 124.
27 Ryrie, *Origins*, 102–3; James K. Cameron, "Catholic Reform in Germany and in the pre-1560 Church of Scotland," *Records of the Scottish Church History Society* 20 (1979): 105–17.

And similarly, when the playwright has his ignorant parish priest boast that "Thocht I preich not, I can play at the caiche. || I wait [i.e., *believe*] thair is nocht ane among yow all || Mair ferilie can play at the fute-ball" (ll. 3440–42), he was picking up on the perceived lack of education and consequent inability to preach among the parish clergy that prompted the Council to endorse and promote Hamilton's catechism, which was produced "considering … that the inferior clergy of this realm and the prelates have not, for the most part, attained such proficiency in the knowledge of the holy Scriptures as to be able by their own efforts rightly to instruct the people in the catholic faith and other things necessary to salvation, or to convert the erring".[28]

4 Reforming Drama

Even a cursory examination of the similarities between the *Satyre* and the reforming initiatives embodied in the statutes of 1549 and 1552 should be enough to suggest the close and detailed relationship between the two. As Lyndsay was writing his play for the 1552 production in Cupar, he seems to have been acutely aware of the discussions in the councils, the second of which concluded only months before, and determined to echo and explore them in his work.[29] The play is shot through with the same issues, and proposes many of the same solutions to them as the council proposed. Its diagnosis of an ignorant, immoral, vainglorious clergy unwilling or unable to understand and communicate the lessons of the Scriptures and the rudiments of the faith to its lay charges is thus not a radical assault on ecclesiastical practice from outside the church but a close reflection of elements of the church hierarchy's view of its own failings articulated in 1549 and reinforced in 1552, and embodied in Hamilton's catechism which would be distributed for public reading to every parish later that year.

At times the play and Hamilton's reforming texts are strikingly similar, both in their vocabulary and their intentions, as in the following passage from the catechism listing among those who offend against the seventh commandment "tham that defrauds or spoulȝeis the com[m]on geir, aganis the com[m]on weill for luf of thair awin pryvate and syngulare weill …"

---

28 Patrick, *Statutes*, 143.
29 Folly's allusion to the St Andrews Paternoster controversy (ll. 4636–41), which had been debated in the 1552 Council, seems further to cement this claim.

> All merchandis that sellis corruppit and evyll stufe for gude, and gyf thay or ony uthir in bying or sellyng use desait, falsate, periurie, wrang metis or weychtis, to the skaith of thair nychtbour, thay com[m]it gret syn agane this com[m]and. Nother can we clenge fra breakyng of this com[m]and all kyndis of craftis men, quhilk uses nocht thair awin craft leillalie and trewlie as [th]ai suld do.[30]

The language of common weal and singular profit, the criticism of corrupt craftsmen and of counterfeit goods, and even the collocation of the three terms, deceit, falsehood, and perjury; these are the common currency of Lyndsay's satire. Indeed, the correlation between deceit, falsehood, and perjury, and Lyndsay's vices, Dissait, Falset, and Flatterie (Gude Counsall names him 'Fals Report' [l. 980]) seems so striking as to suggest a direct echo of the catechism.

Even where Lyndsay's play seems irreverent to the point of heterodoxy, as in its apparent indifference to Papal authority, and its criticisms of the Roman church and curia, it was echoing the strategies and emphases of Hamilton's reforming programme and earlier initiatives by the playwright's former charge and sovereign, James V. The absence of any reference to Rome and the papacy in Hamilton's catechism is, as Ryrie suggests, a striking omission, indicative of the archbishop's frustrations with the politics of the curia and his wish to secure legatine powers for himself.[31] The memorable tirade in the play against 'Rome-runners' voiced by the otherwise reserved Gude Counsall also seems an oppositional statement, aligning Lyndsay with those seeking a break from Rome along English lines. But it too has its roots in the thinking of the Scottish government, in this case in the pragmatic concerns of Lyndsay's former master, James V. For, as Ryrie notes, the king had been equally vocal in his frustrations at the way in which his own authority, and his capacity to exercise patronage over the Scottish church, was not infrequently circumvented by independent lobbying by clerics in Rome for Scottish benefices for which the king had other ideas in mind, or pardons for offences which he wished to punish.[32] Hence an Act had been passed against the practice in 1541, and James repeatedly lobbied the pope himself for the appointment of a *legate a latere* for Scotland, who would be able to exercise papal authority within the realm in the same way that Cardinal Wolsey had in the interests of Henry VIII in England in the 1520s, and so prevent the majority of appeals to Rome. But attempts to nominate first

---

30   *Catechisme*, fols. lviii(v)–lix. See also lix–lix(v).
31   Ryrie, *Origins*, 94 and 99.
32   Ibid., 38.

James's old tutor, Gavin Dunbar, and then Cardinal David Beaton for the role had yielded nothing by the time James died in 1542.[33]

Also rooted in the preoccupations of James's reign was the play's concern with the need for royal justice to be exercised more obviously and consistently in the interests of the poor. James V had proudly fostered the image of himself as 'the poor man's king' through conspicuous acts such as the creation of a legal officer who would plead poor men's cases in the courts pro bono, and the establishment, by Act of the parliament of 1532, of a new College of Justice, created, as the Act declared,

> Because our soverane is maist desyrous to have ane permanent ordoure of justice for the universalle wele of all his liegis and thairfor tendis to Institute ane College of cunning and wise men...for the doing and administracioune of justice.[34]

It is this pragmatic royal initiative that Lyndsay plays upon and extends in the *Satyre*, through the proposal that a second College be established to take the efficient delivery of royal justice into the highlands and the north (ll. 3855–86). The care and detail with which he sets out the structure of this proposed college, with its president and sixteen senators (carefully specifying two more than James's original foundation),[35] the generous terms of their stipends, and the means by which it is to be funded from the revenues of dissolved nunneries, is an index of the significance of the measure for Lyndsay's conception of a reformed Scotland. Similarly James's idealised image of himself as 'the poor man's king', only ever fitfully lived up to in his lifetime, just as surely stands behind the representation of Rex Humanitas in the play summoning the three Estates with a request that any man with a grievance against church or state should appear and present it without hesitation or fear, as does his subsequent willingness to act upon John the Commonweal and Pauper's complaints.

There is, however, a curious paradox, or queasy unease, in Lyndsay's attitude towards spiritual reform in the play. On the one hand he closely echoes the reforms of Hamilton and his allies, combining these with an obvious harking back to the measures pursued by James V in his dealings with Rome and the domestic church leadership, using the image of a divinely-inspired monarch as the vehicle for the suppression of clerical abuses and the reform of society. To this degree, he offers in Rex Humanitas the image of James V *redivivus* as a

---

33   Ibid., 38.
34   *Acts of the Parliament of Scotland*, 12.
35   Edington, *Court and Culture*, 134.

solution to Scotland's ecclesiastical and social problems. Yet, behind that apparent willingness to endorse James V's own thwarted ambitions to be a quasi-absolutist reforming monarch in the model of Henry VIII or François I, there is also evident a profound distrust of kings in general, and of James V in particular, if left entirely to their own devices. Lyndsay knew James and his foibles too well to take him or his successors wholly seriously as the answer to all the nation's problems. Hence, he marshals all the resources of Erasmian humanism to hedge his reforming monarch about with checks and balances, with the formal apparatus of council and parliament, and with the influence of Chastitie, Veritie, Gude Counsall, and Divine Correctioun, all of whom inform him in no uncertain terms of the dangers of tyranny and the importance of surrounding himself with sound advisors, whose guidance must direct his own actions.

A similarly shrewd political wisdom, born of experience, seems to underlie the playwright's treatment of church reform, acting as an undertone of caution beneath the apparently enthusiastic endorsement of the initiatives of the ecclesiastical councils that the play offers. The broad thrust of Lyndsay's satire against worldly, ignorant clergy who do not fulfil their duties would have found a sympathetic hearing among Hamiltonian reformers eager to advance essentially Erasmian reforms. For such men, intent upon reaching a consensual reform of the church from within, what Jane Dawson has called "the worldly cleric grimly defending his privileges seemed a greater obstacle [to reform] than the heretic."[36] Hence they were ready to criticise their failings to the point of "flagellation,"[37] and to envisage reforms that would have placed them dangerously close to Protestantism in their campaign to remove those clergy unwilling or unable to fulfil their duties. But Lyndsay was not averse to pushing the boundaries of this consensus, and nudging his audiences to understand that commitment needed to go beyond idealistic declarations and hopeful enjoinders if reform was to be effective in practice. Dawson notes the lukewarm contemporary response to (and limited effectiveness of) Hamilton's conciliar initiatives:

> Though the decrees were eminently worthy, tightening clerical discipline and providing a limited educational programme to deliver longer-term improvements, they lacked two crucial ingredients for a successful reform programme: religious zeal and a viable method of enforcement.

---

36 Jane E. Dawson, *Scotland Reformed, 1488–1587* (Edinburgh: Edinburgh University Press, 2007), 186.
37 Ryrie, *Origins*, 102.

> Specifically, there was a deafening silence on the subject of visitations, the time honoured method by which Council decrees were implemented. Visiting was essential if changes to the behaviour of the diocesan clergy and the regular orders were to be introduced and monitored.[38]

It is in this context that we should probably read Lyndsay's repeated insistence that the reforms enacted by the three Estates needed to be driven home in practice. The Council of 1549 *had* called for a programme of visitations to investigate and reform both the regular religious houses and the parish clergy. Regarding the former, the council noted that,

> Whereas it is manifest that the discipline of canons-regular and of monks has been weakened and relaxed in great part by the negligence of those whose duty it is to exercise supervision over them, the present convention exhorts in the Lord all and sundry the abbots, priors, commendators, and administrators of exempt monasteries, as far as they collectively and severally can, to strive, as becomes good pastors, to reform the life, morals, piety, and learning of monks, and to bring them back to the first state of the monastic institution, that so piety may flourish in their midst, and the murmers of the outside world be silenced.[39]

They similarly instructed that parish priests be examined regarding their fitness for office.

> Betwixt this and the last day of December next to come, all curates [should] be cited by their local ordinaries to appear before the said ordinaries or their commissaries, deputed or to be deputed thereto, and undergo a due examination in all the requirements of their offices.[40]

Any found wanting should be required to resign at the next synod.

These stipulations are impressive in their commitment to reform, but their exhortatory (rather than compulsory) tone is explicit. The power of visitation remained with the bishops and heads of houses themselves, and so relied upon

---

38   Dawson, *Scotland Reformed*, 186.
39   Patrick, *Statutes*, 94–5. The stress here on visiting those houses exempt from Episcopal authority is echoed in Lyndsay's jibes at the clergy's capacity to claim exemption from Scottish jurisdiction every time they are threatened with reform (see, for example, ll. 2704–06).
40   Ibid., 110.

their commitment to the project for their success. And, since it was often recalcitrant bishops and abbots who were at the root of the problems, the flaw in the system was obvious. Hence, perhaps, the rather different approach to the question of visitations taken in the *Satyre*. There Divine Correctioun and Gude Counsall also insist upon a general visitation of the clergy to root out and replace those who cannot fulfil their duties to preach and teach, which results in the deprivation of the Abbasse, Vicar, Abbot, and Spiritualitie himself. But, strikingly, they invest the responsibility to conduct the visitation, not in the senior clergy but in the king (ll. 3350–72). The failing clergy are then replaced by the educated Doctor and Licents, better able to understand and deliver the agenda of a preaching, teaching ministry.

But Lyndsay does not leave things there. In a pointed reminder to those in authority, both on and off-stage, that reforms need to be followed up if they are to be effective, he gives the last word to Pauper, who, following the grand recitation of the Acts of the Parliament, declares,

I gif yow my braid *bennesoun*,	[blessing]
That hes givin Common-weill a goun.	
I wald nocht for ane pair of *plackis*,	[four-penny coins]
Ye had nocht maid thir nobill Actis.	
I pray to God and sweit Sanct Geill	
To gif yow grace to use them weill:	
Wer thay weill *keipit*, I understand,	[kept]
It *war* great honour to Scotland.	[would (be)]
It had bene als gude ye had sleipit,	[(But) it]
As to mak Actis and *be nocht keipit*.	[(they) be not kept]
Bot I beseik yow for Allhallows,	
To *heid* Dissait and hang his fellows,	[behead]
And banische Flattrie aff the toun,	
For thair was never sic ane loun.	
That *beand* done, I hauld it best	[being]
That everie man ga to his rest.	(ll. 3982–97)

The implication seems clear: high aspirations are one thing, the will to carry them through against indifference and active opposition over time, quite another, so the people will remain vigilant and will react angrily if there is any suggestion of betraying the reforming principles initiated by Correctioun. And, significantly, while Dissait and his fellows are hanged, Flatterie is not banished, but rather goes back into the church, seeking shelter with one of James v's favoured clerics, the hermit of Loreto (ll. 4299–301), and so the potential for continued corruption remains. And the play ends with the sermon of the fool, Folly, whose text, "Infinite are the number of fools" suggest that no one, prince, prelate or pauper, is free from responsibility for the state into which the church and society have got themselves.

All of this suggests a playwright who was determined, not to bring down the established church but to further its reform, who used his play as a means of popularising the reforming agenda behind the Provincial Councils of 1549 and 1552, and of representing the kinds of abuses and resistance that those councils were seeking to uproot in striking and memorable ways. Yet it also suggests, I would argue, a Lyndsay who was not content simply to mirror the agenda of the councils in dramatic form, but was also seeking to intervene in the politics of conciliar reform and its reception in the civic community, and to hold the reforming intentions behind it to account. Mindful of the many slips, compromises, and negotiations necessary to enact reform in the *Realpolitik* of a Scottish minority, he used drama's traditional capacity to speak truth to power to stress the need to do more than simply pass statutes if the intention really was to mend Scotland's broken spiritual commonwealth.[41]

5   Whose Reformation? The Complexities of Reform

The *Satyre's* attitude to ecclesiastical reform is thus more complex and conflicted than an account such as Henry Charteris's would suggest, both closer to the agenda of the church authorities that Lyndsay was satirising than might initially appear and more reflective of the intricacies of contemporary politics. It is a play about the difficulties of reform in an age of Reformation rather than a Reformation play *per se*. It stages the breadth of the contemporary cultural landscape in an exploration of what reform might involve in the current Scottish context, reflecting a range of current opinions from the stereotypes of anticlerical discourse to specific allegations seemingly born of direct local experience. Hence some of the virtuous characters it portrays are more radical in their views than others, and some of the opinions expressed less orthodox than others, without the play as a whole necessarily endorsing them wholeheartedly

---

41   The combination of its dialogic form and affective power, coupled with the tradition of moral drama as a moral 'mirror', gave the interludes and moralities of the sixteenth century a particular capacity to offer their patrons and audiences often quite abrasive good counsel. For examples, see Greg Walker, *Plays of Persuasion: Drama and Politics at the Court of Henry VIII* (Cambridge: Cambridge University Press, 1991) and *The Politics of Performance in Early-Renaissance Drama* (Cambridge: Cambridge University Press, 1998).

or consistently. Thus John the Commonweal argues at one point for the expulsion from the realm of all entertainers, poets, and musicians along with sturdy beggars, charlatans of all kinds, and the regular religious (ll. 2609–15) – a line frequently encountered in legislation and commonwealth writing, but not one Lyndsay himself would seriously have endorsed, and which the play itself does not take further. Similarly, Diligence seems, as we have seen, to have presented the Estates with an Act enabling clerical marriage without their having debated or agreed upon it. The implication is that each character brings to the play, and to the debates in parliament, their own agenda, born of their own particular social position, class, beliefs, and vocation, which complicates the discussion, and the narrative, beyond the simple binaries of conventional moral drama. Religious reform is presented as no simple black and white matter (as it is, say, in the work of John Bale), but as a subject always already implicated in and interconnected with the diverse, conflicted interests of the various groups that make up Scottish civil society.

We see an instance of this diversity at the very start of part two, as the Estates gather for the parliament, and each responds quite differently to the nature of the assembly and the prospect of reform that it offers. Spiritualitie, the first to greet the king, fails even to acknowledge the reforming impetus behind the gathering, treating it as merely another occasion to signal his loyalty to royal authority and affirm the status quo, while taking the opportunity to claim precedence over the secular lords in the determination of affairs (ll. 2359–65). Temporalitie, while ready to acknowledge the reforming agenda behind the summons, nonetheless tries to place conditions and limitations on the scope of the punishment to be meted out, suggesting that his commitment to reform depends upon the use of mercy to temper Correction's reforming zeal ("We are content, but doubt that we may se || That nobill heavinlie King Correctioun, || Sa he with mercie mak punitioun" [ll. 2370–72]). Only Merchand signals a wholehearted enthusiasm for the reforming project and the punishment of "misdoers," but again only in terms that make transparent that he does so in the hope that it will further his own economic wellbeing ("For now I traist wee sall get rest and peace. || Quhen misdoars ar with your sword overthrawin, || Then may leil merchands live upon their awin" [ll. 2377–79]).

It is in this arena dominated by distinct private interests that the reform of the common weal will have to be hammered out under Correctioun's direction. The play at a stroke here both identifies the clergy as the principal barrier to reform, but also suggests that reform itself is a complex and conflicted issue, every bit as political as it is moral and confessional. And this is reflected in the succeeding debates, in which Temporalitie and Merchand join forces to deflect attention from their own failings and abuses (Spiritualitie's passing admission that he pays many noblemen an annual retainer to ensure their loyalty [ll. 3395–98] is not pursued) and ultimately to defeat Spiritualitie by weight of numbers rather than the force of their arguments.

It is this kind of nuanced, politically-aware approach to the pragmatics of reform during a royal minority that provides the context for Veritie's role in the *Satyre*. She carries an English New Testament and she has, like many a heretic and heretical book, come into Scotland from the Continent, having "oversaillit many stormie sey" (l. 1080). But she is not demonstrably doctrinally heterodox. Her primary call is for priests to live a moral life as good examples to their flocks, and she stresses the importance of works and deeds rather than faith – which would seem to align her with traditional catholic rather than protestant teaching.

> *Sic luceat lux vestra coram hominibus ut videat opera vestra bona.*[42]
> And specially ye princes of the preists,
> That of the peopill hes spiritual cuir,
> Dayly ye sould revolve into your breistis
> How that thir haly words ar still maist sure:
> In vertuous lyfe gif that ye do indure,
> The peopill wil tak mair tent to your deids
> Then to your wordis; and als baith rich and puir
> Will follow yow baith in your warks and words.   (ll. 1068–76)

And yet she is readily identified as a heretic by her ecclesiastical persecutors. Significantly, though, the process by which this happens is itself again complex, conflicted, and politicised. On seeing Veritie enter the playing area, Flatterie's initial intention is to flee, believing that he is about to be exposed and that his corrupt game is up. It is only Falset's intervention that persuades him to "ather gang or ryde || To Lords of Spritualitie || And gar them trow yon bag of pryde || Hes spoken manifest heresie" (ll. 1093–96). When Flatterie duly warns Spiritualitie that, "Be scho ressavit, but [i.e., *without*] doubt wee ar bot schent" (l. 1101), the latter too is unsure how best to act, until the Abbot proposes that they imprison her without charge until the third day of the coming parliament and then either "accuse hir of hir herisie || Or than banishe hir out of this cuntrie" (ll. 1116–17), while the Persoun more pointedly encourages him to "go destroy all thir Lutherians, || In speciall yon Ladie Veritie" (ll. 1126–27). Still ignoring the question of doctrine, Spiritualitie then sends the Persoun and

---

42   So let your light shine before men, that they may see your good works, and glorify your Father who is in heaven.

Flatterie in commission to interrogate Veritie, with the instruction that "gif scho speiks against our libertie || Then put hir in perpetuall presoun, || That scho cum nocht to King Humanitie" (ll. 1133–35).

The clerical agenda in the play is thus far from clear or unified. The corrupt priests are determined to maintain their traditional privileges but seem very uncertain about what kind of doctrinal threat, if any, Veritie poses. And indeed, as we have seen, she does not seem interested in the details of doctrine either, being focused on reforming clerical morality rather than disputing the nature of Justification. Hence, when she replies to Flatterie's accusation that her New Testament represents heresy, "Forsuith, my friend, ye have ane rang judgement, || For in this buik there is na heresie, || Bot our Christis word, baith dulce and redolent, || Ane springing well of sinceir veritie" (ll. 1156–59), we might, perhaps, conclude that Lyndsay intended audiences to take her at her word. Such an exchange seems reflective of the blurred lines characteristic of mid-sixteenth century Scottish religious culture, in which the distance between reforming Catholicism and evangelical heresy was not always great or easy to determine, and nothing was quite as clear cut as writers such as Knox or Charteris would subsequently claim.

And the play as a whole seems equally careful – at times even coy – about what exactly constitutes heresy or unacceptable belief. On a number of occasions it signals an alliance with the kind of divisive reform associated with protestant evangelicalism. Diligence begins the second part, for example, with a challenging defence of the action to follow, claiming that "We sall say nathing bot the suith" (l. 2308), but assumes that this will in itself divide the audience. "Gude virtuous men, that luifis the veritie" (l. 2309) will excuse any negligence on the part of the players,

> Bot vicious men, denude of charitie,
> As feinyeit fals flattrand Saracens,
> Howbeit they cry on us ane loud vengeance,
> And of our pastyme mak ane fals report,
> Quhat may wee do bot tak in patience,
> And us refer unto the faithfull sort? (ll. 2311–16)

And the kind of division he envisages is clearly confessional in nature, and likely to lead to allegations of heresy, for he concludes,

> Our Lord Jesus, Peter nor Paull
> Culd nocht *complies* the peopill all,   [please/content]
> Bot sum war miscontent;

> Howbeit thay schew the veritie,
> Sum said that it war heresie,
> Be their maist fals judgement. (ll. 2317–22)

But what the play goes on to deliver is, as we have seen, not as threatening doctrinally as this might suggest. Its critique of the clergy stays well clear of the issues that marked the battle ground between Wittenberg, Geneva, and Rome, and its "Lutherans" are not really very Lutheran at all. We are thus left with the conclusion that Lyndsay was either consciously presenting the play as more radical, theologically, than it actually was, or, conversely, was presenting radical reform in the Hamiltonian mould as actually rather less threatening and divisive than its critics might claim, staging the politics of such a reformation in such a way as to make it appear a self-evidently unifying rather than divisive process for the commonweal. A spectator seeking clarification from the play about the precise nature of those blurred lines between Veritie and heresy was thus unlikely to have come away with any clearer sense of what the issues at stake really were. What they would have emerged with, however, if the *Satyre* had achieved its apparent aims, was a strong sense of the need for the clergy to address their own moral and institutional failings (or have them addressed for them by the civil authorities), and of the critical importance of preaching and teaching to the spiritual health of the commonweal, and also of the very real difficulties that the community as a whole would have to face in order to achieve those aims.

Bibliography

Bible and Holy Scripture Conteined in the Olde and Newe Testament, The. Edinburgh: Alexander Arbuthnot and Thomas Bassandyne, 1579.

Bible and Holy Scriptures Conteyned in the Olde and Newe Testament, The, Translated according to the Ebrue and Greke, and Conferred with the best Translations in Divers Languages. Geneva: Rowland Hall, 1560.

Cameron, James K. "Catholic Reform in Germany and in the pre-1560 Church of Scotland." *Records of the Scottish Church History Society* 20 (1979): 105–17.

———. "Humanism and Religious Life." In *Humanism in Renaissance Scotland*, edited by John MacQueen, 161–77. Edinburgh: Edinburgh University Press, 1990.

Carpenter, Sarah. "Verity's Bible: Books, Texts, and Reading in *Ane Satyre of the Thrie Estaitis*." *Medieval English Theatre* 33 (2011): 58–74.

Catechisme, The: That is to say, ane com[m]one and catholik instructioun of the christin people in matteris of our catholik faith and religioun, quhilk na gud christin man or woman suld misknaw ... St Andrews: [s. n.], 1552.

Charteris, Henry. "Preface to the Reidar." In *The Warkis of the famous and [w]orthie knicht, Sir David Lyndesay of the Mount*, sig ii(v)-iii. Edinburgh: Henry Charteris, 1568.

———. "Adhortatioun of All Estatis To the Reiding of Thir Present Warkis." In ibid., sig. Aii [17–24].

Dawson, Jane E. *Scotland Reformed, 1488–1587*. Edinburgh: Edinburgh University Press, 2007.

Derrick McClure, J. "A Comparison of the Bannatyne MS and the Quarto Texts of Lyndsay's *Ane Satyre of the Thrie Estaitis*." In *Scottish Language and Literature, Medieval and Renaissance*, edited by Dietrich Strauss and Horst W. Drescher, 409–22. Frankfurt am Main: Peter Lang, 1986.

"Douay-Rheims Bible + Challoner Notes" website. Accessed December 11, 2014, <http://www.drbo.org/chapter/61003.htm>.

Edington, Carole. *Court and Culture in Renaissance Scotland: Sir David Lyndsay of the Mount*. Amherst: University of Massachusetts Press, 1994.

Kenneth, Brother. "Sir David Lyndsay, Reformer." *Innes Review* 1 (1950): 79–91.

Patrick, David, ed. *The Statutes of the Scottish Church, 1225–1559: Being a Translation of the Concilia Scotiae*. Publications of the Scottish History Society, 54. Edinburgh: University Press, 1907.

Ryrie, Alec. "Reform without Frontiers in the Last Years of Catholic Scotland." *English Historical Review* 119 (2004) nr. 480: 27–56.

———. *The Origins of the Scottish Reformation*. Manchester: Manchester University Press, 2006.

Walker, Greg. *Plays of Persuasion: Drama and Politics at the Court of Henry VIII*. Cambridge: Cambridge University Press, 1991.

———. *The Politics of Performance in Early-Renaissance Drama*. Cambridge: Cambridge University Press, 1998.

———, ed. *Medieval Drama: An Anthology*. Blackwell Anthologies. Oxford: Blackwell, 2000.

Wright, David. "John Knox's Bible." In *The Bible as Book: The Reformation*, edited by Orlaith O'Sullivan. London and New Castle, DE: The British Library and Oak Knoll Press, 2000.

CHAPTER 3

Play Titles without Play Texts: What Can They Tell Us, and How? An Investigation of the Evidence for the Beverley Corpus Christi Play

Diana Wyatt

Abstract

Beverley, in the historical East Riding of Yorkshire, is known – from extant local manuscript evidence covering almost 150 years – to have had a Corpus Christi play like York, thirty miles to the north-west. The surviving Beverley manuscript records witness a play structure and performance method similar to that of York, though on a smaller scale: up to thirty-six pageants performed by craft guilds and other local groups on wagons at six stations over a route through the town from the North Bar to the port area at the Beckside. But whereas York also provides a play text which the manuscript evidence can support, from Beverley only records survive. This essay investigates the surviving evidence from Beverley itself as well as comparisons with extant play texts from York and elsewhere, and analogous evidence from Biblical subjects depicted in late medieval art, to try to establish how much we can learn from a play-text-less body of evidence about the content and nature of the Beverley play and its performance.

Key words

Beverley – Corpus Christi plays – pageant – labours of Adam and Eve – Seth – oil of mercy

1   Introduction

The absence of any surviving play text may seem an unpromising starting-point for a study of the Corpus Christi cycle of Beverley in the historic East Riding of Yorkshire. Clearly there is much that we simply cannot now discover about the play: the style and length of individual pageants, how (or whether) they were developed or revised over time, their possible resemblance to any surviving texts such as that of York, and any clues about performance style that might be given by stage directions. But a substantial quantity of documentary evidence for the play does survive from Beverley from 1377 to at least 1520,[1] which tells us that it was performed customarily, though not annually, on pageant wagons, by guilds and other local groups, and that it consisted of thirty-six pageants in the early sixteenth century, although the number may have varied over the years of its existence. This essay is an exercise in discovering just how much can be learned from the documentary evidence and analogies in surviving play texts from elsewhere and, failing appropriate textual analogies for specific pageants, from contemporary art.

2   The Pageant-Assignment List in the Beverley *Great Guild Book*

The main documentary focus for this exercise in evidence-based drama history is the only surviving list among the Beverley records of pageant-assignments to guilds, found on fol. 1 of the so-called *Great Guild Book:* not a book of guild documents in fact, but a record book kept by the Beverley town governors, which contains among other important documents many town copies of guild ordinances – hence, probably, its modern name. It was evidently of great importance to the Beverley town government: for many years a body of twelve Governors or Keepers, and from the charter of incorporation in 1573, a Mayor and council. It was kept as a book, not compiled from separate sheets, and datable entries run from 1409 to 1589. Within its own pages and in other contemporary records it is referred to as "the lygger" (ledger) or simply "the register."[2]

The pageant-assignment list is the only text on fol. 1, the front page, of the *Great Guild Book*. It seems to have been written on that page partly because it was empty, and also perhaps to indicate the list's importance: a position on the front page of the book made it easy to locate as well as suggesting a position of priority. Unfortunately no text on this leaf or anywhere else in the *Great Guild Book* (or other extant contemporary documents) tells us precisely why, or even when, the entry was made. Judging by palaeographical comparison with the hands of dated entries

---

[1] Most of the surviving documentary evidence comes from accounts and other records kept by the Governors or Keepers of Beverley, its ruling body until 1573, and thereafter the Mayor and Council appointed by the Elizabethan Charter of Incorporation in 1573. The manuscripts are now held in the East Riding Archives (hereafter ERA) in Beverley.

[2] ERA BC/II/3. For the manuscript list see Fig 3.1. I gratefully acknowledge the permission of the ERA to reproduce the image.

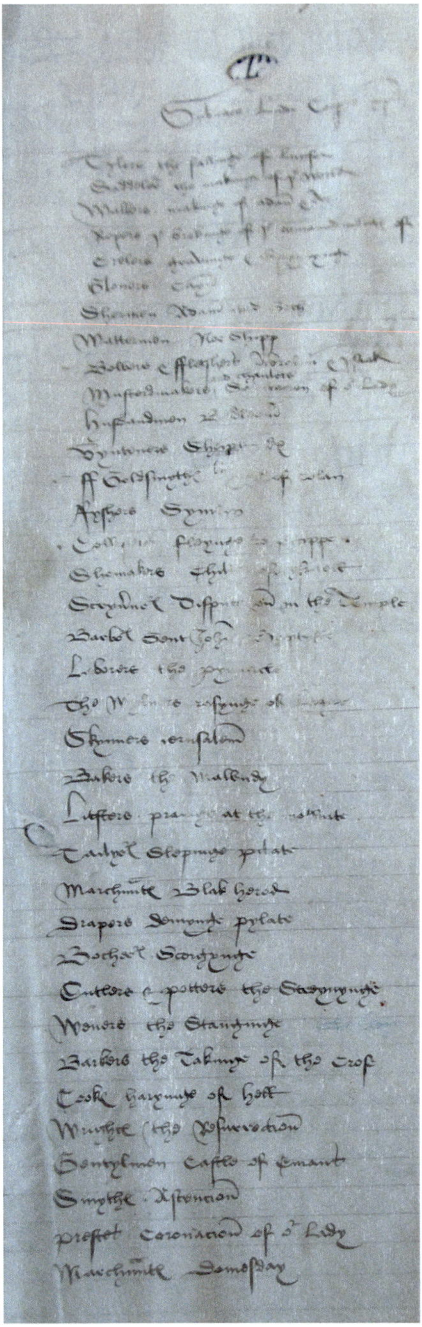

Gubernacio Ludi Corporis Christi

Tylers   the falling of Lucifer
Saddelers   the making of þe World
Walkers   makinge of adaum & eve
Ropers   þe brekinge of þe commandments of god
Crelers   gravinge & spynnynge
Glovers   Cayn
Shermen   Adam and Seth
Wattermen   Noe Shipp
Bowers & ffletshers   Abraham & ysaak
Musterdmakers and chanlers   salutacion of our Lady
Husbandmen   Bedleem
Vynteners   Sheipherdes
Goldsmythes   kinges of Colayn
ffyshers   Symeon
Cowpers   fleynge to egippe
Shomakers   Childer of ysraell
Scryuernoures   Disputacion in the Temple
Barboures   Sent Iohn Baptyste
Laborers   the Pynnacle
The Mylners   rasynge of Lazar
Skynners   ierusalem
Bakers   the Mawndy
Litsters   prainge at the mownte
Tailyoures   Slepinge pilate
Marchauntes   Blak Herod
Drapers   demynge pylate
Bocheoures   Scorgynge
Cutlers & potters   the Streynynge
Weuers   the Stanginge
Barkers   the Takinge of the Crose
Cookes   haryinge of hell
Wrightes   the Resurrection
Gentylmen   Castle of Emaus
Smythes   Ascension
Prestes   Coronacion of our Lady
Marchauntes   Domesday

FIGURE 3.1   *Beverley Pageant Assignments to Guilds, c. 1510–20* (*Great Guild Book*, EAST RIDING ARCHIVES, BC/II/3, FOL. 1ʳ)

of 1508–20, I would date it to the first quarter – maybe even the second decade – of the sixteenth century. As the latest surviving performance record of the Beverley play is from 1520, the list may give us a picture of the state of the cycle and the pageants assigned to guilds in the final stages of the life of the play.[3] My focus will be on a few unusual or puzzling pageant titles in this list and the scope they offer to interpretation, which must necessarily be cautious in the circumstances. But it makes for a useful exercise in comparison; firstly, between the titles in this list and other Beverley references to what appear to be the same pageants, or at least pageants on the same biblical episodes, and secondly, between the Beverley pageants and surviving texts or records of plays on similar subjects. More widely it may offer scope for a consideration of the uses of analogies, from other drama and from contemporary art, in aiming at a greater understanding of the content of a lost cycle. The uniqueness of the *Great Guild Book* pageant list among surviving documents of the Beverley play has in itself stimulated my interest in exploring its informative possibilities. Another stimulus has been an assertion made by Lawrence Clopper, that the terseness of the titles in the list (as well as some other Beverley evidence) prompt us to understand the Beverley pageants as static tableaux rather than dramatic actions.[4] My own understanding of the focused brevity of the titles has always been that they reflect that particular scribe's sense of the theatrical impact, rather than the narrative content, of the pageants; but an alternative

---

3   The last surviving record of performance of the play is in the town account roll for 1520–21 (ERA BC/6//18). No relevant records survive between 1521 and 1536, after which there are no subsequent records of performance. A record of 1547 has recently come to light which suggests the possibility of the Corpus Christi play's survival till later in the century: it is an inserted clause of the Bakers' ordinances, part of a running set of revised and edited clauses copied into the *Great Guild Book* over many years (as was also the case for other guilds). The clause provides that any "foryner" bringing bread to sell at the market in Beverley must pay the guild 4d annually towards "vestur[e] and pageand." However, given the isolation of this record at that period, it may be the result of absent-minded scribal copying from an earlier text (ERA BC/11/3, fol. 74.). For discussion of the revision apparently made to the play text in 1519–20 by William Pyers or Peeris, secretary to the fifth Earl of Northumberland, see Diana Wyatt, "The untimely disappearance of the Beverley cycle: what the records can and can't tell us," *Medieval English Theatre* 30 (2008): 26–38.

4   Lawrence M. Clopper, *Drama, Play and Game: English Festive Culture in the Medieval and Early Modern Period* (Chicago and London: University of Chicago Press, 2001). The existence of two mid-fifteenth-century lists of stations of the Corpus Christi play does suggest that, at that period at least, the pageants had enough dramatic action to justify seven performance stops along the route through the town; but admittedly there is no such evidence for earlier or later dates.

scholarly reading of them is a salutary prompt to consider all the available evidence about them.

2 The *Great Guild Book* New Testament Pageant Titles: Supporting Documentary Evidence and Textual Analogies

To begin with, we can compare the titles in this list with the titles of surviving play texts: much of what it tells us of the content of the Beverley Corpus Christi play is unsurprising, but there are a few apparent eccentricities in both the Old Testament and New Testament parts of the list. One or two are puzzling because their titles are odd (in the Passion sequence, "the Streynynge" and "the Stanginge" stand out); others are intriguing because they are unusual among dramatised biblical topics in English drama. In the Creation-Fall-Expulsion-consequences sequence, the presence of both pageant 5, "gravinge & spynnynge," and pageant 7, "Adam and Seth," is striking. No existing English play manuscript contains a title representing either of these episodes. In structure the Beverley list suggests a cycle more like York than any other: York has a sequence of seven pageants from the Fall of the Angels to Cain, and then moves straight to Noah's building of the Ark. Chester has one pageant for the fall of the angels, and then covers the creation and fall of Adam and Eve, plus Cain's murder of Abel, in a second long pageant of 700 lines before moving on to Noah. The Towneley manuscript has only the Creation followed (admittedly after four missing leaves) by Cain and then Noah. The N-Town manuscript covers the same ground (from the creation and fall of the angels to the end of the Cain story) in what are labelled as four pageants, although we must be careful to avoid assumptions about the conditions of performance in that case – and probably in that of Towneley too. But Beverley compares interestingly with all of these by having seven pageants, including the apparently unique coverage of the labours of Adam and Eve, and the Seth story, before reaching Noah: in splitting the material into so many pageants it most resembles York, although of course York contains no Labours or Seth pageants. However, we can have no idea how long the individual Beverley pageants were, nor indeed whether any of them was related to any equivalent York pageant. And the reasons for splitting of topics in a guild-produced play may reflect various local conditions about which we have no specific evidence, including the numbers and combinations of local crafts at the dates when particular pageant texts were written or revised, and even, perhaps, the interests of local writers.

Between the earliest records of Beverley Corpus Christi pageants and play, in 1377, and the latest surviving performance record of 1520, there are numerous references in local records to the play as a whole and to the individual component pageants, some of which help to shed light on the titles in the *Great Guild Book* list. A few of the puzzles are at least illuminated by reference to earlier records of what appear, on the basis of the guilds responsible in each case and the place of the pageants in the sequence of the play, to be the same episodes. So looking first, briefly, at the New Testament episodes, we find a Passion sequence running:

> Skynners   ierusalem
> Bakers   the Mawndy
> Litsters   prainge at the mownte
> Tailyoures   Slepinge pilate
> Marchauntes   Blak Herod
> Drapers   demynge pylate
> Bocheoures   Scorgynge
> Cutlers & potters   the Streynynge
> Weuers   the Stanginge
> Barkers   the Takinge of the Crose

The first three are clear enough: these terse titles, with their visual rather than narrative focus, reflecting perhaps, as I have suggested above, the scribe's mental picture of each pageant (and perhaps also his awareness of the need to contain the whole list on a single page), can be easily understood as the familiar episodes of the Entry into Jerusalem, the Last Supper and the Garden of Gethsemane. The next pageant, 'Sleeping Pilate', is likely to represent Jesus' first appearance before Pilate who, in the York Tapiters' and Couchers' play which dramatises the same part of the sequence, does indeed sleep in the course of the action.[5] That is followed by the trial before Herod ('black' in character or actually dressed or made up so? Unfortunately, no other extant record sheds any light on how the character was presented in this pageant), and the scourging. The next part of the sequence is, at first glance, puzzling: there is no pageant in the list entitled 'The Crucifixion'. After "Deeming – i.e., judging – Pilate" follow two oddly-titled episodes, "the Streynynge" and "the Stanginge." As they in turn are followed by the "taking of[f] the crose", clearly the Deposition, I suggest that we can reasonably take them to represent two parts

---

5   *The York Plays: A Critical Edition of the York Corpus Christi Play as Recorded in British Library Additional MS 35290*, 2 vols., ed. Richard Beadle, EETS s.s. 23–24 (Oxford: Oxford University Press, 2009–13), 1: 30.

of the Crucifixion sequence.[6] For "the Streyninge" there is some corroborative evidence from earlier local records that the word 'straining' here means the Crucifixion, the action of nailing Jesus to the cross before erecting it. The guilds jointly assigned to "the Streyninge" here are the Cutlers and Potters; records elsewhere in the *Great Guild Book* show us that in 1425[7] and 1433[8] and again much later, in 1476,[9] a group led by the Braziers, and including the Cutlers, was responsible for the Crucifixion (described simply and clearly in the 1425 record as "*pagenda de Crucifixe christi*", a pageant of the crucifixion of Christ). Despite the modern understanding of 'potter' as a worker in ceramics, medieval braziers and potters were all metal-workers, referred to by an overlapping range of occupational names, so it is very likely that 'Cutlers and Potters' represent the same composite guild as 'Braziers'.[10] In the 1433 ordinance the play is described as "*de destriccione Christi in Cruce*" (the stretching of Christ on the cross). The descriptive title in that record adequately explains the list's 'straining', which connotes stretching: the torturers' emphasis on having to stretch Jesus' limbs to fit the cross because, to quote the York *Crucifixion*, "Þe senous are so gone ynne" (the sinews are so gone in).[11] In addition, other surviving play texts offer corroborative evidence that the Beverley scribe responsible for the *Great Guild Book* list might have identified the brutal act of forcing Jesus' wasted body to fit the pre-drilled holes in the cross as the most memorable part of the action. The Towneley *Tortores* spend eighty lines in gruesomely practical discussion and demonstration of the mechanics of attaching ropes and pulling the limbs to

---

6 Perhaps understandably, Rosemary E. Horrox, "Medieval Beverley: The Guilds and their plays," in: *A History of the County of York East Riding*, vol. 6: *The Borough and Liberties of Beverley*, ed. K.J. Allison (Oxford: Oxford University Press, 1989), 47, comments on this apparent absence, but without realising that "the Streyninge" might represent the Crucifixion pageant: "The [Great Guild Book] list … omits the metal workers' play of the Crucifixion … Even if the metal-workers had given it up, it is hard to believe that so crucial an episode had been dropped from the cycle altogether."

7 ERA BC/II/3, fol. 65.

8 Ibid., fol. 71ᵛ.

9 Ibid., fol. 78.

10 See, for example, H.E. Jean le Patourel, "Documentary evidence and the medieval pottery industry," *Medieval Archaeology* 12 (1968): 102. She discusses the complicated terminology applied to metal-workers, noting that 'pots' were likely to be made of various metals including brass (hence the likelihood that the Beverley Braziers and Potters are the same crafts): "Experience suggests that in a town a potter must be considered to be a metal-worker unless there is proof to the contrary." See also Heather Swanson, *Medieval Artisans: An Urban Class in Late Medieval England* (Oxford and New York: Basil Blackwell, 1989), for discussion of the activities and nomenclature of metal-workers.

11 Beadle, *York Plays*, 35.108.

the holes so that they can drive the nails in securely.[12] The N-Town Passion play's four *Judei* engage in an equally graphic, though shorter, discussion:

Tertius Judeus	Gef hese other arm to me!
	Another take hed to hese feet!
	And anon we xal se
	Yf þe borys be for hym meet.
Quartus Judeus	Þis is mete, take good hede!
	Pulle out þat arm to þe, sore!
Primus Judeus	Þis is short, þe deuyl hym sped,
	Be a large fote and more!
Secundus Judeus	Fest on a rope and pull hym long,
	And I xal drawe þe ageyn.
	Spare we not þese ropes strong,
	Þowe we brest both flesch and veyn.[13]

The Chester *Crucifixion* text also dwells on this brutal action, actually using the word 'strain' for the pulling of the limbs:

Primus Judeus	... as mote I thee,
	Shorte-armed is hee.
	To the booringe of this tree
	hit will not well last.
Secundus Judeus	A, therfore care thou nought.
	A sleight I have sought.
	Roopes must be brought
	To strayne him with strenght.[14]

That, though only a small example, shows how one local record may help to illuminate another where no play text survives, with supportive analogous evidence from extant texts on the same topic. However, the following pageant in the *Great Guild Book* list, the Weavers' "The Stanginge," is not explained by any surviving evidence from Beverley; frustratingly, other extant records of the

---

12 *The Towneley Plays*, 2 vols., ed. Martin Stevens and A.C. Cawley, EETS s.s. 13–14 (Oxford: Oxford University Press, 1994), 23.119–99.

13 *The Passion Play from the N. Town Manuscript*, ed. Peter Meredith (London and New York: Longman, 1990), ll. 755–66.

14 *The Chester Mystery Cycle*, 2 vols., ed. R.M. Lumiansky and David Mills, EETS s.s. 3 and 9 (Oxford: Oxford University Press, 1974–86), 16A.181–88.

Weavers' pageant consistently fail to name it. But early citations in the Oxford English Dictionary define the verb 'to stang' as 'to pierce' (cf. 'sting'), and interestingly 'stange' is a northern dialect word for a pole or rod. The pageant comes in the cycle list between the Crucifixion and the Deposition, which suggests that it may feature the apocryphal story of Longinus, the blind man whose sight is restored when he is ordered to pierce Jesus' side with a spear and the blood runs on to his face. The narrative of the blind Longinus, based on John 19, is found in the popular *Gospel of Nicodemus*. The episode is dramatised in the Chester Ironmongers' 475-line pageant covering the crucifixion and death of Jesus,[15] and touched on briefly in the York Butchers' *Mortificacio Christi*[16] and the Towneley *Crucifixion*.[17] No surviving play text, then, features this as a separate episode, but it can easily be imagined as a medium-length pageant in the Beverley cycle, comparable to the York *Mortificacio* though with different emphases, including perhaps some dialogue between John and Mary at the foot of the cross and the death of Jesus as well as the "Stanginge" of the title.

Moving back through the list to the brief Ministry sequence, I want to pause at the play here tersely entitled "the Pynnacle." This is one to which Clopper refers, suggesting that as the temptation of Christ in the desert has, biblically, three parts, and this title suggests only the set for the last of them, the pageant itself may have been little more than a tableau featuring Christ and Satan standing on the pinnacle of the temple but little or no action. It is one of the titles in this *Great Guild Book* list which he thinks "invites us to imagine the Beverley pageants as focusing on one scene, one emblematic tableau, rather than being dramas like those at York, Chester and Coventry."[18] It is of course impossible to produce proof either to support or to refute Clopper's argument, but we may note that the 1451 ordinances of the Labourers who are assigned the pageant in the list describe it more fully as *"pagendam quomodo diabolus assumpsit ihesum & stauit cum eum supra pinnaculum temple"* (a pageant of how the Devil tempted Jesus and stood with him on the pinnacle of the Temple). There might still be only one temptation represented, although 'tempted Jesus *and* stood with him' could perhaps be taken to indicate different stages of a longer action; at any rate this more narrative title does suggest action and dialogue. Here again we can usefully look at analogous cases from surviving play texts. In Chester, for instance, the Butchers' pageant text includes both the Temptation – over 200 lines – and the Woman Taken in Adultery

---

15   Ibid., 16A.372–407.
16   Beadle, *York Plays*, 36.291–312.
17   Cawley and Stevens, *Towneley Plays*, 23.651–64.
18   Clopper, *Drama as Play and Game*, 153.

(another 100 lines), which is recorded in the list preceding the 1539 banns simply as "the pynacle with the woman of canany", so that if only the record survived it might be tempting to suppose that it too was no more than a two-scene tableau.[19] Again I would suggest that this type of record, as in the Beverley *Great Guild Book* list, reflects not a play containing very brief pageants or tableaux lacking dramatic action, but a theatrical, rather than narrative, way of thinking about them (evidently common to particular scribes in both Chester and Beverley).

3 The "Gravinge and Spynnynge" Pageant and the "Adam and Seth" Pageant: The Documentary Background and Related Play Texts

To discuss the final two plays on the Beverley list that I find particularly intriguing, I shall move back again through the sequence to the early Old Testament pageants, and specifically to the Creelers' "gravinge and spynnynge" (pageant 5) and the Shearmen's "Adam and Seth" (pageant 7).

The Adam and Seth play is interesting in that there are few recorded examples of plays in the British Isles on this subject. Beverley's is the only example in English I have come across, and the only other is in Cornish, in the *Origo Mundi*, the first part of the *Ordinalia*, and in the later *Creacion of the World*, in each of which, of course, it is a scene in a single long play rather than a discrete pageant. As Lucy Toulmin Smith, the pioneering editor of the York play, noted long ago, the Beverley Shearmen's pageant presumably dramatises the apocryphal episode of Adam's old age and his sending of his third son Seth (born after Abel's murder) to Paradise to fetch the oil of mercy promised by God after the Fall. Seth returns with three seeds given him by an angel, which he plants under Adam's tongue as instructed. After Adam's death and burial, three holy trees grow from the seeds, from which together the 'oil of mercy' – which is, according to one tradition, the Redemption through the death of Christ on the cross made from the wood of the combined trees – will be provided. The legend itself was well known, and appears in the *Legenda Aurea*, *Cursor Mundi* and the *Northern Passion*, any of which might have been used as source material by the Beverley dramatist. What is curious here is that Beverley should, according to the surviving evidence, have provided the only known English-language dramatisation of the subject; surprising, given the evident popularity

---

19 *Records of Early English Drama: Cheshire Including Chester*, 2 vols., ed. Elizabeth Baldwin, Lawrence M. Clopper and David Mills (Toronto and London: University of Toronto Press and The British Library, 2007), 1: 80.

of the Seth legend.[20] Frustratingly, no other Beverley record survives either of the pageant (or indeed of the Shearmen's Guild in any relevant context), which leaves us with no history of its inclusion in the play, or of the participation of the guild. The general incompleteness of the records makes it impossible to know whether the Shearmen performed this pageant only during the period when the *Great Guild Book* list was compiled, or were responsible for it over many years. In the absence of any documentary evidence, no conclusions can be drawn here, and speculation must be tentative. But if the list was compiled for reasons connected with William Pyers' revision of the Beverley Corpus Christi play, the absence of previous records of the Shearmen's play makes it not impossible that the Seth pageant may have been inserted in the cycle only at that point, as a suitable expansion of the Fall-and-consequences sequence already extended in the Beverley play by the most curious of all the odd titles in this list, the Creelers' pageant of "gravinge & spynnynge."[21]

Given the position of the Creelers' pageant in the sequence, between the Fall pageant ("þe brekinge of þe commandments of god") and the Cain pageant, and given that it was, and is, well known that 'Adam delved and Eve span', we can assume that Adam and Eve are those who are doing this graving (or delving, or simply digging), and spinning – and in fact earlier Beverley records confirm it. There are two earlier extant references to the guild of, in full, Porters and Creelers, both trades involved in carrying loads, particularly of freight shipped from and to Beverley Beck, the port connecting the town with the

20 Seth's only appearance in any extant English text is in the Chester *Harrowing of Hell*, where, as one of those to be redeemed, he recounts his story in a very succinct two-stanza speech. See *Chester Mystery Cycle*, ed. Lumiansky and Mills, 17.73–88.

21 The Shearmen in Beverley did form a separate guild, unlike the position in, say, Coventry, where they were joined with the Tailors in a composite guild. Their ordinances of 1432 (ERA BC/II/3, fol. 71) provide for the erection of their Rogation Day castle but make no mention of a pageant. It is possible that they were already producing 'Adam and Seth' at that date, but that the Governors failed to make a copy of the relevant ordinances. At any rate the Shearmen were among eight crafts assigned to the pageant of Sloth in the 1441 production of the Pater Noster play. However, their Corpus Christi pageant might have been a later acquisition; the insertion of new pageants into the Beverley play, even at a surprisingly late date, is not unknown: the Drapers petitioned the Governors as late as 1493 to become a guild independent of the Merchants, asked to be given whatever pageant the Governors chose, and were assigned "Deming Pilate." While that pageant immediately follows the Merchants' "Blak Herod" in the running order of the *Great Guild Book* list, and may therefore have been an expansion of a scene taken from it, the Seth narrative is too complete in itself to have been developed from the existing Cain pageant of the Glovers, and whenever it was written, must surely have been designed as a separate pageant.

River Hull, the Humber and ultimately the North Sea and continental Europe. In one mid-fifteenth century record the guild is warned by the Governors to have a pageant, unnamed, newly made by the next feast of the Annunciation, ready for performance on the following Corpus Christi Day.[22] The surviving copy of the guild's ordinances in the *Great Guild Book*, entered in 1476, specifies that officers of the guild are to take charge of a certain "*pagendam de Grauing & Spynnyng Ade et Eue in festo corporis Christi ludi consuete in Beuerlaco*" (a pageant of the Graving and Spinning of Adam and Eve usually played in Beverley on the feast of Corpus Christi).[23] That suggests that the guild remained fairly stable, along with its responsibility for that particular pageant, at least from the mid-fifteenth century till the end of the play's known existence. How much further back it may have existed we have no way of knowing, but even seventy-odd years would be a good lifespan for the pageant. What is curious about it is the absence of a surviving play text, or reference to a play, on this subject anywhere else in Britain (including, in this case, Cornwall, although a scene in the *Origo Mundi* and a passage in the York *Expulsion* do offer some suggestions for dramatic development, both of which will be considered below). It is another of the Beverley pageants that Lawrence Clopper mentions as unlikely to have involved more than a tableau, and certainly in this case it is very hard to find any specific source-story for an entire dramatic action devoted to Adam and Eve's labour. What sources are (and were, in the later Middle Ages) known for Adam and Eve's post-lapsarian life and activities will be discussed below.

---

22   ERA BC/II/7/1 (the first *Governors' Minute Book*), fol. 117ᵛ, dated 16 June 1452, after Corpus Christi that year, which suggests that the guild had failed in the production of its pageant on the day. It is not clear from the wording of the entry whether it was the text of the pageant or the wagon itself that was to be "*de nouo factam;*" "*pagenda*" in these records can mean both dramatic material and vehicle. Horrox, "Medieval Beverley", 42, reads 'Annunciation' in the record ("*per festum Annunciationis beate Marie Virginis proximum futurum*" [by the next feast of the Annunciation of the Blessed Virgin Mary]) as the name of the pageant rather than the deadline by which it was to be prepared: "The porters and creelers ... in 1452 ... agreed to play the 'newly made' pageant of the Annunciation on the next feast day."

23   ERA BC/II/3, fol. 78ᵛ.

FIGURE 3.2 *Carvings on the tomb of Henry Fitzroy, Duke of Richmond.*
ST MICHAEL'S, FRAMLINGHAM, SUFFOLK.

4   The 'Gravinge and Spynnynge' Pageant: Evidence from Contemporary Art

However, there is certainly some surviving *visual* evidence that Adam and Eve's carrying out of their Divine sentence to hard labour was considered over a long period to be a discrete episode in the sequence of Fall, Expulsion, and the consequences, including Cain's murder of Abel and the Seth story that prefigures redemption. Available evidence is scarce, but there are wall-paintings in several churches: St Agatha's, Easby, North Yorkshire; Holy Trinity, Bledlow, Buckinghamshire; and All Saints', Broughton, Cambridgeshire. Carvings on one of the splendid tombs in St Michael's, Framlingham, Suffolk – that of Henry Fitzroy, Duke of Richmond, the illegitimate son of Henry VIII, who died at the age of sixteen in 1536 – include a three-panel sequence of Expulsion, Labours, and Cain and Abel. Interestingly the Labours carving depicts, quite clearly, Adam swinging what looks like a pickaxe, while Eve suckles an infant, though she does not hold a distaff.[24]

There is also, interestingly for my present purposes, a carving on the parapet on the south side of Beverley Minster. There are nine carvings along the parapet, originally made in the fourteenth century as an integral part of the building of the parapet itself: they are evidently carved from the same stone. They are very much weathered, and in fact the first two (from the west) date from the eighteenth century and may have replaced corroded medieval carvings. The others appear to represent the sequence of the creation of Adam (though it is too worn to be sure), the creation of Eve, Temptation, Expulsion (at least the

---

24   Dr Carol Rowntree, to whom I hereby express my gratitude, very kindly took the photograph at my request.

FIGURE 3.3 *Adam holding a spade with Mary sitting beside him (carving on the parapet of Beverley Minster).*

expelling angel can be made out), Adam and Eve in shame after expulsion, and then Adam, holding a still-visible spade, with Eve sitting beside him: it is no longer possible to make out either a child or a distaff. (The final carving is too corroded to be identified with any certainty.[25])

The Beverley 'labours' carving is certainly more iconographic than narrative, and in any case is so weathered that some of the detail is no longer visible, but its presence might at any rate suggest the existence of a local interest in the episode, which a dramatist might therefore have found it natural to include in the Corpus Christi play.[26]

---

25   I am very grateful to Dr Barbara English for providing the photograph and information about the carvings. On the dating of the parapet and its carvings, see Nikolaus Pevsner and David Neave, *Yorkshire: York and the East Riding*, The Buildings of England (New Haven and London: Yale University Press, 2005).

26   Peter Happé has very helpfully drawn my attention to the similar inclusion of the Labours of Adam and Eve as an episode in the sequence of Old Testament scenes forming the border of the woodcut on the title page of John Bale's *Three Laws,* printed in Wesel in 1547. Bale had been Prior of the Carmelite house at Doncaster, about forty miles from Beverley, in the 1530s. The geographical connection, taken with the fact that that the woodcut has not been found elsewhere and may therefore have been made especially for that edition,

FIGURE 3.4
Adam delving and Eve spinning (with the Expulsion?).
HOLY TRINITY, BLEDLOW, BUCKINGHAMSHIRE,
C. 1300.

However, none of the other surviving pictorial representations of the topic that I have found comes from Beverley, and none even from Yorkshire except the Easby wall-painting, so no conclusions can be drawn even tentatively about significant local variations in the use of certain Old Testament topics in art. All the wall-paintings I shall discuss, on which she also provides illuminating commentary, are included in Anne Marshall's excellent online resource, *Medieval Wall Painting in the English Parish Church*.[27] On the Bledlow painting, of the early fourteenth century, she notes the scarcity of the subject and wonders whether what may be the hand of God pointing accusingly at Adam suggests that the painting combines Expulsion with subsequent punishment. Interestingly, the combining within a single pageant of Expulsion and at least a hint about Adam's (and to a lesser extent Eve's) labours does occur in York; the closest any existing English play text comes to dramatising a 'graving and spinning' episode.[28]

Marshall also suggests that Eve seems not to be using the distaff she is holding but possibly cradling a baby, although the fading of the paint makes it very hard to see. However, the clarity of the Framlingham tomb carving of the subject, in which Eve is definitely suckling a baby (but not apparently holding a distaff) does add weight to the suggestion. On the Broughton painting, of the

---

   raises an interesting possibility that Bale himself knew of the Minster carvings and of a local interest in the subject.

27 The pictures of wall-paintings from Bledlow and Broughton reproduced to illustrate this article are taken, with permission, from the website: www.paintedchurch.org (accessed 05 December 2014).

28 Beadle, *York Plays*, 6. See below for discussion of the York pageant and the related episode in the Cornish *Origo Mundi*.

FIGURE 3.5
Adam and Eve delving and spinning. ALL SAINTS', BROUGHTON, CAMBRIDGESHIRE, 15TH CENTURY.

fourteenth century, Marshall points out that this painting is on the south wall of the nave below a painting of the Expulsion and close to one of Doomsday, before commenting on the scarcity of representations of the subject:

> Adam and Eve now afflicted by the curse of Labour, as decreed in *Genesis* 3:19, is very seldom found. The heavily-bearded Adam, possibly still dressed in the same 'coat of skin' that God clothed him in, has to drive his spade into the ground, which is littered with stones. Beside him Eve, with a red robe and her long yellow hair loose, spins with a distaff.

Perhaps the best and clearest of the known wall-paintings on the subject is that in St Agatha's, Easby, North Yorkshire, the church of the former St Agatha's Priory. The Labours painting is the last in a fine thirteenth-century Genesis series covering the creation of Eve, Temptation, Expulsion and finally (separated, rather appropriately, from those set in Paradise by a window), the Labours. The paintings were delicately conserved in 1994 (after a previous Victorian restoration which, Anne Marshall remarks, were fortunately *not* "the disastrous travesty that the Victorians inflicted on some medieval paintings"[29]) and are in excellent condition on the whole. The Labours painting shows very clearly the details of Adam's spade, on which he is leaning while engaging in dialogue with an angel overhead (giving instructions?), and Eve's distaff, which she is already using while watching the angel.[30]

All these paintings do suggest possibilities for action and certainly for dialogue, perhaps not very lengthy, but as existing pageant texts have playing

---

29 See Anne Marshall, "Genesis Scenes: Easby, N. Yorkshire (‡*Ripon*) C.13," accessed 5 December 2014, <http://www.paintedchurch.org/easbygen.htm>.

30 I am grateful to Peter Thomas for permission to reproduce this photograph. The *Holkham Bible Picture Book* also includes a scene of Adam apparently being instructed by the angel as Eve, spinning, looks on. (See *The Holkham Bible Picture Book,* with introduction and commentary by W.O. Hassall [London: The Dropmore Press, 1954], fol. 4^v).

FIGURE 3.6
Adam and Eve delving and spinning. ST AGATHA'S, EASBY, NORTH YORKSHIRE, 13TH CENTURY.

times of between ten and thirty minutes, a ten-minute pageant on the topic would be perfectly possible for a competent dramatist.

5   The "Graving and Spynnyng" Pageant: Evidence from English and Cornish Play Texts

What might the action of such a pageant have been? Although there is no known separate English play or pageant on the subject, English dramatisations of the Fall and Expulsion do hint at how Adam and Eve's life out of Eden might be developed dramatically. For instance N-Town incorporates Adam and Eve's acceptance of their punishment into their lament for their sin and their exile from Paradise:

> *Adam:* But lete vs walke forth in to þe londe
> With ryth gret labour oure fode to fynde
> With delving and dyggyng with myn hond
> Our blisse to bale and care to-pynde.
> And, wyff, to spynne now must þu fonde
> Oure nakyd bodyes in cloth to wynde ...[31]

A mixture of lament and recrimination amid efforts to carry out tough and unfamiliar tasks has the potential to be developed into a short play preparing

---

31   *The N-Town Play: Cotton MS Vespasian D.8*, 2 vols., ed. Stephen Spector, EETS s.s. 11–12 (Oxford: Oxford University Press, 1991), 2: 321–26.

the ground, so to speak, for the further results of the Fall: Cain the farmer killing his brother.

Chester moves directly from the Expulsion to the beginning of the Cain and Abel episode within the same pageant, with the passage of time being indicated by the stage direction "Minstrelles playe." When the now grown Cain and Abel join them, both Adam and Eve tell their sons how they have sinned and been punished, though mainly retrospectively and without actually enacting their punishment:

> *Adam*: Nowe for to get you sustenance
> I will you teach without distance.
> For sythen I feele that myschaunce
> of that fruit for to eate,
> my leefe children fayre and free,
> with this spade that yee may see
> I have dolven. Learne yee this at mee,
> Howe ye shall wynne your meate.
>
> *Eve:* My sweete children, darlinges deare,
> Yee shall see how I live heare
> Because enbuxone so wee weare
> And did as God would not wee shoulde.
> This payne, theras had bine no neede,
> I suffer on yearth for my misdeed;
> And of this wooll I will spyn threede by threede,
> To hill mee from the could.
>
> Another sorrowe I suffer alsoe:
> My childrenn must I beare with woo,
> As I have donne both you too;
> And soe shall wemen all.
> This was the divell, our bitter foe,
> That made us out of joy to goe.
> To please, therefore, sonnes bee throwe,
> In sinne that yee ne fall.[32]

Cain then brings in his plough, Abel begins his sacrifice and their parents are directed to exit until Cain has killed Abel.

---

32 Lumiansky and Mills, *Chester Mystery Cycle*, 2.489–512. This long pageant of 704 lines in fact covers Creation and Fall as well as Expulsion and Cain and Abel.

The Towneley manuscript offers no possibility of comparison, because four leaves are missing between the beginning of the Temptation and the beginning of the Cain episode. York does, however, offer an interesting possibility for development, although it is part of the Armourers' pageant of the Expulsion (No. 6) and is too briefly treated to make a complete pageant in itself. York notably devotes its first six pageants to the Creation and the Falls of Lucifer and of Adam and Eve; the seventh is the Glovers' Cain and Abel pageant. The Armourers' version approaches, at least, a dramatisation of digging and spinning. After expelling them, the Angel gives both practical instructions and, even more helpfully, a spade to Adam:

Angelus That while yee wrought vnwittely,
Soo for to greue God almyghty,
And þat mon ye full dere abye
Or þat ye go;
And to lyffe, as is worthy,
In were and wo.

Adam, haue þis, luke how ye thynke,
And tille withalle þi meete and drynke
For euermore.
Adam Allas, for syte why [ne] myght Y synke,
So shames me sore.

Eue Soore may we shame with sorowes seere,
And felly fare we bothe in feere;
Allas, þat euyr we neghed it nere,
Þat tree vntill.
With dole now mon we bye full dere
Oure dedis ille.

Angelus Eve, for þou beswyked hym swa,
Trauell herto shalle þou ta,
Thy barnes to bere with mekill wa -
Þis warne I Þe.
Buxom shalle Þou and othir ma
To man ay be.[33]

---

33 Beadle, *York Plays*, 6.52–74. Beadle notes that a distaff as well as the spade is mentioned in the 1415 *Ordo paginarum* description of the pageant, and suggests that the Angel may hand it to Eve at lines 70–74, although the extant text may differ from the earlier

Later in the pageant comes Adam's actual, frustrated, effort at digging:

> *Adam* A, lorde, I thynke what thynge is þis
> That me is ordayned for my mysse;
> Gyffe I wirke wronge, who shulde me wys
> Be any waye?
> How beste wille be, so haue Y blisse,
> I shalle assaye.
>
> Allas, for bale, what may þis bee?
> In worlde vnwisely wrought haue wee,
> This erthe it trembelys for this tree
> And dyns ilke dele!
> Alle þis worlde is wrothe with mee,
> Þis wote I wele.[34]

Adam's speech notably underscores his anxiety about having nobody to instruct or direct him in these daunting new labours, an anxiety borne out in the second stanza quoted above by his shocked exclamation that the earth trembles at his attempt to dig it, which he assumes is because his sin against nature ("this tree") has turned the whole world against him. The next fifty lines which close the pageant, however, do not follow up the dramatic earth-tremor: both Adam and Eve lament their sin and its harsh consequences, and blame each other; Eve wretchedly wishes herself dead, and the pageant ends with a prayer from Adam to be kept from misery. No help is forthcoming with the digging, and incidentally no speech indicates that Eve actually embarks on her spinning in the course of the pageant, despite the suggestive mention in the *Ordo paginarum* of the distaff (*colo*) as one of the props for the pageant.[35]

It is to Cornwall we must look, again, to see a real dramatic development of the episode. In the *Origo Mundi,* the first day of the three-day *Ordinalia,* the

---

description, and the Angel here specifically mentions only the labour pains of childbirth and her subordination to man as Eve's special punishment. The *Ordo* listing of a distaff, however – "*Adam & Eua, Angelus cum vanga & colo assignans eis laborem*" (Adam and Eve, the Angel with a spade and a distaff, assigning work to them) – is intriguingly suggestive of some spinning by Eve at some point in the action. See *Records of Early English Drama: York*, 2 vols., ed. Alexandra F. Johnston and Margaret Rogerson (Toronto: University of Toronto Press, 1970), 1: 17 and 25 (for the shorter *Ordo* listing), and Beadle, *York Plays*, 2: 31, for discussion.

34 Beadle, *York Plays*, 6.105–16.
35 See note 32.

action is continuous to reflect its place-and-scaffold staging, so the digging and spinning sequence is not, of course, treated as a separate 'pageant', but its treatment is the fullest and most dramatically developed I have found.[36] The Cherubin who expels Adam and Eve from Paradise gives them instructions on their future life of labour:

> [*Cherubin:*] You will [both] proceed to another country and make a new life, you by tilling the soil, your wife by spinning and weaving.

There is no explicit stage direction for the Cherubin to give Adam and Eve their tools but Adam's speech, once they have emerged from the gate of Paradise, clearly implies that he has done so:

> [*Adam:*] With not a stitch to our backs, no roof over our heads, we shall all but perish from cold, astray amid terrors and parted far from the joy and pleasantness that were ours. In our wretchedness, we have no idea where to turn, whether to field or forest. In dire need of food, our bellies empty, we may starve.
>
> Therefore, Eve, take the distaff, spin clothes for us, while with every ounce of my strength I start to work the soil.

The stage direction at this point is highly dramatic in itself, and the startling effect of the earth not simply trembling as in the York *Expulsion*, but protesting vocally, is emphasised by the repetition: *And he shall dig, and the earth cries out; and again he shall dig and the earth cries out.*

Adam is aghast that the earth "won't even let me scratch the surface so that I can raise a little grain." He prays to God, who descends again from the scaffold of the Holy Trinity and commands the earth to let Adam break it "to cut the earth a full spade's length." A fascinating discussion between Adam and God follows, in which Adam gradually talks up God's allowance of earth he may cultivate by pointing out that he needs more than one spade's length for both himself and Eve, and more still if they have a child, and yet more if they have

---

36   All quotations from the *Origo Mundi* are taken from *The Cornish Ordinalia: A Medieval Dramatic Trilogy*, trans. Markham Harris (Washington, DC: The Catholic University of America Press, 1969). The sequence from God's pronouncement of Adam and Eve's punishment to Eve's beginning to spin is at pages 9–14. Both the York earthquake and the Cornish cry of protest from the apparently animated earth pose fascinating questions about stagecraft and production, but neither of the manuscripts offers specific suggestions about theatrical solutions.

several children. God eventually concedes, with an expansiveness that is somewhat unexpected in the circumstances of the recent Fall and Expulsion (though qualified later in the scene):

> [*God the Father:*] Very well, Adam, go and take possession of as much of the world as you desire. You shall find that it serves you well, you and your descendants.

Adam gives thanks and glorifies God, but his exultation to Eve that "the mastery of the world is mine" carries some dramatic irony in its foreshadowing of the behaviour of some of his descendants from Cain onwards. Eve responds by also expressing her gratitude to God for granting permission to cultivate the earth and announces that she will now "take my distaff and begin to make us clothes." Possibly while Adam and Eve make progress in their respective labours, God the Father reminds the audience of Adam and Eve's sin and his continuing anger. He commands Adam to offer a tithe of his produce "as an acknowledgement of what I have done for you," which is to be made "of your free will and without grudging." (More dramatic irony here: once Adam has expressed his obedient acquiescence and God has moved back to the Heaven scaffold, Cain and Abel appear immediately – as soon as God's back is turned, one might say.)

The digging and spinning episode in the *Origo Mundi* is certainly not very long, but with Adam's repeated struggle, the shock of the earth itself protesting, his dismay, and then his successful argument with God about how much land he needs to till, it is genuinely dramatic, as well as unexpectedly and imaginatively comic in Adam's apparently winning the argument with God about how much cultivation of the earth it takes to support a (still hypothetical) family. As Brian Murdoch comments, the active role taken by the earth itself here is comparable to its crying to God in Genesis on the death of Abel; but the Cornish dramatist has used the motif here with daringly comical results. More strikingly, this dramatically original development of the digging and spinning motif is hard to attribute to any known source. Murdoch points out that "it does not appear in any of the apocryphal Adam books, for instance."[37] Interestingly, Murdoch also notes that in various English, Welsh and Cornish versions of the *Vita Adae and Evae*, which apocryphally explore the post-lapsarian story of Adam and Eve, two motifs do generally occur: firstly, Adam and Eve doing penance by standing in rivers (the Jordan for Adam, the Tigris for Eve). In some

---

37 Brian Murdoch, *The Apocryphal Adam and Eve in Medieval Europe: Vernacular Translations and Adaptations of the* Vita Adae et Evae (Oxford: Oxford University Press, 2009).

versions, Satan again successfully tempts Eve, this time to give up her penance too soon. There is no known dramatisation in Britain of this motif, for which we might suggest a number of possible reasons. The very static nature of the water penance is inherently un-dramatic, and in any case the presentation of Adam and Eve standing up to their necks in water is theatrically impracticable. In addition, a second temptation of Eve might be considered too repetitive; but inevitably these suggestions must remain purely speculative. However, the second motif usually included is that of Seth's journey to Paradise in quest of the oil of mercy for the dying Adam (with its linked narrative of the Holy Cross) which is also, as I have noted above, dramatised in the *Origo Mundi,* and, as far as we know, nowhere else in Britain except Beverley.[38]

Unless, by some archival miracle, the text of the full Beverley cycle or of any of its component pageants should turn up, we can never be sure of its length, stylistic qualities, development or dramatic coverage of biblical episodes. Nonetheless, by carefully examining a single piece of documentary evidence – in this case, the *Great Guild Book* pageant assignment list – in the light of other Corpus Christi play records and of textual and visual analogies, we can tease out helpful clues to the narrative content and dramatic possibilities of even its most unusual or oddly-titled pageants.

Bibliography

Baldwin, Elizabeth, Lawrence M. Clopper and David Mills, eds. *Records of Early English Drama: Cheshire Including Chester*, 2 vols. Toronto and London: University of Toronto Press and The British Library, 2007.

Beadle, Richard, ed. *The York Plays: A Critical Edition of the York Corpus Christi Play as Recorded in British Library Additional MS 35290*, 2 vols. EETS s.s. 23–24. Oxford: Oxford University Press, 2009–13.

Clopper, Lawrence M. *Drama, Play and Game: English Festive Culture in the Medieval and Early Modern Period*. Chicago and London: University of Chicago Press, 2001.

Harris, Markham, trans. *The Cornish Ordinalia: A Medieval Dramatic Trilogy*. Washington, DC: The Catholic University of America Press, 1969.

Hassall, W.O., ed. *The Holkham Bible Picture Book,* with introduction and commentary. London: The Dropmore Press, 1954.

---

38   For a full and illuminating discussion of the Latin and vernacular versions of the *Vita Adae et Evae,* see Brian Murdoch, *The Medieval Popular Bible: Expansions of Genesis in the Middle Ages* (Woodbridge: D.S. Brewer, 2003).

Horrox, Rosemary E. "Medieval Beverley: The Guilds and their plays," in: *A History of the County of York: East Riding*, vol. 6: *The Borough and Liberties of Beverley*, edited by K.J. Allison, 42–49. Oxford: Oxford University Press, 1989.

Johnston, Alexandra F., and Margaret Rogerson, eds. *Records of Early English Drama: York*, 2 vols. Toronto: University of Toronto Press, 1979.

Le Patourel, H.E. Jean "Documentary evidence and the medieval pottery industry." *Medieval Archaeology* 12 (1968): 101–26.

Lumiansky, R.M., and David Mills, eds. *The Chester Mystery Cycle*, 2 vols. EETS s.s. 3 and 9. Oxford: Oxford University Press, 1974–86.

Marshall, Anne. "Genesis Scenes: Easby, N. Yorkshire (‡*Ripon*) C.13." Accessed 5 December 2014. <http://www.paintedchurch.org/easbygen.htm>.

Meredith, Peter, ed. *The Passion Play from the N. Town Manuscript*. London and New York: Longman, 1990.

Murdoch, Brian. *The Medieval Popular Bible: Expansions of Genesis in the Middle Ages*. Woodbridge: D.S. Brewer, 2003.

———. *The Apocryphal Adam and Eve in Medieval Europe: Vernacular Translations and Adaptations of the* Vita Adae et Evae. Oxford: Oxford University Press, 2009.

Pevsner, Nikolaus, and David Neave. *Yorkshire: York and the East Riding*. The Buildings of England. New Haven and London: Yale University Press, 2005.

Spector, Stephen, ed. *The N-Town Play: Cotton MS Vespasian D.8*, 2 vols. EETS s.s. 11–12. Oxford: Oxford University Press, 1991.

Stevens, Martin, and A.C. Cawley, eds. *The Towneley Plays*, 2 vols. EETS s.s. 13–14. Oxford: Oxford University Press, 1994.

Swanson, Heather. *Medieval Artisans: An Urban Class in Late Medieval England*. Oxford and New York: Basil Blackwell, 1989.

Wyatt, Diana. "The untimely disappearance of the Beverley cycle: what the records can and can't tell us." *Medieval English Theatre* 30 (2008): 26–38.

CHAPTER 4

The Bible and the *Towneley* Plays of *Isaac* and *Iacob*

Philip Butterworth

Abstract

Of all the individual plays in the collections and cycles of mystery plays in England, there are none that follow the biblical narrative as closely as those of the consecutive *Towneley* plays of *Isaac* and *Iacob*.[1] With the exception of *A newe mery and wittie Comedie or Enterlude, newely imprinted, treating vpon the Historie of Jacob and Esau* (1568), the early seventeenth-century fragment of the pageant of *Jacob* in *The Stonyhurst Pageants* (c. 1610–25) and a fragment of uncertain provenance from the end of the twelfth century that deal with the Isaac and Jacob stories, the *Towneley* plays of *Isaac* and *Iacob* are unique among English mystery plays.[2] This article pursues the question: Why do the *Towneley* plays of *Isaac* and *Iacob* follow the biblical narrative so closely?

Keywords

medieval theatre – *Towneley play of Isaac* – *Towneley play of Iacob*

1 Introduction

The play of *Isaac* consists of 70 lines of text of which 49 lines are directly attributable to the Bible. The play of *Iacob* is composed of 142 lines of text of which

---

1   In this chapter I have not conducted a line by line analysis of the relationship between the biblical narrative and the *Towneley* text. I have selected some lines and passages as indicative examples of the close relationship and left the rest for the reader to examine in Tables 3 and 4.

2   *A newe mery and wittie Comedie or Enterlude, newely imprinted, treating vpon the Historie of Iacob and Esau taken out of the .xxvij. Chap. of the first booke of Moses entituled Genesis* (London: Henrie Bynneman, 1568); *The Stonyhurst Pageants*, ed. Carleton Brown (Göttingen: Vandenhoeck & Ruprecht, 1920); Karl Young, *The Drama of the Medieval Church*, 2 vols. (Oxford: Clarendon Press, 1933), 2: 258–65.

102 may be precisely attributed to the Bible.³ The play of *Isaac* appears to exist as the fragment of a longer play and is presented as a distinct play in the *Towneley* manuscript. Two leaves are missing from the *Towneley* manuscript between folios 15ᵛ and 16ʳ that seemingly contained the beginning of the play of *Isaac* and the end of the previous play of *Abraham*.⁴ The play of *Iacob*, although a short play of 142 lines, appears to be complete in respect of its composition and adherence to the biblical narrative. The play of *Isaac* deals with parts of the biblical narrative contained in Genesis 27:18–28:1 and the play of *Jacob* draws its content from Genesis 28:10–33:4. However, the story of Isaac and his father Abraham does occur in other English mystery plays.⁵

In this chapter I propose to examine the relationship of the *Towneley* text to the Bible and consider this relationship and its implications for theatrical performance.

2 History of Reponses to the *Towneley* Plays of Isaac and Jacob

Nineteenth-century discussion of the close adherence of both plays to the biblical narrative occurs in Bernhard Ten Brink's *History of English Literature*. Ten Brink refers to the play of *Iacob* as the play of *Jacob and Esau*:

---

3 I have previously referred to the composition of the *Towneley* play of *Iacob* and its adherence to the biblical narrative. In this chapter I have adjusted line numbers in relation to Bible verses. These are now more accurate. See Philip Butterworth, "Stage Directions of the Towneley Cycle," M.A. dissertation (School of English, University of Leeds, 1977); idem, "Stage Directions in the Towneley Play of Jacob," in *The National Arts Education Archive: Occasional Papers in the Arts and Education*, 5 vols., ed. A.E. Green (Bretton Hall: The National Arts Education Archive, 1996), 6: 7; idem, *Staging Conventions in Medieval English Theatre* (Cambridge: Cambridge University Press, 2014), 181.

4 San Marino, California, Huntington Library, MS HM1; see also *The Towneley Cycle: A Facsimile of Huntington MS HM1*, ed. A.C. Cawley and Martin Stevens ([Leeds]: University of Leeds, School of English, 1976), Leeds Texts and Monographs, Medieval Drama Facsimiles 2.

5 See *The York Plays: A Critical Edition of the York Corpus Christi Play as Recorded in British Library Additional MS 35290*, 2 vols., ed. Richard Beadle, EETS s.s. 23–24 (Oxford: Oxford University Press, 2009–13), 1: 55–65; *The N-Town Play Cotton MS Vespasian D. 8*, 2 vols., ed. Stephen Spector, EETS s.s. 11–12 (Oxford: Oxford University Press, 1991), 1: 50–58; *The Chester Mystery Cycle*, 2 vols., ed. R.M. Lumiansky and David Mills, EETS s.s. 3 and 9 (Oxford: Oxford University Press, 1974–86), 1: 56–79; *The Towneley Plays*, 2 vols., ed. Martin Stevens and A.C. Cawley, EETS s.s. 13–14 (Oxford: Oxford University Press, 1994), 1: 48–57; *Non-Cycle Plays and Fragments*, ed. Norman Davis, EETS s.s. 1 (Oxford: Oxford University Press, 1970), 32–42 and 43–57; *Records of Early English Drama: Newcastle Upon Tyne*, ed. J.J. Anderson (Toronto: University of Toronto Press, 1982), 57, 63.

> In *Jacob and Esau* the dramatic art is still of a low standard; the situations are not made much use of; the characteristics show little depth or originality. The poet is full of reverence for his subject, and dramatizes faithfully what seems to him its most important traits, without putting to it much of his own originality. He writes in good verses, in simple, vivid language, but hardly ever exerts his powers of invention, and he also evidently requires no special means of excitement to fascinate and affect an audience not spoiled by such exhibitions. But so much greater are the demands he makes on the imagination of his spectators.[6]

The opening sentence of this quotation expresses a judgement seemingly based on an expectation of late nineteenth-century standards. The comment presupposes that there are examples of existing dramatic standards with which to compare *Jacob*. However, the criteria by which Ten Brink is able to make such a statement are not declared. And it appears that he compares the standard of the play with those of his own day and in the process ignores any presumed purpose of the play. He criticises the play for its lack of "depth or originality" without any attempt to determine why this description might be applicable. He similarly criticises the author for not "putting to it much of his own originality" or "powers of invention".[7] These comments may be appropriate if compared with late nineteenth-century or more modern dramatic or theatrical criteria. But they do not attempt to consider the terms of reference by which the play might have originally existed.

---

6 Bernhard ten Brink, *History of English Literature (Wyclif, Chaucer, Earliest Drama, Renaissance)*, 3 vols., trans. Horace M. Kennedy, Wm. Clarke Robinson and L. Dora Schmitz (London: George Bell, 1883–96), 2: 244. Ten Brink's assessment of "the play of *Jacob and Esau*" as one play and not two arises because the play was "originally formed, and, in fact, still forms, one drama, which was produced independently without regard to any cycle of mysteries, and, indeed, earlier than most of the others, probably than all the other parts of the cycle in which it was subsequently incorporated. All this can easily be proved by means now at the disposal of philology, but this is not the place for entering into the subject" (ibid., 3; 274). As with a number of Ten Brink's statements, which may contain accurate elements, he does not provide the evidence to back up his confident certainty. It is quite possible that the plays of *Isaac* and *Iacob* were performed independently and did not formerly belong to a group of plays such as those assembled in the *Towneley* manuscript. Similarly, Ten Brink does not present evidence of his presumed age of the plays. Appropriately, he is more circumspect when attempting to determine the location of performance. Even though the plays of *Isaac* and *Iacob* may be seen to be different plays there is every likelihood that they were written by the same author.

7 Ibid., 2: 244.

However, Alfred W. Pollard in his co-edited (with George England) edition of *The Towneley Plays*[8] does offer some contextual possibilities with regard to the provenance of the plays. Having stated: "I cannot conceive on what occasion, or by whom, an isolated play on *Jacob and Esau* could come to be acted in the vernacular" Pollard later asserts "It is obvious, however, that these two fragments [*Isaac and Iacob*] do belong to a period, whether prae-cyclic or cyclic, at which the narrative and didactic interest of the representation was uppermost ...".[9] He continues this assertion with considerably less authority to suggest "and before the constantly increasing importation of external attractions had produced a distaste for the simpler and more exclusively religious form of drama."[10] With some increased certainty he states that

> I incline strongly to believe that in these plays, and the others which I have mentioned as written wholly or partly in the aa^{4}b^{3}cc^{4}b^3 stanza, we possess part of an original didactic cycle, of much the same tone as the Chester Plays, on to which other plays, mostly written in a more popular style, have been tacked from time to time.[11]

Although Pollard is clearly locked into the late nineteenth- and early twentieth-century assumptions concerning the evolutionary development of English drama,[12] he does offer the purpose and role of didacticism as an explanation of the apparently simple presentation of the plays of *Isaac* and *Iacob*.

John Matthews Manly rationalises his decision to include the plays of *Isaac* and *Iacob* in his two volume *Specimens of the Pre-Shaksperean Drama* by stating "in ten Brink's opinion, they are the most primitive of all the pageants, but also because of their remarkable combination of intensity of conception and phrasing with a simplicity – not to say nakedness – of presentation."[13]

---

8   *The Towneley Plays*, re-edited from the unique manuscript by George England and Alfred W. Pollard, EETS e.s. 7 (London: Kegan Paul, Trench, Trübner & Co., 1897).
9   Ibid., xxv.
10   Ibid.
11   Ibid. See also Charles Mills Gayley, *Plays of our Forefathers and some of the traditions upon which they were founded* (New York: Duffield, 1907), 126, 164.
12   Perceptive dismantling of largely unconscious Darwinian influenced thinking used to rationalise the evolution of 'early medieval drama' was systematically developed by O.B. Hardison Jr., *Christian Rite and Christian Drama in the Middle Ages: Essays in the Origin and Early History of Modern Drama* (Baltimore: Johns Hopkins Press, 1965). See Essay 1 in particular.
13   *Specimens of the Pre-Shaksperean Drama*, 2 vols., ed. John Matthews Manly (Boston: Ginn, 1897), 1: vii.

Pollard and England in their edition of *The Towneley Plays* include the plays of *Isaac* and *Iacob* in a group of old testament plays which Pollard describes as "on the whole very dull."[14] A.P. Rossiter in his *English Drama from Early Times to the Elizabethans: its Background, Origins and Developments* describes the literary qualities of what he considers to be "the older strata" of plays as "insipid to a degree beyond *Hymns Ancient and Modern* at its tritest."[15] Hardin Craig in his *English Religious Drama of the Middle Ages* writes of Ten Brink's views by stating "but no one can deny the soundness of his judgement both as to the language and the dramatic primitivity of those plays."[16]

Thus, the literary and dramatic qualities of the *Towneley* plays of *Isaac* and *Iacob* have been summed up as 'dull', 'insipid', 'of a low standard' and 'primitive'. These accumulated responses are not shared by Martin Stevens and A.C. Cawley in their current *Early English Text Society* volume of *The Towneley Plays*. They challenge the "view that they are remnants of an older drama" and conclude that "There is, however, no basis on which to make this claim."[17] They continue:

> Ten Brink pointed to the choice of subject (ii.244) and the dialect of the rhyme words (iii.274) as the grounds for his opinion; yet neither of these yields any convincing evidence to support his view. The plays are written entirely in couplets and have consequently been thought unsophisticated and primitive. Yet there is nothing inherently simple in either the language or the narrative structure of the two plays, which often elaborate upon the phrasing and details of their Biblical source.[18]

John Gardner in his *The Construction of the Wakefield Cycle* makes a number of loose assumptions concerning the *Towneley Plays* where he corroborates the general drift of literary criticism, initially suggested by Ten Brink, by posing the question: "why should a group of guildsmen who knew these more spectacular pageants, or an audience who had these pageants for comparison, accept several hours of rather dull writing on Isaac, Jacob, the Prophets, and the rest?"[19]

---

14   England and Pollard, *Towneley Plays*, xxix; John Gardner, *The Construction of the Wakefield Cycle* (Carbondale: Southern Illinois University Press, [1974]), 66.

15   A.P. Rossiter, *English Drama from Early Times to the Elizabethans: Tts Background, Origins and Developments* (London: Hutchinson, 1950), 66.

16   Hardin Craig, *English Religious Drama of the Middle Ages* (Oxford: Clarendon Press, 1955), 221.

17   Stevens and Cawley, *Towneley Plays*, 2: 457.

18   Ibid.

19   Gardner, *Construction of the Wakefield Cycle*, 66–67.

Although Gardner's question assumes involvement of 'guildsmen' in the production of the plays it transfers the literary focus into a theatrical one.[20]

3   Comparison of the *Towneley* Narratives with the Wycliffite, Coverdale and Geneva Bibles

Given the long held view expressed by Ten Brink and others that the plays of *Isaac* and *Iacob* represent the "oldest extant English drama"[21] and the more recent views of Stevens and Cawley, I shall consider the texts of the *Towneley Isaac* and *Iacob* plays in relation to the *Wycliffite, Coverdale* and *Geneva Bibles*. More recently, the composition of the *Towneley* manuscript has been considered to belong to a period from 1553–58.[22] Thus, the *Wycliffite Bible* (c. 1382), the *Coverdale Bible* (1535) and the *Geneva Bible* (1560) encompass a time span that covers the potential years of authorship of the plays. The three Bibles each contain roughly the same content but vary in their emphasis on description, reported and direct speech. Just as the *Wycliffite*, the *Coverdale* and the *Geneva Bibles* derive their respective translations from the Vulgate so too is it possible

---

20   Gardner offers the following superficial assumptions/suggestions in answer to his question: "The right answer may well be simply that the writers, guildsmen, and audiences were willing to shrug off a few bad pageants. Nevertheless, certain desperate defences of these pageants can be offered. One is that these pageants involve audience emotions we have lost. Another is that, though dull as written texts, the pageants were interesting as spectacle, making use of theatrical machines and sets not recorded in the written text, and depending on acting styles about which we can only make guesses. A third explanation is that the number of guilds requiring pageants in fifteenth-century Wakefield put the Towneley MS poet or poets in an awkward position; they must provide pageants on minor events in the *Corpus Christi* scheme, yet they must somehow preserve the rhythm of 'the play called Corpus Christi' as a whole" (ibid., 66).
21   Ten Brink, *History of English Literature*, 2: 244; 3: 274; Craig, *English Religious Drama*, 220–21; England and Pollard, *Towneley Plays*, xxv; *The Wakefield Mystery Plays*, ed. Martial Rose (London: Evans, 1961), 143.
22   As part of a forthcoming volume on the *Towneley Plays*, to be edited by Meg Twycross, Alexandra Johnston has contributed a paper over which she and the late Malcolm Parkes corresponded concerning details of Huntingdon MSHM1. The contents of this personal correspondence were made public by Johnston in a paper titled "The Towneley MS (Huntington MS 1): A Paleographical and Codicological Study," 37th International Congress on Medieval Studies, Western Michigan University, Kalamazoo. May 3, 2002. In a letter dated "17.iii.02" to Johnston, Parkes considers the date of the Huntington MSHM1 compilation to have been between 1553–58. The reasons for Parkes' conclusion will appear in Johnston's article.

and likely that the two *Towneley* texts also draw their composition from the Vulgate. However, I have not included the Vulgate for comparison with the *Towneley* text because of the imprecise nature of translation.[23] If the texts of *Isaac* and *Iacob* had been wholly written in Latin then comparison with the Vulgate might have been appropriate.

In order to show the closeness of the *Towneley Plays* to the biblical narrative I have drawn up four tables that demonstrate the relationship. Table 1 (The *Towneley Play of Isaac*) and Table 2 (The *Towneley Play of Iacob*) show the correspondence between lines of the text and verses in the Bible. Tables 3 and 4 show the complete texts of the respective plays set against equivalent bible versions. The *Towneley* text is taken from *The Towneley Plays*, edited by Stevens and Cawley,[24] and the three versions of the Bible are shown as the *Wycliffite Bible* (MS. Bodley 959), the *Coverdale Bible* and the *Geneva Bible*.[25] The information contained in Tables 1 and 3 corresponds as does that in Tables 2 and 4.

The *Towneley* texts of *Isaac* and *Iacob* refer closely to all three Bible accounts. Such closeness may be demonstrated by the opening line of the *Towneley Isaac* which states: "Com nere, son, and kys me." The closest biblical line is from *Coverdale* and is also in the present tense: "Come nye, and kysse me my sonne." Whereas the *Wycliffite* and *Geneva* versions are reported in the past tense as "he come nerre: & kyssid hym" and "And he came nere and kissed him." In each of these versions the content is the same but expressed differently through present and past tenses and direct or reported speech. The *Towneley* lines continue: "The smell of my son is lyke || To a field with flouris or hony-bike." All three biblical sources similarly record the *Towneley* equivalent as direct speech: "lo þe smell of my sonn as þe smell of afull feeld;" "Beholde, the smell of my sonne is as ye smell of the felde;" and "Beholde, the smel of my sonne *is* as the smel of a field." Some five lines later in the *Towneley* text, Isaac says "God gif the plenté grete || Of wyne, of oyll, and of whete" and the three biblical sources state: "plente of whete· & of wyne & of oyle;" "plenteousnes of corne and wyne;"

---

23 Where I have used the Vulgate for comparison I have used *The Vulgate Bible: Douay-Rheims translation*, 6 vols., ed. Swift Edgar (Cambridge, MA–London: Harvard University Press, 2010–13), vol. 1: *The Pentateuch* (2010).

24 See note 5 for details.

25 MS. *Bodley 959: Genesis – Baruch 3.20 in the Earlier Version of the Wycliffite Bible*, 8 vols., ed. Conrad Lindberg, Stockholm Studies in English, 6ff (Stockholm: Almqvist & Wiksell, 1959–97), vol. 1: *Genesis & Exodus*; *Biblia the Byble, that is, the holy Scrypture of the Olde and New Testament, faithfully translated in to Englyshe*, trans. Miles Coverdale ([Southwark]: J. Nycolson, 1535); *The Geneva Bible: A Facsimile of the 1560 Edition*, intro. Lloyd E. Berry (Peabody, MA: Hendrickson, 2007).

and "plentie of wheat and wine." In this instance the *Wycliffite* version is the closest in the repetition of exact words.

The kinds of minor distinctions presented above by the three Bibles in relation to the *Towneley* play of *Isaac* continue to occur throughout both plays. Often, the *Coverdale* and *Geneva* Bibles remove some of the ambiguity of the *Wycliffite Bible* and thus clarify the sense. In *Isaac*, at lines 23–26, Isaac says "Who was that was right now here, || And broght me bruet of a dere? || I ete well, and blyssyd hym; || And he is blyssyd, ich a lym" and the *Wycliffe Bible* says "who þann is he þat now riȝt brouȝte to me huntyng taken· & I *eet* of all befor þat þou come? & I Blysside hym & he schall be blyssid." Isaac has mistakenly blessed Jacob instead of Esau and yet when the error is discovered it is too late to alter the condition – the blessing upon Jacob must remain. This sense is clarified in the *Coverdale* version as: "Who? Where is then the hunter that brought me, and I haue eaten of all afore thou camest, and haue blessed him? And he shall be blessed still."

To what extent do the biblical variations exist in the *Towneley* texts as modifications for theatrical purposes? The opening lines from Deus in *Iacob* (l. 12) address Jacob: "Iacob, Iacob! Thi God I am || Of thi forfader Abraham || And of thi fader Isaac." All three biblical versions present similar wording. *Wycliffe* says: "I am þe lord god of abraham þi fader & god of ysaac." *Coverdale* says: "I am the LORDE God of thy father Abraham, and the God of Isaac" and *Geneva* says: "I am the Lord God of Abrahám thy father, & the God of Izhák." The biblical versions exist as statements. The purpose of these statements is changed in the *Towneley* text to one of theatrical announcement, arrest and explanation by the prefixed address: "Iacob, Iacob!" It is this theatrical purpose that conditions the re-ordered biblical content.

4 The Nature and Purpose of So-called Stage Directions

The play of *Isaac*, however, contains two examples of 'so-called stage directions', written in Latin, that are not dissimilar to those in modern use. The reason for this description of 'so-called stage directions' is that most of them in the *Towneley* play of *Iacob* are not stage directions as we understand the term today. I shall therefore refer to these Latin stage directions as *stage directions*.

The two *stage directions* in *Isaac* are simple announcements for actions to be completed: "Recedet Iacob" (Iacob will leave [l. 18]) and "Et osculatur" (And he kisses [them] [l. 66]). There is no biblical reference to the content of these two *stage directions*. They are thus interpolations created for the theatrical purpose of the *Towneley* text.

There are also two *stage directions* in the play of *Iacob*, similarly written in Latin, which operate in the same way as those in *Isaac* (ll. 34, 130). They too, announce simple actions to be performed. Additionally, there are four Latin *stage directions* that do not operate in the way required of modern stage directions. These are at lines 58, 84, 114 and 122:

l. 34   *Hic [Iacob] vigilet*
        (Here he [Jacob] wakes)
        Vulgate: *Cumque evigilasset Iacob de somno*
        (And when Jacob awaked out of sleep)

l. 58   *Hic egrediatur Iacob de Aran in terram natiuitatis sue*
        (Here Jacob goes out from Harran into the land of his birth)
        Vulgate: *Nunc ergo surge, et egredere de terra hac, revertens in terram nativitatis tuae*
        (Now therefore arise, and go out of this land, and return into thy native country)

l. 84   *Hic scrutetur superlectile, et luctetur angelus cum eo.*
        (Here he shall examine their possessions and an angel shall struggle with him)
        Vulgate: *Transductisque omnibus quae ad se pertinebant, remansit solus, et ecce: vir luctabatur cum eo usque mane*
        (And when all things were brought over that belonged to him, he remained alone, and behold: a man wrestled with him till the morning)

l. 114 *Hic diuidit turmas in tres partes.*
        (Here he divides his company in three parts)
        Vulgate: *divisitque filios Liae et Rahel ambarumque famularum. Et posuit utramque ancillam et liberos earum in principio Liam vero et filios eius in secundo loco Rahel autem et Ioseph novissimos*
        (he divided the children of Leah and of Rachel and of the two handmaids. And he put both the handmaids and their children foremost and Leah and her children in the second place and Rachel and Joseph last)

l. 122 *Et vadat Iacob osculand[o] Esaw; venit Iacob, flectit genua exorando Deum, et leuando, occurrit illi Esaw in amplexibus.*

(And Jacob goes to embrace Esau: Jacob comes, goes down on his knees praying to God, and rising he runs into the arms of Esau)

Vulgate: *Currens itaque Esau obviam fratri suo amplexatus est eum, stringensque collum et osculans, flevit*

(Then Esau ran to meet his brother and embraced him and, clasping him fast about the neck and kissing him, wept)

l. 130 [*Esaw*] *dicit seruis suis*:
(He says to his servants)

The *stage directions* at lines 58, 84, 114 and 122 owe their source directly to the biblical narrative at Genesis 31:13, 32:23–24, 33:1–2 and 33:4 and repeat it. This provides the basis upon which Ten Brink was able to suggest that the author "dramatizes faithfully what seems to him its most important traits without putting to it much of his own originality."[26] So much is clear. But why is this? Why are these *stage directions* included in the text at all? For whose benefit are they included in the manuscript?

I have demonstrated elsewhere that *stage directions* in master copies of play manuscripts known as *regysters, regynalls, originalls, ordinaries, ordinals, game books*, or *play books* were drawn up after the performed event and not before it.[27] The notion that *stage directions* were written after the performed event distinguishes them from most modern explicit stage directions and their purpose. The kind of medieval *stage directions* under examination do not appear to have been written for the player, nor indeed the reader per se. They were written during or after compilation of the text and were devised for and as the record of what had been performed. But is this the case with these four *stage directions* in the *Towneley* manuscript? Do these *stage directions* perform any function(s) over and above that of simply repeating the biblical narrative? Is there any significance to their existence in Latin as opposed to the vernacular of the text?

The first of these four *stage directions* (l. 58) informs the dramatic narrative that "Iacob" shall go from "Aran" (Harran) to the "land of his birth" (Cannan). The text leading up to this *stage direction* involves Deus and Jacob talking to each other. They are still in each other's presence at the point at which the *stage direction* is presented. However, the *Wycliffite, Coverdale* and *Geneva* Bibles record the content delivered by the *stage direction* as an instruction

---

26 Ten Brink, *History of English Literature*, 2: 244.
27 Butterworth, *Staging Conventions*, Introduction.

from God and not simply a narrative description. They state: "Now þann aryse & go out fro þis londe: tornyng aȝeyn in to þe londe of þi byrþe;" "Get the vp now, & departe out of this londe, & go agayne: in to the londe of thy kynred;" "Now arise, get thee out of this countrei & returne vnto the land where thou wast borne." If this instruction had been given by Deus in the *Towneley* text it would have (a) made the story clearer; (b) completed the biblical narrative; (c) completed the dramatic narrative; (d) made for a much more theatrical command/instruction. In this instance the biblical narrative is more dramatic than the *Towneley* text.

The second of these *stage directions* (l. 84) informs the *Towneley* text that "*Hic scrutetur superlectile, et luctetur angelus cum eo*" (Here he shall examine their possessions and an angel shall struggle with him). In the *Towneley* text immediately after the *stage direction* at line 85 Deus says: "The day spryngys; now lett me go." And Iacob replies: "Nay, nay, I will not so." Each of the biblical versions refers to "a man," not Deus, who wrestles with Jacob in his sleep. *Wycliffe* says: "& lo a man wrystyld with hym: vnto þe moru;" *Coverdale* says: "Then wrestled there a man with him vntyll the breake of yᵉ daye" and *Geneva* says: "there wrestled a man with him vnto the breaking of the day." The apparent ambiguity between Jacob's wrestling with a "man" in the Bible and an "angel" in the *Towneley* text is explained by St. Augustine in his *De Civitate Dei*:

> Iacob was also called *Israel* (as I said before) which name his progenie bore after him. This name, the Angell that wrastled with him as hee returned from Mesopotamia, gaue him, being an euident type of *Christ*. For whereas *Iacob* preuailed against him, by his owne consent, to forme this mysterie, is signified the passion of *Christ*, wherein the Iewes seemed to preuaile against him. And yet *Iacob* gotte a blessing from him whom he had ouer-come: and the changing of his name was that blessing.[28]

For theatrical purposes, a clear commitment and statement needs to be made towards the embodiment and portrayal of the personage who wrestles with Iacob. The *stage direction* determines that it is an angel and this is presumably what an audience is intended to witness.

In the third of these *stage directions* the *Towneley* text at line 114 states: "*Hic diuidit turmas in tres partes*" (Here he divides his company in three parts). This announcement provides the bare bones of the necessary action. The three biblical versions of this action each provide more detail than the *Towneley stage*

---

[28] Sᵗ *Avgvstine, The Citie of God with the learned comments of Io. Lod. Vives*, trans. I. H. [= John Healey] (London: George Eld, 1610), 613–14.

direction; they inform of the organisation of the action. Although the content of the *stage direction* is sparse, Iacob's speech at lines 115–22 explains the reasons for his action. His speech paraphrases the biblical narrative at Genesis 33:1–2 but is not directly taken from it:

> Rachell, stand thou in the last eschele,
> For I wold thou were sauyd wele.
> Call Ioseph and Beniamin,
> And let theym not fro the twyn.
> If it be so that Esaw
> Vs before all to-hew,
> Ye that ar here the last,
> Ye may be sauyd if ye fle fast.

The fourth of these *stage directions* at line 122 deals with the same incident as that at Genesis 33:4 but effectively makes a different statement. The *Towneley* text states: "*Et vadat Iacob osculand[o] Esaw; venit Iacob, flectit genua exorando Deum, et leuando, occurrit illi Esaw in amplexibus*" (And Jacob goes to embrace Esau: Jacob comes, goes down on his knees praying to God, and rising he runs into the arms of Esau). The incident recorded in Genesis 33:4 reads as follows in the three Bible accounts: "And so Esau rynnyng to meeten with his broþer·clyppide hym ‖ & streynyng his necke· & kyssyng wepte;" "But Esau ranne to mete him, and enbraced him, and fell aboute his neck, & kyssed him, and wepte;" "Then Esau ran to mete him and embraced him, and fel on his necke and kissed him, and thei wept." The *Towneley stage direction* switches the reconciliation initiative to Iacob. The action of praying to God recorded in the *stage direction* is not contained in the biblical narrative at Genesis 33:4 although a marginal note in the Geneva Bible states: "By this gesture he partly did reuerence to his brother, & partely praised to God to mitigate Esaus wrath" (Genesis 33:3).

5   Deviations of *Towneley* and Biblical Narratives

Given the close adherence of the *Isaac* and *Iacob* texts to the biblical narrative and the dramatic normality that this connection makes upon the composition and character of the plays it may appear unusual to encounter sections in both plays that are not derived from the biblical narrative. However, these are mainly necessary interpolations to lubricate theatrical enactment of the respective stories. They are predominantly concerned with creating transitions in action. The text in *Isaac* at lines 17–18 states:

	Go now wheder thou has to go.
Iacob.	Graunt mercy, syr, I will do so.
	Recedet Iacob[29]

These two lines and the accompanying *stage direction* are needed to bring a conclusion to the scene between Isaac and Iacob and permit the introduction of a scene between Isaac and Esaw. Later, at line 49 Isaac, speaking of Iacob to Rebecca, says "Call hym heder." This direction is taken from Genesis 28:1 but the following *Isaac* lines (ll. 50–57), are not in the Bible. The lines are concerned with Isaac and Rebecca telling Iacob that he must flee to avoid the anger of Esau. Iacob asks, "Whederward shuld I go, dame?" Rachel's reply is, "To Mesopotamean ‖ To my brothere and thyn eme [uncle]." Here, some licence is taken in the *Towneley* text for the person with whom Iacob should hide in Genesis 28:2 is his grandfather and not his uncle. The remainder of the play, from lines 61–70, is not taken from the Bible and is concerned with Iacob saying goodbye to Isaac and Rebecca.

The first seventy-four lines of the play of *Iacob* follow the biblical narrative very closely and it is not until line 75 that a textual diversion occurs through an exchange of lines between Rachel, Iacob and Lya in which Rachel expresses her fear that Esau will kill Iacob when he sees him. In response, Iacob reveals that he intends to offer Esau "many beestys sere present" as recompense in order "his wrath [to] slake." This sequence of lines (ll. 75–84) rejoins the biblical narrative with the *stage direction* at line 84 where Iacob is left alone to wrestle with the angel in his sleep.

Two lines (ll. 113–14) enable Rachel to announce that Esau is near at hand. These lines are not taken from the Bible but they facilitate the theatrical transition into Iacob's organisation of his party. Iacob's instructions to his party (ll. 115–21) are similarly not taken from the Bible. With the exception of the two *stage directions* at lines 114 and 122 which express the content at Genesis 33:1–2 and Genesis 33:3–4 the remainder of the play of *Iacob*, which relates the meeting and reconciliation between Iacob and Esau, does not consist of any closely mirrored biblical narrative detail; it is all dramatic invention.

The relationship between dramatic invention and adherence to the biblical narrative demonstrates the idiosyncratic constitution of these plays. But the principal question remains: why do the *Towneley* plays of *Isaac* and *Iacob* follow

---

29   *Iacob will leave.*

the biblical narrative so closely? Some clues exist in the simplicity of the dramatic organisation of the texts, the verse form, the fact that the *stage directions* are written in Latin, and the apparent purpose to teach the biblical narrative through the plays. The clear and simple arrangements of both plays have been interpreted by earlier scholars, cited above, as simplistic ones. They have been regarded as lacking in dramatic or theatrical understanding. Such assessments have been thought to determine an earlier underdeveloped 'period' of dramatic skill. Some scholars have assumed that simplicity equates with the simplistic and that this quality must therefore have 'evolved' at earlier primitive stages of dramatic or theatrical understanding: the plays are thus considered to be 'inferior'. The assumption they promote is that such simplicity is unconsciously created and is thus naive. However, there are no reasons to denigrate simple theatrical forms, as represented in the plays of *Isaac* and *Iacob*, when simple expression is consciously and deliberately created. Awareness of the value of simplicity is relevant when a teaching motive or didactic purpose is identified. And it seems that such a stance is taken to both of these plays. Hence, the closeness of the dramatic narrative to the biblical narrative; the play script is the biblical script. The presumed audience is intended to go away from performance of these plays knowing the biblical story or, at least, being reminded of it. Given the dependence of both plays on the close relationship between the theatrical personages, neither play demands a large amount of space to fulfil the theatrical needs supplied by the dramatic texts. Consequently, these plays could be played in or on the relatively small space of a pageant vehicle, a platform stage or inside a church. Equally, larger three-dimensional outdoor spaces could be used even though the internal dramatic requirements do not demand such space.

6 The Case for Religious Derivation of the Plays

The simple presentation of these two plays appears to be a conscious one and as such the balance of probability as to their didactic instigation exists within a religious body and a religious motive. Much discussion has taken place as to the identity, attribution and whereabouts of such a religious body in relation to all the *Towneley Plays*. The favoured ascription has been to "a cell of Augustinian canons at Woodkirk,"[30] some four miles north west of Wakefield in the West Riding of Yorkshire.

---

30 Stevens and Cawley, *Towneley Plays*, 1: xx.

Francis Douce, from 1799 to 1811 Keeper of the Manuscripts in the British Museum, appears to have been the first person in modern times to ascribe the *Towneley Plays* to "the Abbey of Widkirk, near Wakefield, in the county of York."[31] This identification is made more fragile by Douce when six years later, in his introduction to *Judicium, A Pageant. Extracted from the Towneley Manuscript of Ancient Mysteries*, the manuscript was presented to the Roxburghe Club by Peregrine Edward Towneley. Douce, writing in the "Introduction," states that the *Towneley* manuscript is "supposed to have belonged to the Abbey of Whalley" near Clitheroe, Lancashire.[32] The preface to the Surtees Society edition of the *Towneley Mysteries* states: "On what foundation either of these suppositions rests we are not informed."[33] However, the ascription to the "Abbey of Widkirk" has prevailed. "Widkirk" is thought to refer to Woodkirk. It is uncertain whether one, both or neither of Douce's attributions are correct.

John Payne Collier calls the *Towneley Plays* the *Widkirk Miracle-plays* in his *History of English Dramatic Poetry*.[34] Like Douce, he too does not present evidence for this ascription but his suggested provenance is no doubt supported by his view that "Miracle-plays were written, and even to a comparatively late period acted, by ecclesiastics."[35] Thus, continued attribution of the *Towneley Plays* to "Widkirk Abbey" does so because of Douce and Collier, who present no evidence for the relationship. The edition of *The Towneley Plays* by England

---

31 The *Towneley Plays* were auctioned in 1814 and Douce wrote the notes to describe them in the auction catalogue. The entry reads as follows: 891 A COLLECTION OF ENGLISH MYSTERIES OR THEATRICAL PAGEANTS. A volume, very fairly written upon vellum, in the reign of Henry VI. or Edw. IV.; and, as it is supposed, formerly belonging to the Abbey of Widkirk, near Wakefield, in the county of York. It contains several *mysteries*, or theatrical *pageants*, constructed from incidents in the Old and New Testaments, differing entirely in language from the celebrated *Chester* and *Coventry Plays*, though agreeing, with some few exceptions, in the subjects. There is very good reason for conjecturing that all the plays of this kind were composed by some ecclesiastical persons for the purpose of being acted in the monastries, as well as by the tradesmen's companies in various populous towns and cities ..." (*Bibliotheca Towneleiana. A Catalogue of the Curious and Extensive Library of the late John Towneley*, [London: R.H. Evans, 1814], 45).

32 *Judicium: A Pageant. Extracted from the Towneley Manuscript of Ancient Mysteries* (London: Richard and Arthur Taylor, 1822), fol. c^r; *The Towneley Mysteries*, [ed. James Raine], Publications of the Surtees Society, 3 (London: J.B. Nichols and Son, 1836), viii.

33 Ibid., viii.

34 John Payne Collier, *The History of English Dramatic Poetry to the Time of William Shakespeare; and Annals of the Stage to the Restoration*, 3 vols. (London: John Murray, 1831), 2: 155.

35 Ibid., 2: 141.

and Pollard iterates the connection of the plays with the abbey at Woodkirk by reprinting much of the introduction to the Surtees Society edition of the plays.

Additionally, considerable discussion has taken place as to the performance location of all the *Towneley Plays*. The town of Wakefield has long been the considered place of performance due to internal manuscript evidence promoted by individual plays.[36] It is known that a *Corpus Christi* play was performed at Wakefield but it is not clear from available evidence that the *Towneley* manuscript, in part or whole, constitutes or represents that play.[37]

The considerable language, dialect and dramatic inconsistencies point to the provenance of the *Towneley Plays* as being a collected edition of plays brought together to resemble a Corpus Christi Cycle of plays.[38] The purpose of

---

36 Pollard in his edition of the plays states: "But we are bound to remember that the connection with Woodkirk is a mere tradition, and that it is quite possible that the whole cycle belongs to Wakefield, which is the only place with which it is authoritatively connected." The so-called "tradition" to which Pollard refers is that created by Douce and Collier earlier in the century. And "Wakefield, which is the only place with which it is authoritatively connected" is only recorded in the titles of plays 1 and 3 in the manuscript. The title of play 1 reads in red: "*In dei nomine Amen Assit principio Sancta maria meo Wakefeld*." Here, the scribe seeks a blessing for his work. However, according to Douce, the "Wakefeld" referred to in the title does not refer to the place but the name of the author. He states: "'In Dei nomine Amen. Assit principio Sancta Maria meo, *Wakefeldus*', we are probably made acquainted with the name of the author, who must have been a member of the above Abbey" (*Judicium*, fol. c^r). This does not prove that the name of the author was *Wakefeldus* or that all the assembled plays were played in Wakefield. However, there are also some local allusions to Wakefield contained in plays 2 (l. 369), 12 (l. 352), 13 (ll. 581, 657), and 30 (l. 186), and thus these localised references, albeit in the imaginative text, permit the additional possibility of a Wakefield attribution to these particular plays. See England and Pollard, *Towneley Plays*, xxviii; Stevens and Cawley, *Towneley Plays*, 1: xix-xxii; *The Wakefield Pageants in the Towneley Cycle*, ed. A.C. Cawley (Manchester: Manchester University Press, 1958), xiv-xx.

37 Proof that a "plaie commonlie called Corpus Christi plaie" was played at Wakefield is contained in a document in the Diocesan Registry at York dealing with the Records of the Diocesan Court of High Commission, "which was, of course, simply an arm of the Privy Council in the North for the settlement of ecclesiastical matters." This document was first published by Gardiner in 1946 and effectively suppressed the "plaie commonlie called Corpus Christi plaie" at Wakefield. See Harold C. Gardiner, *Mysteries' End: An Investigation of the Last Days of the Medieval Religious Stage*, Yale Studies in English, 103 (New Haven: Yale University Press, 1946), 77-78; Cawley, *Wakefield Pageants*, 125.

38 Having directed outdoor performances of twenty-six of the thirty-two plays contained in the *Towneley* manuscript I am well aware of the qualitatively different theatrical demands and needs made by the respective plays. Individual and small groups of plays impose different staging requirements. Useful discussion of the respective groups of plays within

drawing these plays together to create an apparently homogenised collection is uncertain. A.C. Cawley argued that the *Towneley* manuscript provided evidence that it constituted a "'register', i.e. an official text of the cycle, copied from 'originals' of the individual pageants belonging to the various craft-guilds."[39] The 'register', in Cawley's use, relates to a Wakefield civic purpose. Whether Cawley is correct or incorrect in his judgement of the evidence representing a 'register' of civic performance there is the possibility of the evidence contained in the compiled manuscript representing a different kind of formal, legal or quasi-legal record for ecclesiastical purposes.

One of the problems associated with investigation of the provenance of the *Towneley Plays* arises through attempts to locate all the plays in time, space and location as if the collection were of homogeneous origin. Thus, while some suggestions as to the instigation and performance location of some plays may be appropriate they do not fit the circumstances of all the plays. It may therefore be misleading to ascribe all the plays in the *Towneley* manuscript to one place of performance instigated by a given group or groups. Due to the lack of primary evidence that would confirm the auspices and identity of the instigators of the *Towneley Plays* and their place of performance, discussion tends to be convoluted and inconclusive. This condition will remain unless new evidence becomes available.[40]

As far as the *Towneley* plays of *Isaac* and *Iacob* are concerned the close iteration of the biblical narrative appears to be deliberate and not simplistic through lack of dramatic understanding or skill. It is the case that other plays in the *Towneley* compilation, such as those grouped under the authorship of the so-called "Wakefield Master," present more developed dramatic understanding when compared with later dramatic/theatrical criteria. However, such criteria do not tend to take the same kind of account of didactic dramatic/theatrical purpose as demonstrated by the plays of *Isaac* and *Iacob*.

The three Bible accounts to which the *Towneley* plays of *Isaac* and *Iacob* have been compared present few differences in content. However, the language used in the *Towneley* text demonstrates more affinity with that of the *Wycliffite* and *Coverdale Bibles*. Whether such closeness arises directly from these Bibles or translation of the Vulgate is uncertain. Frequently, the *Geneva*

---

    the *Towneley* manuscript is contained in Cawley, *Wakefield Pageants*, xiv-xxx, and Stevens and Cawley, *Towneley Plays*, 1: xxvi–xxxi.

39   Cawley, *Wakefield Pageants*, xii.

40   As I write this work I am conscious that Meg Twycross is working on a volume concerning the *Towneley Plays*. See note 22 above. It is hoped that this work reveals further evidence of the auspices of the *Towneley* manuscript and its relationship to performance.

Bible clarifies the meaning of the earlier Bibles. Recent analysis of the *Towneley* manuscript in respect of paleographical and codicological patterns suggests that its compilation was conducted between 1553 and 1558 – before publication of the *Geneva Bible*. If this is the case then there is every reason to suspect that the codex of the *Towneley* manuscript would be Marian and subject to the influence of official policy to restore the catholicity to the plays. It may be, however, that this point is more applicable to plays other than those of *Isaac* and *Iacob* for the content of these plays does not vary in their narrative affinity to the Vulgate, *Wycliffite*, *Coverdale* or *Geneva* Bibles. The biblical content of these two plays does not appear to have been affected by the different Catholic or Protestant demands. It may be that they 'passed under the wire' of Protestant sensibilities.

TABLE 4.1   *The Townely Play of Isaac – Genesis Table*

ll. 1–4	Genesis 27:26–27	ll. 30–31	Genesis 27:36
ll. 5–6	Genesis 27:18	l. 32	Genesis 27:37
l. 7	no biblical reference	ll. 33–35	Genesis 27:39
ll. 8–10	Genesis 27:28	ll. 36–40	Genesis 27:41
ll. 11–16	Genesis 27:29	ll. 41–42	Genesis 27:46
ll. 17–18	no biblical reference	ll. 43–48	Genesis 27:43–45
ll. 19–20	Genesis 27:30–31	l. 49	Genesis 28:1
ll. 21–22	Genesis 27:32	ll. 50–57	no biblical reference
ll. 23–26	Genesis 27:33	ll. 58–60	Genesis 28:2
l. 27	Genesis 27:34	ll. 61–70	no biblical reference
ll. 28–29	Genesis 27:35		

TABLE 4.2   *The Townely Play of Jacob – Genesis Table*

ll. 1–58	Genesis 28:10–22	ll. 85–112	Genesis 32:26–30
l. 58 s.d.	Genesis 31:13	ll. 113–14	no biblical reference
ll. 59–74	Genesis 32:9–11	l. 114 s.d.	Genesis 33:1–2
ll. 75–84	no biblical reference	ll. 115–22	no biblical reference
l. 84 s.d.	Genesis 32:23–24	l. 122 s.d.	Genesis 33:4
		ll. 123–42	no biblical reference

TABLE 4.3 *The Towneley Play of Isaac*

		Wycliffe MS Bodley 959 (c. 1382)	Coverdale (1535)	Geneva (1560)
[*Isaac*] Com nere, son, and kys me, That I may feyle the smell of the. The smell of my son is lyke To a feld with flouris or hony-bike.		Gen. 27:26–27 he come nerre· & kyssid hym/ & anone þat he feelde þe good smell of his clopes: blyssyng to hym seiþ/ lo þe smell of my sonn as þe smell of afull feeld	Gen. 27:26–27 Come nye, and kysse me my sonne. So he came nye, and he kyssed him. Then smelled he the fauoure of his clothes, and blessed him, and sayde: Beholde, the smell of my sonne is as yͤ smell of the felde,	Gen. 27:26–27 Come nere now, and kisse me, my sonne. And he came nere and kissed him. Then he smelled the fauour of his garments, & blessed him, and said, Beholde, the smel of my sonne *is* as the smel of a field,
Where art thou, Esaw, my son? *Iacob.* Here, fader, and askys youre benyson.	5	Gen. 27:18 ffader my? & he answerede/ I here/ who art þou sonn myn?	Gen. 27:18 And he brought it in vnto his father, and sayde: My father. He answered: here am I, who art thou my sonne:	Gen. 27:18 And whe*n* he came to his father, he said, My Father. Who answered, I am here: who art thou, my sonne?
Isaac. The blyssyng my fader gaf to me,		no biblical reference	no biblical reference	no biblical reference
God of heuen and I gif the: God gif the plenté grete Of wyne, of oyll, and of whete;	10	Gen. 27:28 þe lord blysside/ God ȝ*ife* to þe of þe dew of heuen· & of þe fattnes of þe erþ· plente of whete· & of wyne & of oyle/	Gen. 27:28 God geue the of the fatnesse of the earth, and of the plenteousnes of corne and wyne.	Gen. 27:28 God giue thee therefore of the dewe of heauen, and the fatnes of the earth, and plentie of wheat and wine.
And graunt thi childre all To worship the, both grete and small. Whoso the blyssys, blyssed be he; Whoso the waris, wared be he. Now has thou my grete blyssyng; Loue the shall all thyne ofspryng.	15	Gen. 27:29 be þou þe lord of þi breþeren· & þe sonnes of þy moder· be þey (y)bowid befor þe/ who schall curse to þe: be he (a)cursid: & who schall bli*ssen* to þe· with blyssynges be he fulfyllid/	Gen. 27:29 Be thou lorde ouer thy brethren, and thy mothers children fall downe at thy fote. Cursed be he, that curseth the: and blessed be he, that blesseth the.	Gen. 27:29 be lord ouer thy brethre*n*, and let thy mothers children honour thee. cursed *be he* that curseth thee, and blessed *be he* that blesseth thee.
Go now wheder thou has to go. *Iacob.* Graunt mercy, syr, I will do so. *Recedet Iacob* [Iacob will leave]		} no biblical reference	} no biblical reference	} no biblical reference

THE BIBLE AND THE *TOWNELEY* PLAYS OF *ISAAC* AND *IACOB* 111

	Esaw. Haue, ete, fader, of myn huntyng, And gif me sythen youre blyssyng.	Gen. 27:30–31 Esau come: & soþen meteʒ of þe huntyng: brouʒt'e in to þe fader seyyng/ Aryse fader myn: & ete of þe huntyng of þi sonn þat þi soule bli'sse to me/	Gen. 27:30–31 Esau came from his huntinge, and made meate also, and brought it vnto his father, and sayde vnto him: Aryse my father, and eate of ye sonnes venyson, that thy soule maye blesse me.	Gen. 27:30–31 then came Esau his brother from his hunting, And he also prepared sauourie meat and broght it to his father, and said vnto his father, Let my father arise, and eat of his sonnes venison, that thy soule may blesse me.
20	*Isaac.* Who is that? *Esaw.* I, youre son Esaw, bryngys you venyson.	Gen. 27:32 And ysaac seyde/ who forsoþ art þou? þe which answerde/ I am þi firste goten sonn Esau/	Gen. 27:32 Who art thou? He sayde: I am Esau thy firstborne sonne.	Gen. 27:32 But his father Izhák said vnto him, Who art thou? And he answered, I am thy sone *euen* thy first borne Esau.
25	*Isaac.* Who was that was right now here, And broght me bruet of a dere? I ete well, and blyssyd hym; And he is blyssyd, ich a lym.	Gen. 27:33 who þann is he þat now riʒt brouʒte to me huntyng taken- & I *eet* of all befor þat þou come? & I blysside hym & he schall be blyssid/	Gen. 27:33 Who? Where is then the hunter that brought me, and I haue eaten of all afore thou camest, and haue blessed him? And he shall be blessed still.	Gen. 27:33 Who *and* where *is* he *that* hunted venison, and broght it me, and I haue eat of all before thou camest? and I haue blessed him, therefore he shal be blessed.
	Esaw. Alas! I may grete and sob. *Isaac.* Thou art begylyd thrugh Iacob, That is thyne awne german brother.	Gen. 27:34 roorede wiþ agrete crie:	Gen. 27:34 he cried loude, and was exceadynge sory,	Gen. 27:34 he cryed out with a great crye and bitter, out of measure
30		Gen. 27:35 þi broþer come gylinglich & toke þi blyssyng/	Gen. 27:35 Thy brother came with sotyltie, and hath taken thy blessinge awaye.	Gen. 27:35 Thy brother came with subtiltie, and hathe taken away thy blessing.
	Esaw. Haue ye kepyd me none other Blyssyng then ye set hym one?	Gen. 27:36 '&' wheþer þou hast not reseruyd he seiþ to me (a) þi blyssyng?	Gen. 27:36 Hast thou not kepte one blessynge for me?	Gen. 27:36 Hast thou not reserued a blessing for me?

TABLE 4.3   *The Towneley Play of Isaac* (cont.)

	Gen. 27:37	Gen. 27:37	Gen. 27:37
Isaac. Sich another haue I none;	ysaac answerde,	Isaac answered,	Then Izhák answered,
	Gen. 27:39	Gen. 27:39	Gen. 27:39
Bot God gif the, to thyn handband, The dew of heuen and frute of land; 35 Other then this can I not say.	in þe fattnes of þe erþ· & in þe dew of heuen 'fro' aboun: schall be þi blyssyng/	thou shalt haue a fat dwellinge vpon earth, & of yᵉ dew of heauen from aboue:	Beholde, the fatnes of the earth shalbe thy dwelling place, and *thou shalt haue* of the dewe of heauen from aboue.
	Gen. 27:41	Gen. 27:41	Gen. 27:41
Esaw. Now, alas and waloway! May I with that tratoure mete, My faders dayes shall com with grete, And my moders also; May I hym mete, I shall hym slo. 40	and seide in his herte/ þe days of weyling of my fader schall comme: & I schall slee Iacob my broþer/	and sayde in his herte: The tyme wyll come shortly, that my father shal mourne, for I wil slaye my brother Jacob.	And Esau thoght in his minde, The dayes of mourning for my father wil come shortely, then I wil slay my brother Iaakób.
	Gen. 27:46	Gen. 27:46	Gen. 27:46
Rebecca. Isaac, it were my deth If Iacob weddeth in kynd of Heth.	And Rebecca seide to ysaac/ it anoyiþ me of my lyf for þe douȝt'ris of *heth.* ȝif iacob schall take a wyf of þe lynage of þis lond: I nyll not lyue.	And Rebecca sayde vnto Isaac: I am weery of my life, because of the doughters of Heth: Yf Iacob take a wife of the doughters of this londe, what shall this life then profit me?	Also Rebekáh said to Izhák, I am weary of my life, for the daughters of Heth. If Iaakób take a wife of the daughters of Heth like these of the daughters of the land, what auaileth it me to liue?
	Gen. 27:43–45	Gen. 27:43–45	Gen. 27:43–45
I will send hym to Aran, There my brothere dwellys, Laban; And there may he serue in peasse 45 Till his brothers wrath will seasse. Why shuld I apon a day Loyse both my sonnes? Better nay.	flee to laban my broþer in Aran/ & þou schalt dwelle with hym afewe days · to þe tyme þat þe woodnes of þi broþer reste/ & 'þe' indignacioun of hym ceese/…why schall I be priuyd *eiþer* sonn(s) in o day?	Get the vp, and flye vnto my brother Laban in Haran, and tary there with him a whyle, tyll the furiousnes of thy brother be swaged, and till his wrath agaynst yᵉ be turned from the, and he forget what thou hast done vnto him. So wyll I then sende for the, and cause the be fetched form thence. Why shulde I be robbed of you both in one daye?	Now therefore my sóne, heare my voyce: arise, and flee thou to Harán to my brother Labán, And tary with him a while vntil thy brothers fearcenes be swaged, And til thy brothers wrath turne away from thee, and he forget the things, which thou hast done to him: then wil I send and take thee from thence: why shulde I be depriued of you bothe in one day?
	Gen. 28:1	Gen. 28:1	Gen. 28:1
Isaac. Thou says soth, wife. Call hym heder, And let vs tell hym where and wheder 50 That he may fle Esaw,	ANd so ysaac clepide Iacob·	Then called Isaac his sonne Iacob	Then Izhák called Iaakób

112 BUTTERWORTH

That vs both hetys bale to brew.	} no biblical reference	
Rebecca.		
Iacob, son! Thi fader and I		
Wold speke with the. Com, stand vs by.		
Out of contry must thou fle, 55		
That Esaw slo not the.		
Iacob.		
Whederward shuld I go, dame?		
Rebecca.	Gen. 28:2	Gen. 28:2
To Mesopotamean,	bot go & forþ passe into Mesopotany of Syri to þe house of Batuel þe fader of þi moder.	go into Mesopotamia vnto the house of Bethuel thy mothers father
To my brothere and thyn eme,		
That dwellys besyde Iordan streme; 60		
And ther may thou with hym won,	} no biblical reference	get thee to Padán Arám to the house of Bethuél thy mothers father
To Esaw, myne other son,		
Forget, and all his wrath be dede.		
Iacob.		
I will go, fader, at youre rede.		
Isaac.		
Yei, son, do as thi moder says; 65		
Com kys vs both and weynd thi ways.		
[*Et osculatur*	} no biblical reference	} no biblical reference
[And he kisses (them)]		
Iacob.		
Haue good day, syr and dame!		
Isaac.		
God sheld the, son, from syn and shame.		
Rebecca.	} no biblical reference	} no biblical reference
And gif the grace good man to be,		
And send me glad tythyngys to the. 70		
Explicit Isaac		

TABLE 4.4   *The Towneley Play of Iacob*

	Wycliffe MS Bodley 959 (c. 1382)	Coverdale (1535)	Geneva (1560)
	Gen. 28:10–12	Gen. 28:10–12	Gen. 28:10–12
	þann Iacob gone out to Bᵉersabee ȝede to Aran/ & whenn he was (y) comme to amaner place· & he wolde resten in it: after þe sonne goyng doun: toke of þe stones þat lyen· & vnderputtyng to hys heued: slepte in þe same place/	As for Iacob, he departed from Bersaba, and wente vnto Haran and came to a place, where he taried all night: for the Sonne was downe. And he toke a stone of yᵉ place, & put it vnder his heade, and layed him downe in yᵉ same place to slepe.	Now Iaakób departed from Beer-shéba, and went to Harán, And he came vnto a *certeine* place, & taried there all night, because yᵉ sonne was downe, and toke of the stones of the place and laied vnder his head and slept in the same place.
	Gen. 28:13–15	Gen. 28:13–15	Gen. 28:13–15
	I am þe lord god of abraham þi fader & god of ysaac/ þe lond in which þou slepist: I schall ȝᵗ*ife* to þe & to þi seed/ & þi seed schall be: as þe pouþer of þe erþ/ þou schalt be spred of brode to þe est and west: &	I am the LORDE God of thy father Abraham, and the God of Isaac: The londe yᵗ thou lyest vpon, wyl I geue vnto the, and to thy sede: and thy sede shal be as yᵉ dust of yᵉ earth. And thou shalt sprede forth towarde	I am the Lord God of Abrahám thy father, & the God of Izhák: the land, vpon the which thou slepest, wil I giue thee and thy sede. And thy sede shal be as the dust of the earth, and thou shalt spreade abrod to yᵉ West,

Line numbers: 5, 10, 15

Iacob.
Help me, Lord Adonay,
And hald me in the right way
To Mesopotameam,
For I cam neuer or now where I am;
I cam neuer here in this contré.
Lord of heuen, thou help me!
For I haue maide me, in this strete,
Sore bonys and warkand feete.
The son is downe. What is best?
Her purpose I all nyght to rest.
Vnder my hede this ston shall ly;
A nyghtys rest take will I.

Deus.
Iacob, Iacob! Thi God I am,
Of thi forfader Abraham
And of thi fader Isaac;
I shall the blys for thare sake.
This land that thou slepys in,
I shall the gif and thi kyn.
I shall thi seede multyply,

THE BIBLE AND THE *TOWNELEY* PLAYS OF *ISAAC* AND *IACOB* 115

As thyk as powder on erth may ly:
The kynd of the shall sprede wide,
From eest to west on euery syde,
From the south vnto the north.
All that I say, I shall forth,   20
And all the folkys of thyne ofspryng
Shal be blyssyd of thy blyssyng.
Iacob, haue thou no kyns drede;
I shall the clethe, I shall the fede.
Whartfull shall I make thi gate;   25
I shal the help erly and late,
And all in qwart shall I bryng the
Home agane to thi countré.
I shall not fayll, be thou bold,
Bot I shall do as I haue told.   30

Hic [*Iacob*] *vigilet*.

[Vulgate: *Cumque evigilasset Iacob*]

Iacob.

A, Lord, what may this mene?
What haue I herd in slepe, and sene?   35
That God leynyd hym to a stegh
And spake to me, it is no leghe;
And now is here none otheregate
Bot Godys howse and heuens yate.   40

norþ & souþ· and alle lynageȝ of þe erþ: schullen be blyssyd in þe & *in* þi seed/ & I schall be þi keper whyþer euer þou geest· & I schall bryng þe aȝeyn into þis lond: ne I schall not leue forto I fulfylle alle þe þingeȝ þat I seide/

And whenn Iacob was waken of þe slepe: seide/ forsoþ þe lord is in þis place & I wist not/ & dredyng seid· how feerfull is þis place? here is nonoþer· bot þe house of god: & þe ȝate of heuen/ Arysyng þann erlich toke þe stone· þe which he had*de* vnderputt to his heued/ And arerde

the west, east, north, and south: and thorow the and thy sede shall all the kynreds vpon earth be blessed. And beholde, I am with y^e, and wyll kepe the where so euer thou goest, & wyl brynge the hither agayne in to this lande: for I wil not leaue the, tyll I haue made good, all that I haue promysed the.

Gen. 28:16–22

Now whan Iacob awaked from his slepe, he saide: Surely the LORDE is in this place, and I knew not. And he was afraied, and sayde: How fearfull is this place: here is no thinge els but an house of God, & a gate vnto heau*en*. And Iacob arose early in the mornynge, and toke the stone that

and to the East, and to the North, and to the South, and in thee and in thy sede shal all the families of the earth be blessed. And lo, I am with thee, & wil kepe thee withersoeuer thou goest, and wil bring thee againe into this land: for I wil not forsake thee vntil I haue performed that, that I haue promised thee.

Gen. 28:16–22

Then Iaakób awoke out of his slepe, and said, Surely the Lord is in this place, and I was not aware. And he was afraid and said, How fearful is this place. this is none other but the house of God, and this is the gate of heauen. Then Iaakób rose vp early in the morning, and toke the stone

TABLE 4.4   *The Towneley Play of Jacob* (cont.)

Lord, how dredfull is this stede!		into asyngne of wyrschip: heeldyng oyle aboun … & he auowide auow: seying/ ȝif god were with me- & kepide me in þe way by whyche I go- & ȝ*ife* me loueȝ to eten- & cloþ to be cloþid- & schall be torned aȝeyn's welsumly to þe house of my fader: þe lord schall be to me into (a)god- & þe stone, þat I have arerd(e) into asyngne of wyrschip: schal be clepid þe house of god/ & of all þingeȝ þat þou schalt ȝ*ife* to me: I schal offer dymeȝ to þe/	he had layed vnder his heade, and set it vp, and poured oyle vpon it… And Iacob made a vowe, and sayde: Yf God wyll be with me, and kepe me in this iourney yᵗ I go & geue me bred to eate, and clothinge to put on, and brynge me peaceably home agayne vnto my father: Then shall the LORDE be my God, and this stone that I haue set vp shal be an house of God: and all that thou geuest me, I wyl geue the the tenth therof.	that he had laied vnder his head, and set it vp *as* a piller, and powred oyle vpon the top of it…Then Iaakób vowed a vowe, saying, If God wil be with me, and wil kepe me in this journey which I go, and wil giue me bread to eat, and clothes to put on: So that I come againe vnto my fathers house in safety, then shal the Lord be my God. And this stone, wᶜ I haue set vp *as* a piller, shalbe Gods house: & of all that yᵘ shalt giue me, wil I giue the tenth vnto thee.
Ther I layde downe my hede,			
In Godys lovyng I rayse this stone,			
And oyll will I putt theron.			
Lord of heuen, that all wote, 45			
Here to the I make a hote:			
If thou gif me mete and foode,			
And close to body, as I behoued,			
And bryng me home to kyth and kyn,			
By the way that I walk in, 50			
Without skathe and in quarte,			
I promyse to the with stedfast hart,			
As thou art Lord and God myne,			
And I Iacob, thi trew hyne –			
This stone I rayse in sygne today – 55			
Shall I hold holy kyrk for ay;			
And of all that newes me			
Rightwys tend shall I gif the.			
Hic egrediatur Iacob de Aran in terram natiuitatis sue. [Vulgate: *Nunc ergo surge, et egredere de terra hac, revertens in terram nativitatis tuae*]		Gen. 31:13 Now þann aryse & go out fro þis londe: tormyng aȝeyn in to þe londe of þi byrþe/	Gen. 31:13 Get the vp now, & departe out of this londe, & go agayne: in to the londe of thy kynred.	Gen. 31:13 Now arise, get thee out of this countrei & returne vnto the land where thou wast borne.
A, my Fader, God of heuen, That saide to me thrugh thi steven, 60		Gen. 32:9–11 And Iacob seide/ god of my fader abraham and god of my fader ysaac-	Gen. 32:9–11 Iacob sayde morouer: O God of my father Abraham, God of my father	Gen. 32:9–11 Moreouer Iaakób said, O God of my father Abrahám, and God of my

THE BIBLE AND THE *TOWNELEY* PLAYS OF *ISAAC* AND *IACOB* 117

When I in Aran was dwelland,	þou lord þat seydist to me torne		father Izhák: Lord, which saidest
That I shuld turne agane to land	aȝeyn in to þi lond· & in to þe place		vnto me, Returne vnto thy countrei
Ther I was both fed and born,	of þi birþe: & I schall wel(e) do to		& to thy kinred, and I wil do thee
Warnyd thou me, Lord, beforn,	þe / I am lesse þann all þi mercyes	Isaac, LORDE thou that saydest vnto	good, I am not "worthie of the least
As I went toward Aran	& thi trewþe· þat þou hast fulfyllid	me: Departe agayne to thine owne	of all the mercies & all the trueth,
With my staff, and passyd Iordan; 65	to þi seruaunt / In my staff ich haue	londe and to thy kynred, and I wyl	which thou hast shewed vnto thy
And now I com agane to kyth,	passid þis Iordane: & now with two	do the good: I am to litle for all the	seruaunt: For wᵗ my staffe came
With two ostes of men me with.	companyes I torne aȝeyn / delyuere	mercies and all the trueth that thou	I ouer this Iordén, and now haue
Thou hete me, Lord, to do well with me,	me of þe honde of my broþer	hast shewed vnto thyseruaunt (for	I gotten two bandes. I pray thee,
To multyplye my seede as sand of	Esau· for gretly I drede hym / lest 70	I had no more but this staff whan I	Deliuer me from the hand of my
see;	parauentour co(m)mynge: he smyte	wente ouer this Iordan, and now am	brother, from the hand of Esau: for I
Thou saue me, Lord, thrugh vertew,	þe moders with þe chyldren /	I become two droues) delyuer me	feare him, lest he wil come and smite
From veniance of Esaw,		from yᵉ hande of my brother, from	me, & the mother vpon the children.
That he slo not for old greme		the hande of Esau, for I am afrayed	
These moders with thare barne-teme.		of him, lest he come and smyte me	
		the mother with the children.	
Rachell.			
Oure anguysh, sir, is manyfold, 75			
Syn that oure messyngere vs told	} no biblical reference	} no biblical reference	} no biblical reference
That Esaw wold you slo,			
With foure hundreth men and mo.			
Iacob.			
Forsoth, Rachell, I haue hym sent			
Of many beestys sere present. 80			
May-tyde he will oure giftys take,			

TABLE 4.4 *The Towneley Play of Iacob* (cont.)

		Gen. 32:23–24	Gen. 32:23–24
And right so shall his wrath slake. Where ar oure thyngys? Ar thay past Iordan?	}		}
Lya.			}
Go and look, sir, as ye can.	}		}
Hic scrutetur superlectile, et lucetur angelus cum eo.		'&' ouer lad(de) all þinges þat to hym pertendyn· he dwelte alone/ & lo a man wrystyld with hym: vnto þe moru/	so that all that he had came ouer, and taried him self alone on this syde. Then wrestled there a man with him vntyll the breake of yᵉ daye.	And he toke them, & sent them ouer the river, & sent ouer that he had. When Iaakób was left him selfe alone, there wrestled a man with him vnto the breaking of the day.
[Vulgate: *Transductisque omnibus quae ad se pertinebant, remansit solus, et ecce: vir luctabatur cum eo usque mane*]			
Deus.		Gen. 32: 26–30	Gen. 32:26–30	Gen. 32:26–30
The day spryngys; now lett me go.	85	& he seide to hym/ *leꝼ* me forsoþ now vp steyiþ þe morntyd/ he answerde/ I schall not leue þe: bot ȝif thou bli'*sse* to me/ þenn he seiþ/ what is þe name to þe? he answer 'd*e*/ Iacob/ & he/ no more he seiþ Iacob schall be clepyd þi name: bot i[s]rael/ for ȝif aȝeynst god þou hast ben stronge: mych more aȝeynst men þou schalt haue þe	And he sayde: Let me go, for yᵉ daye breaketh on. But he answered: I will not let yᵉ go, excepte thou blesse me. He sayde: What is thy name: He answered: Iacob. He sayde: Thou shalt nomore be called Iacob, but Israel, for thou hast stryuen with God and with men, and hast preuayled. And Jacob axed him, & sayde: Tell me, what is yʳ name: But	And he said, Let me go, for yᵉ morning appeareth. Who answered, I wil not let thee go except thou blesse me. Then said he vnto him, What is thy name? And he said, Iaakób. Then said he,* Thy name shal be called Iaakób no more, but Israél: because thou hast had power with God, thou shalt also preuaile with men. Then Iaakób demanded, saying, Tel me,
Iacob.				
Nay, nay, I will not so, Bot thou blys me or thou gang; If I may, I shall hold the lang.				
Deus.				
In tokynyng that thou spekys with me, I shall toche now thi thee, That halt shall thou euermore, Bot thou shall fele no sore.	90			

What is thy name? – thou me tell.	maystry/ Iacob askyde hym/ sey to me what name þou ert (y)clepyd?	he sayde: Why axest thou what my name is: And he blessed him there.
Iacob.		
Iacob.	he answerde/ wherto askis þou my name þat is merueylouse? and he blysside hym in þe same place/ And Iacob clepide þe name of þat place phanuel: seying/, I haue (y)seen þe lord: face to face: & my soule is made saufe/ →	And Iacob called the place Peniel, for I haue sene God face to face, & my soule is recouered. →
Deus.	→	→
Nay, bot Israell;	→	→
Syn thou to me sich strengthe may kythe, 95	→	→
To men of erth thou must be stythe.	→	→
Iacob.	→	→
What is thy name?	→	→
Deus.	→	→
Whi askys thou it?	→	→
'Wonderfull', if thou wil wyt.	→	→
Iacob.	→	→
A, blys me, Lord!	→	→
Deus.	→	→
I shall the blys	→	I pray thee, thy name. And he said, Wherefore now doest thou aske my name? And he blessed him there. And Iaakób called the name of the place, Peniél: for, *said he*, I haue sene God face to face, and my life is preserued.
And be to the full propyce, 100	→	→
And gyf the my blyssyng for ay,	→	→
As Lord and he that all may;	→	→
I shall grayth thi gate	→	→
And full well ordeyn thi state.	→	→

TABLE 4.4 *The Towneley Play of Iacob* (cont.)

When thou has drede, thynk on me,		→		
And thou shal full well saynyd be.	105	→		
And look thou trow well my sayes;		→		
And fare well now, the day dayes.		→		
Iacob.				
Now haue I a new name, Israell.		→		
This place shall [hight] Fanuell,	110	→		
For I haue seyn in this place		→		
God of heuen, face to face.		→		
Rachell.		}	}	
Iacob, lo, we haue tythand		} no biblical reference	} no biblical reference	
That Esaw is here at hand!		}	}	
Hic diuidit turmas in tres partes.		Gen. 33:1–2	Gen. 33:1–2	Gen. 33:1–2
[Vulgate: *divisitque filios Liae et Rahel ambarumque ancillam et liberos earum. Et posuit utramque ancillam et liberos earum in principio Liam vero et filios eius in secundo loco Rahel autem et Ioseph novissimos*]		& he *departide* þe sonns of Iya & of Rachel. & of boþe his seruauntez/ & putte eyþer hond mayden & þe free children of hem: in þe bygynnyng/ Lya forsoþ in the secounde place. & þe sonns of here/ Rachell & Ioseph laste/	and he deuyded his children vnto Lea vnto Rachel, and to both the maydens, and set the maydens with their children before, and Lea with hir children after, and Rachel with Ioseph hynder most.	and he deuided the children to Leah, and to Rahél, and to the two maides. And he put the maides, & their children formost, and Leáh and her children after, and Rahél, and Ioseph hindermost.

THE BIBLE AND THE *TOWNELEY* PLAYS OF *ISAAC* AND *IACOB* 121

Iacob.
Rachell, stand thou in the last
    eschele,   115
For I wold thou were sauyd wele.
Call Ioseph and Beniamin,
And let theym not fro the twyn.
If it be so that Esaw
Vs before all to-hew,   120
Ye that ar here the last,
Ye may be sauyd if ye fle fast.

} no biblical reference

*Et vadat Iacob osculand[o] Esaw; venit
Iacob, flectit genua exorando Deum, et
leuando, occurrit illi Esaw in amplexibus.*

[Vulgate: *Currens itaque Esau obviam
fratri suo amplexatus est eum,
stringensque collum et osculans, flevit*]

} Gen. 33:4
And so Esau rynnyng to meeten
with his broþer· clyppide hym/ &
streynyng his necke· & kyssyng
wepte/

} Gen. 33:4
But Esau ranne to mete him, and
embraced him, and fell aboute his
neck, & kyssed him, and wepte

} Gen. 33:4
Then Esau ran to mete him and
embraced him, and fel on his necke
and kissed him, and thei wept.

Iacob.
I pray the, Lord, as thou me het,
That [thou] saue me and my gete.

} no biblical reference

Esaw.
Welcom, brother, to kyn and kyth,   125
Thi wife and childre that comes the with.
How has thou faren in far land?
Tell me now som good tythand.

} no biblical reference

TABLE 4.4 *The Towneley Play of Iacob* (cont.)

Iacob.
Well, my brother Esaw,
If that thi men no bale me brew.   130

[*Esaw*] *dicit seruis suis:*
[He says to his servants]

Esaw.
Wemo! felows, hold youre hend,
Ye se that I and he ar frend;   } no biblical reference
And frenship here will we fulfill,
Syn that it is Godys will.

Iacob.
God yeld you, brothere, that it so is 135
That thou thi hyne so wold kys.

Esaw.
Nay, Iacob, my dere brothere,
I shall the tell all anothere:
Thou art my lord thrugh destyny.
Go we togeder, both thou and I,   140
To my fader and his wife,
That lofys the, brother, as thare lyfe.

} no biblical reference

Explicit Iacob

Bibliography

Anderson, J.J., ed. *Records of Early English Drama: Newcastle Upon Tyne*. Toronto: University of Toronto Press, 1982.

Avgvstine, *The Citie of God with the learned comments of Io. Lod. Vives, S*^{t}, translated by I. H. [= John Healey]. London: George Eld, 1610.

Beadle, Richard, ed. *The York Plays: A Critical Edition of the York Corpus Christi Play as Recorded in British Library Additional MS 35290*, 2 vols. EETS s.s. 23–24. Oxford: Oxford University Press, 2009–13.

Biblia the Byble, that is, the holy Scrypture of the Olde and New Testament, faithfully translated in to Englyshe, translated by Miles Coverdale. [Southwark]: J. Nycolson, 1535.

Bibliotheca Towneleiana. A Catalogue of the Curious and Extensive Library of the late John Towneley. London: R.H. Evans, 1814.

Brown, Carleton, ed. *The Stonyhurst Pageants*. Göttingen: Vandenhoeck & Ruprecht, 1920.

Butterworth, Philip. "Stage Directions of the Towneley Cycle." M.A. Dissertation, School of English, University of Leeds, 1977.

———. "Stage Directions in the Towneley Play of Jacob." In *The National Arts Education Archive: Occasional Papers in the Arts and Education*, 5 vols., edited by A.E. Green, 6: 1–8. Bretton Hall: The National Arts Education Archive, 1996.

———. *Staging Conventions in Medieval English Theatre*. Cambridge: Cambridge University Press, 2014.

Cawley, A.C., ed. *The Wakefield Pageants in the Towneley Cycle*. Manchester: Manchester University Press, 1958.

———, and Martin Stevens, eds. *The Towneley Cycle: A Facsimile of Huntington MS HM1*. Medieval Drama Facsimiles, 2. Leeds Texts and Monographs [Leeds]: University of Leeds, School of English, 1976.

Collier, John Payne. *The History of English Dramatic Poetry to the Time of William Shakespeare; and Annals of the Stage to the Restoration*, 3 vols. London: John Murray, 1831.

Craig, Hardin. *English Religious Drama of the Middle Ages*. Oxford: Clarendon Press, 1955.

Davis, Norman, ed. *Non-Cycle Plays and Fragments*. EETS s.s. 1. Oxford: Oxford University Press, 1970.

Edgar, Swift, ed. *The Vulgate Bible: Douay-Rheims Translation*, 6 vols. Cambridge, MA–London: Harvard University Press, 2010–13.

England, George, and Alfred W. Pollard, eds. *The Towneley Plays*, re-edited from the unique manuscript. EETS e.s. 7. London: Kegan Paul, Trench, Trübner & Co., 1897.

Gardiner, Harold C. *Mysteries' End: An Investigation of the Last Days of the Medieval Religious Stage*. Yale Studies in English, 103. New Haven: Yale University Press, 1946.

Gardner, John. *The Construction of the Wakefield Cycle*. Carbondale: Southern Illinois University Press, [1974].

Gayley, Charles Mills. *Plays of our Forefathers and some of the traditions upon which they were founded*. New York: Duffield, 1907.

Geneva Bible: A Facsimile of the 1560 Edition, The, with an introduction by Lloyd E. Berry. Peabody, MA: Hendrickson, 2007.

Hardison Jr., O.B. *Christian Rite and Christian Drama in the Middle Ages: Essays in the Origin and Early History of Modern Drama*. Baltimore: Johns Hopkins Press, 1965.

Judicium: A Pageant. Extracted from the Towneley Manuscript of Ancient Mysteries. London: Richard and Arthur Taylor, 1822.

Lindberg, Conrad, ed. *MS. Bodley 959: Genesis – Baruch 3.20 in the Earlier Version of the Wycliffite Bible*, 8 vols. Stockholm Studies in English, 6ff. Stockholm: Almqvist & Wiksell, 1959–97.

Lumiansky, R.M. and David Mills, eds. *The Chester Mystery Cycle*, 2 vols. EETS s.s. 3 and 9. Oxford: Oxford University Press, 1974–86.

Manly, John Matthews, ed. *Specimens of the Pre-Shaksperean Drama*, 2 vols. Boston: Ginn, 1897.

Newe mery and wittie Comedie or Enterlude, newely imprinted, treating vpon the Historie of Iacob and Esau taken out of the .xxvij. Chap. of the first booke of Moses entituled Genesis, A. London: Henrie Bynneman, 1568.

Raine, James, ed. *The Towneley Mysteries*. Publications of the Surtees Society, 3. London: J.B. Nichols and Son, 1836.

Rose, Martial, ed. *The Wakefield Mystery Plays*. London: Evans, 1961.

Rossiter, A.P. *English Drama from Early Times to the Elizabethans: Its Background, Origins and Developments*. London: Hutchinson, 1950.

Spector, Stephen, ed. *N-Town Play Cotton MS Vespasian D. 8, The*, 2 vols. EETS s.s. 11–12. Oxford: Oxford University Press, 1991.

Stevens, Martin and A.C. Cawley, eds. *The Towneley Plays*, 2 vols. EETS s.s. 13–14. Oxford: Oxford University Press, 1994.

Ten Brink, Bernhard. *History of English Literature (Wyclif, Chaucer, Earliest Drama, Renaissance)*, 3 vols., translated by Horace M. Kennedy, Wm. Clarke Robinson and L. Dora Schmitz. London: George Bell, 1883–96.

Young, Karl. *The Drama of the Medieval Church*, 2 vols. Oxford: Clarendon Press, 1933.

CHAPTER 5

The Norwich Grocers' Play(s) (1533, 1565): Development and Changes in the Representation of Man's Fall

Roberta Mullini

Abstract

This essay deals with the two versions of the Fall of Man episode, the only surviving play(s) of the lost Norwich cycle of mystery plays (the A and B texts). After discussing their scholarly reception, this article highlights the main differences between the pre-Reformation and the post-Reformation texts, focussing on the endings, perceptibly different because in the Reformed text a more positive and hopeful future for Adam and Eve is substituted to the tone of utter despair of the Catholic version. At the end of the episode, the B text introduces allegorical characters, thus mixing the mystery and the moral play traditions. The relationships and parallels between the Norwich plays and the other extant cycles are then studied, emphasizing the characterization of the protagonists (Adam, Eve, and the devil) and showing how even the attempt at 'reforming' a Catholic play still relies heavily on the old tradition, so much so that prologues are introduced in the B text, in order to justify the legitimacy of a Biblical play (when strictly adhering to the Scriptures) even under the new religion. Despite the efforts of the compiler of the more recent text, the last known performance in Norwich was as early as 1565.

Keywords

biblical drama – English theatre – Norwich cycle – fall of man – reformation; analogues

1 Introduction

While scholars are awaiting the second volume of the *Records of Early English Drama* (REED) devoted to Norwich, which will contain and order all the documents concerning dramatic activities before 1540,[1] the only surviving episode of the cycle performed in this Norfolk town, the Grocers' Play of the Fall of Man, has recently become a touchstone for a general assessment of Tudor drama. In fact, of the two extant versions of the episode, dated c. 1533 (text A) and 1565 (text B) respectively,[2] the latter has led Thomas Betteridge and Greg Walker, the editors of *The Oxford Book of Tudor Drama*, to devote to it the first four pages of the "Introduction" to their volume, where they discuss its relevance as a play featuring the crucial passage from the Catholic to the Protestant milieu in the first years of Queen Elizabeth I: "[i]ts author has sought to turn the traditional form of civic religious drama in a reformed direction, responding ... to protestant objections to the impurities and absurdities of the cycle form."[3] Actually the B text, apart from being dated the very year that saw the last known production of the cycle in Norwich,[4] presents some features that manifest the anonymous playwright's desire to adapt an old tradition to the new Reformist episteme so as to turn a Catholic text into a Protestant (if not Puritan) one, but at the same time not to renounce certain dramatic conventions of the theatre of the past.

What follows, after a necessary assessment of previous studies of the Norwich play, will be an attempt to analyze the two texts in order to highlight the permanence of old aspects of biblical drama on the one hand, and on the other the introduction of new ones. A comparison with the other extant cases of the same episode as present in the major cycles of mystery plays will also be discussed.

---

1   The *Records of Early English Drama* volume of *Norwich to 1540* will be edited, according to the list of the "Collections in progress" provided by the REED site (<http://reed.utoronto.ca/print-collections-2/forthcoming/>, accessed 13 June 2014), by JoAnna Dutka. The years between 1540 and 1642 were published in *Records of Early English Drama: Norwich 1540–1642*, ed. David Galloway (Toronto: University of Toronto Press, 1984). The new volume will collect the various documents now scattered in sundry publications and, hopefully, also reveal so far unknown sources.
2   Here and below in this article the two versions will be called A and B text, following the edition provided in *Non-Cycle Plays and Fragments*, ed. Norman Davis, EETS s.s. 1 (Oxford: Oxford University Press, 1970), from which textual quotations will also be drawn.
3   Thomas Betteridge and Greg Walker, "Introduction," in *The Oxford Handbook of Tudor Drama*, ed. Thomas Betteridge and Greg Walker (Oxford: Oxford University Press, 2012), 3.
4   After the note in the Assembly Minute Books III, for 13 April 1565 – "Also yt ys agreid that Souche pagentes as were wonte to go in the tyme of whitson holydayes shall be Set forthe by occupacions as in tymes paste haue bene vsyd" (Galloway, REED: *Norwich 1540–1642*, 51) – no further mention is made of the performance of the cyclic pageants.

2   The 'State of the Art'

A preliminary question might arise about the nature of the Grocers' plays, given that so far I have presupposed the existence of a Norwich cycle of mystery plays, while the standard edition of the texts is published in a collection entitled "Non-cycle plays." This incongruence is only apparent, though, because the extant documents clearly attest to the existence of a series of Norwich pageants from *Creation* to *The Holy Ghost* in the hands of various town guilds, even though no text survives but the Grocers'.[5] Therefore one can safely talk of "the Norwich cycle," albeit a very 'poor' one in comparison with such collections as York and Chester.

Before the first decade of this century, the study of the Norwich Grocers' play seems to have been concentrated in the 1970s and early 1980s, perhaps as a consequence of Norman Davis's edition of the texts which also republished the then available documents referring to the town, collected by eighteenth- and nineteenth-century antiquarians. It was JoAnna Dutka who mainly focussed her attention on the philological variants of the eighteenth-century transcriptions of the two texts,[6] by comparing their antiquarian sources, Robert Fitch's printed edition ("from a manuscript in [his] possession"), and Osborne Waterhouse's edition.[7] The two latter works are the basis for Davis's version. Some years before, Dutka had presented a general study of the early history of dramatic activities in Norwich, based on pre-1540 documents which testify to the A text being "copied into the Company's records (June 16, 1533)" and performed the following year.[8] In her hypothetical reconstruction of the Norwich plays Dutka polemicizes with Alan Nelson's interpretation of the city documents, especially as concerns the yearly occurrence of performances. In fact Nelson arrives at the conclusion that the biblical plays were performed on Corpus Christi day, whereas Dutka affirms that they were at Whitsun, when the

---

5   See Davis, *Non-Cycle Plays and Fragments*, xxix-xxx.
6   See JoAnna Dutka, "The Lost Dramatic Cycle of Norwich and the Grocers' Play of the Fall of Man," *The Review of English Studies* N. S. 35:137 (Feb. 1984): 1–13. The oldest antiquarian source survives in John Kirkpatrick's early eighteenth-century manuscript papers that had not been discovered before Davis's edition. JoAnna Dutka, "The Fall of Man: The Norwich Grocers' Play," *Records of Early English Drama* 9:1 (1984): 1–11, also made available a facsimile of Kirkpatrick's transcription of the plays.
7   See *Norwich Pageants: The Grocers' Play*, ed. Robert Fitch (Norwich: Charles Muskett, 1856), and *The Non-Cycle Mystery Plays*, ed. Osborne Waterhouse, EETS e.s. 104 (London: Kegan Paul, Trench Trübner & Co., 1909).
8   JoAnna Dutka, "Mystery Plays at Norwich: Their Formation and Development," *Leeds Studies in English* N.S. 10 (1978): 113.

city displayed itself in its major fair.[9] The discrepancies between historians and the fact that documents are spread in various publications make scholars look forward to the issue of the second REED Norwich volume, which will hopefully disentangle problems and resolve disagreement.

In 1981 Kevin J. Harty published an article which analyses the Grocers' play together with its analogues in the N-Town, York, and Chester Cycles.[10] The Protestant shift from the A to the B text is fore-grounded and studied deftly in this contribution as a positive feature of the later version's skilful dramaturgy. The presence of the Reformist aspects of the B text had earlier been spotlighted in Rosemary Woolf's words about the "distinctly Protestant ring" of the play,[11] while it is somewhat overlooked by Dutka, who, as an answer to Woolf's statement, claims that the text "resounds not with what has been called a 'distinctively Protestant ring', but, rather, is an interesting variation on the *felix culpa* theme."[12]

Paul White, in his recent extended study of the play (which he names *Adam and Eve*), depicts a composite picture of the historical context of Protestant Norwich and of the theological complexity of the play.[13] In particular, he stresses the "quintessentially Protestant teaching" about marital relationships as emerging from the B text, and the connection between the play and the contemporary moral interludes.[14] In another contribution, this scholar locates the episode – which he numbers "[a]mong the most staunchly Protestant plays of the early Elizabethan period" – in 1566, even though he does not explain the reason for this change from 1565, and calls the play *Pageant of Paradise*.[15]

---

9   See, respectively, Alan H. Nelson, *The Medieval English Stage* (Chicago: University of Chicago Press, 1974), 121, 131–35, and Dutka, "Mystery Plays at Norwich," 111 and n. 31.

10 Kevin J. Harty, "The Norwich Grocers' Play and Its Three Cyclic Counterparts: Four English Mystery Plays on the Fall of Man," *Studia Philologica* 53 (1981): 77–89.

11 Rosemary Woolf, *The English Mystery Plays* (Berkeley: University of California Press, 1972), 373, n. 41.

12 Dutka, "The Lost Dramatic Cycle," 11. Harty's argument ("The Norwich Grocers' Play," 87–88) about *felix culpa* is not mentioned by Dutka.

13 Paul Whitfield White, "*The Grocers' Play* and the Norwich Cycle Reformed," in Paul Whitfield White, *Drama and Religion in English Provincial Society, 1485–1660* (Cambridge: Cambridge University Press, 2008), 77–88. Harty's contribution does not seem to be acknowledged by White.

14 Ibid., 86 and 87, respectively.

15 Paul Whitfield White, "Interludes, Economics, and the Elizabethan Stage," in *The Oxford Handbook of Tudor Literature*, ed. Mike Pincombe and Cathy Shrank (Oxford: Oxford University Press, 2009), 555. A possible reason for this different name is that a list of the city pageants, which amounted to twelve, assigns "Paradyse" to the Grocers (see the transcription from the *Old Free Book*, fol. 162, in *The Records of the City of Norwich*, 2 vols., ed.

Finally, although it might appear almost extraordinary that the Norwich play, as mentioned earlier, be chosen as the starting point of Betteridge and Walker's "Introduction" to Tudor drama, these authors' decision shows how relevant such a play is in the history of early modern British drama. Its being 'in between' and its having survived in its two versions make of it a keystone for the interpretation of mixed dramatic forms and of the epistemic transition to Elizabethan theatre.

3   The A and B Texts

For brevity, it is certainly convenient to entitle the Grocers' play(s) *The Fall of Man*, according to their analogues in surviving cycles, although we must not forget that they are transcribed in the documents with proper, longer titles. Text A is actually called "The Story of the Creacion of Eve, with the expellyng of Adam and Eve out of Paradyce," whereas text B's original title is "The Storye of the Temptacion of Man in Paradyce, being therin placyd, and the expellynge of Man and Woman from thence, newely renvid and accordynge unto the Skripture, begon thys yere Anno 1565, Anno 7. Eliz."[16] Both titles show that the Norwich texts join more individual biblical episodes in a single play. Waterhouse was the first editor of the play to introduce the distinction between the A and B versions, which he called "Norwich Play, A" and "Norwich Play, B" respectively, while John Manly, who edited the plays in his collection of *Specimens of Pre-Shakespearian Drama*, simply presented them as I and II, labelling them the "Norwich Whitsun Plays."[17]

3.1   *A Synopsis*

Text A starts after Adam's creation. God descends from Heaven "into Paradyce" (l. 9) to create Eve from one of Adam's ribs, after making him fall asleep. The events are somewhat compressed, since soon afterwards Adam praises God,

---

William Hudson and John C. Tingey [London: Jarrold and Sons, 1910], 2: 230; see also Davis, *Non-Cycle Plays and Fragments*, xxix).

16   Davis, *Non-Cycle Plays and Fragments*, 8 and 11.

17   *Specimens of the Pre-Shaksperean Drama*, 2 vols., ed. John Matthews Manly (Boston: Ginn, 1897), 1: 1 and 4. According to Dutka's hypothesis Manly was quite right in avoiding the more usual name of "Corpus Christi Plays," given the city records that testify to the performances taking place, when they did, on Whitsun Monday. See the reproduction of the Assembly Book for 21 September 1527 in Davis, *Non-Cycle Plays and Fragments*, xxvii-viii, and Dutka's ("Mystery Plays at Norwich," 112–16) well-founded hypothesis about the development of the Norwich plays. But cf. Nelson, *Medieval English Stage*.

acknowledges Eve's presence naming her ("virago," l. 20), and receives and accepts the prohibition to eat from "thys tre of connyng" (l. 26). God returns to his "habitacion" (l. 47) and Adam tells Eve, whom he calls "lovely spowse" (l. 48), that he "wyll walk a whyle" for his recreation (l. 50), also because, after all, "In thys place non yll thyng may abyde" (l. 54). Immediately afterwards Serpens addresses Eve without giving any justification for his action, and convinces her to eat "thys apple" (l. 67), assuring her that "To the[e] Almyghty God dyd me send" (l. 68). Eve decides to share the apple with Adam "to please my spowse" (l. 70), and when Adam returns, she explains that "An angell cam from Godes grace || And gaffe me an apple of thys tre" (ll. 74–75). No sooner has she finished speaking than God summons Adam: "Byfore my presens why dost thou not apere?" (l. 80). The manuscript is incomplete from this point till "Musick" is required and a stage direction informs us that *Aftyr that Adam and Eve be drevyn owt of Paradyse they schall speke thys foloyng*," i.e. Adam and Eve both bemoan their sin and, finally, show their despair by singing two doleful final lines (ll. 89–90).

Text B, apart from being preceded by two prologues to be recited according to the occasion,[18] begins almost in the same way as text A: Adam already exists, God first prohibits him to eat of the forbidden tree, then decides to make "an helper" for him (l. 10) after letting him fall asleep, "To comfort one th'other when from you I am gone" (l. 16). Soon after he goes "wher [his] habytacion is" (l. 21). Adam and Eve thank God, then exchange loving words and call each other with tender vocatives: Adam calls Eve "Most lovynge spowse" (l. 28), and "myn owne swete spouse" (l. 34); Eve reciprocates with "swete lover" (l. 29), and "my dere lover" (l. 35). Adam leaves Eve, moved by his "fantasye" "to walke abowt this garden" (l. 32). "*The Serpent speketh*" declares the stage direction soon following: in B, though, the tempter first reveals his plan in a seven-line aside, then speaks to Eve, wheedling her out of her desire to comply with God's rule. On Adam's return, Eve explains to him that God's "angell" has convinced her to eat "this apple" (l. 62). Adam eats and soon discovers their nakedness. After Eve's suggestion to cover it with "fygge-leavis" (l. 69), God calls. Eve reveals that she has been convinced by the Serpent "with that his fayer face" (l. 78), and God asks the latter his reasons. Then follow God's curse against the devil with the menace of future damage to his power ("The womans sede shall overcome the, thus that have I wylde," l. 86),[19] the declaration of the dolorous lot of mankind, and the arrival of an angel who orders Adam and Eve to "Departe from

---

18   See below.
19   God's threat to Satan with the prophecy of Christ's advent is also present in the N-Town and Chester parallel texts, whereas the York Cycle lacks it.

hence at onys from this place of comforte" (l. 100). Man and woman bewail their exile from Eden and are approached by Dolor and Misery, who stress their sorrowful destiny, but also by the Holy Ghost, who consoles them, foretelling salvation through Christ's coming.[20]

Differences and similarities between A and B will be issues of the following paragraphs. Here suffice it to notice the not always recognised reciprocal tenderness of the two spouses in both texts, Satan's presence in B, and, of the utmost relevance, the hopeful ending of B.

3.2   *The Two Prologues to Text B*

That something very important happened between the composition of text A and text B is revealed by the two prologues to text B. A very special feature differentiates the Norwich B text from the majority of other cyclic plays: before the action starts, the text presents two Prolocutors: the first has to speak in case the pageant *"is played withowte eny other goenge befor yt,"*[21] whereas the second only *"yf ther goeth eny other pageantes before yt."*[22] White correctly observes that other figures of Prolocutors are only to be found in John Bale's biblical plays and in the 1560s Protestant interlude *King Darius*,[23] thus stressing the Reformist characteristics of the B text. However, another tradition, still Catholic, has to be remembered, i.e. the frequent roles of Expositors (and/or Doctors) present in the Chester cycle. Both Prolocutors and Expositors are inserted into plays as official voices either of the dramatist, or of orthodoxy, or of religious controversy, their task being multifaceted. "Baleus Prolocutor" is clearly a *persona* of John Bale the Protestant author, summarising the action or polemically interpreting it, while the Expositor who speaks, for example, in the Chester *Abraham* explains "what may this signifye" to the "unlearned standinge herebye," with the intention of making the audience understand the connection between the Old and the New Testament.[24] Whether Protestant or Catholic, both are, in any case, extradiegetic characters, acting as prologues with evident didactic purposes.[25]

---

20   See below. Strictly speaking, the biblical episode occupies 110 lines, while the addition of the two allegories and of the Holy Ghost occupies another 51, so that B consists of 161 lines.

21   Davis, *Non-Cycle Plays and Fragments*, 11; Text B, prologue 1, initial stage direction.

22   Ibid., 12; Text B, prologue 2, initial stage direction.

23   White, *"The Grocers' Play,"* 83.

24   Quotations are drawn from *The Chester Mystery Cycle*, 2 vols., ed. R.M. Lumiansky and David Mills, EETS s.s. 3 and 9 (Oxford: Oxford University Press, 1974–86), 4.113 and 115.

25   Philip Butterworth, *Staging Conventions in Medieval English Theatre* (Cambridge: Cambridge University Press, 2014), 125, summarizes the expositor's function very well: "Such a

In the "Prologues," over and above the indication about the order of the pageants, it is the insistence on "Godes scripture" (prologue 1, l. 2), on the fact that the "stories with the Skriptures most justly agree" (prologue 1, l. 14), and on the precise quotation of "the seconde chapter of Genesis" (prologue 1, l. 17), which shows on the one hand the relevance of a correct correspondence between what is going to be performed and its biblical source, and on the other the supposed knowledge of the Bible itself on the part of the audience. This same care, even more scrupulous, surfaces in the second prologue: not only are the "fyrst" and the "seconde of Genesis" mentioned (prologue 2, ll. 2 and 6), but there is also a further specification of the verse from which the action starts: "From the letter C. in the chapter before saide" (prologue 2, l. 9). The Prolocutor sounds like a preacher in a pulpit, intent on explaining the meaning of the first chapters of the Book of Genesis, and on directing his congregation's attention to the exact wording of the religious text. Clearly such a procedure might have happened in an Anglican church where the *Great Bible* itself was chained to the lectern so that anybody might read it, but not in a Catholic one.[26] The reformed milieu from which text B arises is then defined from the very beginning of the play.

3.3   The Endings

There is also another, more radical, feature which distinguishes the B from the A text and from its analogues in other mystery cycles: the B text, in spite of the presence of the allegorical characters of Dolor and Misery, ends on a positive, hopeful note, because, as the first prologue announces, the terrible consequences of "Mans first disobedience" (as Milton writes) will last "Untyll Godes spright renvid" (prologue 1, l. 28), i.e. the performance will show that man "by God his spright was comforted ageyne," as the second prologue reads (prologue 2, l. 20).[27] The insistence on the biblical text being kept near at hand and

---

figure was able to explain and interpret the religious significance of what an audience had seen and heard, and what it was about to witness. Sometimes, he took on the identity of a personage within the dramatic fiction of the play, and straddled both the inside and outside requirements of the narrative. In other words, he was able to exist and operate in two co-existent realities; one inside the narrative of the play and the other in the consciousness of performance. ... And it is this orientation that enabled him to have a powerful effect upon the didactic nature of the play."

26   For the B text author's reliance on the *Great Bible* see Dutka, "The Lost Dramatic Cycle," 6–7, and White, "*The Grocers' Play*," 83.

27   This is not the place to discuss Milton's possible knowledge of the mystery cycle tradition, especially of the Norwich texts, but see Gordon Campbell and N.M. Davis, "*Paradise Lost* and the Norwich Grocers' Play," *Milton Quarterly* 14:4 (1980): 113–16.

perhaps followed to check its correspondence with the pageant is a distinct signal of the Reformist orthodoxy of the B text, but the addition concerning the positive ending of Man's destiny extends the reach of this reformed adaptation of a Catholic play as far as Calvinism, even though this point comes out clearly only in Adam's last speech, when Adam praises God with these words:

> Nowe fele I such great comforte, my syns they be unlode
> > And layde on Chrystes back, which is my joye and lyght.
> > This Dolor and this Mysery I fele to me no wight;
> No! Deth is overcum *by forepredestinacion*. (ll. 146–49; my emphasis)

Christ is first mentioned by the Holy Ghost, who speaks from line 123 to 143 introducing issues typical of Pauline teaching about Christians' being armoured against evil:[28]

> Theis armors ar preparyd, yf thou wylt turn ageyne,
> > To fyght wyth; take to the, and reach Woman the same;
> The brest-plate of rightousnes Saynte Paule wyll the retayne;
> > The shylde of faythe to quench, thy fyrye dartes to tame;
> > The hellmett of salvacion the devyles wrath shall lame;
> And the sworde of the Spright, which is the worde of God – (ll. 137–42)

Some phrases seem to come directly from the *Great Bible*, which translates St Paul's Epistle to the Ephesians in the following way:

> Wherefore take vnto you y[our] whole armoure || of God, that ye maye be able to resyste in the || euyll daye, and stande perfecte in all things;
> Stande therefore, and youre loynes gyrd || with the trueth, hauynge on the brest plate || of ryghtewesnes, & hauynge shoes on youre || fete, that ye maye be prepared for the Gospell || of peace. Aboue all, take to you the shylde of || fayth, wherwith ye maye quenche all y[our] fyrie || dartes of the wycked. And take the helmet || of saluacyon, and the swearde of the sprete, || which is the worde of God.[29]

---

28   See St Paul, Epistle to the Ephesians, 6:13–17. On this relationship, see Harty, "The Norwich Grocers' Play," 87.

29   *The Bible in Englyshe* (London: Edward Whytchurche, 1539; rpt. 1540), "The epistle of saynct Paul the Apostle to the Ephesyans, The .vi. Chapter, C," fol. lxxviii[r] (<https://archive.org/stream/GreatBible1540/1540GreatBible#page/n505/ mode/1up> [accessed 28 June 2014]).

Man's spiritual suit of armour is completed, first of all, by faith and by the "worde of God," i.e. the foundations of Reformist theology. In his previous words, the Holy Ghost insists on almost the same concept, when he says: "Take owte of the Gospell that yt the requyre, || Fayth in Chryst Jhesu, and grace shall ensewe" (ll. 130–31). Faith is the basis of salvation, and grace follows as a sign of predestination.

Clearly the Norwich B text, through the presence of the Holy Ghost, expresses the basic tenets of the Reformation, in terms not only Lutheran, but, as hinted above, also Calvinist. The process of transformation from the A text certainly shows the attempt of the town (or at least of the Grocers' guild) to 'update' their pageant, to render it more easily tolerated by religious authorities. Evidently, though, this was not enough to guarantee the preservation of performances. Or, the other guilds were not able to change their own texts in the same direction as the Grocers'. In any case, the performance of the cycle, even of 'reformed' plays, was presumably considered to be too redolent of Catholicism and, therefore, no longer acceptable after 1565.

The A text ends with a song of sorrow and Adam and Eve going about the stage wringing their hands, whereas the B text ends with a joyful hymn: "With hart and voyce || Let us rejoyce" (ll. 154–55), sings Adam. We might also surmise that the audience joins him as a united congregation, especially according to the very final lines which sound as an invitation not only to Eve, but to the onlookers: "Lett all our hartes reioyce together, || And lett us all lifte up our voyce, on of us with another" (ll. 160–61).[30]

3.4　　*The Allegories*

Besides the presence of Reformation theology in the B text, what strikes one most when comparing the structure of the two versions of the Norwich Grocers' play is the addition of the two allegories at the end, and of the Holy Ghost. Certainly it is unusual to find allegories in a mystery play, but there are some cases that testify to the dramaturgic possibility of such a mixture. In the N-Town cycle, for example, there are some allegories (Pax, Veritas, Misericordia and Justitia, the Four Daughters of God that also feature in *The Castle of Perseverance*) in the episode of the "Parliament of Heaven" which includes the "Salutation and Conception" (Play 11), together with Spiritus Sanctus, the Holy Ghost, who is present in the Norwich play as well.[31] Therefore, the presence of

---

30　　See Betteridge and Walker, "Introduction," 1–2.
31　　This collection of mystery plays is nowadays considered rather a compilation for private meditation than a set of scripts for performance, in spite of its sometimes very detailed stage directions (see Alan J. Fletcher, "The N-Town Plays," in *The Cambridge Companion to*

the Holy Ghost as a character, i.e. to be impersonated by an actor and not only symbolically represented by a dove or tongues of fire,[32] is not totally new in the English dramatic tradition.[33] In the N-Town cycle itself, Death also appears, in Play 20 ("Slaughter of the Innocents; Death of Herod"), a character who plays a conspicuous role in *The Castle of Perseverance* and in *Everyman*. All these aspects connect the B text both to the early and late fifteenth-century Catholic morality play and to the mid-sixteenth century Protestant moral interludes which also feature allegories (see, e.g., *Nice Wanton* which lists Worldly Shame among its 'personages', besides the Vice Iniquitie, and various Vice figures in other interludes).[34]

Dolor and Misery – 'born' out of the frequent allusions in all Fall of Man episodes to post-lapsarian hopelessness, and directly out of the Norwich A text and its final sorrowful song "Wythe dolorous sorowe, we maye wayle and wepe || Both nyght and daye in sory sythys full depe" (ll. 89–90) – "give both verbal and visual objectification to the psychological and spiritual despair Adam and Eve experience as a consequence of original sin."[35] Dolor invites Adam to "take hold" of him (l. 111), because, as Misery adds, this is "According to desarte thy portion ..., of right" (l. 117). The new psychological perspective of the B text in

---

Medieval English Theatre, ed. Richard Beadle and Alan J. Fletcher [Cambridge: Cambridge University Press, 2008], 183–210).

32 The way the stage direction in the Chester Pentecost Play signals the descent of the Holy Ghost on the apostles at Whitsun seems rather perilous for the actors: "Tunc Deus emittet Spiritum Sanctum in spetie ignis, et ... duo angeli ... projecient ignem super apostolos" (Then God shall send out the Holy Spirit in the form of fire, and ... two angels ... shall throw fire upon the apostles; *Chester* 21.238 s.d.). The English translation is drawn from *The Chester Mystery Cycle: A New Edition with Modernized Spelling*, ed. David Mills (East Lansing: Colleagues Press, 1992), 327. But, unfortunately, "we still have no idea how this was done," even if "the effect was intended to be spectacular" (Pamela M. King, "Playing Pentecost in York and Chester: Transformations and Texts," *Medieval English Theatre* 29 [2007]: 67). See Philip Butterworth, *Theatre of Fire: Special Effects in Early English and Scottish Theatre* (London: Society for Theatre Research, 1998), for the use of fire and gunpowder in English medieval theatre.

33 It is also interesting to remark that the last pageant mentioned in the list of the Norwich plays is *The Holy Ghost,* and that the performance occurred on Whitsun Monday, i.e. that the occasion and the play title, if abbreviated for "Pentecost," coincide.

34 Even if printed in 1560, *Nice Wanton* contains features which suggest a previous date of composition: it deals with children's upbringing and, according to Pamela M. King, "Minority Plays: Two Interludes for Edward VI," *Medieval English Theatre* 15 (1993): 88–89, "on internal evidence, [it] can be attributed incontrovertibly to the period of the brief reign of the child-monarch Edward VI."

35 White, "*The Grocers' Play*," 87.

dramaturgical terms – i.e., the allegories are interiorised although present on stage as individual characters – is well exemplified by Adam's following words: "Thus troublyd, nowe I enter into dolor and miserie" (l. 119).

A similar case occurs in *Apius and Virginia*, a "tragicall comedie" as the full title reads, by an otherwise unknown R. B., which was entered in the Stationers' Register in 1567, even though extant only in a 1575 printed edition. Here Apius, who desires Virginia against her will, is helped in his evil doing by the Vice Haphazard, but – soon after being totally convinced about going on in his mischief, and just after exclaiming "I finde it, I minde it, I sweare that I will, || Though shame, or defame, do happen no skill"[36] – "Conscience and Iustice come out of him" (428 s.d.). They are two allegories, but, before speaking, they are perceived by Apius as inner forces, voices coming from inside himself:

> But out, I am wounded; how am I devided?
> Two states of my life from me are now glided:
> For Conscience he pricketh me contempned,
> And Iustice saith Iudgement wold have me condemned (ll. 429–32)

The Vice accurately interprets the inner nature of Conscience and Iustice and tries to divert Apius' attention by saying: "Why, these are but thoughts, man!" (l. 437). In other words, the allegorical characters are on stage, but they are the simple outward projection of man's soul.

In the Norwich B text, then, the allegorical characters are still useful according to the old structure of religious drama to visualize moods and feelings, but at the same time they are superseded by the new humanist (and Reformist) concept concerning the individual. They are not far-fetched intrusions into a mystery play; on the contrary, they are an integral and coherent part of the revised text, especially of a text revised in 1565.[37]

---

36 All quotations from *Apius and Virginia* are drawn from the text published in *Tudor Interludes*, ed. Peter Happé (Harmondsworth: Penguin, 1972), 271–317.

37 But cf. Woolf, *English Mystery Plays*, 312, for a negative evaluation of the presence of the allegories: "The figures of *Dolor* and *Myserye* who lead man from the Garden of Eden are an ill-placed embellishment." On the other hand Dutka, "The Lost Dramatic Cycle," 10, clearly defends the playwright's choice: "in the Norwich [B] play, the allegory is not superfluous."

4 The Norwich Play(s) and Their Analogues

The events of the creation of Adam and Eve, of the temptation by the devil and the eating of the forbidden fruit from the tree of knowledge, with the consequent exile from Eden, are not equally distributed in all the extant cycles. York divides this material into many episodes: Play 3 contains God's creation of Adam and Eve, Play 4 the prohibition to eat the fruits of "The tree of good and yll" (*York*, 4.56),[38] Play 5 the temptation and the fall, Play 6 the lamentations of Adam and Eve because of their sin, and a first marital strife with Adam accusing Eve of being the cause of their sorrow, since "Allas, what womans witte was light!" (*York*, 6.133).[39] The total length of the four episodes is 533 lines. In Chester, approximately the same narrative material is condensed in Play 2 (704 lines), which also includes the story of Cain and Abel (from line 425, when music signals the passage from Eden to the Earth). The N-Town corresponding play (Play 2) also covers God's creation of the world and arrives at Adam and Eve's expulsion from Paradise (it has 334 lines). It is interesting to notice that in this play Eve asks Adam to kill her because of her inability to resist temptation (*N-Town*, 2.304–08), but Adam comforts his wife and disclaims any idea of punishing her:

> For yf I shulde sle my wyff,
> I sclow myself withowtyn knyff
> In helle logge to lede my lyff
> With woo in wepyng dale. (*N-Town*, 2.318–21)[40]

The episode of the Fall of Man is not contained in the Towneley manuscript: Play 1 displays the whole process of creation, including man's, but leaves out the very material referring to the temptation and the fall. However, the last two lines of this play – "And now ar thay in paradise; || bot thens thay shall, if we be

---

[38] The York plays are cited from *The York Plays: A Critical Edition of the York Corpus Christi Play as Recorded in British Library Additional MS 35290*, 2 vols., ed. Richard Beadle, EETS s.s. 23–24 (Oxford: Oxford University Press, 2009–13).

[39] See Play 6, ll. 129–54. By Adam's quoted speech one is easily reminded of Hamlet's exclamation – "Frailty, thy name is woman" (I.i.146) – about his mother's marriage with Claudius, soon after old Hamlet's death.

[40] The N-Town cycle is cited from *The N-Town Plays*, ed. Douglas Sugano (Kalamazoo, MI: Medieval Institute Publications, 2007). Play 1 includes the creation of the angels and Lucifer's disobedience and consequent fall into hell.

wise" (*Towneley*, 1.266–67) – adumbrate man's destiny in Eden and his expulsion from Paradise, but no dedicated play survives.[41]

From the previous short description, the disparity between other English mystery plays and the Norwich A text is strikingly relevant, if only because of text A's shortness, given that it has only ninety lines, while presenting all the narrative from the creation of man to the expulsion from Paradise. The text is incomplete: it actually lacks the speeches after God's summons of Adam as well as the couple's discovery of their nakedness, God's possible curse of the serpent and his order to the angel to exile Adam and Eve. The text resumes after the gap and God's summons with music and a ten-line speech by Adam. The last two lines are preceded by quite an explicit stage direction; the stage action and the above-mentioned accompanying song are nevertheless suggested by Adam's words themselves:

> Therfor owr handes we may wrynge with most dullfull song.
> *And so they xall syng, walkyng together about the place, wryngyng ther handes.*
> Wythe dolorous sorowe, we maye wayle and wepe
> Both nyght and daye in sory sythys full depe. (ll. 88–90)

Both gesture and words are reminiscent of the final lines of York Play 5, in which the angel's words presuppose a mournful song being started by Adam and Eve, and Adam's own speech must needs be accompanied by a traditional gesture of despair (the same as shown by Eve in Fra Angelico's *Annunciation* in the Prado Museum):

> Adam and Eue, do you to goo,
> For here may yoe make no dwellyng;
> Goo yhe forthe faste to fare,
> *Of sorowe may yhe synge.*
>   Adam
> Allas, *for sorowe and care*
> Oure handis may we wryng. (*York*, 5.171–76; my emphasis)

The feelings of intense suffering and discomfort represented in the phrases "dullful song," "sory sythys," and especially "dolorous sorowe" in the Norwich A text (ll. 88, 89, and 90, respectively) are particularly relevant since the author of

---

41 The Towneley cycle is quoted from *The Towneley Plays*, 2 vols., ed. Martin Stevens and A.C. Cawley, EETS s.s. 13 (Oxford: Oxford University Press, 1994).

text B seems to build the characters of Dolor and Misery on these very words of text A in order to give life to the allegorical figures of his own play. The word "sorrow" often occurs in the other Fall of Man episodes, being reminiscent of God's words to Eve: "tuos in dolore paries filios" (*Vulgata*, Genesis 3:16), which in the *Great Bible* was translated exactly: "In sorowe shalt thou brynge || furth chyldren," also reinforced by God's words to Adam: "In soro= || we shalt thou eate of it [the earth] all the dayes of thy lyfe."[42]

4.1 The Names

The A text still has Adam call Eve (actually Eva in the speech headings) "virago" according to the Vulgate version (Genesis 2:23), thus mirroring Chester Play 2, the only other mystery play where such a word occurs (l. 20: "And *virago* I [Adam] call hyr in thy presens;" Chester, 2.149–50: "Therfore shee shalbe called, iwisse, || 'viragoo', nothinge amisse"). In York Play 3 God himself names the two humans: "Adam and Eue yoour names sall be" (*York*, 3.44), and afterwards along the dialogue, all characters call the woman by this name: from God (4.1; 5.144 and 160), to Satan at the very beginning of the temptation process (5.25), to Adam (5.108, 118, 121, 142), to the Angel (5.171). In the N-Town episode, God gives Adam the power to name all earthly creatures, including the newly-created woman: "Thu geve hem name be thiself alon, || Erbys and gresse both beetys and brake. || Thi wyff thu geve name also" (*N-Town*, 2.24–26); however, no name is mentioned for Adam's mate. Actually, she is only called either "woman" or "wiff" in the whole episode. In the Norwich A text, Eve's personal name never occurs, but it is in the speech headings.

What has been observed so far about the presence of personal names in the Fall of Man episodes is not to be considered superfluous in the light of how the B text deals with the problem. It is true that "virago" is omitted and substituted by "woman" when Adam announces to his mate that "Thow shalte be called Woman, bycaus thow art of me" (l. 26). But in so doing, the author simply draws on the Protestant *Great Bible* (Genesis ii. C: "And man sayde: … She shalbe called woman, because she was taken out of man"), which, in its turn, translates appropriately the Catholic Vulgate sentence "dixitque Adam … haec vocabitur virago quoniam de viro sumpta est."[43] Etymologically, therefore,

---

42   *The Byble in Englishe*, "The fyrst booke of Moses / called in the || hebrue Bereschith: and in the latyn: || Genesis, The .iij. Chapter," fol. ij[r] (<https://archive.org/stream/GreatBible15 40/1540GreatBible#page/no/mode/1up> [accessed 30/09/2014]).

43   And Adam said … this will be called *virago* for she was taken out of *vir*. White, "*The Grocers' Play*," 85, on the other hand, interprets the omission of *virago* as a sign of the B text author's adherence to Calvin.

there is no anti-feminist meaning in the word *virago* (it deriving from *vir*, the Latin word for 'man'), whereas in "woman" there is the echo of a legendary and misogynic merging of 'woe' and 'man'.[44] The B text, furthermore, leaves the personal names Adam and Eve out of the speech headings, which simply name the protagonists "Man" and "Woman," even though somewhat inconsistently. In fact, in the strictly biblical episode "Adam" speaks only once (ll. 72–73), whereas, after the apparition of the two allegories and of the Holy Ghost, all speeches of the male protagonist are attributed to "Adam." The name "Eve," on the other hand, never appears, not even in the headings. These omissions do not seem to have any explanation, unless we surmise that, by using two common names, the playwright intended to generalize even more the concept of Adam and Eve's being the ancestors of all mankind, and to adhere strictly to the letter of Genesis. This hypothesis could be consistent with what was said about the second Prologue, i.e. the author seems particularly attentive to his *readers*, while the absence of the name "Eve" would be absolutely irrelevant to an audience, to whom the identity of the main characters of the play in performance is definitely clear.

4.2   The Protagonists

Among the characters of the Fall of Man episodes the human protagonists and the Serpent seem to deserve deeper analysis, because how they behave in the various cycles can shed light on the permanence of old stylistic and religious features in the Norwich B text on the one hand, and on variations due not only to the Reformation but also to dramaturgical choices on the other. The other characters in the episode, apart from Dolor, Misery and the Holy Ghost (who are present only in the Norwich B text), are common to all the extant cycles and mainly respect a traditional model in the dramatic development of Genesis.

It is especially the relationship between Adam and Eve that is at stake, given the affectionate terms the two exchange in the B text highlighted by recent criticism. Walker and Betteridge underline that "It [text B] emphasizes the companionate, sexual nature of the first couple's marriage in Paradise (where the earlier pageant had glossed over the nature of their relationship, seemingly anxious to promote the idea of celibacy as the highest human virtue)."[45] What the two critics say is acceptable for the B text; nevertheless it seems too harsh for the part concerning text A. Actually, as seen in the Synopsis section above, in the A text Adam addresses Eve with the endearing vocative "O lovely spowse"

---

44   The *Oxford English Dictionary* states the etymology of "woman" from "wife n. + man n.".
45   See Betteridge and Walker, "Introduction," 2.

(l. 48) and sounds protective, if ironical since the devil will soon arrive, when assuring Eve that "Nothyng may hurt us nor do us wronge" (l. 52). On her side, Eve also cares for her man: she wants "to please my spowse" (l. 70), and offers him the apple "for thy pleasure" (l. 77). In the A text there does not seem to be anything hinting at the supremacy of celibacy over married life and, at least in the surviving fragment, no word of reproach is pronounced by Adam for Eve's falling to temptation first. On the contrary, such a nuance can be heard in Adam's words in the B text, when he, answering God's question after the fall "Who so hath cawsyd the?" (l. 74), reveals that the fault is Eve's: "This woman, Lord and God, which thou hast gyven to me" (l. 75). But this answer, beyond coming directly from Genesis 3, has a long dramatic tradition, since it is present (and more widely developed) in the N-Town cycle:

> The woman that thu toke me tylle –
> Sche brougth me therto.
> It was her counsell and her reed:
> Sche bad me do the same deed. (*N-Town*, 2.205–08)

It also appears in the Chester cycle, where Adam directly curses Eve ("Woman, cursed mote thou bee," *Chester*, 2.259) even before God questions him. In the York cycle Adam's accusation occurs as well ("Lorde, Eue garte me do wronge || And to that bryg me brought," *York*, 5.142–43), and is also reinforced in Play 6, when the couple is presented during the first post-lapsarian matrimonial conflict about who was responsible for what, about who should have obeyed whom and, finally, about who is the head of the family (*York*, 6.133–53), so much so that a very misogynic Adam exclaims: "Nowe God late never man aftir me || Triste woman tale" (6.149–50), and pronounces his last rebuke: "Thy counsaille has casten me in care" (6.153).

Certainly the Norwich B text does not develop the issue to its extreme point as York does. However, the Protestant revision of the Catholic A text is not totally exempt from highlighting Eve's responsibility in the fall.[46]

---

46   In the Bible itself Adam's blaming Eve for offering him the forbidden fruit sounds a feeble excuse, since the biblical text tells us that the man accepts the fruit without even asking the woman why she is disobeying God's order. Only to God's question, "hast thou not ea= || ten of the same tre, concernynge the which I || commaunded the, that thou shuldest not eate || of it?", does Adam answer: "The woman, whom || thou gauest to be wyth me, she gave me of || the tree and I dyd eat" (*The Byble in Englishe,* Genesis iii: B, fol. ij^r). In a way, Eve is the one subject to temptation: Adam simply and ambiguously follows suit, so to say, without contradicting her decision.

As hinted above, the A-text devil speaks straight to Eve, thus avoiding that contact with the audience which derives from the use of asides or monologues, while the B-Text devil is dramaturgically more efficacious because he involves the spectators in his guile:

> Nowe, Nowe, of my purpos I dowght nott to atteyne:
>   I can yt nott abyde in theis joyes they shulde be.
> Naye, I wyll attempt them to syn unto theyr payne;
>   By subtyllty to catch them the waye I do well se;
>   Unto this, angell of lyght I shew mysylfe to be;
> With hyr for to dyscemble, I fear yt nott at all,
> Butt that unto my haight some waye I shall hyr call. (ll. 36–42)

In the N-Town Fall of Man play, too, the Serpens addresses Eve without explaining his plans, but the York parallel text (Play 5) starts with a 24-line monologue by Satan, who reveals his envy of God's new creatures and his agenda against them:

> The kynde of man he thoght to take
> And theratt hadde I grete envye,
> But he has made to hym a make,
> And harde to her I wol me hye
> That redy way,
> That purpose proue to putte it by,
> And fande to pike fro hym that pray.
> My trauayle were wele sette
> Myght Y hym so betraye,
> His likyng for to lette,
> And sone I schalle assaye.
> In a worme liknes wille Y wende,
> And founde to feyne a lowde lesynge. (*York*, 5.12–24)

Satan just calls Eve by repeating her name twice, i.e. without using any enticing adjectives, and introduces himself as "a frende" (*York*, 5.25). His persuasive words are first resisted by Eve, to whose question "Why, what-kynne thyng art thou || That telles this tale to me?" (ll. 52–53) he answers: "A worme" (l. 54). And later, when Eve is on the point of giving in and questions him "Is this soth that thou sais?" (l. 74), the playwright makes Satan answer with a speech which borders on comic effects, according to the late medieval concept of the 'comedy of evil:'[47]

> Yhe, why trowes thou noyot me?
> I wolde be no-kynnes wayes
> Telle noyot but trouthe to the. (*York*, 5.75–77)

Eve's following surrender is the immediate sign of Satan's success: "Than wille I to thy techyng traste" (l. 78).

In Chester we can find the most fully developed figure of the tempter: the "Serpens" is given a 48-line monologue, beginning his speech after a very effective stage direction: "*Then the serpente shall come up out of a hole, and the dyvell walkinge shall say*" (*Chester*, 2.160 s.d.).[48] The staging of this moment should require, therefore, an actor with a particular costume, with a snake's tail (for a "serpente"), but allowing free walking movements.[49] At the same time, considering the famous stage direction after line 208 ("*Supremus volucris penna; serpens, pede forma; forma puella*"),[50] the actor should also wear a feminine mask, so as to look more 'friendly' to Eve. As for this aspect, the central boss in the vault of the east nave in Norwich Cathedral shows a maid-faced serpent entwined to the tree of knowledge while offering golden apples to Adam and Eve.[51]

In his monologue he tells the story of his own fall and reveals his envy of this "caytiffe made of claye" (*Chester*, 2.177), so that he wants to tempt him and his wife out of Eden, by approaching Eve and 'teaching' her "a playe" (l. 179). Then the audience is made participant of the first theatrical disguise ever performed on the English stage; the devil announces:

---

47 For this concept, see Charlotte Spivack, *The Comedy of Evil on Shakespeare's Stage* (Rutherford, NJ: Fairleigh Dickinson University Press, 1978).

48 Very probably the wagon for this episode, like others in the cycle, was provided with a trap.

49 Only after God's curse against the devil ("Edder, ... || Upon thou brest shalt goo," l. 297 and 301) will the actor playing Satan possibly crawl on his 'breast', according to the stage direction in manuscript H of the plays: "*Tunc recedet serpens, vocem serpentinam faciens*" (*Chester Mystery Cycle*, eds. Lumiansky and Mills, 1:26 note; translation from Mills, *Chester Mystery Cycle*, 36: Then the serpent shall withdraw, making a noise like a snake). The Norwich Grocers' documents for 1565 list "a cote with hosen & tayle for ye cerpente" (Galloway, *REED: Norwich 1540–1642*, 53).

50 Upper part of the body with feather of a bird; serpent, by shape in the foot; in figure, a girl (translation from Mills, *Chester Mystery Cycle*, 33].

51 Adam's and Eve's creation is represented in two lateral bosses.

> A maner of an edder is in this place
> that wynges like a bryde shee hase –
> feete as an edder, a maydens face –
> hir kynde I will take. (*Chester*, 2.193–96)

After disguising, the devil addresses Eve simply by calling her "Woman," very probably – given his "maydens face" – in a "voyce so small," that is, in a falsetto, according to how the Norwich Serpent describes the pitch of his speech to Eve (l. 43).[52]

From how the devil is presented in York and Chester, it is evident that the Norwich B text comes in the wake of this (very Catholic) tradition which presents the tempter as a forerunner of later Vices or Vice-like figures, i.e. characters that allure the protagonist towards evil, but that are quite open and sincere with the audience. Spectators, for their part, are at once 'tempted' by the Vice's jokes, rhetoric and body language, and made aware of the evil this character represents.[53] The A text, on the other hand, avoids this approach to the character, leaving the spectators out of the dramatic action, therefore not involving them in the temptation process.

Another feature of the B text's devil is worth mentioning, i.e. his answer to God's question why he has beguiled "my creatures and servantes" (l. 80). Satan briefly and curtly replies: "My kind is so, thou knowest and that in every case – || Clene out of this place theis persons to exile" (ll. 81–82). While Diabolus in N-Town Play 2 (the only parallel text which gives Satan an answering speech) explains his reasons in eight lines (*N-Town*, 2.235–42) stating that he has acted out of "gret envy || Of wreth and wyckyd hate" against humans (2.237–38), the Serpent in text B shows not only an efficacious power of synthesis (his goal is achieved, and that is enough), but also, what seems more striking, he relies on God's knowledge of his 'kind', thus refusing to say more. The B Text Serpent sounds as if he were anticipating Iago ("that demi-devil", according to Othello's now knowledgeable definition), who, after the Moor's question to Cassio "Will

---

[52] See White, "*The Grocers' Play*," 85.

[53] Besides the volume by Charlotte Spivack, see L.W. Cushman, *The Devil and the Vice in the English Dramatic Literature Before Shakespeare* (Halle an der Saale: Niemeyer, 1900; rpt. London: Frank Cass, 1970); Bernard Spivack, *Shakespeare and the Allegory of Evil: The History of a Metaphor in Relation to his Major Villains* (New York: Columbia University Press, 1958); Robert Jones, "Dangerous Sport: the Audience's Engagement with Vice in the Moral Interludes," *Renaissance Drama* N.S. 6 (1973): 45–64; J.A.B. Somerset, "'Fair is foul and foul is fair:' Vice-comedy's Development and Theatrical Effects," in *Elizabethan Theatre V*, ed. G.R. Hibbard (London: Macmillan, 1975), 54–75, and Peter Happé, "Deceptions: 'The Vice' of the Interludes and Iago," *Theta VIII-Théâtre Tudor* (2009): 105–24.

you, I pray, demand that demi-devil || Why he hath thus ensnared my soul and body?", answers shortly with: "Demand me nothing: what you know, you know" (*Othello*, V.ii.302–04). The villain-Vice Iago seems to echo the B text devil's words.

A last trait of the two Norwich devils concerns the way they address Eve. In the A text Serpens calls her "O gemme of felicyté and femynyne love" (l. 55), and in B: "Oh lady of felicité" (l. 43), two flattering expressions absolutely absent from the other Fall of Man analogues.[54] Evidently the B text author accepted the seductive power of the A text wording, even though he excised the reference to feminine love (which might be seen as contradictory in a play that modern critics have interpreted as emphasizing "the companionate, sexual nature of the first couple's marriage in Paradise."[55]) Rather, the B text dramatist did not want to leave the idea of 'love' to the devil, and preferred to move it to the two human protagonists who, as mentioned above, call each other "my dere lover" (Eve to Adam; l. 35) and "My love" (Adam to Eve; l. 59).

5. Conclusion

At the end of this analysis one might say that, apart from the prologues and the Holy Ghost's speech, the narrative and much of the wording of the two Norwich plays remain very similar, and in line with the Catholic tradition of the major mystery play cycles. Nevertheless, the care with which the B text underlines the adherence of the play to the Bible and, especially, the Reformist principles introduced by the Holy Ghost show how towns and cities tried to adapt old 'containers' to new 'content' (and vice versa), in order to preserve local traditions which were also profitable for the citizens.[56] But, as the letters of the Puritan preacher Christopher Goodman testify, concerning the changes introduced into the Chester plays in order to make the latter more adherent to Reformist theology, quoting the Scripture was not sufficient for the survival of the mystery plays: more radical transformations would have been necessary to eliminate the 'absurdities' of such plays. But, in the end, was it not better to

---

54 On Eve as a figure of Mary, see Dutka, "The Lost Dramatic Cycle," 9.
55 See Betteridge and Walker, "Introduction," 2.
56 The principal fair in Norwich (at Tombland) took place at Whitsun, and one can imagine how the performances could contribute to the concourse of people to the fair itself (Dutka, "The Lost Dramatic Cycle," 4).

abolish them as "unfitt for this time & Christian commonwealths"?[57] In Chester, performances stopped in 1575, in Norwich the plays are not mentioned any longer in the town documents after 1565. The Puritan attacks against religious plays will soon target the public theatres of Elizabethan London.

Bibliography

Baldwin, Elizabeth, Lawrence M. Clopper, and David Mills, eds. *Records of Early English Drama: Cheshire Including Chester*, 2 vols. London and Toronto: British Library and University of Toronto Press, 2007.

Beadle, Richard, ed. *The York Plays: A Critical Edition of the York Corpus Christi Play as Recorded in British Library Additional MS 35290*, 2 vols. EETS s.s. 23–24. Oxford: Oxford University Press, 2009–13.

Betteridge, Thomas, and Greg Walker, eds. *The Oxford Handbook of Tudor Drama*. Oxford: Oxford University Press, 2012.

Bible in Englyshe, The. London: Edward Whytchurch, 1539 (rpt. S.l.: Edward Whytchurche, 1540).

Butterworth, Philip. *Theatre of Fire: Special Effects in Early English and Scottish Theatre*. London: Society for Theatre Research, 1998.

———. *Staging Conventions in Medieval English Theatre*. Cambridge: Cambridge University Press, 2014.

Campbell, Gordon, and N.M. Davis. "*Paradise Lost* and the Norwich Grocers' Play." *Milton Quarterly* 14:4 (1980): 113–16.

Cushman, L.W. *The Devil and the Vice in the English Dramatic Literature Before Shakespeare*. Halle an der Saale: Niemeyer, 1900; rpt. London: Frank Cass, 1970.

Davis, Norman, ed. *Non-Cycle Plays and Fragments*. EETS s.s. 1. Oxford: Oxford University Press, 1970.

Dutka, JoAnna. "Mystery Plays at Norwich: Their Formation and Development." *Leeds Studies in English* N.S. 10 (1978): 107–20.

———. "The Lost Dramatic Cycle of Norwich and the Grocers' Play of the Fall of Man." *The Review of English Studies* N. S. 35:137 (Feb. 1984): 1–13.

---

57   Christopher Goodman's correspondence concerning his accusation against the performance of "the old Popish plays of Chester" (because "albeit divers have gone about the correction of the same at sundry times & mended divers things, yet hath it not been done by such as are by authority allowed, nor the same their corrections viewed & approved according to order, nor yet so played for the most part as they have been corrected") is reproduced in *Records of Early English Drama: Cheshire Including Chester*, 2 vols., ed. Elizabeth Baldwin, Lawrence M. Clopper, and David Mills (London and Toronto: British Library and University of Toronto Press, 2007), 1: 145–46.

---. "The Fall of Man: The Norwich Grocers' Play." *Records of Early English Drama* 9:1 (1984): 1–11.

Fitch, Robert, ed. *Norwich Pageants: The Grocers' Play*. Norwich: Charles Muskett, 1856.

Fletcher, Alan J. "The N-Town Plays." In *The Cambridge Companion to Medieval English Theatre*, edited by Richard Beadle and Alan J. Fletcher, 183–210. Cambridge: Cambridge University Press, 2008.

Galloway, David, ed. *Records of Early English Drama: Norwich 1540–1642*. Toronto: University of Toronto Press, 1984.

Happé, Peter. "Deceptions: 'The Vice' of the Interludes and Iago." *Theta VIII-Théâtre Tudor* (2009): 105–24.

---, ed. *Tudor Interludes*. Harmondsworth: Penguin, 1972.

Harty, Kevin J. "The Norwich Grocers' Play and Its Three Cyclic Counterparts: Four English Mystery Plays on the Fall of Man." *Studia Philologica* 53 (1981): 77–89.

Hudson, William, and John C. Tingey, eds. *The Records of the City of Norwich*, 2 vols. London: Jarrold and Sons, 1910.

Jones, Robert. "Dangerous Sport: the Audience's Engagement with Vice in the Moral Interludes." *Renaissance Drama* N.S. 6 (1973): 45–64.

King, Pamela M. "Minority Plays: Two Interludes for Edward VI." *Medieval English Theatre* 15 (1993): 87–102.

---. "Playing Pentecost in York and Chester: Transformations and Texts." *Medieval English Theatre* 29 (2007): 60–74.

Lumiansky, R.M., and David Mills, eds. *The Chester Mystery Cycle*, 2 vols. EETS s.s. 3 and 9. Oxford: Oxford University Press, 1974–86.

Manly, John Matthews, ed. *Specimens of the Pre-Shaksperean Drama*. Boston: Ginn, 1897.

Mills, David, ed. *The Chester Mystery Cycle: A New Edition with Modernized Spelling*. East Lansing: Colleagues Press, 1992.

Nelson, Alan H. *The Medieval English Stage: Corpus Christi Pageants and Plays*. Chicago: University of Chicago Press, 1974.

Somerset, J.A.B. "'Fair is foul and foul is fair': Vice-comedy's Development and Theatrical Effects." In *Elizabethan Theatre V*, edited by G.R. Hibbard, 54–75. London: Macmillan, 1975.

Spivack, Bernard. *Shakespeare and the Allegory of Evil: The History of a Metaphor in Relation to his Major Villains*. New York: Columbia University Press, 1958.

Spivack, Charlotte. *The Comedy of Evil on Shakespeare's Stage*. Rutherford, NJ: Fairleigh Dickinson University Press, 1978.

Stevens, Martin, and A.C. Cawley, eds. *The Towneley Plays*, 2 vols. EETS s.s. 13–14. Oxford: Oxford University Press, 1994.

Sugano, Douglas, ed. *The N-Town Plays*. Kalamazoo, MI: Medieval Institute Publications, 2007.

Waterhouse, Osborn, ed. *The Non-Cycle Mystery Plays*. EETS e.s. 104. London: Kegan Paul, Trench Trübner & Co., 1909.

White, Paul Whitfield. *Drama and Religion in English Provincial Society, 1485–1660*. Cambridge: Cambridge University Press, 2008.

———. "Interludes, Economics, and the Elizabethan Stage." In *The Oxford Handbook of Tudor Literature*, edited by Mike Pincombe and Cathy Shrank, 555–70. Oxford: Oxford University Press, 2009.

Woolf, Rosemary. *The English Mystery Plays*. Berkeley: University of California Press, 1972.

CHAPTER 6

Preaching Penance on the Stage in Late Medieval England: The Case of John the Baptist

Charlotte Steenbrugge

Abstract

This essay situates Middle English biblical plays in the context of contemporary ecclesiastical legislation and religious controversy, using the pageants on the Baptism of Christ from the York Corpus Christi Play, the N-Town manuscript, and the Towneley manuscript as a case study and the same episode from various French *mystères* for comparative purposes. The French dramatists included preaching on penance as standard practice for this episode, and were prone to identify these sermons as such; English dramatists, on the other hand, appear to have tried to avoid staging a sermon or mentioning penance. In particular, I argue that the unwillingness by the playwrights of the York and Towneley plays to stage a sermon is due to an atmosphere of anxiety and self-censorship following Arundel's *Constitutions* of 1409, which restricted preaching to specially licensed members of the clergy. The N-Town play does feature a preaching protagonist, unlike the pageants from York and Towneley. However, the truly remarkable insistence on confession in the N-Town pageant, a point of contention between the orthodox authorities and Lollards, serves to make explicit the orthodox affiliation of the play. These references thereby also make the on-stage sermon less controversial for Church authorities. Both the lack of sermons in York and Towneley, and the insistence on confession in N-Town indicate the extent to which medieval English biblical plays were affected by current controversies about who had the right to preach to the laity.

Keywords

John the Baptist – N-Town – Towneley – York – Lollards – penance

1   Introduction

Although John the Baptist was a popular saint in late medieval England, there is reason to assume that plays dealing with this character's preaching of penance and his baptism of Jesus were relatively controversial. Despite the solid biblical background for these episodes (especially Matthew 3:1–12, Mark 1:3–8, Luke 3:2–18), this should not be surprising. The Lollards challenged various sacraments, including at times baptism; the denial of the need of infant baptism by a priest is attested from the late fourteenth century onwards in Lollard trials.[1] A bigger point of contention was the sacrament of penance, Lollards generally being of the opinion that only contrition was necessary for the remission of sins, rather than confession to a priest and priestly absolution: "Þerfore it is certeyn, clerer þanne liȝt, þat synnes ben forȝeuen be contricioun of hert. Hec ibi. Þerfore very contricioun is þe essencial parte of penance, and confecioun of mouþe is þe accidental parte. But naþeles confessioun of hert done to þe hiȝe prest Crist is as nedeful as contricioun."[2] Moreover, in order to contain the Lollard threat, preaching was increasingly controlled and circumscribed, particularly in terms of personnel. The connection between Lollards and vernacular preaching was made early on in the history of the movement, with Leicester Lollards in 1389 maintaining that "any layman can preach and teach the gospel anywhere."[3] The most well-known measures which aimed to restrict preaching are Arundel's *Constitutions* of 1409, but already in 1400 action was taken throughout England to limit preaching to those with a licence from their diocesan and parochial chaplains in their own churches.[4] It is hard to know how strictly these rules were enforced, but people were certainly wary of unauthorized preaching. For instance, in 1417 some chaplains were charged with preaching in contravention of Arundel's *Constitutions* and Margery Kempe had to defend herself to the archbishop of York against accusations of preaching.[5] In fact some Lollards complained that nowadays even as holy a man as John the Baptist would be charged as a Lollard for preaching: "and if ony preche þe trouþe, þe multitude schal aȝenseie him ... þouȝ he were as hooli as euere was seint Ion Baptist, he schulde not faile to be sclaundrid for a

---

1 Anne Hudson, *The Premature Reformation: Wycliffite Texts and Lollard History* (Oxford: Clarendon Press, 1988), 292.
2 Hudson, *Premature Reformation*, 295–99, and "Sixteen Points on which the Bishops accuse Lollards," in *Selections of English Wycliffite Writings*, ed. Anne Hudson (Cambridge: Cambridge University Press, 1978), 21.
3 Margaret Aston, "Lollardy and Sedition, 1381–1431," *Past and Present* 17 (1960): 12.
4 Ibid., 33.
5 John A.F. Thomson, *The Later Lollards, 1414–1520* (London: Oxford University Press, 1965), 117, and *The Book of Margery Kempe*, ed. Lynn Staley (Kalamazoo, MI: Medieval Institute, 1996), Book I, Chapter 52.

cursid Lollard & pursued as an heretik."⁶ Any play dealing with this saint's preaching of penance and baptism of Jesus therefore touched upon controversial material and there is sufficient evidence from the surviving John the Baptist plays from York, N-Town, and Towneley (there is no such play from Chester) to indicate that they were affected by these controversies, most importantly in their depiction of John the Baptist as a preacher.

2   John the Baptist in the French *Mystères*

Before analysing the English plays' presentation of John the Baptist's sermon on penance, I would like to take a brief look at some French *mystères*, which are roughly comparable in date to the composition and/or performance history of the surviving English pageants. This is because France was untroubled by Lollardy and its concomitant legislation, which would argue for greater freedom in presenting a vernacular sermon on penance on the stage.⁷ And this is borne out by the texts: all the French *mystères* I have looked at (*Passion de Semur* [Burgundy, probably fourteenth century], *Passion d'Arras* [Arras, probably early fifteenth century], Gréban's *Mystère de la Passion* [Paris, c. 1450], *Passion d'Auvergne* [Montferrand/Clermont-Ferrand, 1477], and Michel's *Mystère de la Passion* [Angers, 1486]) have a John the Baptist episode, and in all of these he preaches on penance to a greater or lesser degree.⁸ For example, the theme of John's first sermon on the second day of Gréban's play is *penitenciam agite* (do penance) and it counsels, amongst other things,

---

6   *The Lanterne of Liȝt, edited from MS. Harl. 2324*, ed. Lilian M. Swinburn (London: Kegan Paul, Trench, Trübner & co., 1917; rpt. New York: Kraus Reprint, 1971), EETS O.S. 151, 101.

7   There were issues with heterodoxy in France as well but the plays do not stem from a place or time much affected by this issue. Catharism had been all but eradicated by the Albigensian Crusade of the early thirteenth century and the last Cathar was burned in 1326; the Waldensians were more long-lived but had retreated mainly to isolated Alpine valleys of south-eastern France by the fourteenth century. See Chas S. Clifton, *Encyclopedia of Heresies and Heretics* (Santa Barbara: ABC-CLIO, 1992), 30 and 133, and Gordon Leff, *Heresy in the later Middle Ages: the relation of heterodoxy to dissent, c. 1250-c. 1450*, 2 vols. (Manchester: Manchester University Press, 1967), 2: 450 and 482.

8   For the French playwrights' propensity to include sermons in their *mystères*, see also Charles Mazouer, "Sermons in the *Passions* of Mercadé, Gréban and Jehan Michel," in *Les Mystères: Studies in Genre, Text and Theatricality*, ed. Peter Happé and Wim Hüsken, Ludus: Medieval and Early Renaissance Theatre and Drama (Amsterdam: Rodopi, 2012), 247–69.

> ung chascun mette diligence
> de faire en soy les dignes fruiz
> de penitance, car je truis
> et vous adnonce pour certain
> que la regne Dieu est prochain. (ll. 10017–21)[9]

[Let each be diligent to bring forth the noble fruit of penitence because I affirm and tell you for certain, that the reign of God is nigh.]

It also urges

> Et, pout tant, selon l'Escripture,
> vous ay dit et admonnesté:
> *penitenciam agite.*
> Peuple de povre remembrance,
> fais penitence, penitence,
> fais penitence austere et dure
> tant que ta povre vie dure. (ll. 10115–22)

[And, therefore, according to Scripture, I have said and admonished you: *penitentiam agite* (do penance). People of poor remembrance, do penance, penance, do austere and harsh penance, while your poor life lasts!]

The French playwrights are not just willing to insert sermons on penance, they are keen to identify their sermons as such. The speech just cited is announced in the prologue with "Jehan, venez vous advancer || de vostre sermon commancer" (John, come forth and begin your sermon; ll. 10008–09). Perhaps most exciting in this regard are those sermons which have, or claim to have, an overt modern or university sermon structure. In the *Passion d'Arras*, John the Baptist asserts that he is going to preach on the theme *Penitentiam agite, appropinquabit enim regnum celorum* (Do penance, for the kingdom of heaven is at hand; l. 6424):

> Je vous feray cy ung sermon
> En bien briefve collation,
> Mon premier theume exposeray
> Auquel j'ay dit se l'en sievray.
> *Pentitentiam agite*, etc. (ll. 6434–39)[10]

---

9 *Le Mystère de la Passion d'Arnoul Gréban*, ed. Omer Jodogne (Brussels: Académie Royale de Belgique, 1965).

10 *Le Mystère de la Passion: texte du manuscript 697 de la bibliothèque d'Arras*, ed. Jules-Marie Richard (Arras: Société du Pas-de-Calais, 1891).

[I will make you here a sermon in a nice short collation. I shall expound my first theme, concerning which I have said: *Penitentiam agite* (do penance), etc.]

This is a little confused, as a sermon has only one theme, which is then divided: strictly speaking, one cannot have a "premier theume." Still, the intention to have a sermon, and one that would moreover have been familiar and recognisable for a medieval audience in terms of structure, is evident. The first speech by John the Baptist in Michel's play is on the theme *Parate viam Domini, rectas facite in solitudine semitas Dei nostri. Ysaie XL* (Prepare the way of the Lord, make straight the paths of our God in solitude; l. 888), which is given at the start of the sermon; the theme is identified as such and developed with two divisions:

> Et pour tant, au commencement
> de ceste predicacion,
> j'ay prins pour introduction
> le mot d'Isaÿe que je dy:
> *Parate viam Domini.*
> En ce theme icy, je puis prendre
> deux poins bien ayséz a comprendre
> a tout homme de bon vouloir.
> Le premier sera de sçavoir
> comme on doit preparer son cueur
> a la venue de saulveur;
> et cecy nous est denote
> par ce mot icy *Parate.*
> Le second sera par quell œuvre
> la grace de Dieu on requeuvre;
> et est ce noté quant je dy:
> *Rectas facite semitas Dei nostri.* (ll. 902–18)[11]

[At the beginning of this preaching, I have taken as introduction the words of Isaiah, which I pronounce: *Parate viam Domini* (prepare the way of the Lord). In this theme here, I can take two points, very easy to understand for all men of good will. The first will be to know how one must prepare one's heart for the coming of the Saviour. And this is demonstrated to us by the word *Parate* (prepare) here. The second point will be by which work one might receive the grace of God, and this is meant when I say: *Rectas facite semitas Dei nostri* (make straight the paths of our God).]

---

11   Jean Michel, *Le Mystère de la Passion (Angers 1486)*, ed. Omer Jodogne (Gembloux: Duculot, 1959).

These two divisions are then duly developed.

There are two points of interest concerning John the Baptist's sermons on the French stage in relation to the relative dearth of such sermons in the English biblical plays. Firstly, during the saint's sermons there are extra characters on stage who represent Jews from the New Testament in the French *mystères* but seemingly not in the English plays. This possibly has the effect that – as in the York opening speech to an extent (see below) – the spectators of the play are often not the expressed target of the sermon. In Michel's play, for example, the sermon's audience is living at the time of Christ: "Cestui saulveur est ja venu || et est ja sur terre regnant" (The Saviour is already come and is already reigning on earth, ll. 1072–73). But the contemporary spectators of the play are by no means excluded from the lessons of the sermons in the French *mystères*. After Michel's John repeatedly seems to address a New Testament audience, he includes various categories of sinners that map onto medieval society rather well and for which there is no biblical precedent. These fifteenth-century categories are closely interwoven with Luke's account of John's preaching: the bourgeois and merchants are told to give their second cloak and meat to the poor, for example. Evidently, the real audience of the sermons consisted, at least partly, of the spectators watching the play – but it is certainly possible that the actors representing John predominantly addressed other actors on the stage. This has implications for the status of these sermons: the claim to authority of a 'genuine' sermon addressed to a contemporary audience is very different to that of a 'historical' sermon to a historical audience. Secondly, clerics seem to have participated quite actively in French *mystères*, but there is no evidence for clerics acting in the English biblical plays which have survived (although that does not mean that they certainly did not). The delivery of sermons by clerical actors would presumably have made the sermons both more authoritative for the audience and less troublesome for local Church authorities, than if they were delivered by lay actors.

It is in any case clear that the French playwrights included preaching on penance for this episode as standard practice, and were prone to identify these sermons as such. References to a theme and divisions and the consistent use of a Latin opening tag demonstrate how strong was the urge to clothe these speeches in the dress of contemporary sermons. As we shall see, this is very dissimilar from the English situation, where only N-Town contains a preaching John the Baptist and even this John does not employ a thematic sermon.

3   The English John the Baptist Plays

The orthodoxy of the three English plays is evident from their desire to teach their audiences not simply about the baptism of Jesus, but also about the sacrament of baptism. In the York pageant, John explains that "baptyme is tane || To wasshe and clense man of synne" (21.77–78), while Jesus stresses the necessity of baptism for salvation (21.90–91).[12] In N-Town, Jesus announces that he has come to take baptism in order to "conferme þat sacrament þat nowe xal be" (22.64).[13] When the angels restrain the protagonist from going to meet Jesus in the Towneley play, John takes this to mean that infant baptism should happen in church: "By this I may well vnderstand || That childer shuld be broght to kyrk || For to be baptysyd in euery land" (19.85–87).[14] Towneley is the most insistent on the sacramental nature of the event, as Jesus is also anointed "With oyle and creme, in this intent || That men may wit, whereso thay go, || This is a worthy sacrament." (19.194–96). Baptism is also linked to the other sacraments in this play (19.197–200).[15] These pageants present self-conscious, orthodox support for the sacrament of baptism. We do not know how a late medieval audience would have reacted to these assertions, but their controversial nature is indicated by the fact that the whole stanza about the anointment and the seven sacraments in Towneley was cancelled at some point in the manuscript's career.[16] Although this was probably due to Reformist objections to the sacramental system, it is reasonable to assume that these kinds of comments would have been objectionable to many a Lollard as well, and were included to reinforce the audience's orthodoxy.

We might therefore expect that these plays would be equally forceful in their representation of penance as a sacrament, but this is not the case. In fact, only in the N-Town *Baptism* is penance mentioned at all. As there is a fair

---

12   *The York Plays: A Critical Edition of the York Corpus Christi Play as Recorded in British Library Additional MS 35290*, 2 vols., ed. Richard Beadle, EETS s.s. 23–24 (Oxford: Oxford University Press, 2009–13).

13   *The N-Town Play: Cotton MS Vespasian D. 8*, 2 vols., ed. Stephen Spector, EETS s.s. 11–12 (Oxford: Oxford University Press, 1991).

14   *The Towneley Plays*, 2 vols., ed. Martin Stevens and A.C. Cawley, EETS s.s. 13–14 (Oxford: Oxford University Press, 1994).

15   Garrett P.J. Epp, 'Re-editing Towneley', *The Yearbook of English Studies* 43 (2013): 103-04, has argued that the badly formed 'v' of the manuscript may originally have read 'i', which would date the play to the period after the Ten Articles of 1536 and before anointment at baptism disappeared from church ritual in 1552. This would locate the play in a Reformist rather than Catholic setting, but it would still emphatically assert its orthodoxy. The cancellation of the stanza would then relate to Catholic anxieties rather than Reformist objections to the sacramental system.

16   For a discussion on the authenticity of the cancellation see Alexandra F. Johnston, "The Towneley Manuscript: Huntington Library MS HM1" (forthcoming). Garrett P.J. Epp, "The Towneley Plays and the Hazards of Cycling," *Research Opportunities in Renaissance Drama* 32 (1993): 129, points out that "there is a notable lack of similar marginalia and cancelling in the case of other sacramental references in the manuscript."

amount of information about what John preached in the biblical narratives and agreement on the importance of penance for his preaching, this is extremely odd. The York saint does, he says, preach to the people to avoid sin, "Therfore be clene, bothe wiffe and man, || Þis is my reed" (21.39–40), but that is not quite the same thing as penance. Similarly, the Towneley closing speech warns its audience to forsake sin and beware of death, but there is not a single mention of penance.

The reasons for the omission of penance from the pageants in York and Towneley are not evident, and I can only tentatively suggest factors that may have contributed. One possible explanation is that the York and Towneley playwrights preferred to focus on one sacrament, namely baptism, in such a relatively short play. Towneley's mention of the other sacraments (though not by name) makes this perhaps unlikely. Another reason could be that penance was simply too controversial a topic to be dealt with. Admittedly, the sacrament of penance was more strongly contested than that of baptism, and the biblical John's preaching does not really support orthodox stress on private confession and priestly absolution. What exactly the saint meant by penance is not entirely clear, but it does seem to involve baptism and the performance of charitable deeds, neither of which were particularly important in the debates surrounding penance by the time these plays were written and conceived.[17] The fact that Love glosses over John's preaching of penance might support the notion this was truly a dangerous topic; "John baptizing sinfulmen, & miche peple þat was come þider to here his predicacion, for þei helden him at þat tyme as criste," and "For John prechede to sinful men to do penance & baptized hem" is all the information one receives in the eminently orthodox *Mirrour of the blessed lyf of Jesu Christi*.[18] On the other hand, the writer of the N-Town *Baptism* seems to have felt no qualms about dealing with this topic and to have been successful in emphasizing the orthodox aspects of penance. *Wisdom* (c. 1465–70), a so-called morality play, likewise deals with the sacrament of penance in some detail (ll. 957–96).

It is perhaps possible that the playwrights were concerned by the audience's reactions to a sermon on penance on their holiday. Given the didactic nature of the biblical plays this may at first sight seem improbable. These plays are fundamentally serious in intent and an important aim, if not the principal one, of

---

17 For the orthodox discussions see Thomas N. Tentler, *Sin and Confession of the Eve of the Reformation* (Princeton: Princeton University Press, 1977), *passim* but especially 24, 27, 30, 52, 68, 318–19; for the heterodox angle, see Hudson, *Premature Reformation*, 299.

18 Nicholas Love, *The Mirror of the Blessed Life of Jesus Christ: A Full Critical Edition*, based on Cambridge University Library Additional MSS 6578 and 6686 with Introduction, Notes and Glossary, ed. Michael G. Sargent (Exeter: University of Exeter Press, 2005), 66 and 68.

the writers and producers must have been to educate the spectators in moral and religious matters and to stir them to devotion. That much is clear from the content of the plays and from various other records; as mentioned above, these very pageants' insistence on baptism as a sacrament bears this out as well. But messages are not always received as they are intended. To give but two examples from medieval York: the play of Fergus gave rise to more noise and laughter than devotion ("magis risum & clamorem causabat quam deuocionem") which upset its producers.[19] William Melton preached in 1426 about the York Corpus Christi Play. He commended the Play affirming that is was good in itself and most laudable ("affirmando quod bonus erat in se & laudabilis valde"). However, he despaired of the audience because they are given greatly to feastings, drunkenness, clamours, gossiping, and other wantonness ("comessacionibus ebrietatibus clamoribus cantilenis & alijs insolencijs multum").[20] Presumably this refers to only (a small) part of the audience, although one can imagine a vocal one. Here are then two sources which demonstrate that the spectators of the York Corpus Christi Play did not always behave appropriately. Furthermore, we know that sermon audiences were not always well-behaved either, especially if the lesson of the sermon was too specifically targeted at them.[21] If even real preachers during proper sermons encountered all sorts of upsets and antagonism, it is very possible that at least some of the playgoers would object to being subjected to a sermon on the need to repent on their holiday. The fear of an unfavourable reception of such a sermon by the spectators cannot be entirely dismissed. On the other hand, there is a strong didactic element to both the York and Towneley pageants, and evidence from France shows that sermons exhorting penance could be incorporated successfully in plays. And the audience of the N-Town *Baptism* pageant (of which more below) are told to repent. Consequently, consideration for the audience cannot solely explain the lack of preaching on penance in the York and Towneley plays, although it might have been a contributing factor.

---

19 The complaint is noted in 1431–32. Interestingly, one of the Masons' objections to the play appears to have been that the subject of this pageant is not contained in the sacred scripture ("materia pagine illius in sacra non continetur scriptura"), which may indicate certain Lollard tendencies in York. See *Records of Early English Drama: York*, 2 vols., ed. Alexandra F. Johnston and Margaret Rogerson (Toronto: University of Toronto Press, 1979), 1: 47–48, 2: 732.

20 Johnston and Rogerson, REED: *York*, 1: 43, 2: 728.

21 For examples of problematic audience reactions to sermons, see John H. Arnold, *Belief and Unbelief in Medieval Europe* (London: Hodder, 2005), 48–49, and Jacques Berlioz and Marie Anne Polo de Beaulieu, "The Preacher Facing a Reluctant Audience According to the Testimony of Exempla," *Medieval Sermon Studies* 57 (2013): 16–28.

Another possibility is that the link between penance and preaching in relation to John the Baptist was too strong. If penance is mentioned in the spoken text, then the John actor must be preaching, and that in itself would have been controversial. This may seem far-fetched, but given late medieval anxiety about unlicensed preaching, it may well have been an issue. It is probably no coincidence that the one John who mentions penance in the English corpus is the only one to preach.

As mentioned above, preaching without a licence was prohibited by Arundel's *Constitutions* of 1409 and earlier measures intended to circumscribe preaching. It is therefore conceivable that playwrights and producers felt uneasy at the idea of having actors preach to the audiences – and I would like to argue that the plays do indeed display considerable anxiety in their attempts, or lack thereof, to represent John as a preacher.

4   The York *Baptism*

Most intriguing in this regard is the York *Baptism* where the protagonist takes such care *not* to preach to the audience. It should have been relatively straightforward to write a little sermon for the protagonist, and this is indeed what happens normally in the French *mystères*, as we have seen above. However, in the York Corpus Christi Play John's whole speech is ostensibly addressed to God and the more sermon-like part of it is introduced as a recapitulation of the actual preaching event: "Loke þou make þe redy, ay saide I" (21.29). The audience of the play is, of course, at the receiving end of the lesson, despite this device, so the question that needs to be addressed is why the playwright chose to adopt this format of indirect preaching instead of a sermon directly addressed to an (on-stage or off-stage) audience. At the close of this play there is a renewed interest in preaching when John promises, "I schall gar preche" (21.171) but, again, there is no preaching on-stage. It is interesting to see that John Clerke made notes to the effect that John's opening speech had been amended at line 2 ("De nouo facto"), that "a pece newely made for saynt John Baptiste" was missing at the close of John's opening speech (l. 49), and that John's closing speech was also changed and/or augmented ("This matter is newly mayde and devysed || wherof we haue no coppy regystred," after l. 175).[22] It is therefore very possible that by the time John Clerke had access to the manuscript in the sixteenth century the protagonist's intriguing failure to preach penance to the audience had been amended; in any case, it seems clear that

---

22   Beadle, *York Plays*, 1: 166, 167, 171.

the saint's speeches, as they have survived, were at some point felt to be dramatically, and perhaps also theologically, inadequate. Indeed, there does not seem to be any good aesthetic reason for the writer's choice regarding John's opening speech. A speech which directly engages with the audience would surely have greater dramatic potency than the recollection of a sermon. Nor are there so many sermons or sermon-like speeches in the York Corpus Christi Play overall that it would have been too much of a good thing. It is therefore likely that the reasons behind the York playwright's decision not to stage preaching are external to the drama, and the most obvious explanation is that sermons were, in theory at least, strictly policed.

The date of composition of this York pageant is not known. The first record to the Corpus Christi Play dates from 1376 but presumably the cycle grew and evolved over time. Richard Beadle suggests that the text from the mid-1470s is closely related to the performance recorded in the *Ordo Paginarum* of 1415.[23] Meg Twycross has called into question to what extent the *Ordo Paginarum* refers to scripted plays but notes that spoken text is involved in the York Corpus Christi Play by at least 1421–22.[24] There is then some evidence tentatively to suggest that the text evolved after the promulgation of Arundel's *Constitutions* (1409), which forbade unlicensed preaching, and during the archbishopric of Henry Bowet (1407–23), who was so eager to evict the unlicensed teacher (and preacher) Margery Kempe from his diocese.[25] Even if the York *Baptism* text is not to be pinned down so precisely, it is likely that the concern for unlicensed preachers and other Lollard threats would have been an influence. Although the diocese of York appears to have been little troubled by actual cases of Lollardy, most of its archbishops were actively involved in promoting anti-Lollard measures and eradicating Lollardy: for instance, Arundel (1388–96) was one of the foremost anti-Lollard agitators; Scrope (1398–1405) had worked under Arundel; Bowet (1407–23) interviewed Margery Kempe on suspicion of heresy; and Kempe (1426–52) called a convocation to address the danger of Lollardy shortly after his translation to the archdiocese.[26] It is possible that the presence of archbishops with such strong anti-Lollard sentiments created an

---

23   Ibid., 2: 169–70.

24   Meg Twycross, "The *Ordo paginarum* Revisited, with a Digital Camera," in *'Bring furth the pagants': Essays in Early English Drama Presented to Alexandra F. Johnston*, ed. David N. Klausner and Karen Sawyer Marsalek (Toronto: University of Toronto Press, 2007), 111.

25   As far as I am aware, there is no evidence for clerical actors who were also licensed to preach participating in the surviving biblical plays, although we know that a religious institution, namely St Leonard's Hospital, originally brought forth *The Purification of the Virgin* at York (Beadle, *York Plays*, 2: 136).

26   Thomson, *Later Lollards*, 194–97.

atmosphere of self-censorship in which the playwright felt that sermons on the stage, in breach of Arundel's *Constitutions* and other measures, were best avoided. The influence of such bishops over religious life in York may well explain the playwright's choice of indirect preaching for his John the Baptist.

5 The Towneley *John the Baptist*

The York situation is not entirely unique in the English corpus: the long opening speech of the protagonist in the Towneley *John the Baptist* pageant is nothing like a sermon. In fact, this speech is not even particularly concerned with sin or baptism, and focuses more on John the Baptist's identity, the Crucifixion to come, and John's relationship with Jesus. The inclusion of this kind of material is not noteworthy in itself, but the lack of stress on penance is, again, intriguing, as is the saint's failure to preach. At the close of the play, as in York, John departs to preach but before he does so, this John does turn to the audience to give them sage counsel:

> Syrs, forsake youre wykydnes,
> Pryde, envy, slowth, wrath, and lechery.
> Here Gods seruice, more and lesse;
> Please God with prayng, thus red I;
> Bewar when deth comys with dystres,
> So that ye dy not sodanly. (19.275–80)

Though strongly didactic, this speech of fourteen lines does not constitute a sermon: there is no opening prayer, no Latin, no use of authorities, or any other features one would expect in a Middle English sermon, and neither does this speech rely on the biblical accounts of the saint's preaching. Again, there does not seem to be a sound dramatic or literary reason for this decision not to have the protagonist preach (penance) to the audience. The Towneley and York pageants therefore both seem to go against the biblical account in order to avoid preaching on the stage.

The date and location of the composition and performance(s) of the Towneley *John the Baptist* play are unknown, although it is likely that the Towneley manuscript consists of a collection of disparate plays from the West Riding and perhaps Lancashire, plays which may have been performed variously at places such as Wakefield, Pontefract, and Doncaster.[27] It is consequently

---

27 Barbara D. Palmer, "Recycling 'The Wakefield Cycle': The Records," *Research Opportunities in Renaissance Drama* 41 (2002): 88, 95, 108.

impossible to ascertain whether the Towneley lack of overt preaching might similarly be due to close clerical supervision over religious matters, as I have suggested for York, although that is certainly not impossible. There are one or two lines which would suggest some uneasiness about the 'sermonising' – however little it bears resemblance to genuine sermons – of the protagonist at the end of the play. In this speech we encounter the unexpected advice to "Here Gods seruice, more and lesse" (19.277); Peter Meredith has suggested that the second half of the line originally ended in "mes" (mass), which would have enhanced the orthodox message of the speech even more.[28] The playwright appears to be taking some pains to confirm that he is in no way opposing the Church, even though the other advice he gives consists of such bland and utterly uncontroversial statements as "forsake youre wykydnes" (19.275) and "Bewar when deth comys" (19.279). Similarly, when John recommends "Beseche youre God, both euen and morne, || You for to saue from syn that day" (19.283–84) it is interesting to note that you should not pray to God to save you – bypassing the priest and the Church – but merely to prevent you from sinning. These are suggestive indications that even a mildly exhortative speech might potentially be seen as heterodox and that the playwright was well aware of this danger. If such a short and innocuous speech caused this much anxiety, one can readily understand why the playwright avoided staging a sermon.

6   The N-Town *Baptism*

That this presentation of a non-preaching John the Baptist is unusual in medieval drama is demonstrated not just by the French *mystères* but also by the N-Town *Baptism* pageant. The latter play opens with John the Baptist preaching penance to the audience:

> Ecce vox clamantes in deserto. [Here a voice of one crying in the desert]
> I am þe voys of wyldirnese
> Þat her spekyth and prechyth yow to.
> ...
> Pentitenciam nunc agite [Do penance now]
> Appropinquabit regnum celorum: [For the kingdom of heaven is at hand]
> For your trespas penaunce do ȝe

---

28   This whole line seems to be an addition on top of an erasure and is framed with black lines, which again indicates that at some point in the play's or manuscript's history this may have been considered to be controversial. For the "mes" to "lesse" change, see Epp, "Towneley Plays," 147 n. 27.

> And ʒe xall wyn hevyn Dei Deorum. [of the God of Gods]
> ...
> Baptyme I cowncell yow for to take
> And do penaunce for your synnys sake.
> And for your offens amendys ʒe make,
> Your synnys for to hyde. (ll. 1–26)

This is not much like most surviving Middle English sermons, being too short, in verse (with some macaronic lines, which are highly unusual in surviving Middle English sermons), and there is no a theme.[29] Nevertheless, there are clear references to the biblical account of John's preaching, such as lines 14–15 which cite Matthew 3:2 ("paenitentiam agite adpropinquavit enim regnum caelorum" [do penance for the kingdom of heaven is at hand]), and this speech can be taken to constitute a dramatic rendition of a preaching event. And, unlike in York and Towneley, penance is emphatically mentioned. The saint's whole opening speech is in the hand of scribe C (probably late fifteenth or early sixteenth century), and although it may simply be a newer copy of the original text, it may equally be a later reworking.[30] But at the close of the play, John the Baptist has another, longer, sermon-like speech on penance in the hand of the main scribe, which addresses the audience, and which commences "Of penawne do I preche" (22.14) and concludes "Now haue I tawght ʒow penauns" (22.180). Again, this sermon is to some extent based on the biblical accounts of John's preaching: the reference to the felling of the fruitless tree and the disregard for chaff recall Matthew 3:10 and Luke 3:9, and Matthew 3:12 and Luke 3:17 respectively. Although these speeches do not resemble surviving Middle English sermons in many respects, there can be no doubt that they were supposed to be a dramatic rendition of John's biblical preaching on penance.

At first sight, it would therefore seem that the playwright and producers of this pageant felt no particular anxiety about a sermon on penance preached on the stage. Perhaps if we knew more about the locale and date of this play, we could to some degree account for this very different treatment of the biblical sermon on penance by the protagonist in this pageant vis-à-vis the York and Towneley pageants. Nonetheless, the East-Anglian N-Town play would seem to have been created and copied at a time when there was substantial anti-Lol-

---

29   Although the Latin opening line certainly recalls the sermon theme.
30   Spector, *N-Town Play*, 1: xxiii.

lard propaganda.[31] We might consequently expect to find signs that there was some uneasiness about staging preachers, and indeed N-Town's conspicuous emphasis on confession in John's closing sermon in fact shows just that. This unusual and unexpected stress on confession – which the Lollards rejected, of course – shows the playwright's efforts explicitly to endorse orthodoxy and the Church: "I rede þat ʒe ʒow shryve" (22.147), "Shryfte of mowth loke þat ʒe make" (22.155), "God wyl be vengyd on man þat is both dum and mute, || Þat wyl nevyr be shrevyn" (22.162–63), "Schryfte of mowthe may best þe saue" (22.167), and "Whan man in good penauns and schryfte of mowth be sene, || Of God he is wel-belovyd" (22.177–78). Confession is, of course, necessary for the sacrament of penance according to orthodox theology but this playwright almost seems to claim that confession only can save you. This emphasis on confession is indeed remarkable, as can be seen when this sermon is compared to the sermons on penance in the French *mystères* where there is no such insistence on confession; sometimes it is not even mentioned at all, as in Michel's John the Baptist sequence, for instance. The saint's closing speech in the N-Town pageant is then perhaps not so much a sermon on penance but rather a promotion for aural confession and, consequently, the ecclesiastical institution. Again it would seem that there was some anxiety concerning on-stage sermons, and that this playwright, again, went out of his way to affirm his and the play's orthodoxy.

7 Conclusion

Woolf points out that the N-Town *Baptism* play is "exceptional ... in giving emphasis to John the Baptist as preacher."[32] In fact, the N-Town representation of John the Baptist is what one would expect, given the biblical accounts of this event. It is the lack of sermons on penance in York and Towneley which needs to be accounted for, not the inclusion of such speeches in N-Town. The fact that the inclusion of recognisable sermons for John the Baptist is standard practice in the French *mystères* also indicates that the cause for not doing so in York and Towneley is likely to be a peculiarly English issue. The various measures that were enforced in late medieval England to limit preaching to licensed preachers may well have made playwrights and producers wary of staging

---

31 Although no further prosecution was undertaken after Alnwick's Lollard trials of 1428–1431 in Norwich until 1472, there were cases in neighbouring dioceses in the mid and later fifteenth century; Thomson, *Later Lollards*, 120–22, 132–34.
32 Rosemary Woolf, *The English Mystery Plays* (London: Routledge & Paul, 1972), 217.

preaching figures overtly preaching. The unexpected material with a decidedly institutional-Church-supporting slant in both instances of vaguely sermon-like speeches by the N-Town *Baptism* and the Towneley *John the Baptist*, as well as the fact that York's *John the Baptist* emphatically does *not* preach on stage, demonstrates that there was uneasiness in late medieval England about usurping the role of a preacher on the stage – even if the person represented was a popular saint like John the Baptist.

Bibliography

Arnold, John H. *Belief and Unbelief in Medieval Europe*. London: Hodder, 2005.

Aston, Margaret. "Lollardy and Sedition, 1381–1431." *Past and Present* 17 (1960): 1–44.

Beadle, Richard, ed. *The York Plays: A Critical Edition of the York Corpus Christi Play as Recorded in British Library Additional MS 35290*, 2 vols. EETS s.s. 23–24. Oxford: Oxford University Press, 2009–13.

Berlioz, Jacques, and Marie Anne Polo de Beaulieu. "The Preacher Facing a Reluctant Audience According to the Testimony of Exempla." *Medieval Sermon Studies* 57 (2013): 16–28.

Clifton, Chas S. *Encyclopedia of Heresies and Heretics*. Santa Barbara: ABC-CLIO, 1992.

Epp, Garrett P. J. "The Towneley Plays and the Hazards of Cycling." *Research Opportunities in Renaissance Drama* 32 (1993): 121–50.

———, 'Re-editing Towneley', *The Yearbook of English Studies* 43 (2013): 87–104.

Hudson, Anne. *The Premature Reformation: Wycliffite Texts and Lollard History*. Oxford: Clarendon Press, 1988.

———, ed. "Sixteen Points on which the Bishops accuse Lollards." In *Selections of English Wycliffite Writings*, 19–24. Cambridge: Cambridge University Press, 1978.

Jodogne, Omer, ed. *Le Mystère de la Passion d'Arnoul Gréban*. Brussels: Académie Royale de Belgique, 1965.

Johnston, Alexandra F. "The Towneley Manuscript: Huntington Library MS HM1" (forthcoming).

———, and Margaret Rogerson, eds. *Records of Early English Drama: York*, 2 vols. Toronto: University of Toronto Press, 1979.

Leff, Gordon. *Heresy in the later Middle Ages: the relation of heterodoxy to dissent, c. 1250-c. 1450*, 2 vols. Manchester: Manchester University Press, 1967.

Love, Nicholas. *The Mirror of the Blessed Life of Jesus Christ: A Full Critical Edition, based on Cambridge University Library Additional MSS 6578 and 6686 with Introduction, Notes and Glossary*, edited by Michael G. Sargent. Exeter: University of Exeter Press, 2005.

Mazouer, Charles. "Sermons in the *Passions* of Mercadé, Gréban and Jehan Michel." In *Les Mystères: Studies in Genre, Text and Theatricality*, edited by Peter Happé and Wim Hüsken, 247–69. Ludus: Medieval and Early Renaissance Theatre and Drama, 12. Amsterdam: Rodopi, 2012.

Michel, Jean. *Le Mystère de la Passion (Angers 1486)*, edited by Omer Jodogne. Gembloux: Duculot, 1959.

Palmer, Barbara D. "Recycling 'The Wakefield Cycle': The Records." *Research Opportunities in Renaissance Drama* 41 (2002): 88–130.

Richard, Jules-Marie, ed. *Le Mystère de la Passion: texte du manuscript 697 de la bibliothèque d'Arras*. Arras: Société du Pas-de-Calais, 1891.

Spector, Stephen, ed. *The N-Town Play: Cotton MS Vespasian D. 8*, 2 vols. EETS s.s. 11–12. Oxford: Oxford University Press, 1991.

Staley, Lynn, ed. *The Book of Margery Kempe*. Kalamazoo, MI: Medieval Institute Publications, 1996.

Stevens, Martin, and A.C. Cawley, eds. *The Towneley Plays*, 2 vols. EETS s.s. 13–14. Oxford: Oxford University Press, 1994.

Swinburn, Lilian M., ed. *The Lanterne of Liȝt, edited from MS. Harl. 2324*. EETS o.s. 151. London: Kegan Paul, Trench, Trübner & co., 1917; rpt. New York: Kraus Reprint, 1971.

Tentler, Thomas N. *Sin and Confession of the Eve of the Reformation*. Princeton: Princeton University Press, 1977.

Thomson, John A.F. *The Later Lollards, 1414–1520*. London: Oxford University Press, 1965.

Twycross, Meg. "The *Ordo paginarum* Revisited, with a Digital Camera." In *'Bring furth the pagants': Essays in Early English Drama Presented to Alexandra F. Johnston*, edited by David N. Klausner and Karen Sawyer Marsalek, 105–31. Toronto: University of Toronto Press, 2007.

CHAPTER 7

"Have here a Drink full good": A Comparative Analysis of Staging Temptation in the Newcastle Noah Play

Katie Normington

Abstract

The surviving fragment of the Newcastle Flood play unusually shows Mrs Noah being tempted by Satan to disrupt the building of the ark. This essay examines other instances of female temptation by Satan within the extant Corpus Christi plays in order to establish the dramatic principles behind their effectiveness. It concludes that the compilers of the dramatic scenes readily departed from biblical antecedents in constructing the pageants. One reason for this is that they recognised the dramatic potential in staging temptation and were therefore keen to fully exploit the material. This led to accretions to the biblical material, such as the inclusion of Satan in the Flood drama at Newcastle.

Keywords

medieval drama – Newcastle – women – temptation

1   Introduction

Only the Noah play remains as a ghost-like snippet from a lost Newcastle Corpus Christi cycle of some twenty-five pageants.[1] Even then the text is "very

---

1 The oldest reference to the Newcastle plays was to be found in a now lost ordinance of the Coopers dating from 1426 which "enjoined them to go together yearly at the feast of Corpus Christi in procession, as other crafts did, and play their play at their own charge; each brother to attend at the hour assigned him at the procession on pain of forfeiting a pound of wax." John Brand, *The History and Antiquities of the Town and County of the Town of Newcastle upon Tyne*, 2 vols. (London: B. White & Son and T. And I. Egerton, 1789), 2: 344, cited in John Anderson, and A.C. Cawley, "The Newcastle play of *Noah's Ark*," REED *Newsletter* 2:1 (1977): 11.

far from being satisfactory"[2] since the earliest surviving version, printed in 1736, was constructed by Henry Bourne, a curate at All Hallows in Newcastle, from corrupted copies which have now been lost. Evidence of the performance of the Corpus Christi plays exist in the Newcastle Coopers' ordinary (the regulations of the trade craft) of 1427, while the last entry is from 1578, by which point "it seems probable that ... the plays had lost some of their popularity since they had ceased to be played annually."[3] The ordinaries of the Carpenters', Masons' and Joiners' have the last record at 1589.[4]

However, the remains of the text indicate much to admire in the originality of the Noah play. The play, like York, separates the building of the ark and the boarding of it into two dramatic episodes. All that remains is the first scene. The Newcastle version follows much of the pattern of the other extant texts in terms of first depicting God's predicament regarding the disobedience of mankind, resolving to flood the land and then instructing Noah to build the ark. In the Newcastle version an Angel also visits Noah to brief him about the ark. Unusually here Mrs Noah is also involved in the decision to build the ark. In a striking and original scene, Satan attempts to confound the building of the ark and thus the salvation of mankind through tempting Uxor Noah to "drink full good" of a potion that she will also serve to Noah, which will prevent them from completing and boarding the ark. This temptation is of course a trope present at the start of the biblical cycle when Eve is tempted to eat the apple, and it is one repeated on stage in the York cycle when Dame Procula, Pilate's wife, is visited by Satan in a dream where he persuades her to intervene in the sentencing of Christ. This essay will consider the temptation of women by the devil within biblical drama, and specifically within the Newcastle Noah play, to examine how dramatists staged temptation, the techniques they used and the possible effect of this upon their audiences.

The trope of temptation is central to much biblical action, the epitome of this being Christ after forty days in the wilderness, where the devil torments him but is repudiated three times. Christ then declares "You shall not tempt Lord your God" (Matthew 4:7), and this rejection of temptation forms much of the basis of Christian belief. God and the devil are frequently pitted against each other in a demonstration of the perils of temptation. This dynamic forms

---

2   *The Non-Cycle Mystery Plays*, ed. Osborn Waterhouse, EETS e.s. 104 (London: Kegan Paul and Oxford University Press, 1909), xxxv.

3   Ibid., xxxix. Waterhouse argues that the use of Northern spellings "qu" or "quh" in words such as "what" or "when" also locates the text in the region (ibid., xxxvii).

4   *Non-Cycle Plays and Fragments*, ed. N. Davis, EETS s.s. 1 (Oxford: Oxford University Press, 1970), xliii.

the stimulus for visual as well as dramatic representations which survive from the medieval period. Emmerson notes that the Antichrist uses four methods to gain power: false preaching, bribes, persecutions and miracles, and that these are fully represented in the art of the time.[5] In fact so prevalent were images of the devil that Margaret Jennings notes "an ordinary medieval man's concept of the Devil and his wiles may well have been more real to him than the concept of God."[6]

2   Function of the Devil in Drama

John Cox argues that the function of the devils in the Corpus Christi plays has historically been interpreted as two-fold. The first function is that devils are seen as part of the vernaculisation of medieval drama, or as vestiges of folk drama and thus they serve a subversive role often questioning and mocking traditional values.[7] The second view, however, sees the comic interventions made by devils as functionally reinforcing the demonstration of God's order and thus the role served to "reinforce the existing power structure."[8] Cox argues that the study of devils within their theological context suggests that these two functions are allied. The theological reading of the devil means that "One of the major purposes of liturgical participation throughout one's life, from baptism to the last rites, was therefore to reject and defeat the Devil."[9] In this sense, the role that the devil plays in tempting those on stage (and thus the audience) is crucial.

Cox sees the role of the devil within the cycle plays as to define "what community was *not*"[10] and he cites the Towneley Fall of Lucifer as an example of this. He observes that the Devil is an essential part of the social relations within medieval society and believes the fall of Lucifer play "suggest[s] that the demonic destruction of community occurs in repeating the sin of Lucifer, that is, in abuses of power by the powerful."[11] He argues that devils appear relatively

---

5   Richard Kenneth Emmerson, *Antichrist in the Middle Ages: A Study of Medieval Apocalypticism, Art, and Literature* (Manchester: Manchester University Press, 1981), 131.
6   Margaret Jennings, "Tutivillus: The Literary Career of the Recording Demon," *Studies in Philology* 74:5 (Dec. 1977): 83.
7   John Cox, "The Devil and Society in the English Mystery Plays," *Comparative Drama* 28 (1994–95): 407.
8   Ibid., 408.
9   Ibid.
10   Ibid., 410.
11   Ibid., 413.

infrequently in the plays and that "they always appear in keeping with Lucifer's disruption of primordial community."[12]

It is my argument, however, that the staging of temptation was popular because it was innately theatrical, and it is this potential of theatricality that the dramatists, if we may call them that, of the Corpus Christi cycles recognised.[13] Evidence of this is the way in which the dramatists elaborated upon the role of the temptation of women by the devil from biblical source material. Aside from the temptation of Eve which is fully reported within the Old Testament, the temptation of Procula and Mrs Noah are events which are largely embellished or totally fabricated.[14] Matthew mentions the intervention of Procula's dream within Pilate's judgement: "While he was sitting on the judgment seat, his wife sent to him, saying, 'Have nothing to do with that just man, for I have suffered many things today in a dream because of Him'".[15] The translation of this reference into the dramatic scene of the Corpus Christi plays is a large embellishment of this initial event.

The temptation of Mrs Noah by the devil is complete dramatic licence. In fact Mrs Noah receives little attention within the Bible, where it is Noah, after the flood, who is shown as a renegade, falling drunk after cultivating his vines. The origins of the portrayal of Mrs Noah are unknown but Lynette Muir argues that the temptation of Mrs Noah by the devil has Eastern roots.[16] Elsewhere I have noted that Queen Mary's Psalter shows an image of the devil influencing Mrs Noah.[17] Peter Meredith in briefly examining the relationship between the Bible and medieval English drama notes some of the issues in determining the relationship. In particular he observes the likelihood that any reference or quo-

---

12 Ibid., 415.
13 The term 'theatricality' was not recognised within medieval times. It first appears in 1837 (see Thomas Postlewait and Tracy C. Davis, "Theatricality: An Introduction," in *Theatricality*, ed. Tracy C. Davis and Thomas Postlewait [Cambridge: Cambridge University Press, 2003], 2). It can be defined though as "a mode of representation or a style of behaviour characterized by histrionic actions, manners and devices, and hence a practice" (ibid., 1).
14 Similarly, Cox, "The Devil and Society," 28, notes that in Towneley some twelve lines which pertain to the devil from the source material expand into almost 400 lines of playing material.
15 Matthew 27:19.
16 Lynette Muir, *The Biblical Drama of Medieval Europe* (Cambridge: Cambridge University Press, 1995), 73.
17 Katie Normington, *Medieval English Drama: Performance and Spectatorship* (Cambridge: Polity Press, 2009), 86. See for a digitised image of the Queen Mary Psalter Royal MS 2B VII 41r-66v: <http://www.bl.uk/manuscripts/Viewer.aspx?ref=royal_ms_2_b_vii> (Accessed, 30 March 2015). The Psalter also shows an angel speaking to Noah.

tation from the Bible will have been memorised rather than literally transcribed, and thus exact copying is unlikely. He concludes:

> If they wanted to use the Bible text, writers could create scenes from biblical descriptions, could make their characters do what the Bible says where there is an action described, or say it where there is direct speech, or they could use the Bible text to create dialogue out of reported speech or description. They could also make use of the exegetical habit of seeing one part of the Bible as figuring another and transfer sections from one place to another.[18]

It is clear that these moments of temptation caught the dramatists' imagination, and it seems likely they recognised the theatrical potential of these incidents. They also recognised the potential that staging the devil offered, for the dramatists realised that, as Meg Twycross has stated when speaking about the interlude *Mankind*, "Virtue is no fun, vice is."[19]

3   Newcastle Noah Play

Turning now to the Newcastle fragment, it is interesting that the play is seen as a complex arrangement: "In comparison with the first York play and the first part of the Towneley play, the Newcastle version is arranged on a considerably more elaborate scale."[20] This is due in part to the appearance of the Angel, the placement of Noah's wife in the first part of the drama and the appearance of the devil. Waterhouse notes that while "The introduction of the Angel was doubtless intended to increase the spectacular effect – the chief consideration in the early fifteenth century – although at the same time it increased the dramatist's difficulties, since it necessitated God's command appearing twice."[21] The dramatist deals with this by splitting some of the instructions regarding the building of the ship and through having the angel, rather than God, instruct Noah to gather his family. As Noah deliberates the instructions he has received

---

[18]   Peter Meredith, "The Direct and Indirect Use of the Bible in Medieval English Drama," *Bulletin John Rylands Library* 77:3 (1995): 74.

[19]   Meg Twycross, "The Theatricality of Medieval English Plays," in *Medieval English Theatre*, ed. Richard Beadle and Alan J. Fletcher (Cambridge: Cambridge University Press, 2008 [2nd ed.]), 63.

[20]   Waterhouse, *Non-Cycle Mystery Plays*, xxxviii.

[21]   Ibid.

he laments the condition of humankind, "Even wo worth the, fouled sin" (l. 87). Diana Wyatt believes that Noah's reflection and admonition to the audience about the consequences of sin cues the entrance of the devil.[22] This thesis fits with the notion espoused by Cox that within the mystery plays the devil is presented within the confines of traditional religion and is associated with the "disruption of primordial community."[23] It is notable that when the devil enters the stage the verses become more irregular and are rich in alliteration. As Waterhouse asks, "Was this intentional on the part of the writer, and so designed in order to be in keeping with the ranting and unruly behaviour conventionally assigned to this popular stage figure?"[24] Certainly Satan's entrance, "Out, out harro and welaway" (l. 95), encourages loud and unruly ranting from the performer.

The devil's temptation within the Newcastle fragment runs in clear parallel to the Fall in Eden. In fact Wyatt argues that "typologically the play clearly harks back to the Fall."[25] The weakness of Mrs Noah is perceived by Satan from the outset since "In faith she is my friend || She is both whunt and slee" (ll. 111–12). Satan plays a careful game with Mrs Noah, teasing her by not revealing his name but playfully commenting on his "crooked snout," warning her that following her husband's advice will lead to the death of her family. He succeeds in tempting Mrs Noah to take the potion to give to Noah to drink.

As Noah returns from the hard labour of building the ark Mrs Noah greets him warmly, tempting him to sit close to her and tending to his weariness by offering food and crucially drink. The sense of dramatic irony is built as Noah declares "What the devil! What drink is it!" (ll. 156–57). The appearance of the angel frames the end of this episode and counterpoints that of the devil, who opens this sequence. The angel returns to convince Noah that he is right to build the ark, while Mrs Noah questions his wisdom and, acting as an agent of the devil, tries to stop him from completing it. Noah resists the drink and completes the ark. As Wyatt points out, the "Devil's plot, as the text stands, turns out rather a damp squib."[26] Perhaps to compensate for the inconclusive appearance of the devil, it is left for him to provide an ironic caution to the audience in the final epilogue; all those that do not believe in him will be cursed.

---

22 Diana Wyatt, "Arts, Crafts and Authorities: Textual and Contextual Evidence for North-Eastern English Noah Plays," *Yearbook of English Studies* 43 (2013): 55.
23 Cox, *The Devil and the Sacred in English Drama*, 23.
24 Waterhouse, *Non-Cycle Mystery Plays*, xxxvii.
25 Wyatt, "Arts, Crafts and Authorities," 61.
26 Ibid., 66.

Little critical attention has been given to the Newcastle fragment. Rosemary Woolf finds the play to be "a rather confused and mechanical handling of the subject."[27] She argues that the theme of secrecy is confused and that the purpose of the devil's potion is unclear. However, to assess the significance of the devil it is important to consider, as Lesley Wade Soule argues, that characters such as the devil need to be imagined in performance.[28] Soule sees that the personification of the devil within drama can be both "frightening and comic" and that "The voice and figure of the devil as performer, including his grotesque mask and costume(s), were instruments for asserting a powerful and pleasurable performative presence."[29] She goes on to argue that the devil shows traits of an archetypal comic anti-hero in that he is:

> (1) of lower status; (2) ugly and ludicrous; (3) violent but not actually harmful; (4) vainglorious yet cowardly; (5) resentful of and rebellious against authority; (6) amoral and immoral; (7) both impulsive and scheming (i.e. a shrewd fool); and finally (8) outrageous, exhibitionistic, and free of the constraints of either decorum or morality.[30]

She notes that while God remains an allegorical figure in a fixed state the fall allows Satan to become mobile. For example he is able to take on different guises.[31] So while God remains a symbolic entity that rigidly denotes spiritual hierarchy, Satan is able to shape shift, appear in different environments and employ a variety of tactics to reach his goal: "The threat conveyed by masking was an inevitable extension of that implied by concealment, for a creature that is unidentifiable and unpredictable is also frightening."[32] As Soule notes, citing Twycross, devils "play games with the conventions of acting, continually working up illusions and then dropping them."[33]

The devil within the Newcastle fragment employs many of the techniques outlined by Soule. He is a scheming, immoral presence who teases and bates Mrs Noah. It is difficult to discern much about the appearance of Satan from Newcastle and it is here that evidence from other sources is helpful.

---

27   Rosemary Woolf, *The English Mystery Plays* (Berkeley and Los Angeles: University of California Press, 1972), 137.
28   Lesley Wade Soule, "Subverting the Mysteries: The Devil as Anti-Character." *European Medieval Drama* 2 (1998): 278.
29   Ibid., 279 and 283.
30   Ibid., 281.
31   Ibid., 285.
32   Ibid., 286.
33   Twycross, "Theatricality of Medieval English Plays", 73.

4   The Devil's Appearance

Evidence from other forms of medieval drama from both England and the continent provide examples of the stage appearance of the devil. Tydeman notes that it is the "evil and theologically disreputable figures in the plays who have the greatest opportunity for physical activity."[34] He cites the manner in which in the French drama *Le Mystère d'Adam* the devils, after running around the acting area and possibly into the audience, carry Adam and Eve into Hell. This spectacular and physical presence on stage would have been attractive to an audience. Indeed the importance of such performers is indicated in the payments they received. At Perth, for example, in the Fall play Adam and Eve earned 6d for playing in 1518, whereas the devil received 8d.[35]

The costuming of the devil also shows his flamboyancy. For example, the Coventry Drapers 1572 record shows "ij pound of heare for the demons cotts and hose" while the devil in *Le Jour de Jugement* dressed as a dandy with a blue coat with long ermine sleeves almost to the floor and a red hood. Attendant devils were painted red or back with tails and bright shields and pitchforks.[36] Elsewhere, the devil was clad in feathers. At Chester the Midsummer Show records payments for feathers for him, while at Cambridge he wore a black coat.[37] The Cambridge Queens' College Miscellany records of 1547 shows devils sporting capes of yellow and red cloth with masks made from painted linen.[38]

Attention has been paid by Twycross and Carpenter to the masks worn by devils; they comment that they are the only characters who seem to always wear masks and they frequently appear with horns and large animal ears, with fangs and bulbous noses. Some could breathe fire or smoke,[39] although Butterworth notes that the Cornish *Creacion of the World* requires Satan to "be on fire."[40] Even more elaborate is the stage direction from the 1501 Mons play: "Here there comes a smoke and an explosion from under the girl and Fergalus

---

34   William Tydeman, *The Theatre in the Middle Ages* (Cambridge: Cambridge University Press, 1978), 193.
35   Ibid., 209.
36   Ibid., 211.
37   See *Records of Early English Drama: Chester*, 2 vols., ed. Lawrence M. Clopper (Toronto: University of Toronto Press, 1989), 1: 198, and *Records of Early English Drama: Cambridge*, 2 vols., ed. Alan H. Nelson (Toronto: University of Toronto Press, 1989), 1: 161.
38   Nelson, REED: *Cambridge*, 1: 146.
39   Meg Twycross and Sarah Carpenter, *Masks and Masking in Medieval and Tudor England* (Aldershot: Ashgate, 2002), 201–06.
40   Philip Butterworth, *Theatre of Fire : Special Effects in Early English and Scottish Theatre* (London: Society for Theatre Research, 1998), 4.

comes out."[41] Twycross and Carpenter conclude that masking allowed the concealed performer liberties which would not otherwise be afforded to unmasked players.[42]

5   Temptation in Other Cycles

The pattern of temptation utilised at Newcastle is one in which Satan recognises womanly weakness, shifts his identity in a teasing game with Mrs Noah, threatens the loss of her family and personal circumstances and eventually succeeds in tempting her to become his agent. It is a similarity shared with other temptation scenes within the Corpus Christi plays.

The York Fall of Man opens with Satan's direct address to the audience in which he displays his anger at God's behaviour, and his envy towards mankind for being chosen by God. Satan plots to steal God's pleasure from him by approaching Eve. The second scene shows him disguised as a serpent and constructing a lie: "founde to feyne a lowde leasing" (5.24).[43] As Satan approaches Eve he pretends that he is "a frende" and is acting "for thy gude" (5.27–28). He manipulates Eve into revealing the existence of the forbidden fruit and then coaxes her to taste it so that she can equal God and "Shall have knowing as well as he" (5.51). Eve attempts to discern the nature of her tempter and for a moment seems to see through his deceit:

> Why, what kynne thyng art þou
> þat telle þis tale to me? (5.52–53)

It is here that Satan has to draw upon the full mastery of his conceit. Just as Eve has seemingly seen through his guise he retaliates pointing out he is a mere worm and that she will be 'worshipped' should she taste the forbidden tree. He tempts Eve with advanced status. In fact the very thing that caused Satan to overreach and that led to his own fall. As Eve is finally persuaded to eat the apple, she is instructed by Satan to ensure that Adam also eats it, at which point Satan "recedet" (5.82). The York tempter is duplicitous, playful, and pushes the boundary of his discovery. This is very different from the N-Town tempter who is direct, rapid and faces a harder challenge.

---

41 Ibid., 7.
42 Twycross and Carpenter, *Masks and Masking*, 213.
43 References to the York Corpus Christi plays are taken from *The York Plays: A Critical Edition of the York Corpus Christi Play as recorded in British Library Additional MS 35290* ed. Richard Beadle, 2 vols., EETS s.s. 24 and 34 (Oxford: Oxford University Press, 2009–13).

In the N-Town version, some material found at the end of the Creation pageant at York begins the N-Town Fall. As a result the play starts with God's creation and shows Adam and Eve in bliss before the serpent appears. The serpent immediately flatters Eve and moves straight to the point:

> Heyl, fayr wyff and comely dame!
> This frute to ete I thee cownselle.
> Take this appyl and ete this same!
> This frute is best as I thee telle. (2.87–90)

Eve fully understands the consequences of eating the fruit: she has been warned by God that they will be expelled from the garden and will die should they venture to taste it. It makes Satan's task of temptation somewhat harder than at York, where Eve had only a vague idea as to why the fruit was forbidden. Satan offers power over the world to Eve:

> Sunne and mone and sterrys bryth,
> Fysch and foule, boȝe sond and se,
> At ȝoure byddyng bothe day and nyth:
> Allthynge xal be in ȝoure powsté.
> Ȝe xal be Goddys pere! (2.104–08)

Satan tempts Eve by first trying to get her to hold the apple, then asking her to bite it and then tempting Adam to eat the fruit. In N Town Satan uses rhetoric very effectively to persuade Eve of all the riches she will inherit when she is equal to God; the temptation is almost exactly repeated by Eve to Adam and is effective for a second time.

At Chester the creation and fall are dramatised in one pageant. The plotting of the episode is carried out with some aplomb and the dramatist manages to carefully manipulate the situation so that Satan skilfully tempts Eve into willingly eating the apple. Following the creation of Adam and Eve the stage direction mentions that "the serpente shall come up out of a hole, and the deyvell walkinge shall say ..."[44] which suggests that the devil dressed as a serpent enters from a hell's mouth beneath the stage. Satan rails against his fallen state and declares that he will "teach his wiffe a playe" (2.179) and that "hir hoppe I will begylle" (2.184). Satan devises his plot around Eve's innocence and ability to be beguiled, as well as the unruliness of her gender: "That woman is forbydden to doe|| for anythinge the will therto" (2.185–86). Satan designs a

---

[44] *The Chester Mystery Cycle*, 2 vols., ed. R.M. Lumiansky and David Mills, EETS s.s. 3 (Oxford: Oxford University Press, 1974), 2: 161.

disguise for himself whereby he will have a serpent's body but the face of a maiden; in other words "hir kynde I will take" (2.196). In order to tempt Eve into believing him he will represent himself as something familiar to her. Satan remains confident his plan will work given women's "licourouse" or pleasure-seeking nature. Satan proceeds to put on an "edders coate," his snake disguise. The description inserted into the text provides a rare glimpse into the precise detail of the costume here which Walker translates as an "Upper part with bird's feathers; serpent shaped in the foot, in a figure a girl."[45]

As Satan approaches Eve he immediately questions her as to why God forbad them from eating the fruit within Paradise. Eve corrects this, saying it is only the fruit of one tree they cannot eat and they will die if they do. Satan then tempts Eve with knowledge and power, declaring she shall be as wise as God and that God has intentionally kept her from this. Drawing on the delicious taste of the fruit, "Yt is good meate" (2.234), he offers her the chance to "bee like godes" (2.238). Eve rationalises that the tree looks healthy, the fruit sweet and that if it will elevate her status she will take only one apple at which point she "shall take of the fruite of the serpente" (2.248).

In Towneley the temptation of Eve is conducted in a manner which stresses a variety of her features, her innocence, which makes her gullible, her pride and therefore openness to flattery, her hedonism, which draws her to taste the sweet food, and lastly the predisposition of women to be disobedient. It is a pattern which, as I note below, is largely reproduced in Procula's dream at York. The Towneley plays sets up Eve's obedience to her husband as well as to God since Adam reminds her of her obligation before the visitation of Satan:[46]

> Bot luke well, Eue, my wife,
> That thou negh not the tree of life; (1.242–43)

Eve promises him that she will not be disobedient: increasing the sense of dramatic irony for the audience who are only too aware that she will, of course, sin. Satan laments his position but the rest of the scene is missing so it is difficult to anticipate his *modus operandi*.

The other moment of temptation of a woman by Satan is in Procula's dream. The York Christ Before Pilate 1: The Dream of Pilate's Wife was sponsored by the Tapiters and Couchers, whose tapestries and ornamental cloths may well have been represented in Procula's bed place. In a sort of double plot, Satan

---

45   *Medieval Drama: An Anthology*, ed. Greg Walker, Blackwell Anthologies (London: Blackwell, 2000), 28 n. 4.

46   References to the Towneley plays are taken from *The Towneley Plays*, ed. Martin Stevens and A.C. Cawley, 2 vols., EETS s.s. 13 (Oxford: Oxford University Press, 1994).

ironically appears this time to attempt to save Christ's life so that he cannot find glory through his Crucifixion and Resurrection nor threaten Satan's power in Hell. Walker notes that "Procula represents an interesting variant on a misogynistic type, combining elements of the sexual temptress (in her dealings with her husband) with the abusive instincts of the scold (evident in her responses to the Beadle)."[47]

Procula's entrance to the scene is enhanced by Pilate himself who declares his wife to be "worthely" and "semely." Pilate's attention is repaid as his wife praises his own lineage as a judge connected to the aristocracy. She warns that to ignore his judgements can lead to death, and anyone would be ill served to drive him to a rage. Pilate's wife then spends a stanza indulging in self-praise:

> All welle of all womanhede I am, wittie and wise,
> Consayue nowe my countenaunce so comly and clere. (30.39–40)

She boasts of her beauty, her fine robes and the love of her husband. Pilate's wife's bragging is useful dramatically not so much for the establishment of her colourful character, but more for her pride and vanity, which Satan can then easily attack. The Pilates unashamedly kiss and flirt in public and demonstrate their very fallen state. Pilate even confides in an aside to the audience that his wife "In bedde is full buxhome and bayne" (30.52). The juxtaposition of Pilate as a womaniser and a legal authority sets up the moment when he will later have to decide between his 'head' and judgemental role against his 'heart' and the biddings of his wife.

Procula is shown to be short-tempered and tempestuous through her treatment of the Beadle who interrupts her and Pilate. Her shortness is commented upon by Pilate who asks her "Do mende you madame, and youre moode be amendand" (30.64). The portrayal of Procula is shown as someone who is liable to fluctuations in emotion; a facet that Satan will exploit. As the day draws to a close, the Beadle calls upon Pilate to, as the law dictates, spend the night alone before he preside over the court. Meanwhile Procula is sent back to their private quarters, although Pilate will only allow this once she and Pilate have refreshed themselves with wine. The luxuriousness of their drinking reminds the audience of the state of affairs that has been achieved since the fall of man. There is vulnerability in the way Procula is sent into the evening away from the courts of justice back home accompanied by her maid and a boy. Once Procula is in her night attire she rudely dismisses her servants: "Now be yhe in pese, both youre carpyng and crye" (30.157) dismissing them for their noisiness. The preamble to the visitation of the devil depicts Procula as vain, proud, ill-tem-

---

47   Ibid., 99.

pered and impatient: in other words she would be unlikely to have found much sympathy within the audience.

It is likely that Satan would have been heard before he was seen as he shouts "Oute! Harrowe!" (30.157a). Here no disguise is needed as Procula is asleep during the visitation, however it may have been more convincing for an audience were he to be disguised. He laments that Christ's sacrifice and the Harrowing of Hell will end Satan's power over hell and thus conspires to affect Pilate's judgement through his wife. Satan uses Procula's vanity to warn her that if the death of Christ is sanctioned by Pilate there will be repercussions which will cause the loss of their power and wealth. As Procula wakes she is "drecchid with a dreme full dredfully to dowte" (30.176). Procula dispatches a reluctant messenger into the night to warn Pilate, emphasising in her missive that she was visited by the dream as she slept naked; a point which draws her closer still to the image of the pre-fallen Eve. The warning is immediately seized upon by Caiaphas as 'witchcraft' but it determines Pilate to fairly hear the case, though the intervention is in the end unsuccessful.

6   Dramatic Theory and Staging Temptation

The Newcastle fragment and this evaluation of the temptation of women by Satan need to be set within the context of dramatic presentation. The presentation of temptation is ideally suited to the stage because in order to elucidate the issue for an audience a number of dramatic devices come into play. In considering these devices I draw upon the theoretical analysis of Aristotle. I am using this as a framework for the taxonomy of dramatic devices rather than arguing that Aristotelian theory was known to the scribes or dramatists at the time. In his *Poetics* Aristotle argues that tragedy "has six elements on the basis of which it is evaluated, namely the story, the moral element, the style, the ideas, the staging, and the music."[48] The aim of representing action on stage has, for Aristotle, the purpose of "effecting, through pity and fear, the purification [*katharsis*] of such emotions."[49] Kenny in his edition of *Poetics* argues that

> Aristotle does not mean that tragedy cleanses the soul or purges the emotions, in the sense of getting rid of them altogether ... The translation of *katharsis* as 'refining' is closer to Aristotle's meaning. A courageous man

---

[48]   Aristotle, *Poetics*, transl. by Anthony Kenny (Oxford: Oxford University Press, 2013), 24.
[49]   Ibid., 23.

is one who fears what it is right to fear, at the right time, and in the right proportion.[50]

Applied to the notion of temptation, this would mean the person who realises what it is to be tempted but resists is more courageous than the one who avoids understanding it entirely.

The act of representing temptation immediately draws upon a number of Aristotle's dramatic elements. The plot, or *muthos*, is seen by Aristotle as the most important element as it displays action and reveals moral character often through the dramatisation of characters being faced with choices. Read in this manner, the intervention of Satan in the Newcastle Noah play casts Noah as hero against the weak-willed villainy of Mrs Noah and Satan's temptation of Noah. The text focuses on the choice that Noah will make: will he choose to drink the potion or not?

Staging temptation also draws upon other Aristotelian elements such as *dianoia* (thought or ideas) and *opsis* (scenography). *Dianoia* is central to any temptation scene; in the Wilderness it is the polemic of the ideas of Christ and that of the devil which drives the momentum of the incident. Staging temptation brings into play at least two characters on stage who hold a polarity of motivation and objectives. The rhetorical display of one trying to persuade another who is unwilling forms the basis of a dramatic element, for it foregrounds the notion of the debate.

The use of scenography including costumes and objects is seen by Aristotle as having secondary importance. However, he perhaps neglected to consider that when action is placed on the stage as opposed to the page visual aspects take on a strong association for the audience. The staging of temptation often goes beyond words and requires tangible objects which form the focal point for the temptation. This is exemplified in Lewis Carroll's *Alice in Wonderland* when the young girl is tempted to 'eat me' and 'drink me' by having labelled food and drink placed in front of her. It is also present in the Tudor interlude *Mankind* when New Guises displays the latest fashion to Mankind in order to tempt him to follow Titivillus. In the Noah play a drink becomes the focus of the temptation, replacing Eve's apple from the Fall of Man scenes.

Aristotle's emphasis on *catharsis* as the important outcome of drama is something that is particularly apposite for a medieval audience. Kenny's definition cited above that reads catharsis as more of an emotional balance is one that is helpful here. A display of temptation on stage is likely to lead the audience to recognise the event; they too have been tempted in the past. Through

---

50   Ibid., xxv.

this process of identification it is likely they experience a moment of catharsis. Their fears of being tempted are expunged and overcome, instead allowing them to be appropriately 'God fearing'. The dramatists of these temptation scenes clearly realised the dramatic potential of playing these scenes on stage, but also were aware of the affect that such moments would have on the sensibilities of the audience, who like the characters would learn the better way is to avoid temptation. In tempting Mrs Noah to 'drink full good' the Newcastle devil tests the audience.

Bibliography

Anderson, John, and A.C. Cawley. "The Newcastle play of *Noah's Ark*." REED *Newsletter* 2:1 (1977): 11–17.

Aristotle. *Poetics*, translated by Anthony Kenny. Oxford: Oxford University Press, 2013.

Beadle, Richard, ed. *The York Plays: A Critical Edition of the York Corpus Christi Play as recorded in British Library Additional MS 35290*, 2 vols. EETS s.s. 23–24. Oxford: Oxford University Press, 2009–13.

Brand, John. *The History and Antiquities of the Town and County of the Town of Newcastle upon Tyne*, 2 vols. London: B. White & Son and T. And I. Egerton, 1789.

Butterworth, Philip. *Theatre of Fire: Special Effects in Early English and Scottish Theatre*. London: Society for Theatre Research, 1998.

Clopper, Lawrence M., ed. *Records of Early English Drama: Chester*, 2 vols. Toronto: University of Toronto Press, 1989.

Cox, John. "The Devil and Society in the English Mystery Plays." *Comparative Drama* 28 (1994–95): 407–38.

———. *The Devil and the Sacred in English Drama, 1350–1642*. Cambridge: Cambridge University Press, 2000.

David, Alfred. "Noah's Wife's Flood." In *The Performance of Middle English Culture: Essays on Chaucer and Drama*, edited by James J. Paxson, Lawrence M. Clopper and Sylvia Tomasch, 97–109. Cambridge: D.S. Brewer, 1998.

Davis, Norman, ed. *Non-Cycle Plays and Fragments*. EETS s.s. 1. Oxford: Oxford University Press, 1970.

Emmerson, Richard Kenneth. *Antichrist in the Middle Ages: A Study of Medieval Apocalypticism, Art, and Literature*. Manchester: Manchester University Press, 1981.

Jennings, Margaret. "Tutivillus: The Literary Career of the Recording Demon." *Studies in Philology* 74:5 (Dec. 1977): 83–95.

Lumiansky, R.M., and David Mills, eds. *The Chester Mystery Cycle*, 2 vols. EETS s.s. 3 and 9. Oxford: Oxford University Press, 1974–86.

Meredith, Peter. "The Direct and Indirect Use of the Bible in Medieval English Drama." *Bulletin John Rylands Library* 77:3 (1995): 61–77.

Muir, Lynette. *The Biblical Drama of Medieval Europe.* Cambridge: Cambridge University Press, 1995.

Nelson, Alan H., ed. *Records of Early English Drama: Cambridge*, 2 vols. Toronto: University of Toronto Press, 1989.

Normington, Katie. *Medieval English Drama: Performance and Spectatorship.* Cambridge: Polity Press, 2009.

Postlewait, Thomas, and Tracy C. Davis. "Theatricality: An Introduction." In *Theatricality*, edited by Tracy C. Davis and Thomas Postlewait, 1–39. Cambridge: Cambridge University Press, 2003.

Soule, Lesley Wade. "Subverting the Mysteries: The Devil as Anti-Character." *European Medieval Drama* 2 (1998): 277–91.

Spector, Stephen, ed. *The N-Town Play: Cotton MS Vespasian D. 8*, 2 vols. EETS s.s. 11–12. Oxford: Oxford University Press, 1991.

Stevens, Martin and A.C. Cawley, eds. *The Towneley Plays*. 2 vols. EETS s.s. 13. Oxford: Oxford University Press, 1994.

Twycross, Meg. "The Theatricality of Medieval English Plays." In *Medieval English Theatre*, edited by Richard Beadle and Alan J. Fletcher, 26–74. Cambridge: Cambridge University Press, 2008 (2nd ed.).

———, and Sarah Carpenter. *Masks and Masking in Medieval and Tudor England.* Aldershot: Ashgate, 2002.

Tydeman, William. *The Theatre in the Middle Ages.* Cambridge: Cambridge University Press, 1978.

Walker, Greg, ed. *Medieval Drama: An Anthology.* Blackwell Anthologies. London: Blackwell, 2000.

Waterhouse, Osborn, ed. *The Non-Cycle Mystery Plays.* EETS e.s. 104. London: Kegan Paul and Oxford University Press, 1909.

Woolf, Rosemary. *The English Mystery Plays.* Berkeley: University of California Press, 1972.

Wyatt, Diana. "Arts, Crafts and Authorities: Textual and Contextual Evidence for North-Eastern English Noah Plays." *Yearbook of English Studies* 43 (2013): 48–68.

CHAPTER 8

Dramatizing the Resurrection

Peter Happé

Abstract

This essay is a comparison between ways of dramatizing the Resurrection in England and France. It establishes a core of items which are incorporated in many versions, short and long, as well as non-biblical elements which are frequently attached to the scriptural details. The experience of possible audiences who must have drawn upon existing recollected items is considered as well as the inclusion of musical and visual referents. The dramatic structure and development of the chosen plays are reviewed in order to illustrate the variety of the theatrical elements. Attention is paid to the reasons for including the Resurrection, which for some plays was a matter of defining, rehearsing or sustaining belief. Such material is relevant to the central item in Resurrection sequences, the moment when Christ rises from the tomb, and the way this is presented in the dramatic texts. The reticence with which this is treated is found to be one of the essential aspects of the dramatizations, which are largely influenced by versions in the Scriptures but are not entirely determined by them. This aspect of the plays is shown to be performed in ways which sustain the mystery inherent in it, and this is seen against a background of belief in what was familiar though it had a sustained spiritual reference.

Key words

biblical versions – belief – mystery – staging – audience response – paradramatic elements

1   The Scope of This Enquiry

The presentation of the Resurrection in medieval plays is remarkable for its copiousness, for its variety and for its central function in the narrative of salvation which informs many plays of the period. But this plenitude presents us with some ambiguous and paradoxical aspects which lead to questions about the means by which the episodes in the scriptural accounts were developed into dramatic form and how the dramatization was used to further the experience of the Bible. In this complex process we may, however, find indications of the nature and function of the religious drama in medieval society and of the ways in which the audiences were induced to take part in an experience which was at the same time religious and theatrical. To consider these matters we shall here look at a selection of dramatic texts which feature the biblical narrative of the Resurrection, but which embody dramatic experience in different ways. The plays chosen include some which are free standing, and some which form part of larger theatrical and religious structures and so function in the light of the context into which they were created. There are also differences in scope as one of them, *Le Mystère de la Résurrection* (Angers, 1456) is a three-day version of some 19,895 lines, whereas others are much shorter, sometimes because they have to fit in with the requirements of urban processional performance, or in a church within a ceremony.

In itself the Resurrection could have been seen as a culmination of the history of salvation as it was the moment of triumph when Man was saved through Christ's redemption. Yet most of the texts that survive are remarkably limited in what they reveal about how this climactic moment was shown to the audiences. In many ways it remains mysterious because the texts are often frustratingly brief. In part this may be due to the need to indicate that something mysterious was being suggested, and some of the psychological effect lay in the necessity to show that Christ was both present and absent at the critical moment.[1] As far as the narrative was concerned, the episode marked a change in his status: he was transformed here from a vulnerable human being into a triumphant divinity who still retained human characteristics, and it was necessary to see him in these two different aspects. An interpretation of how these processes worked must largely depend upon the nature of the surviving texts and their relationship to what can be deduced about different kinds of performance and the varying relationship with those participating. In the light of some aspects of modern scholarship these texts need careful appraisal. Along with this, we need to consider the narrative core which is at the heart of the dramatizations and is largely derived from the gospel accounts, supplemented as it is by a number of non-scriptural elements.

The plays under consideration here are:

La Seinte Resureccion
York   38 The Resurrecton
     39 Christ's Appearance to Mary Magdalene

---

[1] Sarah Beckwith, *Signifying God: Social Relation and Symbolic Act in the York Corpus Christi Plays* (Chicago: University of Chicago Press, 2001), 73.

Chester	18 The Resurrection
Towneley	26 Resurrection
N-Town	34 The Burial, The Guarding of the Sepulchre
	35 The Harrowing of Hell (Part II), Christ's Appearance to Mary, Pilate and the Soldiers
	36 The Announcement to the Three Marys, Peter and John at the Sepulchre
	37 The Appearance to Mary Magdalene

Le Mystère de la Résurrection (Angers 1456)
Christ's Burial and Christ's Resurrection (MS Bodley e Museo 160: 'Digby')
The Resurrection of Our Lord.[2]

These are but a sample of the surviving plays treating the Resurrection, but it is hoped that they can each yield something distinctive to the discussion here.[3] It is apparent from this list that the coverage of the Resurrection could be presented and divided in a number of different ways, a variety which is closely related to different approaches of staging.

2   Core Events in the Resurrection

The events which comprise the narrative of the Resurrection are remarkably consistent in many dramatic versions of the episode. They are determined largely by the accounts in the four gospels even though individually there are

---

[2] References are to these editions: *La Seinte Resureccion*, ed. T.A. Jenkins, J.M. Manly, M.K. Pope and J.G. Wright (Oxford: Blackwell, 1943); *The York Plays: A Critical Edition of the York Corpus Christi Play as recorded in British Library Additional MS 35290*, ed. Richard Beadle, 2 vols., EETS s.s. 23–24 (Oxford: Oxford University Press, 2009–13); *The Chester Mystery Cycle*, ed. R.M. Lumiansky and David Mills, 2 vols., EETS s.s. 3 and 9 (Oxford: Oxford University Press, 1974–86); *The Towneley Plays,* ed. Martin Stevens and A.C. Cawley, 2 vols., EETS s.s. 13 (Oxford: Oxford University Press, 1991); *The N-Town Play: Cotton Vespasian D.8*, ed. Stephen Spector, 2 vols., EETS s.s. 11 (Oxford : Oxford University Press, 1991); *Le Mystère de la Résurrection (Angers 1456)*, ed. Pierre Servet, 2 vols. (Geneva: Droz, 1993); *Christ's Burial* and *Christ's Resurrection* in *The Late Medieval Religious Plays of Bodleian MSS. Digby 133 and e Museo 160*, ed. Donald C. Baker, John L. Murphy and Louis B. Hall Jr., EETS 283 (Oxford: Oxford University Press, 1982); *The Resurrection of Our Lord,* ed. J.D. Wilson, B. Dobell and W.W. Greg, Malone Society Reprint (Oxford: Oxford University Press, 1913).

[3] Alexandra F. Johnston has a valuable review of the dating and distribution of Resurrection plays in "The Emerging Pattern of the Easter Play in England," *Medieval English Theatre* 20 (1998): 3–23. Many of these items are references without a text, but their frequency and popularity cannot be doubted.

differences between these primary witnesses.[4] But there are also elements not found in the Bible but which are associated with the narrative and are often part of it. It appears that there was a commonly held accumulation of events which the dramatists were able to draw upon. This core comprises the following:

> The Harrowing of Hell carried out by Anima Christi
> Joseph asks Pilate for Christ's Body in order to bury it
> The Centurion's affirmation that Christ is the Son of God
> Longinus pierces the body and his sight is restored
> Recall by Pilate and others of Christ's prophecy that the Resurrection would occur on the third day
> The burial watched by the women
> Fear of the High Priests, alleging that the disciples would steal Christ's body
> The Watch set with Pilate's agreement
> The Resurrection itself [which is not described in detail]
> The Watch overcome
> Earthquake and other signs
> The stone is rolled away from the tomb
> The Marys come to the tomb where they see the Angel or Angels who confirm that the Resurrection has happened and that Christ has gone away into Galilee
> The Angel or Angels send the women to tell the disciples
> Christ's speech after the Resurrection
> Christ visits his mother
> Peter and John run to the tomb and enter it
> Mary Magdalene, lamenting, sees the empty tomb and meets Christ, mistaking him at first for a gardener
> The Watch reports the Resurrection and their response to the High Priests and Pilate, and are bribed to blame the disciples for stealing the body.

Of these events only the Harrowing of Hell, Christ's speech after the Resurrection, and his visit to his mother are not in the biblical accounts.[5] As it stands this list is roughly chronological, but it is apparent that the order of events could be altered. For example, in the more common version to be found

---

4   See Matthew 27:51–66, 28:1–15; Mark 15:39–47, 16:1–10; Luke 23:47–56, 24:1–12; and John 19:31–42, 20:1–18.
5   Longinus is not actually named in the gospels and he is not described as being blind, there being no mention of his miraculous restoration; see John 19:34.

in the York Plays, the arrival of the Marys at the tomb comes before the report of the Watch to Pilate, whereas these are reversed in Chester.

In considering how these events were presented to the audiences, it cannot be doubted that there was a great deal of direct exposure to the language of the Bible and, whatever the level of understanding of Latin by individuals, familiarity with the words of the Bible must have been high. Yet there remains an issue over how far congregations could understand all that they heard, as the controversy over the need for vernacular versions illustrates. The development and dissemination of the Wycliffite Bible and the response against it embodied in the *Constitutions* of Archbishop Arundel in 1409, very close in time to the beginnings of mystery cycles, are pertinent indications of the importance of this problem. Possibly the prohibitions in the *Constitutions* were a stimulus to innovation.[6] Other vernacular sources were evolved to explain, and make more accessible the details of the biblical account, as was indeed the case for many other parts of the biblical record apart from the Resurrection. The apocryphal *Gospel of Nicodemus*, *The Northern Passion*, and Nicholas Love's *Mirror of the Blessed Life of Jesus Christ* can all be seen as contributing to accessibility and they contain details which are taken over in the process of dramatization.[7] In spite of the constraint on altering the Bible in Arundel's *Constitutions*, Love makes the case for imaginative reconstruction of scriptural events and he appears to have been convincing at the time and to have been accepted by Arundel. Love's heading for Easter Sunday implies a need to explain his departure from what is found in the Bible: "Of þe gloriouse resurrexion of oure Lorde Jesu & how he first apered to his modere as it may be reasonably trowede."[8] The result is that the core account of the Resurrection was embellished by what came to be thought of as well-known additions, even though a formal record was not written down: it would have remained understood and expected in spite of the absence of a textual record. The fact that this material came to

---

6 Pamela M. King, *The York Mystery Cycle and the Worship of the City* (Cambridge: Brewer, 2006), 16. See Peter Happé, "Genre and the Fifteenth-century Drama: The Case of Thomas Chaundler's *Liber Apologeticus*," *Medium Aevum* 82 (2013): 66–80.

7 See *The Middle-English Harrowing of Hell and Gospel of Nicodemus*, ed. William Henry Hulme, EETS e.s. 100 (London: Kegan Paul, 1907), ll. 1699–1812; *The Northern Passion*, ed. Frances A. Foster, EETS o. s. 147 (London: Kegan Paul, 1916), ll. 1917–2072: *Nicholas Love's Mirror of the Blessed Life of Jesus Christ: A Critical Edition based on Cambridge University Library MSS 6578 and 6686*, ed. Michael G. Sargent (New York and London: Garland, 1992), 199–208.

8 Sargent, *Love's Mirror*, 195.

be used in visual representations of the Resurrection must have increased its familiarity and given it further interest.[9]

3 Experiencing the Resurrection

Awareness of and response to the scriptural accounts of the Resurrection will have informed the process of dramatization. We can approach this by considering some aspects of the information which had to be communicated. As the core of events incorporated in Resurrection drama suggests, the scriptural accounts contain elements of a different nature. The following interpretations are possible, working from the core outlined above. The significance of the Harrowing which immediately precedes the Resurrection is that it shows Christ as supernatural, triumphantly saving the faithful from the damage of the Fall and overcoming Satan. But the human body of Christ has to be buried, a contrasting moment of great sorrow, and this is done in the worldly circumstances of his suffering and death in the corrupt human world, without awareness of the Resurrection, even though it had been prophesied in the biblical account. The worldly context may account for the enlargement of the vernacular details in the raising of the Watch and the subsequent exposure of the corruption of truth which the narrative of the Watch develops in its second phase, with the active participation of Pilate. Such a corruption is the obverse of the need to ensure that the truth of the Resurrection is known and sustained. The portrayal of corruption, however, did not necessarily take the same form. Thus we find that the York Pilate is more cunning, more inclined to temporize than his boastful and bombastic counterpart in Towneley. In *The Resurrection of Our Lord* Pilate appears even more hesitant than in York, asking at one point "howe coulde I, I praye you, have Donne more for hym || then this?" (ll. 39–40). In the context of this earthly corruption, faith in Christ's divinity has to be asserted through the unlikely witness of the Centurion who might have been expected to be a hostile and incredulous stranger. His testimony and the evidence of disturbances in the natural world have to be presented. He also represents the dissemination of belief beyond Christ's immediate circle. After the burial the moment of Resurrection has to be accounted for, and then there is another

---

9 For the Protestant view that sight was superior to hearing if it allowed one to see through objects rather than at them, see Arthur F. Marotti, "In Defence of Idolatry: Residual Catholic Culture and the Protestant Assault on the Sensuous in Early Modern England," in *Redrawing the Map of Early Modern English Catholicism*, ed. Lowell Gallagher (Toronto: University of Toronto Press, 2012), 29.

supernatural intervention as the Angel(s) are given the role of confirming the truth of the Resurrection to the Marys. These characters have to convey something of broad significance in their emotional reaction which starts with sorrow and is eventually turned to joy. Once the certainty of the Resurrection is established, the Marys are told to spread the news of it by the Angel and there follows the process by which this dissemination is achieved, as well as having due attention to the continuing spread of certainty through Christ's own appearances to his followers and others.

The need to be faithful to the scriptural texts must have meant that these differing elements had to be presented in the dramatization and this has led to decisions about how to communicate the events concerned. Traditional non-dramatic modes were available through the liturgy and this meant that the common experience of the music in the liturgy could be used by dramatists to help realise the performance. Such material would have powerful emotional connotations and these would have helped to make the events more accessible. However, the accretion of non-scriptural material was also available and this was used in particular for the images of worldly corruption which sought to inhibit the worthy spread and contemplation of the central events as well as the mystery of the Resurrection. The effects of the Resurrection on the corrupt world as well as upon the followers of Christ are essential for the presentation of its significance.

Besides the impact of the Scripture itself the decisions of the dramatists must have been affected by the music of the liturgy as well as by many elements embedded in iconographic tradition. Many of these would have been familiar experiences whenever people went to church and they would have been appreciated by the very fact of their familiarity. It is interesting that dramatists made extensive use of such material even though they modified it.[10] Moreover, it has been pointed out that contact with the Bible, reading it, hearing it read, hearing it sung can be seen as an act of worship.[11] Such acts frequently, even usually, depend largely upon the recreating of what is familiar and reassuring. Drama works at different levels and whilst at one level an

---

10   For the musical background see Richard Rastall, *Music in Early Religious Drama*, 2 vols., (Cambridge: Cambridge University Press, 1996–2001). For location of iconographic details, especially at York, see Clifford Davidson, "Memory, the Resurrection, and Early Drama," in Idem, *Selected Studies in Drama and Renaissance Literature* (New York: AMS Press, 2006), 3–37. Sarah Beckwith, "Absent Presences: The Theatre of Resurrection in York," in *Medieval Literature: Criticism and Debate*, ed. by Holly A. Crocker and D. Vance Smith (London and New York: Routledge, 2014), 450, describes "an interaction between memory and performance" and "perpetually re-lived and always present enaction."

11   King, *The York Mystery Cycle*, 31.

onlooker may be pleased or intrigued by the way a narrative turns out, at another level a repetition of what is familiar can be exciting and indeed involve powerful emotional experience: this would be particularly true for the lamentation of the women over Christ's death which was regularly presented *in extenso* before the Resurrection could be appreciated. Such renewal with the familiar could be musical, but it would also be capable of a strong visual impact in the appearance of the three women dressed in black for mourning.

After this preparation we come to what might be the central item in these plays, the Resurrection itself. Most of the dramatic versions under review here are extraordinarily limited in what they tell us about how this central event was performed.[12] In some cases dialogue after the event by the Angels and the Watch give some details in retrospect, and it could be that performing the moment when Christ rose from the tomb was so obvious that it needed nothing to be said about it. But mystery remains.[13] Some versions refer to a musical performance at this critical moment. Because such items were familiar from such liturgical ceremonies as the Easter Sepulchre, the interaction of these well-known elements with the present physical manifestation within the minds of onlookers must have been significant. It may well be that the drama of such an event is potent because it is a moment when the ritual comes to life.[14]

There is little doubt that the Holy Week liturgy, comprising the musical items in the *depositio*, the *elevatio*, the *visitatio* and the *Peregrini* would be much in the minds of those watching a Resurrection Play.[15] We should also notice that church rituals involved processions and the impact of these would be another feature likely to have an effect upon Resurrection drama. In both cases there was a separation of the participants from the onlookers, but it is apparent that the dynamics of the two were somewhat different. Because at

---

12 Lynette R. Muir, *The Biblical Drama of Medieval Europe* (Cambridge: Cambridge University Press, 1995), 139, has noted that in some German plays an Angel summons Christ to rise. This may be the result of an urge to make the action more realistic.

13 Interpreting a stage direction Rosemary Woolf, *The English Mystery Plays* (London: Routledge, 1972), 274 and n. 14, suggested that in Arnoul Gréban's *Le Mystère de la Passion* a successful dramatic moment was achieved by having Christ arise from the tomb in complete silence.

14 Meg Twycross, "Playing 'The Resurrection,'" in *Medieval Studies for J.A.W. Bennet aetatis suae LXX*, ed. P.L. Heyworth (Oxford: Clarendon Press, 1981), 290. See also Pamela M. Sheingorn, *The Easter Sepulchre in England* (Kalamazoo, MI: Medieval Institute Publications, 1987), 55–58.

15 Karl Young, *The Drama of the Medieval Church*, 2 vols. (Oxford: Clarendon Press, 1927), 1: 201–539, documents liturgical plays associated with Easter.

York and Chester the dramatic events were presented through an experience of procession, and some French and German cycles contained procession within their action it seems that such elements were valued. In the case of York the procession of the plays was closely associated with the Corpus Christi Procession which eventually took place in the sixteenth century on the day after the performance of the plays.[16]

4   Individual Dramatizations

In considering the central moments of the Resurrection itself we find many similarities which suggest common purposes, but there are differences which may be revealing. As noted, the varying status of individual texts affects how we can interpret the decisions of dramatists on how to present the events.

La Sainte Resureccion has survived in two fragments in Anglo-Norman, one from Canterbury in the late thirteenth century and one from Paris slightly later. Working from the stage directions, the editors have made a case for the twelfth-century original to have been a dramatic text which appears to have been modified for meditational purposes. The Prologue, which was probably written after the change of purpose, sets out requirements for "lieux" and "mansions" implying an ample acting area, with fixed structures for certain characters, but with locations designated at places in between. The stage directions are presented in rhymed verse which suggests that they might have been recited. If that is so, it might have been envisaged that a dramatic performance would be circumscribed by some kind of director, a "meneur de jeu" perhaps, managing the presentation. However, the grammar of these directions uses imperatives and the future tense, suggesting that they really were meant to tell the actors what to do.

The two fragments overlap with many details the same, and they end at roughly the same point in the Resurrection narrative when the Watch has been set up and Joseph of Arimathea is arrested on suspicion of unauthorised removal of the body. The staging requirements in the Prologue, however, indicate that Heaven and Hell were to be set up, together with a crucifix, a place for Pilate, one for the Marys and the disciples, and Galilee and the "castle" at Emaus (ll. 11–34, Canterbury text). These indicate that the whole play must have gone on to include many items characteristic of the Resurrection story.

---

16   For the relationship at York between the Corpus Christi Procession and that embodying the plays see Alexandra F. Johnston, "The Procession and Play of Corpus Christi in York after 1426," *Leeds Studies in English* NS 7 (1973–74): 55–62.

There are notable differences in the status of the texts in the four English cycles. In *York* there is no doubt that for many years performances took place on the feast of Corpus Christi on pageant wagons which stopped at ascertainable locations around the city. The surviving text is a register of the plays compiled in about 1476–77 which was subsequently used as a check on performances each year. Some of the changes are marked on it by the town clerk.[17] The overall narrative, substantially, but not entirely biblical, was divided into sections for performance by craft guilds. Because of the dynamic of the procession which had to be completed in one day, the individual sections could not be very long and thus long sequences like the Nativity or the Passion were subdivided, with individual guilds performing segments. Chester presents some parallels in that craft guilds performed episodes of comparable size on pageant wagons drawn through the streets but the relationship of the surviving cycle texts to performance is much more problematic. For one thing there were many changes, probably from year to year, and the versions of the whole cycle that have come down to us are all later than 1590, some years after performances had ceased. Crucially there is very little information available about the contents of performances before 1521. This means that the survivals are more likely to be informative about the sixteenth century rather than earlier. Whereas the earlier York Register was an official record of performance, as far as it could be written down, we do not have a text of similar authority for Chester.

In *Towneley* and *N-Town* the function and purpose of the surviving texts differ further. They are both collections of plays from different provenances, and there is very little to suggest that either was ever performed in the form presented in the manuscripts. The *Towneley* texts are a retrospective collection with different origins and authors, some of them from before 1500, put together in the sixteenth century, possibly during the reign of Queen Mary. The status of the surviving manuscript (HM1 at the Huntington Library) may be slanted more towards it being a document for reading and contemplation rather than a register of what was actually performed year by year in Wakefield streets. Five of the individual plays are closely associated with corresponding items in York, the Harrowing and the Resurrection among them.[18] Whilst we can be sure that there was a performance on wagons in the streets at York, there is no certainty about how the whole *Towneley* text was presented – if it ever was.

---

17   Peter Meredith, "John Clerke's Hand in the York Register," *Leeds Studies in English* NS 12 (1981): 245–71.
18   Peter Happé, *The Towneley Cycle: Unity and Diversity* (Cardiff: University of Wales Press, 2007), 28–29.

In *N-Town* the texts of the Resurrection sequence are independent of the other three cycle versions. Though the structure of events is broadly similar to that at York, Christ visits his mother after the Resurrection in a joyful encounter (35.97–136). Some indication of the separateness of parts of the Resurrection sequence is apparent in the verse forms and stage directions.[19] The Resurrection sequence, spread over four separate plays, forms a part of Passion Play 2, itself a distinct sequence which begins with its own introduction by Contemplacio. Marginal additions indicate that a Resurrection play might have been extracted for a separate performance.[20]

We find that the text of the *York* version at the critical moment of the Resurrection is tantalizingly brief. Once the Watch is set, there is the ambiguous stage direction *"Tunc Jesu resurgente"* (38.186), followed immediately by the beginning of the speech of the first Mary as she approaches the tomb, which is a shift in time to an event afterwards. It is apparent from what ensues that the Resurrection takes place at the moment covered by the stage direction.[21] The latter may suggest that the Easter antiphon *Jesus resurgens* (Jesus Rising) be sung, but, alternatively, the grammar of the direction, in the ablative case, may carry the sense that Mary does not speak until Christ has risen to the accompaniment of the song. This textual obscurity is of long standing because the Town Clerk later in the sixteenth century added *"Tunc Angelus cantat Resurgens"* in the margin (38.186 s.d) and in the present tense, indicating that for a performance he saw, there is no doubt that the Angel (a "ʒonge childe" [boy], 38.225) sang the antiphon. Our interpretation of the physical detail of what actually happened on the stage has to rely upon conjecture, but there is some help from iconographic parallels. Traditionally Christ is shown rising from the tomb, carrying a cross staff with a pennant, and as he climbs out he steps upon one of the sleeping soldiers. Later the First Soldier says that he "wente his way" (38.332) perhaps suggesting that he came down from the wagon and walked away through the crowd in the York street. Christ here is conspicuously silent unlike some of the other versions we have noticed. There

---

19 Peter Meredith, *The Passion Play from the N-Town Manuscript* (London and New York: Longman, 1990), 245.

20 The marginal notes "Incipit hic" (34.158) and "finem [prim]a die Nota" (below 35.304) suggest a possible structure and the second implies that when extracted the sequence was performed on more than one day. One note referring to Cain (34.40) and another for a devil (34.64) indicate that additional speeches were written or proposed for the extract, but no text has survived (Meredith, *The Passion Play*, Appendix 5, 252–54).

21 There is no precedent for showing the actual Resurrection in the liturgical drama (Beadle, *York Plays*, 2: 364).

is, however, a retrospective mention of a "melodie" by the Fourth Soldier (38.385) which may confirm that there was a musical element.

The differences between the dramatizations of the Resurrection in the *York* and *Towneley* texts are intriguing because the *Towneley* text is plainly derived from the *York* version, with some additions. *Towneley* 26 has a different, more boastful introductory speech by Pilate (ll. 1–35), a more elaborate declaration by the Centurion of Christ's divinity, including reference to signs of it in nature (ll. 51–75), and a monologue by Christ after the Resurrection which draws attention to his sufferings on the cross and is closely related to lyric poems with this emphasis (ll. 230–350). At the end the *Towneley* dramatist has added a scene between Mary Magdalene and Christ, differing from the separate version in *York* 39 (ll. 579–659). These changes are highlighted by prosodic differences. If the compilation of *Towneley* does indeed date from the reign of Queen Mary these alterations may be motivated by ideological objectives relevant to her intention to prompt a return to traditional catholic values. There are some hints of uncomfortable comedy in the performance of the Watch as there appears to be some jostling around the tomb (26.221) and in the exaggeration of the alleged intruders (26.485). At the point of Resurrection the stage direction is more specific than at York: "*Tunc cantabunt angeli 'Christus resurgens', et postea dicet Iesus:*" (26.229 s.d.; Then Angels shall sing "Christ Rising," and afterwards Jesus shall say). Once again the text and directions are sparse about details of what was actually shown. Here there appears to be an abrupt transition from the setting of the Watch to the subsequent action, except that Jesus speaks his added lyric presentation of his physical suffering. This may suggest that the wounds from the crucifixion are visible, and it might be associated with catholic rather than protestant sentiment. The comments of the Watch show that they were confused by what happened to them. The Second Soldier claims that he saw Christ go (26.478), as might have been the case in York, but the Third is afraid that they shall have to admit to Pilate that they were sleeping when Christ left (26.477–78). A possible explanation for this contradiction comes from iconography in which some images show the Watch asleep, but with open eyes so that they witness what is happening.[22]

In *Chester* there are again touches of humour in the Watch episode and in Pilate who speaks terrible French (18.1–8) and uses lumpy alliteration. The soldiers are given pretentious chivalric names (which have not been successfully identified) and they are ridiculously boastful. One wonders how comic lines like this threat might have seemed:

> For and he ones have up his head

---

[22] Meredith, *The Passion Play*, 222, n. 1560–67.

>   but that he be soone dead,
>   shall I never eate more bread. (18.118–20)

The crude rhyming prevents serious belief. At another point Pilate comes out with an egregiously inappropriate oath in the circumstances: "by Jesu that dyed on roode" (18.74). In this version the stage direction at the point of Resurrection specifically requires that the two Angels shall sing "*Christus resurgens a mortuis*" and then Christ shall arise.[23] In some variant texts the direction requires that he shake the Soldiers with his foot, as in the visual imagery.[24] When they awake, the dramatist returns to their ambiguous state of consciousness. The First Soldier says his eyes were blind, while the Third says he had no power to rise upright and fight the "two beastes" (18.214). This implies that he did see something of the arrival of the Angels. The account is further embroidered when they report to Pilate, as the Third Soldier claims:

>   Hee rose up, as I saye nowe.
>   And lefte us lyenge, I wott nere howe,
>   all bemased and in a swoone
>   as we had binne stycked swine. (18.262–65)

However comic this may have been for many of the onlookers it must have been measured against the serious account in Matthew which says that the keepers shook for fear and became as dead men (Matthew 28:4). The dramatist takes the interesting step of putting this sequence about the reactions of the Watch immediately after the speech by Jesus, and before the arrival of the weeping Marys raises the emotional pitch, first to sorrow and then joy.

In *N-Town* the dramatization was made for different staging arrangements, which had several locations for individual characters in a place and scaffold configuration. The Resurrection sequence has plenty of directions about movement as the action switches between the locations or scaffolds and characters are brought into the action. Thus Pilate allows Joseph to take down the body and place it in the tomb. Mary thanks Joseph for having done this, and he and Nicodemus go away leaving the women at the tomb. Attention shifts to Pilate who sets up the Watch, and the Knights go to the tomb and take their places. They are followed by Pilate, Annas and Cayphas who seal the tomb and return to their own scaffolds while the Knights are overcome with sleep. Anima Christi leads Adam and the other souls from hell, binds Beliall and returns to

---

23   The use of *Christus Resurgens* in three texts underlines its value in performance.
24   Lumiansky and Mills, *Chester Cycle*, 18.152 s.d. and textual notes 1: 345.

the tomb. The stage direction embodies sequential action: "*Tunc transiet Anima Christi ad resuscitandum corpus; quo resuscitato dicat Jesus*" (35.72 s.d.; Then the Spirit of Christ shall go to the resurrection of his body;[25] when it is resurrected Jesus shall say.)

The Knights wake up, recalling the disturbance in nature and immediately recognise that the Resurrection has occurred even though they were apparently asleep (35.137–52). They go to Pilate and their report to him puts the Resurrection beyond doubt: "on ground on lyve he goth, || Qwycke and levynge man" (35.179–80). Believing them, Pilate holds a council and he bribes the Knights with gold to say that the disciples stole the body (35.275–79). The bribery is scriptural (Matthew 28:12), but there it is the chief priests who provide the money and the change fits with Pilate's crafty character in this dramatization.

The manuscripts of the Digby plays of *Christ's Burial* and *Christ's Resurrection* reveal a state of transition from primarily a meditative document to one related to performance. The first heading is for "The prologe of this treyte [treatise] or meditation ..." (fol. 140ʳ), while at the end of the Prologue there is a direction in red which begins: "This is a play to be played, on[e] part on Gud Friday afternone, and þe other part opon Ester Day after the resurrection in the morowe" (fol. 140ᵛ). Signs of the change of purpose are apparent in the excision of narrative material and the fact that speakers' names and stage directions are cramped until *Burial* 435, after which they are neatly spaced.[26] Several features of the manuscript make clear that the objective was performance, albeit that it was going to be one in which liturgical elements had a dominating effect. For example once Christ, mistaken for a gardener, appears to Mary Magdalene there is not much action and there is a musical dialogue between the Marys and three disciples, as is detailed in an extensive stage direction, showing how the words of the liturgical sequence *Victimi Pascali* are to be divided between the singers voices (*Resurrection* 690 s.d.). The text does, however, contain notable indications of "spectakille" (*Burial* 101) and some of the dialogue indicates that there was a visual representation of the crucifixion on the stage.[27] Mary Magdalene has a major part in both these plays and there is much emphasis upon the extent and persistence of her sorrows, musically and otherwise, but eventually the joyful news of the Resurrection is celebrated (*Resurrection* 755 s.d.). In the staging of *Christ's Resurrection* the action does not include the

---

25 The grammatical construction of the Latin here expresses purpose.
26 Baker, Murphy and Hall, *Late Medieval Religious Plays*, lxxxix, n. 1, remark: "The materials here were never a play or there would have been no need to turn them into one."
27 "he hinges here" (*Burial* 71), "com nere" (ibid., 85), "beholde and see" (ibid., 89), "this rood" (ibid., 128).

Resurrection itself and Christ himself does not appear until he speaks to Mary Magdalene "*in specie ortulani*" (l. 601 s.d.), which implies that he dressed as a gardener here, rather than that Mary mistook him for one. This narrative is largely dependent upon the gospels in that the Resurrection is referred to as having happened when the Marys are informed by the Angel (l. 137).

By contrast the larger scope of the Angers *Mystère*, with its many stage directions, provides a much more detailed presentation of the key moments of the Resurrection than any of the others considered here. Attributed to Jean du Prier, the extant manuscript was created in the mid-fifteenth century at a time when plays on a large scale lasting for several days became popular in France. This text comprises a three-day scheme, with the first concentrating on the Harrowing of Hell; the second and largest contains the bulk of the Resurrection narrative; and the third, including the Ascension and Pentecost, is substantially an affirmation of faith conveyed through sermons.[28] There was a performance in Angers on 29–31 May 1456, but the extant text does not necessarily refer directly to it. A complex staging area is required, with separate named locations. Of the plays under review here this version gives us the fullest detail of how the moment of Resurrection was enacted because of the necessity to explain how this set was to be used. The didactic stance of this work involves much address to the audience and the didactic mode is highlighted by Christ's address to his mother after the Resurrection when he sits her by his side and speaks a "lay" on love (ll. 6658–783). Remarkably the didactic function and the need to preach the faith is emphasized at the end of the third day by recital of versions of the Creed in Hebrew, Greek (text omitted), and Latin by Peter, and in French, German and Breton by John.

From the stage directions it is possible to gain an impression of how the action was managed and how it flowed. Pierre Servet, the editor, considers that this dramatization follows the common French pattern for large-scale plays having a series of "mansions" for individual characters. He shows that they must have been arranged in a straight line or a curved semi-circle with a space behind separated from the audience and beyond their view, though they could see into the mansions themselves as well as outside them.[29] This is made more likely because, some directions indicate that actors were to go under the ground ("Jhesus ... doit aller par dessoubz terre," l. 6252 s.d.) from

---

28 Sermons were a distinctive feature of the French *Passions*: see Charles Mazouer, "Sermons in the *Passions* of Mercadé, Gréban and Jean Michel," in *Les Mystères: Studies in Genre, Text and Theatricality*, ed. Peter Happé and Wim Hüsken (Amsterdam and New York: Rodopi, 2012), 247–69.

29 Servet, *Mystère*, 61–63.

DRAMATIZING THE RESURRECTION

one location to another. The directions do not reveal how these passageways were constructed.[30]

The plentiful and elaborate stage directions which describe the action in some detail reveal the following sequence:[31]

> – Magdalene and three women leave the mother of Jesus to go to the tomb, with ointments, and wait secretly until it is time to go forward. "And Jesus, dressed in white, with bare feet and accompanied by three Angels, that is, Michael, Raphael and Uriel, must suddenly and subtly burst from the ground near to the tomb by a little wooden trap door covered with turf and grassy earth, which re-closes so that it cannot be seen." There is an earthquake and the four guards fall flat, unable to move until they go to tell the Jews of the Resurrection. Jesus speaks sitting on the tomb (l. 6235 s.d.).
> – Kneeling, the three Angels sing as Jesus sits on the tomb. Jesus accompanied by the Angels walks about the place ("champ") and then goes under the ground to his mother who is alone in the cenacle, ready to appear at the appropriate time. God speaks to Gabriel who is dressed in white and has a red face ([a mask?]; l. 6252 s.d.).
> – [God instructs Gabriel to go and move the stone and tell the women that Jesus is already risen (in dialogue).]
> – Gabriel descends from heaven, removes the stone and sits on the right of the tomb before the women arrive (l. 6294 s.d.).
> – The Mother of Jesus kneels, alone in the cenacle (l. 6370 s.d.).
> – Jesus appears to his Mother and speaks (l. 6427 s.d.).
> – Jesus with the three Angels goes back under the ground (l. 6913 s.d.).
> – The women, on their way to the tomb, kiss the ground and the cross where Jesus suffered (ll. 6995 s.d., 7013 s.d., 7021 s.d., 7027 s.d., 7043 s.d.).
> – The women go to the tomb where Gabriel, described again, speaks to them (l. 7075 s.d.).
> – The women leave the tomb to go to the disciples in Jerusalem, at a different place from the cenacle where the Mother is (l. 7095 s.d.). This is repeated when they reach the disciples (l. 7363 s.d.).

---

30 Possibly there was a system of tunnels under the main acting area: Donald Clive Stuart, *Stage Decoration in France in the Middle Ages* (New York: Colombia University Press, 1910), 137.

31 I have paraphrased these extensive directions, translating one particular quotation. The events of the Resurrection of Carinus and Leonicus, which are interwoven with the narrative about Christ, are ignored here.

– John and Peter run to the tomb where they find the empty shroud and bandages, but no Angels because they have hidden themselves under the ground (l. 7477 s.d.).
– Peter and John enter the tomb (l. 7495 s.d.).
– John goes back to the other disciples but Peter returns to the hole ("fosse") where he had been and speaks as he goes in the field (l. 7571 s.d.).

This presentation of the Resurrection sequence is close to the gospel accounts, but it indicates that by managing features of the stage layout a sequence of theatrically appreciable events could be shown and made to interact. Though the events are shown in imagined detail, it is clear that this dramatization has a close relationship with the other shorter versions noticed here. It is striking that such a parallel should arise a between different countries and differing theatrical traditions.

The speech made by Christ before the coming of the Marys functions in different ways in several plays. Sometimes this is made in connection with a visit to his mother, but not always. In the *Towneley* version the dramatist has added a speech for Christ, calling upon a lyric tradition which dwells upon the physical pains endured on the cross. Although the speech is not biblical it clearly is an allusion to the words previously spoken by Christ on the cross and thus it does have a kind of scriptural dimension.[32] Though the text is very close to the lyric versions it does provide several opportunities for visual gesture as Christ invites the onlookers: "Lo, how I hold myn armes on brade, || The to saue ay redy mayde!" (20.325–6).

The dynamic of the *Chester* text works rather differently, in part because the order of events here moves the biblical Marys sequence to after the Soldiers' report to Pilate. The resurrected Christ addresses the audience directly as though they were in his presence. However, his speech concentrates upon the sacrament itself and this may well be a reflection of the relatively late date of this cycle, whose surviving texts can be seen to take some account of the role of the Eucharist which became controversial under the impact of protestant revaluation.[33] The preceding stage direction requires that Christ shakes the sleeping soldiers as he rises from the tomb and he immediately tells earthly

---

32 The lyric parallel was noted by George C. Taylor, "The Relation of the English Corpus Christi Play to The Middle English Religious Lyric," *Modern Philology* 5 (1907): 26–27): see also Carleton Brown, *Religious Lyrics of the Fifteenth Century* (Oxford: Clarendon Press, 1952), 151–56, no. 102.

33 For the Puritan opposition to the plays see David Mills, *Recycling the Cycle: The City of Chester and its Whitsun Plays* (Toronto: University of Toronto Press, 1998), 145–52.

man to "awake out of thy sleepe" (18.155). Perhaps this is a protestant prompt, but the dramatist appears rather cautious in what follows, as the editors have noticed. More than two of Christ's four stanzas in this speech are devoted to his body as the "verey bread of life" and he seems to hint at the controversy over transubstantiation when he asserts that his flesh "becomes my fleshe through your beleefe" (18.174). The fact that he refers to bread, but not wine may also be a reflection of controversy because of the protestant insistence upon communion of both kinds.

In *N-Town* Christ's speeches combine the concern about the Eucharist with a visit to Mary. The latter is not scriptural and there is a link with Nicholas Love's *Mirror* where the visit is also included.[34] The first lines of his speech are close in wording to a passage in The Harrowing of Hell.[35] Like *Chester*, this version associates Christ's suffering with his flesh made into bread: "For man I haue mad my body in brede, || His sowle for to fede" (35.83–84). But the conversation with his mother is concerned with her worship, suggesting that this episode was meant to support catholic devotion to Mary. It is developed emotionally, striking a joyful mood for the first time (35.104, 118), and there is a sense of new life: "For deth is deed and lyff doth wake" (35.119, echoed at l. 126).[36] The insertion of this episode in *N-Town*, unlike the *York* version, has a structural impact. It is followed by the report of the Watch, and then by the approach of the three Marys at the beginning of Play 37.

Returning to the *Mystère*, we find that Christ appears to his Mother in response to her begging that he will fulfil the prophecy he had made to her. When he does, he turns her sorrow into joy and he speaks at length about the power of love and how that has been his main motivation. She kneels before him, but he raises her to sit by his side and prophesizes her future role as mediator (ll. 6371–913).

In *The Resurrection of Our Lord*, which survives from 1530–60 in four fragments amounting to 1151 lines, the dramatist's protestant allegiance shows itself in persistent attention to biblical detail, including marginal notes giving biblical sources. The play was arranged for a two-day performance. It covers a sequence of episodes from the Centurion's description of events at the time of the crucifixion, through much detail concerning the setting of the Watch, followed by the four Marys being told of the Resurrection by two Angels, to reach

---

34 There is a specific verbal echo at 35.89 in the salutation *Salve, sancta Parens*, noted by Audrey Davidson as the Introit for the Lady-Mass; see Spector, *N-Town*, 521.
35 Spector, *N-Town*, 521.
36 As Meredith, *The Passion Play*, 221, notes, this is an adaptation of an antiphon for Holy Saturday.

a conclusion in the overcoming of the doubts of Thomas. The dramatization is paced by Appendix, a commentator who emphasizes the spiritual life and who makes a number of significant comments about Scripture in relation to what is performed. The dialogue and characterization are noticeably realistic, as though prioritizing a credible representation of real life. Notably Appendix is articulate in defence of the material which is not directly scriptural, and he draws attention to what is invented and seeks to justify the exercise of "ymagenation" (ll. 525, 530). He is particularly concerned with a rejection of what is old and past and he looks forward to walking anew (l. 272), identifying a church of the faithful elected to God (ll. 717–18).

5 Conclusion

Though there are didactic elements in the Resurrection plays, including the exposure of worldliness, the religious experience comprised much that was already familiar and largely justified by biblical precedent. If, as I have suggested, the Resurrection itself was presented somewhat indirectly in the gospels and in the dramatizations, it is likely that memory and recall were also significant. This retrospective aspect is derived from the gospels themselves where the bulk of the information about the Resurrection comes after it has happened through the words of the Angel(s) and at a supernatural level to begin with. This is supplemented by the report of the Watch in Matthew 27:11–15, though in the plays their testimony is somewhat contradictory. The Angel's testimony is more exactly supported by Christ's appearances to Mary Magdalene, Luke and Cleophas at Emmaus, and finally and conclusively to Thomas in the presence of the other disciples. Thus we see that the gospel narrative is preoccupied with establishing and confirming the truth of the Resurrection rather than actually describing it and the dramatists fall in with this for the most part and construct their narrative accordingly.[37] This fidelity includes the impact upon the disciples and the world in general. But the concern we have noticed about justifying the use of the imagination, which is traceable in Nicholas Love's work as well as in *The Resurrection of Our Lord*, suggests that the dramatization of the event induced both musical and visual additions to the rather spare gospel narrative. These elements were stimulated and supported by the use of memory in respect of liturgical practices, and

---

37   For the limits of verbal persuasion about the evidence of the Resurrection see Chester N. Scoville, *Saints and the Audience in Middle English Biblical Drama* (Toronto: University of Toronto Press, 2004), 10–17.

especially in the recall of details of the Passion and its emotional impact on the Marys, and by drawing upon what had been made familiar by non-dramatic imagery and the associations it has generated, such as Christ stepping on the prostrate Soldiers. Among the influences here there could have been the ceremony of the Easter sepulchre which used visual items including carrying the cross and the sacrament in procession. In Pamela Sheingorn's account it is clear that musical elements were also common.[38]

There is a striking contrast between the realistic dialogue of Pilate, the High Priests and the Watch which often has some comic aspects and is commonly satirical, and the use of liturgical elements to express the responses of the Marys which are largely sorrowful, though there is also a modulation into joy and even triumph at times. One of the main thrusts is the concern with credibility because it was necessary to leave no doubt about the actuality of the Resurrection. This accounts for the linguistic concern with legal language which has been found in the text and which substantially contributes to the worldliness and contains social criticism.[39] But whenever doubt was raised about whether Christ had risen, that in itself would presumably have helped to generate a re-affirmation for the onlookers who would tend to separate themselves from the doubts, distancing themselves from what was experienced by the characters in the plays. In the end, however strong the need to remain close to the biblical treatment with its reliance upon memory and the urge to make what was on offer something memorable, it would seem most likely that dramatization inevitably required something spectacular and impressive to give a sensory reality to what was inherently a mystery. Perhaps to dramatize meant realizing a mystery and making it accessible.

Bibliography

Baker, Donald C., John L. Murphy and Louis B. Hall Jr., eds. *The Late Medieval Religious Plays of Bodleian MSS. Digby 133 and e Museo 160.* EETS 283. Oxford: Oxford University Press, 1982.

---

[38] Pamela Sheingorn, *The Easter Sepulchre in England,* 59, and for musical elements see 249, 349, and 364.

[39] See especially the consideration of the word 'maintenance' by Olga Horner, in "'Us Must Make Lies': Witness, Evidence, and Proof in the York *Resurrection*", *Medieval English Theatre* 20 (1998): 24–76.

Beadle, Richard, ed. *The York Plays: A Critical Edition of the York Corpus Christi Play as recorded in British Library Additional MS 35290*, 2 vols. EETS s.s. 23–24. Oxford: Oxford University Press, 2009–13.

Beckwith, Sarah. *Signifying God: Social Relation and Symbolic Act in the York Corpus Christi Plays*. Chicago: University of Chicago Press, 2001.

———. "Absent Presences: The Theatre of Resurrection in York," 441–54. In *Medieval Literature: Criticism and Debate*, edited by Holly A. Crocker and D. Vance Smith. London and New York: Routledge, 2014.

Brown, Carleton. *Religious Lyrics of the Fifteenth Century*. Oxford: Clarendon Press, 1952.

Davidson, Clifford. "Memory, the Resurrection, and Early Drama." In Idem, *Selected Studies in Drama and Renaissance Literature*, 3–37. New York: AMS Press, 2006.

Foster, Frances A., ed. *The Northern Passion*. EETS o. s. 147. London: Kegan Paul, 1916.

Happé, Peter. *The Towneley Cycle: Unity and Diversity*. Cardiff: University of Wales Press, 2007.

———. "Genre and the Fifteenth-century Drama: The Case of Thomas Chaundler's *Liber Apologeticus*." *Medium Aevum* 82 (2013): 66–80.

Hulme, William Henry, ed. *The Middle-English Harrowing of Hell and Gospel of Nicodemus*. EETS e.s. 100. London: Kegan Paul, 1907.

Jenkins, T.A., J.M. Manly, M.K. Pope and J.G. Wright, eds. *La Seinte Resureccion*. Oxford: Blackwell, 1943.

Lumiansky, R.M., and David Mills, eds. *The Chester Mystery Cycle*, 2 vols. EETS s.s. 3 and 9. Oxford: Oxford University Press, 1974–86.

Johnston, Alexandra F. "The Procession and Play of Corpus Christi in York after 1426." *Leeds Studies in English* NS 7 (1973–74): 55–62.

———. "The Emerging Pattern of the Easter Play in England." *Medieval English Theatre* 20 (1998): 3–23.

King, Pamela M. *The York Mystery Cycle and the Worship of the City*. Cambridge: Brewer, 2006.

Marotti, Arthur F. "In Defence of Idolatry: Residual Catholic Culture and the Protestant Assault on the Sensuous in Early Modern England." In *Redrawing the Map of Early Modern English Catholicism*, edited by Lowell Gallagher, 27–51. Toronto: University of Toronto Press, 2012.

Mazouer, Charles. "Sermons in the *Passions* of Mercadé, Gréban and Jean Michel." In *Les Mystères: Studies in Genre, Text and Theatricality*, edited by Peter Happé and Wim Hüsken, 247–69. Amsterdam and New York: Rodopi, 2012.

Meredith, Peter. "John Clerke's Hand in the York Register." *Leeds Studies in English* NS 12 (1981): 245–71.

———. *The Passion Play from the N-Town Manuscript*. London and New York: Longman, 1990.

Mills, David. *Recycling the Cycle: The City of Chester and its Whitsun Plays.* Toronto: University of Toronto Press, 1998.

Muir, Lynette R. *The Biblical Drama of Medieval Europe.* Cambridge: Cambridge University Press, 1995.

Rastall, Richard. *Music in Early Religious Drama,* 2 vols. Cambridge: Cambridge University Press, 1996–2001.

Sargent, Michael G., ed. *Nicholas Love's Mirror of the Blessed Life of Jesus Christ: A Critical Edition based on Cambridge University Library MSS 6578 and 6686.* New York and London: Garland, 1992.

Servet, Pierre, ed. *Le Mystère de la Résurrection (Angers 1456),* 2 vols. Geneva: Droz, 1993.

Sheingorn, Pamela M. *The Easter Sepulchre in England.* Kalamazoo, MI: Medieval Institute Publications, 1987.

Spector, Stephen, ed. *The N-Town Play: Cotton Vespasian D.8,* 2 vols. EETS s.s. 11. Oxford: Oxford University Press, 1991.

Stevens, Martin and A.C. Cawley, eds. *The Towneley Plays,* 2 vols. EETS s.s. 13. Oxford: Oxford University Press, 1991.

Stuart, Donald Clive. *Stage Decoration in France in the Middle Ages.* New York: Colombia University Press, 1910.

Taylor, George C. "The Relation of the English Corpus Christi Play to The Middle English Religious Lyric." *Modern Philology* 5 (1907): 1–38.

Twycross, Meg. "Playing 'The Resurrection'." In *Medieval Studies for J.A.W. Bennet aetatis suae LXX,* edited by P.L. Heyworth, 273–96. Oxford: Clarendon Press, 1981.

Wilson, J.D., B. Dobell and W.W. Greg, eds. *The Resurrection of Our Lord.* Malone Society Reprint. Oxford: Oxford University Press, 1913.

Woolf, Rosemary. *The English Mystery Plays.* London: Routledge, 1972.

Young, Karl. *The Drama of the Medieval Church,* 2 vols. Oxford: Clarendon Press, 1927.

CHAPTER 9

Seeing and Recognizing in the Sacred and New: The Latin Scriptural Plays of Nicholas Grimald

Elisabeth Dutton and Stephanie Allen

Abstract

Nicholas Grimald (1519–62) was the author of six Latin plays, including a nativity play and plays about St Stephen and Athanasius. Two of his plays have survived: the scriptural dramas *Christus Redivivus* (1543) and *Archipropheta* (1548). Grimald participated in the 'Christian Terence' movement which sought to adapt classical models to Christian purposes. In his Latin scriptural drama, Nicholas Grimald yokes the classical with the scriptural, Plautus with Seneca, and the devil with the pagan underworld. His stories are scriptural but he translates scripture from the Latin of the Vulgate into the Latin of Virgil. This essay examines Grimald's use of classical Latin resources in his scriptural plays. It focuses on the themes of seeing and testimony in his two surviving plays, plays that everywhere question whether the human senses and reason can guide their characters to a happy outcome.

Keywords

Nicholas Grimald – *Christus Redivivus* – *Archipropheta* – University drama – Latin scriptural drama – Christian Terence – rhetoric

1 Introduction

Nicholas Grimald is probably best known for his contributions to *Tottel's Miscellany* and an influential translation of Cicero's *De Officiis*. He is also remembered as 'the Judas of the Reformation', a recanter who betrayed the Oxford martyrs Latimer, Cranmer and Ridley to their deaths.[1] John Bale's catalogue of Grimald's works in his *Index Britanniae Scriptorum* offers a different side to the story, portraying an industrious Humanist scholar and translator,

---

1   See L.R. Merrill, "Nicholas Grimald, the Judas of the Reformation," *PMLA* 37 (1922): 216–27.

a prolific academic playwright, and an enthusiastic writer and collector of English poetry.[2] Bale includes six Latin plays in his list of Grimald's works, including a nativity play and plays about St Stephen and Athanasius, now lost.[3] Two of Grimald's plays were printed in Germany and have survived: the scriptural dramas *Christus Redivivus* (1543) and *Archipropheta* (1548). The newness of Grimald's dramatic project is announced by the title page of *Christus Redivivus*, which declares that the play is "comoedia tragica, sacra & nova."[4] Though novelty, or invention, was valued in humanist rhetoric, "newness still had to be vindicated against the unquestionably greater authority of the old as endorsed by the classical models."[5] Andreas Höfele argues further that a "demand for newness arose with the attempt to adapt these models for Christian purposes, to reshape, for example, the classical school author of Latin comedies, Terence, into 'Christian Terence'."[6]

If Grimald's *Christus Redivivus* is "comoedia tragica, sacra & nova," the pairings are suggestive: as comedy is in tension with tragedy, is the sacred in tension with the new? Höfele cites John Foxe, for whom innovation is "almost a synonym for anarchic disorder."[7] If Catholics accused Protestants of 'innovation', the reformers' retort was always that they sought the restitution of the Church's first true state – not the new, but renewal. In this context, 'newness' is a virtue only when it escapes the movement of history, or defies the "changing manners, customs or religious observances" and achieves "a haven of permanence." Thus the sacred and the new may appear oxymoronic but in fact define each other very precisely, just as the tensions of the 'tragi-comic' create a precise generic term which was pioneered by the Protestant writers of Latin scriptural drama: Foxe, Grimald, Thomas Kirchmeyer.[8]

Christian writers commonly deploy paradox, oxymoron, and the yoking of opposites to reveal religious truth. This is perhaps unsurprising given the central Christian tenet of the incarnation, a God-Man, whose Crucifixion is a victory – a *tragi*comedy indeed. But even the most striking paradox can become

---

2   *Index Britanniae Scriptorum quod ex variis bibliothecis non paruo labore collegit Iohannes Baleus, cum Aliis*, ed. Reginald Lane Poole and Mary Bateson (Oxford: Clarendon Press, 1902), 301–04.
3   Ibid.
4   *The Life and Poems of Nicholas Grimald*, ed. L.R. Merrill (New Haven: Yale University Press, 1925), 90. All references to Grimald's plays will be to this edition.
5   Andreas Höfele, "John Foxe, *Christus Triumphans*," in *The Oxford Handbook of Tudor Drama*, ed. Thomas Betteridge and Greg Walker (Oxford: Oxford University Press, 2012), 127.
6   Ibid., 127.
7   Ibid., 128.
8   Ibid.

familiar and the task of the evangelical writer may be to defamiliarise, to make her/his audience look anew at the paradoxical truth using all the resources of literary language, genre, tradition. In his Latin scriptural drama, Nicholas Grimald yokes the classical with the scriptural, Plautus with Seneca, and the devil with the pagan underworld. His stories are scriptural but he translates scripture from the Latin of the Vulgate into the Latin of Virgil. We will examine Grimald's use of classical Latin resources in his scriptural plays, asking how he uses them, and why. In order to focus these huge questions carefully, this essay will focus on the themes of seeing and testimony in *Christus Redivivus* and *Archipropheta*, plays that everywhere question whether the human senses and reason can guide their characters to a happy outcome.

2   Theories of Seeing

Grimald's interrogation of human sight must be set in the context of a long tradition of epistemological doubt about the reliability of the eye as an instrument to understand the world.[9] Sight was the sense accorded the greatest practical and rational power by Aristotle's doctrine of visible *species* in *De Anima* III.7; the philosopher's influential articulation that 'the soul never thinks without an image' established the centrality of a form of vision to every act of understanding.[10] Robert Burton testifies to the traditional hegemony of the sight in acts of perception in his digression on human anatomy, in which he states that "Of these five senses, sight is held to be the most precious, and the best, and that by reason of his object, it sees the whole body at once. By it we learn, and discern all things, a sense most excellent for use."[11] But disagreement with the Aristotelian concept of the process of seeing as rational, straightforward and consistent began as early as Greek antiquity, and in early modern Europe varied intellectual forces contributed to a crisis of confidence in the reliability of the eye. The perceived power of human vision was matched by its vulnerability:

---

[9]   See Stuart Clark, *Vanities of the Eye: Vision in Early Modern European Culture* (Oxford: Oxford University Press, 2007). See also Arnold Hunt, *The Art of Hearing: English Preachers and their Audiences, 1590–1640* (Cambridge: Cambridge University Press, 2010), 23–60.

[10] See Michelle Karnes, *Imagination, Meditation, and Cognition in the Middle Ages* (Chicago: Chicago University Press, 2011), 24–74.

[11] Robert Burton, *The anatomy of melancholy: what it is. VVith all the kindes, cavses, symptomes, prognostickes, and severall cvres of it. In three maine partitions with their seuerall sections, members, and svbsections. Philosophically, medicinally, historically, opened and cvt vp by Democritvs Iunior. With a satyricall preface, conducing to the following discourse* (Oxford: Iohn Lichfield and Iames Short, 1621), 33.

the eye, the sensory organ confounded by dreams, delusions, optical illusions and the dangerous idols of Catholicism, came to be seen as vulnerable, easily misled, and above all, concerned with the shallow and distracting surfaces of things.[12] Grimald's preface to his translation of Cicero presents seeing as an unstable process, easily overpowering the reason required to distinguish inner truth from outward appearance:

> Yet is the selfsame minde by the felouship, and companie of the senses, and desires, many a time called awaie from that principall office [i.e. the worship of God], to consider these unstable, and mutable things ... and sometime to view things sensible, that can in no wise bee sondered from the materiall substance: as elementes, beastes, herbes, trees, metalls, stones, and such like: all the which must needes be sensed, & fortified *with* the trade of debating doutes, and discerning of trouth from untrouthe: which is the art of Logik, the verie rule of reason, and instrument of all discourse.[13]

These characteristics of sight are important to Grimald and other early modern writers, because the vulnerability of the eye to the fanciful and fictive grants the rhetorician an important power: that of manipulating the vision of his audience. For Quintilian, the use of visual and emotive language to direct the 'mind's eye' of an audience was the means by which rhetoric graduated from being merely narrative or argumentative to become compelling: the rhetorician is not using his full powers if he appeals only to hearing: "non enim satis efficit neque, ut debet, plene dominatur oratio, si usque ad aures valet atque ea sibi iudex, de quibus cognoscit, narrari credit, non exprimi et oculis mentis ostendi" (or if the judge merely feels that the facts on which he has to give his decision are being narrated to him, and not displayed in their living truth to the eyes of the mind).[14] Quintilian identifies the *phantasia*, the unreal images that the mind creates, and which can interrupt the process of apprehending the world through the eye, as the sources of the orator's power to effect this control of the vision:

---

12 See Clark, *Vanities of the Eye*, 1–52.
13 Nicholas Grimald, *Marcus Tullius Ciceroes thre bokes of duties, to Marcus his sonne, turned out of latine into english* (London: Richard Tottel, 1556), 12.
14 Quintilian, *The Orator's Education*, 5 vols., ed. and trans. Donald A. Russell, Loeb Classical Library, 124–27, 494 (Cambridge, MA: Harvard University Press, 2002), 3:8.4.62–63. All future references to and translations of Quintilian will be from this edition.

> There are certain experiences which the Greeks call *phantasiai* and the Romans *visiones*, whereby things absent are presented to our imagination with such extreme vividness that they seem actually to be before our very eyes. It is the man who is really sensitive to such impressions who will have the greatest power over the emotions ... And it is a power which all may readily acquire if they will. When the mind is unoccupied or is absorbed by fantastic hopes or day-dreams, we are haunted by these visions of which I am speaking to such an extent that we imagine that we are travelling abroad, crossing the sea, fighting, addressing the people, or enjoying the use of wealth that we do not actually possess, and seem to ourselves not to be dreaming but acting. Surely, then, it may be possible to turn this form of hallucination to some profit. I am complaining that a man has been murdered. Shall I not bring before my eyes all the circumstances which it is reasonable to imagine must have occurred in such a connection? Shall I not see the assassin burst suddenly from his hiding-place, the victim tremble, cry for help, beg for mercy, or turn to run? Shall I not see the fatal blow delivered and the stricken body fall? Will not the blood, the deathly pallor, the groan of agony, the death-rattle, be indelibly impressed upon my mind? From such impressions arises the *enargeia* which Cicero calls *illuminatio* and *evidentia*, which makes us seem not so much to narrate as to exhibit the actual scene, while our emotions will be no less actively stirred than if we were present at the actual occurrence.[15]

It is through harnessing the illusory power of his own vivid *phantasia*, Quintilian argues, that the orator can imbue his oration with *enargeia*, the quality of rhetorical 'vividness' proper to the Grand Style, by which the orator, poet or artist lent force and vigour to a narrative. His practical instructions for the creation of *enargeia*, moreover, make two claims that will be crucial to our study of Grimald. First, he implies that rhetoric constitutes a mode of seeing: the skilful orator can turn the inner eye of his audience to view in colourful detail that which is in his own mind. Second, the orator's control over the inner eye of his audience extends far beyond the realm of the merely visual, encompassing in addition the manipulation of the emotions.

---

15   Quintilian, *Orator's Education*, 3:6.2.29.

3 *Archipropheta*: Rhetoric and Sight

Grimald wrote *Archipropheta*, about the death of John the Baptist, for performance in late 1547, in support of his application for membership of Christ Church, Oxford.[16] In conspicuous contrast to near-contemporary John the Baptist plays by George Buchanan and John Bale, scriptural narrative here finds dramatic realisation not in the form of Roman or medieval comedy; instead, Grimald makes the striking decision to figure the story as a Senecan tragedy. Briefly, *Archipropheta, Tragoedia* combines the Gospel accounts of the life of John the Baptist, and his murder at the hands of Herod the Tetrarch, with the details of Herod's vexed and incestuous family life in Josephus's *Antiquities of the Jews*, to create a five-act tragedy that culminates in John's death, gruesomely represented onstage as his severed head is presented to the audience on a platter. Grimald fits the Biblical story to his Senecan medium, imagining it as one of thwarted love, jealousy and a governing, irresistible *furor* set at the court of Herod Antipas. He constructs the *agon* of the play around the account in Matthew and Mark that "Herod had taken John, and bound him, and put him in prison for Herodias' sake, his brother Philip's wife. For John said unto him, it is not lawful for thee to have her."[17] When John the Baptist, newly arrived in Galilee after years of preaching in the wilderness, advises the king that his marriage to his wife is unlawful in the eyes of God, Herodias persuades her husband to disregard the words of the preacher and throw him into prison. The second half of the play follows the queen as, consumed and ruled by a desire to see her adversary dead, she contrives an elaborate feast and spectacle on Herod's birthday in order to trick her resistant husband into agreeing to John's murder.

Archipropheta, then, is a tragedy of humankind's entanglement in sin and inability to distinguish the will of God from our own depraved impulses. The story of Herod and Herodias denies the power of human sight to discern God: Herod and his wife resemble the doomed sinners described in Grimald's influential preface to his translation of Cicero's *De Officiis* (1556), "that alonely serue theyr senses" and are "overmuch enclined to paumpering, and pleasing of the vitall portion ... all bent to gather good, and holly given to gaine ...".[18] John's language, moreover, repeatedly evokes the Biblical parable of the sower, for

---

[16] See Merrill, *Life and Poems of Nicholas Grimald*, 232.
[17] *The Bible and Holy Scriptvres Conteyned in the Olde and Newe Testament. Translated according to the Ebrue and Greke, and conferred with the best translations in diuers languages* (Genève: Rowland Hall, 1560), Matthew 14: 1–12 (henceforth: *Geneva Bible*).
[18] Grimald, *Marcus Tullius Ciceroes thre bokes of duties*, 13.

example where he likens himself to a cultivator of fruit who must root up and cut out useless weeds, thorns, tares, burrs, wild oars and thistles, before he ventures to commit to the unfit earth his chosen seeds ("Tanquam frugi colonus herba' inutiles || Tribulos, lolium, lappas, auenas, carduos || Runcare ac demetere prius fere solet").[19] In the parable, Christ numbers among those who do not correctly apprehend the word of God, and are therefore barred from salvation, those who hear the word but become distracted from salvation by their earthly preoccupations.[20] The allusive references to the parable throughout the play undermine the characters' repeated claims that the act of seeing is in part an act of judgment or discernment, and by extension, that sight leads to understanding.

Grimald offers his audience a reliable, sanctioned authority in the form of the testimony of John. He points and emphasises the language of testimony that pervades his biblical sources: John repeatedly defines his role as the 'witness' or 'herald' (he is variously *praesagius*, *praeco* and *nuntius*)[21] of Christ, asserting that the men he has baptised represent an "indicium certum atque testificatio,"[22] a sure sign and testimony, of the soul's purification from sin, while his Disciples summarise that "testimonium || Praebebas"[23] (You bore testimony) to Christ. The trope of John as witness is a scriptural one: the Gospel of John omits biographical detail of the Baptist's life and engages with him only as a witness to Christ, recounting that, "He came as a witness to testify concerning that light [of the world, i.e. Christ]: he himself was not the light; he came only as a witness to the light."[24] Again, in John 1:15, the Baptist 'testifies' about Christ who will surpass him; quizzed by the Jewish leaders he 'confesses freely' that he is not Elijah, nor the Messiah, but is the 'voice of one crying the wilderness' about the coming of the Messiah, as mentioned in Isaiah.[25] In fact, all the gospels identify John with this passage in Isaiah, and cite John's assertions that, while he baptizes with water, the Messiah will offer a more powerful, redeeming baptism. In the gospels, John is emphatically a witness offering testimony. All four gospels show Jesus being baptized by John: at the moment of baptism, the descent of the Holy Spirit in the form of a dove, and the words

---

19   Merrill, *Life and Poems of Nicholas Grimald*, 278.
20   See *Geneva Bible*, Matthew 13:4–23, Mark 4:1–29, Luke 8:4–21.
21   Merrill, *Life and Poems of Nicholas Grimald*, 318; 328; 396.
22   Ibid., 284.
23   Ibid., 306.
24   *Geneva Bible*, John 1:6–7.
25   Ibid., John 1:19–23.

from heaven: "This is my own Son, with whom I am well-pleased," offers the most authoritative testimony – the direct witness of the divine voice.

In the play's third act, Herodias seeks to undermine John's testimony in a series of debate scenes in which the opponents vie to persuade Herod to opposite courses of action. Christian insight and truth are here opposed to the display and deception of classical oratory: in addition to the psychological, inward focus that *Archipropheta* takes from its Senecan models, it also takes their thematic concern with rhetoric, and anxiety about the power of persuasive speech. But this is not to say that the play constitutes a decisive rejection of the monuments of classical knowledge by the loving translator of Cicero's *De Officiis*. In fact, Grimald's didactic purpose depends upon his audience responding sympathetically towards Herodias and her husband, and appreciating that they embody, albeit in exaggerated form, our own fallen nature and impulse towards the sensuous and sinful. The distinctively classical elements of *Archipropheta* come to represent valiant human attempts to understand, and assert themselves in the face of a terrifying universal blindness.

In *Archipropheta*, Grimald presents human sight as disastrously frail, and vulnerable to the control of persuasive speech: to convince someone of something is to manipulate their vision. John and Herodias deploy contrasting models of rhetoric in their respective quests to win the soul of Herod; but what the two have in common is their habitual appeal to the visual. John suggestively offers numerous accounts of the method or reason behind the style of his preaching throughout the play. He explains to Herod that he teaches the presence of God, which can only be perceived by engaging the rational, divine part of man's soul, "Per summam rerum harunce similitudinem || Quae sub oculos cadunt" (by means of the great likeness to those things which are visible to the eyes).[26] The audience sees this method at work repeatedly, for example when the preacher bids his gathered disciples, "Prae oculis habete primus quo statu parens || Patratum post scelus fuerit" (to hold before (their) eyes the state in which our first parent was in after he had sinned).[27] John here follows Quintilian's instructions for creating *enargeia* precisely: he recognises that a speaker must capture the inner eye of his audience in order truly to arrest and persuade them of what he says, and, moreover, couches emotional manipulation in visual language. What John elliptically places before the eyes of his disciples is much more than a picture – his words summon to mind a story loaded with poignant emotion. For Grimald's audience, to picture the aftermath of the fall of Adam would not in fact have required much imaginative

---

26 Merrill, *Life and Poems of Nicholas Grimald*, 282.
27 Ibid., 244.

effort: it was to remember a familiar story, and to feel the sense of profound loss and entanglement in sin that characterised Reformed religious life. In fact, John portrays vision as the essential tool for true understanding throughout the play, attempting, for example, to impress the significance of Herod's error in choosing Herodias upon the king with an appeal to his sight: "quid agas vide" (look to what you do).[28] Crucially, though, like the men who hear the word of Christ in the parable of the sower, or the man in Grimald's preface to Cicero who must regulate the impressions of his senses with 'the rule of reason', John's audience must actively participate to reach true understanding, weighing his testimony and interpreting his images for themselves.

The forensic rhetoric deployed by Herodias, by contrast, with all its intellectual and emotional manipulation, seeks to control both the vision and the understanding of its audience, testifying to the unreliability of a model of knowing based on the sight. The queen's speech is consciously and conspicuously that of the courtroom; she describes the fight to save her marriage, for instance, as a *causam*,[29] the word used for legal cases in classical rhetorics. Herodias, superficially similar to John, equates seeing and understanding. She imagines proof and authority in pictorial terms: after hearing the disciples' account of the works of John the Baptist she affirms to her husband that "O mi vir, haec quidem nobis oratio || Clare depingit hospitem minime malum" (This speech, my husband, clearly described to us a guest not at all evil).[30] The first meaning of the verb *depingere* is 'to paint',[31] while the adverb *clare* also carries a prominent visual meaning, 'brightly', 'shining' or 'clearly'.[32] For Herodias, to describe is to paint a vivid verbal picture. The queen also repeatedly plays on the multiple meanings of the verb *cernere*: the *Oxford Latin Dictionary* lists its first sense as "to sift," its second as "to distinguish, separate," its third "to decide" and only its fifth as "to discern with the eyes, distinguish, see."[33] In Act III Scene vii, having won the assurance that her husband will not desert her, Herodias further demands of him, "potes hunc adhuc uultu remisso cernere?" (Are you able to look upon this man with patience?).[34] Merrill's English translation, "Can you look upon this man [i.e. John] with patience?" flattens the layers of meaning contained in the verb and thus misses the point of the

---

28 Ibid., 298.
29 Ibid., 296.
30 Ibid., 274.
31 P.G.W. Clare, *Oxford Latin Dictionary*, 2 vols. (Oxford: Oxford University Press, 2012), 1:569.
32 Ibid., 1:365.
33 Ibid., 1:331.
34 Merrill, *Life and Poems of Nicholas Grimald*, 298

queen's language: Herodias, in essence, insists that her husband identify John in a manner that suits her, as a boorish, impudent fraud; she insists that he allow her to manipulate his vision, and relinquish his own reason and capacity for interpretation.

The queen makes extensive use of two rhetorical techniques to undermine John's testimony and refashion Herod's vision according to her desire. The first is intimately connected with discernment or identification, and was variously termed 'substituting *res pro re*', *distinctio, meiosis* and *paradiastole* in classical rhetorics. According to Quintilian, this technique is of particular use to the judicial orator when he is at his most deliberately deceptive, attempting to combat the accusation of an opponent which he cannot hope to deny, and which has left the judges 'roused' ("exasperavit") and 'full of anger against us' ("plenos irae reliquit").[35] The orator's defence must then consist in restating the facts of the case, but in such a way as to lend them a different moral complexion: 'luxury will be softened down into generosity, avarice into economy, carelessness into simplicity' ("luxuria liberalitatis, avaritia parsimoniae, neglegentia simplicitatis").[36] Elsewhere, Quintilian demonstrates that the figure might equally be used to blacken the character of an adversary, and points at the means of heightening its emotional force:

> This method of amplification can be increased and made more manifest if the words of greater force are explicitly compared with those we propose to substitute ...: "We have brought before you for judgment not a thief but a plunderer, not an adulterer but a rapist, not a committer of sacrilege but an enemy of everything sacred and religious, not an assassin but someone who has actually butchered fellow-citizens and allies with the utmost cruelty."[37]

While early modern discussions of the figure tended to borrow heavily from Quintilian's account, the sixteenth century saw a gradual rejection of *paradiastole* as a figure that habitually and disturbingly sacrificed truth to eloquence:[38]

---

35   Quintilian, *Orator's Education*, 2:4.2.75.
36   Ibid., 3:4.2.78.
37   "Hoc genus increscit ac fit manifestius si ampliora verba cum ipsis nominibus pro quibus ea posituri sumus conferantur ... 'non enim furem sed ereptorem, non adulterum sed expugnatorem pudicitiae, non sacrilegum sed hostem sacrorum religionumque, non sicarium sed crudelissimum carnificem civium sociorumque in vestrum iudicium adduximus'" (Ibid., 3:8.4.2.)
38   See Quentin Skinner, *Reason and Rhetoric in the Philosophy of Hobbes* (Cambridge : Cambridge University Press, 1996), 172–81.

indeed, in the second edition of his *Garden of Eloquence* (1593), Henry Peacham condemned re-description as a "faultie tearme of speech" which "opposeth the truth by false tearmes and wrong names," and could only really be a technique for "the better maintenance of wickednesse."[39] Given the terms of the suspicion that accrued around *paradiastole* in the sixteenth century, it is perhaps not surprising that Grimald associates the technique so firmly with Herodias, the play's principal deceiver.

The queen uses *paradiastole* throughout the scene of rhetorical contest with John to undermine the preacher's testimony and manipulate her husband's vision, fashioning it according to her desire. Where Herod informs her that "connubium hoc nostrum nefas putat || nouum hospes" (Our new guest considers our marriage unlawful), Herodias inverts the terms of the accusation, asserting that "Est hostis, haud hospes, vir acceptissime" (He is an enemy, not a guest, my husband).[40] The preacher's 'invincible arguments' ("invictis rationibus") become 'harsh words' ("dicta ... tristia") and later, 'wicked speech' ("iniqua oratio").[41] Finally, the queen persistently refigures John's asceticism and devotion to Christ as crude, distasteful poverty: the preacher becomes 'this barbarian' ("istum barbarum"), an 'ignorant, low-born, boorish, worthless fellow' ("inepti, obscuri, agrestis atque; ignobilis || Homuncionis"), and a 'wretch' ("sceleste").[42] Throughout the scene, in her scandalous treatment of the venerable ancient preacher, Herodias performs the early modern anxiety that the figures of mitigation, and especially *paradiastole*, represented "the point at which the equivocal nature of the relationship between truth and eloquence revealed itself most alarmingly."[43] Simultaneously, though, the technique of re-description works to force Herodias' audience to view her opponent with a kind of double-vision, as her reading of John vies for prominence with his own claims about himself. Herodias demands that we confront her story, one-dimensionally didactic in the Bible, through new eyes; criticism of the queen's arrogance, materialism and short-sightedness necessarily involves the recognition that she is not in possession of all the facts.

The second figure upon which the queen relies is commonplace. She uses a host of literary *topoi* about the betrayed and abandoned woman to create

---

39 Henry Peacham, *The Garden of Eloqvence, Conteining the most excellent Ornaments, Exornations, Lightes, flowers and forms of speech, commonly called the Figures of Rhetorike* (London: R.F. for H. Iackson, 1593), 169.

40 Merrill, *Life and Poems of Nicholas Grimald*, 294.

41 Ibid., 294–96.

42 Ibid., 296–98.

43 Skinner, *Reason and Rhetoric in the Philosophy of Hobbes*, 174.

emotional force and refashion her own image in the eyes of her husband and audience. She invokes the previous marriage she abandoned for Herod, her ruined modesty and reputation, the vows of love, marriage and fidelity Herod has made to her, and the certainty of her suffering at the hands of the spurned Philip should her husband take John's advice. Her speech reads like an impressionistic rendering (or *aemulatio*, in the terms of the humanist doctrine of imitation) of that of Virgil's Dido, at the point in Book Four of the *Aeneid* at which the Carthaginian queen confronts Aeneas, knowing he intends to abandon her for Italy. Grimald's recognisable allusions to Virgil's language focus the attention of his audience on Herodias's intertextuality, and status as an echo of the archetypal scorned and abandoned woman; but his playful revisions of that language at once resist absolute identification with Dido, and impress the commonplace nature of Herodias's emotional appeals.

Grimald everywhere rewords, reorders and shifts the emphases of his source text; thus, for example, Dido's "te propter eundem ‖ extinctus pudor" (The modesty I forsook on account of you; *Aen.* 4.321–2) becomes "ergone te propter spretae pudiciae ‖ non ulla habetur cura aut ratio"[44] (Shall there be no thought or care for her who spurned modesty for your sake?); "nec te noster amor nec te data dextera quondam ‖ nec te moritura tenet crudeli funere Dido" (Can't our love, or the hand you once gave me, or the cruel death of Dido make you delay?; *Aen.* 4.307–308) becomes "Data haec est dextera?" (Is this the hand you gave me?).[45] Herodias, eschewing specificity in favour of the universal relevance offered by the commonplace, exploits a long tradition of classical literature sympathetic to the painful, emotional and female consequences of grand male narratives.

Alison Thorne argues that commonplace, principally among other rhetorical techniques, affords language the capacity "to function as a rhetorical equivalent or analogue of perspective."[46] She examines early modern conceptions of the commonplaces as physical or material places, store-houses or hiding-places for ready-made arguments, alongside the numerous visual tropes embedded in commonplace theory, to argue that topical invention affords the rhetorician or dialectician "virtually an Argus-eyed view or any subject of discourse." Characters such as Jacques in *As You Like It* embody Shakespeare's understanding that if, as theorists from Agricola to Puttenham put it, the places

---

44   Merrill, *Life and Poems of Nicholas Grimald*, 296. Merrill reads *pudiciciae* instead of *pudiciae*, but this must be an error.
45   Ibid., 296.
46   Alison Thorne, *Vision and Rhetoric in Shakespeare: Looking Through Language* (Basingstoke: Macmillan, 2000), xiv.

contained within them "each thing and every possible argument," then they must also contain all the possible intellectual perspectives on a given object or topic. Finally, "perception is so deeply informed by our linguistic habits that it itself is a product of discourse."[47] One obvious implication of Thorne's argument is the idea that the persuasive, pictorial or topical language of one person or character might be used to manipulate the vision of another – and indeed, this is what Herodias achieves through her use of literary commonplaces. Her sustained allusions control our appreciation of her character, adding colour and detail even as they complicate and deceive. As Herodias assumes the guise of a wronged and betrayed literary woman, she challenges any straightforward conception that she is a manipulator and villain, forcing her husband and audience to view her in her own terms, and to recognise their own sense of the importance of the worldly values to which she appeals.

Perhaps Grimald's most poignant denial of the power of sight is found in the repeated instances of mistaken recognition and identification that occur throughout the play. The play's anxieties about the disastrous vulnerability of human vision and understanding converge on the word *agnoscere* and its cognates, which appear repeatedly only to be undermined and redefined. John uses *agnoscere* in its straight sense, as recognition, telling his disciples that he preaches "Ut quisque in agnitionem adducatur sui" (So that each man might be lead to a knowledge of himself),[48] and impressing upon Herod that "Suum mens aegra debet morbum agnoscere" (The sick soul ought to know his own disease),[49] while an angel sent by God tells John's parents that their unborn son will cause men to recognise their own sin ("scleribus agnitis"[50]). But for Grimald's earthly characters, by contrast, recognition is almost without exception comically mistaken. Gelasimus, the wise fool whose words eerily and elliptically anticipate and echo those of John throughout the play, summarises man's difficulty when he asks:

> Quid cuique nostrum scire difficillimum est? ...
> Certe ego puto, ut suum quis agnoscat patrem. (p. 280)

[What seems to each one of you to be the most difficult thing to know? ... I certainly think it is, how one is to know his own father.]

---

47 Ibid, 17.
48 Merrill, *Life and Poems of Nicholas Grimald*, 244.
49 Ibid., 278.
50 Ibid., 268.

Against the context of the play's depiction of female lust and immorality, and Grimald's promise in the epistle that he will provide opportunities to 'note the wantonness of women' ("Nec abs re fuerit, animadvertere muliebrem petulantiam"),[51] the lewd, vulgar implication of the fool's observation is most immediately obvious. But the statement is simultaneously an accurate diagnosis of the crux of the tragedy; in Grimald's world, even John's disciples mistake the preacher for Jesus, and are unable to distinguish his secondary importance, while Herod, his wife and the Pharisees everywhere confuse moments of genuine insight with the promptings of their natural impulses towards lust and greed.

Herod, comically weak and buffoonish, characterised by his vulnerability to the persuasion of whoever has spoken last, enacts misrecognition most frequently, and with the most ruinous consequences. Grimald's major thematic revision to the tragic plot inherited from Seneca is that ultimately, the outcome of the play depends not on the *furor* that possesses Herodias, but rather Herod's vulnerability to persuasion. Emerging from conversation with the preacher, Herod uses *agnoscere* in the sense articulated by John, as the identification and appreciation of one's own sin, telling the audience that he 'recognises' that he has sinned gravely in marrying Herodias:

> Sane pudet (fatebor) pigetque is poenitet:
> Et agnosco me iam intulisse iniurias
> Thalamo germani. (p. 292)

[Truly I confess that I am ashamed. I am sorry, and I repent. Now I see that I have wronged my brother's marriage bed.]

But in the very next scene, the king allows his wife to convince him that he has misread John, stating confusedly:

> Huccine putam, uxor, a gradu constantiae
> Posse unquam deijci? Modestiam audaciam
> Videor agnoscere audacem & modestiam.
> O quanto in illo maius est, quam se refert? (pp. 294–96)

[Did you imagine, wife, that he, going forth from our palace, can ever be turned from the path of constancy? I seem to recognise his modesty as audacity, and his audacity as modesty. How much more there is in that man than appears!]

---

51   Ibid., 234.

Herod momentarily views John with the uneasy double-vision created by the two equally compelling, but conflicting rhetorical accounts he has heard. The king's contorted language expresses his inability to accommodate the opposite views of the preacher offered by John himself and Herodias respectively. But disastrously, he is unable to judge between them.

With our privileged knowledge of the truth contained in the Bible, the play's moral order, vindicating John's account of himself and indexing Herod and his wife as villains, is clear to the audience. But flat dichotomy is troubled by our awareness that the figure onstage does not share our knowledge, and embodies, albeit in exaggerated form, our own fallen nature and natural impulse towards the sensuous and sinful. Herodias's means of deception are, at first sight, deceptively similar to John's method of teaching; the path to true faith looks bewilderingly like the fallen and flawed ways of knowing that distract Herod, and block his ears to the word of God. The same qualities that make rhetoric powerful have always constituted the basis of its criticism.

The play's conclusion provides Grimald's final statement of the weakness of the human eye. In the banquet scene and its aftermath, Grimald stages two contrasting modes of seeing; the tragic vision of the worldly characters is opposed to the prophetic assurance of Jehovah, whose vision transcends physical and temporal boundaries to perceive that "modus extat definitus, ordoque; stabilis || Qui nostris continuatur in actionibus' (There is a definite method and fixed order that is continued in all our actions):[52] namely, a universal pattern of paradox according to which worldly folly teaches holy wisdom; debasement and suffering at the hands of humankind prefigure heavenly glory, and a display of weakness on earth demonstrates the supreme power of God. Men, Jehovah asserts, have failed adequately to recognise John, who is vindicated and assured of salvation against this pattern: "Secus tecum est Iohannes, quam homines putant" (O John, it is otherwise with thee than men think).[53]

Grimald focuses the attention of his audience on the processes of seeing and recognising throughout the banquet scenes. The characters' vision is emphatically that of Senecan tragedy: Scene IV.XII resounds with echoes of the Thyestean feast as Herod is tricked, his vision clouded by greed and lust as he is ensnared in his wife's trap, and finally presented with John's severed head, the gruesome evidence of his ruin. In his Senecan imagining of the scene, Grimald focuses our attention on the spectacle of the head as evidence of the violence done to John, and the human interpretation of that spectacle.

---

52 Ibid., 348.
53 Ibid., 346.

The language of looking and seeing pervades the scene: the Chorus of servants who present the head to Herodias enter with the command "ecce caput" (behold the head),[54] and the queen's first action is to gather an audience for her spectacle. Conspicuously echoing Atreus in Seneca's *Thyestes* (l. 909), who throws the doors of the banquet-hall open for all to see its contents after his brother's feast, she commands that her guests enter into the palace, and vows that the whole of Idumea will be welcome to see the terrible sight. A nameless Syrian girl, a few lines later, can engage with the crime only in its visual dimension, lamenting that "non ista poscit hoc tempus spectacula" (the time demands no such sight as this).[55] In Scene V.III the girl again emphasises the visual aspect of the crime, wailing "Atrocem O regem: flebile O spectaculum" (O cruel king! O doleful spectacle), and recoils from "istae epilae ... istae, quas intuerier || Vix potui" (these feasts ... these, which I could scarce bear to look upon).[56] The Chorus demand that the audience, 'huc, huc osculos vertite vestros' (here, here turn your eyes):[57] only through confrontation of the shocking sight will the audience learn the moral lessons the play provides. Later, John's disciples, finding the Baptist's bloody trunk lying elsewhere in the sand, along with a Chorus of Syrian people interpret the sight as the emblem of an unforgivable wrong, and react to it with angry despair. The disciples ask: "Quis hanc || Speciem cernendo a lachrymis sibi temperet" (Who, looking on such a sight, can refrain from tears?)[58] while the Chorus repeat their diagnosis that the death is 'much to be lamented' ("O deflenda nimis funera, funera").[59]

The play's final act, then, stages a range of stock tragic responses to the gruesome spectacle of John's head, which, we are told, sits vividly at the centre of the banquet table throughout. Gruesome desire to feast the eyes is juxtaposed with shock and revulsion, and finally the impulse to generalise and moralise. But the words of Jehovah, immediately following John's murder, expose the worldly characters' tragic interpretations of the head as mistaken, a final misrecognition of the preacher and his significance. John's head cannot finally be said to provide testimony – it is an arresting, appalling and ultimately misleading construction of human vanity, its function analogous to that of classical rhetoric in the play. The sacred truth contained in the Bible offers a redemption from tragic narrative that Grimald's characters are unable to see. Classical

---

54   Ibid., 344.
55   Ibid. This line is a quote from *Aeneid* VI, 37.
56   Ibid., 350.
57   Ibid., 346.
58   Ibid., 356.
59   Ibid.

paradigms of knowledge are reassessed against the assurance of this faith, and found wanting.

4 *Christus Redivivus*: Seeing and the Body

By contrast with *Archipropheta*, reaching a climax in the image of John's severed head, Grimald's earlier Latin scriptural play, *Christus Redivivus*, has at its heart the image of the empty tomb. By his own account, Grimald wrote the play in the winter of 1541, to fill time upon his arrival in Oxford while he waited for his books to arrive.[60] Details of the play's performance are uncertain, though the young author speaks in his dedicatory epistle of a pressure to stage and publish the play, leading Merrill to speculate that it was performed in the Easter of 1542.[61]

In *Christus Redivivus*, it is possible that Grimald is drawing much more heavily on the vernacular English tradition of scriptural drama than he does in *Archipropheta*, although once again his treatment of the scriptural narrative is heavily mediated by classical tropes, and his language richly laced with echoes of classical texts. The quartet of soldiers who so spectacularly fail to guard Christ's tomb are the most critically discussed aspect of Grimald's *Christus Redivivus*:[62] their interest lies in their New Comedy pedigree for each one is a Plautine *miles gloriosus*, boastful but ultimately cowardly, all talk and no trousers. The Gospels tell us very briefly that Jesus' tomb was guarded, that after the Resurrection these guards reported to the chief priests all that had happened, and that the elders bribed the guards to say the disciples had stolen the body.[63] Grimald is not the first to make the soldiers four in number, and to make them comically boastful: that this had already happened in the vernacular tradition of scriptural drama is evident in the *N-Town* Plays.[64] It seems likely that the vernacular scriptural tradition was here also imitating Plautus, and it is of

---

60 Ibid., 92.
61 Ibid., 94.
62 See George Coffin Taylor, "The Christus Redivivus of Nicholas Grimald and the Hegge Resurrection Plays," PMLA 41 (1926): 840–59. See also Nicholas Grimald, *Christus Redivivus* (*printed 1543*), *Archipropheta* (*printed 1548*), prepared with an introduction by Kurt Tetzeli von Rosador (New York: G. Olms, 1982), 9.
63 *Geneva Bible*, Matthew 27.
64 See N-Town Passion Play 2: Burial and Guarding of the Sepulchre: N-Town Pilate and Soldiers, in *The N-Town Plays*, ed. Douglas Sugano (Kalamazoo, MI: Medieval Institute Publications, 2007), 275–84, 287–92. Grimald's use of N-Town is discussed in Taylor, "The Christus Redivivus," but his arguments are not conclusive.

course possible that Grimald's direct source here was not Plautus but *N-Town*.[65] But it is certain that Grimald would have studied Roman Comedy too, and it is certain that his Latin medium enables him to develop fully the humour of these Plautine characters in a manner much more extended than that of *N-Town*, for surely the mere fact of low characters from the vernacular tradition speaking in Latin must itself have been comical, precisely because they are not in a Plautine comedy but instead are juxtaposed with the Virgilian and the Senecan.

But their principal comic effect is of course as the braggards who fail dismally to live up to their boasts. When we first meet the quartet, they are describing their valour, comically concluding that in order to guard the tomb of Christ they will bravely use their arms against the unarmed and feeble:

Dromo: Haud frustra, mento bene barbato aetas mea
          Voltum ornauit, praesertim cum mihi mascula
          Corda nequaquam desint ... (p. 140)
Sangax: ... Quid in hoc corpore desideretur? Siue quis
          Proceritatem siue magnitudinem,
          Siue optime compacta membra expenderit? (p. 144)
Brumax: ... Armati nudos, strenui infirmo' ac debiles ... (p. 146)

[*Dromo*: Time has not adorned my face with a well-bearded chin to no purpose, especially since I do not lack a manly heart ... *Sangax*: ... What is lacking in this body, whether one considers height, or size, or limbs well set up? *Brumax*: ... Armed against the unarmed, vigorous against the weak and feeble ...]

Why does Grimald choose to develop so extensively the boasting of the *miles gloriosus* in his four tomb guards? Is it just for comical effect? Or is it also that the comedy of the boasts highlights the puniness of human resistance to the will of God? Strikingly, comical as the soldiers are their words are laced with arguments and *sententiae* which echo rhetorical debate: "ars, quod inchoat natura, perficit" (art perfects what nature begins),[66] Sangax declares, for example, after an erudite summary of *Aeneid* VIII, 416–38.[67] Dorus provides a lengthy

---

65   The English and French vernacular traditions in presenting the Resurrection are discussed in Peter Happé's essay, "Dramatizing the Resurrection," in this volume.
66   Merrill, *Life and Poems of Nicholas Grimald*, 144.
67   "Arma illorum, quos exteri celebres habent, Puto Cyclopum esse fabricata manibus" (The arms of those whom foreigners consider famous were, I think, made by the hands of the

and rhetorically elegant justification of the superiority of the mind over the body, arguing with the Stoics that our bodies are just like those of dumb beasts, but our minds make us godlike, ready to rise above the stars.[68] Although his arguments are self-promoting, because he is physically punier than his companions, they are also elegant and potentially even perhaps heroic. They present a question about the importance of the bodily which will be resoundingly answered by Grimald's resurrected Christ.

Vitally, then, the play presents Christ's Resurrection, and the reason for this focus must first be briefly considered. A Prologue emphasizes the material nature of the Resurrection by alluding to biological functioning:[69] Christ took up again the organs of the body ("organa … corporis"), and made this manifest ("manifestis declarauit") by various signs, here "testimonijs," including eating and offering his body to the touch of others. After the Prologue has recounted the gospel accounts of the bodily appearances of *Christus Redivivus*, additional examples of bodily Resurrection are invoked, along with other very material miracles: on the way to embalm Christ's body, Mary Magdalene and Cleophis tell each other about Christ turning water into wine, walking on water, stilling the sea-storm, healing the sick, as well as raising the centurion's son and Jairus' daughter.[70] When Brumax is sceptical about the possibility of the bodily Resurrection, he echoes the Prologue in referring to death as the ceasing of bodily functions:

> Ecquando a corporeis functionibus
> Qui deficiuntur semel, ab irremeabili, &
> Clauso barathro suum reducent halitum? (p. 146)

[Shall they whose bodily functions have once ceased ever bring back their breath from the closed pit from which there is no returning?]

and Dromo, recovering from the shock of the power manifested as Christ is raised, comments that the his bodily functions ("functiones"[71]) are not yet ready to do their work. The resurrected Christ immediately tells the audience that the mortal body is now made immortal:

Cyclops; ibid.).
68 Merrill, *Life and Poems of Nicholas Grimald*, 142.
69 Ibid., 116.
70 Ibid., 152–60.
71 Ibid., 172.

> Ergo, quod dissolubile modo corpu' extitit,
> Quod conditionem habuit, ut posset mori,
> Aeternitate iam imbutum, renascitur. (p. 150)

[This body, which but a while ago was subject to dissolution, and was of such a nature that it could die, is now born again imbued with life eternal.]

But it is most certainly a resurrected mortal body, a material reality: when Peter gives his account of meeting the risen Christ, his testimony recounts the bodily nature of the proofs Christ lays before him, inviting him to gaze on ("cernite") his hands, side and feet, and to handle His body ("trectate dicit corpora"), eating fish and honey. It is a testimony of inescapable physical evidence. These events are of course scriptural, not Grimald's invention, but by his selection, arrangement and extrapolation of material he provides a particular emphasis on the Resurrection of Christ's body as that which makes most clearly visible God's love, and which we should see and celebrate:

> Si ergo hic dei tanta elucet benignitas,
> Quantam non cuncta opera ostentant caetera:
> Certe nullum spectrum uberiore gaudio
> Christiadum poterit pertentare pectora. (p. 116)

[If, therefore, the loving kindness of God shines forth more brightly here (that is, in the Resurrection) than it does in all his other works, surely no sight can pervade the hearts of the sons of Christ with more abundant joy than this.]

This might perhaps be contrasted with the presentation of Christ in the (essentially pre-Reformation) mystery plays, which tends to emphasize the Crucifixion as the event on which we should meditate, Christ's suffering as the evidence of his love which should bring us joy. In Grimald's play the emotive language of medieval contemplation is used by Mary Magdalene to condemn the actions of the 'unjust Jews' ("iniqui Iudaei") in crucifying Christ:

> Tu uulnificis, heu, sertis inflictum caput,
> Tu palmas traiectas acuta cuspide,
> Tu clauis confossos pedes
> Alta in pinu ac tristi pendenteis machina:
> Tu, tu, dico, exultans respexti hostiliter. (p.120)

[Thou didst gaze on that head smitten and wounded with the crown of thorns on the palms pierced with the sharp nails, on the feet of Him, transfixed by spikes, who hung from the lofty tree, the cruel cross – thou, thou I say, exulting in enmity.]

Whereas in the York Crucifixion, for example (Play 35, ll. 253–64), Christ invites the audience to contemplate the wounds of his body and recognize their implicit guilt in causing Christ's suffering through their sins, in Grimald Mary uses the same language to indicate the actual, historical guilt of those who crucified Christ, and suggests that contemplation of his wounds gives them perverse pleasure. It is true that in Grimald Mary's own contemplation of the memory of the Passion is at the heart of her mourning of Christ:

> Verum, quoties tenax repetit memoria,
> Punctum corolla spinifera sinciput
> Manus adfixas, ferro contrusos pedes,
> Turpatos crineis, barbam cretam sanguine,
> Illusum, pulsatum, ignominiose pendulum,
> Vna cum pessimae notae latronibus,
> Deiectos oculos, ora morientia,
> Et etiam hastam cruore intepuisse lateris:
> Toties, eheu, cur non licitum erit mihi,
> Sic caesum insontem, saltem lamentarier? (p. 126)

[But as often as memory recalls the head pierced by the crown of thorns, the hands nailed to the cross, the feet fastened together with iron, locks befouled, beard clotted with blood – Him mocked, beaten, hanging in dishonour, together with robbers of most evil repute, eyes cast down, dying lips, and the spear, too, warm with the blood from His side, why should I not be permitted at least to lament the innocent thus slain?]

But this mourning is challenged by Nicodemus, firstly on the pragmatic grounds that it increases grief rather than bringing consolation, and secondly on the logical grounds that, since Christ was able to perform so many superhuman feats for the general good ("res totius publicae"[72]) he could have saved himself had he wished: therefore the Crucifixion must be understood to have been part of his plan. Nicodemus here perhaps exemplifies a Protestant belief in the ability and indeed the responsibility of each individual not only to see but to interpret for him- or herself what is seen in scripture, to respond not just emotively but also intellectually. Nicodemus recalls that Christ had told him that he must be 'lifted up' just as Moses' bronze serpent was lifted up in the

---

72   Ibid., 126.

desert, although he acknowledges that he does not clearly understand ("non plane intelligo"[73]) the meaning of these events – his dialectical logic has enabled him to see the nature of the questions about Christ's power raised by the Crucifixion, but he does not yet have the vital piece of argument –: the testimony of the Resurrection.

It seems likely that confessional differences are driving dramatic focus: Grimald is indeed here attacking traditional contemplations of the Passion, and with them the mystery cycles' focus on the Crucifixion, arguing instead for the centrality to reformed faith of Christ's Resurrection, and creating a drama which reflects this. However, despite the theologically motivated differences between the mystery plays and Grimald's play, both the Crucifixion and the Resurrection are crucially *bodily* events, physical and material, not primarily spiritual. They are therefore both ripe for dramatic treatment, since the power of theatre stems from its embodiment – the words and actions of the protagonists repeated through the words and actions of actors. Of course, the audience of a play know that the actor they see eating bread or inviting Thomas to touch his side is not in fact the risen Christ, but (in this case, most likely) a fellow Oxford undergraduate. But he is crucially *alive*, capable of eating and being embraced, and thus may present truthfully the essential quality of Christ in Grimald's play. Drama is therefore Grimald's appropriate medium.

As the Resurrection is itself the testimony of God's love, so it is announced through the testimony of a variety of witnesses, and interrogated by a number of other characters within Grimald's play.[74] So Peter's response to the sight of the empty tomb is to declare that he must discover the sources of these events and the reasons they have happened: "Equidem hercle operam dabo, ut unde & quorsum haec fiant, intelligam" (By Hercules, I will try to learn from what sources, and to what end, these things happen).[75] John immediately declares that he will believe that Christ has risen, presenting this as the logical interpretation of the evidence before him, but Peter maintains scepticism even in the face of Cleophis' testimony that she has been greeted by Christ himself, and his doubt is based on the lack of precedent:

---

[73] Ibid., 128.
[74] The vernacular tradition of Resurrection plays shares with Grimald a "linguistic concern with legal language:" in the vernacular tradition this is motivated by a desire to "leave no doubt about the actuality of the Resurrection" (Happé, "Dramatizing the Resurrection," 201). See also Olga Horner, "'Us Must Make Lies': Witness, Evidence and Proof in the York Resurrection," *Medieval English Theatre* 20 (1998): 24–76.
[75] Merrill, *Life and Poems of Nicholas Grimald*, 160.

> Multa audiui, multa inspexi, multa didici,
> Multa memini: nihil post hominum memoriam
> Tale accepi; nihil omni aetate huiusmodi
> Cognoui: unde induci non queo, ut adsentiar. (p. 178)

[I have heard many stories, seen many sights, learned many things, and remember many, but I have never heard of anything like this within the memory of man; nothing like it in any age I have known: therefore I cannot be brought to regard these things as true.]

Nonetheless, he is willing to investigate, and suggests that they go to see the tomb. After meeting the risen Christ himself, Peter's testimony is in turn examined by a sceptical Thomas, who condemns his narrative as a silly story ("surdo fabellam"):[76] Cleophis then summarizes the evidence of the Old Testament prophecies which Christ has recounted on the road to Emmaus, and declares that they recognized the risen Christ when he broke bread:

> E uestigio mens nobis est reddita.
> Agnoscimus & colimus aperta numina. (p. 206)

[Instantly our eyes were opened. We recognised and worshipped the Deity disclosed.]

But Thomas' reply challenges this revealed truth, declaring it to be instead beautiful, persuasive rhetoric which has no basis in reality. Of course, Thomas' declaration that he will only believe when he sees and touches Christ for himself is scriptural, but Grimald has here developed the scriptural moment into a questioning of the value of elegant words, which can be deceitful:

> Dixti pulchre. Sed tam impossibile facinus,
> Nemo homo quamuis uehemens, facundus, & eloquens,
> Quamuis limatule & polite pinxerit
> Orationem, mihi persuadere poterit,
> Eum ipsum his oculis nisi praesentem uidero,
> Hijsque; auribus nisi praesentis uocem hausero, &
> Nisi hisce manibus uolnera praesentia
> Reuera & indubitanter contrectauero. (p. 206)

---

76   Ibid., 200.

[Thou has told thy story beautifully. But no man, however forcible, fluent, and eloquent, however polished and elegant his portrayal, will be able to convince me of so impossible a thing, unless with these eyes I shall see Him Himself, unless in His presence with these ears I drink in His voice, and unless with these hands I really and undoubtedly touch His wounds.]

Indeed, Grimald seems to have focused and developed his version of scriptural events in such a way as to set up rhetorical spin in opposition to dialectical ideas of testimony as based on true events. It is thus significant that Thomas is not condemned for his mistrust of elegant words: it is important to distinguish between empty rhetoric which can persuade but also deceive, and true testimony describing facts. Thus Grimald's Christ declares, as he does scripturally, that they are blessed who, unlike Thomas, have not seen and yet have believed, but adds a commendation that Thomas has spoken and acted rightly: "Verum tu tamen || Recte & facis, & loqueris."[77]

The need to weigh the evidence of testimony is demonstrated by the false witness of the four soldiers who had been set to guard the tomb: they are bribed by Caiaphas at the persuasion of Alecto, servant to Cacodemon, a demon of the underworld, and the diabolical origins of deceit are thus laid bare. Grimald's treatment of the underworld is one of the most intriguing and egregious aspects of this play: the mystery plays develop spectacular, though largely non-scriptural, scenes of Christ harrowing hell, terrifying the devils who dwell there and rescuing souls from limbo, and Grimald follows the vernacular tradition by including such scenes, but translates them into Latin Senecan tragedy. Senecan tragedies invariably feature a dark, tormented character from a sinister, ghostly world which threatens to spill over into the earthly world of the protagonists; Grimald creates the character of Cacodemon, who dwells in a dark underworld which threatens earth but is itself now threatened by a terrible light:

O o caelum, o tellus, prata o Neptunia,
Vos Plutonem recipite, quem tartarus euomit.
Date locum, in quem me liceat abstrudere:
Donec lux tanta, meis resedit sedibus
...
Oh, iam splendet nouis aer fulgoribus.
Oh, uolitant agminatim ad caelum caelites.
Nunc uisam apud nos commotas tragoedias.   (pp. 146–48)

---

[77] Ibid., 210.

[O heaven, O earth, O meadows of Neptune, receive Pluto, whom Tartarus spews forth. Give me a place in which I may hide myself as long as so great a light remains in my abode... Oh, now the air gleams with unwonted brightness; oh, the inhabitants, of heaven are flying in their ranks upward to the sky! Now I behold the disaster that has come upon us.]

Cacodemon is never personified in classical drama; he is an internal daemon, a manifestation of an individual's character, a personal fate. He does not belong to the underworld. Grimald may be the first to personify the Greek term and connect him with Satan in hell, as a devil in the Christian tradition. His Senecan character in Grimald is seen in the content and the form of his speeches, in this passage including apocalyptic action, references to Neptune and Pluto, and the vivid verb "euomit," and he describes the events as "tragoedias" – which of course for him they are. His identity within Christian tradition is clear from his account of being driven from heaven by a God who preferred the human race to us ("nobis anteponeret Hominum genus"), of having tainted Adam's offspring with sin and banished him from the garden of Paradise ("horto Paradisiaco"), though the way from the Christian Paradise is across the classical "stygios lacus."[78] Because this Cacodemon is also Satan, he is active in trying to undo God's work of redemption through the resurrected Christ, and so it is he who persuades the Jewish high priests to concoct a lie about the empty tomb. He tells them to bribe the soldiers who have guarded the tomb to say that the body has been stolen. But he does not do this himself; rather he sends another demon, this time Alecto, one of the classical Furies.

Alecto punishes moral crimes against others: she relates to the external fate of the individual; she is sent by the gods to make things happen, including, very often, to drive an individual crazy – as for example in Seneca's *Hercules Furens* in which she drives Hercules to a madness in which he kills his own wife and children. She truly belongs in the underworld. In Book 7 of the *Aeneid*, it is Alecto who, at Juno's command, appears to Turnus in a dream and persuades him to begin the Trojan war. That she is sent to the high priests is therefore not unsurprising, though that she is sent by Cacodemon, and that he describes her as "mens mea," my soul, is more striking: Grimald has made her some infernal messenger and some sort of outward manifestation of the inner demon. But she is also here equated not with the drive to homicide, as in classical tragedy, but with the drive to suicide. She is an analogue of the morality figure of Mischief, who offers the protagonist a rope as the means of self-destruction in,

---

[78] Ibid., 182.

for example, *Mankind* and Skelton's *Magnyfycence*. Grimald's Alecto says of herself:

> Num tibi restim
> Ipsa ferebam
> Perdite Iuda? (p. 184)

[Lost Judas, did not I myself bring thee the rope?]

It is this destructive figure who persuades Caiaphas to bribe the soldiers through praise of a personified King of Money: "Nummus rex, rex nummus, quid non facere potest In omnibus negocijs?" (Money the King, King Money, what can he not do in all affairs?).[79] The silver, filling a purse, is described by Caiaphas as what lies hidden within ("intus latet"[80]); it can work miracles and drive men's hearts, and indeed in this scene it turns the four witnesses entirely. Interrogated by Caiaphas as to whether Christ is resurrected, each soldier asserts in turn that this is indeed the case, and Dromo claims further that he has given proofs of this thing ("rei argument") which were evident ("apertum").[81] In a comically abrupt change of heart, however, once offered money the soldiers equally emphatically declare, each in turn, that the Christ's body was instead stolen while they slept.

The soldiers even congratulate themselves on their good sense in accepting the bribe, in *sententiae* that embrace the royal personification of money and comically expose the corruption of worldly wisdom:

> Nemo tam nulla mente, uel tam nullius
> Est consilij, qui respuat pecunias.
> Conspiranteis animos, tam concinnat cito
> Nihil, quam haec regina sacro sancta pecunia. (p. 194)

[No one is of so little understanding, or so lacking in sense, as to reject money. Nothing so quickly joins together congenial souls as this most sacred Queen, money.]

In humanist pedagogy, *sententiae* were the available riches of Seneca, Plautus and Terence and other classical writers, ripe for reaping and a way of relating

---

79   Ibid., 186.
80   Ibid., 188.
81   Ibid., 190.

the specific action of a play to universal moral truths: by contrast, Grimald here creates aphorisms which instead reflect the immorality of the characters speaking them; the 'wisdom' of the soldiers' *sententiae* does indeed appear universal, but also cynical, and the corruptability of the human outlook is thus exposed.

Strikingly, at the moment of commission, Cacodemon tells Alecto that she must make the soldiers deny what they have seen ("se uidisse pernegent") because there is great need of proofs and deception ("testamentis .... Ac fallacijs").[82] Testimonies can be false, rhetoric can be deceitful, proverbial wisdom can fail and become demonic: through his dramatic intermingling of the classical and the scriptural Grimald perhaps shows that classical wisdom is lightweight in the face of scriptural truth. But how, then, is the truth to be discovered?

Sight is essential to the process. The Angels urge Cleophis to come near, to look inside the empty tomb, to see the place and behold the abandoned grave clothes, explaining that, if words cannot persuade her, then these sights should give her faith:

> Accedite, adsistite, oculis omnem locum
> Perlustratote, qui uacuus cadauere,
> Signum etiamdum effigiemque; sepulti corporis
> Retinet. Et exuuias, quibus implicatus est.
> Si non facile adduci potestis, ut mihi
> Credatis, nec persuadeat oratio mea,
> Vobis praesentia praesentem haec facient fidem. (p. 166)

[Come near, see all the place, which, though empty, still retains the marks and traces of the buried body. Behold the cloths in which He was wrapped. If ye cannot easily be led to believe me, and my speech does not convince you, these, the present sights, will give you ready faith.]

But, as we have seen in Quintilian, and in *Archipropheta*, and as Peter here protests, the eyes can be deceived, as by images in a dream.[83] What is visible may be only part of the truth; as Caiaphas's purse suggests, what lies within, hidden, may be demonically powerful, since money has the power to corrupt the testimony of the soldiers. Or what lies hidden may be the truth that even the devil has to acknowledge: Cacodemon talks of God hidden under the dis-

---

[82] Ibid., 184. Merrill actually has *tentamentis*, but this is presumably an error.
[83] Ibid., 172.

guise of a human form ("humana sub nube & imagine Deus occultatus").[84] To see truly therefore vitally requires also interpretation. Grimald's dramaturgy makes this clear: his play requires only one piece of scenery, one specific visual clue: an empty tomb. The disciples and the women and the soldiers see this sign, and then offer testimonies which interpret it, whether truthfully or deceitfully.

To see and to interpret accurately is to *recognize* – as in *Archipropheta*, the verb *agnoscere* rings throughout the play. When Mary Magdalene first sees the resurrected Christ he is in the form of an unknown gardener ("ignoti sub hortulani schemata") and so she sees him but does not correctly interpret what she sees. It is when he speaks that she recognizes him, by his voice: "Agnoui ex uoce,"[85] and it is this recognition which leads to illumination, as Mary delivers an extended simile of the light of day revealed by a wind dispelling clouds.[86] Whereas in *Archipropheta* Grimald defrocks *agnoscere* and its cognates, exposing the claim of the human senses to offer a reliable understanding of the world, in *Christus Redivivus agnoscere* is the term chosen by both Mary and Cleophus to describe a moment of both sight and insight, recognition beyond doubt, supported by the irrefutable testimony of Christ's risen physical body. As Thomas exemplifies, all individuals must see, weigh and interpret this evidence for themselves; in the divine comedy of the Resurrection human insight checked by providence can find the truth. In the tragic, pre-Resurrection world of *Archipropheta*, Herod becomes the negative exemplar of a harsher didactic truth, that it is because human sense cannot be trusted, and indeed can be perverted by rhetoric, that he is blessed who has not seen and yet has believed.

5   Conclusion

In the Epistle with which he dedicates his play to Archdeacon Gilbert Smith, Grimald is keen to emphasize the enormous scholarly demands of scriptural study: in order to understand the philosophy of the Bible, a man must master Greek and Hebrew, and must make great efforts of comparison and synthesis ("singular inter se loca studiose contulerit"[87]). These great intellectual labours Grimald then compares to his own labours in presenting a play of the Resurrection:

---

84   Ibid., 182.
85   Ibid., 174.
86   Ibid., 174–76.
87   Ibid., 94.

> Tum de Christi a mortuis exurrectione, quam sic ante constituere, quasi si res iam ageretur, contendo, haud paucis difficultatibus, inuoluta historia est. (p. 94)

[So the account of the Resurrection of Christ, which I am trying to set before you as if it were now taking place, involves a great many difficulties.]

There are some, he notes, who feel that the young, like himself, should not be permitted to study scripture at all, or should only be permitted to approach it as listeners, but not to expound it ("quidem accede re patiuntur, ut interpretem autem nullo modo"). Grimald explains that, in addition to the difficulty of understanding scripture, he encounters the difficulty of clothing it in appropriate diction ("digna oratione uestire"): to the philosophical challenge of perceiving and noting in each instance what is proper ("re decorum perspicere & obseruare") a subject treated by scholars of Ethics ("in Ethica"), is added the rhetorical challenge of fashioning diction in harmony with the matter and characters ("consentaneam rebus & personis orationem adfingere").[88] The generic shift by which Grimald fashions drama from the scriptural narrative, changing the 'matter', grants the playwright a certain freedom in adapting the word of God. Thus his task as author combines the work of the Christian divine with that of the classical rhetorician, just as the drama he produces translates Christian narrative into neo-classical Latin, shot through with quotation from the works of the classical greats.

The reader of Grimald, like the audiences of his plays, must correctly recognize the learned elements of his work in order to grasp his message. Similarly, many of the characters within his plays are presented with challenges of recognition. In *Christus Redivivus* and in *Archipropheta* both words and deeds must be scrutinized, weighed, and judged, and the testimony of witnesses compared, one among the others, just as in the work of scriptural scholars. Grimald, a university man schooled in rhetoric and dialectic, appears to explore the Resurrection as the vital divine testimony which must evaluated by dialectic, and which can challenge the rhetoric of worldly wisdom. The difficulty for Herod and Herodias is that they live in a world before this testimony, and the audience of *Archipropheta* must interpret instead the prophet's severed head.

---

88   Ibid.

Bibliography

Bible and Holy Scriptvres Conteyned in the Olde and Newe Testament, The. Translated according to the Ebrue and Greke, and conferred with the best translations in diuers languages. Genève: Rowland Hall, 1560.

Burton, Robert. *The anatomy of melancholy: vvhat it is. VVith all the kindes, cavses, symptomes, prognostickes, and severall cvres of it. In three maine partitions with their seuerall sections, members, and svbsections. Philosophically, medicinally, historically, opened and cvt vp by Democritvs Iunior. With a satyricall preface, conducing to the following discourse.* Oxford: Iohn Lichfield and Iames Short, 1621.

Clare, P.G.W. *Oxford Latin Dictionary*, 2 vols. Oxford: Oxford University Press, 2012.

Clark, Stuart. *Vanities of the Eye: Vision in Early Modern European Culture.* Oxford: Oxford University Press, 2007.

Grimald, Nicholas. *Marcus Tullius Ciceroes thre bokes of duties, to Marcus his sonne, turned out of latine into english.* London: Richard Tottel, 1556.

———. *Christus Redivivus (printed 1543), Archipropheta (printed 1548)*, prepared with an introduction by Kurt Tetzeli von Rosador. New York: G. Olms, 1982.

Höfele, Andreas. "John Foxe, *Christus Triumphans*." In *The Oxford Handbook of Tudor Drama*, edited by Thomas Betteridge and Greg Walker, 124–43. Oxford: Oxford University Press, 2012.

Horner, Olga. "'Us Must Make Lies': Witness, Evidence and Proof in the York *Resurrection*." *Medieval English Theatre* 20 (1998): 24–76.

Hunt, Arnold. *The Art of Hearing: English Preachers and their Audiences, 1590–1640.* Cambridge: Cambridge University Press, 2010.

Karnes, Michelle. *Imagination, Meditation, and Cognition in the Middle Ages.* Chicago: Chicago University Press, 2011.

Merrill, L.R. "Nicholas Grimald, the Judas of the Reformation," PMLA 37 (1922): 216–27.

———, ed. *The Life and Poems of Nicholas Grimald.* New Haven: Yale University Press, 1925.

Peacham, Henry. *The Garden of Eloqvence, Conteining the most excellent Ornaments, Exornations, Lightes, flowers and forms of speech, commonly called the Figures of Rhetorike.* London: R.F. for H. Iackson, 1593.

Poole, Reginald Lane, and Mary Bateson, eds. *Index Britanniae Scriptorum quod ex variis bibliothecis non paruo labore collegit Iohannes Baleus, cum Aliis.* Oxford: Clarendon Press, 1902.

Quintilian. *The Orator's Education*, edited and translated by Donald A. Russell, 5 vols. Loeb Classical Library, 124–27, 494. Cambridge, MA: Harvard University Press, 2001.

Skinner, Quentin. *Reason and Rhetoric in the Philosophy of Hobbes.* Cambridge: Cambridge University Press, 1996.

Sugano, Douglas, ed. *The N-Town Plays*. Kalamazoo, MI: Medieval Institute Publications, 2007.

Taylor, George Coffin. "The Christus Redivivus of Nicholas Grimald and the Hegge Resurrection Plays." *PMLA* 41 (1926): 840–59.

Thorne, Alison. *Vision and Rhetoric in Shakespeare: Looking Through Language*. Basingstoke: Macmillan, 2000.

CHAPTER 10

Staging and Liturgy in *The Croxton Play of the Sacrament*

David Bevington

Abstract

The present essay asks why this unusual play was written when it was written, and how its remarkable staging devices, including an oven that is riven asunder to reveal the speaking image of Christ, are deployed to convey its homiletic idea. The essay argues that theatre and liturgy coalesce in a way that, while characteristic of other medieval religious plays, is here given a sharpness of focus that may owe its sense of urgency to then-current debate over the Real Presence of Christ in the Mass. We encounter in this play a striking ambiguity as to whether the audience is witnessing a theatrical fiction or a liturgical celebration of the 'truth' of the Real Presence. Although liturgy and theatrical mimesis are theoretically incompatible with each other, since liturgy insists on the Real Presence of Christ in the Mass rather than a metaphorical or historical remembrance, *The Play of the Sacrament* erases the distinction between liturgy and *imitatio*. The action may conclude in an actual church with a Bishop presiding over a ceremony of conversion and baptism of the Jews.

Keywords

medieval drama – Croxton Play of the Sacrament – East Anglia – staging – liturgy – *imitatio* – Jews – conversion

1   Introduction

The fifteenth-century *Play of the Conversion of Ser Jonathas the Jew by Miracle of the Blessed Sacrament* is remarkable in many ways.[1] It is a kind of saints' play, in that it presents the story of a miraculous conversion, and its staging methods

---

1   Citations from *The Play of the Conversion of Ser Jonathas the Jew by Miracle of the Blessed Sacrament* are from *Medieval Drama*, ed. David Bevington (Boston: Houghton Mifflin, 1975; rpt. Indianapolis/Cambridge, MA: Hackett Publishing Company, 2012), 754–88.

may have resembled those employed for example in *The Castle of Perseverance* or *The Conversion of St. Paul* and *Mary Magdalen* from the Digby MS.[2] And yet its narrative is in no way biblical and it makes no use of allegorical figures like Humanum Genus, Avarice, Backbiter, Humility, and Perseverance. It is instead a theatrical demonstration of the Real Presence of Christ in the Christian Mass. Its story proceeds by analogy: Jonathas and his fellow Jews who torment the Host in this play are enacting an updated version of the crucifixion of Christ. Their refusal to believe that a priest at a Christian altar can, "by the might of his word" (l. 202), transform a mere "cake" (l. 200) into the "flessh and blode" of him "that deyed upon the rode" (ll. 202–04) is manifestly a representation of pagan scepticism about the central miracle of the Christian faith. Their swearing "by Machomete so mighty" (l. 209) generalizes their anti-Christian scepticism to embrace other pagan religions and attitudes. To these Jews, Christian faith is "fals" (l. 213) when it declares that a loaf of bread can be "He that on Calvery was kild" (l. 214). The mock crucifixion they enact is designed to prove exactly their point, that the bread of the Host is no more than bread. When they strike the Host with their knives, they say, "we shall know if he have eny blood" (l. 452). When they *"prik ther daggerys in four quarters"* (l. 468 s.d.) with Jonathas as the fifth Jew striking in the centre, they are reenacting the torment of Christ on the cross. The bleeding of the Host at this moment recalls Christ's bleeding on the cross while at the same time manifesting the truth they wish to deny, that Christ is present in the Host when the celebrant of the Mass intones, *Hoc est enim corpus meum* (For this is my body). When the Jews undertake to boil the Host in the oven for "three howrys" (l. 488), the text may be alluding indirectly to the three days that Christ spent in the tomb and descent into hell.

By the same analogy, Aristory, the Christian merchant who steals the Host out of a church in return for a payment of "twenty pownd" (l. 282) from the Jews, an offer later extended to "an hundder pownd" (l. 312), is enacting a role like that of Judas Iscariot, the disciple who betrayed Christ in the Garden of Gethsemane to the chief priests for twenty pieces of silver.

The present essay asks why this unusual play was written when it was written, and how its remarkable staging devices, including an oven that is riven

---

2   Elisabeth Dutton, "The Croxton *Play of the Sacrament*," in *The Oxford Handbook of Tudor Drama*, ed. Thomas Betteridge and Greg Walker (Oxford: Oxford University Press, 2012), 55–71, argues persuasively for a flexible approach to staging: the play may well have been written for a travelling troupe, but the use of multiple scaffolds may not always have been practical, and performance at a fixed location may also have taken place at some point. This view is espoused too by David Lawton, "Sacrifice and Theatricality: The Croxton *Play of the Sacrament*," *Journal of Medieval and Early Modern Studies* 33 (2003): 281–309. Lawton provides a useful survey of criticism on the play.

asunder to reveal the speaking image of Christ, are deployed to convey its homiletic idea. My argument will be that theatre and liturgy coalesce in a way that, while characteristic of other medieval religious plays, is here given a sharpness of focus that may owe its sense of urgency to then-current debate over the Real Presence of Christ in the Mass. We encounter in this play a striking ambiguity as to whether the audience is witnessing a theatrical fiction or a liturgical celebration of the 'truth' of the Real Presence.

2   Patterns of Stage Movement

I should like to begin by tracing patterns of stage movement in this play in its original theatrical location, as called for in the stage directions and other indications in the dialogue. The play is notably attentive to such matters, like its much larger near neighbour and near contemporary, *The Castle of Perseverance*. Like Gail Gibson, Victor Scherb, William Tydeman, Marianne Briscoe, John Coldeway, and others,[3] I hold to the view that *The Croxton Play of the Sacrament* (hereafter *Sacrament*) is visibly East Anglian in dialect and staging conception, and that the play's place-and-scaffold staging is presumably crucial to its devotional effects. The banns, resembling those of *The Castle of Perseverance*, are an advertisement for a performance to take place "At Croxston on Monday" (l. 74), or at some other time if a change was called for. Among the various Croxtons to be found in England's midlands at the time, the town in question is very likely to have been the one near Thetford in Suffolk and thus in the vicinity of Bury St. Edmunds, near "Babwell Mill" mentioned familiarly in line 621, and also Tolcote, if that is how we are to interpret "colkote" in line 620. The banns, and the indication that *"Nine may play it at ease,"* suggest itinerant performances by professional players in a number of nearby locations, though not necessarily so. As John Sebastian argues, a casting chart of this sort would be of great practical benefit to an itinerant company; on the other hand, nine is

---

3   Gail McMurray Gibson, *The Theater of Devotion: East Anglian Drama and Society in the Late Middle Ages* (Chicago: University of Chicago Press, 1989; rpt. 1994); Victor J. Scherb, *Staging Faith: East Anglian Drama in the Later Middle Ages* (Madison: Fairleigh Dickinson University Press; London and Cranbury: Associated University Press, 2001); William Tydeman, *English Medieval Theatre, 1400–1500* (London and New York: Routledge, 1994); *Contexts for Early English Drama*, ed. Marianne G. Briscoe and John Coldeway (Bloomington: Indiana University Press, 1989). More recent scholars that are cited in this essay, notably Elisabeth Dutton, John T. Sebastian, and David Lawton, are substantially in agreement about the play's East Anglian provenance.

rather a large number for such a touring company active at this time.[4] The invitation issued by the second Vexillator or banner-bearer to the "S[o]vereyns" (l. 9) who are present to "here the purpoos of this play || That [is] representyd now in yower sight" (ll. 9–10) seems to suggest that the announcing of the banns was accompanied by a brief miming of the play's story by actors in costume. Minstrels are demonstrably there to add to the festive nature of the occasion; the second Vexillator concludes his pitch with "Now, minstrell, blow up with a mery stevyn!" (i.e., sound; l. 80).

Gail Gibson argues that the play was originally produced at Bury St. Edmunds on Corpus Christi Day "by one or more confraternities of priests and pious laymen," perhaps in the "open market square at Angel hill, just in front of the parish church of St. James, which could have served as the church setting for the Episcopus scenes." Gibson further hypothesizes that a copy was then made by "R. C.," whose initials appear in the manuscript, for a performance "at the small neighbouring Norfolk village of Croxton, perhaps, as was so often the case in East Anglian villages, to raise money for the parish church." R. C. might then be Robert Cooke, a local vicar and collector of manuscript playbooks, acting here as scribe to provide Croxton with a play script.[5] Alternatively, R. C. might be the printer Robert Copeland. Gibson's arguments in favour of Bury St. Edmunds as a centre of performance have not won universal acceptance, but they do offer an intriguing scenario.

The text calls for three acting locations plus platea or open acting area: a scaffold for Aristory the Merchant, another for Jonathas the Jew and his fellows, and a church. John Sebastian would like to place the scaffold of Aristory at the centre, envisioning him as the first and perhaps central figure in a kind of psychomachia drama with the demonic Jonathas on one side and the church on the other.[6] Just as plausibly, I think, one might suppose the church to be the

---

4 John T. Sebastian, *Croxton Play of the Sacrament: Introduction.* Published online by Robbins Library Digital Projects, 2012. Accessed December 6, 2014, <http://d.lib.rochester.edu/teams/text/sebastian-croxton-play-of-the-sacrament-introduction>. Prepared from Dublin, Trinity College MAS F.4.20 and the facsimile edition of the play in *Non-Cycle Plays and the Winchester Dialogues*, ed. Norman Davis, Medieval Drama Facsimiles 5 (Leeds: University of Leeds, School of English, 1979).

5 Gibson, *Theater of Devotion*, 40.

6 Sebastian, "Staging the Croxton Play of the Sacrament," in ibid., *Croxton Play: Introduction.* As Dutton, "Croxton *Play of the Sacrament*," 64, notes, the word scaffold does not in fact appear in the original manuscript; see the text in *Non-Cycle Plays and Fragments*, ed. Norman Davis, EETS s.s. 1 (London: Oxford University Press, 1970). To be sure, Jonathas is directed to "*goo do[w]n of[f] his stage*" (l. 228 s.d.), which I take to require something more than the simple step that Dutton proposes; "stage" can certainly mean "platform".

most imposing central structure, especially if, as some scholars have speculated, the final action of the play is to take place (at least in some performances) inside the church. The Bishop issues what may well be an invitation to the spectators to accomplish exactly this. The Holy Sacrament, he orders, is to be borne "to chirche with sole[m]pne procession" (l. 837). "Now folow me, all and summe!" he cries. "And all tho that bene here, both more and lesse, || This holy song, *O sacrum convivium*, || Let us sing all with grett swetnesse" (ll. 838–41). Although that word "all," twice uttered, could be addressed to the players assembled on stage, the familiar "both more and lesse" seems intended more broadly for the socially inclusive group of local citizens who are both well-to-do and less so. That is surely the thrust of the Vexillators' pronouncing the banns in *The Castle of Perseverance*, when they address "all the ryall[ys] of this revme ... And all the goode comowns of this towne that beforn us stonde || In this place" (ll. 7–9), or Mercy in *Mankind* when he addresses "ye soverens that sitt, and ye brotheryn that stonde right uppe" (l. 29).

Earlier, too, in *Sacrament*, the Bishop has urged "all ye peple that here are" to go barefoot "In the devoutest wise that ye can" in solemn procession to the Jews' house (ll. 810–13). An itinerant processional event for the laity present, along with the clergy, would signal unmistakably the sacramental and liturgical way in which all those present are to celebrate two ecclesiastical missions: the veneration of the Host as central to the entire Christian mystery (a celebration that would make great sense on Corpus Christi Day), and the conversion of the Jews to Christianity. These tasks are so momentous in liturgical terms that the role of the Bishop is seemingly transformed before our very eyes from a part enacted by a player in costume to the actual presence of the Bishop himself. The device thereby enacts in theatrical language the mystery of the Real Presence, as embodied in the sacred Mass. Theatre becomes liturgy.

3 Actors' Movements

Pursuing this line of investigation, then, let us follow the actors as they mount and dismount platforms and proceed on foot from one place to another across the platea or open acting area situated between and among the scaffolds. Such a platea was readily available in the space lying before the west door of the church, whether St. James in Bury St. Edmunds or All Saints' in Croxton. We begin with Aristory boasting to be "of all Aragon ... most mighty of silver and of gold" (l. 87). His vaunt marks him as worldly and arrogant, in the theatrical vein of Herod. Clearly he speaks on his scaffold, from which point his clerk, Peter Paul, must then *"withdrawe him"* (l. 148 s.d.) on orders from his master to search

"Thorowght all Eraclea" (i.e., Heraclea, the city of Hercules, in Aragon; l. 138) for merchants from "Surrey" (i.e., Syria) or "Sabé" (i.e., Sabia; l. 140) with whom Aristory can barter. On the platea, this *"merchant[ys] man"* will shortly *"mete with the Jewes"* (l. 236 s.d.). We know that this happens in the open space between the scaffolds, since Jonathas the Jew is instructed, after he has delivered from his own "stage" or scaffold *"his bost"* (l. 148 s.d.) in a ranting style like that of Aristory, to *"goo do[w]n of[f] his stage"* (l. 228 s.d.), that is, to descend from his scaffold to the platea and thus encounter Peter Paul. The action of ascent and descent is repeatedly put to use. The platea is explicitly called *"the place"*: *"Here shall the lechys man come into the place"* (l. 524 s.d.).

Once Jonathas has indicated to Peter Paul that he would be interested in bargaining with Aristory, the clerk is instructed to *"goon to ser Aristory"* (l. 248 s.d.) and presumably does so by mounting that scaffold, where he is then set to work by his master hanging the parlour with "pall" or rich cloths "As longeth for a lordis pere" (ll. 264–65) so as to impress the Jewish visitors with Aristory's wealth and might. Presumably this scaffold provides means for such decorative arrangements, and also affords a way for the clerk and the Clericus or chaplain, "ser Isodere" (l. 344), who is one of Aristory's retainers, to retire out of sight on that scaffold when the priest is bidden to go to bed or when Aristory calls *"his clarke to his presens"* (l. 355 s.d.). Peter Paul also retires and then reappears when he is bidden by his master to bring wine and a "lofe of light bred" (l. 342).

When Aristory has, reluctantly at first, acceded to Jonathas's request that he steal from the church "Yowr God, that is full mythety, in a cake" (i.e., the Host; l. 285), in return for "twenty pound" (l. 282; compare the twenty pieces of silver paid to Judas for betraying Christ) and has raised the price to "an hundder pound" (ll. 315), *"Here goeth the Jewys away"* (l. 335 s.d.), whereupon Aristory proceeds on foot to the church. *"Here shal he entere the chirche and take the hoost"* (l. 367 s.d.). The church could be another scaffold, but there is no need or indication for this; indeed, the scaffolds for Aristory and the Jews require elaborate scenic arrangement (more on this shortly), whereas the church throughout is simply *"the chirche."* The taking of the Host, if done out of view of the spectators, would be all the mysterious for that, and done in such a way as to avoid the potential blasphemy of seeing a secular person robbing the sepulchre of its sacred treasure. At this point the Host is arguably still a stage prop, not some holy bread actually removed from the sacristy of the church. Best to have it so, since it is to be tortured and desecrated by the Jews.

Aristory, with the purloined Host in his hand, thus emerges from the church door, now visible to the spectators, allowing them to surmise the enormity of what he has done. Here he encounters Jonathas: "Me thinketh I him see" (l.

376). Where has Jonathas been in the meantime? He could retire to his scaffold, but I would guess instead that he has been hovering about in the platea, rubbing his hands in anticipation while the robbery is being perpetrated. At any rate, after Jonathas has received the stolen Host from Aristory and has wrapped it in cloth so that "no wight shall the[e] see" (l. 384), Aristory goes *"his waye,"* which I take to mean back to his scaffold, while *"Jonathas and his servauntys shall goo to the tabill"* (l. 384 s.d.). Clearly, though no stage direction specifies that he ascends to his scaffold, he must do so, since the table is a central feature of this stage edifice. It adumbrates, by profane analogy, the holy altar of a Christian church were Mass is said. We, as readers today, are left to gather to what extent this table was in fact make to look like such an altar, but at the very least it had to provide a means for Jonathas to mime the breaking of the bread and give it to his cohorts as he recites an English translation of that central moment of the Mass itself: "He brake the brede and said, 'Accipite' (i.e., take and eat), || And gave his disciplys them for to chere" (ll. 399–400). Jonathas then blasphemously intones the immortal words of the Mass through which the great miracle of the Christian religion is accomplished: *"Comedite, [hoc est] corpus meum"* (l. 404).

The more this blasphemous re-enactment of the Lord's Supper on the Jews' scaffold is made to look as though it takes place at a church altar, the more the audience will perceive the resemblance to the actual church standing before them in the acting arena. If, as I argue, the play is to end (at least in some performances) with a procession into the church where the audience can witness a ceremony of conversion and baptism on the feast of Corpus Christi, the more striking will be this visual and theatrical juxtaposition of two locations. Perhaps it will somewhat resemble the *Second Shepherd's Play*'s visual pairing of Mak and Jill's ruined cottage with the lowly manger in Bethlehem where Jesus was born.

I once attended a demonstration Mass in Kalamazoo Michigan's Episcopal Church during a medieval conference there in which the Roman Catholic priest who had agreed to take the part of the celebrant was told by Episcopalian authorities that under no circumstances would he be allowed to utter those sacred five words, *Hoc est enim corpus meum*, lest the demonstration Mass transform itself into the real thing. Indeed, despite this precaution, as the event proceeded the many members of religious orders who were there all stood or knelt at the appropriate times as the Mass was sung, so that one could never be sure whether one was beholding a Mass or a theatrical event. My argument here is that something like that moment of theatrical daring and ambiguity must have occurred in the staging of *The Play of the Sacrament*.

4   The Paradoxical Use of Stage Illusion to Depict the Real Presence

This ambiguity is key to what then follows in the play. The Jews' scheme is to torment the stolen Host (which the audience understands has already been mystically transformed inside the church into Christ's body and blood) in order to determine whether this bread is the ordinary loaf that it appears to be or is truly Christ's body and blood. "Iff that this be he that on Calvary was mad[e] red," says Jason, "Onto my mind, I shall kenne yow a conceit good": let us seize on "this bredde" with our daggers and "clowtys" in order to determine "if he have eny blood" (ll. 449–52). They do so, ferociously, picking their daggers "*in four quarters*" (l. 468 s.d.), with Jonathas striking "In the middys" (l. 480). "*Here the [h]ost must blede*" (l. 480 s.d.). And so the business proceeds as they nail the sacrament to a post representing the cross. The Host refuses to let go of Jonathas's hand, whereupon Jonathan's arm and hand (still stuck fast to the Host) pulls away from his body and remains nailed to the post. When Jason plucks out the nails and shakes the hand into the cauldron (l. 660 s.d.), the Host is removed from the blood-red cauldron and is cast into the oven (l. 700 s.d.). Finally, the oven "*must rive asundere and blede owt at the cranys, and an image appere owt with woundys bleding*" (l. 712 s.d.). The "*image*" is made to "*speke to the Jews*" (l. 716 s.d.), upbraiding them for having tortured "yowr king" (i.e. Christ, l. 720).

This astonishing sequence, ending in the conversion of the Jews to Christianity, was clearly intended as a demonstration of the Real Presence in the Mass, a dogma being emphasized by the Papacy in the fifteenth century as central to the Feast of Corpus Christi or Corpus Domini, the Body of Christ. The feast, which had become universal in 1317, celebrated the crucial importance of the Eucharist to the entire history of Christianity. Coming as it did in midsummer, when the liturgical calendar was not busy as it had been earlier with Advent, Christmas, Lent, Easter, and still more, the feast could serve as a way of bringing the liturgical year to a triumphant close. It could serve as a bulwark against the threat of heresy posed by the Lollards and other heretical sects that were increasingly active and worrisome. It could reassure the faithful at a time when the Papacy was subjected to sustained criticism for pluralism, simony, luxurious living, and other corruptions. The Feast of Corpus Christi also proved to be an especially suitable occasion for accepting converted Jews into the Christian communion. Numerous miracles in the fifteenth and early sixteenth centuries attested to a living tradition, as when witnesses affirmed that they had seen the body of the crucified Christ hovering over the altar table while the celebrant sang Mass.[7]

---

7   See Albrecht Dürer's woodcut, "The Mass of St. Gregory," 1511. A copy is located in the National Gallery of Canada. The woodcut is based on the twelfth-century "Life of St. Gregory the Great,"

For our purposes as theatre historians, this sequence also provides a brilliant illustration of the ambiguous and disappearing line between drama and liturgy that is an essential part of the story of Western religious drama from the earliest days of *Quem quaeritis*. Drama and liturgy are, in theory, incompatible. One is fictional, the other stoutly defended by many church authorities as literal. Conservative opponents of Bishop Honorius of Autun insisted on that point in their disapproval of his theatrical interpretation of the Mass itself (in *Gemma Animae*, c. 1100). Yet the language of rubrics in early texts repeatedly manifests an understandable tendency to employ what we can interpret as dramatic language. In the *Visitatio Sepulchri* from the *Regularis Concordia of St. Ethelwold* at Winchester, c. 965–75, the three monks who are to approach the altar are instructed to do so "*cappis induti, turibula cum incensu manibus gestantes ac pedemptim ad simulitudinem quaerentium quid*" (vested in copes, bearing in their hands thuribles with incense, and haltingly, in the manner of seeking for something). "*Aguntur enim haec ad imitationem angeli sedentis in monumento*" (These things are done in imitation of the angel seated on the tomb), and so forth. A Good Friday ceremonial from the same monastery employs similarly theatrical language: "*Sit autem in una parte altaris, qua vacuum fuerit, quaedam assimilatio sepulchri, velamenque quoddam in gyro tensum quod*" (Let there be on one part of the altar, where there is room, a likeness of the sepulchre, and a curtain stretched around it). The three brethren are to approach the place of the sepulchre, "*depositque cruce, ac si Domini nostri Jhesu Christi corpore sepulto*" (and when the cross has been laid therein, as if the body of our Lord Jesus Christ has been buried), they are to sing the antiphon "*Sepulto Domino*" (The Lord having been buried), and so on.[8] The theatrical nature of such rubrics increases in the eleventh and twelfth centuries, by which time a number of these liturgical ceremonials have been collected in what can be called playbooks, in Fleury and in other monasteries.

In *The Play of the Sacrament*, the ambiguous boundary between theatre and Christian miracle dissolves entirely if, as I have been supposing, the show ends with a ceremonial procession of actors and audience into the church. There,

in which Christ appeared to Pope Gregory as he was celebrating the Mass in St. Peter's Basilica in Rome, after an assistant had doubted the Real Presence of Christ in the bread and wine of the Holy Communion. The woodcut shows Christ rising out of his tomb on the altar table, surrounded by the instruments of his Passion and attended by angels. The woodcut is featured on the dust cover and as frontispiece illustration for O.B. Hardison Jr., *Christian Rite and Christian Drama in the Middle Ages: Essays in the Origin and Early History of Modern Drama* (Baltimore: Johns Hopkins Press, 1965).

8 Texts of these early ceremonials are available in Bevington, *Medieval Drama*, 9–29. For more extensive coverage, see Karl Young, *The Drama of the Medieval Church*, 2 vols. (Oxford: Clarendon Press, 1933).

the figure identified in the stage directions and speech prefixes as *"Episcopus"* presides over what has now becomes a service. He lays the Host *"u[p]on the autere"* (l. 865 s.d.), intones a liturgical passage from Revelation 20, metes out harsh penance to those who have transgressed, receives their confessions, absolves them, and christens them *"with gret solempnité"* (l. 951 s.d.). He uses the language of the liturgy to bless them "with the water of baptime" (l. 953), delivers a brief homily on the Ten Commandments, and closes the proceedings, as he would a service in the church, with singing of *Te Deum Laudamus*. Are we at a religious service, or are we watching a play?

5   *Imitatio* and Ritual

The Play of the Sacrament approaches *imitatio* in a way that today may seem awkward but nonetheless instructive. The production offers itself, in the language of the *Regularis Concordia* at Winchester, "for the strengthening of the faith of the unlearned multitude and of neophytes." Those witnessing the play are to find their Christian faith affirmed and bolstered by the dramatization of a miracle demonstrating the truth of the Real Presence in the Mass. Yet the means of staging this miracle are transparently mechanical. An oven bursts asunder and Christ's image appears, "with wo[u]ndys all bloody" (l. 942). When the play was produced by students at the University of Chicago in the 1970s, the audience at this moment collapsed into hysterical laughter. The original fifteenth-century production of the play took place in an age of faith, to be sure, but even so we are bound to wonder today how this could have worked then. The answer, perhaps, is that the mechanical means of producing a miracle through quasi-dramatic representation was no less evident to the monks at Winchester in the tenth century taking part in their *Depositio* and *Quem Quaeritis* ceremonies for Good Friday and Easter Sunday. They could not have been ignorant of the arrangement by which the Host had been 'reserved' or removed from the sepulchre, its regular place of containment in the chancel. The removal was essential to the whole process of darkening the church on Good Friday and then 'discovering' that the Host was absent from its regular place on Easter morning. That moment of recognition, when (as at Winchester) the Angel must lift the veil *"ostendatque eis locum cruce nudatum"* (and show them [i.e., the three brethren-disciples] the place bare of the cross), demonstrates the miracle of the Resurrection. It is to be done *"ac veluti ostendentes, quod surrexit Dominus et iam non sit illo involutus"* (as if demonstrating that the Lord has risen and is not now wrapped in) the "shroud" used to wrap the Host.

The veil is lifted, the place is bare of the cross. Behold, the Lord is risen! *Surrexit Dominus de sepulchro!*[9]

The staged miracle in *Sacrament* calls upon the same act of faith in great things that are unseen. The more improbable or impossible this is to ordinary sense, the more one's faith is called into service. One learns to believe "because it is absurd or impossible." "*Credo quia absurdum est*," wrote the first- and second-century church father Tertullian in *De Carni Christi*, 5, 4; "*Certum est, quia impossibile*" (It is certain because it is impossible); "*Credibile est, quia ineptum est*" (It is credible because it is ridiculous). Tertullian's task was to refute the Gnostic docetism of Apelles and others who argued that Christ put on the appearance but not the reality of being human. Tertullian contended that the body of Christ was a real human body, born from the Virgin Mary without human procreation. Here, then, was the central 'impossibility' of Christian faith. *Sacrament* is squarely in this tradition.

6   The Comic Interlude

One question not yet addressed in this essay is what to make of the comic interlude involving Colle "*the lechys man*" (l. 524 s.d.) and the doctor he serves, Master Brundiche of Brabant, identified as "magister phisicus" in 'The Namys and Numbere of the Players." This episode occurs, surprisingly, right in the midst of the Jews' tormenting of the Host. Things are not going well for the Jews at this point: Jonathas has seized the Host in order to throw it into their cauldron, only to have the Host cling to his hand, prompting Jonathas to run "*wood*" (i.e., run mad; l. 503 s.d.). When his fellows manage to catch him and nail the Sacrament to a post, their frantic attempts to pull Jonathas away from the Host result in their plucking away his arm without his hand, which remains with the Host: "*Here shall thay pluke the arme, and the hand shall hang still with the sacrament*" (l. 515 s.d.). Jonathas, paradoxically, begins to take on the role of the one who is being persecuted and crucified, no longer just the agent of those atrocities. He even begins to speak in language reminiscent of Christ's last words. When Jonathas cries out, "Ther is no more; I must enduer!" (l. 520), we can hear echoes of Christ's "My God, my God, why hast thou forsaken me?" and "I thirst" and "It is finished" (Matthew 27:46, Mark 15: 34, John 19:28, 30). The Jews in *Sacrament* thereupon retire to "owr chamber" on their scaffold, "Till I may get me sum recouer" (l. 521–22), as Jonathas explains to them. This move

---

[9] Bevington, *Medieval Drama*, 27–29, and Young, *Drama of the Medieval Church*, 1: 249.

appears to be a stage device to clear the acting arena so that Colle, the doctor's servant, may "*come into the place*" (l. 524 s.d.) and begin the comic interlude.

But why have such an interlude at all? It is fairly extensive: 128 lines out of a total of 1007. It is an almost entirely separate action: Colle and Master Brundiche play no part in the re-enactment of the crucifixion. They come into the playing area only after the Jews on their scaffold have retired to their "chamber," where seemingly they are no longer visible to the audience. The only brief interaction of the clownish characters with the Jews is at the end of the episode: Master Brundiche, having learned from Colle that a Jew named Jonathas has "lost his right hond" (l. 629) and "nedethe helpe of a phesisician" (l. 623), goes to Jonathas, presumably through some doorway ("the gate is here"; l. 631) at the Jews' scaffold. Here Brundiche offers his professional services, only to be abused for the intrusion. Even Colle's insistence that his master has "savyd many a manes life" (l. 643), along with an offer to analyze a urine sample "In a pott if it please yow to pisse" (l. 648), fails to persuade the enraged Jonathas. Jonathas orders his friends to "Brushe them hens bothe" (l. 651). "*Here shall the four Jewys bett away the leche and his man*" (l. 653 s.d.). The play returns to the painful business of Jason's plucking out the nails and shaking the hand into the cauldron.

Meantime, the comic episode itself is full of local colour and comic shtick. Colle's opening declamation, like the banns of the play proper, announces who and what the audience is to behold. Master Brandiche, Colle mockingly declares, is "a man of all sience" (l. 529) whose chief occupation appears to be that "He sitteth with sum tapstere in the spence" (l. 531), keeping company with a female tapster who is evidently amenable to his approaches. "His hoode there will he sell" (l. 532); he would sell the very hood off his back, presumably for wine. He "seeth as wele at noone as at night" (l. 537), that is, his vision is equally imperfect whether by day or night; his "judgiment" or medical opinion is equal in value to a person "that hathe noon eyn" (l. 539–40), cannot see. He is a "boone-setter", and "I knowe no man go the better!" (ll. 541–42) says Colle, using a familiar Chaucerian formula of mock praise. He runs up debts in every tavern. A lady patient of his will never be heard to tell tales against him – presumably because she is no longer living. "He spekit[h] never good matere nor purpoose" (l. 571) and deserves no less than pillorying, Colle concludes.

Master Brundiche, unobserved at first by Colle as he enters, presumably overhears some of Colle's raillery. They spar, with Colle in the venerable stage tradition of cheeky servant, chaffing with his master. When Brundiche insists that the patient last under his "medicament" did "never fele annoyment" (l. 582–83), Colle has the suitable riposte: "Why, is she in hir grave?" (l. 584). Evidently Brundiche devotes most of his professional attention to women patients. When he boasts, "I have savid many a mannys life," Colle corrects his indication of gender: "On widowes, maidese, and wife || Yowr conning yow have nyh[e] spent" (ll. 594–96). The potions he has administered to one woman patient, "a drinke made full well || With scamoly and with oxennell, || Lettuce, sauge, and pimpenelle," earns sardonic praise from Colle: "Nay, than she is full save" (i.e., out of danger because no longer breathing, ll. 585–88). Scamole or scammony is a strong purgative and oxymell a concoction of vinegar and honey, in the usual catalogue of rostrums used by doctors to cure the body by the use of violent emetics. Brundiche bids his servant make a proclamation to the "grete congregacion" (l. 601) that is present, bidding them have recourse to this great doctor who "will never leve yow till ye be in yow[r] grave," whether you suffer from "the canker, the collike, or the laxe [i.e., diarrhea], || The tercian, the quartan, or the brynnin[n]g axs [i.e., burning fever]," or "wormys ... grindi[n]g in the wombe or in the boldyro" [i.e., perhaps, the genitals, ll. 611–14], and so on in a bravura list of medical ailments. The conclusion is anything but reassuring: "Thow[g]h a man w[e]re right heyle [i.e., hale, healthy], he cowd soone make him sek[e]!" (l. 619). Local references presumably add comic immediacy to this satirical skit: Master Brundiche's prospective patients are to "Inquire to the colkote, for ther is his logging, || A lityll beside Babwell Mill, if ye will have und[er]stondin[g]" (ll. 620–21). Colkote may be a copying error for Tolcote, as indicated earlier; both Tolcote and Babwell Mill are in the vicinity of Croxton near the border of Norfolk and Suffolk.

What has all this to do with Jonathas and the assault on the Host in the main plot? 'Comic relief' is too easy a nostrum, though this episode certainly serves in that capacity: it breaks in two the sequence of tormenting the Host, giving time for the Jews to retire to their "chamber" on their scaffold and look after Jonathas's physical distress, and for the audience to reflect on what has happened thus far. The connection between comic interlude and main plot is given a plausible if thin justification, in that Jonathas's condition does seem to call for a physician, even if Brundiche is comically the wrong doctor.

More substantially, the two stories are linked by the way in which Jonathas's agony is taking on ludicrous dimensions. We cannot be sure if laughter is intended in a play nearly six hundred years old, but a reasonable guess is that his losing of his hand to the tenacious Host is meant to be funny. It is not unlike the comic business in Marlowe's *Doctor Faustus* when the Horse-courser or horse-dealer, having been conned by Faustus into paying forty dollars for a horse that then turns into a bundle of hay when ridden into the water, attempts to get his money back by pulling on the sleeping Faustus's leg until it comes away in his hands. The B-text's fulsome spinning out of this joke, more deftly and briefly presented in the A-text (IV.i), attests as an item of stage history to the irresistibly comic nature of an actor losing a limb or part of one.

Dismemberment of this sort is a fine sight-gag on stage, especially since it depends on a *trompe-l'oeil* effect: Faustus presumably lies under a cloak, with the extra stage leg ready to be pulled out by the Horse-courser. A similar crude stagecraft must apply in *Sacrament*: Jonathas seizes the Host, it refuses to let go when he tries to throw it into the oven, Jonathas's fellow Jews desperately nail the Sacrament to a post, and the Host still refuses to relinquish its grasp. When the Jews "*pluke the arme, … the hand shall hang still with the sacrament*" (l. 515 s.d.). It is at this point that Jonathas disconsolately retires out of sight on his scaffold with his friends, leaving the acting arena to Colle entering into "*the place*" (l. 524 s.d.). The Host, tenaciously clinging to Jonathas's hand, remains in plain sight throughout the comic interlude of doctor and roguish servant. At the end of this episode, the hand and Host are still there; they provide visual justification for Master Brundiche's ascending the Jews' scaffold to offer his medical expertise, and they are there to provide visual continuity as the main plot proceeds: "*Here shall Jason pluck owt the nailys and shake the hand into the cawdron*" (l. 660 s.d.).

If the jesting about dismemberment is recognizably hoary with stage tradition, it fits the business of Jonathas's running mad and falling into comic desperation. That action is a ludicrous parody of Christ's suffering and crucifixion. It employs the kind of daring juxtaposition one often finds in medieval religious drama, as, famously, in *The Second Shepherd's Play* already mentioned above, when the holy episode of the nativity is introduced by a hilarious yarn about a sheep-stealer and his wife trying unsuccessfully to hide their stolen sheep by concealing it beneath clothes in a crib. The sheep is a type of the infant Christ. The ragged clothes in which it lies are like the swaddling clothes used to warm the newborn child; they also invite the audience to think of the "shroud" used to wrap the Host in the sanctuary "tomb" when the Angel holds up the empty grave clothes as he says, by way of demonstrating the great truth of the Resurrection, "*Venite et videte locum ubi positus erat Dominicus*" (Come and see the place where the Lord had been laid; The Raising of the Host from the Sepulchre, *St. Gall*).[10] Another example of daring and nearly blasphemous juxtaposition is to be found in many versions of the troubles of Joseph, when he learns that his wife is pregnant without his agency and falls at once into the comic stereotype of the *vieux jaloux*, the jealous husband (the Towneley cycle offers a piquant instance).

Risible jesting of this sort is a staple of medieval art of all sorts, including of course the drama. The episode of Master Brundiche and Colle is in this tradition. It invites, by comparison, laughter at Jonathas's ridiculous attempts to

---

10 Bevington, *Medieval Drama*, 17.

ridicule the sacred Host. He is his own worst enemy, a braggart, a Herod figure on stage, blustering, ultimately self-defeating. This is the comic strategy of medieval religious art more generally to portray the way in which the devil and his numerous worshippers among men are destined to fall into their own traps. This is the *Divina Commedia* of medieval religious drama; in *Sacrament*, as in Dante and indeed universally in medieval Christian art, the painful story of suffering and sacrifice is the prelude to a story of spiritual triumph. Adam and Eve fall from grace so that Christ's coming will be the necessary completion of God's great plan of salvation. The cruel and shocking physical violence in *Sacrament*, together with its grotesque comedic effects, link this play to the great tradition that informs the cycle plays. We should not be surprised to find in *Sacrament* an episodic instance of this paradoxically comic suffering in the little story of Master Brundiche and his servant. The parallelism between the ineffectual ridiculousness of Master Brundiche and that of Jonathas invites satirical laughter at those who would foolishly deny the miracle of the Host in the little story of Master Brundiche and his servant.

7   The Jews and Conversion

What then does the play make of the fact that Jonathas and his cohorts are Jews? The first obvious answer, of course, is that they are likened to the Jews who crucified Christ; they are his torturers, his betrayers. They are in league with the great Enemy whose fixed purpose it is, in the N-Town cycle for instance, to determine that Christ was in fact a human being and only that; as such, he can be hunted down and destroyed. The N-Town cycle dramatizes, at its core, the motif of the beguiler beguiled. Driven on by his obsessive desire to prove that Christ was a man only, the devil in that cycle visits Pilate's wife in a dream, urging her to prevail upon her husband to abort the crucifixion of Christ. He does this because he has realized, too late, that the crucifixion will set in motion the salvation of the human race. Earlier, the devil has urged Judas to betray his master as part of the devil's plan to kill the human Christ and thereby undo all that Christ had taught. Now it is too late for his fatal miscalculation. Curses, foiled! The devil is the engineer of his own undoing.

And thus it is with Jonathas and his fellow Jews, until the miracle of the flaming oven occurs. Their great sin, in the playwright's view, is their unwillingness to leave their benighted scepticism and embrace the truth of the new dispensation offered by Christianity. This is a sin that is easily remedied if they are ready to convert to the true religion. The history of persecution of the Jews throughout this period and indeed throughout history testifies to a deeper and irrational hatred, of course, but theologically the guilt of the Jews in medieval drama has nothing to do with culture and ethnicity.

This reading of Jewish history is remarkably consistent in the religious drama of Western Europe from the tenth century onward. The language of early *Visitatio Sepulchri* texts is offensive to our modern sensibilities for the most pertinent of reasons, as when, in the twelfth-century Fleury playbook, the three Marys approach the tomb intoning, "*Heu! Nequam gens Judaica, || quam dira frendet vesania. || Plebs execranda!*" (Alas! Wretched Jewish people, whom an abominable insanity makes frenzied. Despicable nation!; ll. 7–9). Clifford Flanigan and other scholarly producers at Indiana University of the *Ludus de Nativitate* from Benediktbeuern, sung in Latin, had to cancel a planned visit to New York City in the 1960s, during the era of John Lindsay's mayoralty, once the Anti-Defamation League had discovered and publicized an English translation of its script, including "*Judaea misera, || sedens in tenebris, || repelle maculam || delicti funebris*" (Wretched Judaea, dwelling in shadows, cast off the stain of mortal transgression), etc.[11]

Sacrament follows suit: "*O mirabiles Judei, attendite et videte || Si est dolor sicut dolor meus!*" (O ye strange Jews, behold and see if there is any sorrow like unto my sorrow; ll. 717–18, borrowing a line from Lamentations 1:12), says Jesus when his image appears in the bursting oven. Offensive such language undeniably is, but the remedy is at hand, and is immediately effective in this play. Jonathas and his fellows at once kneel down and cry out "with sorow and care and grete weping" (l. 746), "*Lacrimis nostris conscientiam nostram baptizemus!*" (with our tears may we baptize our conscience; l. 749). They greet Jesus as "thow my Lord God and Saviowr ... || Thow King of Jewys and of Jerusalem || ... thow mighty, strong Lion of Juda" (ll. 778–80), acknowledging that Jewry is now folded into the kingdom of Christ.

This is essentially a philosemitic view of Jewish history, in which the Old Testament is integral to the story of salvation; it is often endorsed today by many fundamentalist Christians, like Tom Delay of Texas, formerly Republican Party House Majority Leader in the US Congress.[12] The only problem the Jews have is that they are benighted and headed straight for eternal damnation. They are ideal candidates for conversion.

---

11 *Ludus de Nativitate*, ll. 19–22 (Bevington, *Medieval Drama*, 181). For the quotations from the Fleury *Service for Representing the Scene at the Lord's Sepulche,* see ibid., 39–44, especially ll. 7–9.

12 See Tom D. Delay, *No Retreat, No Surrender: One American's Fight* (New York: Sentinel, 2007).

The play ends, therefore, with a group conversion and baptism that is highly ceremonial, featuring a singing procession as the Host is escorted to the church (l. 841 s.d.). All persons present, including, it would seem, the spectators, are to follow the Bishop and sing *O sacrum convivium*, a Latin text written by Thomas Aquinas as an antiphon for the feast of Corpus Christi to honour the Blessed Sacrament: "*O sacrum conviviam, || in quo Christus sumitur: || recolitur memoria passionis eius: || mens impletur gratia: || et futurae gloriae nobis pignus datur*" (O sacred banquet at which Christ is received and consumed, the memory of his Passion is renewed and recalled, our souls are filled with grace, and the pledge of future glory is given to us). The rubrics specify that the Bishop "*shall entre the chirche and lay the [h]ost u[p]on the autere*" (l. 865 s.d.), as he sings "*Estote fortes in bello et pugnate cum antico serpente, || Et accipite regnum aeternum, et cetera*" (Be valiant in battle and fight with the old serpent, and receive the eternal kingdom, and so on). This text, taken from Revelation 20:2, provides a favourite motet for feasts of apostles and evangelists, set in more recent years by noted composers like Tomás Luis de Victoria and Carlo Gesualdo. The Bishop christens the Jews "*with gret solempnité*" (l. 951 s.d.), intoning in translation the wording of the baptismal ceremony:

> with the watere of baptime I shall yow blisse ...
> In the name of the Father, the son, and the Holy Gost,
> To save yow from the devillys flame,
> I cristen yow all. (ll. 954–59)

The altar, the water, the Bishop, all are provided for by the sacristy in which this dramatic ceremonial concludes.

This final ceremonial, and the play preceding it, belong authentically in the tradition of medieval religious drama, both as theatrical performance and liturgical celebration.

Bibliography

Bevington, David, ed. *Medieval Drama*. Boston: Houghton Mifflin, 1975; rpt. Cambridge, MA: Hackett Publishing Company, 2012.

Briscoe, Marianne G., and John Coldeway, eds. *Contexts for Early English Drama*. Bloomington: Indiana University Press, 1989.

Davis, Norman, ed. *Non-Cycle Plays and Fragments*. EETS, s.s. 1. London: Oxford University Press, 1970.

———. *Non-Cycle Plays and the Winchester Dialogues*. Medieval Drama Facsimiles, 5. Leeds: University of Leeds, School of English, 1979.

Delay, Tom D. *No Retreat, No Surrender: One American's Fight*. New York: Sentinel, 2007.

Dutton, Elisabeth. "The Croxton *Play of the Sacrament*." In *The Oxford Handbook of Tudor Drama*, edited by Thomas Betteridge and Greg Walker, 55–71. Oxford: Oxford University Press, 2012.

Gibson, Gail McMurray. *The Theater of Devotion: East Anglian Drama and Society in the Late Middle Ages*. Chicago: University of Chicago Press, 1989; rpt. 1994.

Hardison Jr., O.B. *Christian Rite and Christian Drama in the Middle Ages: Essays in the Origin and Early History of Modern Drama*. Baltimore: Johns Hopkins Press, 1965.

Lawton, David. "Sacrifice and Theatricality: The Croxton *Play of the Sacrament*." *Journal of Medieval and Early Modern Studies* 33 (2003): 281–309.

Scherb, Victor J. *Staging Faith: East Anglian Drama in the Later Middle Ages*. Madison: Fairleigh Dickinson University Press; London and Cranbury: Associated University Press, 2001.

Sebastian, John T. *Croxton Play of the Sacrament: Introduction*. Published online by Robbins Library Digital Projects, 2012. Accessed December 6, 2014, <http://d.lib.rochester.edu/teams/text/sebastian-croxton-play-of-the-sacrament-introduction>.

Tydeman, William. *English Medieval Theatre, 1400–1500*. London and New York: Routledge, 1994.

Young, Karl. *The Drama of the Medieval Church*, 2 vols. Oxford: Clarendon Press, 1933.

CHAPTER 11

Herod's Reputation and the Killing of the Children: Some Theatrical Consequences

Bob Godfrey

Abstract

From the story of the Epiphany in Matthew's Gospel this chapter offers a brief account of the evolution of Christian attitudes to Herod the Great and how the slaughtered Innocents became subjects of devotional attention, the first martyrs for Christ. Taking then a variety of examples of how the story of the Epiphany captured the imagination of Christian poets and liturgical and religious playmakers the discussion proceeds to an examination of two plays from the Towneley collection, *The Offering of the Magi* and *Magnus Herodes*. Focussing on the character of Herod as presented there it is shown how his character can be interpreted as both violently threatening and yet obviously absurd. This ambivalence is brought out most strongly in *Magnus Herodes* where the Wakefield Master skilfully manages audience reception to see Herod as a character in a play, an entertainment in his own right, as much as a target for Christian vindictiveness. Herod's *envoi* in the Towneley play is cheeky since it foregrounds the character's humanity as against his culpability. In comparison with other examples this playwright seems to have been reluctant to join the almost universal moralising and condemnation of Herod in favour of a perfectly theatrical outcome.

Keywords

Epiphany – innocents – Towneley – Magi – Herod – tragicomic

1   Introduction

My aim in this chapter is to offer performance readings of the Epiphany sequence from the Towneley collection of plays contained in *The Offering of the Magi* (14) and the *Magnus Herodes* (16), the second of which is of greatest interest. I shall also make occasional reference to other versions of this sequence in plays nearly contemporary with Towneley but only in so far as they offer distinctly different motifs or emphasise different approaches to the story. The representation of Herod is of singular importance, but at the same time it is essential to examine the context of promise and miracle within which his story is contained. What matters most is the ways in which the playwrights have chosen to transform the biblical story and thereby work to influence audience reception.

2   The Biblical Account of the Epiphany

The dramatisation of the Epiphany sequence takes its cue from the time of the Gospel of Matthew where Herod first gained his reputation as enemy of Christ. Herod came, therefore, to be cast in the role of a main protagonist in this series of plays. The Gospel, quoted from the King James Bible, begins the narration of the familiar story:

> Now when Jesus was born in Bethlehem of Judaea in the days of Herod the king, behold, there came wise men from the east to Jerusalem, Saying, Where is he that is born King of the Jews? for we have seen his star in the east, and are come to worship him. When Herod the king had heard these things, he was troubled, and all Jerusalem with him. (Matthew 2:1–3)

In purely political terms, therefore, Herod's concern begins when he realizes that his position as king may be threatened by a young pretender. A rival king would be no small matter in the business of the state, a factor that is underlined by Matthew's comment that not only Herod but "all Jerusalem" was troubled by the news. In particular Herod was not himself a natural Jew, though his father had converted, and he had become king only by being chosen by the Romans to rule the Jewish kingdom. In such circumstances, in the eyes of the Jewish people, a child of the house of David would represent a genuine challenge to Herod's position. Furthermore, in the following verses of Matthew's Gospel, we are told that the birth had been anticipated by the prophets of the Old Testament. Without wishing to excuse him of his atrocity all of this adds weight to an historical understanding of Herod's trouble. So it follows that, when he heard of their arrival in Judea seeking a King of the Jews, Herod summoned the "wise men" to him to explain their journey through his territory. After some consultation he asked them to "diligently enquire" after Jesus so that he himself might later go and pay homage to the child. The urgency of the word "diligently" further expresses Herod's state of mind regarding his own insecurity and that of his kingdom.

The Magi, as the story tells us, did go and find Jesus but, as we remember, divine intervention subsequently warned them against returning to Herod with the information he required. The consequence of their deceit was the action that immortalised Herod for succeeding generations of Christians and made him a main protagonist in the Epiphany dramas:

> Then Herod, when he saw that he was mocked of the wise men, was exceeding wroth, and sent forth, and slew all the children that were in Bethlehem, and in all the coasts thereof, from two years old and under, according to the time which he had diligently inquired of the wise men. (Matthew 2:16)

Fortunately for Christianity, as the Gospel makes clear, by the time of this order Jesus was safely in Egypt. The Holy family had fled there, guided, as the Magi had been, by divine intervention. They later returned to Israel but only after the death of Herod.

3 The Character of Herod in History

This Biblical account of the incidents that surrounded the killing of the children forms the basis for the plays I wish to consider and in itself adds up to a serious indictment of Herod. But Herod's character at large, as represented, for instance, in the first century AD by historian Josephus, was seen to be of a piece with this act. Even though Josephus makes no mention of the slaughter of the children he does indicate that during his life Herod on occasion had to deal with what he suspected were challenges to his authority. To be fair the situation in Judea under Roman occupation was politically uneasy at best and Herod often felt driven to act ruthlessly, even and especially with regard to his own family. Finally, in the *Antiquities of the Jews*, Josephus draws a moralistic conclusion to Herod's story in the account of his quite horrible death. The historian reports that "It was said by those who pretended to divine, and who were endued with wisdom to foretell such things, that God inflicted this punishment on the king on account of his great impiety."[1] Furthermore Josephus says that as Herod came nearer to his death "he grew so choleric, that it brought

---

1 Flavius Josephus, *The Antiquities of the Jews*, trans. William Whiston, Book XVII, Chapter 8, Paragraph 5, reproduced through Project Gutenberg as EBook #2848, produced by David Reed and David Widger, 2009–13, accessed 24 May 2015, <http://www.gutenberg.org/files/2848/2848-h/2848-h.htm>.

him to do all things like a madman."[2] Altogether it is small wonder that the Roman Church felt able to make capital out of Herod's soiled reputation.

4 An Early Representation of the Epiphany Story

So it came about that in the fifth century when the Roman poet Prudentius was moved to write a hymn in celebration of the Epiphany, he included a dramatised, and to some extent, a sensationalised account of Herod's part in the story:[3]

> Distraught, the tyrant base doth hear
> That now the King of Kings draws near
> To reign in David's seat of state
> And Israel's empire dominate.
>
> "Betrayed are we," he maddened cries,
> "Our throne's usurper doth arise:
> Go, soldiers, go with sword in hand
> And slay all babes within my land.
>
> "Spare no male child: each nurse's robe
> Your scrutinizing steel must probe:
> Spare not the suckling infant, though
> O'er mother's breast its life-blood flow.
>
> "On Bethlehem our suspicion falls,
> On every hearth within its walls:
> Lest mothers with love's tender zeal
> Some manly scion may conceal." (ll. 93–108)

The hymn continues with a graphic evocation of the slaughter of the children by Herod's soldiers, the juxtaposed images of sword blades and "silken fragile" throats, of tender bones dashed against jagged stones, mangled limbs, sighs

---

[2] Ibid.
[3] Aurelius Clemens Prudentius, "Hymn for the Epiphany", in Idem, *The Hymns of Prudentius*, trans. R. Martin Pope (London: J.M. Dent, 1905), Project Gutenberg Ebook ≠14959, produced by Ted Garvin, Stephen Hutcheson, et al., 2005, accessed 24 May 2015, <http://www.gutenberg.org/files/14959/14959-h/14959-h.htm>.

and sobs and broken cries creating a vivid picture of the effects of the atrocity.[4] The evil act perpetrated by Herod is coloured by images of vulnerable flesh and Prudentius exploits that to significant emotional effect. Prudentius also makes clear that the sufferings of the children make a strong parallel with the sufferings of Christ himself, he who is held to have died on mankind's behalf. The identification of Herod as the enemy of Christ grows even more pointed in Prudentius's Hymn when he goes on to describe the slaughtered children as "Ye flowers of martyrdom" (l. 125), "Ye first fruits of Christ's bitter pain!" (l. 130). The status of martyrs that these children acquired was the Christian answer to the horror of the deed. Thus, Prudentius's question in the hymn, "Of what avail is deed so vile?" (l. 133) set against the certainty of the doctrine of Christ's promise of resurrection serves to suggest the impotence of Herod, and other tyrants like him, to outface the Christian God's plan for mankind.

5 Developing Dramatisations of the Epiphany Events

While there seems to be no direct line forward in time to the liturgical dramas that make a documented appearance from the tenth century onwards, nevertheless it is clear that the Epiphany story was taken up as much for its dramatic potential as for its appropriateness to the Christmas festivals. It is even the case that the Fleury playbook, attributed to the monastery of Saint-Benoit-sur-Loire, contains an *Ordo ad Repraesentandum Herodem*[5] that is certainly a direct dramatisation of the events as recorded in Matthew's Gospel. The play of Herod ends with the decision by the Kings to return home another way. There follows the sequel *Ordo ad Interfectionem Puerorum*[6] which begins exactly where Herod finds out that he has been deceived, and falls into a rage; an act guaranteed to appeal to the theatrical imagination. Thus it may be seen that the Fleury drama mainly follows Matthew's account including, perhaps appropriately for the liturgical setting, the Gospel's motif of Rachel weeping over the children who have died. Dramatically this motif contrasts with the appalling nature of the Slaughter and, as in the case of Prudentius, establishes the credentials of the children as the first martyrs of the Christian Church.

More developed than the liturgical dramas is the *Ludus de Nativitate* from Benediktbeuern, a church play of the twelfth century.[7] It presents the whole of

---

4 Ibid., ll. 109–24.
5 *Medieval Drama*, ed. David Bevington (Boston: Houghton Mifflin, 1975), 57–66.
6 Ibid., 67–72.
7 Ibid., 178–202.

the Epiphany story but gives it a wider context adding, for instance, a procession of Old Testament Prophets who, through their predictions of the coming of the child Christ, seek to emphasise how the actions of Herod that follow are indeed contrary to divine purposes. Additionally an anti-Semitic element is introduced through a figure called Archisynagogus whose role is indicative of the Jewish rejection of Christ. In debate with the Prophets represented by St Augustine Archisynagogus first denies the validity of the virgin birth. The figure is then instrumental in persuading Herod to make use of the Magi in searching out the child. Opposition to the Christian message is thus represented in a powerful way through this double action. The Benediktbeuern play dramatises this opposition to Christ further in showing the Shepherds, 'simple minded folk', caught between an angel and a devil as they decide whether or not to go to Bethlehem to worship the child in the stable. What becomes clear from these earliest attempts to dramatise the episodes in the childhood of Christ is that the creators of religious drama found material in the story of Herod that was irresistible and that lent itself to imaginative amplification. The final scene of the Benediktbeuern play shows Herod dying, in retribution for his evil act, "*corrodatur a vermibus*" (gnawed to pieces by worms),[8] a representation undoubtedly derived from Josephus's account of the tyrant's suffering and death.

6 *The Offering of the Magi* (Towneley 14)

By the time we reach the period of the medieval civic plays, therefore, it can be confidently asserted that Herod's place in the Epiphany story has a well-established tradition behind it. It also becomes clear that the various playwrights responsible for bringing the story to the public stages felt free to amplify and extend their material to suit the theatrical demands of their time. The essence of the narrative remains the same but with different emphases, sometimes with regard to the sequencing of scenes but especially with regard to the manner of the characterisation and, in some cases, the death of Herod. As I have said, I have chosen to look in detail at the Towneley versions of *The Offering of the Magi* (14) and the *Magnus Herodes* (16).[9]

Each of these plays could be played outdoors or in, there being no precise indication of performance place in the texts. However, in *The Offering* there are

---

[8] Ibid., 200.
[9] Line references are to *The Towneley Plays*, ed. Martin Stevens and A.C. Cawley, EETS s.s. 13 (Oxford: Oxford University Press, 1994), 158–77 and 183–204 respectively.

indicators strongly suggestive of an outdoor location which might be a market place or other town station, a church yard, a convenient field, all such spacious enough to accommodate the travelling action. But first of all there must be a platform for Herod which should be dressed appropriately according to his regal status. This platform has to be large enough to provide seats for the three Magi whom at one point Herod invites to sit down (14.392). There must also be provision for action that takes place away from the stage and we must presume that this is in the space normally identified as the *platea*, a flat area down from but adjacent to the staging. Certainly the Magi arrive "equitans" (on horseback) and the messenger meets them on their horses before introducing them at Herod's Court. Similarly, after they have left Herod's Court, the Magi come off the platform to recover their horses.

But the play must also provide for a Stable to house the holy family. This must be either on a second platform or on a resetting of the existing stage. In this regard there is a hint in the text that an interval of theatrical time is created by the Magi's concern that the Star has disappeared. They decide to dismount again and kneel where they are to pray (14.504–22). At the end of this interlude of prayer the Star reappears and seems to be standing over where the Stable is located, now close by. This interlude would undoubtedly give sufficient time in which to change the scene on the platform and audiences could be easily persuaded to accept such a change. Whatever the case, a second platform or a redressed one, it would show good theatrical sense to have the solemn and deeply meaningful scene of the offering also raised on a stage provided it was distinguishable from Herod's Court. Further suggestion of the playmakers' awareness of the use of simultaneous staging is suggested by the fact that, following on from the offering scene, the Magi emerge from the Stable to discover "a lytter redy cled" (14.590). It is the scenic space where they will be able to take their rest and sleep and receive the angel's message that they should avoid returning to Herod. A litter is of course a portable item and could easily be introduced into the scene but most likely at ground level. So it becomes clear that the playmakers were alert to a range of staging possibilities demanded by the narrative of their play and we must presume had the means to effect them. This part of the narrative ends with the Magi, once awakened, consulting together and deciding to return home directly, ignoring Herod. They then remount their horses and depart in their several directions.

The dynamic of this piece is thus constructed around the playing space, and can be seen to emphasise above all the visitation of the Magi. Their first meeting together is treated fully; their consultation with Herod, amplified with his search in Scripture for prophesy confirming the advent of a King of the Jews, also serves to foreground the significance of their quest. After the Magi leave

Herod's Court, which has dominated the play to this midpoint, the play then focuses securely on the Stable and the offering of the Magi as the act of homage it is intended to be.

However, even acknowledging the way in which the play remains true to its main theme it is impossible to ignore the manner in which the playwright has chosen to characterise Herod, arch enemy of Christ, both in his own words and in those of the Messenger and of the Magi who visit him. The play is written throughout in a six line stanza with rhyme scheme *aaabab* achieving a kind of tail rhyme effect. For the opening six stanzas, however, the playwright has chosen to give the form a sophistication using linked verses, so that last and first lines offer a repeat of a motif. Herod's claim that "Of all this warld, sooth, far & nere, || The Lord am I" (14.5–6) is taken up as "Lord am I of every land" in the second stanza (14.7). The fourth stanza ends "The feynd, if he were my fo, || I shuld hym fell' (14.23–24) followed by "To fell those fatures I am bowne, || And dystroy those dogys in feyld and towne || That will not trow on Sant Mahowne, || Oure god so swete" (14.25–28). While the speech offers a picture of a king whose self-aggrandisement and threatening behaviour may mask a major insecurity, the decorous manner of these stanzas gives him some dignity. However, for whatever reason, the playwright abandons the device of linking after those first six stanzas and the play evolves further unadorned in this way to its end.

Herod's opening words, here as in other plays on this theme, demand silence under the threat of death. As a theatrical device this always suggests that by custom his entry onto the scene would be greeted far from respectfully. So we may conclude that, while at one time this could have been an improvised response to crowd heckling, it was so regularly the case that it came to be incorporated into the later recorded written text. That in itself is a hint at the way in which the plays, as frequent and familiar events in the towns in which they were presented, may have invited such behaviours to grow up round their performance. So, Herod proceeds with this introductory speech, and as he does so, it becomes even clearer that he is protesting too much. The frequent threats of death to all opponents, public and private, the vanity of his appeal to the ladies, his frequent invocation of his divine leader Mahowne, all go to create a *persona* that is, at one level, laughable because so extreme. However, because of his physical presence and proximity, Herod is also distinctly and genuinely threatening. The playwright works on this ambivalence to create a figure whose threatening physical presence produces sufficient substance to create dramatic tension in the development of the drama.

After this passage of self-aggrandisement Herod sets the action of the play going by despatching his messenger into the countryside to check to see that there's no-one secretly planning to challenge either himself or his god,

Mahowne. Perhaps in an attempt to represent the indoor and outdoor world of the play the messenger now comes forward and speaks to the audience directly, as if they may not have been privy to Herod's own speech. He repeats the request for "All peasse, lordyngys, and hold you styll" (14.73), gaining a silence in which he repeats in précis what Herod has been saying at length:

> He commaundys you everilkon
> To hold no kyng bot hym alon,
> And othere god ye worship none
>   Bot Mahowne so fre;
> And if ye do, ye mon be slone –
>   Thus told he me. (14.79–84)

Apart from giving the messenger an individual authority with the audience to act on Herod's behalf it does seem a strange redundancy until it becomes apparent that, while he takes no speaking part in the scene of the meeting of the Magi that follows, he must be present. Where he is placed remains a puzzle but the Magi arrive, as I have said, "equitans," on horseback and, so we must imagine, meet on the *platea*. The messenger, therefore, must be placed conveniently close to overhear what goes on and to be seen by the audience doing that as the second sequence of action in the play begins.

The dignified, formal and gentle speeches of the Magi form a direct contrast with the braggart tone and brusqueness of Herod's speech. They each arrive on a mission to find the explanation of the portent of the Star. The first of them, *primus rex* in the text, adds to his search a plea that he may be granted the "grace of company, || That I may have som beyldyng by || In my travayll" (14.92–95) and sure enough *secundus rex* is at hand to fulfil that part of his wish. They exchange greetings and names, Melchor from Araby and Jasper from Tarsas. The arrival of a third, *tercius rex*, completes the picture. He notices the other two immediately and quietly addresses them:

> Lordyngys, that ar leyf and dere,
> I pray you tell me with good chere
> Wheder ye weynd on this manere,
>   And where that ye have bene;
> And of this starne that shynys thus clere,
>   What it may mene. (14.145–50)

The tone and temper of his speech characterises the whole of this exchange between the three Magi. *Tercius rex* soon also gives his name, Balthesar from

Saba, and they agree to ride on together. The motif of the Star is now enthusiastically observed, to such an extent that it surely must have been present to the Magi and to the audience. Indeed throughout this scene the Star must have been present in a form that lived up to the descriptions of brightness and glory to which they give expression. They use the terms "yonde" and "this starne" to indicate its presence. Regrettably the actual nature of this wondrous star has been lost but it is not difficult to imagine perhaps a kind of processional cross with its head in the form of a great star, gilded and possibly more extravagantly decorated, or even an ornamental torch flaming, carried and positioned appropriately by a player suitably costumed for the best effect.

The Star features prominently in the scene, therefore, as the present herald of the child Jesus. As a material scenic device it is put to use to influence the audience's reception of the performance. The playwright deploys the emblem of the Star both for its spectacular impact and for its dramatic effect which is reinforced by the words of *tercius rex*, "yond starne betokyns, well wote I, || The byrth of a prynce, syrs, securely" (14.199–200) followed by his assertion that if it were otherwise then "the rewlys of astronomy || Dissauys me" (14.203–04). The importance of all this is underlined when *primus rex* introduces the prophecy of Balaam as confirmation of the significance of their quest. This sequence of discussion around the Star concludes with these words by *secundus rex*:

> Now is he borne that se and sand
> > Shall weyld at wyll:
> That shewys this starne, so bright shynand
> > Vs thre untyll. (14.225–28)

The Star is the emblem that supports these successive expressions of the divinity and power of Christ. One further effect of this scene of the Magi is to provide an important counterpoise to Herod's bombastic braggart authority and it is brought to a conclusion when *primus rex* proposes that they journey forward together. It remains only for them each to speak of their offerings of gold, as token of the child's kingship, of "rekyls" (incense) as token of his divinity, and myrrh as token of his death. Then they depart the scene, still on horseback it seems, not to "rest, even nor morne, || unto we com ther he is borne" (14.253–54) and to "Felowe this light – els be we lorne" (14.255). The Star is their guiding light. The scene has been a calm, quietly formal and even ceremonial interlude. It has conveyed all the necessary elements of the doctrine of the Nativity as borne by the Magi. Theatrically it sets up the audience to witness the following scene in a new light.

Although conceptually divisible into sequences of action the play is continuous and Herod's next appearance is occasioned by the Messenger's return from his foray into the country seeking out, on behalf of his master, secret plots and challenges. The messenger greets his king politely "My lord, Syr Herode, the saue and se!" (14.260), but he is met with a bad tempered insult – "Where has þou bene so long fro me, || Vyle stynkand lad?" (14.261–62). The Messenger replies reasonably that he has only been doing what was asked of him, to which Herod replies "Thou lyys, lurdan, the dewill the hang!" (14.265). So the third sequence of action opens and immediately the atmosphere returns to one of verbal violence in which Herod's shifting and aggressive moods frame what is to follow. The messenger now reveals that he has been witness to the meeting of the Magi and reports their conversation to Herod in some detail. The news he brings, that the Magi are seeking a child who shall be King of the Jews, seems completely to undo Herod. He rants against the child, the Magi and the world at large coming eventually as he sees it, to his own desperate situation:

> Those lurdans wote not what thay say;
> Thay ryfe my hede, that dar I lay;
> Ther dyd no thythyngys many a day,
>   Sich harme me to!
> Fo[r] wo my wytt is all away;
>   What shall I do? (14.295–300)

This pattern of self-regarding anxiety mixed with various threats against the child and the Magi grows over five stanzas into a crescendo of angry, even frustrated complaint so that, by inference, the audience are presented with an absurdly flawed figure of power. He cannot command their respect even though he may physically be able to intimidate them. Nor is this characterisation merely a sketch: it is a carefully and knowingly developed piece of dramatic writing intended to invoke in its audience a sense of evil that reveals itself as dangerous even though, in the larger picture, it may be shown to be impotent. The quick shift from the temper of this tirade into the polite welcome of a sovereign eager to have news of the expedition of the Magi develops a new characteristic, Herod's capacity for deceit. The impression of charm is soon overturned, however, as the scene develops. In response to the Magi's reports of mystical occurrences Herod invites his own advisers to search Scripture for any inkling of this new born king. The prophesy of Isaiah is now cited foretelling of the virgin birth. Once again and even in the presence of the Magi, as the prophesies are read out to him, Herod responds in the exaggerated fashion of the first scenes. In some plays Herod takes the Scriptures and throws them to the floor, his reputation for raging extended by the playwrights to this occasion. Here he simply is beside himself, his rage reflected in his voice alone:

> Shall he have more pausté then I?
> A, waloway.
> Alas, alas, I am forlorne!
> I wold be rent and all to torne! (14.431–34)

And a shortly after he curses his scholar advisers "The dewill hang you high to dry || For this tythyng!" (14.455–56). His whole style is exclamatory but as ever with that edge of self pity. His final remarks are a kind of capitulation:

> Alas, that ever I shuld be knyght,
> Or holdyn man of mekyll myght,
> If a lad shuld reyfe me my right
>   All thus me fro! (14.475–78)

With that he turns again to the Magi, all courtesy and smiling, another change from harsh to soft demeanour, and offers them safe conduct with the small proviso that they come back to give him news of the new born king. His genial remark "Ye shall me fynd a faythfull freynd, || If ye do swa" (14.485–86), would leave the audience clear about his duplicity. The Magi, once outside and going to mount their horses, immediately express their own doubts about Herod. They attribute the temporary disappearance of the Star from the sky to Herod's bad influence. Indeed *tercius Rex* voices the problem:

> Wo worth Herode, that cursyd wyght!
> Wo worth that tyrant day and nyght!
> For thrugh hym have we lost that sight,
>   And for hys gyle,
> That shoyn to vs with bemys bright. (14.499–503)

As I have indicated briefly before, the Magi, emerging from Herod's court, mount their horses as if to ride off and almost immediately, according to a stage direction "*Here lyghtys the kyngys of thare horses*" (14.504) in order to kneel and pray. After which interlude the Star returns now standing over the Stable where the holy family are set. The succeeding action is of a formal, ritualised, quasi-liturgical representation of the Magi's offering of their gifts. They hail the child, each speaking a different quality: "Hayll be thou, maker of all kyn thyng, || That boytt of all oure bayll may bring!" (14.541–42), "Hayll, overcomer of kyng and of knyght, || That fourmed fysh and fowyll in flyght!" (14.547–48), "Hayll, kyng in kyth, cowrand on kne! || Hayll, oonefold God in persons thre!" (14.553–54). They make their offerings of gold, frankincense and myrrh and Mary replies on behalf of her son:

> Syr kyngys, make comforth you betweyn,
> And mervell not what it may mene.
> This chyld, that on me borne has bene,
>   All bayll may blyn;
> I am his moder, and madyn clene
>   Withoutten syn. (14.559–64)

Thus the identity of the child and the religious significance of the birth are encapsulated in these words and are honoured in the nature of the enactment. It is an entirely positive dramatic contrast to the preceding action that has been overshadowed by the domineering behaviour of Herod. The audience are given the inescapable impression first, that the images of the offering have conformed to the symbolic truth of the gospel and then, theatrically, are given the satisfaction of an anticipated action accomplished. The play then concludes with the image of the sleeping Magi, all tucked up in their "lytter" to be visited by the angel who warns them against returning to Herod. Finally they take leave of each other to return directly home to their own lands. It may be that the shadow of Herod still hangs over this last action but, in spite of that, the play has completed its task of foregrounding and celebrating the occasion of the Nativity with its profound message of hope for sinning mankind.

7 The *Magnus Herodes* (Towneley 16)

In the recorded sequence of Towneley plays the *Offering* (14) is followed by *The Flight into Egypt* (15), a part of the story that is usually and logically inserted in the Innocents tale between Herod's order and the actual killing. It is a short piece that stands on its own but it remains an issue that if it were played in sequence where it is it would anticipate Herod's decision to kill the children. Furthermore, in its independent status, *The Flight* is expanded to display both comedy and seriousness showing, as it does, Joseph fed up with being ordered around by angels, feeling too old to travel to Egypt and warning young men of the troubles of marriage. Mary, too, has much to say about protecting her child and worrying about where to go and how to get there. At one point Joseph says in rebuke "Now, leyfe Mary, be styll; || This helpys noght. || It is no boytt to grete"

(15.90–92), and again later "We! leyf Mary, lett be" (15.161) as her pitiful exclamations delay their preparations to depart. However, the play retains its atmosphere of imminent danger, anxiety for the future and a sense of the pressure of time. Thereby it could be argued that it fulfils a theatrical function in providing a strong anticipatory link with the play that follows. Herod as the tyrant king maliciously pursuing his intent to eradicate all challenge to his status and authority is indeed a threatening figure for the Christ child and his parents.

In dramatic terms the *Magnus Herodes* (16) is certainly quite special. We encounter a playwright of distinct character who, by critical agreement, is referred to as the Wakefield Master, and whose style of writing is robustly individual. While the manuscript representation of the verse form seems to show an eight line stanza the most recent editors have demonstrated that that is a contracted, possibly space saving form, and that it is written in a thirteen line stanza that offers an opening of full eight lines, rhyming *abababab*, with a tail rhyme echo that spans over three further rhyming short lines *cdddc*.[10] The verse is loosely held together with variable stresses that to some extent sound out as speech rhythms. The effect of the tail rhyme is to summarise and effect a pause in the flow of the speech for emphasis. The language too is strong and expressive of the varied moods of the *personae*. All these usages invite the actor to speak in a vigorous and intense way supported by both form and expressive meanings. The writing gives a vigorous structure and promotes a sound-scape that invades the senses of the spectators. The messages of the play are thus conveyed both conceptually and sensually.

The staging in this play is more limited than that of the *Offering* creating a focus that makes a more direct demand upon the audience's attention. Herod's seat of majesty has to be provided with an open area in which he can confront his knights or soldiers. This could easily be represented on a single raised stage. However, the action, as in the *Offering*, seems to extend into a second area most likely located as a *platea* in front and below the staged area. It is a space where the children will be butchered in the very face of the audience and would almost certainly be at ground level. Otherwise no further locations are required.

To fill this straightforward staging plan the play has been constructed in what can be described as seven movements each of which focuses differently on Herod's involvement with the atrocious act of the Slaughter of the Innocents. We begin with Nuncius who provides a Prologue to the main action. He seems to speak from the front of the platform area providing him with a dominant

---

10   Stevens and Cawley, eds., *Towneley Plays*, xviii-xxxi.

position in relation to the audience, an authority that he is asked to exploit. Nuncius's first words invoke Mahowne who, we then learn, is Herod's own mentor and guiding light. By virtue of the authority vested in him by Mahowne Herod is to be respected and feared. The audience is to receive him in lowly fashion. The Nuncius moves on then to speak of how Herod is troubled because of a "boy that is borne herby" (16.38) who is called a king. But, of course, the official message is that there is no king but Herod himself. Indeed his rule extends widely across the world as a subsequent alliterative and suggestive listing of distant and exotic locations implies. Turkey and Tuscany, Paradise and Padua, India and Italy, Normandy and Norway, all bow to his rule. Both the manner and the content of this listing has an absurdity about it which undermines the claims of omnipotence. It is absurd in its exaggeration, an absurdity that is made even more pointed by the inclusion of a place, Kempton, obviously English and just as obviously not only inappropriate but also seemingly non-existent. A.C. Cawley suggests that it could be a satirical reference to the city of York infamous at this time for its absentee Archbishop John Kempe.[11] If that were the case it would indicate that the playwright was playing to his audience who might be expected to understand the full implication of this satirical aside. It is certainly a characteristic tactic associated with the work of the Wakefield Master.

Thus, while apparently building Herod up as a potentate without equal, the speech of the Nuncius subtly undermines any such reception of this phoney king. So when the Nuncius proclaims Herod "Here he commys now, I cry, || That lord I of spake!" (16.92–93) the audience have been prepared to be sceptical, a response confirmed in large measure by the reception they seem expected to give him and which requires him not only to call for silence, but repeatedly so for two whole stanzas. There he stands threatening the audience with awful retribution if they do not show proper respect. When he begins "Stynt, brodels, youre dyn – || Yei, euerychon!" (16.118–19) we must know, as before, that the audience has greeted the character noisily. He goes on to say "if I begyn, || I breke ilka bone, || And pull fro the skyn || the carcas anone" (16.122–25) a bloodcurdling threat that, for the audience at any rate, is never followed up. But more such horror is invoked as Herod has a second time to ask for silence. This time "Styr not bot ye have lefe, || For if ye do, I clefe || You small as flesh to pott" (16.141–43). While its apparent hyperbole seems to make the claim both vain and weak the scenes of slaughter they anticipate are here graphically represented to the imagination of the audience.

---

[11] [11] A.C. Cawley, *The Wakefield Pageants in the Towneley Cycle* (Manchester: Manchester University Press, 1968), 115, n. 47.

As the noisy interactions subside the playwright allows Herod a long solo passage in a continuing vein of threatened violence. But now the object of his ire is "that lad" (16.153) who threatens his claim to the throne of Jewry. Brandishing his sword he swears to break all the bones in his body. He thinks he will burst "For anger and for teyn" (16.171), and he claims that "It mefys my hart right noght || To breke his nek in two" (16.181–82). His second anger is directed at the Magi whom he learns from his Knights have passed him by. Now the anger explodes in a sequence of exclamations that strongly suggests vehement action: "We! outt! for teyn I brast! || We! fy! || Fy on the dewill!" (16.216–18) and much more of the same. These expressions of violent anger are repetitive in form but singularly inventive in their variety. In a flurry of paranoid frustration Herod then turns on the knights and blames them roundly for letting the Magi slip away. He even beats them. They complain at the treatment "Thus should ye not thrett us, || Vngaynly to bete us" (16.231–32). They get only further abuse for their pains "Fy, losels and lyars, || Lurdans ilkon, || Tratoures and well wars! || Knafys, bot knyghtys none!" (16.235–38). Herod's tantrums are very active ones: "I wote not where I may sytt || For anger and for teyn" (16.248–49). While this section of Herod's raging produces a maybe alarming, even horrifying, effect it seems intended overall to present the audience with an absurd picture of a man out of control and includes the farcical knockabout sequence of belabouring the knights. It is thus of a piece with other representations of the king as an altogether unpredictable, bullying and braggart character. After these outbursts the knights do attempt to excuse themselves with some misplaced fawning. They claim loyalty to the king and assert how they would have stopped the Magi in their tracks if they had caught up with them. Herod is apparently somewhat calmed by their febrile excuses but then dismisses them in order to consult with his privy council.

Thus the play proceeds to sequence three and the development of Herod's response to the threat of the newborn challenge. The king himself opens the conversation saying that he has heard "A wonderfull talkyng" in his ear that a "madyn shuld bere || Anothere to be kyng" (16.287–90). He goes on to command his counsellors to "inquere / In all wrytyng" (16.291–92) that includes the rather unlikely authors, Virgil and Homer, but excludes legend, epistles, graduals, mass and matins. We are obviously not meant to enquire too closely into Herod's command of the detail of such research. What the counsellors reveal to Herod are the prophesies of Isaiah that a maiden will bear a child who will be called Emanuel, and that other authorities have said that "Of Bedlem a gracyus || Lord shall spray" (16.317–18) and that he will be honoured by king and emperor. This news, predictably, throws Herod into another rage. He accuses the counsellors of seeking to anger him deliberately and abuses them vigorously:

> Outt, thefys, fro my wonys!
> Fy, knafys!
> Fy, dottypols, with youre bookys –
> Go kast thaym in the brookys!
> With sich wylys and crokys
> My wytt away rafys. (16.333–38)

He finishes this tirade with a self-referential "War! I say, lett me pant" (16.345), referring presumably to the fact that all this shouting makes him out of breath. As an aside, possibly spoken directly to the audience, it further reinforces the idea that Herod's rage partakes of farce even as it apparently threatens other characters and the audience. As it happens the counsellors are quick to quiet the king and offer him a solution to his troubles. Why not, they suggest, send out soldiers to kill all "knave-chyldren" of two years and under and living around Bethlehem? Herod is charmed by this idea which he describes immediately as "A right nobyll gyn" (16.377) and the rewards he offers of land and riches must satisfy the counsellors as they withdraw.

The play proceeds to sequence four, the command given to the knights to kill the children. Nuncius summons the soldiers and there is yet again a hint of humour at Herod's expense as they question whether they need to be in shining armour, to be dressed well to meet their monarch and to be ready for his commands. They hail their king with due deference saying they are ready to do his will and they find that Herod's mood is conciliatory, very different from that that they experienced before. The knights are welcome, they are given their horrendous task and the promise of good rewards, and in the tail rhyme of the speech are urged to:

> Spare no kyns bloode,
>   Lett all ryn on floode;
> If women wax woode,
>   I warn you, syrs, to spede you. (16.452–55)

The knights' response is all enthusiasm for the task.

Immediately we are transported into the fifth sequence of the play, the actual killing of the children. It is abruptly introduced and, it would appear, as in the previous play of the *Offering of the Magi*, that the subsequent action occurs at ground level, away from Herod's court, though not at too great a distance. The soldiers make a boast before departing and then enter upon a formally choreographed sequence of slaughter. Each of the three soldiers addresses one of three mothers each carrying a child. The action of the whole scene is one of conflict, violence and pathos with the soldiers seeking to kill the children and the mothers desperately trying to protect them. The contrasting words of cruelty and suffering emphasise the horror of the moment. The mothers are represented as helpless though resistant. They try to run, the soldiers catch up with them. They hit out with their fists to no effect. Their words express their intent with a cogent intensity and despite the fact that the children will be represented by dolls there is nevertheless a great show of blood to which every mother refers: "Outt, alas, my chyldys bloode!" (16.493), "My child that was me lefe! || My luf, my blood, my play, || That never dyd man grefe!" (16.524–26), "God forbede! || Thefe, thou shedys my chyldys blood!" (16.542–43), a display in sound and action that will create a vivid effect for an audience positioned perhaps not very far from the scene. Once the deed is done the mothers cry out at the atrocity with graphic exclamation of how their children are "al to-torne" (16.500), "Thy body is all to-rent" (16.564), the prefix 'to-' showing the intensity of feeling. And the first four lines of each mother's speech is deployed to cry vengeance upon Herod and his men. The second mother is given a tail rhyme to add emphasis to the cry:

> Veniance I cry and call
> On Herode and his knyghtys all;
> Veniance, Lord, apon thaym fall,
> And mekyll warldys wonder! (16.530–34)

The scene ends abruptly as the mothers are cursorily chased off stage by the soldiers and the violence of the scene is over, but it will have left upon the audience an effect of terror and gross injustice as well as of horror and suffering.

We now have sequence six in which, first, the soldiers brag about what they have done and, as they return to Herod, compete for the title of who did best. Unrepentant, therefore, for the slaughter, and full of insolence in their celebration of success they report back to Herod who, naturally, is overjoyed at the result. He rewards his knights royally with women "to wed at [their] wyll" (16.624–26), with "A hundreth thowsand pownde" (16.642) and "castels and towres, || Both to you and to youres, || For now and evermore" (16.648–50). Although they have doubts about the sincerity of Herod's promises the sequence ends with the soldiers hailing Herod as lord and king in what seems to be a travesty of the greeting offered by the Magi to the Christ child.

Herod sends the soldiers off with a blessing from Mahowne who has shadowed the actions of this play throughout. Sequence seven follows in which Herod alone speaks a kind of *envoi* directly to the audience. He begins with a sigh "Now in peasse may I stand – || I thank the, Mahowne" (16.664–65), and explains that he now feels quite secure. He promises a thousand marks to members of the audience whom he treats as his subjects. But when he goes on to brag about the pleasure of shedding "so mekyll blode" (16.679) the text suggests that the audience react in a by now familiar way that requires Herod once again to demand silence. Nevertheless he expresses further delight and lack of feeling for the suffering he has caused. He can laugh and suggest that he is truly happy:

> A, Mahowne,
> So light is my saull
> That all of sugar is my gall!
> I may do what I shall,
> And bere vp my crowne. (16.685–89)

He goes on to admit that the news of the birth made him afraid but, by his own efforts as he claims, he is assured now that his crown is safe. He further boasts of the 144.000 that are dead as his great achievement and a guarantee of his reputation when he is dead. He also makes threats to "tech knavys || Ensampyll to take" (16.716–17) should they even think in future of challenging his rule. Once again it is suggested that here the audience responds to his boasting and threats so that he must needs quiet them and, indeed, having just offered them rewards, now he has to threaten them with punishments unless they keep their mouths shut:

> For if I here it spokyn
> When I com agayn,
> Youre branys bese brokyn;
> Therfor be ye bayn.
> Nothyng bese vnlokyn;
> It shal be so playn.
> Begyn I to rokyn,
> I thynk all disdayn
> For-daunche. (16.729–37)

As I have suggested earlier there is an absurdity about Herod's continual bragging and threatening which presents him as what might be termed at one level, a pantomime villain. He demands the attention of the audience and is given the solo speeches to achieve that effect. However, the self-presentation is written in such a way that his authority is undermined and his actions, therefore, diminished. This comic status with which the playwright endows Herod allows the audience to experience a sense of superiority even while being startled and possibly horrified by the matter and manner of the slaughter itself.

Herod's final words in this play of the Wakefield Master are enigmatic:

> Syrs, this is my counsell:
> Bese not to cruell.
> Bot adew! – to the deuyll!
> I can no more Franch. (16.738–40)

To give the audience advice not to be too cruel when they have witnessed one of the grossest acts of cruelty instigated by the man himself sounds seriously out of place. It amounts to a stepping out of character and, therefore, out of the play. It has a flippancy that is startling since his "adew" here is one of the very few occasions on which Herod has used any French in the course of his performance. Perhaps it is an attempt to place the performance in a context of 'play', a context that queries any aspiration for the incidents portrayed to be taken seriously. What will become, therefore, of the cries of the mothers for vengeance, a sentiment with which audience members could understandably sympathise? Herod, it would seem from this abdication, has got away with the massacre and is here cocking a snoop at the moral judgement to which he might be subject. This ending certainly questions the audience's assumptions regarding the dominant Christian narrative about how good must and will always triumph over its opponents. Herod's disturbing challenge to the message of comfort carried by the Nativity story remains 'live' in this moment, an open wound, rather than being neatly packaged away, shut down, as it is in other plays on this subject.

8 A Question of Endings

Whatever we choose to make of the Towneley ending in other respects the 'Master' in essence diverts very little in his representation of the character of Herod from a shared Christian tradition. Likewise, all the playwrights of the civic plays attempted to do justice to his character as they understood it. In every case his extravagant behaviour becomes his common signature. Even though he is sometimes represented in his dealings with the Magi as courteous and cunning, nevertheless he makes outrageous and sometimes blasphemous claims concerning his power to create and rule the world, the weather even, and to command the loyalty of his subjects whether kings or commoners. The playwrights give him moments of ranting and panting, and staves and swords to brandish or destroy in his passion. He rages at the words of prophecy that foretell the advent of the child king and destroys the books in which the prophecies are written. He rages at the deception of the kings and makes them carry some responsibility for the killing of the children. He vaunts endlessly against the boy who seeks to usurp him and will break all his bones or chop off his head, and cause him suffering in as many ways as he can. He will brook no opposition. He threatens or persuades his soldiers, even sometimes against their will, to commit the dire deed of massacre. The scene between the soldiers and the mothers, the act of slaughter, serves to promote in the audience feelings of terror, tenderness or horror, even when it offers to descend for a moment into knockabout farce. But the slaughter is always accomplished with differing degrees of cruelty and always in Herod's absence, so that, when the soldiers report back that the deed has been accomplished, the king's sense of triumph is at least distasteful but most often monstrous in the extreme.

But it is in the matter of the endings that there is the greatest disparity between the playwrights. They all have at hand the history of Josephus and materials from *The Golden Legend* from which to construct an appropriate theatrical *dénouement*. In the two plays of York and Coventry, for instance, the ending, as in the case of the Wakefield play, is left open, but neither of them is equivocal in the same way. In each of them Herod becomes aware of the escape of the Holy Family and so leaves the stage at the end of both plays threatening to pursue them into Egypt. There is unfinished business to attend to. Herod's frustration and anger is apparent but nothing like the off-hand abandonment of responsibility which marks out the Towneley piece. The remaining endings, however, are all focused on what must be considered a just retribution for Herod's appalling crime against humanity and especially against Christ.

In the Digby play of *The Killing of the Children*,[12] for instance, the soldiers returning to report their achievement also report, through the foolish character of Watkyn, that the mothers are crying out against the atrocity and against Herod himself such that he is told:

---

12 Line references are to "The Killing of the Children" in *The Late Medieval Religious Plays of Bodleian MSS Digby 133 and e Museo 160*, ed. Donald C. Baker, John L. Murphy and Louis B. Hall Jr., EETS 283 (Oxford: Oxford University Press, 1982), 96–115.

>   thei crie in every stede:
> 'A vengeaunce take Kyng Herode, for he hath our children sloon!'
> And bidde 'A myscheff take hym!' both eveyn and morn;
> For kyllyng of ther children on you thei crie oute,
> And thus goth your name alle the cuntre abought. (ll. 360–64)

The playwright thus shows Herod cornered in a social environment that has become hostile to him. The king is given a remarkable response when first he says:

> Oute! I am madde! My wyttes be ner goon!
> I am wo for the wrokyng of this werke wylde!
> For as wele I have slayn my frendes as my foon!
> Wherfor, I fere, deth hath me begyled! (ll. 365–68)

He goes on to say that he is not sure he has killed the actual child Christ and as a result his heart now begins to quake. He falls ill even to the extent that he fears he is about to die: "What! Out,out! Allas! I wene I shalle dey this day! || My hert tremelith and quakith for feere!" (ll. 381–82) and indeed in the next eight lines he dies and falls upon the stage. Thus the news of his bad name is shown to bring on a fit of madness and an admission of guilt, both of which are linked to the sudden onset of death. It makes for a dramatic ending that emphasises Herod's actual guilt with his own bad faith and bad conscience. The play ends there quite abruptly, the point having been made.

In the Chester Cycle the playwright provides an equally dramatic death scene but with two additional twists of the knife of retribution.[13] The first is that one of the women turns out to be the nurse to whom Herod's own son has been entrusted. The king's own child has been killed; an example of rough but obviously deserved justice offering some assurance to the audience that God is, after all, on the side of right. But the second element is the arrival of the Devil sent "to fetch this kinges sowle here present || into hell, there to bringe him, there to be lent, || ever to live in woe" (10.443–45). These two devices provide a formally acceptable climax to the play embracing the concept of justice and judgement within the frame of the dominant narrative of the Christian church. The final twist is to bring Herod's sin into alignment with those of the

---

[13] Line references are to Play X, *The Goldsmiths Play*, in *The Chester Mystery Cycle*, ed. R.M. Lumiansky and David Mills, 2 vols., EETS s.s. 3 and 9 (Oxford: Oxford University Press, 1974–86), 1: 185–204.

present audience, though apparently in a peculiarly topical and immediate way:

> No more shall you trespas. By my lewtye,
> That filles there measures falselye
> Shall beare this lord companye. (10.450–52)

What we must take to have been a besetting sin in Chester at the time of these plays becomes the focus of an *envoi* from the devil with an edge to it for knowing members of the audience.

Possibly even more extravagant is the ending created for the N-town *Death of Herod* play.[14] It is worked up by the dramatic expedient of having Herod create a celebratory dinner on stage for himself and his soldiers. As they are invited to sit down at the table the action is interrupted by the arrival of *Mors*, Death, skeletal, no doubt, and apparently dripping worms from the remnants of his flesh. He is a horrific presence. Since the royal party remains innocent of Death's arrival it must be assumed that at first he speaks from some distance away from the stage action of the feast, something that is confirmed by "Ow! Se how prowdely ʒon kaytyff sytt at mete! || of deth hath he no dowte: he wenyth to leve evyrmore!" (20.194–95). The whole of Death's speech here is about Herod's presumption in challenging God's will who has "sent me here || ʒon lordeyn to sle, withowtyn dwere || For his wykkyd werkynge" (20.178–80). But Death is also given time to develop the idea that nothing on earth, man, beast or even the mighty oak tree can resist his power. While Death falls silent for a space, Herod and his soldiers gloat over their great success, the king satisfied that he is now safe from rivalry and the soldiers celebrating the killing when "þe boys sprawlyd at my sperys hende" (20.220). Out of this the playwright has created a dramatic climax which comes just as Herod commands a fanfare of trumpets in joyous celebration. For the 'heroes' it might just as well be the sounding of the last trump, for Death, in that instant, strikes at them all and the stage direction reads "*Mors interficiat Herodem et duos milites subito.*" The force of that "*subito*" cannot be overestimated especially in association with the sound of the trumpet fanfare. It is surprising, dynamic and climactic in a wholly theatrical way. But there is a further surprise in store. Enter directly, the Devil, crying:

---

14 Line references are to Play 20, *The Death of Herod*, in *The N-Town play: Cotton MS Vespasian D.8*, ed. Stephen Spector, EETS s.s. 11 (Oxford: Oxford University Press, 1991), 187–97.

> All oure! All Oure! þis catel is myn!
> I xall hem brynge on to my celle.
> I xal hem teche pleys fyn,
> *and* shewe such myrthe as is in helle! (20.233–36)

If it takes two such extreme characters to bring about his end that is a telling enhancement of the narrative of Herod's atrocity. Such dramatic amplification of the story shifts our perspective on Herod's character. He becomes an even greater and substantial threat to Christian values than one had ever dreamed of. As it is, the Devil expeditiously carries the souls off to hell while the character of Death remains to give an explicit sermon to the audience reflecting first on Herod's pride and fall but naturally proceeding to a moralistic warning to the audience there assembled:

> I xal ȝow make ryght lowe to lowth
> And nakyd for to be.
> Amonges wormys, as I ȝow telle,
> Undyr þe erth xul ȝe dwelle
> And þei xul etyn both flesch and felle,
> As þei have don me. (20.279–84)

So once again the formal moral warning is evident both in the word and the action of this ending. But the dramatic effect is far more poignant even than that of the Chester or the Digby plays. The finality of the action is one thing, a sense of having arrived, a sense of closure, maybe, but the manner of its accomplishment creates an unavoidable occasion for moral reflection through the characters of both Death and the Devil. It presses insistently for a moral and eschatological understanding of the consequences of sin. Herod is shown to be an epitome of evil unequivocally condemned to a deserved damnation, a damnation that can readily be avoided. A position, as performed, quite different from that evoked by the mischievous Towneley Herod with his dismissive advice to be not too cruel and the throw away ending about having no more French.

9. Conclusion

Through analysis of the performative aspects of the Towneley *Offering of the Magi* and *Magnus Herodes* this paper gave first an account of the character of Herod that may be found in essence in all of the plays concerned with his part in the Epiphany story. The playwrights showed Herod, in all his bragging, laying claim, as G.R. Owst tells us, to "all those gifts of kind, fortune and grace which the preachers specified as the ground of human pride."[15] Of course, the sin of pride can lead to crimes against other human beings, as it did with Herod. There is that aspect of Herod's character, his rages, that suggest he is in the hold of the sin of Wrath. Finally, his paranoia regarding the Christ Child could well be associated with Envy of the boy's alleged power and his destiny to rule in Herod's place. So, viewed in that way, Herod represents all those sins which might be identified as they are in *The Castle of Perseverance* as "the Develys chyldryn three."[16] Thus it may be argued that Herod, by some of these playwrights, was justifiably treated as a profoundly satanic figure whose destiny was to take him without question and directly into the fires of hell where he belonged. It is remarkable, therefore, that the Wakefield Master, while giving him all of the attributes to which I have drawn attention, nevertheless avoids the more extreme possibilities of a moralised ending. Herod is allowed to address his audience with a familiarity and directness that endows him with a cheekiness that disarms judgement. He leaves the stage just as wicked a man as he has shown himself to be throughout the play, but a man nevertheless, and free, bearing his sins with him, in common with the audience he leaves behind. The challenge this parting leaves behind, it may be argued, is possibly more demanding than the sermons and threats of death and hell that other playwrights have chosen to deploy. It may be seeks to escape the constraints of the dominant Christian narrative and to see the killing of the children as simply an act of *Realpolitik*. The Wakefield Master is, maybe, saying to us that while one can never excuse Herod, and history suggests that he came to a bad end, nevertheless his story commands our understanding as much from a human point of view as from a religious and moral one. Herod's cheeky departure seems to insist that although guilty of horrors unspeakable he remains flesh and blood, one of us and, not least, let us remember that his performance has highly entertained us.

---

15   G.R. Owst, *Literature and Pulpit in Medieval England* (Oxford: Blackwell, 1966), 494.
16   *The Macro Plays*, ed. Mark Eccles, EETS 262 (Oxford: Oxford University Press, 1969), 29, l. 894.

Bibliography

Baker, Donald C., John L. Murphy and Louis B. Hall Jr., eds. *The Late Medieval Religious Plays of Bodleian MSS Digby 133 and e Museo 160*. EETS 283. Oxford: Oxford University Press, 1982.

David Bevington, ed. *Medieval Drama*. Boston: Houghton Mifflin, 1975.

Cawley, A.C. *The Wakefield Pageants in the Towneley Cycle*. Manchester: Manchester University Press, 1968.

Eccles, Mark, ed. *The Macro Plays*. EETS 262. Oxford: Oxford University Press, 1969.

Josephus, Flavius. *The Antiquities of the Jews*, trans. William Whiston. Reproduced through Project Gutenberg as EBook ≠2848. Produced by David Reed and David Widger, 2009–13. Accessed 24 May 2015, <http://www.gutenberg.org/files/2848/2848-h/2848-h.htm>.

Lumiansky, R.M., and David Mills, eds. *The Chester Mystery Cycle*, 2 vols. EETS s.s. 3 and 9. Oxford: Oxford University Press, 1974–86.

Owst, G.R. *Literature and Pulpit in Medieval England*. Oxford: Blackwell, 1966.

Prudentius, Aurelius Clemens. *The Hymns of Prudentius*, trans. R. Martin Pope. London: J.M. Dent, 1905. Project Gutenberg Ebook ≠14959. Produced by Ted Garvin, Stephen Hutcheson, et al., 2005. Accessed 24 May 2015, <http://www.gutenberg.org/files/14959/14959-h/14959-h.htm>.

Spector, Stephen, ed. *The N-Town play: Cotton MS Vespasian D.8*. EETS s.s. 11. Oxford: Oxford University Press, 1991.

Stevens, Martin, and A.C. Cawley, eds. *The Towneley Plays*. EETS s.s. 13. Oxford: Oxford University Press, 1994.

CHAPTER 12

Passion Play: Staging York's *The Conspiracy* and *Christ before Annas and Caiaphas*

Philip Crispin

Abstract

In March 2013, I directed two Passion Pageants from the York Mysteries – *The Conspiracy* and *Christ before Annas and Caiaphas* (hereafter *Conspiracy* and *Annas and Caiaphas*). Each of them is both sacred and profane, devotional and political, providing an arena for social contestation. I analyse the two pageants through the prism of festive drama and play: the ludic interrogation of society, power and violence in both word and ritual. My interdisciplinary approach ranges from the carnivalesque and anthropology to Christian hermeneutics and art history; and I examine key discourses, rituals and plot developments nourished by both religious and secular sources.[1] I proceed to apply the performance theories of Jerzy Grotowski and Jacques Lecoq, two twentieth-century theatre-makers, to the pageants; their thoughts and observations (alongside Walter Benjamin's theory of history and anachronism) complement medieval theatre scholarship and further inform how to approach the performance of this drama, in terms of theatricality, performance practice and acting styles. Informed by all the above, I discuss how I approached my own production in terms of staging, performance and interpretation.

Key words

passion – performance – play – ritual – anachronism – carnivalesque

1   Introduction

"The Word was made flesh and dwelt amongst us" (John 1:14)
"And the world knew him not" (John 1:10)

---

[1] Biblical references come from the Passion and Holy Week liturgy readings.

"The Son of Man must suffer many things and be rejected" (Mark 8:41)
"And give his life as a ransom for many" (Matthew 20:28)

In *The Conspiracy*, the Temple authorities demand that Pilate put Christ to death, and Judas Iscariot offers to betray him for thirty pieces of silver. In *Annas and Caiaphas*, Jesus – disowned by a wretched Saint Peter – is hauled in front of the chief priests, subjected to brutal questioning, mocked and tortured.[2] Both plays are set at night, in an atmosphere of tension and confusion, and feature corrupt and worldly authorities, scapegoating and ritual abuse. They are remarkable for their arresting, alliterative language, communication of emotion, and dramatic potency.

Christ's all too human suffering and eventual agonising death at others' hands is at the heart of the Passion narrative, and this leads, as in the plays here, to a focus upon the power-wielders and regimes who sanctioned such violence. The Christian mystery of the Incarnation, according to which transcendent and ineffable God, the divine Word, took on human fresh and frailty, has a particular resonance in theatre, where the word does indeed become enfleshed in embodied performance. In terms of religious theatre, and Passion plays in particular, this incarnational discourse is all the more resounding (not least because of the compassion aroused by Christ's physical agonies): like the cycle plays in general, *Conspiracy* and *Annas and Caiaphas* are both sacred and secular; devotional and political. At the Last Supper, Christ enjoined his followers: "Do this in memory of me" (Luke 22:19). He spoke truth to power with a prophetic voice, a suffering witness to that truth. To honour his memory is to honour his political courage – and to consider how he is distinguished thematically and dramatically from all others in these pageants. Furthermore, as Christ came into a fractured world which failed to recognise his coeval divinity, the two pageants are a dialogic and agonistic forum of dissonant voices and human agents. Government, whether temporal or ecclesiastical, in which institutions jostle for pre-eminence, is held up to scrutiny. Medieval York was a patchwork of jurisdictions – those of the city authorities, powerful monasteries, the Minster, the King's Council in the North – and audiences might have registered the painful similarities between their situation and the representation of hegemonic struggle in first-century Palestine.

---

2   All citations from the two plays, respectively 26, *The Cutteleres*, and 29, *The Bowers and Flecchers*, are taken from *The York Plays: A Critical Edition of the York Corpus Christi Play as Recorded in British Library Additional MS 35290*, ed. Richard Beadle, 2 vols., EETS s.s. 23–24 (Oxford: Oxford University Press, 2009–13), 1: 213–23; 241–55.

Just as the medieval craft-guilds employed anachronism and bi-focal references (first-century chief priests are fifteenth-century bishops; imperial Roman procurator Pilate is the King's man on the Council of the North), so did I: remembering (and re-membering) the past, via historical and mythological framing references, informed by and with the urgencies of the actual. Both plays offer preoccupying resonances for today: such as occupation, scapegoating and the abuse of human rights. Benjamin enjoins: "Seize hold of a memory as it flashes up at a moment of danger" (Thesis 6).[3] My own specific and topical cultural responses sought to do just that, in order to realise, like the medieval players, an active, not passive, relationship with history, to seize hold of it as a living provocation.

2 Festive Drama

"Festivals and feast day celebrations can be considered among the most significant cultural phenomena of any society and in any period in history."[4] Festival is the symbolical arena in which opposing cultural traditions clash with most dramatic force. In the same way, these two pageants refer to the hegemonic relations of the different complexes of order (religious, legal, political) in the medieval polis. To analyse the motors of play within these two Passion pageants, I draw upon the theories of Mikhail Bakhtin's carnivalesque and Victor Turner's cultural anthropology.[5] Ritualised festivity occurs during a liminal crack in time, such as seasonal change or a rite of passage. In medieval York on the feast of Corpus Christi, a religious holy day co-existed alongside a playing holiday; the sacred mingled with the secular and profane. At such sanctioned moments, perceptions are projected in liminal space when "people 'play' with the elements of the familiar and defamiliarize them."[6]

---

3   Walter Benjamin, "Theses on the philosophy of history" [1940], in Idem, *Illuminations: Essays and Reflections*, ed. Hannah Arendt, trans. Harry Zohn (New York: Shocken Books, 1969), 253–64. Because the theses are so short and are widely anthologised, reference is made to the number of thesis cited.
4   Anu Mänd, *Urban Carnival: Festive Culture in the Hanseatic Cities of the Eastern Baltic, 1350–1550* (Turnhout: Brepols, 2005), 1. The author (ibid., 1–7) provides a perceptive overview of recent research trends into medieval festivals and the carnivalesque.
5   Mikhail Bakhtin, *Rabelais and His World*, trans. Hélène Iswolsky (Bloomington: Indiana University Press, 1984); Victor Turner, *From Ritual to Theatre: The Human Seriousness of Play* (New York: Performing Arts Journal Publications, 1982); Idem, *The Anthropology of Performance* (New York: Performing Arts Journal Publications, 1987).
6   Turner, *From Ritual to Theatre*, 27.

These ludic performances played out along the margins of central institutions (such as the crown and church) and were plural, fragmentary and experimental in character – a useful way to describe the episodic pageants of the assorted craft guilds which, although tied to an officially sanctioned script, were open to topical resonance, satire and improvised reference. Bakhtin's carnivalesque examines the complex, protean and opportunistic popular-festive life of the period which engages with and refashions life "according to a certain pattern of play."[7] Festival suspended customary hierarchical rank and prohibitions and licensed the craft-guilds to imitate, quite possibly parodically, high status roles, transgressing boundaries in a symbolic violation of the social order from below. The carnivalesque made possible "a second world and a second life outside officialdom;" a utopian alterity, a referential doubleness, "a critical, historical consciousness."[8] Opposing dogmatism, it communicated through ritual confrontation, yoking together antinomies such as the sacred and the profane, the proud and the humble. The carnivalesque provided a strategic nexus between the popular and the powerful, combining literate and learned discourse such as political and legal theory and theology alongside traditional ritual performance.

3 Performances of Power

The two pageants contain notable examples of the three elements Bakhtin identifies as integral to carnivalesque performance: comic and parodic verbal compositions; various genres of billingsgate: curses, oaths, popular blazons; and ritual spectacles.[9] The first of these, comic verbal compositions, the boastful opening speeches of Pilate and Caiaphas are examples of 'pomping'. Their pride is on display and both provide fulsome *curricula vitae*, indicative of character, ripe for satire and contention. Pilate is the representative of royal power: "Undir þe ryallest roye of rente and renowne, || Now am I regent of rewle" (26.1–2). The Council of the North resided in York. Annas and Caiaphas are 'bishops': York Minster was the seat of the Archbishop of York.

Both plays show authority figures obsessed with the recognition and exercise of their power and prerogatives.[10] In *Conspiracy*, Pilate needs to reassert

---

[7]   Bakhtin, *Rabelais and His World*, 7.
[8]   Ibid., 5, 9–10.
[9]   Ibid., 5.
[10] For a further discussion of the power politics, contemporary discourses and topical resonances, see: J.W. Robinson, "The Art of the York Realist," *Modern Philology* 60 (1963): 241–51; Lawrence Clopper, "Tyrants and Villains: Characterization in the Passion

constantly, "Obeye unto bidding bud busshoppis me bowne" (26.3) as the prelates demand that Christ be prosecuted. Pilate is markedly jealous of his status – "The dubbing of my dingnite may noȝt be done downe" (26.7) – and he insists that traitors will be pursued in summary fashion: "traytoures tyte will I taynte" (26.6). For all his claims of philosophical mastery and exercise of detached reason in jurisprudence, Pilate is a peremptory overlord who brooks no complaint in his ruthless will to power. Describing himself a "perelous prince," he warns dissidents: "Be ware, for wyscus I am. ... He schall full bitterly banne þat bide schall my blame, ... For sone his life shall he lose, or left be for lame" (26.14, 19, 21).

From the outset then, and for all Pilate's boast of ruling over a peacetime dominion ("þis region in reste", 26.2), there is a clear understanding that authority depends upon the threat, and if necessary, the exercise of violence, and superior force of arms. Pilate commands, "bolde men þat in batayll makis brestis to breste" (26.4). The procurator's boast is, in fact, characterised by a prevailing sense of insecurity. The whole notion of manhood, and the concepts of hierarchy and order within patriarchy, were based upon violence which was essential for the regulation (and subversion) of male relationships. "An important key to the understanding of violence in medieval plays can be found in the relationship between *violentia*, *vis*, and *potestas* (violence, force and power), the three possible meanings of the German term *Gewalt*. Medieval plays – and especially religious plays – normally do not present violence as an isolated feature, but rather represent it as an expression or a means of power, and as a mode to discuss the legitimacy of power."[11]

This key-note of violence and its constant menace, introduced from the very beginning of the play, flares up throughout *Conspiracy* and notably when Pilate, the viceroy, is rattled by the allegations of Christ's claims to kingship:

> And if so be, þat borde to bayll will hym bring,
> And make hym boldely to banne þe bones þat hym bare.
> For-why þat wrecche fro oure wretthe schal not wryng,
> Or þer be wrought on hym wrake.
> ...

Sequences of the English Cycle Plays," *Modern Language Quarterly* 41 (1980): 3–20; Robert A. Brawer, "The Characterization of Pilate in the York Cycle Play," *Studies in Philology* 69 (1972): 289–303; Pamela M. King, "Contemporary Cultural Models for the Trial Plays in the York Cycle," in *Drama and Community: People and Plays in Medieval Europe*, ed. Alan Hindley (Turnhout: Brepols, 1999), 200–16.

11 Cora Dietl, "Preface," in *Power and Violence in Medieval and Early Modern Theater*, ed. Cora Dietl, Christoph Schanze and Glenn Ehrstine (Goettingen: V&R Academic, 2014), 7.

> For kende schall þat knave be to knele. (26.117–20, 124)

It is well known that one of the functions of ritual violence (dramatic or otherwise) was to reinforce the social hierarchy by instilling a sense of security and 'consubstantiality'.[12]

As for Caiaphas – mocked in *Annas and Caiaphas* for his obsession with bourgeois etiquette and decorum, and penchant for alcohol – there is an explicit unquietness and contention referred to in the very first line of his opening boast: "Pees, bewshers, I bid no jangelyng ʒe make" (29.1). He asserts his primacy in law and worldly wisdom (29.14–17), yet this assertion runs counter to his emotive intervention in due process. In *Conspiracy*, Pilate, the temporal ruler, sardonically detached from the confessional gripes against Jesus, discerns the viciousness of the bishops and their retinue: "I here wele ʒe hate hym; youre hartis are on heght … ʒoure rancour is raykand full rawe … Forsothe, ʒe ar over-cruell to knawe." (26.35, 93, 95)

Rhetoric was not "a quiet and peaceable art."[13] Forensic rhetoric was considered dangerous because of its perceived emphasis on the histrionic over the epistemological. Classical and medieval commentators considered forensic argumentation to be the verbal analogue of violent confrontation.[14] Note the inflammatory and insulting terms used in these pageants to describe Jesus which may be summarised under the following categories: mad-fool-idiot; sorcerer-heretic-traitor; villain-worthless individual-boy; Jew. In similar fashion, in *Annas and Caiaphas*, the apostle Peter is likened to an ape, badger and owl. Here we are in the realms of Bakhtin's various genres of billingsgate – curses, oaths and flyting – that serve to demonise and dehumanise. The Woman pursues and interrogates Peter whom she accuses of being a spy (29.94):

---

12   Kenneth Burke, *The Philosophy of Literary Form: Studies in Symbolic Action* (Berkeley: University of California Press, 1973), 107–9. 'Consubstantiality', derived from theology, literally means 'being of the same substance', hence a very strong sense of identity politics, of communal solidarity.

13   Tacitus, *Dialogus de oratoribus,* 40. Cited in Jody Enders, *Rhetoric and the Origins of Medieval Drama* (Ithaca: Cornell University Press, 1992), 89.

14   "Legal and legalistic disputation might be resituated within the larger ludic-agonistic context of a medieval society that literally plays itself out in its magic, rituals, tournaments, and military sports" (Jacques Le Goff, *La Civilisation de l'Occident médiéval* [Paris: Arthaud, 1967], 444). Cited in Enders, *Rhetoric and the Origins of Medieval Drama,* 90. Alan Knight, *Aspects of Genre in Late Medieval French Drama* (Manchester: Manchester University Press, 1983), 31, recalls late medieval theatre's similar structure to the Old Comedy of Aristophanes, where, in Northrop Frye's words, "the distinguishing feature is the *agon* or contest."

Thou caytiffe, what meves þe[e] stande
So stabill and stille in þi thoght?
Þou hast wrought mekill wronge in londe,
And wondirfull werkis haste þou wrought.

A lorell, a leder of lawe,
To sette hym and suye has þou soght. (29.109–14)

Her edgy questions stress how identity is formulated through allegiance, inclusion and social positioning. People were highly sensitive to disorder and displacement because they were so concerned with the hierarchies and group identities that defined and preserved their position in the universe. Prevailing cultural identity attained its sense of corporate force from a set of invoked contraries. The pageant enacts a brutal paranoia that derives a febrile, triumphalist force from the invocation of a heretical Other perceived as an invasive threat to the prerogatives of the authorities. Annas accuses Jesus of performing his life-restoring miracles by the "myghtis of Mahounde" (29.267).[15] During this period, social groups defined themselves by inclusion and exclusion, by the opposition between identity and alterity. "Alterity is first and foremost the inversion of identity" (settled citizens as opposed to spies; the orthodox as opposed to heretics).[16] Jesus and Peter are the excluded Other, deemed to hail from a subversive anti-world, distinct and separate from the socio-political and cultural orthodoxy. "Othering" is a term, advocated by Edward Said, which refers to the act of emphasising the perceived weaknesses of marginalised groups as a way of stressing the alleged strength of those in positions of power.[17]

The incursion of the "foreign" Galilean Peter into Caiaphas's inner courtyard ruffles the sense of domestic security: hence the accusation that he is a spy. The medieval control and codification of space was territorial: Jerusalem (like York) is a "towre begon towne" (26.5).[18] Safe domestic spaces contrasted with the dangerous territories outside such as the forest or wilderness. As with Hereford's *Mappa Mundi*, most models of the cosmos and society were circular and centripetal; God was at the centre of the medieval panopticon. Medieval world

---

15 Here "Mahounde" means a false god or demon, as it was used in the Christian west, indicative of the 'othering' of Islam. Ironically, Annas swears by "Beliall bloode and his bonys" (29.288) just a few lines later.
16 Jelle Koopmans, *Le théâtre des exclus au moyen âge: hérétiques, sorcières et marginaux* (Paris: Editions Imago, 1997), 97, my translation. See Koopmans for a rich examination of dramatised Others and the rituals and discourses surrounding them.
17 Edward W. Said, *Orientalism* (Harmondsworth: Penguin, 2003).
18 Cf. 29.237–38.

maps portray a centrifugal space for ejecting the vile outcasts of society: the further things err from Jerusalem (the centre), the more monstrous and alien they become. There was, furthermore, a clear moral divide between good and evil in this spatial demarcation.[19] In *Conspiracy*, when Pilate and the Temple authorities retire to discuss the fate of Jesus within the palace, Judas, "the traitor," seeks to gain access to them from without. First of all, he harangues the spectators with a self-pitying and damning tirade – an unashamed rant of thwarted greed: in particular, a stymied scam to steal the tithe, just as Cain does in *Cain and Abel*, coupled with a heartless disregard for the suffering of the poor: one of the corporal works of mercy. He vows vengeance against a "lathe" [vile] Jesus (26.128) whom he accuses of having deprived him of his intended ill-gotten gains:

> Wherfore for to mischeve þis Maistir of myne
> Perfore faste forþe will I flitte
> The princes of prestis vntill,
> And selle Hym full sone or þat I sitte,
> For therty pens in a knotte knytte. (26.148–52)

His attempt to gain admission to "þis prowde place" (26.155) is initially blocked by the porter who, as a representative of natural humanity, recognises something monstrously deviant about Judas, providing further choice examples of billingsgate abuse in the process:

> ... þou glorand gedlyng, ...
> Thy glyfftyng is so grimly þou gars my harte growe.
> ... I fele by a figure in youre fals face
> It is but foly to feste affeccioun in ʒou.
> ... Say, bittilbrowed bribour
> ... Þou arte combered in curstnesse.
> ... on-hanged harlot
> ... brethell, ...
> Þou chaterist like a churle þat can chyde. (26.157–83)[20]

---

19 See Koopmans, *Théâtre des exclus*, 27.

20 Cf. the deformed *grylli* in medieval art who represented ignoble instinct. Ugliness and deformity, institutionalized in court dwarfs and buffoons, signified a grotesque distortion of divinely created nature. See Michael Camille, *Image on the Edge: The Margins of Medieval Art* (Cambridge, Mass: Harvard University Press, 1992), 14, 138; Timothy Hyman, "A Carnival Sense of the World," in Timothy Hyman and Roger Malbert, *Carnivalesque*

Once again, a turning point comes when Judas claims that the security and preservation of the hegemonic power is at stake – "thurgh my dedis youre dugeperes fro dere may be drawe" (26.182) – and, with his claim to be privy to crucial intelligence, he gains entry. This is a liminal moment *par excellence* – on the very threshold of Pilate's palace – when the fate of humanity hangs in the balance. Judas goes about his nefarious business at night on the eve of Passover (Matthew 26:14–15), the Old Testament precursor to Christ's own paschal sacrifice, significantly commemorated at the Feast of Corpus Christi, itself a festival of early summer. "Good things of day begin to droop and drowse, || while night's black agents to their preys do rouse" (*Macbeth*, III.ii.52–3).

Judas the traitor is "cladde in a cope" (26.202). In other words, sporting a hooded cloak, he is disguised. This masking emphasises his false nature, his hypocrisy; the master of such disguises could only be the Devil, the Prince of Lies.[21] The etymology of hypocrite is 'actor'. In *Conspiracy*, I Miles is outraged how "þis losell [Judas] laykis with his lord" (26.239). In *Annas and Caiaphas*, The soldiers recall and parodically re-enact Judas's dark pantomime of loyalty. He "feyned to be his frende, as a faytour, || This was þe tokenyng before þat he tolde us" (29.232–33). And Caiaphas opines: "Nowe trewly, þis was a trante of a traytour" (29.234). The performance of the kiss is a theatrical fiction. Taking their cue from Saint Augustine, medieval anti-image writers attacked such false representations and drew an analogy with actors' masks disguising reality as paradigmatic of the idolatrous falseness of perception. They warned against becoming enslaved by representation itself, delighting in fictions like "the obscenities of the stage, which modesty detests."[22] Masking, in the broad sense of disguise and deception, is a preoccupation in medieval theatre. The duplicitous, sheep-stealing trickster Mak, in the *Second Shepherds Play*, who makes a blasphemous prayer to Pontius Pilate, and is in effect a comic devil-figure, dons a cloak to disguise himself. In *Wisdom*, the actors who represent Perjury wear

---

(London: Hayward Gallery Publishing, 2000), 32–39. The porter's words make elliptical reference to Judas's reported suicide by hanging. They also exemplify the demonizing, scapegoating and Othering of Judas, the chief priests and the 'Jews': a vicious irony (given the concerns of the Gospel) which contemporary Christianity sanctioned, for the Jews were deemed en bloc guilty of deicide.

21   Karin Ueltschi, *La Mesnie Hellequin en conte et en rime: Mémoire mythique et poétique de la recomposition* (Paris: Honoré Champion, 2008), 556–57. See also Olga Anna Dull, *Folie et rhétorique dans la sottie* (Geneva: Droz, 1994), 255, for a discussion of the Christian condemnation and prohibition of masking "fausse semblance" as spawn of the Devil. One etymology of vice comes from the Old French *vis*, meaning visage, seeming.

22   Michael Camille, *The Gothic Idol: Ideology and Image-making in Medieval Art* (Cambridge: Cambridge University Press, 1989), 36–38, 62–69.

masks of two faces, and in John Skelton's *Magnificence* (1515–18), the character Cloaked Collusion (reminiscent of the cloaked conspirator Judas here) hides two faces under his hood.[23]

As for the 'Judas kiss', itself, it is framed as a grotesque perversion of the natural order. In *Annas and Caiaphas*, III Miles recounts ironically how: "[Judas] markid us his maistir emang all his men || And kyssid hym full kyndely his comforte to kele" (29. 224–25). In late medieval culture, a kiss was a visual sign of concord and harmony. An actual public ritual, the love-day embrace, was used to confirm the achievement of private peace settlements through a ritualistic exchange of the kiss of peace. Europe was full of male-male embraces, both in dramatic representation and in real life. Such embraces served to reinforce 'homosocial' bonds, what Eve Kosofsky Sedgwick calls "male 'homosocial' desire ... the affective or social force, the glue ... that shapes an important relationship."[24] Consider the Benedictine Rupert of Deutz's dream of Christ on the cross in which he craved closer union with the Lord: "I held him, I embraced him, I kissed him for a long time. I sensed how seriously he accepted this gesture of love when, while kissing, he himself opened his mouth that I might kiss more deeply."[25] The Janitor astutely remarks that Judas is "uncomely to kys" (26.201); his "kene," wolvish face makes him a devil figure, a potential practitioner of the impure '*osculum infame*'.

The most socially significant of medieval male-to-male kisses was that exchanged by the monarch or feudal overlord and vassal or retainer in the ritual of the verification of loyalty: the 'homage'. It is Judas's willingness to betray his master in such a hypocritical way – an inversion of the homage – that infuriates the soldiers who are, themselves, bound by an oath of loyalty: "Take þer of, a traytour tyte!" (26.237). Rather than being a spiritual obligation, loyalty, it transpires, is something which is bought. *Conspiracy* casts a cold eye on royal and urban power-broking. During the Cousins' War, success at the summit depended on a flexibility and a willingness to slide from one great patron to another. In a significant departure from the Biblical narrative, where it is the chief priests who pay, here it is Pilate who secures Judas's services. The

---

[23] See Leigh Winser, "*Magnyfycence* and the Characters of *Sottie*," *Sixteenth Century Journal* 12 (1981): 85–94; Jelle Koopmans, "'Et doit avoir un faux visage par derrière': Masques et apparences dans le théâtre profane français (1450–1550)," *L'immagine riflessa* N.S. 9 (2000): 267–83.

[24] Eve Kosofsky Sedgwick, *Between Men: English Literature and Male Homosocial Desire* (New York: Columbia University Press, 1985), 2.

[25] Mary Wack, *Lovesickness in the Middle Ages: The* Viaticum *and Its Commentaries* (Philadelphia: University of Pennsylvania Press, 1990), 24. For a general overview, see *The Kiss in History*, ed. Karen Harvey (Manchester: Manchester University Press), 2005.

pragmatic governor skirts over the disciple's treachery, "For it is beste for oure bote" (26.271), and makes him his creature: "Judas, to holde þi behest, be hende for our happe, || And of us, helpe and upholde we hete þe[e] to have" (26.282–3). *Conspiracy* examines the crown's surveillance and intelligence-gathering as well as its use of force to preserve hegemony. The monarchy's pre-eminent power was based upon overwhelming financial and military resources, and legislative scope. Ironically, while the Woman identifies Peter as a "spie" in *Annas and Caiaphas* (29.92), it is Judas who is the double-agent and this momentous Gospel moment of betrayal is commemorated on "Spy Wednesday" in Holy Week. "By force and by law [the man of sorrows] was taken" (Isaiah 53:8). Pilate, Judas and the Temple Authorities combine privily to pervert justice. In carnivalesque 'play', the law becomes the subject of interrogation. Indeed, official law could be seen from this perspective as a form of *disorder*. All this takes place at the bar. Judas transacts on the threshold, a liminal double-dealer. Thus, the inner sanctum is not soiled by the grubby transaction, the "knotte knytte" – the polar opposite of the New Covenant of Christ's blood which redeems humanity with grace. Traditionally, and in our production, Pilate throws the money down onto the ground, and Judas participates in his moral degradation in grovelling to pick it up: "And therefore, Judas, mende þou thy mone, || And take þer þi silvere all same" (26.276–77).

4   Passion Play

The upshot of Judas's betrayal is the arrest, interrogation and torture of Christ. Enraged by Jesus's testimony, the chief priests sanction his 'buffeting' by the soldiers – a carnivalesque ritual of mockery, humiliation and exclusion comparable to the festive, ridiculous thrashings meted out in the market square and on the scaffold in a highly developed rhetoric of violence. III Miles announces that he and his fellow soldiers will "play popse for þe pages prowe" (29.358). This turns out to be a sadistic, choreographed variation of the children's game hoodman-blind (blindman's buff):

IV MILES		Late see, who stertis for a stole?
		For I have here a hatir to hyde hym.
I MILES		Lo, here is one full fitte for a foole,
		Go gete it and sette þe[e] beside hym.
II MILES		Nay, I schall sette it myselffe and frusshe hym also.
		Lo, here, a shrowde for a shrewe, and of shene shappe.
		(29.356–61)

FIGURE 12.1 *Jesus blindfolded and seated on a low stool.*

They blindfold Jesus, quite possibly with the aid of a hangman's noose ("hatir") and seat him on a low stool before raining down blows upon him (Fig. 12.1):

> III MILES   Playes faire, in feere, I schall fande to feste it
> With a faire flappe, and þer is one! [*strikes Jesus*], and þer is ii;
> And ther is iij; and there is iiij.
> Say nowe, with an nevill happe,
> Who negheth þe[e] nowe? Not o worde? No!
> IV MILES   Dose noddill on hym with neffes, that he noght nappe.
> (29.362–67)

I Miles replies: "Nay, nowe to nappe is no nede, || Wassaille! Wassaylle! I warande hym wakande" (29.371–72). "I was the song of drunkards" (Psalm 69): it has been mooted that here the soldiers toast each other in a festive drinking game. However, I Miles's belief that Jesus is not napping but awake following his cries of "Wassail" suggests another possibility. The blows to Christ's head could certainly have led to his being concussed, even knocked out. I Miles might well utter, "I warande hym wakande," after dousing Christ in liquid. Certain illustrations of this scene depict a torturer upending a chamber pot over the Saviour's head, a viciously ironic wassail bowl (Fig. 12.2). Clerical commentators like Pope Innocent III considered spittle, urine and excrement as the "vile ignobility of human existence."[26] Christ is also spat upon in the

---

26   Lamentations 4:5. For excrement, see Camille, *Image on the Edge*, 111–14, Timothy Hyman, "A Carnival Sense," 32, and Stephen J. Greenblatt's acute essay "Filthy Rites" in his *Learning*

FIGURE 12.2 *A torturer upending a chamber pot over the Saviour's head.*

Biblical narratives of this encounter (such as Mark 14:65), and Isaiah's suffering servant makes no resistance against insult and spittle (Isaiah 50:6).[27] The defenceless Christ is defiled (Figs. 12.2 and 12.3):

II MILES	3a, and bot he bettir bourdis can byde,
	Such buffettis schall he be takande.
III MILES	Prophete, Y saie, to be oute of debate,
	Quis te percussit [Who struck you], man? Rede, giffe þou may. (29.370–73)

Jesus does not offer 'better sport' and suffers for it. Such 'sporting' is a constant and troubling leitmotif throughout this pageant. Caiaphas has ordered the tracking down and arrest of Christ "halfe for hethyng" (29.33), and II Miles, likewise, presents the bound Jesus to him with the words, "here is layke, and ȝou list!" (29.192). Both Caiaphas and Annas describe Christ and his detention-and-interrogation as a "game" (29.206, 207, 290), with Caiaphas telling Christ: "Boy, be not agaste if we seme gaye" (29.291).

---

to Curse: Essays in Early Modern Culture (**New** York: Routledge, 1990), 59–79. In *Mankind*, the vice figure Nought urinates over his foot and laments, "My fote ys fowly ouerschotte" (l. 786), just as, morally, things turn ugly.

27   In our performance, our soldiers spat on him here, too. I was inspired by Fra Angelico's *The Mocking of Christ*.

FIGURE 12.3 *Christ defiled*

"Whatever material you're working with, games amplify action and bring it alive."[28] This is certainly true of the torture of Christ. At the same time, the jarring discordance between a light-hearted and innocent children's game and its refashioning as a wilfully violent adult amusement is disturbing.[29] The late medieval devotional practice of affective piety inculcated a compassionate, deeply felt identification with Christ's human suffering.[30] Imagine, as a person of faith, playing in the Passion sequences or knowing someone who was.[31]

28 John Wright, *Why is that so Funny? A Practical Exploration of Physical Comedy* (London: Nick Hern Books, 2011), 38.
29 According to Jean-Claude Schmitt, "Les images de la dérision," in *La dérision au Moyen Age: De la pratique sociale au rituel politique*, ed. Elisabeth Crouzet-Pavan and Jacques Verger (Paris: Presses de l'Université Paris-Sorbonne, 2007), "A limited number of texts – in the Bible essentially – inspired the essential of the medieval iconography of mockery" (267) and "none rivalled the Mockery of Christ" (272). As the editors note in their introduction, "The scenes of the mockery of Christ multiply in the art of the late Middle Ages; the sufferings of the Passion rouse not mockery but emotion and pity" (10).
30 On affective piety, see Clifford Davidson, "Suffering and the York Cycle Plays," in Idem, *Festivals and Plays in Late Medieval Britain* (Ashgate: Aldershot, 2007), 141–67. See also the essays by Alexandra Johnson, Margaret Rogerson and Jill Stevenson in *The York Mystery Plays: Performance in the City*, ed. Margaret Rogerson (Woodbridge: York Medieval Press, Boydell and Brewer, 2011). Stevenson turns to cognitive theory to explore affective piety's ongoing relevance in terms of "lived bodiliness," empathic neural activity, visceral connection and imaginative engagement.
31 Meg Twycross, "Beyond the Picture Theory: Image and Activity in Medieval Drama," *Word and Image: A Journal of Verbal/Visual Enquiry* 4 (1988): 591, discusses the emotionally

There is a symbolic fall from grace here. J.W. Robinson comments that the grim games afoot show both the sinfulness of the Israelites and the effect of sins committed by audience members.[32] He proceeds to discuss the rich polysemy of the word 'game': variously scheme, trick or plot and, in some contexts, an "ill-advised scheming to dominate." The 'game' in the Passion pageants is essentially a cruel hunting down, seizing and torturing of the prey – a process begun in *Conspiracy*. Christ is 'game' in this sense, too – a hunted creature: "Itt is no burde to bete bestis þat are bune" [There is no fun in beating a bound beast; 29.243], "like a lamb that is led to the slaughter-house" (Isaiah, 53:7).[33] The Middle English word *game* also has its modern sense of 'childish amusement'. The Chief Priests possess a fundamental lack of spiritual profundity and discernment. Caiaphas's demonstrated predilection for whimsical play runs counter to his boast of judicial gravitas and is, rather, all of a piece with his emotive intervention in legal process. In the morality play *Mankind*, the devil Titivillus crows: "Farwell, everychon, for I have don my game, || For I have brought Mankynde to myscheff and to schame" (ll. 605–06). A game, which can also mean a play, is, in this context, something inherently insincere and trivial. It is opposed to right conduct, decorum and ethical control.[34] Such frivolity, in which Jesus is both prey and a play*thing*, connotes both a lack of empathy and a sadistic distancing.

In *Conspiracy*, I Miles says of Judas Iscariot: "Late no man wete || How þis losel laykis with his lord" (26.238–39). Judas breaks his sacred bond of fealty and is, as previously discussed, a false and insincere player with a greed for gain who is only too happy to set the trap and who relishes the prospect of physical violence:

---

stirring quality of affective piety and notes how plays scored over painting, quoting from the *Tretise of Miraclis Pleyinge*: "betere they be holden in mennus minde and oftere rehersid by the pleyinge of hem than by the peintinge, for this is a deed bok, the tother a qu[i]ck."

32   J.W. Robinson, *Studies in Fifteenth-Century Stagecraft* (Kalamazoo, MI: Medieval Institute Publications, 1991), 192. There is also the chance that some spectators might be caught up in the mob-violence – a dramaturgical trip-up. Cf. Psalm 68: "It is for you that I suffer taunts, ... That I have become a stranger to my brothers ... I looked in vain for compassion, for consolers; not one could I find."

33   As is Peter, the baited badger (26.117–18). See Robinson, *Studies in Fifteenth-Century Stagecraft*, 192–93, for a discussion of the Biblical discourse around game/prey; hunting as a sign of sinfulness, and the satirising of clerics who hunted.

34   Like Christ, here, Mercy in *Mankind* is pilloried by the vices because "ye mak no sport."

JUDAS	For tytte schall þat taynte be tone,
	And þerto jocounde and joly I am.
	...
	I schall bekenne ȝou his corse in care for to clappe.
	(26.279–83)

Such predators dehumanise those they scapegoat and upon whom they prey. Judas entered *Conspiracy* seething against Jesus whom he judged to be "lathe." Further insights into this marginalisation may be gleaned through the appreciation of Christ being cast as an abject figure and through an analysis of the processes of this abjection.[35]

The literal sense of abjection is 'the state of being cast off' – essentially what Judas does to Christ. The word has connotations of degradation and baseness, but the abject has been explored as that which inherently disrupts conventional identity and cultural models. The concept of abjection can be summarised as the process by which social groups separate their sense of self – variously physical, social and cultural – from that which they consider intolerable and which infringes upon their self. The abject is, as such, the 'me that is not me', that which is both rejected by and disturbs social reason – the communal consensus that underpins a social order. Abjection disturbs identity, system and order. Crucially, abjection occurs through language, both on the micro-level of individual speaking beings (and their subjective dynamics) and on the macro-level of society, through language as a common and universal law. Three times, Christ's interrogators bid him to speak, and three times he remains silent ("Harshly dealt with, ... he never opened his mouth," Isaiah 53:7). This silence and lack of language provokes a gamut of responses – frustration, anger, mockery – but in each case, Jesus is identified as an abject.

CAYPHAS	And tell us som tales, truly to traste.
ANNA	Sir, we might als wele talke tille it tome tonne.
	I warande hym witteles, or ellis he is wrang wrayste.
	(29.246–48)
III MILES	Prophete, Y saie, to be oute of debate,
	Quis te percussit, man? Rede, giffe þou may.
IV MILES	Those words are in waste, what wenes þou he wate?
	It semys by his wirkyng his wittes were awaye.

---

35 I draw upon Julia Kristeva, *Powers of Horror: An Essay on Abjection* (New York: Columbia University Press, 1982), for the following discussion.

> I Miles   Now late hym stande as he stode in a foles state.
>   (29.372–76)[36]

The abject is an object which is violently cast out of the cultural world, having once been a subject ("a thing despised and rejected by men, a man of sorrows and familiar with suffering, ... and we took no account of him", Isaiah 53:3).[37]

> Cayphas   Do telle to sir Pilate oure pleyntes all pleyne,
>   And saie þis ladde with his lesyngis has oure laws lorne.
>   And saie þis same day muste he be slayne,
>   Because of Sabott day þat schal be tomorne.
>   ...
>   [To Jesus] Sir, youre faire felawschippe we betake to þe fende,
>   Goose onne nowe, and daunce forth in þe Devyll way.
>   (29.386–95)

Social groups use rituals, specifically those of defilement, to attempt to maintain clear boundaries between that deemed socially acceptable and that deemed socially transgressive, paradoxically both excluding and renewing contact with the abject in the ritual act. There is a physical proximity in the striking of Christ but this very closeness can only come about through a perverse emotional distance – a negation of the bonds of common humanity.[38] Christ's torturers seek to trump his dissident subjectivity by rendering him both an object and an abject.

For Kristeva, the sense of the abject stands both in binary opposition to and complements the existence of the "superego," the representative of culture, of the symbolic order: here the chief priests, inflexible and obdurate in their piety and their hypocritical legalism.[39] Abjection is often used to describe the state

---

36 On the scapegoating of fools and 'heretical fools', see Jacques Heers, *Fêtes des fous et carnavals* (Paris: Fayard, 1983), 142–49, and Koopmans, *Théâtre des exclus*, 53–60.

37 Cf. also Psalm 31:12: "I am like a dead man, forgotten in men's hearts, like a thing thrown away."

38 Consider Bosch's painting, *The Mockery of Christ*, with its pack-like quartet of anachronistic, contemporary torturers; and cf. Psalm 21:17, "For many dogs have encompassed me."

39 See Clopper, "Tyrants and Villains," 11: "Their stated reason for their antagonism toward Christ in all the cycles is that they fear the loss of their law, and the charges they bring against Him are violations of the Judaic law." He lists all of their motivations from the cycle plays. There is a sabbatarian bathos in their lament that Jesus heals and resurrects etc. Christ has come of course to fulfil the Old Law with the New.

of marginalised outgroups, labelled as revolting figures, for they revolt against their abject identity. Christ shakes the Temple authorities' sense of identity (and authority) to the core.

5 Theatrical Insights and Continuities

The theories, insights and observations of two key modern theatre makers and teachers can be applied to the performance styles and types appropriate to these two Passion pageants. Firstly, Christ's torturers resonate with the satirical and infantile *bouffons* of Jacques Lecoq who underline the grotesque aspects of all hierarchies of power and profane the sacred. They delight in violence, live in gangs, and hark back to the devils, vices and vicious fools of medieval theatre.[40] Secondly, all of Jesus's opponents, with their overblown rhetoric, volubility and histrionics, resemble what Jerzy Grotowski dubs "courtesan actors" whose collection of skills he refers to a as a "box of tricks." Conversely, Christ, appropriately enough, is a perfect exemplar of Grotowski's "holy actor."[41] Christ makes his statement, his witness, with utter serenity and calm, in defiance of the corrupt law, and becomes a kind of provocation for the spectator. The Greek word for witness is *martus* (whence 'martyr') and integral to Christ's testimony is the offering up of his suffering body. Grotowski describes Holy Actors as sacrificial figures who give themselves "fully, humbly and without defence."[42] The decisive factor is humility, a spiritual predisposition: not to *do* something, but to *refrain* from doing something. Such actors make a total gift of themselves, in "a complete stripping down, the laying bare of [their] own intimity – all this without the least trace of egotism or self-enjoyment."[43] With these players, there is an urge towards intimate, solemn revelation. They are a source of 'spiritual light' and their very silence is to be filled with meaning.[44]

In terms of the Gospel narrative, Christ will shortly embark on his *via dolorosa* to Calvary, though clearly his journey of suffering has already started by the start of *Annas and Caiaphas*. The holy actor, similarly, is, in Grotowski's phrase, embarked on a *via negativa*: not a collection of skills, the courtesan

---

40 Jacques Lecoq, *The Moving Body: Teaching Creative Theatre*, trans. David Bradby (London: Methuen, 2002), 104, 124–33.
41 Jerzy Grotowski, *Towards a Poor Theatre* (London: Methuen, 1969), 35.
42 Ibid., 38.
43 Ibid., 16.
44 Ibid., 20.

actor's 'box of tricks', but an eradication of blocks to the truth.[45] Christ, the suffering servant, is the Logos – both speech and reason, the enfleshed Word – resisting the overblown rhetoric, babel-babble and hurly burly with truth in testimony, composure in bearing and eloquent silence. Jesus's silence in these plays anticipates Beckett and Pinter where silence and hiatus in dialogue operate as a receptacle for the audience's own thoughts and meditations, a space to consider the subtext: what is left unsaid. Further, the actor playing Christ resembles an ordained priest in that both are *in persona Christi*. In their mediating role, they are sacramental vectors: an outward sign of an inward grace.

I made the decision for our company to deliver the Middle English script in Middle English pronunciation.[46] The challenge of being understood furthered my appreciation of gestural acting, as identified in the rubrics of the twelfth-century Anglo-Norman *Jeu d'Adam*: "All persons ... shall speak composedly and shall use such gestures as become the matter whereof they are speaking."[47] Grotowski notes, "We know that the text *per se* is not theatre, that it becomes theatre only through the actors' use of it – that is to say, thanks to intonations, to the association of sounds, to the musicality of the language."[48] Again, Lecoq's insights, as laid out in his appropriately entitled *Moving Body*, provide theoretical insight into our approach. He advocates setting the text free inside the body. "We consider words as living organisms which carry within themselves the dynamics of movement." Actors translate scripts through "mimodynamics," a gestural translation of words and highly apt for present-day delivery of unfamiliar Middle English.[49] This involves the miming body in the recognition and understanding of reality, seeking forms rooted in real life. This gestural translation is based upon natural dynamics and action gestures, but, in a highly structured technique of theatrical transposition, it goes beyond pure imitation and is given the expressiveness of play.[50] "In the theatre, making a movement is never a mechanical act but must always be a gesture that is justified. Its jus-

---

45   Ibid., 17.
46   As Carl Heap warned, during our post-performance discussion, "When the scripts are modernised, they can sound trite, jingly, awkward. This plays into the hands of all those who believe that medieval performers were mere rude mechanicals. By taking the risk that we may only partially understand the language, we can better appreciate the foreignness of the medieval culture; we lean forward and try harder."
47   *A Source Book in Theatrical History*, ed. A.M. Nagler (Mineola: Dover Publications, 1959), 45. I am grateful to Carl Heap for this note.
48   Grotowski, *Towards a Poor Theatre*, 21.
49   Lecoq, *The Moving Body*, 50, 51, 107.
50   Ibid., 45, 173.

FIGURE 12.4
An example of gestural acting

tification may consist in an indication or an action, or even an inward state."[51] Similarly, Grotowski's "extra-daily," heightened acting style has something of the iconic, the "sculptural," harking from the spiritual realm of churches and cathedrals[52] (Fig. 10).

Apart from words and gestures, performance also involves actors, audience, props, space, and the complex dynamics between them at any particular moment. The medieval staging of the Passion cycle on the feast of Corpus Christi established a clear relationship between the sacrificial human Christ present in the pageants and the projected sacramental 'real presence' of Christ in the consecrated host paraded in a monstrance for the purposes of adoration. Our Passion pageants were staged during Lent, in the run-up to the Christian celebration of the Passion, Death and Resurrection of Jesus Christ. The location of our performance was highly symbolical. Rather than the narrow streets of York, the two pageants were played in the chancel of Hull's Holy Trinity Church, a sacred precinct which led up to the high altar. The Eucharistic images over this again served as a reminder (certainly to the symbolically literate among any Christian faithful present) of the link between the sacrificial

---

51   Ibid., 69.
52   Grotowski, *Towards a Poor Theatre*, 39.

suffering of the actor playing Christ and the re-enactment of the Last Supper within the same space.

Grotowski notes that the Middle Ages produced the idea of "sacral parody" and identified the ritual roots of "the dialectics of mockery and apotheosis" within his own theatre.[53] The torture and crucifixion of Christ were staged at stations around York, certainly familiar with corporal and capital punishment. Staging these Passion pageants within Holy Trinity linked the spiritual space with a temporal violence at the outset of the Christian story, creating, conceivably, a sacrilegious *frisson*: a violation of the house of God just as the temple of Christ's body was violated. The spectators in medieval York were ritual participants in the Mystery cycle: part of the body of Christ, themselves, no less. (Similarly, "Carnival does not acknowledge any distinction between actors and spectators ... Everyone participates."[54]) This medieval *communitas* is seized upon by Grotowski in his acknowledgement of the medieval effects of his own "Poor Theatre": theatre's riches lie not in seeking to emulate the technical advances of visual media but in "the closeness of the living organism." Theatre "cannot exist without the actor-spectator relationship of perceptual, direct, live communion."[55] It is necessary to abolish the distance between actors and audience. An encounter and confrontation are necessary, brought about by actors who are athletes of the heart. Similarly, Lecoq seeks out 'complicity': a shared understanding between actors, or between actors and audience.[56]

Grotowski provides scenographic instructions for his ritual theatre, embodying communion in physical arrangements which include spectators in the architecture of action: "Once spectators are placed in an illuminated zone, or in other words become visible, they too begin to play a part in the performance."[57] This live communion and complicity is of inestimable value, and one of the gifts of early theatre. We played with electric lights on – it was dark outside – and our audience faced each other from choir stalls across the chancel. Hence there could be direct communication between actors and spectators. The chancel's width equated to the breadth of York's narrow streets, so a suitable intimacy was maintained. For example, in seeking to evade the accusatory Woman, Peter takes evasive action into the crowd: "Thruste in yone thrawe" (29.115). Our traverse playing space resembled the *platea* in front of the pag-

---

53   Ibid., 22, 18.
54   Bakhtin, *Rabelais and His World*, 7.
55   Ibid., 41, 19.
56   Ibid., 34, 174.
57   Ibid., 20.

eant wagon (a couple of trestles for us). Peter was able to run up a short passageway between the choir stalls and spectators.

Before a discussion and analysis of my *mise-en-scène* of the two pageants, further consideration of the theories and theatrical philosophies of Grotowski, Lecoq, and also Walter Benjamin, serve to situate my directorial approach and provide fascinating insights into dynamic theatre-making – not least medieval theatre – in their own right. Grotowski declares:

> The theatre, with its full-fleshed perceptivity, has always seemed to me a place of provocation. It is capable of challenging itself and its audience by violating accepted stereotypes of vision, feeling, and judgment – more jarring because it is imaged in the human organism's breath, body and inner impulses. ... The violation of the living organism, the exposure carried to outrageous excess, returns us to a concrete mythical situation, an experience of common human truth.[58]

As I have discussed above, theatre tells a story and bears witness. Put another way, it recounts and re-enacts history. Its memorial function, coupled with its embodied actuality – acting out in the here and now, its 'live' presence – are fundamental. Christ enjoined his disciples: "Do this in memory of me." In terms of the York cycle, its players and producers were honouring the mystery of the incarnation, the enfleshment of the Word, and its irruption into history. The Christian myth, then, is both sacred and secular: the foundational narrative of Western civilisation is inextricably bound up with the cultural history of its people. These pageants have a memorial function. Like Christ, they bear witness, but the witness is not only to the Biblical past but also to the present. There is a relationship between the performance event and social and political reality. The work can still shake audiences into attending to the silencings and oppressions of the present as well as the past.

Walter Benjamin's *Theses on the Philosophy of History* provide insights into the significance of anachronism and topical references in theatre. He argues that history is never over or in any sense complete. Benjamin conceived history as a text, as a series of events which 'will have been'. Their meaning, their historical dimension, is decided afterwards, through their inscription in the symbolic network. There is retroactivity of historical meaning. Hence, historical conditions can be endowed with contemporary relevance and a significance after the fact. Benjamin asks of history: "To seize hold of a memory as it flashes up at a moment of danger" [Thesis 6]. Anachronism is no error but

---

58   Ibid., 21–3.

by juxtaposing first-century Biblical history (as also re-enacted anachronistically in medieval York) with the contemporary, the latter is thrown into relief.[59] Historical and topical events become framing references, a mosaic of historical juxtapositions in a form of montage effect. According to Benjamin, such historical references or "quotation," whether in the guise of gesture, costume, delivery or ritual, is a form of guerrilla warfare with the ruling culture, a quasi-anarchistic technique which explodes, and in every sense arrests, interrupts and fragments the continuity of ideologies, texts, biographies and periods, resisting dominant narratives and the closure of discourse. This fragmentary and episodic technique – which chimes with Bertolt Brecht's episodic and defamiliarizing "dialectical theatre," and with late medieval festive drama, not least the episodic mystery plays – provokes questions and responsive engagement, eschewing heritage theatre or mere scholarly archaeology. As Lecoq writes:

> There is always a danger that students will rely on the cultural references which come with these dramatic territories. Each of us has our own way of imagining the past ... No reading of reference books can substitute for creative work, renewed each day ... Beyond styles or genres, we seek to discover the motors of play ... so that it may inspire creative work. And this creative work must always be of our time.[60]

6 The Hull Production

We performed from the medieval script but, just as York's craft-guilds 'inhabited' first-century Palestine and their own time, so did we. Our Pilate donned the be-medalled military dress uniform of many a modern dictator from around the world. He sported dark glasses as did his unsmiling and inscrutable security detail. The shades signified that they were not open to dialogic communication but masked and closed off, the eyes being the mirrors of the soul. In removing his glasses with a slow and studied flourish at the start of his harangue, Pilate chose to address the audience strictly on his one-way terms.

---

59   Cf. Twycross, "Beyond the Picture Theory," 591, and her discussion of the medieval theory of the relationship of visual images, including those realised in theatre, to memory. She cites Durandus, *"Per picturam quidem res gesta ante oculos ponitur"* [For by a picture, a historical event is placed before your eyes], and remarks: "It seems the function of pictures was reckoned to be two-fold: to recall actual events to your mind, whether you were actually there or not (the newsreel effect), and to leave you with a vividly memorable image for future use."
60   Lecoq, *The Moving Body*, 104.

FIGURE 12.5 *An electric torch shining blindingly onto Christ.*

Overall, I adopted an eclectic, '*bricolage*' approach to costume. The guards and soldiers wore military fatigues (black boots, combat trousers and leather jackets) and were armed with truncheons – the boot-boys of any dictatorial regime – and electric torches, shone blindingly onto Christ (Fig. 12.5). Pilate, himself, brandished a revolver when he warned, "Be ware, for wyscus I am" (26.14), an early marker of his might-is-right, "fascist" politics. The medieval script has several references to halter as a favoured method of execution: a comparable anachronism. Religious figures wore a variety of flowing robes and vestments as they still do in Jerusalem, with Annas and Caiaphas sporting respectively a skull-cap and a peaked, mitre-esque bonnet: plausible indicators of both Christian bishops and Jewish high priests. They strode on with ceremonial crosses which they used as gestural aids. Judas, "clad in a cope," wore a cowled black habit, both monk-like and evocative of a *djellaba*: biblical scholarship identifies Judas as a member of the radical zealots. Jesus wore a simple white robe, signifying priesthood (like a priest's alb), purity, but also denuded vulnerability, and folly.[61]

Our Jesus (Monde Sibisi) was a black South African, in one way irreducibly Other from the first moment of visual contact, as the rest of the cast were white. His ethnic identity lent a specific racialised resonance to the frequent

---

61   Christ is dressed in white by his tormentors for the purpose of mockery in the York Cycle's *Christ before Herod* (ll. 336–50).

references to him as a "boy", "in a bande boune." Not only is *boy* a pejorative and racist signifier of inferiority, it was also used as a substantive for men in colonial service or servitude. In a post-performance discussion, a British mixed-race audience member said the bound "boy" Jesus reminded her of the toxic racism and lynchings in the southern states of the United States of America. Sibisi responded by referring to multiple colonial and post-colonial layers in Christ's dramatic identity, chiming with Benjamin's historical "collage" of references, not least to apartheid South Africa. (Pilate was, of course, an occupying Roman governor.) He added, "This makes the violence resonate more with a current audience. If you feel uncomfortable, that is a good thing. Jesus was uncomfortable."

I added further recent and topical geopolitical markers in the torture scene. The soldiers first placed a black paramilitary-style balaclava over Christ's head, though with the narrow eye-slits on the opposite side. Then they tied a *keffiyeh*, the Palestinian scarf, over this. A gamut of references and resonances were at play here. Annas and Caiaphas, whether prelates or chief priests, were forbidden to authorise Christ's execution. Says Annas to his incensed son-in-law, "Nay, sir, þan blemysshe yee prelatis estatis, || ȝe awe to deme no man to dede for to dynge" (29.338–39), and yet they are shown to exult in his cruel torture and anticipate his death with avidity. The double-speak of games and joy for violence and pain connoted for me the similar dissonance between recent western leaders crowing about civilised western values and denouncing 'terrorists' while their own security forces conspired in extra-judicial, 'extra-ordinary rendition' which often involved torture in third-party countries, often situated in the Middle East. Christ's bearing of the Palestinian scarf evoked the ongoing occupation of the Palestinian territories and blockade of Gaza with all the concomitant violence and bitterly contested rule of law that accompanies this. Not only is Christ a victim of 'extra-ordinary rendition' and false witness, passed from judicial pillar to post between power-wielders of spurious legitimacy, he is also subjected to water boarding: "Wassail!" Christ was in my production a composite representative of the 'wretched of the earth', yet, for all the torture, unbowed and uncowed: "I am untouched by the insults. So, too, I set my face like flint; I know I shall not be shamed" (Isaiah 50:7).

In terms of space, there was a hierarchy of height. Pilate lorded it over everyone from the trestle-stage (placed where the pageant wagon would reside); ditto the chief priests in the second play. The Janitor guarded the entrance to Pilate's palace from a "watch-tower" (the chancel pulpit), removing his dark glasses to reveal his character in his altercation with Judas.[62] What of the challenges of playing in the platea, on ground level? In Medieval York, visibility and

---

62   In *Conspiracy*, Pilate describes Jerusalem as a "towre-begon towne" (l. 5).

FIGURE 12.6 *Blocks in the traverse ground-level space to allow the public to remain involved in the action.*

audibility must have presented problems, even if only playing before a crowd of a hundred or so at certain stations. I placed a few blocks in our traverse ground-level space onto which actors could leap, possibly leaping from one block to another during longer speeches, so that no section of the public was kept at too much of a remove for too long (Fig. 12.6). Actors also needed to revolve in the "platea" in order to play to spectators on three sides, both flanks of the traverse and some at the far end. It was important to create a dynamic scenographic geometry: "the arrangement of groupings on stage that avoid the inert precision of the military parade ground, achieving organic rhythm."[63]

A couple of higher blocks were placed directly below the trestle, and were most often populated by Annas and Caiaphas in *Conspiracy*. Actors on these and the trestle needed to adopt a different performance style, dubbed 'front of curtain' playing by Carl Heap, the founder and artistic director of the Medieval Players, a reference to the old-time music-hall comedians who would banter with the audience from front of curtain while the set was changed behind it. This outward-projecting and stylised acting style demands a clear focus, with actors addressing their lines to the spectators in front of them, rather than to their dramatic interlocutors alongside. Nods to the latter could be made during punctuation breaks. Meanwhile the interlocutors would generally focus on the speaker. Actors in the platea could engage in a much more 'up close and personal' way with the audience, in a manner evocative of pantomime. Apart from

---

[63] Lecoq, *The Moving Body*, 175.

FIGURE 12.7 *An example of iconic 'framing': Pilate with the Temple authorities flanked on either side.*

Peter dashing into the crowd, the soldiers menaced from close quarters (with enlivening interaction with younger audience members); Judas paced up and down, fretting before Pilate's return; and the vitriolic and virulent Temple delegation sought to whip up the crowd, driving a wedge between them and their colonial overlord, to achieve their aim of Christ's destruction – ironically, precisely what they accused Jesus of doing: "To mort hym for movyng of men" (26.77). I had them cry out "A mort! A mort!" here, as if on Caiaphas's cue. Who knows what extra-textual elements were improvised in the Middle Ages.

Certain moments in the pageants lent themselves to *tableaux* and iconic 'framings'. Just prior to Judas's entrance, Pilate beckoned the delegation to follow him further into the palace's inner sanctum. He sat upon his throne, situated just in front of the high altar, flanked on either side, with Annas and Caiaphas to his immediate right and left, with a body guard looking on: a pyramidal frieze of temporal authority (Fig. 12.7). Christ was an emblem of patience and a 'spectacle' of suffering at key moments. Both plays ended in silence – the latter with Christ being dragged off to Pilate for his next interrogation – evocative of the silence after the Good Friday liturgy and its memorial of the Passion.

7 Conclusion

"The words that I have spoken to you are spirit and life" (John 6:63). The spiritual resources of the Bible are complemented by its 'incarnational' relevance, its application to the secular domain. My interpretation of these two Passion pageants has underlined the riches of the biblical source: mythical, narrative, devotional, political and dramatic. In both pageants – under lip-service to reason, loyalty, and the due process of forensic examination – there is a constant threat of duplicity, violence, maltreatment and torture. This certainly runs contrary to a dispassionate exercise of objective justice. The authority figures will resort to any means to defend their standing. Carnivalesque and festive performance increased the awareness of the existing order, but also subverted order by increasing the awareness of its weaknesses. Jesus – the abject; the political prisoner of conscience – is the supreme scapegoat who is sacrificed to maintain the hegemonic status quo. The performance of the sufferings of the incarnate Christ are a "tangible laceration," a radical challenge to our common humanity.[64] The sadistic, carnivalesque play of violence to which he is subjected is brought into further sharp relief through anachronistic allusion to contemporary scandals and abuses of power. The witness of Christ, the 'holy actor', invites understanding and compassion, making it clear, too, that there is no escape from politics. My directorial experience convinces me that medieval theatre's vivifying and enfleshed ludic transpositions – the re-framings and re-shapings of its myths and histories, according to contemporary exigencies – remain a vibrant template now, and the theatrical riches of medieval theatre and performance are a priceless resource for theatre-making across the ages.

Bibliography

Bakhtin, Mikhail. *Rabelais and His World*, translated by Hélène Iswolsky. Bloomington: Indiana University Press, 1984.

Beadle, Richard, ed. *The York Plays: A Critical Edition of the York Corpus Christi Play as Recorded in British Library Additional MS 35290*. 2 vols. EETS s.s. 23–24. Oxford: Oxford University Press, 2009–13.

Benjamin, Walter. "Theses on the Philosophy of History," 253–64. In Idem. *Illuminations: Essays and Reflections*, edited by Hannah Arendt, translation Harry Zohn. New York: Shocken Books, 1969.

Brawer, Robert A. "The Characterization of Pilate in the York Cycle Play." *Studies in Philology* 69 (1972): 289–303.

Burke, Kenneth. *The Philosophy of Literary Form: Studies in Symbolic Action*. Berkeley: University of California Press, 1973.

---

64   Artaud employs the term "tangible laceration" when describing his Theatre of Cruelty: the compelling of an audience to face up to unpalatable truths, recoiling in sympathetic horror at the enactment of physical cruelty on stage.

Camille, Michael. *The Gothic Idol: Ideology and Image-making in Medieval Art.* Cambridge: Cambridge University Press, 1989.

———. *Image on the Edge: The Margins of Medieval Art.* Cambridge, Mass: Harvard University Press, 1992.

Clopper, Lawrence. "Tyrants and Villains: Characterization in the Passion Sequences of the English Cycle Plays." *Modern Language Quarterly* 41 (1980): 3–20.

Davidson, Clifford. "Suffering and the York Cycle Plays," 141–67. In Idem, *Festivals and Plays in Late Medieval Britain.* Ashgate: Aldershot, 2007.

Dietl, Cora. "Preface," 7–10. In *Power and Violence in Medieval and Early Modern Theater,* edited by Cora Dietl, Christoph Schanze and Glenn Ehrstine. Goettingen: V&R Academic, 2014.

Dull, Olga Anna. *Folie et rhétorique dans la sottie.* Geneva: Droz, 1994.

Enders, Jody. *Rhetoric and the Origins of Medieval Drama.* Ithaca: Cornell University Press, 1992.

Greenblatt, Stephen J. "Filthy Rites," 59–79. In Idem, *Learning to Curse: Essays in Early Modern Culture.* New York: Routledge, 1990.

Grotowski, Jerzy. *Towards a Poor Theatre.* London: Methuen, 1969.

Harvey, Karen, ed. *The Kiss in History.* Manchester: Manchester University Press, 2005.

Heers, Jacques. *Fêtes des fous et carnavals.* Paris: Fayard, 1983.

Hyman, Timothy. "A Carnival Sense of the World,"32–39. In Timothy Hyman and Roger Malbert, *Carnivalesque.* London: Hayward Gallery Publishing, 2000.

King, Pamela M. "Contemporary Cultural Models for the Trial Plays in the York Cycle," 200–16. In *Drama and Community: People and Plays in Medieval Europe,* edited by Alan Hindley. Turnhout: Brepols, 1999.

Knight, Alan. *Aspects of Genre in Late Medieval French Drama.* Manchester: Manchester University Press, 1983.

Koopmans, Jelle. *Le théâtre des exclus au moyen âge: hérétiques, sorcières et marginaux.* Paris: Editions Imago, 1997.

———. "'Et doit avoir un faux visage par derrière': Masques et apparences dans le théâtre profane français (1450–1550)," *L'immagine riflessa* N.S. 9 (2000): 267–83.

Kosofsky Sedgwick, Eve. *Between Men: English Literature and Male Homosocial Desire.* New York: Columbia University Press, 1985.

Kristeva, Julia. *Powers of Horror: An Essay on Abjection.* New York: Columbia University Press, 1982.

Lecoq, Jacques. *The Moving Body: Teaching Creative Theatre,* translated by David Bradby. London: Methuen, 2002.

Le Goff, Jacques. *La Civilisation de l'Occident médiéval.* Paris: Arthaud, 1967

Mänd, Anu. *Urban Carnival: Festive Culture in the Hanseatic Cities of the Eastern Baltic, 1350–1550.* Turnhout: Brepols, 2005.

Nagler, A.M., ed. *A Source Book in Theatrical History.* Mineola: Dover Publications, 1959.

Robinson, J.W. "The Art of the York Realist." *Modern Philology* 60 (1963): 241–51.
———. *Studies in Fifteenth-Century Stagecraft*. Kalamazoo, MI: Medieval Institute Publications, 1991.
Rogerson, Margaret, ed. *The York Mystery Plays: Performance in the City*. Woodbridge: York Medieval Press, Boydell and Brewer, 2011.
Said, Edward W. *Orientalism*. Harmondsworth: Penguin, 2003.
Schmitt, Jean-Claude. "Les images de la dérision," 263–74. In *La dérision au Moyen Age: De la pratique sociale au rituel politique*, edited by Elisabeth Crouzet-Pavan and Jacques Verger. Paris: Presses de l'Université Paris-Sorbonne, 2007.
Turner, Victor. *From Ritual to Theatre: The Human Seriousness of Play*. New York: Performing Arts Journal Publications, 1982.
———. *The Anthropology of Performance*. New York: Performing Arts Journal Publications, 1987.
Twycross, Meg. "Beyond the Picture Theory: Image and Activity in Medieval Drama." *Word and Image: A Journal of Verbal/Visual Enquiry* 4 (1988): 589–617.
Ueltschi, Karin. *La* Mesnie Hellequin *en conte et en rime: Mémoire mythique et poétique de la recomposition*. Paris: Honoré Champion, 2008.
Wack, Mary. *Lovesickness in the Middle Ages: The* Viaticum *and Its Commentaries*. Philadelphia: University of Pennsylvania Press, 1990.
Winser, Leigh. "*Magnyfycence* and the Characters of *Sottie*." *Sixteenth Century Journal* 12 (1981): 85–94.
Wright, John. *Why is that so Funny? A Practical Exploration of Physical Comedy*. London: Nick Hern Books, 2011.

CHAPTER 13

"Alle out of hir self": Mary, Effective Piety and the N-Town *Crucifixion*

James McBain

Abstract

Critics have often noted the inclusion of Marian lament in medieval biblical drama and how playwrights draw upon the affective conventions of *Planctus Mariae* lyric poetry to develop a compelling narrative from bare scriptural sources. Whilst demonstrating an influential relationship with an affective tradition, most notably developed from a study of elements of Nicholas Love's *The Mirror of the Blessed Life of Jesus Christ*, this essay argues that the portrayal of Mary in the N-Town *Crucifixion* play both performs affective piety and also importantly considers, challenges, and refines its use. In addition to providing a close study of the play and a comparison of N-Town with similar extant examples, the essay seeks to engage with Mary's complex theological and literary reception, within which she has been described as demonstrating the impossible synthesis of both 'perfection' and 'realism'.

Keywords

Virgin Mary – crucifixion – affective piety – N-Town – Nicholas Love's *Mirror of the Blessed Life of Jesus Christ* – Marian lament/*Planctus Mariae*

1   Introduction

The seeds for this essay were sown when I had the privilege of supervising an outstanding extended essay on affective piety.[1] The initial focus was on Aemelia Lanyer's representation of the Virgin Mary in *Salve Deus Rex Judaeorum* (1611) but the work subsequently, and brilliantly, ranged to much wider theological,

---

1   Charlotte Clark, "'Will he weep when the speaker's eyes are dry?" (Unpublished Extended Essay), University of Oxford: Faculty of English, 2013.

philosophical, and literary ground, with memorable brief sections on medieval drama, early modern tears poetry, and Kristeva's analysis of Holbein's *Dead Christ*. Within the tight word limit, there was insufficient space for a detailed consideration of the depiction of Mary in the N-Town *Crucifixion* play, however, which thankfully provided this opportunity. My aim here is to consider how the N-Town dramatist(s), or rather the author of the Passion Play section of it,[2] chose to develop sources and conventions not merely to perform affective piety through the figure of Mary, but importantly also to consider, explore, and represent that use. Alexandra Johnston, in what I think is the most significant account of Mary's role in the N-Town *Crucifixion* to date, states that "other dramatic versions of the Passion treat Mary differently than she is portrayed in N-Town," and I agree entirely.[3] In fact, as I will argue, when considered alongside other examples of dramatic Marian lament, the portrayal is even more different than Johnston allows.

Aemelia Lanyer provides a productive starting point, not least because of the perspective from which she could consider earlier literary and artistic traditions. She represents an early modern 'reader' of the tradition of Marian lament as much as a contributor to it.[4] As modern readers, we can in turn seek to appreciate the choices that Lanyer makes in shaping a narrative based upon the spare details of Gospel account – it is important to remember that only John positively places Mary at the Cross, and even then simply 'standing' as a witness (19:25) – and also to weigh the possible, sometimes competing, frames of reference from which those elements gain their significance. To give just one example of what I mean: in a central episode of the Passion, Lanyer draws upon significant meditative convention when she depicts the Virgin Mary as swooning in response to Christ's impending death:

> His woefull Mother wayting on her Sonne,
> All comfortlesse in depth of sorow drowned;
> Her griefes extreame, although but new begun,
> To see his bleeding body oft shee swouned;
> How could shee choose but thinke her selfe undone,

---

2 See *The Passion Play From The N. Town Manuscript*, ed. Peter Meredith (London: Longman, 1990).

3 Alexandra F. Johnston, "Acting Mary: The Emotional Realism of the Virgin Mary in the N-Town Plays," in *From Page to Performance: Essays in Early English Drama*, ed. John A. Alford (East Lansing: Michigan State University Press, 1995), 87.

4 For an excellent and wide-ranging collection of essays dedicated to the *Salve Deus Rex Judaeorum*, see *Aemelia Lanyer: Gender, Genre, and the Canon*, ed. Marshall Grossman (Kentucky: University of Kentucky Press, 1998).

He dying, with whose glory shee was crowned?[5] (ll. 1009–14)

Mary's swoon will be at the heart of my later discussion, an extreme physical reaction that might be seen to support her virtue; the swoon apparently serves as evidence of a sincere and natural reaction to her beholding of the scene before her. In this way, Lanyer's Mary might be understood as intended to serve as an affective role model to readers 'beholding' the poem, both in terms of how they should comprehend Mary's part in the Passion narrative, but also how they should react to it. We might remember Rosemary Woolf's description of how Marian affective piety functioned here, that "a description of the Virgin's distress enabled the mediator to be stirred through sympathy with the internal sufferings of Christ" and that "the Virgin's grief is both an incentive to the mediator's and also a measure of what his should be."[6] Indeed, this is the reading identified by Gary Kuchar, who argues that, it is "the deeply human, physically anguished dimension of Mary's grief that best expresses the Virgin's exemplarity."[7]

A reading such as Kuchar's is, of course, neither the only response available, nor a conclusive one, however. It is entirely plausible that Lanyer self-consciously uses the swoon in order to confront and exploit a misogynistic characterization of excessive grief as "uncomly and wommanishe," for example.[8] Indeed here, as throughout Lanyer's poem, her poetic strategy is to use details of her account to emphasise the centrality of women in Gospel narrative

---

5   *The Poems of Aemelia Lanyer: Salve Deus Rex Judaeorum*, ed. Susanne Woods (Oxford: Oxford University Press, 1993), 94.
6   Rosemary Woolf, *The English Religious Lyric in the Middle Ages* (Oxford: Oxford University Press, 1968), 241.
7   Gary Kuchar, "Aemelia Lanyer and the Virgin's Swoon: Theology and Iconography in the *Salve Deus Rex Judaeorum*," *English Literary Renaissance* 37 (2007): 50.
8   Elizabeth M.A. Hodgson, "Prophecy and Gendered Mourning in Aemelia Lanyer's *Salve Deus Rex Judaeorum*," *Studies in English Literature* 43 (2003): 103; see also Katharine Goodland, "Inverting the Pietà in Shakespeare's *King Lear*," in *Marian Moments in Early Modern British Drama*, ed. Regina Buccola and Lisa Hopkins (Aldershot: Ashgate, 2007), 47–74. Gendered condemnation of excessive grief was also related more broadly to opposing systems of faith, but Brian Cummings, *Literary Culture of the Reformation: Grammar and Grace* (Oxford: Oxford University Press, 2007), 333, warns against a simplistic attribution of affective work to Catholicism in noting that, "having originated in a need to counter Reformation forms of spirituality, this catholic literature in turn filled a gap among protestants ... Calvinist England, whilst always alert to any whiff of popery, proved a receptive home for a literature of sentiment which it could not produce for itself." For a fascinating discussion of Grimald's meta-dramatic use of crucifixion scenes, "in which confessional differences are driving dramatic focus," see the essay by Dutton and Allen in this volume.

in order to confront misogynistic prejudice.[9] But such a focus on Mary's naturalness and humanity risks undermining her status as co-redemptrix, since it is an obvious point to make that there is nothing exceptional about someone who is just like the rest of us; one can certainly imagine being "comfortlesse," "drowned," and "undone" by grief, but they all significantly develop from passivity and a forced understanding of events as being far beyond our control.

For its affective potential, and its ability to serve as theological emblem, Mary's swoon was depicted in visual art with increasing frequency from the thirteenth century onwards, to indicate "her compassion, her maternity, and her sacrifice."[10] Indeed, as Harvey Hamburgh observes, the depiction became so powerfully prevalent that the Catholic Church felt the need to develop an official position from which to consider it against more traditional depictions of an 'upright' saint. The key text in what came to be known as the "*lo spasimo*" debate was provided in 1506; written for Pope Julius II by Thomas de Vio, Cardinal Cajetan, it concluded that Mary did not in fact swoon, as this would have been contrary to the Gospel since John states that she "stood near the Cross," and also that any hint of emotional incapacity would also be contrary to her role:

> It is necessary to deny such a bodily defect in her because it would have impeded this plentitude and perfection of grace. It is plain that grief which would have made her 'beside herself' would have impeded her use of reason at that moment when it was the time for her to meditate most intensely and intelligently on the passion ... It was more pleasing to God that Mary should have shared in the passion of her Son not only in her feelings but also in her mind since that is the nobler part of man in which merit and grace properly reside.[11]

---

9 In the paratextual epistle, "To the Vertuous Reader," Lanyer exclaims that "[I]t pleased our Lord and Saviour Jesus Christ ... to be begotten of a woman, borne of a woman, nourished of a woman, obedient to a woman; and that he healed women, pardoned women, comforted women: yea, even when he was in his greatest agonie and bloodie sweat, going to be crucified, and also in the last hour of his death, tooke care to dispose of a woman ... All which is sufficient to inforce all good Christians and honourable minded men to speak reverently of our sexe, and especially of all virtuous and good women" (*Salve Deus Rex Judaeorum*, ed. Woods, 49–50: ll. 39–56).

10 See Amy Neff, "The Pain of Compassio: Mary's Labor at the Foot of the Cross," *The Art Bulletin* 80 (1998): 255.

11 Quoted in Harvey E. Hamburgh, "The Problem of *Lo Spasimo* of the Virgin in Cinquecento Paintings of the Descent from the Cross," *The Sixteenth Century Journal* 12:4 (1981): 46.

Cajetan's conclusion is an attempt to punctuate both theological and artistic history, although later statements with similar impetuses suggest that it should be seen as a comma rather than the full stop it aspired to be. Almost regardless of its efficacy, however, the point to take about the statement is how it seeks to tread carefully between active meditation and passive reception, between the 'perfection' of Mary's divinity and the natural physicality that links her to the rest of humanity.

To return briefly to Lanyer with this in mind, the interpretative challenge invited by the passage from her poem is therefore how we might comprehend and subsequently judge Mary's physical response. On the one hand, we might view her swoon as autonomic, that is, an automatic and unconscious physical reaction to the gory stimulus of Christ's wounds. But, on the other hand, we are told that Mary is thinking here, even if the scope of her thoughts is understandably limited by the vision before her. We have a complicated and polysemous final question that could be read either as: 'she had no option but to think that she was undone, since he was dying and it was through his glory that she was crowned'; or alternatively, 'what other choice was there but to think herself [to become] undone, since he was dying and it was through his glory that she was crowned'; or indeed, 'since she was undone, with him dying etc., how could she do anything other than think'. In the second and third readings, Mary 'thinks' herself into a physical, somatic response – a willing swoon – and indeed, the fourth line from the quotation provided above offers alternative interpretative possibilities, that either 'numerous sights of his bleeding body caused her to swoon', or that 'she swooned a number of times, seeing his bleeding body'. In both cases, however, the swoon(s) result(s) from a decision to behold the grisly spectacle before her and our complex reaction to the poem ultimately depends upon our similar willingness to comprehend and engage with affective writing on its own terms. That said, it is difficult to understand precisely what terms we are asked to accept, unless they are clearly articulated by the writer. In the N-Town *Crucifixion* and significantly also in one of its (probable) major sources, Nicholas Love's *Mirror of the Blessed Life of Jesus Christ*, I will argue that those terms are very clearly laid out.

2   *"For hem I offre my self"*: Alternative Versions of Affect

The close relationship between Love's *Mirror* and the N-Town plays has often been stressed, for example by Richard Beadle, to the extent that some sections seem to have been written with the text not simply in mind but rather to hand.[12] Love's writing exploits numerous features that render it proto-dramatic, particularly the use of the rhetorical skill of *enargaia* to enable a reader or hearer to imagine and 'behold' the scene 'in their mind's eye' which is necessary to invoke a compassionate response.[13] Coupled with the frequent insistence on editorial/narratorial presence, the author seeks to present himself as a reliable 'witness' to the scene, bringing Gospel history into the present tense, but also as an authority, one who can be relied upon to direct our attention to a particular understanding of the narrative he shares. This can be illustrated by a passage from the Friday of the Passion, immediately before, "Howe oure lorde Jesus was dampnet to þe deth of þe crosse."[14] Throughout the narration of Jesus' trial before Pilate, Love employs apostrophe to address Jesus, "Oo lorde Jesu, who was he so || fole hardye þat dorst despoile þe?" (169/14–15); Christ's tormentors, "Oo wrecches, how dredeful sal þat hede apere at þe laste || to ʒow þe which ʒe smyten now so boldly" (170/1–2); and most often, the readers or audience, "Now with inwarde compassion beholde him here in maner || as I seide before" (171/1–2); "Take now here gude hede by inwarde meditacion of alle || hees pey nes abidyngly, & bot þou fynde þi herte melte in to || sorouful compassion" (169/6–8).

In addition to being able to interpret events on our behalf, Love also states that he has 'invented' extra-biblical details. In the Proem to the *Mirror*, Love employs patriarchal sanction, from St Bernard, to support his imaginative depictions:

> And so what tyme or in what place in þis boke is writen þat þus dide or þus spake oure lorde Jesus or oþer þat bene spoken of, & it mowe not be prevet by holi writ or grondet in expresse seying of holy doctours: it sal be

---

12 Richard Beadle, "'Devoute ymaginacioun' and the Dramatic Sense in Love's *Mirror* and the N-Town Plays," in *Nicholas Love at Waseda: Proceedings of the International Conference, 20–22 July, 1995*, ed. Shoichi Oguro, Richard Beadle and Michael G. Sargent (Cambridge: D.S. Brewer, 1997), 1–17. Beadle provides parallel texts of the N-Town "Salutation and Conception" and the relevant section of *The Mirror* to prove remarkable similarity.

13 Equating "Ocular Demonstration" with *enargaia*, the author of the *Rhetorica ad Herennium* explains how it occurs "when an event is so described in words that the business seems to be enacted and the subject to pass vividly before our eyes." (Cicero, *Ad C. Herennium Libri IV: De ratione dicendi*, transl. by Harry Caplan [Cambridge, MA: Harvard University Press, 1954], 405, IV:68.)

14 Nicholas Love, *The Mirror of the Blessed Life of Jesus Christ*, ed. Michael G. Sargent (Exeter: Exeter University Press, 2004), 170/16. Subsequent references will be cited within the main text. I have used a colon to denote a *punctus elevatus* throughout.

> taken none oþerwyes þan as a devoute meditacion, þat it miȝt be so spoken or done. (11/5–9)

Beadle has written persuasively about Love's repeated appeal to "devout imagination," a neologism that, together with its equivalents (devout meditation, devout contemplation, devout compassion), essentially authorise the details provided by the text.[15] But it is important to emphasise that these 'devout' utterances also authorise the affective nature of the text too; Love stresses the 'devout' nature of his imaginative processes, since it is this devoutness, and only this, that renders them theologically acceptable. As is the case with the defence of extra-biblical details here, Love essentially provides limitations to his affective piety by insisting on sound and correct interpretation.

A further assertion of control over affective potential might well be seen in the comparative use of possible sources. Critics had previously observed that the pseudo-Bonaventuran *Meditationes vitae Christi*, and thereafter Love's text too, provides alternative versions of the mechanics of the Crucifixion and Sarah McNamer has recently extended that observation in an important argument about the text's composition.[16] In a section of her thoughtful and compelling consideration of affective writing that deals particularly with the *Meditationes*, McNamer draws attention to two differing, and in her terms 'competing', accounts of Jesus' ascent of the cross.[17] Since Nicholas Love includes both versions in his *Mirror*, I quote from his text here. First of all, we have an account which is compelling, in every sense:

> Now take gude hede to alle þat foloweþ. Oure lorde þanne was compellede & beden fort go vp one þat laddre to þe crosse, & he mekely doþe alle þat þei bedene him. And when he came vp to þe ouerest ende of þat short laddre: he turnede his bakke to þe crosse, & streyht out one brede þoo kynges armes, & hese fairest handes ȝafe vp to hem þat crucifiede him. And þan liftyng up hees louely eyene to heuen seide to þe fadere in þees maner wordes, Loo here I am my dere fadere as þou woldest þat I sholde lowe my self vnto þe crosse, for þe sauacion of mankynde, & þat is pleisyng & acceptable to me, & for hem I offre my self: þe which þou woldest

---

15 Beadle, "Devoute ymaginacioun", 9.
16 Vincent Gillespie, "Vernacular Books of Religion," in *Book Production and Publishing in Britain, 1375–1475*, ed. Jeremy Griffiths and Derek Pearsall (Cambridge: Cambridge University Press, 1989), 324, suggests that the differences attest to an 'unstable' text.
17 Sarah McNamer, *Affective Meditation and the Invention of Medieval Compassion* (Philadelphia: University of Pennsylvania Press, 2010), 96–97.

> sholde be my || breþerne. Wherefore also þou fadere take gladely þis sac-
> rifice for hem of me, & now heþen forwarde be plesede & wele willede to
> hem for my love, & alle olde offense & trespasse forȝive & wipe awey, &
> put aferre alle vnclannes of sinne fro hem. For soþely I offre here now my
> self for hem & hir hele.
>
> And þan he þat was on þe laddere behynde þe crosse: takeþ his riht
> hande & naileþ it fast to þe crosse. And after he þat was on þe lift side
> draweþ wiþ alle his miht þe lift arme & hande,& driveþ þerþorh a noþere
> grete naile. After þei comen done & taken awey alle þe laddres & so
> hangeþ oure lorde onely by þoo tweyn nailes smyten þorh hees handes
> without sustenance of þe body, drawyng donwarde peynfully þorh þe
> weiht þerof.
>
> Herewiþ also a noþer harlote renneþ to, & draweþ done hese feete
> with alle his miht, & anoþer anone driueþ a grete longe naile þorh boþe
> hese feete ioynede to oþer. (174/36–175/20)

At this point, the narrator re-introduces himself into the story and acknowledges the possibily of an alternative account:

> Þis is one maner of his crucifiying after þe opinione of sume men.
>
> Oþere þere bene þat trowen not þat he was crucifiede in þis manere:
> bot þat first liggyng þe crosse on þe gronde: þei nailede him þere vpon, &
> after with him so hangyng þei liften vp þe crosse & festen it done in [to]
> þe erþe.
>
> And if it were done in þis manere: þan maist þou se, howe vileynsly þei
> taken him as a ribaude & kasten him done vp on þe crosse, & þan as wode
> þefes drowen on boþe sides first hees handes & after hees feete, & so
> nailede him fast to þe crosse, & after with alle hir miht liften vp þe crosse
> with him hangyng als hye as þei miht & þan lete it falle done in to þe
> morteise.
>
> In þe which falle as þou may vnderstande, alle þe senewes to breken,
> to his souereyn peyne. Bot wheþer so it be in one maner or in oþere: soþe
> it is þat oure lorde Jesus was nailede harde vpon þe crosse, hande & foote,
> & so streynede & drawen: þat as he himself seiþ by þe prophete Dauid,
> þat þei mihten telle & noumbre alle hees bones. (175/21–38)

I have quoted at length because the two accounts are so radically different in their 'affective' treatment of details. In the first instance, Jesus willingly and knowingly submits "mekely" in full view of an audience of onlookers, obeying the commands of his torturers and, more broadly, the will of his Father. He ascends regally, turns his back to the cross and offers his open hands, before turning his "louely eyene" upwards and articulating his calm knowledge of the purpose of his fate and the role that the crucifixion must come to play in Christian soteriology. That is not at all to dismiss the corporeal cruelty described immediately afterwards, as the soldier stretches Christ's left arm "woth alle his miht," or the suffocating stretch of Christ's body "drawyng donwarde peynfully," exaggerated with the pendant pull of "a noþer harlot," but ultimately Jesus' martyrdom is paramount. In the second account, by contrast, Jesus is a victim of a villainous and unworthy assault, in which the pain of torn sinews is "souereyn," rather than the dignified figure of the "kyng." Put crudely, Christ is forced into the shape of the cross rather than assuming the symbol by his own free will.

As McNamer argues, whilst the "recumbent" crucifixion invokes pathos, the Ascension scene, which is notably given more space in the text, instead "dilutes" simplistic pathos with an alternative response: "the scene thus encourages the reader to adopt a stoical stance; to 'see through' the violence of the Passion to its larger purpose in the scheme of salvation, just as early medieval renderings of the crucifixion had done."[18] Indeed, McNamer argues persuasively that the Ascension scene is a later interpolation into the 'original' version of the *Meditationes*, and that, far from evidence of a lack of concern for historical accuracy – the editorial commentary upon the two competing accounts that is maintained in Love's 'translation' above – the text comes to facilitate and support a restrained and meek affective vision. To refine McNamer's analysis slightly, whilst the two versions are theologically at odds, when put together in the text, they do not so much compete in my view, as that the interpolated account serves to modify and supplement the original. The narrator breaks into the narrative even as it is being delivered and draws attention to the way in which an affective account should be performed, with the effect being that the 'original', or second account of the Crucifixion, is not seen to be theologically sufficient in and of itself. It should be emphasised that the shock of vivid violence is no less in the 'corrective', supplementary account, and the author certainly does not spare us from gory details. But the purpose and ultimate theological significance of those horrific images are brought to mind immediately and, in the editor's view, more effectively as didactic performance than would be the case from a purely pathetic response.

The interpretative distinctions available between a dignified ascent and recumbent crucifixion are a fascinating means by which to consider the performance of the Passion in cycle drama. In N-Town, for example, the inclusion

---

18 McNamer, *Affective Meditation*, 98.

of the apocryphal detail of Veronica wiping blood and sweat from Jesus' face with her "kerchy," thereby creating a sacred relic,[19] creates a sharp contrast with the stage direction that immediately follows, in which Christ is stripped and brought to the ground:

> *Þan xul þei pulle Jesu out of his clothis and leyn them togedyr; and þer þei xul pullyn hym down and leyn hym along on þe cros, and aftyr þat naylyn hym þeron.* (32.48 s.d.)

The dialogue that ensues between the Jews reinforces both physical and metaphorical fall: "Cast hym down here, in þe devyl way || How long xal he standyn on his fete? || Pul hym down, evyl mote he the!" (32.49–51); before then descending into cruel farce as they narrate the need to stretch Christ's arm to fit the holes and delight in the breaking of "both flesch and veyn" (32.68). There is a degree to which the narration of sinewy detail is necessary for performance; the Jews describe what they are doing for those that cannot see, so that the cruel rhetorical skills of the playwright conjure both the events and consequent pain 'before their eyes' instead. But, in the light of the available alternatives in Love's *Mirror* one should acknowledge simultaneously the decision to stage Christ being degraded and attacked from an affective perspective, that he is denied the dignified ascent to the Cross and equally the initial agency that it entails.[20]

The same is almost true of the York Crucifixion; the soldiers boast, at the end of *The Road to Calvary*, that Jesus is "boune as beeste in bande, || That is demed for to dye" (34.341–42), but as the soldiers open the following play,

---

19 *The N-Town Play: Cotton MS Vespasian D. 8*, ed. Stephen Spector, 2 vols., EETS s.s. 11 (Oxford: Oxford University Press, 1991), 1: 32.48. Subsequent references will appear in the main text. As Beadle notes, the similar "vernicle" created in York 34.183–89 might well have been assigned to III Maria for reasons of dramatic economy. (See *The York Plays: A Critical Edition of the York Corpus Christi Play as recorded in British Library Additional MS 35290*, ed. Richard Beadle, 2 vols., EETS s.s. 23–24 [Oxford: Oxford University Press, 2009–13], 2:314–15.) Subsequent references will appear in the main text. Kerstin Pfeiffer, "Passionate Encounters: Emotion in Early English Biblical Drama" (PhD diss., University of Stirling, 2011), 163, makes the excellent point that Veronica serves to "provide the play with an embodied opposite to the mourning of the daughters of Jerusalem. Her compassion manifests itself in action rather than in streams of tears," which serves equally well as a contrast to the particular portrayal of Mary.

20 Christ is similarly nailed to the Cross in a recumbent position on the ground in both the Chester *Passion* and Towneley *Crucifixion*, without the opportunity to speak between Pilate's command that he be "spoyled" and the raising of the Cross.

Crucifixio Christi, and discuss how best to undertake the killing, Christ is given precisely the same opportunity to speak and accept his fate as with the ascent in the *Meditationes* and *Mirror*:

> JESUS   Almyghty God, my fadir free,
> Late þis materes be ma[rke]d in mynde:
> þou badde þat I schulde buxsome be
> For Adam plyght for to be pyned. (35.49–52)

As Rosemary Woolf observes, "Christ's free offering of Himself (he suffered *quia ipse voluit*) is then confirmed by Christ's action of laying himself upon the Cross."[21] Ironically adopting the meditative invitation to 'behold', the third soldier invites his peers to take note of Jesus' actions, "Byhalde, hymselffe has laide hym doune, || In lenghe and breede as he schulde bee" (35.75–76).

Pamela King has written convincingly in spatial terms about how the "interstitial relationship between Christ and the audience is 'radically altered' as the cross is later raised from the *platea* to the *locus* of the wagon."[22] But in terms of audience response, the affective waters have already been muddied, so to speak, by Christ's earlier utterance and his willing performance of spatial submission. From the raised Cross, which serves metaphorically to reflect Jesus' godhead, and powerfully visible to all, Christ invites his audience to engage affectively with his wounds and unprecedented physical suffering:

> Beholdes myn heede, myn handis, and my feete
> And fully feele nowe, or ȝe fyne,
> Yf any mournyng may be meete,
> Or myscheve mesured vnto myne. (35.255–58)

But the reminder that then follows, that his pain has been for mankind's salvation, ultimately serves to reinstate, rather than add, Christ's 'superhuman' willing martyrdom that was espoused whilst he was physically associated with the audience at ground level, symbolic of humanity. Just as with the supplementation of a version of the crucifixion that might be seen to rely on pathos with one that also speaks of a stoic acceptance in the *Meditationes* and *Mirror*, so the York dramatist provides a scene that links affective and justificatory

---

21   Rosemary Woolf, *The English Mystery Plays* (London: Routledge, 1972), 261.
22   Pamela M. King, "Spatial Semantics and the Medieval Theatre," in *The Theatrical Space*, ed. James Redmond, Themes in Drama, 9 (Cambridge: Cambridge University Press, 1987), 56.

performances. As before, my point is not that the details of the violence inflicted upon Christ are not intended to be affective, but rather that the affective nature of a possible audience response is mediated through an enforcement of his willing martyrdom. Affective piety is being directed even as it is being performed.

3   "Alle out of hir self": Exemplary Mary

Whilst Love and the author(s) of the *Meditationes* before him provide two competing accounts of the Crucifixion, it is striking that Mary is seen to be consistent throughout the text. It is equally clear that a consistent affective reading is provided too. Love establishes Mary's role as exemplary early on, when he explains how, whilst visited by Gabriel, she responded with meek silence:

> Here þan maizt þou take ensaumple of Marie, first to love solitary praiere & departyng fro men þat þou mowe be worþi angeles presence, & forþermore, lore of wisdome to here or þou speke, & fort kepe silence & love litil spech, for þat is a ful gret & profitable vertue. For Marie herde first þe angele twis speke or she wold answere ones azeyn.   (24/40–25/5)

In case the point about exemplary self-control is missed by his meditative audience, Love adds shortly afterwards, "Lerne þou þen by ensaumple of hire to be shamefast/vertuesly & meke" (27/2–3). Meek silence continues when we turn to the narrative of the Passion; Love describes how Mary rushed, with John and others, to meet with Jesus on his way to Calvary, but that her grief and compassion rendered her silent:

> And when she mette with him, without þe zate of þe Cite, þere as tweyne weyes meten to gedire, & sauhe him charget & overleide with so grete a tre of þe crosse, þe which she sawe not before: she was alle out of hir self, & half dede for sorowe, so þat neiþer she miht speke to him one worde nor he to hir bycause of þe grete haste of hem þat ladden him to the iewes. (171/33–38)

If we relate this to Lanyer's Mary and the effects of her grief, we might suggest that Love's Mary undoubtedly experiences an autonomic, physical response that renders her silent. However, it is important to observe that, whilst unwilled and uncontrolled, her bodily reaction nevertheless supports the initial virtue of her silence as a manifestation of meekness; her loss of control, so to speak, is ironically supportive of her earlier self-restraint.

With the pattern established, we can see that Mary is again 'struck dumb' with grief at the Crucifixion:

> Aa lorde in what sorowe is hir soule nowe? Soþely I trowe þat she miht not speke one worde to him for sorowe. But she miht do no more to him nor help him. For if she miht without doute she wolde. (174/24–27)

Following the accounts of the cruelty of the Crucifixions considered above, and a reference to the compassion that Christ suffers for his mother, we come to the core of Marian lament, when Mary seems to invoke her own death in response to the degree of sorrow experienced:

> And alle þese reproves, blasfemies & despites ben done, seynge & heryng his most sorowful modere, whose compassion & sorowe made him hir sone to have þe more bitter peyne.
>
> And on þat oþere halfe she hange in soule with hir sone on þe crosse & desirede inwardly raþer to have diede þat tyme with him: þan to have lyvede lengire. (176/10–15)

It is clear that Mary is doing more than silently grieving – Jesus can hear her laments as well as see her sorrow – and the sense of her grief affecting the dying Christ as "bitter peyne" is desperately powerful. But it is equally clear that Mary is far from self-centred here; to "hange in soule" is a precise and poignant expression of compassion and the desire for death is something that she keeps 'inward'. The mutual compassion is similarly emphasised when we are then told how, standing by the cross, "she turnede neuer hir eyene || fro him, she was full of anguysh as he was also" (176/17–18). And the prayers that each articulates are importantly reciprocal pleas to God for the other to be released from pain:

> And she preide to þe fadere at þat tyme, with alle hir herte seying þus, Fadere & god without ende it was pleisyng to 3ow þat my sone sholde be crucifiede: & it is done. It is not now tyme to aske him of 3owe a3eyn, bot 3e seene nowe in what anguish is his soule. I beseke 3ow þat 3he wille ese his peynes, gode fadere I recommende to 3ow in alle þat I may my dere sone. (176/18–24)

There are a number of points here that help develop Mary's particular portrayal. The mutual relationship helps establish Mary as co-redemptrix and, over and above her grief, she is significantly aware and able to articulate the meaning of Christ's sacrifice. Thinking again of Cajetan's conclusion about the 'perfect' Mary, that she "should have shared in the passion of her Son not only in her feelings but also in her mind", it would seem that this is very much the kind of role-model he had hoped to identify. Her selfness-ness is seen to be characteristic, even within her sorrow.[23] From a reader's perspective, Mary serves here both to allow us to understand and meditate upon the depth of grief suffered by her, but also to rationally and cogently understand her loss. That said, there are certainly moments, such as with Mary's earlier autonomic silence, when she suffers the physical 'incapacity' that Cajetan denies. From the very moment of Jesus' death, we have the following account:

> Oo lorde god in what state was þat tyme his modere soule, whan she sawh him so peynfully faile, wepe & dye? Soþely I trowe þat for þe multitude of anguishes she was alle out of hir self & unfelable made as half dede, & þat now mich more: || þan what tyme she mette with him, beringe þe crosse as it is seide. (178/32–36)

Clearly Mary swoons here and Love explains it as a passive and natural reaction to the onslaught of suffering. We might again suggest that this is an autonomic and unwilled response, not least because there is no reason to reach any other conclusion. But surely that is to diminish Mary's status and to see her portrayal as bordering on the human rather than the divine? Happily, in terms of a desire for a consistent treatment, Love provides a second instance of swooning that allows us an alternative conclusion. When the soldiers come to remove the bodies from the crosses, and following Mary's unsuccessful appeals for kindness Longinus, "despisyng hir wepyng & praieres," pierced Christ's side:

> & made a grete wonde, oute of þe which anone ranne to gedire boþe blode & water. And þerwiþ oure lady felle done in swowhen half dede, bytwix þe armes of Maudelyn. (180/34–36)

---

[23] Similarly, following Christ's death and when the soldiers come to break the crucified men's legs, Mary prays meekly and earnestly to them for compassion, an appeal that Love describes as "travaile in vayne" (180/30), but certainly not vainly done.

The precise timing of "þerwiþ" may initially seem confusing, as if Mary might be seen to be swooning at the sight of the streaming blood and water, much as Lanyer's Mary might well have swooned at the sight of Christ's "bleeding body." Once we acknowledge that the swoon clearly activates the scriptural prophecy of Luke (2:35), that "a sword shall pierce through thy own soul also," it is clear that what we really have in the instances of Mary's swoons are an enforcement of compassion and scriptural precision through rigorous synchronicity. Mary suffers a wound at precisely the same time as Christ, so that her natural reaction to it, which might be seen as incapacity were the timing not so precise, is instead evidence of her divinity rather than merely her humanity. Ironically, those moments at which Mary is seen to be "alle out of hir self" become the moments at which she is most powerfully herself. By carefully ensuring that scriptural and theological reason accompanies the gory details of Christ's wounds or the emotional depths sounded by Mary's grief, Love ensures that his affective piety is didactic and effective, rather than merely and solely pathetic.

4   "Self-centred grief": N-Town Mary

In between Love and Lanyer, in temporal terms at least, N-Town's Mary (in) famously swoons too, which is all the more remarkable because, whilst Woolf notes that the Virgin swoons "as so often in fifteenth-century art," it actually seems to be a relatively unusual choice in English drama.[24] The Digby *Christ's Burial and Resurrection* has Mary swooning a number of times, but it occurs exclusively subsequent to Christ's death, which renders it materially different to the other examples considered here.[25] Furthermore, the Digby play also serves almost as an accreted checklist of possible compositional elements for Marian lament and it is significant that the more selective authors of relevant plays from the York, Towneley, and Chester cycles choose not to depict Mary's swoon.[26]

---

24   Woolf, *English Mystery Plays*, 265.
25   *The Digby Plays*, ed. F.J. Furnivall, EETS e.s. 70 (London: Kegan Paul, Trench, Trübener & Co., 1896).
26   In his foundational study George C. Taylor, "The English 'Planctus Mariae'", *Modern Philology* 4 (1907): 605–37, provides a helpful "Table of Motives," a systematic list of available elements from the extant laments, both dramatic and non-dramatic, and also draws links between lyric poems and biblical drama where available. It is striking that the Digby play shows twenty-one of Taylor's thirty-three possible elements, which is rather more than the other plays considered here. Taylor notes of Marian laments in N-Town, that "there is sufficient number of conventional planctus motives to enable one to say with certainty

It has been written that "the Virgin steals the limelight from Christ during the [N-Town] Crucifixion"[27] precisely through "'a melodramatic series of swoons, weeping and laments with the Virgin clinging to the Cross and refusing to be led away'".[28] If it is true that Mary dominates the scene, and I would support that reading, such a judgement is testament to a remarkably powerful, if concise, portrayal.[29] Woolf observes that the N-Town *Crucifixion* "lacking a complaint" – by which she means a formal set-piece *Planctus* – "gives to the Virgin only brief snatches of impassioned outcry ... [which] vary from the rhetorically chill to the touching,"[30] whilst Johnston provides statistical evidence, such as that Mary's "lines make up 44 percent of the entire episode" of the Digby play to support her account of the distilled power of Mary's utterances in N-Town.[31] On the one hand, she is seen to serve as a focus of recognition for female audience members, "a woman whose experiences and sufferings have been shared by many women."[32] And on the other hand, her performance brings together numerous 'traditional' and 'familiar' elements from both ancient and medieval literature and art.[33] As I suggested at the beginning of this essay, perhaps the best account of Mary, informed by personal performance of the part within the N-Town *Crucifixion*, remains Johnston's tracking of Mary's emotional trajectory within the scene, with elements of "anger, shock, shame, self-pity, [and] self-centered grief." As Johnston continues, "there is nothing controlled here, nothing cerebral. The character of Mary is completely given over to hysterical grief."[34]

that they belong to the planctus type, but in them more than in York, Towneley, Chester, or Digby, is introduced matter not typical of the planctus ... [They] are therefore more unlike the independent lyrics than those of any other plays" (624).

[27] Katie Normington, *Gender and Medieval Drama* (Cambridge: D.S. Brewer, 2004), 98.

[28] Christine Richardson and Jackie Johnston, *Medieval Drama* (London: Macmillan, 1991), 77 (Quoted in Normington, *Gender and Medieval Drama*, 98).

[29] Gary Waller, *The Virgin Mary in Late Medieval and Early Modern English Literature and Popular Culture* (Cambridge: Cambridge University Press, 2011), has surprisingly little to say about the N-Town *Crucifixion*, despite often discussing Mary elsewhere in the text throughout the relevant chapter of his monograph study. In Chapter 3, "The Virgin's body in late medieval poetry, romance, and drama," Waller remarks, that "Mary tends to be a side player in the Crucifixion and Resurrection plays – but though small, her role is crucial ... She is presented as beside herself with grief" (64).

[30] Woolf, *English Mystery Plays*, 265.

[31] Johnston, "Acting Mary," 87.

[32] Ibid. See also Sue Niebrzydowski, "Secular Women and Late-Medieval Marian Drama", *Yearbook of English Studies* 43 (2013): 121–39.

[33] Spector, *The N-Town Play*, II. pp. 513–515.

[34] Johnston, "Acting Mary", p. 89.

It is an obvious point to make that the Mary described here, which Johnston notes is "hardly the hieratic Mary of the iconographic tradition,"[35] is also far from the sanctioned role-model put forward by Love. But whilst it is entirely plausible that the portrayal of Mary's grief is both naturalistic and affecting, something to which audience members are forced to relate, particularly those who have buried children, I wonder whether the depiction of Mary is intended to be valorised? If we do not have the depiction of Mary that Love provides here, or rather, if our reception of Mary does not depend upon similarities to but rather differences from Love's portrayal, perhaps the shorter, more brutal account of the Crucifixion in Love's *Mirror* is a helpful way to consider her? 'Uncerebral' and apparently unconscious of the wider theological significance of the scene for much of it, Mary's depiction instead relies upon raw and vivid emotion to affect us. Following this reading, we might hope to have additional text to 'supplement' the portrayal in order to mediate and control its affective nature and, albeit brief, I would argue that we have just that.

Within the *Crucifixion* play, Mary's entrance is marked by her first swoon as she sees her son upon the cross:

> *Here þe sympyl men xul settyn up þese ij crossys and hangyn up þe thevys be þe armys. And þerwhyls xal þe Jewys cast dyce for his clothis, and fytyn and stryvyn. And in þe menetyme xal oure Lady come with iij Maryes with here and Sen Johan with hem, settyng hem down asyde afore þe cros, oure Lady swounyng and mornyng.* (32.92 s.d.)

Immediately, therefore, we have the invocation of powerful affective grief, but Mary's swoon is a physical reaction that is not linked with theological precision to an authorising 'intertext', whether that is gospel sanction or the iconographic tradition of Mary swooning under the pain of contractions of which she had been innocent when giving birth.[36] At the very least, given that Love's Mary swoons for the first time at the moment of Christ's death, the depiction here represents an emotional escalation. Mary then has the first of her 'impassioned outcries' and initially addresses her Jesus, before turning her anger towards herself:

> MARIA   A, my good Lord, my sone so swete!
> What hast þu don? Why hangyst now þus here?
> Is þer non other deth to þe now mete

---

[35] Ibid., p. 88.
[36] See Neff, "The Pain of Compassio".

> But þe most shamful deth among þese thevys fere?
> A, out on my hert – whi brest þu nowth?
> And þu art maydyn and modyr, and seyst þus þi childe spylle!
> How mayst þu abyde þis sorwe and þis woful þowth?
> A, deth, deth, deth! Why wylt þu not me kylle? (32.93–100)

As the target of Mary's apostrophe in the second stanza shifts quickly – from her heart, to herself, and then to death – it is difficult to know precisely how we should receive these lines. Whilst certainly drawing elements from the conventions of the *Planctus Mariae*, ultimately Mary pleads here for a somatic response that cannot be performed. And, rather than merely wishing to die, and it notably is not a wish to die in Christ's place as an active martyr as elsewhere in the tradition, Mary would be the passive victim of death here. It is certainly true that the audience would have already had a longer and more detailed lament from Mary; Woolf identifies N-Town as "the only English cycle [sic] to draw upon the meditative treatment of the Virgin for the first part of the Passion sequence"[37] and indeed she is given some thirty-two lines in response to Mary Magdalene informing her of Christ's arrest. But whilst the initial lament is broader in focus, addressing God as well as Christ, equally more cognitive of theological context, and whilst *epizeuxis* is used, either a symptom of pain: "A! A! A!" (28.161), or as an apostrophe to her son rather than death: "A, Jesu, Jesu, Jesu, Jesu!" (28.165), the fundamental difference might well be that Mary is not yet 'self-centred'. Lamenting the fact that Christ is innocent, for example, Mary wonders whether she is somehow guilty, "I suppoce veryly it is for þe tresspace of me" (28.171). The conclusion of the scene, indeed, has Mary accepting her son's martyrdom and adding herself, almost as an afterthought, to the rest of mankind whom Christ will redeem:

> Now, dere sone, syn þu hast evyr be so ful of mercy
> Þat wylt not spare þiself for þe love þu hast to man.
> On all mankend now have þu pety –
> And also thynk on þi modyr, þat hevy woman. (28.188–91)

To return to the *Crucifixion*, having pleaded for death, we are told by a stage direction that Mary swoons again. The same stage direction informs us that Jesus then speaks. Whilst an audience would clearly not have the play-text before them, the caesura in the middle of the line almost suggests that both actions carry equal weight and there is certainly an imposition of order here

---

37   Woolf, *English Mystery Plays*, 263.

– first Mary swoons and then Christ speaks: *"Here oure Lady xal swonge aʒen, and ore Lord xal seyn thus"* (32.101 s.d.). It is remarkable then that Christ does not even acknowledge his mother's presence, let alone the extent of her grief and the physical toll it is taken on her. Instead he sticks to a scriptural text, as it were, performing the (non-affective) role that the Gospel has provided for him.

In a second plea for his attention, Mary then speaks again, complaining that Jesus has engaged with everyone else there – even the Jews:

> MARIA   O my sone, my sone, my derlyng dere!
> What! Have I defendyd þe?
> Þu hast spoke to alle þo þat ben here,
> And not o word þu spekyst to me.
>
> To þe Jewys þu art ful kende:
> Þu hast forgove al here mysdede.
> And þe thef þu hast in mende:
> For onys haskyng mercy, hefne is his mede.
>
> A, my sovereyn Lord, why whylt þu not speke
> To me þat am þi modyr, in peyn for þi wrong?
> A, hert, hert, why whylt þu not breke,
> Þat I wore out of þis sorwe so stronge! (32.133–44)

Remarkably, Mary's position has now radically altered from her earlier lament and guilt is now firmly ascribed to Christ, who is furthermore blamed for hurting her – Mary is "in peyn for þi wrong." Finally, Mary returns again to literal and metaphorical self-centred grief, with a repetition of her desire for death to end her suffering.[38] As Alexandra Johnston notes, "Christ's next speech is a direct rebuke of her selfish extravagance;"[39] the repetition of "woman" certainly seeming rather more condescending than the compassionate generosity

---

[38] Pfeiffer, "Passionate Encounters," 167, astutely notes that the Towneley Mary also speaks of Christ's silence, but that she does not share N-Town's Mary's articulation of disappointment. Whilst certainly true, there are similarities available and it is perhaps a question of degree; Jesus asks Mary to "chaunge thi chere!" because of the negative effect her articulated sorrow might have on him: "Sease of thi sorow and sighyng sere; || It syttys vnto my hart full sore." (See *The Towneley Plays*, ed. Martin Stevens and A.C. Cawley, 2 vols., EETS s.s. 13 (Oxford: Oxford University Press, 1994), 23: ll. 503–05.

[39] Johnston, "Acting Mary," 88.

suggested by Love.[40] In fact, if this is the moment at which Mary 'becomes' a mother again, with Christ's commitment of John to her, the emphasis is strikingly rather on her childish forgetfulness of the significance of his martyrdom:

> JESUS A, woman, woman, beheld þer þi sone,
> And þu, Jon, take her for þi modyr.
> ...
> And, woman, þu knowyst þat my fadyr of hefne me sent
> To take þis manhod of þe, Adamys rawnsom to pay.
> ...
> Now syn it is þe wyl of my fadyr, it xuld þus be.
> Why xuld it dysplese þe, modyr, now my deth so sore?
> And for to suffre al þis for man I was born of the,
> To þe blys þat man had lost, man aӡen to restore.
> (32.145–46, 149–50, 153–56)

Having observed Christ's rebuke, Johnston rightly notes that Mary ignores his words and rushes to embrace the cross and also that Mary Magdalene and John attempt to take her away. Johnston does not include the fact that Magdalene also rebukes Mary and suggests that, far from serving any positive purpose, the affecting display of grief is both detrimental to the rest of them and also an infliction of further pain upon Jesus:

> MARIA A, good lady, why do ӡe þus?
> MAGDALENE Ӡoure dolfol cher now cheuyth us sore.
> And for þe peyne of my swete Lord Jesus,
> Þat he seyth in ӡou, it peyneth hym more. (32.157–60)

This is an important, and particularly condemnatory, interjection for a number of reasons. Sarah McNamer's fundamental argument about Marian lament develops from a recognition of a powerfully and cohesively gendered discourse; "compassion, as scripted through Middle English meditations on the Passion, is largely a function of gender performance: to perform compassion is to feel like a woman."[41] N-Town's Magdalene would clearly dissent from this view. Likewise, in the York *Mortificacio Christi* Play, the other example in which

---

40 "He clepede hir not at þat || tyme, *modere*, lest she sholde þorh feruent tendirnes of love haue || bene more sorye" (177/13–15).

41 McNamer, *Affective Meditation*, 119.

a woman interjects to respond to Mary's laments, it usually being John or Jesus alone who do so, Maria Cleophas offers compassionate concern for the Virgin's sorrow, rather than direct criticism of the further pain caused to Jesus:[42]

> MARIA CLEOPHE A, Marie, take triste unto þe,
> For socoure to þe will he sende
> þis tyde.
> ...
> It dose hir pyne
> To see hym tyne.
> Lede we her heyne,
> Þis mornyng helpe hir ne maye. (36.181–83, 270–73)

Mary is subsequently removed from the cross and Christ dies, having first addressed the audience to explain the scriptural basis of the scene before them. Even as he dies and utters his final words "Nunc consummatum est" (32.221), however, Mary returns to her lament and again exclaims that her heart is broken, which cannot but seem like an empty metaphor when contrasted with the corpse before her:

> MARIA Alas! Alas! I leve to longe,
> To se my swete sone with peynes stronge
> As a theff on cros doth honge,
> And nevyr ʒet dede he synne!
> Alas, my dere chyld to deth is dressyd!
> Now is my care wel more incressyd!
> A, myn herte with peyn is pressyd –
> For sorwe myn hert doth twynne! (32.222–29)

For all the tenderness here, there is a tragic poignancy in the immediate focus shifting very quickly to one of those left behind: "Now is my care wel more incressyd!" John attempts to console Mary by reminding her of Jesus' willing sacrifice and also of the mutual care he had commanded of them, but her

---

42 In the Chester *Passion* Play, whilst Mary is the principal mourner, arriving at the cross in tears, the laments are shared between the four Marys present and the degree of suffering is indistinct – Maria Jacobi shares (Virgin) Mary's desire for death, for example: "Helpe me, Jesu, with some thinge ... or elles slaye me for anything || and stynt me of this stryffe." (See *The Chester Mystery Cycle*, ed. R.M. Lumiansky and David Mills, 2 vols., EETS s.s. 3 [Oxford: Oxford University Press, 1974], XVIA: ll. 277–80).

response focuses instead on the physical degradation of the body, as if explicitly performing ekphrastic affective piety, which is somewhat odd for an audience that have seen it all for themselves, rather than engaging in meaningful dialogue with her new 'son':

> MARIA   Thow he had nevyr of me be born,
> And I sey his flesch þus al to-torn,
> On bak behyndyn, on brest beforn,
> Rent with woundys wyde,
> Nedys I must wonyn in woo,
> To se my frende with many a fo
> All to-rent from top to too,
> His flesch withowtyn hyde. (32.238–45)

John attempts to persuade Mary to comprehension once again, urging her to be "mery in hert" (32.253), but although she now begins to remember and understand, she closely aligns her grief with the visual 'beholding' of Christ's body. In other words, it is the sight of the wounds that affects her, rather than her loss *per se*, and equally the affective vision that diminishes rather than supports her ability to appreciate the anticipated truth of the Gospel resurrection to follow. John clearly articulates this distinction when he urges her to remove herself from the sight of her son's body:

> JOHANNES   Now, dere lady, þerfore I ʒow pray,
> Fro þis dolful dolour wende we oure way;
> For whan þis syght ʒe se nought may,
> ʒoure care may waxe more lyght. (32.258–61)

Mary acknowledges that she should remove herself from the gory sight, but pauses to kiss Christ's feet and lament once again, "Al joye departyth fro me" (32.269). At this point, and for a final time, Mary swoons once more and falls 'half-dead' to the ground. When she awakes, at John's bidding, it is as though her self-control has been restored and she asks to be taken to the temple, a locus that will enable her, as Pfeiffer suggests, to "transform grief into [a] devotionally useful offering to God."[43] One might add the obvious point that as well as being useful, prayer is controlled and cerebral. When we next see Mary, once Christ's body has been taken from the cross and placed on her lap in an enactment of the *pietà*, her articulation of *Planctus* convention in remembering her

---

43   Pfeiffer, "Passionate Encounters," 171.

maternity is hugely affective, but particularly so because she is simultaneously in full control of the meaning of her scene, "A, mercy, Fadyr of Hefne, it xulde be so"(34.133). As Johnston superbly puts it, rather than a "self-centered" performance of grief, "here the figure of Mary finds again the centre of her being and finally accepts Christ's death."[44] At the centre of Mary's being, of course, is her divinity, that which makes her more than merely an 'everywoman', and so her return is simultaneously a reinstatement of a portrayal that maintains theological significance at its core too.

A reading of Mary's portrayal that suggests an internal criticism within the play of her detached embodiment of powerful affective piety might seem at odds with what makes the scene so striking. But it is remarkable, as I have argued, that N-Town provides both a Mary at the *Crucifixion* whose grief is more particularly self-centred than other extant plays on the same theme and also more precise reproaches for that behaviour from those around her. Mary's swoons might well affect the audience, but it is worth observing the degree to which the other characters within the play are unmoved by the physical manifestation of her suffering.[45] Within the broader discourse of the *Planctus Mariae*, critics have often written of an increasing disjunction of affect and theological value as the 'genre' develops. Woolf, for example, contrasts an earlier portrayal of Mary's grief, "the balancing of distress with faith and with modesty," with a later tradition, represented by the Digby play, which she categorises as "monotonous excess," an "indiscriminate copiousness of lamentation," "an unmodulated battering upon the emotions."[46] C.W. Marx notes similarly "that the "dominant impression" left by late medieval laments "is one of an extreme emotionalism which easily becomes monotonous."[47] Significantly, Woolf is careful to argue that a modern rejection of such affect is not simply anachronistic distaste, but is also evident in contemporaneous criticism of emotive performances that fail to simultaneously provide "a substantial theological frame of reference, which could control invention and feeling."[48] Among the many differences between the N-Town *Crucifixion* and the examples considered here is this very insistence that whilst emotion can, of course, be powerfully affective, it needs to be controlled, directed and used properly for compassion to be effectively mediated and invoked.

---

44   Johnston, "Acting Mary," 90.
45   By contrast, Mary's swoon at the initial sight of Christ's body in the Digby play is conspicuously met with alarm from both Mary Magdalene and Joseph (see ll. 459–63).
46   Woolf, *English Religious Lyric*, 241, 265.
47   Quoted by McNamer, *Affective Meditation*, 157.
48   Woolf, *English Religious Lyric*, 272.

Bibliography

Beadle, Richard. "'Devoute ymaginacioun' and the Dramatic Sense in Love's *Mirror* and the N-Town Plays," 1–17. In *Nicholas Love at Waseda: Proceedings of the International Conference, 20–22 July, 1995*, edited by Shoicho Oguro, Richard Beadle and Michael G. Sargent, 1–17. Cambridge: D.S. Brewer, 1997.

———, ed. *The York Plays: A Critical Edition of the York Corpus Christi Play as recorded in British Library Additional MS 35290*, 2 vols. EETS s.s. 23–24. Oxford: Oxford University Press, 2009–13.

Cicero. *Ad C. Herennium Libri IV: De ratione dicendi*, translated by Harry Caplan. Cambridge, MA: Harvard University Press, 1954.

Clark, Charlotte. "'Will he weep when the speaker's eyes are dry?'" Unpublished Extended Essay, University of Oxford: Faculty of English, 2013.

Cummings, Brian. *Literary Culture of the Reformation: Grammar and Grace*. Oxford: Oxford University Press, 2007.

Furnivall, F.J., ed. *The Digby Plays*. EETS e.s. 70. London: Kegan Paul, Trench, Trübener & Co., 1896.

Gillespie, Vincent. "Vernacular Books of Religion," 317–44. In *Book Production and Publishing in Britain, 1375–1475*, edited by Jeremy Griffiths and Derek Pearsall. Cambridge: Cambridge University Press, 1989.

Goodland, Katharine. "Inverting the Pietà in Shakespeare's *King Lear*," 47–74. In *Marian Moments in Early Modern British Drama*, edited by Regina Buccola and Lisa Hopkins. Aldershot: Ashgate, 2007.

Grossman, Marshall, ed. *Aemelia Lanyer: Gender, Genre, and the Canon*. Kentucky: University of Kentucky Press, 1998.

Hamburgh, Harvey E. "The Problem of *Lo Spasimo* of the Virgin in Cinquecento Paintings of the Descent from the Cross." *The Sixteenth Century Journal* 12:4 (1981): 45–75.

Hodgson, Elizabeth M. A. "Prophecy and Gendered Mourning in Aemelia Lanyer's *Salve Deus Rex Judaeorum*." *Studies in English Literature* 43 (2003): 101–16.

Johnston, Alexandra F. "Acting Mary: The Emotional Realism of the Virgin Mary in the N-Town Plays," 85–98. In *From Page to Performance: Essays in Early English Drama*, edited by John A. Alford. East Lansing: Michigan State University Press, 1995.

King, Pamela M. "Spatial Semantics and the Medieval Theatre," 45–58. In *The Theatrical Space*, edited by James Redmond. Themes in Drama, 9. Cambridge: Cambridge University Press, 1987.

Kuchar, Gary. "Aemelia Lanyer and the Virgin's Swoon: Theology and Iconography in the *Salve Deus Rex Judaeorum*." *English Literary Renaissance* 37 (2007): 47–73.

Love, Nicholas. *The Mirror of the Blessed Life of Jesus Christ*, edited by Michael G. Sargent. Exeter: Exeter University Press, 2004.

Lumiansky, R.M. and David Mills, eds. *The Chester Mystery Cycle*. 2 vols. EETS s.s. 3. Oxford: Oxford University Press, 1974.

McNamer, Sarah. *Affective Meditation and the Invention of Medieval Compassion*. Philadelphia: University of Pennsylvania Press, 2010.

Meredith, Peter, ed. *The* Passion Play *From The N. Town Manuscript*. London: Longman, 1990.

Neff, Amy. "The Pain of Compassio: Mary's Labor at the Foot of the Cross." *The Art Bulletin* 80 (1998): 254–73.

Niebrzydowski, Sue. "Secular Women and Late-Medieval Marian Drama." *Yearbook of English Studies* 43 (2013): 121–39.

Normington, Katie. *Gender and Medieval Drama*. Cambridge: D.S. Brewer, 2004.

Pfeiffer, Kerstin. "Passionate Encounters: Emotion in Early English Biblical Drama". PhD diss., University of Stirling, 2011.

Richardson, Christine and Jackie Johnston. *Medieval Drama*. London: Macmillan, 1991.

Spector, Stephen, ed. *The N-Town Play: Cotton MS Vespasian D. 8*. 2 vols. EETS s.s. 11. Oxford: Oxford University Press, 1991.

Stevens, Martin and A.C. Cawley, eds. *The Towneley Plays*. 2 vols. EETS s.s. 13. Oxford: Oxford University Press, 1994.

Taylor, George C. "The English 'Planctus Mariae'". *Modern Philology* 4 (1907): 605–37.

Waller, Gary. *The Virgin Mary in Late Medieval and Early Modern English Literature and Popular Culture*. Cambridge: Cambridge University Press, 2011.

Woods, Susanne, ed. *The Poems of Aemelia Lanyer: Salve Deus Rex Judaeorum*, Oxford: Oxford University Press, 1993.

Woolf, Rosemary. *The English Religious Lyric in the Middle Ages*. Oxford: Oxford University Press, 1968.

———. *The English Mystery Plays*. London: Routledge, 1972.

CHAPTER 14

Memory and Remembering: Sacred History and the York Plays

Clifford Davidson

Abstract

The York Corpus Christi play cycle was a remarkably long-lived civic event requiring concerted and enthusiastic local effort. The plays dramatized sacred history from Creation to Doomsday. Sponsored by the city Corporation rather than the Church, they were designated as a work of charity for the benefit of the spectators. Their object was not didactic but rather a representation of salvation history that would be held in the memory of participants and spectators for their spiritual benefit. Designed to make the past present, they were expected to reinforce cultural memory of the Christian narrative, especially the events at the centre of history (the time of Jesus the Saviour). A goal was the formation of civic identity as catholic Christians. The plays, using canonical and other sources available to the authors of the texts, provided a view of the past from biblical history that would make the central events of past salvation history to be present for spectators. In conclusion, the Doomsday play brought to mind that which was expected to come at the end of history.

Keywords

civic performances – collective memory – Corpus Christi plays – identity formation – memory theory – non-biblical sources

1   Introduction

The York mystery plays represent a unique survival of a cycle of Corpus Christi pageants that were staged on wagons in the streets of this medieval English city along the same route over a centuries-long period, albeit much remains unknown about them over the time of their survival up to their suppression in 1569. The outlines of their history are documented by fragmentary records, still remaining in archives mainly at York itself, that have been edited by Alexandra

F. Johnston and Margaret Rogerson.[1] Of the cycle's inception in the late fourteenth century Richard Beadle has plausibly suggested a community effort "on such a scale" that would have required "a high degree of consensus among all those involved; and its continuity must have relied on a continuous process of constructive negotiation and cooperation among everyone who had a stake in it."[2] His conclusions concerning the texts of the plays now indicate their collection and entry into a single manuscript, the "Register" (British Library Add. MS. 35,290), by around 1476–77.[3] But if there is much yet unknown about the earliest status of the cycle, the records are clear in indicating performance already at a dozen sites throughout a route leading from the gates of Holy Trinity Priory, near the great entrance to the city at the head of Micklegate, to the city centre and to the open space at the Pavement before the church of All Saints.[4] Further, by 1415 an official list, the *Ordo paginarum*, had been drawn up that would specify the names of guilds and their responsibilities with regard to pageant production.[5]

The purpose of the present study, however, is to return to a topic that has long interested me, that is, the manner in which the plays set out sacred episodes derived from the Bible and tradition in order to help establish and

---

1   *Records of Early English Drama: York*, 2 vols., ed. Alexandra F. Johnston and Margaret Rogerson (Toronto: University of Toronto Press, 1979), hereafter REED: *York*.

2   *The York Plays: A Critical Edition of the York Corpus Christi Play as Recorded in British Library Additional MS 35290*, 2 vols., ed. Richard Beadle, EETS s.s. 23–24 (Oxford: Oxford University Press, 2009–13), 2: xxii-xxiii. Citations to the York plays in the present study are to this edition. For the necessity of guild enthusiasm about performance for the continuance of the cycle, see Clifford Davidson, *Corpus Christi Plays at York: A Context for Religious Drama*, AMS Studies in Middle English, 30 (New York: AMS Press, 2013), 7–32.

3   See Beadle, *York Plays*, 1: xii-xviii, and Beadle's more detailed discussion in "Nicholas Lancaster, Richard of Gloucester and the York Corpus Christi Play," in *The York Mystery Plays: Performance in the City*, ed. Margaret Rogerson (Woodbridge: York Medieval Press, 2011), 31–52. Earlier estimates of the dating suggested 1463–77.

4   Meg Twycross, "'Places to hear the play': Pageant Stations at York, 1398–1572," *REED Newsletter* 3: 2 (1978): 10–33, and Eileen White, "Places for Hearing the Corpus Christi Play in York," *Medieval English Theatre* 9 (1987): 23–63. For a map showing the route, see Davidson, *Corpus Christi Plays at York: A Context*, 89 (fig. 4).

5   REED: *York*, 1: 16–24, and a subsequent list, by some scholars dated 1422, at ibid., 25–26. The *Ordo paginarum*, however, represents a frequently corrected text, and hence cannot be regarded a complete record. Plays and guild participation were subjected to change. See especially Meg Twycross, "The *Ordo paginarum* Revisited, with a Digital Camera," in *"Bring furth the pagants": Essays in Early English Drama Presented to Alexandra F. Johnston*, ed. David N. Klausner and Karen Sawyer Marsalek (Toronto: University of Toronto Press, 2007), 105–31.

maintain a collective memory of salvation history.[6] My approach will be more theoretical than has been my usual practice, since it will be necessary to cast my net wide in order to suggest (1) how the experience of remembering in the plays depends on conceptions of sacred time, and to suggest (2) how the play texts absorb the biblical story in the canonical scriptures, the apocrypha and other heterodox writings.[7] The latter must include accretions over many centuries that found their way into the tradition to appear in such sources and analogues as, for example, the *Meditations on the Life of Christ* and Nicholas Love's adaptation of this work, *The Mirror of the Blessed Life of Jesus Christ*; the *Stanzaic Life of Christ*; *The Northern Passion*; and the *Revelations* of St. Birgitta of Sweden. These sources were ultimately derived from eyewitness accounts, early written testimony and interpretation, hearsay, visionary experience, and pure fantasy, all of it a rich mixture of traditional matter that was to be found locally in the libraries of York, particularly in the vast library of the Augustinian canons, whose priory was located next to the seat of civic government.[8] Alexandra Johnston has even plausibly suggested that the writers of the texts were the canons of this establishment.[9]

A good example of extra-biblical material added to the canonical text involves Pilate's wife, Percula (Procula), found only in a single verse, Matthew 27:19, in which she "sent to him," asking him to desist from condemning Jesus, "that just man," for on his account she has "suffered many things this day." She becomes a major figure in a presumably mid-fifteenth-century addition to the York plays of the trials before Pilate.[10] The principal source is the apocryphal *Gospel of Nicodemus*, even announcing her experience of demonic inspiration in words lifted from the English translation of this work: "I have ben dreched

---

[6] In no sense should my approach in this paper be regarded as excluding other approaches to the plays, for example, the excellent but quite different analysis of cycle form in Peter Happé, *Cyclic Form and the English Mystery Plays*, Ludus: Medieval and Early Renaissance Theatre and Drama, 7 (Amsterdam: Rodopi, 2004).

[7] In introducing the Nag Hammadi papyri in 1979, Elaine Pagels, *The Gnostic Gospels* (New York: Random House, 1979), was able to show, in a book for the general public, how diverse early Christianity proved itself to be in spite of efforts to contain the biblical message to an 'orthodox' core represented by the canonical texts and the creeds.

[8] The catalogue of this vast library is extant; see *The Friars' Libraries*, ed. K.W. Humphreys (London: British Library, 1990).

[9] Alexandra F. Johnston, "*The York Cycle* and the Libraries of York," in *The Church and Learning in Late Medieval Society: Essays in Honour of R.B. Dobson*, ed. Caroline Barron and Jenny Stratford, Harlaxton Medieval Studies, 11 (Donington: Shaun Tyas, 2002), 355–70.

[10] Because Percula is not listed as present in the 1415 *Ordo paginarum* in the *York Memorandum Book A/Y*, the addition of this character to the text at a later date seems certain.

with dremes so || all this nyght" becomes "I am drecchid with a dreme" (30.176).[11] Further, an important connection in the play of the devil's role with the temptation in the Garden of Eden was noticed by Rosemary Woolf to have been derived from another source, the *Glossa Ordinaria*,[12] certainly an inspired choice that allowed the remarkably frivolous figure of Percula to connect the Passion story with that earliest of catastrophic events in the history of the human race. Percula's story in time is thus linked to a larger vision, the condition of all humankind from the beginning and its need for the remedy – that is, the Crucifixion – which she, as she is tempted by the devil, attempts to prevent.

2   Framing the Narrative

With regard to the handling of temporality, we need to keep in mind that the plays were structured to recall the past from a particular perspective, treating time in its beginnings, mid-point, and also its end, its culmination in the Last Judgement (*Doomsday*, play 47), the latter powerfully reconstructed from prophetic sacred texts. In this project, as Pamela King has shown, special importance was attributed by the writers to the lessons attached to the Church Year that, read on the appointed days in the liturgy, formed an aggregation of material that was accessed for structuring the play cycle.[13] This, along with other sources, canonical and non-canonical, established the groundwork for telling of sacred story and its visualization through the speeches memorised by the actors and their gestures. Significantly, the pageants were presented on Corpus Christi, a special feast established on Thursday after Trinity Sunday to honour the Holy Sacrament, itself believed to be existing in sacred time, simultaneously in past, present, and eternity.[14] So too the plays set out to make past history present, for in these dramatizations the spectators were to feel as if they were living contemporaries of the characters peopling the events being

---

11   *The Middle-English Harrowing of Hell and Gospel of Nicodemus*, ed. William Henry Hulme, EETS e.s. 100 (London: Oxford University Press, 1907), 35 (British Library Add. MS. 16,165). For the introduction of the devil's role into the story from Comestor's *Historia Scholastica*, see Beadle, *York Plays*, 2: 251.

12   Rosemary Woolf, *The English Mystery Plays* (Berkeley: University of California Press, 1972), 245.

13   Pamela M. King, *The York Mystery Cycle and the Worship of the City*, Westfield Medieval Studies, 1 (Woodbridge: D.S. Brewer, 2006).

14   For the establishment of the feast, see Miri Rubin, *Corpus Christi: The Eucharist in Late Medieval Culture* (Cambridge: Cambridge University Press, 1991).

shown – events being made visible for the people's edification as devotional experience, outside of duration, that is, ordinary time.[15]

By way of a local example of an object of devotion, a relic of the Passion exposed in York Minster may further illuminate the above. One of the most ugly scenes in the cycle is the brutal Crowning with Thorns scene in the Tilemakers' *Second Trial before Pilate* when Jesus is beaten, mocked, clothed as a mock king, and "kyndely" crowned "with a brere." In fact, the crown has been cruelly forced down on his head so that "His brayne begynnes for to blede" (33.389, 401). The Crown of Thorns was brought to Paris in 1239, two thorns later being acquired by Archbishop Thomas Arundel, who presented these relics to York Minster along with a reliquary for them.[16] The relics, since they were on display, could thus be seen and venerated as a way for worshippers to come as if into the presence of the torturing of Jesus in biblical times. Relics were a potent stimulus for making the past present, but only if their meaning had been made plain through a narrative revealing their significance. Such a narrative was presented in the Tilemakers' play, which provided a lively, and horrifying, demonstration of the biblical event in which the thorns present in this very city had played a role.

At the head of the first play in the York cycle stands the extra-metrical motto, "Ego sum Alpha et O[mega], vita, via, || Veritas primus et nouissimus," words assigned to God the Creator.[17] Already in this play the text seems to signal that the pageants are not to be principally didactic but are to function generally in quite another manner than to teach the articles of faith.[18] Rather, it is clear that the plays are to inform and allow actors and audiences alike to participate vicariously in the whole history of the world from even before its physical cre-

---

15   For useful comments about sacred time as distinguished from duration, see Mircea Eliade, *The Sacred and the Profane: The Nature of Religion* (New York: Harcourt and Brace, 1959), 68–104.

16   Sarah Brown, *York Minster: An Architectural History, c 1220–1500* (Swindon: English Heritage, 2003), 170. For a late fourteenth-century thorn reliquary in the British Museum, see *Treasures of Heaven: Saints, Relics, and Devotion in Medieval Europe*, ed. Martina Bagnoli et al. (London: British Museum Press, 2011), 94–95 (no. 54).

17   These words echo, or are echoed by, the motto ("Ego sum alph[a] et [Ω]") on the Book of Creation held by the Creator God in the top panel in the tracery of the Great East Window of York Minster; see Thomas French, *York Minster: The Great East Window*, Corpus vitrearum Medii Aevi, Great Britain, 2 (Oxford: Oxford University Press, 1995), 16–17.

18   See Hans-Jürgen Diller, "Theological Doctrine and Popular Religion in the Mystery Plays," in *Religion in the Poetry and Drama of the Late Middle Ages in England*, ed. Piero Boitani and Anna Torti (Woodbridge: D.S. Brewer, 1990), 199–213, for a strong case against seeing the mysteries as essentially didactic.

ation to its end and dissolution in the Doomsday drama. In the course of its historical sweep, the action presented in these plays is situated along the streets, passing the churches and the Minster, a local topography saturated in images, many of them representing the same events to be imprinted on the collective memory by the scenes in the cycle.[19] The first pageant wagon, sponsored by the Barkers (Tanners), will mount the story of a familiar non-biblical event from pre-history, prior to the beginning of time, "ab initio temporis," in St. Augustine's words.[20] This will be the creation of the angels and the splitting of their number into those who remain loyal to the Good and those who succumb to evil, especially dramatizing the role of Lucifer, his hubris, and his fall along with those that followed him into the depths of a stinking hellmouth. The story involved the mythic interpretation of the origin of evil that, allowed to be set loose in the cosmos, would be catastrophic for all subsequent centuries. The narrative, given prominence by St. Augustine in *The City of God* where it is pieced together from a small handful of disconnected biblical verses,[21] was foundational, an explanation of the source of evil and suffering that would affect humankind very quickly in primordial time after Adam and Eve were given the "gast of lyffe" by God (*The Fall*, 5.43). The fall of Lucifer still may be seen in painted glass panels in the East Window of York Minster (1405–08) and in a window in the church of St. Michael Spurriergate (1400–25), the latter affixed with a motto apparently adapted and abbreviated from Isaiah 14:12: "How thou art fallen from heaven, O Lucifer, who didst rise in the morning, how art thou fallen to the earth that didst wound the nations."[22]

---

19 For the relevance of the religious imagery present in churches located along the pageant route and corresponding to scenes in the plays, see Davidson, *Corpus Christi Plays at York: A Context*, 87–125.

20 Woolf, *English Mystery Plays*, 107, citing Augustine, *The Literal Meaning of Genesis*, 11.16.

21 St. Augustine, *The City of God*, trans. Marcus Dods et al. (New York: Modern Library, 1950), book 11.14–17, attempting to explain 1 John 3:8: "the devil sinneth from the beginning." Woolf, *English Mystery Plays*, 107, notes that Augustine's view was rejected by orthodox commentators such as St. Thomas Aquinas in favour of placing the fall of Lucifer at an instant at the beginning of time, not before.

22 Clifford Davidson and David E. O'Connor, *York Art: A Subject List of Extant and Lost Art, Including Items Relevant to Early Drama* (Kalamazoo, MI: Medieval Institute Publications, 1978), 20, revised as "Early Drama, Art, and Music" website (2003): <http://scholarworks.wmich.edu/early_drama/4/> (accessed 7 December 2014); Barbara Palmer, *The Early Art of the West Riding of Yorkshire: A Subject List of Extant and Lost Art, Including Items Relevant to Early Drama*, Early Drama, Art and Music Reference Series, 6 (Kalamazoo, MI: Medieval Institute Publications, 1990), 156, 288–90.

The spectacular fall of Lucifer into the pit of hell, from which he and a cohort emerge commenting on the intolerable heat, filth, and stench of that place (1.97–112), serves along with the pageants of the Creation and Fall of Adam and Eve in the beginning to function as a bookend for the York cycle, while the other bookend, bracketing the end, was the pageant of *Doomsday* that was presented by the Mercers, the most affluent and powerful of the city's guilds. More is known about the staging of this pageant than about any other play on account of the survival of a 1433 indenture, which reveals properties consistent with illustrations of the scene in large representations in English art such as the restored Doom paintings at Holy Trinity Church in Coventry and St. Thomas of Canterbury, Salisbury. However, no examples of this iconography originating from York exist aside from two manuscript illuminations and a Doom, painted glass of 1340, by Master Robert of York in the tracery of the East Window at Selby Abbey.[23] The inventory in the indenture reports a wheeled pageant wagon, a mechanism for Jesus to descend to sit in judgement upon a rainbow constructed from two pieces of wood, angels with the instruments of the Passion as well as other angels, costumes and masks, trumpets, and two groups of "saules," split into the damned and those who will be received into heaven by St. Peter.[24] Unlike the Apocalypse panels in the Great East Window of York Minster, the scene in the pageant is dependent mostly on Matthew 25:31–46, stressing a binary division of 'souls' in accord with their performance of the Corporal Acts of Mercy – that is, acts of charity that are obligatory in the devotional practice demanded by traditional religion.[25] For those who have failed this test, devils emerge onto the stage with hope of capturing their prey. But Jesus will intercede for his "chosen childer" (47.365–68), for whom he has come to display his bleeding wounds as signs of his mercy. The Day of Wrath at the end of the world will come without warning and will spare only those who have shown devotion to him and have proven their spiritual sincerity by their charitable deeds in this life. The scene in the pageant, projected as a vision of the future, needs simultaneously to be seen as a remembering of Jesus' commands in Matthew's gospel that must be followed if men and women wish not to be consigned to the place of "exterior darkness" where there is sighing and weeping without end (Matt. 25:30). Thus the cycle is bracketed by plays showing the origin in primordial time of everything that exists and by a final pageant

---

23 York Minster Library, MS. Add. 2 (Bolton Hours), fol. 208, and MS. VI.K.6, fol. 31 (initial).
24 *REED: York*, 1: 55–56.
25 See the chapter "Theater and Charity," in Davidson, *Corpus Christi Plays at York: A Context*, 165–88, and, for the Works of Mercy, Eamon Duffy, *The Stripping of the Altars: Traditional Religion in England, c. 1400-c. 1580* (New Haven: Yale University Press, 1992), 357–62.

that projects memory up to the end of time when all will be dissolved except heaven, where the saved will be invited to sing in joy among the angels in the bright presence of God, and hell, where unendurable pain will be felt eternally by denizens of the place of darkness.

That such framing is critical for the establishment of collective memory has been emphasised by Maurice Halbwachs, whose early work on the subject has been a starting point for more recent sociological studies of the phenomenon. "No memory," he wrote, "is possible outside frameworks used by people to determine and retrieve their recollections."[26] Further, in the process he emphasises the importance of religion, which is dependent on remembering the sacred narrative[27] and locating oneself in relation to the eternal verities – that is, finding one's place in the scheme of things. The Fall of Lucifer and the Creation on the one hand, and the Last Judgement on the other establish the limits of the human story, and not only in the York cycle but also elsewhere in depictions of the Christian story. These are the cosmic events explaining origins, in this case catastrophic, and of time's conclusion, with permanent effects in the hereafter for those who live in the temporal world. We find, for example, the same framework in the illustrations in the fourteenth-century *Holkham Bible Picture Book*,[28] which in a miniature on fol. 2 begins the narrative with the famous illustration of God as an architect holding a set of compasses in the centre of the as yet unfinished cosmos (the heavens, with sun and moon, are all that are in place), and above him Lucifer arrogating a seat on a throne while being worshipped by his followers at his left. The loyal angels at his right turn away. Below the circle designating the cosmos-in-progress is the mouth of hell and the flames that will shortly swallow up the rebel angels and their leader. On the verso will then be the creation of all living things, followed by the creation of Adam and Eve, their fall into disobedience, and their expulsion from Paradise. The next scene will be the murder of Abel by Cain (fol. 5v), a splitting of human beings into the good and the bad that will foreshadow the binary division of the race at the end of time. This is shown on the final folio of the *Holham Bible Picture Book*, with human figures below at the Judge's right being welcomed into bliss by St. Peter, and on the other side souls being tortured and

---

26   Maurice Halbwachs, *On Collective Memory*, ed. and trans. Lewis A. Coser (Chicago: University of Chicago Press, 1992), 43.
27   See ibid., 84–119.
28   *The Holkham Bible Picture Book*, introduction and commentary by W.O. Hassall (London: Dropmore Press, 1954).

taken toward hellmouth,[29] itself positioned under two cauldrons (one hanging above the other, which stands on legs), both containing souls suffering from the flames below (fol. 42v).

3 The Charitable Project

The official reasoning behind performance of the York Creation to Doom cycle is laid out in the *York Memorandum Book A/Y* as early as 1399, when the purpose of playing the plays, presumably already ranging from the fall of Lucifer to the Doomsday, was implied to be a work of charity ("ouvere de charitee"), an enterprise for the good of the people. It is affirmed that the said pageants are maintained and supported by the commons and the craftsmen of the city "en honour & reuerence nostreseignour Iesu Crist" as well as for the "glory and benefit of the same city."[30] More or less the same formula was repeated in 1417 as well as in 1422, when it was noted that the cycle was made for the cause of devotion and the extirpation of vice and reformation of customs ("deuoticionis causam et extirpacionem morumque reformacionem").[31] In 1415, more than half a century before the collecting of individual play scripts in a comprehensive Register, the city clerk's deputy arranged for an official listing, the *Ordo paginarum*, designating the order and content of the pageants, all of them noted in order and naming their characters, and identifying the guilds responsible for producing them.[32] Quite firmly the document ordered under threat of loss of privileges or imprisonment that neither the pageants nor the civic Corpus Christi procession which as yet occurred on the same day was to be hindered by a disturbance of any kind, hence, for example, prohibiting the carrying of swords among the citizens.[33] On account of the pageants' official status and also their sacred content, it would have been a civic and Christian duty to present edifying performances in a manner reflecting well on the honour of the city. The Corporation, which rather than the Church served as the ultimate sponsor of the plays, was insistent on its authority and promulgated such strict rules to ensure that the mode of performance would be satisfactory, even worshipful, though, as we are able to surmise, this clearly did not mean

---

29 Some are being ferried to the place of punishment in a wheelbarrow; for comment, see ibid., 155–56.
30 *REED: York*, 1: 11, 2: 697–98.
31 Ibid., 1: 37, 2: 722.
32 Ibid., 1: 16–25.
33 Ibid., 1: 24.

the lack of all humour or certainly of vitality in acting style. However, if the Corporation exercised power to control and see that a proper respect be enforced in the re-enactment of sacred history, the evidence is that the guilds were on the whole genuinely enthusiastic, for otherwise it is not credible that the pageants could have been continued as long as they did. The city elite and the other citizens would seem to have been well aware of the plays' charitable function and their importance to them. This was so even after the rise of Protestantism and after the consequent attack on Purgatory, which had long underpinned the Catholic doctrine of good works as directly associated with deferred rewards for them after death. Following the plays' suppression, citizens' voices were raised in vain attempts to re-establish their tradition, and a number of guilds continued for many years to maintain their pageant houses for storage of their wagons and playing gear. There can be no doubt that the pageants had been a significant element in the formation of their identity as individuals, as guilds, as citizens of the city of York, as Catholic Christians.

Identity formation,[34] then, is a consequence of a successful establishment of collective memory – a memory program which, in the case of the York plays, projects visual and aural representation that erases the lines between the seen (the physical plays) and the 'real'. The words and images delivered in the plays are (in Ernst Cassirer's words) "endowed with real forces."[35] Some may see the process to be brought to mind, borrowing Heidegger's terminology, as the "deconcealment of Being"[36] or, more responsibly with St. Paul's words concerning "the invisible things" of God that "from the creation of the world are clearly seen, being understood by the things that are made" (Romans 1:20). The intended result is the promotion of understanding, of knowing the origins and

---

34 A useful discussion of the relation between memory, identity, and history may be found in Aleida Assmann, *Cultural Memory and Western Civilization: Function, Media, Archives* (New York: Cambridge University Press, 2011), 118–34. Memory culture and identity formation are also discussed in very perceptive ways by Jan Assmann, *Cultural Memory and Early Civilization: Writing, Remembrance, and Political Imagination* (New York: Cambridge University Press, 2011). Identity, as in the instance of the York guild members in connection with their pageants, has also been seen in anthropological terms introduced by Mary Douglas; see Clifford Davidson, "Positional Symbolism and Medieval English Drama," *Comparative Drama* 25 (1991): 66–76.

35 Ernst Cassirer, *The Philosophy of Symbolic Forms*, vol. 1: *Language*, trans. Ralph Manheim (New Haven: Yale University Press, 1953), 42.

36 Martin Heidegger, "The Origin of the Work of Art," in *Poetry, Language, Thought*, trans. Albert Hofstadter (New York: Harper & Row, 1971; rpt. 1975), 15–87, esp. 39ff. This is not to suggest that Heidegger's philosophy, essentially materialist, was based on a medieval view of the Creation or of history.

meaning of life itself, and this is felt to result from the heavy investment by dedicated community effort and involvement as well as appropriate audience response. Very substantial financial expense and the physical effort certainly were present in the process, as the dramatic records indicate. However, the experience of participating in this type of play production cannot today be replicated except partially since the social and intellectual basis in which it was rooted has changed utterly. In such a secular environment as in the West of the twenty-first century, where the collective memory has been suppressed and is not likely to be revived as a part of the social identity, it should nevertheless be our task to come to terms with the manner in which religious plays, repeated annually or nearly so, were once embedded in the collective life of the community. Because our ancestors believed, our contemporaries today do not necessarily believe, or if they do, their manner of believing cannot be the same. Tradition, which links, in Danièle Herview-Léger's words, a "body of representations, images, theoretical intelligences, behaviours, attitudes and so on that a group or society accepts in the name of the *necessary* continuity between past and present,"[37] has been fractured, broken. The ability to effect an "absent present," to experience the full power of the forces originally felt in watching the plays, will have been largely lost, albeit without the loss of a very powerful personal sense of aesthetic enjoyment in seeing the same plays. In re-capturing the Middle Ages in play, and this can be very successful, the absent present cannot be expected to be identical to what medieval spectators experienced.[38]

4   The Shape of Salvation History

But it is necessary to look further at the pageants as an aggregate, to see that the invocation of the "honour and reverence of our Lord Jesus Christ" in the official record in fact suggests further a powerful dynamic in the cycle within

---

37   Danièle Hervieu-Léger, *Religion as a Chain of Memory*, trans. Simon Lee (New Brunswick, NJ: Rutgers University Press, 2000), 87.

38   This is not at all to denigrate modern performance, and I agree that it is important in performing medieval drama not to fall into the mistake of creating an imitation of an imitation, a complaint that was directed by Hans-Georg Gadamer and others at the performance practice of early music during the beginning years of the revival; see Gadamer's *Truth and Method* (London: Sheed and Ward, 1975; rpt. New York: Seabury Press, n.d.), 107. Many, including myself, saw the 1998 production of the York plays at Toronto as an absolutely thrilling experience, but even for modern Christians it was in fact the perception of medievalism – that is, of 'heritage' – that sometimes stood between them and religious experience.

which salvation history is shown. The incarnate Christ is indeed at the centre, the plays concerning his life forming the exact emotional and theological centre. A movement that draws the viewer to that centre is revealed – a centre at which there resides a remedy for the fractured condition of humanity. The rich Old Testament pageants, effective drama in themselves as they call to memory the events from mythical and early Jewish ages of history, are chosen because they are forward looking. The Glovers' play of the killing of Abel by Cain, albeit incomplete in the Register, reports a terrible and long-lasting effect of the Fall that comes into history, but because memory of the death of Abel is also connected with sacrifice it looks forward to the sacrifice which is the death of Jesus on the cross at the historical centre of time. Then, the pageants of the Flood anticipate not only the centre but the end, when the ship which is the Church will have deposited the faithful in safety. Quite significantly, the Fishers and Mariners' pageant of the Flood concludes with Noah's explanation that eventually the earth shall "be waste with fyre || And never worþe to world agayne," but only hundreds of years in the future (9.301–02, 307–08). In the Parchmentmakers and Bookbinders' play, Abraham's willingness to sacrifice Isaac at God's command is a commitment from which he is released by the appearance of the angel who calls out for him to spare his son and substitute "a schepe [for] thy offerand" (10.303–04), foreshadowing the *Agnus Dei*, the substitute who is the Son of God. Finally, the Hosiers' *Exodus*, which has a strong presence in the Lenten liturgy, foreshadows the *Harrowing of Hell* (play 37). In this pageant as in the visual arts, Anima Christi rescues the souls of the predeceased righteous from the hellmouth. The pattern established in the cycle should now be more clear: after only eleven of the forty-seven plays, the cycle already approaches the core events toward which the frame directs the spectators. These events will exist at the dividing line, the mid-point of history, which introduces the New Age.[39] It is the point at which God has come into time.

The Annunciation dramatised in the next pageant, by the Spicers, is intended to call to mind the Incarnation, believed to be effected at the very time that the angel Gabriel announces to Mary that she will be the Mother of God, a role affirmed by the Council of Ephesus in 431 A.D. In the Bolton Hours (York Minster Library, MS. Add. 2, fol. 35v), Gabriel kneels, holding a scroll containing "Ave Maria gratia plena" while rays from heaven carrying a

---

39   See Oscar Cullmann, *Christ and Time: The Primitive Christian Conception of Time and History*, trans. Floyd V. Filson (Philadelphia: Westminster Press, 1964), 81–93. St. Augustine saw the present age, comparable to old age in the life of a human, as extending from the Advent of the Lord until the end of time; see Elizabeth Sears, *The Ages of Man: Medieval Interpretations of the Life Cycle* (Princeton, NJ: Princeton University Press, 1986), 58.

dove and a small soul like a small child come down toward her. In painted glass in a window of c. 1420 given by Archbishop Henry Bowet in the choir of York Minster, the lily which separates the Virgin and Gabriel contains a crucifix, a reminder that the Annunciation already implies the Crucifixion, believed to have occurred on the same day of the year, March 25.[40] With the Pewterers and Founders' *Joseph's Trouble about Mary* (play 13), based on only two verses in Matthew's gospel (1:19–20) and the much expanded account in the apocryphal *Protoevangelion* as well as the *Meditations on the Life of Christ*, the story of the Nativity and early life of Jesus continues, again often depending on such extra-biblical sources. For the moment of the birth itself in the Tilethatchers pageant, the author is indebted to the account in the *Revelations* of St. Birgitta, whose vision of the arrival of the baby Jesus, which omitted the midwives of the Byzantine iconography and the account in the *Protevangelium*,[41] provided a highly theatrical episode of Mary, alone, experiencing the birth without pain as she kneels in a prayerful posture.[42] As a central point of doctrine from which to deviate was considered heretical, the Child thus born is affirmed to be both divine and human, "our brother," as St. Anselm insisted in *Cur Deus Homo*, perfect and without sin and so prepared to serve as a sacrifice without blemish for sin-stained human beings.

The Nativity plays continue for another five pageants[43] before the episode, lively and terrifying, of the *Slaughter of the Innocents* (play 19), with only the pageant of Spurriers and Lorimers' *Christ and the Doctors* following before coming to Jesus' adulthood and initiation to his ministry in the Barbers' *Baptism* (play 21). The latter is a dramatization ostensibly of the gospel lesson for the first Sunday after the octave of Epiphany but with reliance on such sources as the *Lay Folks Catechism* (1357), the handbook prepared by order of Archbishop Thoresby of York and containing matter that every Christian was obliged to learn and remember for his or her salvation. In the Baptism pageant, the Holy Spirit having descended upon Jesus, he will accept his role as the one

---

40 Davidson and O'Connor, *York Art*, 39–40; cf. W.L. Hildburgh, "An Alabaster Table of the Annunciation with the Crucifix," *Archaeologia* 74 (1923–24): 203–34.

41 *The Apocryphal New Testament: Being the Apocryphal Gospels, Acts, Epistles and Apocalypses*, trans. Montague Rhodes James (Oxford; Clarendon Press, 1924; rpt. 1980), 47; one midwife is mentioned, named Salome, but iconography later tended to adopt two, as in the Master of Flémalle's Dijon Nativity; see J.W. Robinson, *Studies in Fifteenth-Century Stagecraft* (Kalamazoo, MI: Medieval Institute Publications, 1991), fig. 1.

42 Birgitta of Sweden, *Life and Selected Revelations*, ed. Marguerite Tjader Harris, trans. Albert Ryle Kezel (New York: Paulist Press, 1990), 202–04.

43 Of these, the Hatmakers, Masons, and Labourers' *Purification* (play 17) was added to the Register at a later date.

who will defeat the "dragons poure" and save "mankynde, saule and body, || Fro endles payne" (21.157–61).[44] This he will indeed already begin to accomplish in the next pageant, the Smiths' *Temptation*, when he has a direct confrontation with the Devil, whom he will order to the "pyne of helle" (22.159). The scene shows a crucial testing of the Saviour's resolve in preparation for his final struggle on the cross. In the Register, the Ministry series that follows is short, omitting the formerly extant *Marriage at Cana and the Feast at Simon's House*, but including the Curriers' *Transfiguration* (play 23), the Cappers' *Woman Taken in Adultery* (based on a post-Patristic addition to the canonical text of the Bible) and *The Raising of Lazarus* (play 24), the latter a story appearing in the lectionary as a Lenten lesson but foreshadowing the Resurrection of Christ.

Only the Skinners' *Entry into Jerusalem* (play 25) with its triumphant singing of *Osanna [to] þe sone of Dauid*, unnamed in this pageant but identified subsequently (30.343),[45] now remains before the core episodes of salvation history are advanced, many of the pageants of the Passion dramatizing the utmost cruelty of treatment of Jesus so that, in the words of Nicholas Love, by the time he had arrived at the cross on Golgotha, his appearance was consistent with the prophecy in Isaiah 53:4: "*þere was none semlynesse nor beuty in hym, and we helde him as foule as a leprose manne þat were smitene do[w]ne and made lowe of God*."[46] For a comparison, albeit extreme, we may think of the horrific depictions of the crucified Saviour and Burial in the Isenheim Altarpiece, painted by Matthias Grünewald, where Jesus is shown in death, wounded over every inch of his body.[47] Such representations were at the heart of late medieval mystical experience, and worshippers were advised to keep all of the Passion in memory, not only the crucifixion on the cross but also all the events commemorating Jesus' arrest and torture. Nicholas Love indeed insisted on the necessity for one's salvation of meditating on these events, "makyng hym self as present in alle þat befelle aboute þat passion and crucifixione" with "gostly gladnes."[48]

In the York cycle, the extended block of eleven plays divides the Passion into discreet episodes, the Register at one time including the dramatisation of the

---

44 King, *York Mystery Cycle*, 42 43, 170–73.
45 See Richard Rastall, *The Heaven Singing*, Music in Early English Religious Drama, 1 (Cambridge: D.S. Brewer, 1996), 34–35.
46 Nicholas Love, *Mirror of the Blessed Life of Jesus Christ: A Critical Edition Based on Cambridge University Library Additional MSS 6578 and 6686*, ed. Michael G. Sargent (New York: Garland, 1992), 171.
47 See Andrée Hayum, *The Isenheim Altarpiece: God's Medicine and the Painter's Vision* (Princeton: Princeton University Press, 1989), pl. 7, and passim for further illustrations and commentary.
48 Love, *Mirror*, 162.

establishment of the Eucharist. However, the Bakers' *Last Supper* (play 27) is incomplete due to the loss of a leaf (following fol. 132 in the manuscript), an unfortunate occurrence since representation of the consecration of communion bread and wine, however it was done, would have been critical.[49] This would have involved the institution of an action which is central to the obligatory Christian experience of remembering commanded in Luke 22:19 ("This is my body, which is given for you. Do this for a commemoration of me") and in virtually identical words in 1 Corinthians 11:24. Memory was embedded in the Eucharistic rite in a symbolic re-enactment of the sacrifice of Jesus (*anamnesis*), a rite believed to be participation in the reality of the event itself, as had been taught by the Church Fathers.[50] Sometimes after the consecration the celebrant mimicked the outstretched arms of the victim on the cross.[51] Such remembering erased linear time, made the absent present, and indeed even further offered an entry into sacred time, in which temporality, the then and the now, exists as if contemporary for the participant.[52] Paradoxically, sacred time is all-inclusive, taking into itself all temporal time, as we have seen, making even the last days of history to be present, again an absent present in which the events of the end time participate as well as the first. Hence, in the Eucharist, participants are able to have a foretaste of the heavenly banquet promised to the faithful.[53] But a play, however ritualistic and religious, is not the Mass, and any depiction of the rite must be seen as a "representation of a representation,"[54] not a sacramental remembering.

The Cutlers' *Conspiracy* (play 26) and the other pageants that follow[55] move the action closer and closer to the direct showing of the Trials and the Crucifixion in a full display of the bullying of officialdom and its brutality.[56]

49 One possibility is that the leaf might have been removed before the text was turned over to the Archbishop for inspection to keep the authorities from seeing an exposition of the Catholic view of the Eucharist that had been suppressed under Protestantism.
50 See J.R. Halliburton, "The Patristic Theology of the Eucharist," in *The Study of Liturgy*, ed. Cheslyn Jones, Geoffrey Wainwright and Edward Yarnold (London: SPCK, 1978), 205–09.
51 Josef A. Jungmann, *The Mass of the Roman Rite: Its Origins and Development* (*Missarum Sollemnia*), 2 vols., trans. Francis A. Brunner (New York: Benzinger, 1951–55; rpt. Westminster, MD: Christian Classics, 1986), 1: 142.
52 Halliburton, "Patristic Theology," 206.
53 Jean Daniélou, *The Bible and the Liturgy* (Notre Dame, IN: University of Notre Dame Press, 1966), 129.
54 For this terminology I am indebted to Gadamer, *Truth and Method*, 107.
55 The episode of driving the moneychangers from the Temple courtyard is omitted.
56 See Clifford Davidson and Sheila White, "Bullying in York's Plays: A Psycho-Social Perspective," in Davidson, *Corpus Christi Plays at York: A Context*, 189–209.

These events are meant to mark themselves on the memories of viewers indelibly, all the more powerfully because they could hear *and see* them. In the common understanding of the sense of sight inherited from Greek philosophy, they could experience these events as *touch* through direct contact of the eyes, whereupon the images were received and imprinted as if on the wax tablets of the memory,[57] and indeed, all the more forcefully surely because in the case of plays the scenes were repeated nearly every year. Furthermore, since originality in production was evidently not an issue, many of the scenes were in this regard strengthened by familiarity with depictions in the visual arts and vice versa. For example, representations of both the Agony and the Betrayal still exist in extant glass in York Minster and parish churches, and there is evidence of more such images that have been lost. Still, in regard to the significance of depictions such as the Arrest in the glass from the (now closed) church of St. Martin-cum-Gregory (showing the kiss of Judas at the centre but also the figure of Malcus, whose ear has been cut off by Peter, who is sheathing his sword), this is only a single dramatic moment. It is not the lively scene brought to life in the Cordwainer's pageant (play 28), for which its text depended on a variety of other sources to create a vivid picture of the event. The pageant, as no image in painted glass could do, is able to provide a narrative account far more explicable and memorable *as story* to the lay person unable to comprehend the Latin of the Holy Week lessons of the lectionary.

The "tournament" that Jesus has announced he must endure in the Cordwainers' play (28.90)[58] is elaborated at considerable length in the following pageants from the relatively brief biblical accounts in the Holy Week gospel lessons. Its most remarkable feature is the depiction of Jesus as an isolated and silent centre of the frenetic activity and speech of his enemies,[59] both Jewish and Roman, throughout the Trial pageants. This continued further to the cross and his gasping of the words, borrowed from Psalm 30:6 (AV: 31:5), commending his "spirite" into his Father's hands, "*in manus tuas*" (36.259–61). As one who

---

57   Francis Yates, *The Art of Memory* (Chicago: University of Chicago Press, 1966), 33–37, citing Aristotle, Plato, et al.; Davidson, *Corpus Christi Plays at York: A Context*, 37–40; Mary Carruthers, *The Book of Memory: A Study of Memory in Medieval Culture* (Cambridge: Cambridge University Press, 1990), passim; Bob Scribner, "Popular Piety and Modes of Visual Perception in Late-Medieval and Reformation Germany," *Journal of Religious History* 15 (1989): 448–69.

58   See the discussion of the tournament metaphor in Rosemary Woolf, "The Theme of Christ the Lover-Knight in Medieval English Literature," *Review of English Studies* n.s. 13 (1962): 1–16.

59   This important motif is discussed in Alexandra F. Johnston, "'His language is lorne': The Silent Centre of the York Cycle," *Early Theatre* 3 (2000): 185–95.

would ultimately be the *Christus victor* he is remarkably passive, for he does not meet violence and bullying with aggression. Nicholas Love explained that "his wil was to suffre þe hardest deþ and most soroufal peynes, for þe redempcion of mankynde."[60] He has become throughout, as in the *Meditations* and in Love's *Mirror of the Blessed Life*, a supreme example of a holy victim, indeed the holiest, sacred beyond the martyrdom endured by the saints, some of whom, like St. Erasmus or St. Lawrence, gruesomely had their bodies invaded in a deadly game performed by their torturers. Jesus' blood is itself salvific, and the desired audience reaction was sympathy, not engagement with his enemies' acts.[61]

Much has been made of empathy neurons and their function in spectators' viewing of the theatrical scene, but research has shown that response is determined by one's pre-existing attitude, for example, to a character under torture. Empathy with Nazi soldiers who victimize Jews and others during the Holocaust is absolutely taboo, considered by most to be a sign of a very unhealthy mind. A sympathetic character such as a saint and martyr, or especially Jesus, suffering for the sins of all people, could not, we might add, be played in a carnivalistic reversal demanding empathy for the 'wrong side'. Jesus' blood in particular was venerated, specimens of it when acquired highly valued as relics, as at Hayles Abbey and Bruges, the latter a city that would have been familiar to traders from York who had a presence in that location in the Low Countries.[62] Even depictions of the wounded heart, feet, and hands, or individual drops, were the focus of pious meditation and prayer involving requests to be merged in spirit with the victim, to feel what he felt. Indeed, as Nicholas Love advised in his *Blessed Life*, one should feel what Jesus felt in his Passion: "haue trewe ymaginacion and inwarde compassion of þe peynes and þe passion [suffering] of Oure Lorde Jesu verry God and man. ..."[63] Thus *remembering* the Passion, even shedding tears while watching such pageants as if present in person at the events, is verified by the *Tretise of Miraclis Pleyinge*, albeit the

---

60   Love, *Mirror*, 161.
61   See my chapter, "Sacred Blood and the Late Medieval Stage," in Clifford Davidson, *History, Religion, and Violence: Cultural Contexts for Medieval and Renaissance Drama*, Variorum Collected Studies Series (Aldershot: Ashgate, 2002), 124–48.
62   For information concerning the York-Bruges connection I am indebted to James Murray. The cult of the *Heilig Bloed* at Bruges continues to this day, along with an annual procession. Veneration of the Holy Blood at Hayles Abbey was suppressed at the Reformation. This relic is discussed by Nicholas Vincent, *The Holy Blood: King Henry III and the Westminster Blood Relic* (Cambridge: Cambridge University Press, 2001), 137–50.
63   Love, *Mirror*, 161.

authors of this work did not approve of religious drama.[64] The plays leading up to and including the Crucifixion inhabit the centre of the story and of the York Corpus Christi cycle – indeed, plays that dramatise events at the centre of history – undoubtedly would have received the most intense attention of all by members of the audience. Within the frame established in the York drama cycle, encompassing the beginning and the end of history, this is the part of the story that mattered most, that was required most to be imprinted in the spectators' memories, retrieved by the imagination, and meditated upon.[65] But of course this is not the full story, since audience reaction was certainly not uniform. Those watching the scene were *bystanders*, in some sense therefore complicit in the deeds of torture, bullying, and desecration being committed by the actors. They are witnesses to the subversion of legitimate boundaries. Bystanders were after all necessary participants in this action and hence were involved in a level of engagement with the perpetrators of violence, who are shown on stage (remembering the description in the Passion psalm) as like the roaring bulls, lions, and the "many dogs" that "encompassed" the sacred person of Jesus (Psalm 21:13–14, 17, 22; *AV*: 22).[66]

The specificity of detail in the delineation of the Passion of Jesus in the York plays, extending beyond the canonical writings, is indicative of the richness of textual traditions that ultimately derive from many sources, as for example the detail of being pulled apart by ropes intended to attach him to the cross so that "all his synnous go asoundre" in the Pinners' *Crucifixio Christi* (35.132). This again echoes Psalm 21 (*AV*: 22), the Passion psalm, recited each year as part of the Holy Week liturgy, but the use of ropes was also an abiding tradition that would be remembered and passed on by the *Meditations*.[67] Ropes in fact had already been mentioned in the mid-fourth century by Hilary of

---

64 *A Tretise of Miraclis Pleyinge*, ed. Clifford Davidson (Kalamazoo, MI: Medieval Institute Publications, 1993, rev. rpt. 2011), 102.

65 For a useful discussion, see the chapter "The Aesthetics of Suffering: Figuring the Crucified Jesus in Manuscripts and Wall Paintings," in Ellen M. Ross, *The Grief of God: Images of the Suffering Jesus in Late Medieval England* (Oxford: Oxford University Press, 1997), 41–94.

66 See especially the discussion in Davidson and White, "Bullying in York's Plays," 199–207, and also Jill Stevenson's very useful comments in "Embodied Enchantments: Cognitive Theory and the York Mystery Plays," in Rogerson, *York Mystery Plays*, 91–112, though her article does not in my view treat all the deeper cultural and psychological structures of complicity and guilt involved.

67 *Meditations on the Life of Christ: An Illustrated Manuscript of the Fourteenth Century, Paris, Bibliothèque Nationale Ms. Ital. 115*, trans. and ed. Isa Ragusa and Rosalie B. Green (Princeton, NJ: Princeton University Press, 1961; rpt. 1977), 333–34.

Poitiers, as F.P. Pickering has noted.[68] Details such as this added substantially to the plain story and would remain in memory for centuries. Indeed, many such oral and written accounts of the Christian story that had circulated in the early centuries of the Church were never forgotten, none more visibly, perhaps, than the apocryphal *Gospel of Nicodemus*, which would provide a narrative for the Saddlers' *Harrowing of Hell* (play 37). From a single verse in 1 Peter, stating that Jesus had preached "to those spirits that were in prison" (3:19), and augmented by prophetic passages in Isaiah and Psalm 23 (AV: 22), speculation was enabled to fill in the missing story of events between the Crucifixion and the Resurrection. The *Descensus ad Inferos*, with its story of the rescue of souls of the righteous from Limbo in a defeat for the devil, was well accepted, and was in fact acknowledged in two antiphons in the Holy Saturday liturgy in the York Breviary.[69] The Harrowing was considered important, an elaboration of the "He descended into hell" clause of the Apostles' Creed,[70] but additionally comforting in providing circumstantial support for the doctrine of Purgatory. The Creed was of course an article of faith, obligatory for all Christians to have in memory as part of the basic knowledge demanded of them by the *Lay Folks' Catechism*. As an inscription on a fourteenth-century font at Bradley, Lincolnshire, explains, the essentials were three: "Pater Noster, Ave Maria, Creide || Lernen þe childe yt is nede."[71]

5   The Concluding Pageants of the Cycle

In the Carpenters' *Resurrection* (play 38), the triumph of Christ is complete, the basis for the most important feast of the Christian year, Easter, in which his rising from the tomb is remembered and commemorated. Since no text accompanies the actual rising from the tomb in the pageant and a misleading rubric concerning music has been a cause of confusion, the manner of understanding the scene has been the subject of some discussion. Was there

---

68   F.P. Pickering, *Literature and Art in the Middle Ages* (Coral Gables, FL: University of Miami Press, 1970), 244, and for Gerard David's painting of the Nailing to the Cross with the cross on the ground, ibid., fig. 24.

69   King, *York Mystery Cycle*, 157–58.

70   The clause seems to have appeared initially in fourth-century Arian creeds, then gradually spread to the Western Church; see "Descent of Christ into Hell," in *The Oxford Dictionary of the Christian Church*, eds. F.L. Cross and E.A. Livingstone (Oxford: Oxford University Press, 1997 [3rd. ed.]), 472. It is also found in the Athanasian Creed.

71   Francis Bond, *Fonts and Font Covers* (London: H. Frowde, 1908), 113; also cited by Duffy, *Stripping of the Altars*, 53.

a "great earthquake" when the stone was removed from the tomb, as had been indicated in Matthew 28:2? Music, almost certainly the traditional *Christus resurgens* ("Christ having risen from the dead," etc.), seems what is indicated by a later rubric.[72] But the fact that Jesus' rising is unseen by the witnesses, the holy women, who only are able to take the word of the angel and accept as evidence the empty tomb, is a reminder that the Resurrection event had long been contentious, among pagans a source of disbelief and among some early Christians a matter of fierce debate.[73] Elaine Pagels, in her survey of the controversy concerning Christ's rising from the dead, cites Origen's complaint in his commentary on 1 Corinthians excoriating those who object that having belief in the Resurrection is a "faith of fools."[74] But by the late thirteenth century the *Northern Passion* reports that a blessing will be granted to the person who hears or reads the Passion and Resurrection narratives, and that for so doing he will receive a hundred days of pardon in Purgatory.[75] Easter indeed ushers in a new age, believed to be the age when salvation has become available to all who will believe and act accordingly. But it is also a period of senectitude, when the world has fallen into old age.[76] At the end of this age all history will collapse into the eternal present, when time shall be no more.

The cycle now takes up the Appearances of the Resurrected Christ (plays 39–41), beginning with the *Hortulanus* scene, presented by the Winedrawers – a scene of *mis-recognition*, then recognition, at first mistaking the Resurrected Christ for a gardener – followed by the attractive Woolpackers and Woolbrokers' *Travelers to Emmaus*, also identified as *Apparicio Christi peregrinus* in an early list of the pageants, and the Scriveners' *Doubting Thomas*. The latter, the only play that also exists in a separate copy apart from the Register,[77] is based on the Gospel lesson for the first Sunday after Easter (John 20:31). Here Jesus appears with wounds still bleeding (41.175), and Thomas has the honour to touch his "blessid blode" (l. 184). These are plays designed to confirm the bodily resurrection of Jesus for remembering by Christians, for it is proof that, since his blood

---

72 Rastall, *Heaven Singing*, 189.
73 Samuel Byrskog, *Story as History – History as Story: The Gospel Tradition in the Context of Ancient Oral History* (Tübingen: Mohr Siebeck, 2000; rpt. Leiden: Brill, 2002), 75, 79, comments on the lack of credibility of women, who may also have been present at the Trial of Jesus but, except for Mary Magdalen, were removed from the story in written texts.
74 Pagels, *Gnostic Gospels*, 11.
75 *The Northern Passion*, ed. Frances A. Foster, vol. 1: *The Parallel Texts*, EETS o.s. 145 (London: Oxford University Press, 1913; rpt. Millwood, NY: Kraus, 1971), 249.
76 Cf. the chapter on the "Ages of History," in Sears, *Ages of Man*, 54–58.
77 "The Sykes MS of the York Scriveners' Play," ed. A.C. Cawley, *Leeds Studies in English* 7–8 (1952): 45–80. The manuscript is in the York City Archives.

is still wet and not coagulated, he retains the signs of his life, even after his death on the cross. Now only the *Ascension* and *Pentecost* (plays 42–43) will need to be included in order to finish this group of plays.

The remaining pageants, leading up to the Last Judgement, are concerned with the conclusion of the life of the Virgin Mary (plays 44–46),[78] all of which would be suppressed with England's turn to Protestantism. These are extra-biblical, with sources in tradition, in such works as the *Golden Legend* of Jacobus de Voragine, and apocryphal writings. Their status, while fostering faith in the Son whose incarnation, *agon*, and Resurrection formed the centre of the cycle as the events that also formed the centre of history, was rooted in the veneration of the Virgin. The cult of Mary, which, as Barbara Newman has shown, gave her a favoured position within the holy family, absorbed her into worship, allowing her to be venerated like a goddess, even like a goddess who seems to transform the Trinity into a quaternity, at the Assumption and Coronation even becoming something of a Queen Mother and the sister-bride of the Song of Songs.[79] Newman cites Adam of St. Victor's sequence *Salve mater Salvatoris*, which, reflecting a shrine of the Virgin enclosing the Trinity as if within her womb, refers to her as the "noble banqueting hall of the whole Trinity."[80] She is the Wisdom of the Old Testament, and the goddess of love transformed into its mystical essence; and, as the Mother, her milk, symbol of mercy, will flow until the Last Judgement, the time when her Son's blood will also cease flowing.[81] Her veneration was ubiquitous throughout late medieval Europe, including the city of York. The Coronation of the Virgin was indeed a supremely popular image appearing in the religious art of the city, many examples of which surprisingly survive either in their entirety or in fragments.[82] It is no surprise, then, that the Coronation of the Virgin in the Weavers' *Assumption* (play 45) is an ecstatic and triumphant assertion of her accomplishment as the Mother of God, the facilitator of the work of salvation in time through her own work of motherhood. In the splendid polyphonic choral music for this pag-

---

78　One of these plays, the apparently seldom performed *Funeral of Mary* or "*Fergus*," was not copied into the Register. It was based on the apocryphal *Transitus Beatus Mariae*. See Mark R. Sullivan, "The Missing York Funeral of the Virgin," in *The Dramatic Tradition of the Middle Ages*, ed. Clifford Davidson (New York: AMS Press, 2005), 150–54.

79　Barbara Newman, *God and the Goddesses: Vision, Poetry, and Belief in the Middle Ages* (Philadelphia: University of Philadelphia Press, 2003), 245–90.

80　Ibid., 271, 394–95, quoting *Analecta Hymnica*, 55 vols., ed. Guido Maria Dreves (Leipzig: O.R. Riesland, 1854–1909), 54: 383–84.

81　Newman, *God and the Goddesses*, 275, 396, n. 90 (citing Mechtild of Magdeburg).

82　See the listing in Davidson and O'Connor, *York Art*, 107–10.

eant, requiring young musicians of the greatest skill,[83] she is the "container of life," the Bride of the Song of Songs, now reunited with the Sponsus who is her Son and crowned Queen of Heaven as she has passed out of profane time entirely and entered into sacred space. Onlookers are as if lifted up by the twelve treble voices of the song of angels into the heavenly spheres as witnesses to the crowning of Mary, regarded as friend and intercessor.

So too will the saved be rescued from temporality and taken into eternity in the final pageant of *Doomsday*, though, alas, not for those destined for the other place, where they too will be released from duration, only into a permanent state of punishment. Herein the frame in which the plays are placed is completed, the book of memory closed so far as the pageants were concerned, until the next performance through the streets of York.

Bibliography

Apocryphal New Testament: Being the Apocryphal Gospels, Acts, Epistles and Apocalypses, The, translated by Montague Rhodes James. Oxford: Clarendon Press, 1924; rpt. 1980.

Assmann, Aleida. *Cultural Memory and Western Civilization: Function, Media, Archives*. New York: Cambridge University Press, 2011.

Assmann, Jan. *Cultural Memory and Early Civilization: Writing, Remembrance, and Political Imagination*. New York: Cambridge University Press, 2011.

Augustine, St. *The City of God*, translated by Marcus Dods et al. New York: Modern Library, 1950.

Bagnoli, Martina et al., eds. *Treasures of Heaven: Saints, Relics, and Devotion in Medieval Europe*. London: British Museum Press, 2011.

Beadle, Richard. "Nicholas Lancaster, Richard of Gloucester and the York Corpus Christi Play." In *The York Mystery Plays: Performance in the City*, edited by Margaret Rogerson, 31–52. Woodbridge: York Medieval Press, 2011.

———, ed. *The York Plays: A Critical Edition of the York Corpus Christi Play as Recorded in British Library Additional MS 35290*, 2 vols., EETS s.s. 23–24. Oxford: Oxford University Press, 2009–13.

---

83 There is detailed discussion of the music in Rastall, *Heaven Singing*, 121–37, and see the useful discussion of the *Assumption* by the Master of the St. Lucy legend in the National Gallery, Washington (ibid., 380–81). The folios containing music notation for the songs included in the *Assumption* in the Register are reproduced in colour in *The York Play: A Facsimile of MS Additional 35290, together with a facsimile of the* Ordo Paginarum *Section of the* A/Y Memorandum Book, ed. Richard Beadle and Peter Meredith (Leeds: University of Leeds School of English, 1983).

———, and Peter Meredith, eds. *The York Play: A Facsimile of MS Additional 35290, together with a facsimile of the* Ordo Paginarum *Section of the* A/Y Memorandum Book. Leeds: University of Leeds School of English, 1983.

Birgitta of Sweden. *Life and Selected Revelations*, edited by Marguerite Tjader Harris, translated by Albert Ryle Kezel. New York: Paulist Press, 1990.

Bond, Francis. *Fonts and Font Covers*. London: H. Frowde, 1908.

Brown, Sarah. *York Minster: An Architectural History, c 1220–1500*. Swindon: English Heritage, 2003.

Byrskog, Samuel. *Story as History – History as Story: The Gospel Tradition in the Context of Ancient Oral History*. Tübingen: Mohr Siebeck, 2000; rpt. Leiden: Brill, 2002.

Carruthers, Mary. *The Book of Memory: A Study of Memory in Medieval Culture*. Cambridge: Cambridge University Press, 1990.

Cassirer, Ernst. *The Philosophy of Symbolic Forms*, vol. 1: *Language*, translated by Ralph Manheim. New Haven: Yale University Press, 1953.

Cawley, A.C., ed. "The Sykes MS of the York Scriveners' Play." *Leeds Studies in English* 7–8 (1952): 45–80.

Cullmann, Oscar. *Christ and Time: The Primitive Christian Conception of Time and History*, translated by Floyd V. Filson. Philadelphia: Westminster Press, 1964.

Daniélou, Jean. *The Bible and the Liturgy*. Notre Dame, IN: University of Notre Dame Press, 1966.

Davidson, Clifford. "Positional Symbolism and Medieval English Drama." *Comparative Drama* 25 (1991): 66–76.

———. "Sacred Blood and the Late Medieval Stage." In idem, *History, Religion, and Violence: Cultural Contexts for Medieval and Renaissance Drama*, 124–48. Variorum Collected Studies Series. Aldershot: Ashgate, 2002.

———. *Corpus Christi Plays at York: A Context for Religious Drama*. AMS Studies in Middle English, 30. New York: AMS Press, 2013.

———, ed. *A Tretise of Miraclis Pleyinge*. Kalamazoo, MI: Medieval Institute Publications, 1993 (rev. rpt. 2011).

———, and David E O'Connor. *York Art: A Subject List of Extant and Lost Art, Including Items Relevant to Early Drama*. Kalamazoo, MI: Medieval Institute Publications, 1978, revised as "Early Drama, Art, and Music" website, 2003. Accessed December 7, 2014, <http://scholarworks.wmich.edu/early_drama/4/>.

———, and Sheila White. "Bullying in York's Plays: A Psycho-Social Perspective." In Clifford Davidson, *Corpus Christi Plays at York: A Context for Religious Drama*, 189–209. New York: AMS Press, 2013.

Diller, Hans-Jürgen. "Theological Doctrine and Popular Religion in the Mystery Plays." In *Religion in the Poetry and Drama of the Late Middle Ages in England*, edited by Piero Boitani and Anna Torti, 199–213. Woodbridge: D.S. Brewer, 1990.

Duffy, Eamon. *The Stripping of the Altars: Traditional Religion in England, c. 1400-c. 1580*. New Haven: Yale University Press, 1992.

Eliade, Mircea. *The Sacred and the Profane: The Nature of Religion.* New York: Harcourt and Brace, 1959.

Foster, Frances A., ed. *The Northern Passion*, vol. 1: *The Parallel Texts.* EETS o.s. 145. London: Oxford University Press, 1913: rpt. Millwood: Kraus, 1971.

French, Thomas. *York Minster: The Great East Window.* Corpus vitrearum Medii Aevi, Great Britain, 2. Oxford: Oxford University Press, 1995.

Gadamer, Hans-Georg. *Truth and Method*, translated by Garrett Barden and John Cumming. London: Sheed and Ward, 1975; rpt. New York; Seabury Press, n.d..

Halbwachs, Maurice. *On Collective Memory*, edited and translated by Lewis A. Coser. Chicago: University of Chicago Press, 1992.

Halliburton, J.R. "The Patristic Theology of the Eucharist." In *The Study of Liturgy*, edited by Cheslyn Jones, Geoffrey Wainwright and Edward Yarnold. London: SPCK, 1978.

Happé, Peter. *Cyclic Form and the English Mystery Plays.* Ludus: Medieval and Early Renaissance Theatre and Drama, 7. Amsterdam: Rodopi, 2004.

Hassall, W.O., ed. *The Holkham Bible Picture Book,* with introduction and commentary. London: The Dropmore Press, 1954.

Hayum, Andrée. *The Isenheim Altarpiece: God's Medicine and the Painter's Vision.* Princeton, NJ: Princeton University Press, 1989.

Heidegger, Martin. *Poetry, Language, Thought*, translated by Albert Hofstadter. New York: Harper & Row, 1971; rpt. 1975.

Hervieu-Léger, Danièle. *Religion as a Chain of Memory*, translated by Simon Lee. New Brunswick, NJ: Rutgers University Press, 2000.

Hildburgh, W.L. "An Alabaster Table of the Annunciation with the Crucifix." *Archaeologia* 74 (1923–24): 203–34.

Hulme, William Henry, ed. *The Middle-English Harrowing of Hell and Gospel of Nicodemus.* EETS e.s. 100. London: Oxford University Press, 1907.

Humphreys, K.W., ed. *The Friars' Libraries.* London: British Library, 1990.

Johnston, Alexandra F. "'His language is lorne': The Silent Centre of the York Cycle." *Early Theatre* 3 (2000): 185–95.

———. "*The York Cycle* and the Libraries of York." In *The Church and Learning in Late Medieval Society: Essays in Honour of R.B. Dobson*, edited by Caroline Barron and Jenny Stratford, 355–70. Harlaxton Medieval Studies, 11. Donington: Shaun Tyas, 2002.

———, and Margaret Rogerson, eds. *Records of Early English Drama: York,* 2 vols. Toronto: University of Toronto Press, 1979.

Jungmann, Josef A. *The Mass of the Roman Rite: Its Origins and Development (Missarum Sollemnia)*, translated by Francis A. Brunner, 2 vols. New York: Benzinger, 1951–55; rpt. Westminster, MD: Christian Classics, 1986.

King, Pamela M. *The York Mystery Cycle and the Worship of the City.* Westfield Medieval Studies, 1. Woodbridge: D.S. Brewer, 2006.

Love, Nicholas. *Mirror of the Blessed Life of Jesus Christ: A Critical Edition Based on Cambridge University Library Additional MSS 6578 and 6686*, edited by Michael G. Sargent. New York: Garland, 1992.

Meditations on the Life of Christ: An Illustrated Manuscript of the Fourteenth Century, Paris, Bibliothèque Nationale Ms. Ital. 115, translated and edited by Isa Ragusa and Rosalie B. Green. Princeton: Princeton University Press, 1961; rpt. 1977.

Newman, Barbara. *God and the Goddesses: Vision, Poetry, and Belief in the Middle Ages*. Philadelphia: University of Philadelphia Press, 2003.

Oxford Dictionary of the Christian Church, The, edited by F.L. Cross and E.A. Livingstone. Oxford: Oxford University Press, 1997 [3rd ed.].

Pagels, Elaine. *The Gnostic Gospels*. New York: Random House, 1979.

Palmer, Barbara. *The Early Art of the West Riding of Yorkshire: A Subject List of Extant and Lost Art, Including Items Relevant to Early Drama*. Early Drama, Art and Music Reference Series, 6. Kalamazoo, MI: Medieval Institute Publications, 1990.

Pickering, F.P. *Literature and Art in the Middle Ages*. Coral Gables: University of Miami Press, 1970.

Rastall, Richard. *The Heaven Singing*. Music in Early English Religious Drama, 1. Cambridge: D.S. Brewer, 1996.

Robinson, J.W. *Studies in Fifteenth-Century Stagecraft*. Kalamazoo, MI: Medieval Institute Publications, 1991.

Ross, Ellen M. *The Grief of God: Images of the Suffering Jesus in Late Medieval England*. Oxford: Oxford University Press, 1997.

Rubin, Miri. *Corpus Christi: The Eucharist in Late Medieval Culture*. Cambridge: Cambridge University Press, 1991.

Scribner, Bob. "Popular Piety and Modes of Visual Perception in Late-Medieval and Reformation Germany." *Journal of Religious History* 15 (1989): 448–69.

Sears, Elizabeth. *The Ages of Man: Medieval Interpretations of the Life Cycle*. Princeton: Princeton University Press, 1986.

Stevenson, Jill. "Embodied Enchantments: Cognitive Theory and the York Mystery Plays." In *The York Mystery Plays: Performance in the City*, edited by Margaret Rogerson, 91–112. Woodbridge: York Medieval Press, 2011.

Sullivan, Mark R. "The Missing York Funeral of the Virgin." In *The Dramatic Tradition of the Middle Ages*, edited by Clifford Davidson, 150–54. New York: AMS Press, 2005.

Twycross, Meg. "'Places to hear the play': Pageant Stations at York, 1398–1572." *REED Newsletter* 3:2 (1978): 10–33.

———. "The *Ordo paginarum* Revisited, with Digital a Camera." In *"Bring furth the pagants": Essays in Early English Drama Presented to Alexandra F. Johnston*, edited by David N. Klausner and Karen Sawyer Marsalek, 105–31. Toronto: University of Toronto Press, 2007.

Vincent, Nicholas. *The Holy Blood: King Henry III and the Westminster Blood Relic.* Cambridge: Cambridge University Press, 2001.

White, Eileen. "Places for Hearing the Corpus Christi Play in York." *Medieval English Theatre* 9 (1987): 23–63.

Woolf, Rosemary. "The Theme of Christ the Lover-Knight in Medieval English Literature." *Review of English Studies* n.s. 13 (1962): 1–16.

———. *The English Mystery Plays.* Berkeley: University of California Press, 1972.

Yates, Francis. *The Art of Memory.* Chicago: University of Chicago Press, 1966.

CHAPTER 15

Audience Responses and the York Corpus Christi Play

Margaret Rogerson

Abstract

In arguing for possible reactions to the pageants of the York Corpus Christi Play in the early-fifteenth century, this essay looks at a range of material, not all of it contemporary with the period under consideration. It investigates evidence from sermons and other religious writing, memoirs of spiritually-inspired women, a letter from the year 600 written by Gregory the Great, pictorial narrative in the twelfth-century *St. Albans Psalter*, and civic documents, including records from York relating to two pageants for which no texts survive, *The Hanging of Judas* and *The Funeral of the Virgin (Fergus)*. Much of this material has been examined before by theatre scholars, but consolidated re-examination here allows for further speculation. While it is impossible to define audience reception of theatrical events in any age or any culture with anything approaching precision, this discussion takes into account the social and spiritual nature of the York Play to suggest ways in which the ruling civic authorities and the guilds that had responsibility for the financing and presentation of the pageants may have attempted to shape audience responses to their Play, and in turn, may have shaped their Play in response to perceived audience reactions.

Key words

anti-theatricality – audiences – *imitatio Christi* – laughter – tears – time constraints

1 Introduction

Investigations into the pageants performed in York on Corpus Christi Day and, indeed, discussions of English biblical theatre more generally, are cautious on the topic of original audiences. The past must be ever elusive and the identification of reactions experienced by medieval spectators at such events is fraught with uncertainty. Barbara Newman reminds us of one essential difficulty common to the study of all aspects of the period:

Sacred and secular coexist in our world ... just as they did in the Middle Ages. But for us, the secular is the normative, unmarked default category, while the sacred is the marked, asymmetrical Other. In the Middle Ages it was the reverse.[1]

Allowances can be made for this, but the question remains as to whether anyone living in the twenty-first century can escape the 'default category' entirely, especially in the context of theatre history. Caution must prevail as we attempt to disengage our theatrically-attuned worldview and align our thinking with what we assume was, back then, a more ritually- and devotionally-attuned means of processing the 'theatre' of the York streets. Any conclusions reached through such a study must remain tentative, and the prologue to this essay reiterates some well-known caveats: no single performance of any play is identical to the next; no audience member responds to any performance exactly as any other person present; and, in speculating about audiences in York in the early-fifteenth century, the period on which I focus here, we should be wary of following leads from other places and other times. This said, I propose to take some fairly generous lee-way with the material I present below.

2   Medieval and Modern Audiences

John McKinnell encourages us to trust our instincts as we watch revival productions of biblical theatre, suggesting that we should not "exaggerate the differences between medieval and modern audiences" because "human nature does not alter all that much."[2] Others have advised against exaggerating similarities. Clifford Davidson, commenting on the public display of scenes from the Passion, makes this point firmly:

> audience response to religious drama in the fifteenth and early sixteenth centuries would be difficult if not impossible to replicate today. While the encouragement of strong identification with the suffering Christ in plays of the Passion resulted in the presentation of a character who would appear to be beaten until wounded from his head to his feet, the response

---

1 Barbara Newman, *Medieval Crossover: Reading the Secular against the Sacred* (Notre Dame: University of Notre Dame Press, 2013), viii.
2 John McKinnell, "Modern productions of medieval English drama," in *The Cambridge Companion to Medieval English Theatre*, ed. Richard Beadle and Alan J. Fletcher (Cambridge: Cambridge University Press, 2008 [2nd ed.]), 321.

of a modern audience ... is likely to be one of revulsion rather than sympathy.[3]

Davidson concludes that 'revulsion' was not the expected response "in England and other Northern countries in the late Middle Ages," and complains that twentieth-century productions were nervous about "extensive use of stage blood," resulting in an "anemic presentation of effects" that worked against the texts.[4]

Kerstin Pfeiffer also considers audience reactions to plays on the Passion. Her contention is that although "[a]t first sight, few things would appear more elusive to us than the thoughts and feelings of a fifteenth-century spectator," modern neuro-imaging studies offer "a key ... to the inner lives of historical others watching another person being beaten, scourged, humiliated and crucified on stage."[5] She suggests that the emotions experienced by the soldiers who nail Christ to the cross in the York *Crucifixio Christi* prompt "similar responses in the audience" and that one such response is "laughter."[6] This is a complex situation that Pfeiffer describes as encouraging "the emotional convergence of the audience with the merciless tormentors of Christ," which "ultimately contributes to the spectator's overall emotional experience of the pageant."[7] I return to the issue of possible medieval responses to this pageant later to argue, as Davidson does, that plays that presented scenes of the Passion encouraged audience engagement "on the side of Christ and against his executioners."[8] Further, I suggest that this form of engagement could encourage the practice of *imitatio Christi*.[9]

---

3 Clifford Davidson, "Sacred Blood and the Late Medieval Stage," *Comparative Drama* 31 (1997), 437.
4 Ibid., 439, 441.
5 Kerstin Pfeiffer, "Feeling the Passion: Neuropsychological perspectives on audience response," *Postmedieval: A Journal of Medieval Cultural Studies* 3 (2012): 331.
6 Ibid., 337, 338.
7 Ibid., 338.
8 Davidson, "Sacred Blood," 448.
9 See also Glenn Ehrstine, "Passion Spectatorship between Public and Private Devotion," in *Thresholds of Medieval Visual Culture: Liminal Spaces*, ed. Elina Gertsman and Jill Stevenson (Woodbridge: Boydell & Brewer, 2012), 304, who claims that German medieval Passion plays "allowed the faithful to engage in an inner pilgrimage designed to transform their daily lives in an imitation of Christ" and elicited "*compassio*."

3   Medieval Documentation from York

The establishment view of the York Play promoted by the city's governing elite in the late-fourteenth and early-fifteenth centuries was that the performance on Corpus Christi Day was a devotional act. In 1399, the *A/Y Memorandum Book*, the local council's most formal record of its internal affairs, describes the pageants as being presented *"en honour & reuerence nostreseignour Iesu Crist & honour & profitt de ... la Citee"* (in honour and reverence of our Lord Jesus Christ and for the glory and benefit of ... the city).[10] The nature of the value to York is not precisely delineated, but the connection between *"honour & reuerence,"* the worship of Christ on the feast day, and the *"honour & profitt"* of the city suggests that this value can be interpreted in spiritual terms. Although it did undoubtedly bring commercial advantage to those engaged in the tourist and victualling trades, the implication is that this aspect of the festival was not one that the council sought to emphasise.[11]

In 1422 an even more elaborate description was included in the *Memorandum Book*, again proclaiming the devotional nature of the undertaking:

> *cuius institucio ob magnam deuocionis causam & viciorum extirpacionem morumque reformacionem antiquitus facta.*

[the institution of which was made of old for the important cause of devotion and for the extirpation of vice and reformation of customs].[12]

This is only to be expected of the proud city of York in the early-fifteenth century, when it was a thriving centre of commerce and culture, notable for the piety of its lay people.[13] The official statement in 1422 of the devotional, moral,

---

10   *Records of Early English Drama: York*, 2 vols., ed. Alexandra F. Johnston and Margaret Rogerson (Toronto: University of Toronto Press, 1979), hereafter REED: *York*, 1: 11 (translation 2: 697). A similar description is recorded in 1417, ibid., 1: 28, (translation 2: 697).

11   For medieval drama devised for economic profit see David Mills, "Who are our Customers? The Audience for Chester's Plays," *Medieval English Theatre* 20 (1998): 104–17. Stephen K. Wright, "Religious Drama, Civic Ritual, and the Police: The Semiotics of Public Safety in Late Medieval Germany," *Theatre Annual: A Journal of Performance Studies* 51 (1998): 7, notes that in 1518 the Friedberg bakers asked the civic authorities to forbid "foreign bakers" from bringing bread into the town to sell at the time of a performance of the Corpus Christi Play but that the request was denied "despite the obvious advantages to the baker's guild and to the local economy as a whole."

12   REED: *York*, 1: 37 (translation 2: 722).

13   D.M. Palliser, *Medieval York, 600–1540* (Oxford: Oxford University Press, 2014), 218–20.

and life-changing potential of the Play speaks of the esteem in which the city fathers wished their theatrical undertaking to be held and, to some extent, of the desired responses from the audience. We cannot be certain, however, that all or any of the various audiences for the Play understood it in this way or, themselves, measured up to the council's expectations.

4 Friar Melton in York: A Reliable Eye-Witness?

Four years later, around the time of Corpus Christi in 1426, a Franciscan friar, William Melton, came to York to preach. As Richard Homan has pointed out, Melton's mission was to instruct his hearers in the proper observance of holy days and to persuade them of the need to "expel prostitutes and procurers from the city."[14] Although he came to speak of public morality rather than to offer a critique of the Corpus Christi Play, he was forced to mention it in the course of his sermonizing because of its place in the local observance of the feast honouring the real presence of Christ in the Eucharist, one of the holiest of days in the late-medieval calendar. To maximize his impact, he may have timed his arrival deliberately to coincide with the large influx of people gathering for the festival, which was celebrated on 30 May 1426, just over a week before the record of the friar's visit in the *Memorandum Book*, dated 6 June. What he is reported to have said about the Play is of major interest to theatre scholars, but the official account may be a paraphrase of his comments rather than verbatim quotation. We cannot even be sure that it represents his personal reflections as an eye-witness or simply what he gleaned from others: he may not have seen the Play at all:

> *frater Willelmus melton … famosissimus predicator … in suis sermonibus diuersis ludum … populo commendauit affirmando quod bonus erat in se & laudabilis valde.*

[Brother William Melton … a most famous preacher … has commended the … play to the people in several of his sermons, by affirming that it was good in itself and most laudable.][15]

---

14   Richard L. Homan, "Old and new evidence of the career of William Melton, O.F.M.," *Franciscan Studies* 49 (1989): 29.
15   *REED: York*, 1: 43 (translation 2: 728).

Melton's commendation of the Play as 'good in itself and most laudable' could be interpreted as praise, but perhaps his words of approbation were not as strong as they should have been given the favourable light in which the city fathers presented the enterprise in their record keeping. Rather than applauding the Play, could he be damning it with faint praise? Immediately following these words, there is a telling *"tamen"* (nevertheless) and a list of complaints against some less salubrious aspects of the festival that foreground the friar's interest both in promoting the proper observance of holy days and upright behaviour in general:

> tamen ... ciues predicte ciuitatis & alij forinseci in dicto festo confulentes ad eandem non solum ipsi ludo ... verum eciam comessacionibus ebrietatibus clamoribus cantilenis & alijs insolencijs multum intendunt seruicio diuino officij ipsius diei minime intendentes & quod dolendum est ea de causa amittunt indulgencias in ea parte per felicis recordacionis vrbanum papam quartum graciose concessas.

[nevertheless ... *the citizens of the aforesaid city and the other foreigners* coming in to it during the said festival, *attend not only to the play* ... but also greatly to *feastings, drunkenness, clamours, gossipings, and other wantonness*, engaging *the least in the divine service of the office* of that day and that, alas, for that cause, they *lose the indulgences* granted to them in that matter by Pope Urban IV of happy memory (my emphasis).]

But Melton had a simple remedy in mind for this parlous situation of lax morality and poor church attendance. In 1426, the Play followed hard on the heels of a religious procession on the festival day, both activities being organized under the auspices of the city council;[16] the friar's practical suggestion was that the procession alone should grace the feast, while the Play could be presented separately on another occasion. He was hoping, perhaps, that the solemn liturgical practice of the procession, involving members of the Corpus Christi Guild as well as representatives of the civic hierarchy and of some of the trading guilds, would draw the citizens and visitors to York in its wake, taking them off the streets and into the churches, short-circuiting the urge to

---

16   For discussion of Corpus Christi processions in York see Douglas Cowling, "The Liturgical Celebration of Corpus Christi in Medieval York," *Records of Early English Drama Newsletter* 1.2 (1976): 5–9, and Erik Paul Weissengruber, "The Corpus Christi Procession in Medieval York: A Symbolic Struggle in Public Space," *Theatre Survey* 38 (1997): 117–38.

commit the enormities he had noted, and opening up opportunities for them to avail themselves of the indulgences on offer.[17]

We might be tempted to read what follows the 'nevertheless' in the 1426 record as Melton's subtle reclassification of the Play as evil, despite being 'good in itself', a community activity tainted by association with wanton behaviour that is clearly not consistent with the description of its purpose in the 1422 document cited above. Although there is nothing in the 1426 *Memorandum Book* entry to confirm that it is specifically the Play that drives people to the excesses Melton objects to, Pfeiffer appears to read it as such, interpreting the tendency of playgoers to indulge in such activities as "[i]nappropriate audience response."[18] Similarly Hans-Jürgen Diller congratulates the York council on being "quite capable of assessing the mass psychological consequences of a theatrical performance" in their apparent acquiescence to Melton's demands.[19] As it happens, however, despite the fact that, at the time, the civic officers solemnly agreed to move the performance to the Wednesday immediately before the Thursday of Corpus Christi Day, the preacher's advice actually went unheeded. It was not until 1476 that the Play and the procession were separated and then it was the procession that was moved (to the Friday after the feast), while the Play remained the sole civic marker of the holy day.[20] Either the council only pretended to submit to Melton's criticism in early June 1426 or they thought better of their decision later when he and his stern influence had left the city. Perhaps they knew their Play best and were convinced that, with efficient handling of the performance, the capacity for promoting 'devotion …

---

17   For discussion of indulgences for attendance at the office and for participation in the Corpus Christi procession see Miri Rubin, *Corpus Christi: The Eucharist in Late Medieval Culture* (Cambridge: Cambridge University Press, 1991), 211–12. R.N. Swanson, *Indulgences in the Pre-Reformation Diocese of York* (York: Borthwick Institute, 2011), 18, notes that in 1453 members of the York Guild of Corpus Christi were granted an indulgence of forty days by William Booth (Archbishop of York, 1452–64) for taking part in the Corpus Christi procession. Wright, "Religious Drama," 6, comments that just over ten thousand indulgences were sold to spectators in 1502 at a performance of a Passion Play at Calw in the Black Forrest. For indulgences granted to playgoers in Chester see Margaret Rogerson, "Affective Piety: A 'Method' for Medieval Actors in the Chester Cycle," in *The Chester Cycle in Context, 1555–1575: Religion, Drama, and the Impact of Change*, ed. Jessica Dell, David Klausner, and Helen Ostovich (Farnham: Ashgate, 2012), 100–01.

18   Pfeiffer, "Feeling the Passion," 333.

19   Hans-Jürgen Diller, "Laughter in Medieval English Drama: A Critique of Modernizing and Historical Analyses," *Comparative Drama* 36 (2002): 5.

20   See Alexandra F. Johnston, "The Procession and Play of Corpus Christi in York after 1426," *Leeds Studies in English* n.s. 7 (1973–74): 55–62.

the extirpation of vice and reformation of customs' as recorded in 1422 outweighed the dangers implied by Melton.

There was always a danger of unruly behaviour at the York Play. This is clear from the 1415 Proclamation that was read on the eve of the festival, but although this document is headed "Proclamacio *ludi* corporis Christi" (my emphasis) in the *Memorandum Book*, its warnings against disruption are applied equally to the "kynges pees & þe play" and to "þe processioun."[21] It appears that the danger was that unauthorized persons might come into the city with weapons and that public order could be compromised, not caused directly by the Play, but something that could attend any unusually large gathering of people.[22]

5 Medieval Documentation from Chester

Melton is not the only medieval preacher to have spoken against biblical plays. His complaints, although considerably less aggressive, are similar to the considerably later and much more pointed criticism of Christopher Goodman and other Protestant preachers who were campaigning against the Whitsun Plays in Chester in 1571–72:

> we (i.e. the citizens of Chester) should rather prepare us to humble our hearts with true repentance earnest prayers & fasting, than to attend upon vanities, to solace our selves ... with feasting, infecting of friends & strangers with vain & superstitious plays.[23]

Theatrical events are classified unequivocally here with other forms of wanton behaviour; plays are not for a moment to be considered as 'good in themselves'. In a draft letter to the mayor, John Savage, in 1574–75, Goodman expanded on the evils of the Chester Play, commenting that the recent loss of a ship, *The Bear*, should provoke public mourning, fasting and prayer instead of "feastiuite interteninge of frendes & vaine plays."[24] He argues that plays should be allowed

---

21 REED: *York*, 1: 24.
22 Wright, "Religious Drama," 3–6, discusses this issue in relation to German plays.
23 *Records of Early English Drama: Cheshire, Including Chester*, ed. Elizabeth Baldwin, Lawrence M. Clopper, and David Mills, 2 vols. (Toronto: University of Toronto Press, 2007), 1: 145.
24 Ibid., 1: 169. Goodman did not send the letter but spoke privately with the mayor before the performance took place and afterwards "prached against the plays" (ibid., 1: 170).

only if an impossible set of conditions was met. If the city was not beset by calamities and if all public works were completed, and, further,

> [y]f wickednes & sin were suppressed, & disolute persons broght to good order. Yf the Citie were so hable to cast away so moche monie as by occasion of thes plays wilbe vainely wasted, or elles coulde not bestow it better: than myght you seme to haue som pretence & leasure to play.[25]

The theme of excess, waste, vanity, and sin, is clear in Goodman's fulminations. His rhetoric pretends to offer some openings for the enjoyment of theatrical events, but only to slam the door on them.

6   Anti-theatricality and the *Tretise of Miraclis Pleyinge*

A similar approach is adopted in the early-fifteenth century *Tretise of Miraclis Pleyinge*, where the arguments in favour of biblical plays are put forward as a prelude to their severe demolition. The first of the two clerical authors of this work does not deny that the plays under discussion are recreational, but his point is that they do not constitute a proper or desirable form of recreation to be indulged in on holy days. Rather than attendance at plays, he says, the recreation "men shulden have on the haliday after theire holy contemplacion in the chirche ... shulde ben in the werkis of mercy to his neiebore."[26] Like Melton and Goodman, this author claims that the observance of religious festivals should be marked only by pious reflection, church attendance, and charitable deeds.

The second of the *Tretise* authors also alludes to wasteful expenditure on plays and, like Melton in York in 1426, to bodily excess. In this case, performance is aligned with several of the seven deadly sins:

> miraclis pleyinge is verre wittnesse of mennus *averice* and *coveytise* ... for that that they shulden spendyn upon the nedis of ther negheboris, they spenden upon the pleyis ... and also to han wherof to spenden on thes miraclis and to holden felawschipe of *glotenye* and *lecherie* in siche dayes

---

25   Ibid., 1: 169.
26   *A Tretise of Miraclis Pleyinge*, ed. Clifford Davidson (Kalamazoo, MI: Medieval Institute Publications, 1993), 104.

of miraclis pleyinge, they bisien hem beforn to more gredily bygilen ther neghbors in byinge and in selling (my emphasis).[27]

To echo McKinnell's view noted at the beginning of this essay, 'human nature' has not changed very much between the time that the *Trestise* was written (c. 1380–1425) and the 1570s, when Goodman and his associates took up their fight against the Chester Play. Even though the religious climate had changed dramatically, the opponents of theatrical enterprises are concerned with the same set of ills. And although it would be an exaggeration to align Melton with his near contemporaries, the authors of the *Tretise*, or with Goodman, operating over a century later, his hostility to the York Corpus Christi Play, muted though it may be in comparison, should not go unnoticed, nor should the fact that the good citizens of York refrained from acting on his advice.

7   Tears, the *Tretise*, Margery Kempe, and Angela of Foligno

Two other points made by the *Tretise* are of relevance here. The first is the charge that tears indulged in by spectators at a performance of a biblical play are improper because they are not shed in worship of God or for their own sins or for the sins of their children; they are self-indulgent, outward-looking tears, linked to bodily pleasure and are not to be mistaken as the result of inward-looking spiritual contemplation.[28] The 'famous' preacher, William Melton, who spoke in York in 1426, also had problems with tears, at least with those of Margery Kempe of Lynn, who was, prior to his encounter with her, famous locally for her violent responses to any reminders of the Passion narrative. When he visited the town around 1420,[29] Melton was warned that Margery was likely to have a noisy and tearful response to his performance in the pulpit, and he was advised to suffer it patiently. On the first occasion, when he spoke of the Passion, he tolerated her outbursts, but thereafter he barred Margery from his sermons, saying that she disrupted the proceedings for others. This made him popular with those for whom her behaviour was, indeed, annoying, but when he later preached actively against her, complaining about her conduct, there were others who felt less warmly towards him. The account of this conflict between Margery and Melton is recorded in her autobiography, hence its tenor

---

27   Ibid., 111.
28   Ibid., 102.
29   *The Book of Margery Kempe*, ed. Barry Windeatt (Harlow: Pearson, 2000), 287, dates the visit to *c.* 1420.

is favourable towards her rather than the preacher, in fact, the account of the Melton contretemps leads into a fervent vindication of her copious weeping at the Passion drama that regularly played out in her mind.

Margery Kempe was not the first spiritually intense woman to record violent physical reactions when contemplating the Passion. The thirteenth-century Italian mystic, Angela of Foligno, explains in her *Memorial* that she was similarly afflicted: gazing at paintings of scenes of the Passion would result in fever and sickness so terrible that her supporters, fearing for her health, tried to prevent her seeing such imagery.[30] But as Angela's spiritual progress continues, she exhibits other, perhaps even more alarming, reactions. As Kathleen Kamerick notes, while "[v]ision could provoke bodily fever" in Angela, it "could also spiritually inflame her."[31] This is certainly true of her experience as a spectator at a Passion Play in the piazza of her home town in 1292–93:

> the moment when *it seemed to me one should weep* was transformed for me into a very joyful one, and *I was miraculously drawn into a state of such delight* that when I began to feel the impact of this indescribable experience of God, *I lost the power of speech and fell flat on the ground. I tried to move a little way away from the persons around me*, and I considered it a miracle that I was able to withdraw a little ... It seemed to me that *I had indeed entered at that moment within the side of Christ. All sadness was gone and my joy was so great* that nothing can be said about it (my emphasis).[32]

Angela knows that her behaviour as a member of the audience is out of step with that of those around her. Such contrariety was her frequent practice; Joy Schroeder points out that "under the impact of a eucharistic vision, she stands when the others in the congregation are kneeling" and while other pilgrims are processing, "she faints, collapses, or stands entranced at the sanctuary's threshold."[33] At the play, Angela tries to 'withdraw' from her fellow spectators because she knows that she should react with tears of grief, as we might assume others in the piazza do, but she is filled with great delight because she has

---

30 *Angela of Foligno: Complete Works*, trans. by Paul Lachance (Mahwah, NJ: Paulist Press, 1993), 131.

31 Kathleen Kamerick, "Art and Moral Vision in Angela of Foligno and Margery Kempe," *Mystics Quarterly* 21 (1995): 150.

32 Angela, *Complete* Works, trans. Lachance, 176.

33 Joy Schroeder, "Sacred Space and Sacred Time in the Religious Experience of Angela of Foligno" (PhD thesis, University of Notre Dame, 1999), 33.

become one with Christ, a heightened form of *imitatio Christi* that she has been training herself for over a good many years through the "thirty steps of her mystical ascent."[34] Margery Kempe's tearful anguish in reaction to the Passion, then, extreme though it was, was clearly more normal than Angela's mute and debilitating joy; perhaps further evidence that tears rather than the laughter that is argued by Pfeiffer, were a common and expected response among medieval audiences at plays that presented this central moment of the Christian narrative.

8 Gregory the Great, the *Tretise*, the *St. Albans Psalter*, and *Imitatio Christi*

The second point from the *Tretise* that is relevant to the current discussion is its reference to the defence of painted images by Gregory the Great, who authorized religious painting as a means of facilitating the reading of "the wille of God and his mervelous werkis" by the unlettered:

> sithen it is leveful to han the miraclis of God peintid, why is not as wel leveful to han the miraclis of God pleyed ...? And betere they ben holden in mennes minde and oftere rehersid by the pleyinge of hem than by the peintinge, for this is a deed bok, the tother a quick.[35]

The impact of religious painting, exemplified in exaggerated form by Angela of Foligno, is not to be doubted, and the *Tretise* extends Gregory's appealing metaphor of such art as a 'book' for devotional reading into the even more vibrant metaphor of a religious play as a 'living book' as opposed to the 'lifeless book' of the static image. But, true to form, the *Tretise* author counters this argument. While approving of "peintinge," perhaps in deference to St. Gregory, he dismisses plays even more sternly than he did the self-indulgent tears of their audiences. Plays were definitely sinful books tending to evil, motivated by a desire "to deliten men bodily ... quike bookis to *shrewideness* more than to godenesse" (my emphasis).[36] This clearly delineates the connection between plays and vice that Melton left ambiguous in York in 1426.

Gregory's positive estimation of painted images was expressed in a letter dated to the year 600 and addressed to Serenus, Bishop of Marseilles; this letter

---

34 Angela, *Complete* Works, trans. Lachance, 23.
35 Davidson, *Tretise*, 98.
36 Ibid., 104.

became "the most commonly cited authority on the subject throughout the Middle Ages."[37] One such citation appears in the *St. Albans Psalter*, a work described by Kristen Collins as "one of the most important illuminated manuscripts from twelfth-century Europe."[38] This artefact predates the theatre of the York streets and the "miraclis" under attack in the *Tretise*, but its use of Gregory's defence of images is, nonetheless, instructive. A paraphrase of Gregory's words appears twice, once in Latin and then, immediately afterwards, in Old French, in the St. Alexis Quire "seen by many scholars as the keystone for understanding the book as a whole."[39] Gregory's letter itself has been regarded "as a commentary on the book's pictures,"[40] an impressive array of forty full-page illustrations of events from the Old and New Testaments: the Fall of Adam and Eve, the Expulsion, the Annunciation, the Visitation, eleven scenes from the Nativity through to the Return from Egypt, and twenty-three scenes from the Baptism through to Pentecost (with a strong focus on the Passion). The Alexis miniature, which follows Pentecost and introduces a poem on the life of the saint, is followed by three illustrations of the Emmaus narrative: the meeting with Christ on the road, the supper at Emmaus, and Christ's disappearance. With the exception of the Alexis material, this pictorial narrative bears a considerable likeness to the dramatic narrative in the 'living book' of the York Corpus Christi Play.

Of greater importance here, however, is what the *St. Albans* paraphrase of Gregory's defence of images tells us about the response the Psalter sought to produce in its audience:

> *Aliud est picturam adorare aliud rationem de picturis interroganti per picture historiam quid sit adorandum addiscere. Nam quod legentibus scriptura hoc ignotis prestat pictura qua in ipsa ignorantes vident quid sequi debeant.*

[It is one thing to worship a picture; another to learn, through the story of a picture what is to be worshipped. For the thing that writing conveys to those

---

37 Morgan Powell, "The visual, the visionary and her viewer: media and presence in the Psalter of Christina of Markyate (St Albans Psalter)," *Word and Image* 22 (2006): 340.
38 Kristen Collins, Peter Kidd, and Nancy K. Turner, *The St. Albans Psalter: Painting and Prayer in Medieval England* (Los Angeles: The J. Paul Getty Museum, 2013), 9.
39 Ibid., 36.
40 Ibid., 39.

who read, that is what a picture shows to the illiterate; *in the picture itself those who are ignorant see what they ought to follow* (my emphasis).]⁴¹

Gregory argues that pictures show their readers 'what is to be worshipped' and 'what they ought to follow'. In the context of the Psalter's picture cycle, then, the suggestion is that those who read the pictures should practice *imitatio Christi*, that they should follow the example of the Christ. St. Alexis, whose narrative is recorded in close proximity to the St. Gregory material, like all saints, derived his "sainthood ... entirely from his position as an *imitator Christi*."⁴² This is what is being urged on those who contemplate the pictures of the Psalter; as Collins notes, "twelfth-century picture cycles" were "meant to spark a visual meditative process ... (and) to promote active and audible prayer."⁴³ We can take this further and assume that the ultimate aim with regard to the unlettered was to promote action in the physical life of this world.

It is my contention that a similar form of *imitatio Christi* was being urged on the audiences for the York Corpus Christi Play. Katherine Walker, using medieval theories of optics, has stressed the notion of an "educative devotional gaze" in the Play, "one that involves remembering and reconstructing the events of Christ's Passion."⁴⁴ For Walker, medieval audiences attended the York pageants in a way that was "more than passively witnessing an entertainment or engaging in an act of devotion:" the experience prepared them for "future devotional meditation."⁴⁵ But what the original audiences saw, particularly in the Life and Passion of Christ sequence that formed the bulk of the presentation, was more than a focus for "future devotional meditation," it was an inspiration for subsequent *imitatio Christi* in the conduct of their own lives.

9   A Sermon Exemplum for Good Friday and *Imitatio Christi*

A late-fourteenth century sermon exemplum also presents the argument for *imitatio Christi*, in this case through the metaphor of a performance of a Crucifixion play in which the actor playing Christ provides a model for the

---

41 Based on the transcription and translation of the Latin version of the letter on the *St. Albans Psalter* website (<http://www.abdn.ac.uk/stalbanspsalter/english/>), accessed 17 February 2016.
42 Powell, "The visual," 344.
43 Collins, Kid and Turner, *St. Albans Psalter*, 54.
44 Katherine Walker, "Spectatorship and Vision in *The York Corpus Christi Plays*," *Comitatus* 45 (2014): 171.
45 Ibid., 171, 173.

congregation. Siegfried Wenzel explains that the exemplum "appears in a Good Friday sermon on the *thema* ... 'Christ has suffered for us, leaving you *an example that you may follow in his footsteps*,' 1 Peter 2.21" (my emphasis).[46] Its aim, in line with St. Gregory's comments about the purpose of painted images, was to encourage *imitatio*:

> *Si ergo pendeas cum Christo in cruce et derideraris et tormenta paciaris, quamuis nullus te consoletur nec tecum contristetur et quamuis rideant de tormentis tibi factis, non mireris, ex quo hec facta sunt Christo in cruce pendenti.*

[Therefore, if you hang on the cross with Christ and are mocked and suffer torments, even if no one comforts you and has compassion and people laugh at the torments inflicted on you, you must not be astonished, because these things were done to Christ when he hung on the cross.][47]

When the actor playing Christ determines to abandon the role, complaining that it is too arduous and humiliating, he is told that playing 'Christ's pageant' (*Christi pagyn*)[48] necessarily entails suffering and that this is why so many prefer to play the roles of torturers and devils. He is told that if he continues to imitate Christ, he will be happy at the end of the 'play' when he steps outside the metaphor and finds himself in the company of the blessed at the Last Judgment. The desired reaction on the part of the audience for the sermon is the application of the metaphor to their lives as they follow Christ by practicing *imitatio*.

There is further advice for the auditors of the sermon in a brief comment about the conduct of the spectators at this imaginary play. Wenzel suggests that the exemplum implies that there may have been "some audience participation," basing this speculation on "the tired actor's remark that 'he who could make them (i.e. the devils and the tormentors of Christ) drink and eat was well pleased' – perhaps the audience would offer the players beneath the cross food and drink and urge them on in their taunts."[49] But this reference to audience response is not to be taken literally; it is better interpreted as secondary metaphor within the central metaphor of the playing of Christ's

---

46   Siegfried Wenzel, "'Somer Game' and Sermon References to a Corpus Christi Play," *Modern Philology* 86 (1989): 276.
47   Ibid., 278 (translation, 279).
48   Ibid., 279.
49   Ibid., 282.

pageant. If any member of the audience in the exemplum gave food and drink to the devils and tormentors of Christ, they would, to use a metaphor from a fourteenth-century Wycliffite tract, be playing "a pagyn of þe deuyl," the devil's role being one that entailed "syngynge songis of lecherie, of batailis and of lesyngis, & crie as a wood man & dispise goddis maieste & swere by herte, bonys & alle membris of crist."[50] It is this role that the congregation is being urged to reject.

Just as the sermon audience is directed metaphorically to play the pageant of Christ rather than that of the devil, it is unlikely that a response that aligned the medieval audience with the soldiers would have been encouraged or expected by the presenters of the York *Crucifixio Christi*. Not all spectators at a play on the subject of the Passion will react in the same way, as is evident in the *Memorial* of Angela of Foligno, but if, as I have suggested, tears were regarded as the appropriate reaction in the Middle Ages, it seems unlikely, although not impossible, that many would have responded derisively and disrespectfully towards the actor playing Christ in York. As mentioned above, some scholars, such as Pfeiffer, have argued that in the process of identification with the soldiers in the York pageant, medieval audiences would have laughed at their antics, behaviour that would then trigger contrition as a result of their understanding of their implication in this impious act. Paul Hardwick likewise suggests that "medieval plays frequently attain dramatic gravitas through the juxtaposition of low humour and spiritual insight," citing "the shock with which we find ourselves in sympathetic complicity with the bickering soldiers as they stretch Christ on the cross."[51]

10 Audience Laughter

A number of the texts of the York pageants imply laughter as an expected response, including *Joseph's Trouble about Mary*, where the Virgin's elderly spouse is perplexed by the obvious signs of his wife's condition. Gaëlle Branford sees laughing at Jospeh "as a manifestation of superiority over" him in

---

50   *The English Works of Wyclif Hitherto Unprinted*, ed. F.D. Matthew, EETS o.s. 74 (London: Trübner, 1880), 206. Also quoted in Glending Olson, "Plays as Play: A Medieval Ethical Theory of Performance and the Intellectual Context of the *Tretise of Miraclis Pleyinge*," *Viator* 26 (1995): 212.

51   Paul Hardwick, "Making Light of Devotion: The Pilgrimage Window in York Minster," in *Medieval English Comedy*, ed. Sandra M. Hordis & Paul Hardwick, Profane Arts of the Middle Ages, 3 (Turnhout: Brepols, 2007), 80.

his initial failure to recognise the Virgin's holiness.[52] This laughter can also be construed through "incongruity theory," an eighteenth century interpretation hinging on recognition of "incongruous features of the world" rather than through "superiority theory," which relates to "the motives of the person who laughs."[53] What could be more incongruous to the Middle Ages than Joseph's determined misinterpretation of the Mary's pregnancy?

Hans-Jürgen Diller has pointed out that "[l]aughter about somebody else's misfortunes ... *Schadenfreude* ... even triumphant derision ..., seems to be the intended reaction" to the "terrible fate that awaits the damned" presented in the Last Judgment pageant.[54] Sinners are reaping what they have sewn, their torment and terror as they are condemned to endless pain is just what they deserve. But would medieval spectators laugh at the unjust punishment of Christ or agree with the brutally insensitive soldiers raising the cross in the York *Crucifixio Christi* that he deserved it? If they did, they would be metaphorically playing a pageant of the devil rather than the pageant of Christ. Such a reaction would, surely, have been incongruous in the context of an event that honoured Christ and that was performed as a devotional act on Corpus Christi Day.

11 The Funeral of the Virgin (*Fergus*), Laughter (*Schadenfreude*), Disruption, and the Timing of the Performance

There is one instance in which we know, almost certainly, that medieval audiences in York did laugh at seeing a figure on stage being tormented because the

---

52 Gaëlle Branford, "Laughter in *Joseph's Trouble* (York Cycle): Visual Strategies and Mystical Revelation," in *Tudor Theatre: For laughs (?) / Pour rire (?): Puzzling Laughter in Plays of the Tudor Age / Rires et problèmes dans le théâtre des Tudor*, Theta, 6 (Bern: Peter Lang, 2002), 42.

53 Michael Billig, *Laughter and Ridicule: Towards a Social Critique of Humour* (London: Sage, 2005), 57. For the application of incongruity theory to early religious writing, see Kelly R. Iverson, "Incongruity, Humor, and Mark: Performance and the Use of Laughter in the Second Gospel (Mark 8.14–21)," *New Testament Studies* 59 (2013): 2–19. Christopher E. Crane, "Superior Incongruity: Derisive and Sympathetic Comedy in Middle English Drama and Homiletic Exempla," in *Medieval English Comedy*, ed. Hordis and Hardwick, 49–52, argues for a combination of the "superiority" and "incongruity" theories in relation to the York *Joseph's Trouble* pageant. Ingvild Sælid Gilhus, *Laughing Gods, Weeping Virgins: Laughter in the History of Religion* (London: Routledge, 1997), 90, notes briefly that the *Second Shepherds' Play* operates through "the simple comical technique of incongruity."

54 Diller, "Laughter," 2.

presenters of the pageant of *The Funeral of the Virgin* (*Fergus*), complained of this in 1431–32.[55] The *Fergus* episode is described in the 1415 *Ordo paginarum*, but the text was not recorded in the council register of the Play.[56] In the *Ordo* four apostles are listed as carrying Mary's bier, on which Fergus, a Jew who attacks it, hangs suspended, and there are two other Jews and an angel.[57] Richard Beadle notes that the "Scottish name" is "bizarrely attributed to the Jew" here and in another northern text, the *Northern Homily Cycle*, "probably where the dramatist found it," suggesting, further, that original audiences might have "understood" it "as ironic or grimly humorous."[58] The irony could have been enhanced further by the physical staging of the pageant, where as a Jew, Fergus would possibly have worn a red wig, red hair then being synonymous with Jewishness (and Judas), synonymous also with the Scots, resulting in a composite figure who represented an 'otherness' that was quite close to home in a physical sense as well as the 'otherness' of the biblical Jew.

In 1431–32, the Masons, at that time responsible for the pageant *vbi ffergus fflagellatus erat* (in which Fergus was beaten), complained that audiences were more likely to become disruptive and to laugh than to attend to the performance in a devotional manner and that sometimes disagreements and fights broke out and caused delays. According to legend, the Jew who attacks Mary's bier remains fixed to it, suspended by his hands, as detailed in the *Ordo*, until miraculously released through the power of Christ, but in this pageant, he is also beaten, an element that according to Beadle is not found elsewhere.[59] This on-stage violence may have provoked violence in the audience and derisive laughter, although there may be a number of reasons for these disruptions.[60] Could it be that the special effects required to deal with the suspended hands were inept or faulty and so failed to convince the audience that they had witnessed a miracle? Did some of them laugh derisively at theatrical failure and were the presenters of the pageant and their supporters affronted, leading to

---

55   REED: *York*, 1: 47–48 (translation 2: 732–33).
56   See *The York Plays: A Critical Edition of the York Corpus Christi Play as Recorded in British Library Additional MS 35290*, ed. Richard Beadle, 2 vols., EETS s.s. 23–24 (Oxford: Oxford University Press, 2009–13), 2: 424–29 for a history of the pageant.
57   REED: *York*, 1: 23 (translation 2: 709).
58   Beadle, *York Plays*, 2: 424–25.
59   Ibid., 2: 429.
60   See also Philip Butterworth, "Substitution: Theatrical Sleight of Hand in Medieval Plays," *European Medieval Drama* 9 (2005): 211–15. Beadle, *York Plays*, 2: 429, suggests that the Fergus role "seems likely to have been one that an actor could tear a cat in," opening up the possibility that audiences would laugh at his (over)acting as modern audiences do at Bottom's performance in *A Midsummer Night's Dream*.

physical conflict? But could it be that audience members laughed simply because they saw the Jew getting his just deserts, not only because he was suspended ignominiously from the bier awaiting the miracle, but also because he was being beaten like a common criminal? Medieval reactions to the torments of malefactors, whether it be execution or lesser punishments such as public humiliation by sentencing to the stocks or pillories,[61] were met by at least some spectators, to use Diller's words again, with "laughter about somebody else's misfortunes." Was this what was happening in the case of Fergus, an outburst of 'triumphant derision'? And could there have been a more violent reaction? As James Masschaele suggests, public humiliation "carried the potential threat of physical retribution, depending on the degree of public animus toward the offender;"[62] medieval crowds in York may have deemed it appropriate, especially in the absence of the later tradition of the theatrical 'fourth wall', to join in the beating that they saw performed in the pageant.

We cannot know what the intended reaction to *Fergus* was, but in a city like medieval York, where the veneration of the Virgin remained strong even through the fluctuations in religious affiliation during the Tudor monarchy, we might venture to assume that they were meant to focus closely on the miracle of Fergus the Jew's restoration rather than being carried away by the humiliation of Fergus the Scot.[63]

Another complaint that the Masons brought against *Fergus* was that the disruptions caused by inappropriate audience responses held up the performance so that they could not complete the appointed route through the city during daylight hours. Beadle has dismissed the time issue as being "of scant substance,"[64] but in the 1430s this argument may have held some weight with the city council.

---

[61] For comment on medieval punishments see, for example, Trevor Dean, *Crime in Medieval Europe, 1200–1550* (Harlow: Longman, 2001), 124–29, 130.

[62] James Masschaele, "The Public Space of the Marketplace in Medieval England," *Speculum* 77 (2002): 400.

[63] For discussion of the devotion to Mary in York as evidenced by the history of the Corpus Christi Play see Claire Cross, "Excising the Virgin Mary from the Civic Life of Tudor York," *Northern History* 39 (2002): 279–84.

[64] Beadle, *York Plays*, 2: 428.

12 The Timing of the Performance, *The Hanging of Judas*, and Laughter

Time was certainly an issue in 1399 *Memorandum Book* entry, referred to at the beginning of this essay, in which it was stated that the places where the pageants were to be seen were strictly limited so that the performance would not overrun the span of the day allotted to them. It is also clear in the 1422 entry proclaiming the devotional aspects of the York Play that timing was important. This record attests to the desirability of shortening the playing time "*commodius ludencium oracula audienti populo*" (profitably for the people hearing the holy words of the players).[65] In this instance *The Stretching and Nailing of Christ* and *The Raising of the Cross* were condensed into one pageant to benefit the spectators, who would have, it is implied, a greater chance of reaping the spiritual benefits of attendance at the Play if the overall performance was shorter. The same impulse may be behind the amalgamation of *The Hanging of Judas*, *The Condemnation of Christ by Pilate*, *The Flagellation*, and *The Dicing for Christ's Garments* as a single pageant (*Condempnacio Christi*) in 1432,[66] around the same time that the *Fergus* complaint was under consideration.

Like *Fergus*, *The Hanging of Judas* has disappeared without a trace, although remnants of the other pageants amalgamated in 1432 can be found in the text as recorded in 1476–77.[67] The account of the betrayer's suicide in the *Golden Legend*, where it is embedded in the St. Matthias narrative, explains that when Judas was hanging from the tree, his body opened up and his viscera spilled out. Could it be that the Saucemakers, the presenters of the pageant, were concerned about the dangers of simulating a hanging on stage,[68] or that the small membership of their guild made it difficult to raise the funds required for the production?[69] Is it possible that audiences in York laughed at this pageant, and if they did, could it have been a special effects issue, as suggested above for *Fergus*? Jonathan Harris argues that "sauces" could have been used

---

65 REED: *York*, 1: 37 (translation 2: 722).
66 REED: *York*, 1: 48–50 (translation 2: 733–34).
67 Richard Beadle, "Nicholas Lancaster, Richard of Gloucester and the York Corpus Christi Play," in *The York Mystery Plays: Performance in the City*, ed. Margaret Rogerson (York and Woodbridge: York Medieval Press, 2011), 31–52, argues for this date.
68 See Jody Enders, *Death by Drama and other Medieval Urban Legends* (Chicago: University of Chicago Press, 2002), 61–64, for an account of the near death of an actor playing Judas in Metz in 1437.
69 Beadle, *York Plays*, 2: 277–78, discusses the history of this lost pageant and comments, note 525, that in England the subject appears only "perfunctorily in dumb show in the N-Town Passion, and briefly in the Cornish Passion."

to "represent Judas's exploding viscera ... to ... grotesque effect," while other scholars have suggested that 'sausages' were used in this instance.[70] Could either of these props have been risible, or, again as I have suggested in the case of the red-headed Fergus, could the audience have been laughing derisively as the red-headed betrayer got his just deserts?

13 Conclusion

Audiences in medieval York remain enigmatic, but what does seem clear is that the council and the guilds responded to their responses, attempting to enhance the spiritual impact by shortening the Play and by removing elements that proved to be conducive to disruptive conduct. In these attempts they were shoring up the reputation of the Play as a devotional act appropriate to the observance of the holy day and conducive to the practice of *imitatio Christi*. While scholars have lauded the way in which the biblical past was made present in the pageants of medieval York, perhaps there were times, as in the case of Fergus, and possibly Judas, when the present overshadowed the past and tended to obscure the mission behind the Play as a social and spiritual event.

Bibliography

Angela of Foligno. *Complete Works*, translated by Paul Lachance. Mahwah, NJ: Paulist Press, 1993.

Baldwin, Elizabeth, Lawrence M. Clopper, and David Mills, eds. *Records of Early English Drama: Cheshire, Including Chester*, 2 vols. Toronto: University of Toronto Press, 2007.

Beadle, Richard. "Nicholas Lancaster, Richard of Gloucester and the York Corpus Christi Play." In *The York Mystery Plays: Performance in the City*, edited by Margaret Rogerson, 31–52. York and Woodbridge: York Medieval Press, 2011.

———, ed. *The York Plays: A Critical Edition of the York Corpus Christi Play as Recorded in British Library Additional MS 35290*, 2 vols. EETS s.s. 23–24. Oxford: Oxford University Press, 2009–13.

Billig, Michael. *Laughter and Ridicule: Towards a Social Critique of Humour*. London: Sage, 2005.

---

[70] Jonathan Gil Harris, "Properties of Skill: Product Placement in Early English Artisanal Drama," in *Staged Properties in Early Modern English Drama*, ed. Jonathan Gil Harris and Natasha Korda (Cambridge: Cambridge University Press, 2002), 61, n. 35.

Branford, Gaëlle. "Laughter in *Joseph's Trouble* (York Cycle): Visual Strategies and Mystical Revelation," 41–60. In *Tudor Theatre: For laughs (?) / Pour rire (?): Puzzling Laughter in Plays of the Tudor Age / Rires et problèmes dans le théâtre des Tudor*. Theta, 6. Bern: Peter Lang, 2002.

Butterworth, Philip. "Substitution: Theatrical Sleight of Hand in Medieval Plays." *European Medieval Drama* 9 (2005): 209–29.

Collins, Kristen, Peter Kidd, and Nancy K. Turner, *The St. Albans Psalter: Painting and Prayer in Medieval England*. Los Angeles: The J. Paul Getty Museum, 2013.

Cowling, Douglas. "The Liturgical Celebration of Corpus Christi in Medieval York." *Records of Early English Drama Newsletter* 1.2 (1976): 5–9.

Crane, Christopher E. "Superior Incongruity: Derisive and Sympathetic Comedy in Middle English Drama and Homiletic Exempla." In *Medieval English Comedy*, edited by Sandra M. Hordis & Paul Hardwick, 31–60. Profane Arts of the Middle Ages, 3. Turnhout: Brepols, 2007.

Cross, Claire. "Excising the Virgin Mary from the Civic Life of Tudor York." *Northern History* 39 (2002): 279–84.

Davidson, Clifford. "Sacred Blood and the Late Medieval Stage." *Comparative Drama* 31 (1997): 436–58.

———, ed. *A Tretise of Miraclis Pleyinge*. Kalamazoo, MI: Medieval Institute Publications, 1993.

Dean, Trevor. *Crime in Medieval Europe, 1200–1550*. Harlow: Longman, 2001.

Diller, Hans-Jürgen. "Laughter in Medieval English Drama: A Critique of Modernizing and Historical Analyses." *Comparative Drama* 36 (2002): 1–19.

Ehrstine, Glenn. "Passion Spectatorship between Public and Private Devotion." In *Thresholds of Medieval Visual Culture: Liminal Spaces*, edited by Elina Gertsman and Jill Stevenson, 302–20. Woodbridge: Boydell & Brewer, 2012.

Enders, Jody. *Death by Drama and other Medieval Urban Legends*. Chicago: University of Chicago Press, 2002.

Gilhus, Ingvild Sælid. *Laughing Gods, Weeping Virgins: Laughter in the History of Religion*. London: Routledge, 1997.

Hardwick, Paul. "Making Light of Devotion: The Pilgrimage Window in York Minster." In *Medieval English Comedy*, edited by Sandra M. Hordis & Paul Hardwick, 61–82. Profane Arts of the Middle Ages, 3. Turnhout: Brepols, 2007.

Harris, Jonathan Gil. "Properties of Skill: Product Placement in Early English Artisanal Drama." In *Staged Properties in Early Modern English Drama*, edited by Jonathan Gil Harris and Natasha Korda, 35–66. Cambridge: Cambridge University Press, 2002.

Homan, Richard L. "Old and new evidence of the career of William Melton, O.F.M." *Franciscan Studies* 49 (1989): 25–33.

Iverson, Kelly R. "Incongruity, Humor, and Mark: Performance and the Use of Laughter in the Second Gospel (Mark 8.14–21)." *New Testament Studies* 59 (2013): 2–19.

Johnston, Alexandra F. "The Procession and Play of Corpus Christi in York after 1426." *Leeds Studies in English* n.s. 7 (1973–74): 55–62.

——— and Margaret Rogerson, eds. *Records of Early English Drama: York*, 2 vols. Toronto: University of Toronto Press, 1979.

Kamerick, Kathleen. "Art and Moral Vision in Angela of Foligno and Margery Kempe." *Mystics Quarterly* 21 (1995): 148–58.

Masschaele, James. "The Public Space of the Marketplace in Medieval England." *Speculum* 77 (2002): 383–421.

Matthew, F.D., ed. *The English Works of Wyclif Hitherto Unprinted*. EETS o.s. 74. London: Trübner, 1880.

McKinnell, John. "Modern productions of medieval English drama." In *The Cambridge Companion to Medieval English Theatre*, edited by Richard Beadle and Alan J. Fletcher, 287–325. Cambridge: Cambridge University Press, 2008 (2nd ed.).

Mills, David. "Who are our Customers? The Audience for Chester's Plays." *Medieval English Theatre* 20 (1998): 104–17.

Newman, Barbara. *Medieval Crossover: Reading the Secular against the Sacred*. Notre Dame: University of Notre Dame Press, 2013.

Olson, Glending. "Plays as Play: A Medieval Ethical Theory of Performance and the Intellectual Context of the *Tretise of Miraclis Pleyinge*." *Viator* 26 (1995): 195–221.

Palliser, D.M. *Medieval York, 600–1540*. Oxford: Oxford University Press, 2014.

Pfeiffer, Kerstin. "Feeling the Passion: Neuropsychological perspectives on audience response." *Postmedieval: A Journal of Medieval Cultural Studies* 3 (2012): 328–40.

Powell, Morgan. "The visual, the visionary and her viewer: media and presence in the Psalter of Christina of Markyate (St Albans Psalter)." *Word and Image* 22 (2006): 340–62.

Rogerson, Margaret. "Affective Piety: A 'Method' for Medieval Actors in the Chester Cycle." In *The Chester Cycle in Context, 1555–1575: Religion, Drama, and the Impact of Change*, edited by Jessica Dell, David Klausner, and Helen Ostovich, 93–107. Farnham: Ashgate, 2012.

Rubin, Miri. *Corpus Christi: The Eucharist in Late Medieval Culture*. Cambridge: Cambridge University Press, 1991.

Schroeder, Joy. "Sacred Space and Sacred Time in the Religious Experience of Angela of Foligno." PhD thesis, University of Notre Dame, 1999.

Swanson, R.N. *Indulgences in the Pre-Reformation Diocese of York*. York: Borthwick Institute, 2011.

Walker, Katherine. "Spectatorship and Vision in *The York Corpus Christi Plays*." *Comitatus* 45 (2014): 169–90.

Weissengruber, Erik Paul. "The Corpus Christi Procession in Medieval York: A Symbolic Struggle in Public Space." *Theatre Survey* 38 (1997): 117–38.

Wenzel, Siegfried. "'Somer Game' and Sermon References to a Corpus Christi Play." *Modern Philology* 86 (1989): 274–83.

Windeatt, Barry, ed. *The Book of Margery Kempe*. Harlow: Pearson, 2000.

Wright, Stephen K. "Religious Drama, Civic Ritual, and the Police: The Semiotics of Public Safety in Late Medieval Germany." *Theatre Annual: A Journal of Performance Studies* 51 (1998): 1–14.

CHAPTER 16

"Be ye thus trowing": Medieval Drama and Make-Belief

Garrett P.J. Epp

[N]o man may be convertid to God but onely by the ernestful doyinge of God and by noon vein pleying, for that that the word of God worchith not ne his sacramentis, how shulde pleyinge worchen that is of no vertue but ful of defaute? (*A Tretise of Miraclis Pleyinge*)[1]

∴

Therfor be ye thus trowyng
When all is endid fully. (Towneley 29.135–36)[2]

∴

Abstract

While the Wycliffite *Tretise of Miraclis Pleyinge* famously condemns religious theatre as sinful idleness and 'signs without deed,' biblical drama has the potential to be highly productive, as a form of performative theology. Much like the meditative mode of affective piety, likewise common in the later Middle Ages, when undertaken seriously by or for those who believe in what it represents, the performance of biblical drama can cre-

---

1 *A Tretise of Miraclis Pleyinge*, ed. Clifford Davidson (Kalamazoo, MI: Medieval Institute Publications, 1993; rev. rpt. 2011), 102. While the term "miraclis pleyinge" could designate a wide variety of entertainments, the *Tretise* explicitly condemns "the pley of Cristis passioun" in ways that suggest a familiarity with and antipathy to the sort of biblical drama associated with the civic cycles of York and Chester and with the Towneley and N-Town collections, even if the extant play texts postdate the *Tretise* itself (by up to two centuries in the case of the Chester manuscripts).

2 *The Towneley Plays*, 2 vols., ed. Martin Stevens and A.C. Cawley, EETS s.s. 13–14 (Oxford: Oxford University Press, 1994), 1: 391. Subsequent references to the Towneley plays are given parenthetically by play and line number.

ate rather than merely represent theological meaning. This paper examines a variety of texts and performances, medieval and modern, in order to demonstrate how religious belief and theatrical make-believe can intertwine.

Keywords

biblical drama – performativity – theology – affective piety

1 Introduction

The *Tretise of Miraclis Pleyinge* condemns religious theatre – "miraclis pleyinge" – as "contrarious to the worschipe of God ... Bothe for these miraclis pleyinge been verrey leesing as they ben signis withoute dede and for they been verrey idilnesse as they taken the miraclis of God in idil after theire owne lust."[3] Indeed, the *Tretise* argues that, as an essentially physical act that puts the body on display, encouraging or even forcing the involvement "of oure fleyss, of oure lustis, and of oure five wittis," theatre leads to lechery rather than to holiness.[4] For the Wycliffite author, theatre and theology are thus necessarily opposed: "And sithen miraclis pleyinge is of the lustis of the fleyssh and mirthe of the body, no man may efectuely heeren hem and the voice of Crist at onys, as the voice of Crist and the voice of the fleysh ben of two contrarious lordis."[5] I have argued elsewhere that theatre is indeed necessarily and even distractingly fleshly, as the *Tretise* asserts, but that this can serve a theological end in relation to the theatrical representation of Jesus.[6] Here, however, my focus is on the description of biblical theatre as "signis withoute dede" and thus "verrey idilnesse." While theatre certainly can serve as idle entertainment, the production of biblical drama can also be "ernestful doyinge," as a means of performative theology.

---

3   Ibid., 99.
4   Ibid., 94.
5   Ibid., 96.
6   Garrett P.J. Epp, "Ecce Homo," in *Queering the Middle Ages / Historicizing Postmodernity*, eds. Steven F. Kruger and Glenn Burger (Minneapolis: University of Minnesota Press, 2001), 346–66.

2   Performative Theology

Modern critical use of the term 'performative' is rooted in the speech act theory of John Searle and J.L. Austin, where it refers to utterances that effect or produce what they declare, as in 'I apologize' or 'I promise'. Of course, performance context matters. When God says "Let there be light" in the biblical account of creation (Genesis 1:3), his utterance is performative – he creates light by naming it – while the theatrical equivalent would be at most a stage cue, however effectively carried out. Orthodox Catholics might echo their Wycliffite opponents in considering the onstage utterance of the phrase "*hoc est enim corpus meum*" to be a problematic 'sign' in contrast to a crucially earnest 'deed' because of its performative power in the mass to effect transubstantiation. Those who disbelieve in transubstantiation would consider the same phrase to be but a sign in any case, but might still object to its being stated outside a proper, properly earnest, ecclesiastical context. It is thus unsurprising that representation of the sacraments was banished from the sixteenth-century English stage, along with representation of God, as evident in the often quoted 1576 decree by the Ecclesiastical Commissioners of York regarding Wakefield's "plaie commonlie called Corpus Christi Plaie," ordering "that in the said playe no Pageant be vsed or set furthe wherin the Maiestye of god the father god the sonne or god the holie ghoste or the administration of either the Sacramentes of Baptisme or of the lordes Supper be counterfeyted or represented."[7] When Shakespeare's Celia is asked to perform a mock marriage between Rosalind (playing Ganymede playing Rosalind) and Orlando, regardless of whatever feelings she might have about the relationship itself, she has good reason to declare, "I cannot say the words;"[8] the phrase that would declare the two married is a legally-restricted performative utterance.

Despite its rootedness in speech act theory, however, the term is now most closely associated with contemporary theories of gender and sexuality, thanks mostly to the work of Judith Butler, who described gender identity as being "instituted through a *stylized repetition of acts*."[9] By repeatedly performing the conventions of gendered behaviour, we naturalize them, for ourselves and for others. We follow a social script, literally embodying its codes and conventions,

---

7   Quoted in *The Wakefield Pageants in the Towneley Cycle*, ed. A.C. Cawley (Manchester: Manchester University Press, 1958), 125.
8   William Shakespeare, *As You Like It*, 4.1.109, in *The Norton Shakespeare*, ed. Stephen Greenblatt (New York: Norton, 2008, 2nd ed.), 1641.
9   Judith Butler, "Performative Acts and Gender Constitution: An Essay in Phenomenology and Feminist Theory," *Theatre Journal* 49 (1988): 519.

often unaware that there is a script at all; what we think of as real, natural, and immutable is ultimately an earnest sort of play, "a performative accomplishment which the mundane social audience, including the actors themselves, come to believe and to perform in the mode of belief."[10] Butler was focussed on social actors, not on theatre. However, when undertaken "in the mode of belief," the performance of medieval biblical drama becomes performative theology, creating the theology that it purportedly represents. And that includes both medieval and modern performance: in my own experience as an actor, audience member, director, and producer of contemporary productions of medieval plays, I have seen many whose involvement with medieval drama was very explicitly undertaken "in the mode of belief," from church groups who take on production of a particular pageant for a cycle performance, to audience members who follow Christ to the cross on their knees. Even when undertaken for purely secular reasons (including in-class productions for university courses), the performance of medieval biblical drama can be theologically productive for any that are inclined to believe it thus.

All performance constitutes interpretation both of the dramatic text and of its subject. The performance of biblical drama constitutes an interpretation of scripture and of theological concepts, but also thereby performs theology. This is of course not quite the same thing as performative theology, in which, as Simon Coleman has stated, "the focus is on the self-constituting dimension of 'lived' theological discourse."[11] A "'lived' theological discourse" is not the same as scholarly or priestly or personal interpretation of biblical texts, much less dramatic representation. On the other hand, much like dramatic representation, a "'lived' theological discourse" requires more than textual discourse and interpretation. As theologian Nicholas Lash has stated, "serious theological investigation is never purely a matter of inference and deduction; never merely a matter of the reasoning mind. It is also a matter of the mind and heart at prayer. There is a sense in which all good theology is done on one's knees."[12] However, most discussion of performative theology does deal with the textual interpretation of scripture. Richard Valantasis has described the extra-canonical Gospel of Thomas as containing or constituting

---

10   Butler, "Performative Acts," 520.
11   Simon Coleman, "An Anthropological Apologetics," *South Atlantic Quarterly* 109 (2010): 795.
12   Nicholas Lash, "I watch my language in the presence of God – Theology in the modern university," 2011, Faraday Papers, online: <https://www.faraday.st-edmunds.cam.ac.uk/Issues_Lash.php> (accessed 14 February 2015).

> a performative theology whose mode of discourse and whose method ... revolves about effecting a change in thought and understanding in the readers and hearers (both ancient and modern). The sayings challenge, puzzle, sometimes even provide conflicting information about a given subject, and in so confronting the readers and hearers force them to create in their own minds the place where all the elements fit together. The theology comes from the audience's own effort in reflecting and interpreting the sayings ...[13]

This is not to say that an audience has free rein in its interpretation; much as in Judith Butler's account of gender, one's performative choices are always limited. Butler writes, "Embodiment clearly manifests a set of strategies or what Sartre would perhaps have called a style of being or Foucault, 'a stylistics of existence'. This style is never fully self-styled, for living styles have a history, and that history conditions and limits possibilities."[14] Theology and theological texts, including medieval play texts, likewise have histories that condition and limit interpretative and performative possibilities.

In an article aptly entitled "Performing the Scriptures: Interpretation through Living," Nicholas Lash states that, "as the history of the meaning of the text continues, we can and must tell the [story] differently. But we do so under constraint: what we may *not* do, if it is *this* text which we continue to perform, is to tell a different story."[15] Yet the biblical story itself did and does change, at least in some particulars, even between canonical gospel accounts, not to mention between these and the various apocryphal accounts and, of course, staged representations. Christopher Goodman's 1572 list of 'absurdities' in the Chester plays clearly indicates his objection to "The sacrament made a stage play," but also to various non-biblical narrative elements, such as "The miracle of drying up of Salomes hands & the restoring of the same," "A fable of Seth begging oyl in paradise to anoint Adam when he was sick," and "Michael bringing the fathers out of hell with the cross hanging upon the theef"s back," not to mention the simultaneously anti-Semitic and anti-Islamic tactic of having "The Iews swear by Mahound."[16] Such narrative elements, too, for better and for

---

13   Richard Valantasis, *The Gospel of Thomas*, New Testament Readings, 5 (London: Routledge, 1997), 7.
14   Butler, "Performative Acts," 521.
15   Nicholas Lash, "Performing the Scriptures: Interpretation through Living," *The Furrow* 33 (1982): 473.
16   *Records of Early English Drama: Cheshire Including Chester*, 2 vols., ed. Elizabeth Baldwin, Lawrence M. Clopper, and David Mills (Toronto and London: University of Toronto Press and The British Library, 2007), 1: 147.

worse, perform theology. The letter to the Archbishop of York from Goodman and his co-signatories, Robert Rogerson and John Lane, much like the *Tretise*, argues that "we should rather prepare us to humble our hearts with true repentance earnest prayers & fasting, than to attend upon vanities," then expresses the hope

> that in the name of the Lord Iesus your wisdoms may take such order with the said plays, as by your authority they may either be corrected, allowed, & authorized (if god by any such indirect means will have his gospell furthered where ordinary preaching wanteth not) or els by the same your authority utterly defaced & abolished for ever as pastimes unfitt for this time & Christian commonwealths.[17]

Dramatic performance may not be "ordinary preaching" but it is implicitly treated as preaching nonetheless, and as a means, however imperfect, of furthering the gospel, if (and only if) these absurdities can be corrected.

3   Needful Recreation

As Clifford Davidson has pointed out, Thomas Aquinas among others deemed theatre an acceptable form of recreation,[18] a view that the *Tretise* explicitly rejects, stating that "miraclis pleyinge ne the sighte of hem is no verrey recreasion but fals and worldly," and suggesting that any good Christian should already know "that his recreacioun shulde ben in the werkis of mercy to his neiebore and in diliting him in alle good comunicacion with his neibore ... and in alle othere nedeful werkis that reson and kinde axen."[19] The only acceptable forms of recreation, apparently, are those that are theologically "nedeful." When I teach these plays, I normally ask – indeed, require – my students to perform some of them. While the exercise is not graded, nor is it idle recreation; I deem it academically *nedeful*. Performance is crucial to understanding these plays as plays, but understanding can come by unexpected means, unexpected performance choices.

One year, over a decade ago, my students chose to produce the N-Town Nativity, which like the Chester version includes the midwives episode from the *Protoevangelion* of James. Two Muslim women who had hardly spoken in

---

17   Ibid., 1: 145.
18   Davidson, *Tretise*, 19–20.
19   Ibid., 103, 104.

class throughout the term took on the roles of the two midwives, later telling me that, while both the apocryphal story and theatrical performance itself were new and strange to them, the play's insistence on the sanctity of the Virgin Mary accorded with Islamic tradition and spoke to them, personally. They undertook their roles 'in the mode of belief,' and their performance provoked less the expected laughter, even at the withered hand, than something akin to reverent awe. Yet such reactions do not necessarily depend upon the piety of the performers. A few years earlier, a male student with an interest and some training in *onnagata* roles for the kabuki theatre eagerly took on the part of Mary for an in-class production of the York Nativity pageant. There were no costumes, *per se*, but he strapped a shoe box over his stomach, which provoked laughter on first appearance. However, at the moment of the miraculous birth, he opened the box, took out a small doll, and in the unexpectedly silent classroom he spoke Mary's lines from York 14.55–56: "Jesu my sone þat is so dere, || Nowe borne is he."[20] In attempting to stage this central moment, he had unwittingly echoed the medieval tradition of the *vièrge ouverte* – statues of Mary that open to reveal the infant Jesus – and in the process made me rethink how this moment might originally have been staged; more importantly, perhaps, while he himself espoused no belief in the subject, he had also cited and performed the theology of the virgin birth itself. In the discussion afterward, I explained what a *vièrge ouverte* was and why I found the performance interesting, which clearly interested the group as a whole, but for a few it meant something more: this performance was a profoundly spiritual moment, not merely reflecting or representing but creating theological meaning.

Little clear evidence survives as to the actual effects of such plays on medieval audiences, aside from those audience members opposed to their performance. Still, Carol M. Meale has suggested various ways in which seeing the York plays impacted Margery Kempe's visions of the Nativity (in which she serves as midwife) and the Passion. The particular details of her visions have often been tied to narrative works that she clearly knew, such as Nicholas Love's *Mirror of the Blessed Life of Jesus Christ* and pieces by Richard Rolle. She never mentions drama, but almost certainly saw York's biblical plays, having been in the city the day of their performance in 1413. Meale convincingly argues "that the nature of Kempe's devotion and, indeed, elements of her *Book*'s structure and expression, manifest the effectiveness of the dynamics of performance

---

20   *The York Plays: A Critical Edition of the York Corpus Christi Play as Recorded in British Library Additional MS 35290*, 2 vols., ed. Richard Beadle, EETS s.s. 23–24 (Oxford: Oxford University Press, 2009–13), 1: 97. Subsequent references to the York plays are given parenthetically by play and line number.

upon an individual consciousness."[21] Unsurprisingly, specific striking details such as the means of crucifixion are remembered and represented, but perhaps more important is her sense of playing a role in the scenes she describes, as active participant rather than passive audience member. For example, as Meale explains, having spoken with the Virgin in her vision, Margery "proceeds to accompany Mary on her visit to Elizabeth, begs the latter to intercede with Mary so that she might continue to serve her, then performs the role of midwife at the nativity, all the while begging for lodgings, swaddling clothes, and food."[22] Thus Margery does not so much imitate the physical action she has witnessed onstage as enact the theology that informs that action; indeed, she is doing – if only in her imagination – precisely the sort of work the authors of the *Tretise* define as proper recreation.

4   Devout Imagination

In the middle ages, of course, enacting the life of Christ himself, physically, emotionally, or through what Nicholas Love termed "devout imagination," was a common meditative practice. In an essay that takes its title in part from Love's phrase, Richard Beadle has commented on "how far Love's *Mirror* as a whole possesses a distinct dramatic flavour."[23] In affective piety, the imitation and contemplation of Christ serves as a kind of dramatic incarnation, making Christ present to the meditating subject, if always, necessarily, with individual, personal differences. In her book *Putting on Virtue: The Legacy of the Splendid Vices*, in what she calls an "Excursus: Performative Theology," Jennifer A. Herdt states, "Christ's exemplarity is ... constantly open to interpretation, endlessly re-enacted, but not reiterated, in the lives of the saints. There is indeed

---

21   Carol M. Meale, "'This is a Deed Bok, the Tother a Quick': Theatre and the Drama of Salvation in the *Book* of Margery Kempe," in *Medieval Women: Texts and Contexts in Late Medieval Britain. Essays for Felicity Riddy*, in Jocelyn Wogan-Browne et al., eds. (Turnhout: Brepols, 2000), 49–67; see 52. On Kempe as performer, see Sheila Christie, "'Thei stodyn upon stoyls for to beheldyn hir': Margery Kempe and the Power of Performance," *Studia Anglica Posnaniensia* 38 (2002): 93–103.
22   Meale, "This is a Deed Bok," 58.
23   See Richard Beadle, "'Devoute ymaginacioun' and the Dramatic Sense in Love's *Mirror* and the N-Town Plays," in *Nicholas Love at Waseda: Proceedings of the International Conference, 20–22 July, 1995*, eds. Shoichi Oguro, Richard Beadle, and Michael G. Sargent (Cambridge: D.S. Brewer, 1997), 6. See also Carol M. Meale, "'oft siþis with grete deuotion I þought what I miʒt do pleysyng to god': The Early Ownership and Readership of Love's Mirror, with Special Reference to its Female Audience," in ibid., 19–46.

something creative about imitatio Christi."[24] The *Tretise* implies that any such creative variation is at best problematic, in that it "giveth credence to many mengid leesingis for othere mengid trewthis."[25] As part of its argument against recreation as pleasure, the *Tretise* notes that "of Cristis lawghing we reden never in holy writt, but of his myche penaunse, teris, and scheding of blod, doying us to witen therby that alle oure doing heere shulde ben in penaunce, in disciplining of oure fleyssh, and in penaunce of adversite."[26] To show Christ laughing, in this view, would not simply be a lie but would lead others astray precisely because it would theologize laughter, valorizing laughter and indeed pleasure as inherently holy.

Meale's article on Margery Kemp takes its title from a line in the *Tretise* describing a defense of theatre as better able to represent the will and works of God to the illiterate than painting, "for this is a deed bok, the tother a quick." Unsurprisingly, the *Tretise* itself favours pictorial stasis over fleshly movement:

> we seyn that peinture, yif it be verry withoute menging of lesingis and not to curious, to myche fedinge mennis wittis, and not occasion of maumetrie to the puple, they ben but as nakyd lettris to a clerk to riden the treuthe. But so ben not miraclis pleyinge that ben made more to deliten men bodily than to ben bokis to lewid men.[27]

The sheer physicality of theatre is indeed one of its delights, and – even aside from its potential erotic dimensions – can prove distracting. Human actors are fallible; performance conditions for outdoor theatre in particular can be highly unpredictable. Onstage accidents, missed lines and gestures, audience interference, and more, often prove not simply distracting but productive of meaning, for better or for worse. Misdirection or simple miscasting – an all too common problem in amateur theatrics especially – can alter interpretation. A Christ that at crucial moments appears to lack confidence, whether due to actual lack or to particular performance choices, might not inspire confident faith. On the other hand, that apparent lack might well inspire a certain human (or even Christ-like) sympathy on the part of some audience members.

Such a dynamic accounts in part for the diversity of reactions to the 1973 film version of the musical *Jesus Christ Superstar*, which like the recording and

---

24 Jennifer A. Herdt, *Putting On Virtue: The Legacy of the Splendid Vices* (Chicago: University of Chicago Press, 2008), 165.
25 Davidson, *Tretise*, 103.
26 Ibid., 95.
27 Ibid., 98, 104.

stage productions before it was denounced by many as blasphemous, although others responded with devotion. Ted Neeley, who played Jesus in the film, has stated,

> It wasn't Jesus Christ there, it was me, a human being, dressed and looking like the character we all seem to know and letting people see that that person, too, is a human being and had to deal with daily problems, just like we do. And it worked. For years I have gotten word from all around the world where, "You made me understand who Jesus really was."[28]

On the other hand, as the authors of the *Tretise* would be quick to point out, belief and devotion can be misplaced. Neeley, who has continued to perform the role on stage, notes that some who have seen the show treat him as if he really is Jesus: "People come up and tell me things about their lives. There are people who honestly believe I've cured them from cancer just by hugging them, by saying hello."[29] Yet Neeley himself grew up in a strongly religious environment, and appears to have undertaken the role in a spirit of identification more akin to Love's "devout imagination." He tells for example a story of taking a quiet moment off the film set in Israel to meditate:

> When I opened my eyes, there were a bunch of children sitting in front of me, staring at me. Little Israeli children. I don't know where they came from. I could not speak their language, they could not speak mine. I opened my eyes and saw them. They just stared at me. So I thought, Okay, what would Jesus do? I stood up, I opened my arms, they came to me, it was the most genuinely sweet, loving group hug I've had in my life at that time. And they walked away and I went back to the set.[30]

This, too, is a moment of performative theology.

---

28   Interview with Shawna Hansen Ortega, "Jesus Christ Superstar: Ted Neeley Tells the Inside Story," online at <http://www.songfacts.com/blog/writing/jesus_christ_superstar_ted_neeley_tells_the_inside_story/> (accessed 31 January 2015).
29   Ibid.
30   Ibid.

5 Enacting Virtue

The figure of Christ is central to affective piety, biblical drama, and Christian theology alike, yet other characters and characterisations can be equally important precisely because of their relationships to him, and to Christian virtue. This is true not only for obvious role models and objects of devotion such as his mother Mary, but also for those who oppose them. A particularly vicious or inept-seeming torturer might inspire sympathy or identification with Christ, regardless of how the latter is portrayed, while apparent reluctance or sympathy on the part of a torturer might inspire a different sort of identification. According to the *Tretise*, however, all biblical theatre effectively performs the equivalent of torturing Christ: "sithen thes miraclis pleyeris taken in bourde the ernestful werkis of God, no doute that ne they scornen God as diden the Jewis that bobbiden Crist, for they lowen at his passioun as these lowyn and japen of the miraclis of God."[31] And those who do not laugh (*lowen*) but weep over representations of Passion, are said to weep not out of identification with Christ's suffering, and "not principaly for theire oune sinnes ne of theire gode feith withinneforthe, but more of theire sight withouteforth …".[32] According to such a view, the physicality and inherent falsity of theatre can align it – and its actors and audience – only with evil. Yet inspiring the proper reaction to dramatic representation clearly mattered to many. York's play of the Funeral of the Virgin was ultimately suppressed because of laughter over its representation of the disbelieving Jew who finds his hand miraculously stuck to the funeral bier: "the Masons of this city have been accustomed to murmur among themselves about their pageant in the Corpus Christi Play in which Fergus was beaten because the subject of this pageant is not contained in the sacred scripture and used to produce more noise and laughter than devotion."[33] The Masons were granted new responsibilities and the offending play was never registered; no known copy exists. While they might well have had some concern for their own reputation, it does appear that they took the plays – and scriptural authority – very seriously as well. Their aim was devotional, and virtuous.

---

31 Davidson, *Tretise*, 97.
32 Ibid., 102.
33 *Records of Early English Drama: York*, 2 vols., ed. Alexandra F. Johnston and Margaret Rogerson (Toronto: University of Toronto Press, 1979), 2: 732. ("Cementarij huius ciuitatis murmurabant inter se de pagina sua in ludo corporis christi vbi ffergus fflagellatus erat pro eo quod materia illius in sacra non continetur scriptura & magis risum & clamorem causabat quam deuocionem." Ibid.1: 47–48.) See also the essay by Margaret Rogerson in this volume.

Jennifer Herdt devotes a chapter of her book to the idea of enacting virtue in order to become virtuous, specifically in the Jesuit theatrical tradition, arguing that "Virtue is performative insofar as it is acquired through acting virtuously. It is also theatrical: persons are moved by observing virtue in action and thus inspired to emulate that virtue. Moreover, identity – our sense of our own character – is formed in large part by others' perceptions of ourselves as actors."[34] She goes on:

> it is also true that theatre, like the novel, will have a tendency to exceed any particular moral that might be drawn from it. It cannot be used purely to present exemplary models for imitation, since in order to enact a story it must portray conflict and change, and thus departures from the ideal. The Jesuit embrace of theatre meant a willingness to accept a certain degree of ambiguity – the Jesuits were willing to depict, and allow children to act the parts of, bad characters as well as good. On the other hand, they made certain that good and bad were clearly evident as such and that each received their just desserts. One of the notable ways in which Jesuit dramatists sought to rein in the "excess" of dramatic example in various ways was by depicting the response of spectators-on-stage … in an effort to model an ideal audience reaction.[35]

This is to some extent true for medieval biblical drama as well: the York Entry into Jerusalem, for a classic example, has representative citizens offer praise, devotion, and a hearty "Hayll, and welcome of all abowte, || To owre ceté" (25.543–44). Richard Beadle has noted how

> [i]n the English mystery plays … the beginnings and endings are commonly stylized by having the actors speak directly to the audience in such a way as to make them feel they are actively present as bystanders whilst the events depicted in the drama are taking place, rather than passive spectators at an artificially arranged spectacle. The essence of the technique is to include the audience within the illusion of the play, and sometimes even to implicate them directly in what is going on in it.[36]

Beadle draws a parallel in this respect between the plays and Nicholas Love's *Mirror*, remarking on "the extent to which the set meditative passages that

---

34 Herdt, *Putting On Virtue*, 147–48.
35 Ibid., 148.
36 Beadle, "Devoute ymaginacioun," 12.

[Love] habitually offers as 'devout imaginations' are intended not only to induce love and compassion for Christ, but also to teach moral thought and action, so that the reader or hearer can go forth and enact in their own lives the examples of virtue set out in the gospels."[37]

Yet the doctrinal necessity of the crucifixion effectively renders virtuous not merely the fall of Adam and Eve, but also the actions of the torturer who nails Christ to the cross. As even the *Tretise* argues,

> we seyen that right as a vertuous deede is othere while occasioun of yvel, as was the passioun of Crist to the Jewis, but not occasioun given but taken of hem, so yvele dedis ben occasioun of gode dedis othere while, as was the sinne of Adam occasioun of the coming of Crist, but not occasion given of the sinne but occasion takun of the grete mercy of God.[38]

The presumption here, of course, is that God's mercy would be no more available to those involved in dramatic performance, whether as actor or as audience, than to those who tortured Christ. Still, the *Tretise* treats no biblically-sanctioned action or role as being any more or less objectionable than any other, but recognizes that good and evil alike play roles in divine history – the history represented in medieval biblical drama. All things can point to God. Already *c.* 1100, in his *Gemma animae*, Honorius of Autun compared a priest to an actor, referring to him as a *tragicus* who represents Christ and his Passion in the celebration of Mass.[39] In raising the host at the consecration, the priest arguably plays the part of the executioner rather than (or as well as) the suffering victim raised on the cross. Yet that comparison goes both ways: in raising the cross on a pageant-wagon stage, the actor-torturers elevate the host, not hidden in the accidents of bread and wine, but visibly incarnate, as a flesh-and-blood actor.

6   Directing the Audience

In *Sacred Players: The Politics of Response in the Middle English Religious Drama* – a book whose very title contradicts the presumptions of the *Tretise* – Heather

---

37   Ibid., 14.
38   Davidson, *Tretise*, 100.
39   For contextualization and a different reading of this oft-cited analogy see Lawrence M. Clopper, *Drama, Play, and Game: English Festive Culture in the Medieval and Early Modern Period* (Chicago and London: University of Chicago Press, 2001), 50–52.

Hill-Vásquez argues that the York plays call upon actors and audience alike to see their labour as sacred:

> Connecting the space of his body to city and audience, Christ indicates the presence of the sacred in the streets of York and reminds his spectators of their role in enacting that presence. Directed to contemplate – indeed, to "measure" – the very parts of Christ's body that the soldiers have just labored to nail to the cross, the audience are invoked as workers in their own right, enabling the significance and power of the Crucifixion to span a time and space that includes their own streets, homes, and storefronts. Past and present, divine and human meet as all actors of the drama are expected to participate in a merger of the mundane and sacred labor necessary for spiritual enlightenment and salvation.[40]

If labour is sacred, beyond the list of serious good works sanctioned by the *Tretise*, labour itself becomes a sort of performative theology, potentially leading both to understanding and to salvation. However, as Hill-Vásquez notes,

> in the Chester cycle, whose pageants cover a similar range of sacred history, expectations for audience involvement can seem quite different. In contrast to the temporal and spatial continuity encouraged by Christ and other audience-attentive figures like him in the York cycle, Chester offers a different model of response. A designated "Expositor" figure, acting as a readerly interpreter, sets himself and his audience apart from the time and space of sacred history ...[41]

She then quotes the Expositor's first speech from the Chester play of Abraham, in which – having entered on horseback, breaking whatever frame the performance might have implicitly created – he states:

> Lordinges, what may this signifye
> I will expound yt appertly –
> the unlearned standinge herebye
> maye knowe what this may bee.
> This present, I saye veramente,
> signifieth the newe testamente

---

40   Heather Hill-Vásquez, *Sacred Players: The Politics of Response in the Middle English Religious Drama* (Washington, DC: Catholic University of America Press, 2007), 1.
41   Ibid., 2.

that nowe is used with good intente
throughout all Christianitye.[42]

The speech effectively shifts responsibility for correct interpretation away from the 'unlearned' audience to the Expositor himself. This authoritative 'readerly' model also represents a shift away from the performative theology of York and other examples of medieval biblical drama, including other parts of Chester. As Hill-Vásquez explains, an emphasis on "uncovering sacred truths through attentive interpretation rather than participatory engagement" is largely limited to the plays in which the Expositor figure appears, likely as "a conscious Reformation addition:" "Expositor thus serves as a model for the proper approach to the plays that will, as the late Banns insist, illustrate how the plays align with Protestant thought."[43] David Mills has described various ways, both verbal and visual, in which the Chester audience may have been "made unusually aware of an action mediated by the play-book from the God-book, the Bible."[44] However, he too emphasizes the "disruptive function" of the Chester Expositor who "stands between the performers of the historical action and the audience, objectifying the action to them and creating a meditative distance between the audience and players within the close and intimate space of the street-theatre."[45] The Expositor thus functions as a sort of Brechtian *Verfremdungseffekt*, emotionally distancing the audience from the action in order to emphasize meaning,[46] but also leaving little room for any other interpretation. The explicit didacticism sets this approach apart from performative theology, reducing the audience to passive observers and consumers of a particular, highly textual interpretation rather than active interpreters engaged in a "'lived' theological discourse."

Such an approach has obvious advantages in regard to uniformity of doctrine, and renders the actual performance less important to the interpretive

---

42　*The Chester Mystery Cycle*, 2 vols., ed. R.M. Lumiansky and David Mills, EETS s.s. 3 and 9 (Oxford: Oxford University Press, 1974–86), 1: 62, ll. 113–20. Subsequent references to the Chester plays are given parenthetically by play and line number.

43　Hill-Vásquez, *Sacred Players*, 27.

44　David Mills, "Brought to Book: Chester's Expositor and his Kin," in *The Narrator, the Expositor, and the Prompter in European Medieval Theatre*, ed. Philip Butterworth (Turnhout: Brepols, 2007), 311. Several essays in this collection are notably relevant to the current topic.

45　Ibid., 314.

46　For my earlier, somewhat different thoughts on relations between Brechtian dramaturgy and medieval biblical theatre, see Garrett P.J. Epp, "Visible Words: The York Plays, Brecht, and Gestic Writing," *Comparative Drama* 24 (1991): 289–305.

process, although not to any extent that would please the authors of the *Tretise*: the unpredictable, highly dynamic aspects of theatrical performance almost necessarily work against static interpretation. Each performance varies, however slightly, while different audience members will notice and respond differently to different things, even within a single performance. An observer who is overly conscious of the performance *as* performance might well not be moved to devotion by the drama, whether that consciousness is due to distraction by some production detail, or to identification with the actor as actor (as a friend or relative might well do, then as now), or something else entirely. Following J.L. Austin we might refer to such conditions as "infelicities" or failed performatives.[47] On the other hand, the negative reaction of one who is highly conscious of the performance as an embodiment of theological difference or error, such as a Wycliffite or a Puritan might be, nonetheless is or could be a form of performative theology: in such cases, the stage performance confirms by its inadequacy, its palpable falsehood, what one already believes, while one's adverse reaction both confirms and demonstrates to others – preaches to others – one's sense of the inherent wrongness of performance itself as a means of conveying theological truth.

7 Belief Communities

Theatre is always contingent. One's interpretation of an individual performance of a medieval biblical play, then as now, depends upon one's own prior understanding of and familiarity with the material, the performance context, and even the performers themselves, as well as on what actually happens in that particular performance. Theatre is also a communal event, and the diverse audience reactions to a play – negative and positive, emotional, intellectual, physical, and spiritual – affect the meaning of the performance for each individual involved. If one believes (as many clearly do and have done) that theological truth is and must be utterly singular, especially in situations in which a singular truth appears to be under threat, theatre will almost inevitably appear threatening, as it did in Reformation England.[48] Yet a belief community can itself provide a sense of singularity, of oneness, that allows

---

47 J.L. Austin, *How to Do Things with Words*, eds. J.O. Urmson and Marina Sbisà (Cambridge, MA: Harvard University Press, 1975, 2nd ed.), 14.
48 See Garrett P.J. Epp, "To 'Play the Sodomits': A Query in Five Actions," in *The Ashgate Research Companion to Queer Theory*, eds. Noreen Giffney and Michael O'Rourke (Farnham: Ashgate, 2009), 181–97.

theatrical performance to flourish, its accidents and infelicities forgiven. So indeed can an academic environment such as a class in which students of diverse backgrounds are united in their will to understand the workings of medieval drama. But a unified community or community effort can also provide a sense of authority – a sense that a particular belief or an interpretation is correct because it is (or appears to be) shared. Performative theology can help build a sense of community and communal authority precisely because its truths are apparent through performance, not merely asserted; interpretation is visibly communal, and does not depend on a single authoritative figure who ostensibly understands the truth and can "expound yt appertly" like Chester's Expositor – or indeed like the instructor of a medieval drama course. This can of course worry those who believe strongly in the importance of centralized or hierarchical authority. But performative theology – unlike any class exercise, or secular theatre – also depends upon faith. One can be moved or inspired in an academic sense by a performance of the Nativity as *vièrge ouverte*, but such a performance will clearly mean different things – will mean differently – to those who believe that a virgin gave birth to the son of God. It will demand a different response.

Nicholas Lash argues "that the fundamental form of the Christian interpretation of Scripture is the life, activity and organisation of the Christian community, construed as performance of the biblical text."[49] To illustrate his point, he draws analogies with other texts – specifically, Shakespeare's *King Lear* and Beethoven's late string quartets – as "texts that only begin to deliver their meaning in so far as they are 'brought into play' through interpretative performance." Both biblical texts and works of art such as these also require collaborative communities of interpretation, including but not limited to "the indispensable but subordinate academic interpreters."[50] Yet his essay also differentiates between theological and artistic performance. Lash notes that "an outstanding performance of *King Lear*" might lead an individual audience to both "self-discovery and the discovery of fresh meaning in the text" for the individual audience member;[51] still, the text remains a thing apart. Moreover,

> at the end of a performance of *Lear*, the actors leave the stage, remove their costumes, 'return to life'. But, for each Christian actor, the performance of the biblical text ends only at death. The stage on which we enact our performance is that wider human history in which the Church

---

49 Lash, "Performing the Scriptures," 474.
50 Ibid., 470.
51 Ibid., 470.

exists as the 'sacrament', or dramatic enactment, of history's ultimate meaning and hope.[52]

In the later middle ages, the audiences of biblical drama had reason to understand those theatrical performances as directly related to that "wider human history," and not merely representative of it. Mere attendance could ostensibly confer grace, applicable at the end of time: the 1531–32 proclamation for the Chester plays refers to an ecclesiastical indulgence granted to "euery per*son* resortyng in pecible man*ner* with gode devoc*io*n to here & se the s[aid plays] frome tyme to tyme asoft as they shalbe plaied within this Citie."[53] But "gode devoc*io*n" also implies response. To paraphrase what Richard Valantasis states regarding the Gospel of Thomas and its readers, quoted earlier, performative theology emerges from the actors' and audience's responses to what happens onstage. We do not know what playing Christ or torturer actually meant to any particular medieval actor, nor what seeing the plays might have meant to a particular audience member, but clearly the host itself meant different things to a Catholic and to a Wycliffite or Puritan, and so, typically, did theatre. To some, both the Eucharist and theatre were incarnational, word becoming flesh, whereas to others such a thought was an abomination, and a blasphemous distraction from truth. Such differing reactions to biblical drama in performance – devotion and outrage – are not merely theological in basis but may also perform theology, however differently.

8   "Therfor Be Ye Thus Trowyng"

In the York Crucifixion, Christ effectively both upbraids those in the audience who might identify too closely with him, and forgives his – and by extension the play's – detractors:

> Al men þat walkis by waye or strete,
> Takes tente ȝe schalle no trauayle tyne.
> Byholdes myn heede, myn handis, and my feete,
> And fully feele nowe, or ȝe fyne,
> Yf any mournyng may be meete,
> Or myscheue mesured vnto myne.
> My fadir, þat alle bales may bete,

---

52   Ibid., 474.
53   Baldwin, Clopper, and Mills, *REED: Cheshire*, 1: 72.

> Forgiffis þes men þat dois me pyne.
> What þei wirke, wotte þai noght;
> Therfore, my fadir, I craue,
> Latte neuere þer synnys be sought,
> But see þer saules to saue. (35.253–64)

At the Last Judgement, Christ again calls attention to his wounded body prior to dividing the saved from the damned; indeed, in the Chester version he (repeatedly) emphasizes that the audience "shall appertlye see ‖ freshe blood bleede" from his wounds (24.421–22) in what was clearly a highly anticipated stage effect. However, in all its versions, the staging of the Last Judgment enacts rather than simply represents judgment, ritually and performatively creating a new world through anticipation of what is to come. In the Preface to the 1999 anniversary issue of her book *Gender Trouble*, Judith Butler wrote:

> I originally took my clue on how to read the performativity of gender from Jacques Derrida's reading of Kafka's "Before the Law." There the one who waits for the law, sits before the door of the law, attributes a certain force to the law for which one waits. The anticipation of an authoritative disclosure of meaning is the means by which that authority is attributed and installed: the anticipation conjures its object.[54]

A pageant of the Last Judgement, for anyone who believes that such an event might eventually take place, almost necessarily does just this, performing the anticipated judgement of good and evil. In the closing lines of the York version, God – Father and Son, together, played by the same actor – addresses good- and evil-doers, dramatic devotees and detractors alike, promising that "þei þat mendid þame whils þei moght ‖ Shall belde and bide in my blissing" (47.379–80). Again, the play explicitly demands response – a lived theological response.

When reformer Christopher Goodman compiled his list of "absurdities" in the Chester plays, he included "The words. And therto a full ryche messe, in bred myn one bodie, & that bred I you gyve, your wyked lyffe to amend, becomen is my fleshe, throgh wordes 5 betwyxt the prestes handes."[55] As David Mills has pointed out, the last of these lines in the extant Ascension play are slightly but significantly different:

---

[54] Judith Butler, *Gender Trouble: Feminism and the Subversion of Identity*, 10th Anniversary Edition (New York: Routledge, 1999), xiv-xv.

[55] Baldwin, Clopper, and Mills, REED: *Cheshire*, 1: 148.

> And that bread that I you give,
> your wicked life to amend,
> becomes my fleshe through your beleeffe
> and doth release your synfull band.[56]

This later, clearly revised text lacks all reference to those five Latin words, while the performative power of priestly utterance is effectively transferred to the faithful audience.

In the Towneley Ascension pageant, Christ speaks to the gathered disciples, and to the audience, saying,

> Ye haue harde me say full playnly,
> I go and to you am I commyng.
> If ye luf me forthi,
> Ye shuld be glad of this doyng....
> Therfor be ye thus trowyng
> When all is endid fully. (29.127–30, 135–36)

Not all in the audience – any audience, at any time – can be counted on to respond to a performance gladly or faithfully, "trowing" either the performance or what it represents. But in explicitly calling for such a response, the play and its actors engage less in a world of theatrical make-believe than in the performance of an act of make-belief, for the audience and for themselves – that is, performative theology.

Bibliography

Austin, J.L. *How to Do Things with Words*. Edited by J.O. Urmson and Marina Sbisà. Cambridge, MA: Harvard University Press, 1975 (2nd ed.).

Baldwin, Elizabeth, Lawrence M. Clopper and David Mills, eds. *Records of Early English Drama: Cheshire Including Chester*, 2 vols. Toronto and London: University of Toronto Press and The British Library, 2007.

Beadle, Richard. "'Devoute ymaginacioun' and the Dramatic Sense in Love's *Mirror* and the N-Town Plays." In *Nicholas Love at Waseda: Proceedings of the International Conference, 20–22 July, 1995*, edited by Shoicho Oguro, Richard Beadle, and Michael G. Sargent, 1–17. Cambridge: D.S. Brewer, 1997.

---

56   See David Mills, *Recycling the Cycle: The City of Chester and Its Whitsun Plays* (Toronto: University of Toronto Press, 1998), 182, quoting Chester 18.174–77.

———, ed. *The York Plays: A Critical Edition of the York Corpus Christi Play as Recorded in British Library Additional MS 35290*, 2 vols. EETS s.s. 23–24. Oxford: Oxford University Press, 2009–13.

Butler, Judith. "Performative Acts and Gender Constitution: An Essay in Phenomenology and Feminist Theory." *Theatre Journal* 49 (1988): 519–31.

———. *Gender Trouble: Feminism and the Subversion of Identity*. 10th Anniversary Edition. New York: Routledge, 1999.

Cawley, A.C., ed. *The Wakefield Pageants in the Towneley Cycle*. Manchester: Manchester University Press, 1958.

Christie, Sheila. "'Thei stodyn upon stoyls for to beheldyn hir': Margery Kempe and the Power of Performance." *Studia Anglica Posnaniensia* 38 (2002): 93–103.

Clopper, Lawrence M. *Drama, Play, and Game: English Festive Culture in the Medieval and Early Modern Period*. Chicago and London: University of Chicago Press, 2001.

Coleman, Simon. "An Anthropological Apologetics." *South Atlantic Quarterly* 109 (2010): 791–810.

Davidson, Clifford, ed. *A Trctise of Miraclis Pleyinge*. Kalamazoo, MI: Medieval Institute Publications, 1993 (rev. rpt. 2011).

Epp, Garrett P. J. "Visible Words: The York Plays, Brecht, and Gestic Writing." *Comparative Drama* 24 (1991): 289–305.

———. "Ecce Homo." In *Queering the Middle Ages / Historicizing Postmodernity*, edited by Steven F. Kruger and Glenn Burger, 346–66. Minneapolis: University of Minnesota Press, 2001.

———. "To 'Play the Sodomits': A Query in Five Actions." In *The Ashgate Research Companion to Queer Theory*, edited by Noreen Giffney and Michael O'Rourke, 181–97. Farnham: Ashgate, 2009.

Greenblatt, Stephen, ed. *The Norton Shakespeare*. New York: Norton, 2008 (2nd ed.).

Herdt, Jennifer A. *Putting On Virtue: The Legacy of the Splendid Vices*. Chicago: University of Chicago Press, 2008.

Hill-Vásquez, Heather. *Sacred Players: The Politics of Response in the Middle English Religious Drama*. Washington, DC: Catholic University of America Press, 2007.

Johnston, Alexandra F., and Margaret Rogerson, eds. *Records of Early English Drama: York*, 2 vols. Toronto: University of Toronto Press, 1979.

Lash, Nicholas. "Performing the Scriptures: Interpretation through Living." *The Furrow* 33 (1982): 467–74.

———. "I watch my language in the presence of God – Theology in the modern university," 2011. Faraday Papers, online: <https://www.faraday.st-edmunds.cam.ac.uk/Issues_Lash.php> (accessed 14 February 2015).

Lumiansky, R.M., and David Mills, eds. *The Chester Mystery Cycle*, 2 vols. EETS s.s. 3 and 9. Oxford: Oxford University Press, 1974–86.

Meale Carol, M. "'oft siþis with grete deuotion I þought what I miȝt do pleysyng to to god': The Early Ownership and Readership of Love's Mirror, with Special Reference to its Female Audience." In *Nicholas Love at Waseda: Proceedings of the International Conference, 20–22 July, 1995*, edited by Shoichi Oguro, Richard Beadle, and Michael G. Sargent, 19–46. Cambridge: Boydell & Brewer, 1997.

———. "'This is a Deed Bok, the Tother a Quick': Theatre and the Drama of Salvation in the *Book* of Margery Kempe." In *Medieval Women: Texts and Contexts in Late Medieval Britain. Essays for Felicity Riddy*, edited by Jocelyn Wogan-Browne, Rosalynn Voaden, Arlyn Diamond, Ann Hutchison, Carol M. Meale, and Lesley Johnson, 49–67. Turnhout: Brepols, 2000.

Mills, David. *Recycling the Cycle: The City of Chester and Its Whitsun Plays*. Toronto: University of Toronto Press, 1998.

———. "Brought to Book: Chester's Expositor and his Kin." In *The Narrator, the Expositor, and the Prompter in European Medieval Theatre*, edited by Philip Butterworth, 307–25. Turnhout: Brepols, 2007.

Stevens, Martin, and A.C. Cawley, eds. *The Towneley Plays*, 2 vols. EETS s.s. 13–14. Oxford: Oxford University Press, 1994.

Valantasis, Richard. *The Gospel of Thomas*. New Testament Readings, 5. London: Routledge, 1997.

Index

Abraham's Sacrifice 24
Adam of St. Victor 354
Aeneas 215
Agricola, Rudolph 215–16
Allen, Stephanie 8
Angela of Foligno 369–71, 375
Annunciation 79, 138, 345–46, 372
Anselm of Canterbury 346
Antichrist 168
Apius and Virginia 136
Apelles 245
Aquinas, Thomas 251, 339, 389
Aristophanes 284
Aristotle 178–79, 206, 349
Artaud, Antonin 306
Arundel, Thomas 3, 7, 149–50, 158–60, 186, 338
Ascension 70, 196, 317, 354, 402–03
Ashton, Thomas 21–22
Athanasius of Alexandria 204–05, 352
Atkin, Tamara 25
Augustine (Saint) 102, 258, 287, 339, 345
Austin, J.L. 386, 399

Babwell Mill 237
Bakhtin, Mikhail 281–82, 284
Bale, John 20, 23–24, 46–47, 63, 131, 204–05, 209
Bannatyne Manuscript 45
Beadle, Richard 6, 86–87, 159, 313, 315, 318, 335, 377–79, 391, 395
Beaton, David 58
Beckett, Samuel 297
Benjamin, Walter 279, 281, 300–01, 303
Bernard (Saint) 314
Bethlehem 70, 241, 258, 269
Betteridge, Thomas 126, 129, 140
Beverley 2–3, 6
 Corpus Christi Play 68–90
 Great Guild Book 69–79, 90
 Minster 80–82
Bevington, David 8
Beza, Theodorus 24
Biblical figures
 Abra 32
 Abraham 6, 70, 93, 99, 114, 116

Adam and Eve 6, 72, 78–90, 125, 128–30, 134–35, 137–38, 140, 143, 173, 175, 249, 340–41, 372, 396
Adam and Seth 70, 72, 77–79
Ahasuerus 27
Aman (Haman) 27–28
Annas 22, 48, 194, 279–306
Balaam 262
Belial 194, 285
Caiaphas (Cayphas) 22, 178, 194, 227, 229–30, 279–306
Cain and Abel 70, 72, 78, 80, 85–86, 89, 137, 192, 286, 341, 345
Centurion 185, 187, 193, 199, 222
Daniel 35–36
David 254
Deborah 19, 33
Elizabeth 391
Esther 26–28
Gabriel 197, 320, 345–46
Herod (King) 9, 78, 135, 249, 253–77
Herod Antipas 70, 73, 78, 209–19, 231–32, 239
Herodias 209, 211–19, 232
Hester 4–5, 25–28
Hezekiah 19
Holy Ghost 131, 133–35, 140, 145
Isaac 6, 70, 92–122, 345
Jesus Christ 9, 14, 21, 73–74, 76, 150–51, 155, 160, 186, 192–95, 197, 210, 217, 220, 241, 243, 250, 254–55, 262, 280, 284–86, 289–98, 302–06, 309, 312–22, 325–29, 334, 336, 338, 340, 344–53, 363, 385, 390, 392–93
Jacob and Esau 4, 19, 24–25, 31–35, 92–122
Joachim 36
John (apostle) 76, 184–85, 196, 198, 310, 312, 320, 328–30
John the Baptist 7, 21, 70, 149–64, 209, 212
Joseph 248, 265, 331, 346, 375–76
Joseph of Arimathea 185, 190, 194
Josiah 19
Judas Iscariot 204, 236, 240, 249, 280, 286–89, 293–94, 302–03, 305, 349, 360, 377, 379–80

Biblical figures (cont.)
    Lazarus   70
    Leah (Lya)   100, 104, 120
    Longinus   76, 185, 322
    Lucifer   70, 86, 137, 168–69, 339–42
    Magi   253, 255, 258–65, 268–70, 272, 276
    Malcus   349
    Maria Cleophas   200, 329
    Maria Jacobi   329
    Mary Magdalene   4, 29–31, 183–85, 193, 195–96, 200, 222–23, 231, 236, 326, 328, 331, 353
    Michael   48, 197, 388
    Moses   20, 224
    Nicodemus   194, 224
    Noah   7, 70, 72, 166–80, 345
    Noah's Wife   7, 166–67, 169–72, 174, 179
    Paul (apostle)   32, 44, 133, 343
    Peter (apostle)   22, 184–85, 196, 198, 223, 225–26, 230, 280, 284–85, 289, 293, 299–300, 305, 340–41, 349
    Philip (apostle)   209, 215
    Pontius Pilate   7, 70, 73, 78, 167, 169, 176–78, 184–87, 190, 193–95, 198, 201, 220, 249, 280–84, 286–89, 295, 301–03, 305, 314, 318, 336, 338, 379
    Procula   167, 169, 176–78, 336
    Rachel   100, 104, 117, 120–21, 257
    Raphael   197
    Rebecca   33–34, 104, 112–13
    Salome (midwife)   346, 388
    Susanna   4, 35–37
    Symeon   70
    Thomas (apostle)   22, 200, 225–27, 231, 353
    Three Marys, the   184–86, 188, 190, 194–96, 198–99, 201, 250, 329
    Uriel   197
    Veronica   318
    Virgin Mary   9, 76, 79, 81, 159, 184–201, 224, 245, 250, 265–66, 309–31, 345–46, 354–55, 360, 375–78, 390–91, 394
Birgitta of Sweden (Saint)   336, 346
Bledlow, Holy Trinity   80, 82
Book of Common Prayer   29
Books of the Bible
    Genesis   32–33, 83, 89, 93, 101, 103–04, 132, 139–41, 386
    Isaiah   210, 263, 268, 289, 291, 293–95, 303, 339, 347, 352
    Lamentations   250
    Psalms   290, 293, 295, 349, 351–52
    Matthew   150, 162, 167, 169, 194–95, 200, 209, 245, 253–55, 257, 280, 287, 336, 340, 346, 353
    Mark   150, 209, 245, 280, 291
    Luke   150, 154, 162, 200, 280, 323, 348
    John   76, 185, 210, 245
    Epistles of Paul   32, 133
    Romans   343
    1 Corinthians   348, 353
    1 Timothy   44
    1 Peter   352, 374
    Revelation   244, 251
Bosch, Hieronymus   295
Bourne, Henry   167
Bowet, Henry   159, 346
Bradley   352
Branford, Gaëlle   375–76
Brecht, Bertolt   301, 398
Briscoe, Marianne   237
Broughton, All Saints'   80, 82–83
Bruges   350
Bucer, Martin   4
Buchanan, George   25, 32, 209
Burton, Robert   206
Bury St. Edmunds   237–39
Butler, Judith   386–88, 402
Butterworth, Philip   6, 131–32, 173

Calvin, John   4, 6, 30–31, 34, 133–34, 139, 311
Cambridge   4, 173
Canterbury   190
Cassirer, Ernst   343
Carruthers, Jo   27
Carpenter, Sarah   4–5, 42–45, 173–74
Carroll, Lewis   179
Carpenter, Sarah   4–5, 42–45, 173–74
Castle of Perseverance, The   134–35, 236–37, 239, 277
Cawley, A.C.   96–98, 108, 267
Charteris, Henry   43, 45, 62, 65
Charteris, Robert   44
Chaucer, Geoffrey   246
Chester Plays   2–4, 10, 21–22, 72, 85, 95, 106, 127–28, 130, 141, 145–46, 151, 173, 186, 190–91, 276, 323–24, 363, 366–69, 384, 388–89, 397–98, 400–02
    Fall of Lucifer   72, 175

INDEX

Adam and Eve / Cain and Abel   72, 139, 141, 143–44
Abraham   131
   Slaugher of the Innocents   274–75
   Temptation of Christ / Woman Taken in Adultery   76–77
   Crucifixion   75–77
   Passion   318, 329
   Harrowing of Hell   70, 78, 193–94
   Resurrection   184, 194, 198–200
   Ascension   402
   Pentecost   135, 21
Chicago   244
Cicero   204, 207–09, 211–12, 314
Clitheroe   106
Clopper, Lawrence   71, 76, 79, 295
Coldeway, John   237
Collier, John Payne   106–07
Collins, Kristen   372–73
Coleman, Simon   387
Cologne   55
Cornish *Creation of the World*   77, 173
Cornish *Ordinalia*   77, 88
Cornish *Origo Mundi*   77, 79, 88–90
Cornwall   79, 88
Corpus Christi Day   79, 127, 166, 191, 238–39, 241–42, 251, 281, 287, 298, 337, 342, 360, 363, 366, 376
Council of Basel (1431)   50
Council of Trent (1545–63)   55
Coventry   2, 76, 78, 106, 173, 273, 340
Coverdale Bible   6, 46, 97–99, 101–02, 108–22
Cox, John   168, 171
Craig, Hardin   96
Cranmer, Thomas   15, 17–18, 28, 204
Crispin, Philip   9
Cromwell, Thomas   20, 23
Crucifixion   8, 73–76, 160, 176, 193, 195, 199, 205, 223, 225, 236, 246, 248–49, 299, 309–31, 337, 346–48, 351–52, 373, 391, 396–97, 401
Croxton   237–39, 247
Croxton Play of the Sacrament   8, 235–51
Cummings, Brian   311
Cupar   45, 56
Cursor Mundi   77

Dante Alighieri   249

David, Gerard   352
Davidson, Clifford   10, 250, 361–62, 389
Davis, Norman   127
Dawson, Jane E.   59
Delay, Tom   250
Depositio crucis   189, 244
Deposition   73, 76
Descensus ad Inferos   352
Devil   76, 125, 130, 137, 141–45, 167–79, 192, 204, 206, 230, 249, 274–76, 287, 337, 347, 352, 375–76
Dido   215
Digby plays   276
   Killing of the Children, The   273
   Mary Magdalen   236
   Christ's Burial and Resurrection   184, 195, 323–24, 331
   Conversion of St. Paul, The   236
Diller, Hans-Jürgen   366, 376, 378
Doncaster   81, 160
Doomsday   10, 70, 83, 334, 337, 339–40, 342, 355
Douce, Francis   106–07
Dürer, Albrecht   242
Dunbar, Gavin   55, 58
Dutka, JoAnna   127–29, 136
Dutton, Elisabeth   8, 236, 238

Easby, St Agatha's   80, 82–84
East-Anglia   162, 235, 237–38
East Riding   68
Edinburgh   44–45, 49
Edward VI   4, 15, 19, 25–26, 135
Ehrstine, Glenn   362
Elevatio crucis   189
Elisabeth I   4, 126
Emmaus   70, 190, 200, 226, 353, 372
Emmerson, Richard Kenneth   168
Enargaia   314
England, George   95–96, 106–07
Entry into Jerusalem   73
Epp, Garrett P.J.   10, 155
Erasmus (Saint)   350
Erasmus, Desiderius   15, 17, 30, 47, 59
Everyman   135
Expulsion   72, 79–86, 88–89, 137–38, 341, 372

Fitch, Robert   127

Fitzroy, Henry (Duke of Richmond)   80
Fleury playbook   243, 250, 257
Foucault, Michel   388
Foxe, John   205
Fra Angelico   138, 291
Framlingham, St Michael's   80, 82
François I   59
French *mystères*   7, 149, 151–54, 158, 161, 163
Frye, Northrop   284

Gadamer, Hans-Georg   344
Gaza   303
Garden of Gethsemane   73, 236
Gardner, John   96–97
Garter, Thomas   35–36
Geneva   46
Geneva Bible   6, 44–45, 97–99, 101–03, 108–22, 209–10, 220
Gesualdo, Carlo   251
Gibson, Gail McMurray   237–38
Glasgow   55
Glossa Ordinaria   337
Godly Queen Hester   5, 25–28
Godfrey, Bob   9
Good Friday   243–44, 305, 373–75
Goodman, Christopher   4, 10, 145–46, 367–69, 388–89, 402
Gordon, Bruce   19
Gospel of Nicodemus   76, 186, 336, 352
Gospel of Thomas   387, 401
Gréban, Arnoul   5, 151–52, 189
Gregory the Great (Pope)   242–43, 360, 371–73
Grimald, Nicholas   8, 25, 32, 204–32, 311
Grotowski, Jerzy   279, 296–300
Grünewald, Matthias   347

Halbwachs, Maurice   341
Hamburgh, Harvey   312
Hamilton, John   42, 49–50, 53–59, 66
Happé, Peter   7, 81
Hardwick, Paul   375
Harris, Jonathan   379–80
Harrowing of hell   78, 178, 184–87, 191, 196, 199, 227, 345, 352
Harty, Kevin J.   128
Heap, Carl   297, 304
Heidegger, Martin   343

Henderson, Frank   29
Henry VIII   3, 12–15, 19, 26–27, 57, 59, 80
Hercules   228, 240
Herdt, Jennifer A.   391, 395
Hereford   2, 285
Hervieu-Léger, Danièle   344
Hilary of Poitiers   351–52
Hill-Vásquez, Heather   397–98
Höfele, Andreas   205
Holbein, Hans (the younger)   310
Holkham Bible Picture Book   83, 341
Homan, Richard   364
Homer   268
Honorius of Autun   243, 396
Horrox, Rosemary E.   74, 79
Hull   9, 298, 301–05
Hussee, John   23
Hutson, Lorna   36

Imitatio Christi   10, 362, 371–75, 380, 392
India   267
Innocent III (Pope)   290
Islam   285, 388, 390
Italy   267

Jacob and Esau   24–25, 31–35, 92–99
Jacobus de Voragine   77, 273, 354, 379
James V   49, 57–59, 61
Jean du Prier   196
Jennings, Margaret   168
Jerusalem   70, 73, 197, 254, 285–86, 302, 318, 347, 395
Jesus Christ Superstar   392–93
Jeu d'Adam   297
Jews   8, 27, 154, 197, 209, 223, 235–36, 239–42, 245–51, 254–55, 259, 263, 287, 318, 327, 350, 377
John Clerke   158
John of Thoresby (archbishop)   346
Jonson, Ben   35
Johnston, Alexandra   97, 184, 310, 324–25, 327–28, 331, 334–36
Josephus, Titus Flavus   209, 255, 258, 273
Jour de Jugement, Le   173
Judea   254–55
Julius II (Pope)   312
Juno   228

Kalamazoo 241
Kamerick, Kathleen 370
Katherine of Aragon 26–27
Kempe, John 267
Kempe, Margery 150, 159, 369–71, 390–91
Kempton 267
Kenny, Anthony 178–79
King, Pamela 319, 337
King Darius 25, 131
King James Bible 254
Kirchmeyer, Thomas 205
Knight, Alan E. 284
Knox, John 20–21, 46–47, 49, 65
Kosofsky Sedgwick, Eve 288
Kristeva, Julia 295, 310
Kuchar, Gary 311

Lancashire 106, 160
Lane, John 389
Lanyer, Aemelia 309–13, 320, 323
Lash, Nicholas 387, 400
Last Supper 73, 280, 299, 348
Latimer, Hugh 204
Lawrence (Saint) 350
Lawton, David 236–37
Lay Folks Catechism, The 346, 352
Lecoq, Jacques 279, 296–97, 299–301
Leicester 150
Le Patourel, H.E. Jean 74
Lincoln 2
Lindsay, John 250
Lisle, Lord and Lady 23
Lollards 149–51, 155, 157, 159, 163, 242
Love, Nicholas 6, 9, 14, 16–17, 156, 186, 199–200, 309–28, 336, 347, 350, 390–91, 393, 395–96
Ludus de Nativitate (Benediktbeuern) 250, 257
Luther, Martin 24, 27, 64, 66, 134
Lyndsay, David 5, 42–66
Lynn 369

Mahounde 285
Mankind 170, 179, 229, 239, 291, 293
Manly, John Matthews 95, 129
Marlowe, Christopher 247
Marx, C.W. 331
Mary Tudor 16

Marshall, Anne 82–83
Masschaele, James 378
Master Robert (York) 340
McBain, James 9
McKinnell, John 361, 369
McNamer, Sarah, 315, 317, 328
Meale, Carol M. 390–92
Meditationes vitae Christi (*Meditations on the Life of Christ*) 14, 16, 18, 315–20, 336, 346, 350–51
Melton, William 157, 364–71
Meredith, Peter 161, 169, 199
Merrill, L.R. 212, 220
Michel, Jean 5, 151, 153–54, 163, 196
Mills, David 398, 402
Milton, John 132
Muir, Lynette 169, 189
Mullini, Roberta 6–7
Murdoch, Brian 89
Mystère d'Adam, Le 173
Mystère de la Résurrection 183–84, 196, 199
Mystères, French 7, 149, 151–54, 158, 161, 163

N-Town Plays 2, 7, 22, 72, 128, 130, 134–35, 149, 151, 154, 184, 191, 194, 199, 220–21, 249, 313–14, 384
  Adam and Eve 84, 137, 139, 141–42, 144, 174–75
  Nativity 389
  Death of Herod 275–76
  Baptism of Christ 155–57, 161–64
  Crucifixion 309–31
  Christ's Appearance to Mary 192
  Passion 9, 75, 379
Narveson, Kate 16, 34
Nativity 191, 204–05, 248, 262, 265, 272, 346, 372, 389–91, 400
Neeley, Ted 393
Nelson, Alan 127
Neptune 228
Newe mery and wittie Comedie or Enterlude, newely imprinted, treating vpon the Historie of Jacob and Esau, A 92
Newman, Barbara 354, 360
Newcastle-upon-Tyne 2, 7, 166–80
  Noah Play 7, 166–80
Nice Wanton 33, 135
Normandy 267

Normington, Katie   7
Northern Homily Cycle   377
Northern Passion, The   77, 186, 336, 353
Norway   267
Norwich, 2, 5, 125–28, 163
    Cathedral   143
    Grocers' Play   6, 125–46

Ordo ad Interfectionem Puerorum   257
Ordo ad Repraesentandum Herodem   257
Oswestry   21
Oxford   8, 204, 209, 220, 225
Owst, G.R.   277

Padua   267
Pagels, Elaine   336, 353
Palestine   280, 301
Paradise   77, 83–84, 88, 90, 128, 137–38, 140, 176, 228, 267, 341
Paris   51, 190, 338
Parkes, Malcolm   97
Passion   9, 21, 24, 72–75, 79, 191–92, 201, 224–25, 243, 251, 279–306, 310–12, 314, 317, 320, 326, 328–29, 336–38, 340, 347, 350–51, 353, 361–62, 369–75, 390, 394, 396
Passion d'Arras, Le   151–52
Passion d'Auvergne, Le   151
Passion de Semur, Le   151
Peacham, Henry   214
Pentecost   135, 196, 354, 372
Peregrini   189
Perth   173
Pfeiffer, Kerstin   318, 327, 330, 362, 366, 371, 375
Pickering, F.P.   352
Pinter, Harold   297
Planctus Mariae   309, 323–24, 326, 330–31
Plautus   204, 206, 220–21, 229
Pluto   228
Pollard, Alfred W.   95–96, 107
Pontefract   161
Protoevangelion   346, 389
Prudentius, Aurelius Clemens   256–57
Puttenhem, George   215
Pyers, William   71, 78

Queen Mary   4, 169, 191, 193

Queen Mary's Psalter   169
Quem quaeritis   243–44
Quintilian   207–08, 211, 213, 230

Reformation   1, 3, 8, 12–37, 42–66, 125, 134, 140, 204, 223, 311, 350, 398–99
Regularis Concordia   243–44
Resurrection   7, 8, 21, 29, 70, 176, 182–201, 220–23, 225, 231–32, 244, 248, 257, 298, 323–24, 330, 347, 352–54
Resurrection of Our Lord, The   6, 21, 184, 187, 199–200
Rhetorica ad Herennium   314
Ridley, Nicholas   204
Rogerson, Margaret   10, 335
Rogerson, Robert   389
Rolle, Richard   390
Rome   3, 57–58, 66, 243
Rome-Raker, Robert   54
Rossiter, A.P.   96
Rupert of Deutz   288
Ryrie, Alec   48–50, 55, 57

Sabia (Sabé)   240
Said, Edward   285
Saint-Benoit-sur-Loire   257
Sartre, Jean-Paul   388
Sarum   29
Satan   7, 35, 76, 90, 130–31, 139, 142–44, 166–167, 171–79, 187, 228, 277
Savage, John   367
Sawyer, Karen Elaine   21
Scherb, Victor   237
Schroeder, Joy   370
Scrope, Richard   159
Searle, John   386
Sebastian, John   237–38
Second Shepherd's Play   241, 248, 287, 376
Seinte Resureccion, La   183, 190
Selby   340
Seneca   204, 206, 209, 211, 217–19, 221, 227–29
Serenus (Bishop of Marseilles)   371
Serpent   130, 138, 140, 143–44, 174–76, 224, 251
Servet, Pierre   196
Shakespeare, William
    As You Like It   215, 386
    King Lear   400
    Hamlet   137

    Macbeth 287
    Othello 144–45
Sheingorn, Pamela 201
Shrewsbury 21
Skelton, John 229, 288
Smith, Gilbert 231
Soule, Lesley Wade 172
South Africa 302–03
St. Albans Psalter 360, 371–73
Stanzaic Life of Christ 336
Steenbrugge, Charlotte 7
Stephen (Saint) 204–05
Stevens, Martin 96–98
St. Gall 248
Stirling 20
Stonyhurst Pageants, The 92
Syria (Surrey) 240

Taylor, George C. 323
Te Deum Laudamus 244
Ten Brink, Bernhard 93–97, 101
Terence 25, 32, 204–05, 229
Tertullian 245
Thetford 237
Thomas de Vio, Cardinal Cajetan 312–13, 322
Thorne, Alison 215–16
Tolcote 237, 247
Tomás Luis de Victoria 251
Toulmin Smith, Lucy 77
Towneley plays (see also Wakfield) 2, 6–7, 9, 72, 74, 86, 96–97, 105–09, 137, 149, 151, 248, 253, 323–24, 327
    Creation, The 138, 176
    Fall of Lucifer 168–69
    Noah and the Ark 170
    Isaac 92 122
    Jacob 92–122
    Offering of the Magi, The 253, 258–65, 276
    Flight into Egypt, The 265
    Herod the Great 253, 265–73, 276
    John the Baptist 155–57, 160–64
    Crucifixion 76, 318
    Resurrection 184, 187, 191, 193, 198
    Pilgrims 384
    Ascension of the Lord 403

Tretise of Miraclis Pleyinge, A 293, 350–51, 368–73, 384–85, 389, 391–97, 399
Turkey 267
Turner, Victor 281
Turnus 228
Tuscany 267
Twycross, Meg 36, 108, 159, 170, 172–74, 301
Tydeman, William 173, 237
Tyndale, William 14, 17–19, 24, 27, 31–32, 46

Udall, Nicholas 17

Valantasis, Richard 387–88, 401
Van Beethoven, Ludwig 400
Vaux, Robert 13–14
Vice (stage character) 25, 28, 35–36, 42, 135–36, 144–45, 291
Victimi paschali 195
Virgil (Publius Vergilius Maro) 204, 206, 215, 221, 268
Visitatio sepulchri 189, 243, 250
Visitation 372
Vita Adae and Evae 89–90
Vulgate 3, 5, 14, 44–46, 97–98, 100–01, 108–09, 115–16, 118, 120–21, 139, 204, 206

Wager, Lewis 28–31
Wakefield 97, 105–08, 160, 191
    Corpus Christi Plays (see also Towneley) 96, 107, 273, 386
Wakefield Master 108, 253, 266–67, 272, 277
Walker, Greg 5, 126, 129, 140, 176–77
Walker, Katherine 373
Waterhouse, Osborne 127, 129, 170–71
Watson, Thomas 25, 32
Wenzel, Siegfried 374
West Riding 105, 160
Whitfield White, Paul 1, 30–31, 34, 128, 131
Whitsun 21, 127, 129, 135, 145, 367
Winchcombe (Hayles Abbey) 350
Winchester 243–44
Wisdom 156, 287
Wolsey, Thomas 5, 26–28, 57
Woodkirk 105–07
Woolf, Rosemary 128, 136, 163, 172, 189, 311, 319, 323–24, 326, 331, 337, 339
Wright, David 46
Wright, Stephen K. 363, 366–67

Wyatt, Diana   6, 171
Wycliff, John   3, 6, 97–99, 101–02, 108–10, 114, 186, 375, 384–86, 399, 401

York Corpus Christi Plays passim
   Memorandum Book A/Y   342, 363–64, 366–67, 379
   Ordo paginarum   86–87, 159, 335–36, 342, 377
   The Creation   175
   Fall of Man   138, 142–43, 174
   Expulsion from Eden   79, 86, 88
   Baptism of Jesus   158–60, 164
   Dream of Pilate's Wife   73, 167
   Trial before Herod   73
   Mortification of Christ   76
   Crucifixion   74, 224
   Ascension   354
   Pentecost   354
York Minster   282, 338–40, 346, 349

Zealots   302

Printed in the United States
By Bookmasters